Blackstone's Statutes on

CONTRACT, TORT & RESTITUTION

To Josephine

Blackstone's Statutes on

CONTRACT, TORT & RESTITUTION

Eighth Edition

Edited by

F. D. Rose MA, BCL, PhD, MA

of Gray's Inn, Barrister-at-Law
Professor of Commercial and Common Law, University of Buckingham

This edition published in Great Britain 1995 by Blackstone Press Limited, Aldine Place, London W12 8AA. Telephone: 0181-740 2277

© F D Rose, 1987

First edition 1987
Second edition 1989
Third edition 1991
Fourth edition 1993
Fifth edition 1994
Sixth edition 1995
Seventh edition 1996
Eighth edition 1997

ISBN: 1 85431 660 5

British Library Cataloguing in Publication Data.
A CIP catalogue record for this book is available from the British Library

Typeset by Montage Studios Limited, Tonbridge, Kent
Printed by Livesey Ltd, Shrewsbury, Shropshire

All rights reserved. No part of this book may be reproduced or transmitted in any form or by any means, electronic or mechanical, including photocopying, recording, or any information storage or retrieval system without prior permission from the publisher.

CONTENTS

Preface xi
Preface to the Fourth Edition xiii
Preface to the First Edition xv

PART I STATUTES
Limitation Act 1623 1
Statute of Frauds 1677 1
Fires Prevention (Metropolis) Act 1774 1
Libel Act 1792 2
Statute of Frauds Amendment Act 1828 2
Parliamentary Papers Act 1840 2
Libel Act 1843 3
Gaming Act 1845 4
Libel Act 1845 4
Mercantile Law Amendment Act 1856 4
Offences against the Person Act 1861 5
Apportionment Act 1870 5
Law of Libel Amendment Act 1888 6
Factors Act 1889 6
Slander of Women Act 1891 7
Gaming Act 1892 8
Marine Insurance Act 1906 8
Law of Property Act 1925 11
Reservoirs (Safety Provisions) Act 1930 12
Third Parties (Rights against Insurers) Act 1930 12
Law Reform (Miscellaneous Provisions) Act 1934 14
Law Reform (Married Women and Tortfeasors) Act 1935 15
Law Reform (Frustrated Contracts) Act 1943 16
Law Reform (Contributory Negligence) Act 1945 17
Crown Proceedings Act 1947 18
Law Reform (Personal Injuries) Act 1948 19
National Parks and Access to the Countryside Act 1949 20
Arbitration Act 1950 20
Reserve and Auxiliary Forces (Protection of Civil Interests) Act 1951 21
Defamation Act 1952 21
Occupiers' Liability Act 1957 22
Public Bodies (Admission to Meetings) Act 1960 24
Law Reform (Husband and Wife) Act 1962 24
Plant Varieties and Seeds Act 1964 25
Nuclear Installations Act 1965 25
Criminal Law Act 1967 29
Misrepresentation Act 1967 30

Parliamentary Commissioner Act 1967 31
Civil Evidence Act 1968 31
Theatres Act 1968 32
Theft Act 1968 32
Trade Descriptions Act 1968 33
Employer's Liability (Compulsory Insurance) Act 1969 34
Employers' Liability (Defective Equipment) Act 1969 35
Administration of Justice Act 1970 35
Equal Pay Act 1970 36
Taxes Management Act 1970 36
Animals Act 1971 39
Carriage of Goods by Sea Act 1971 43
Mineral Workings (Offshore Installations) Act 1971 50
Unsolicited Goods and Services Act 1971 50
Defective Premises Act 1972 53
Powers of Criminal Courts Act 1973 56
Supply of Goods (Implied Terms) Act 1973 57
Consumer Credit Act 1974 61
Health and Safety at Work Act 1974 68
Rehabilitation of Offenders Act 1974 71
Solicitors Act 1974 72
Guard Dogs Act 1975 74
Petroleum and Submarine Pipe-Lines Act 1975 75
Sex Discrimination Act 1975 75
Unsolicited Goods and Services (Amendment) Act 1975 77
Congenital Disabilities (Civil Liability) Act 1976 78
Dangerous Wild Animals Act 1976 80
Fatal Accidents Act 1976 81
Race Relations Act 1976 83
Resale Prices Act 1976 83
Protection from Eviction Act 1977 84
Torts (Interference with Goods) Act 1977 85
Unfair Contract Terms Act 1977 91
Civil Liability (Contribution) Act 1978 98
State Immunity Act 1978 100
Customs and Excise Management Act 1979 100
Pneumoconiosis etc. (Workers' Compensation) Act 1979 101
Sale of Goods Act 1979 102
Vaccine Damage Payments Act 1979 120
Highways Act 1980 121
Limitation Act 1980 122
British Telecommunications Act 1981 138
Contempt of Court Act 1981 138
Supreme Court Act 1981 138
Administration of Justice Act 1982 140
Civil Aviation Act 1982 141
Forfeiture Act 1982 142
Insurance Companies Act 1982 143
Supply of Goods and Services Act 1982 143
International Transport Conventions Act 1983 150
Mental Health Act 1983 151
Building Act 1984 151
Data Protection Act 1984 152

Inheritance Tax Act 1984. 152
Occupiers' Liability Act 1984 152
Police and Criminal Evidence Act 1984 153
Telecommunications Act 1984 155
Administration of Justice Act 1985 156
Business Names Act 1985 156
Companies Act 1985 157
Housing Act 1985 159
Landlord and Tenant Act 1985 160
Surrogacy Arrangements Act 1985 160
Agricultural Holdings Act 1986 161
Building Societies Act 1986 161
Financial Services Act 1986 162
Insolvency Act 1986 165
Latent Damage Act 1986 165
Banking Act 1987 167
Consumer Protection Act 1987 167
Crown Proceedings (Armed Forces) Act 1987 197
Minors' Contracts Act 1987 198
Pilotage Act 1987 198
Criminal Justice Act 1988 198
Housing Act 1988 204
Income and Corporation Taxes Act 1988 205
Landlord and Tenant Act 1988 208
Malicious Communications Act 1988 209
Road Traffic Act 1988 209
Road Traffic (Consequential Provisions) Act 1988 217
Children Act 1989 217
Companies Act 1989 217
Electricity Act 1989 218
Employment Act 1989 218
Finance Act 1989 219
Human Organ Transplants Act 1989 219
Law of Property (Miscellaneous Provisions) Act 1989 220
Prevention of Terrorism (Temporary Provisions) Act 1989 221
Security Service Act 1989 222
Access to Health Records Act 1990 222
Broadcasting Act 1990 222
Contracts (Applicable Law) Act 1990 223
Courts and Legal Services Act 1990 224
Environmental Protection Act 1990 225
Food Safety Act 1990 241
Human Fertilisation and Embryology Act 1990 241
National Health Service and Community Care Act 1990 241
Town and Country Planning Act 1990 242
Child Support Act 1991 242
Coal Mining Subsidence Act 1991 244
Land Drainage Act 1991 245
Property Misdescriptions Act 1991 245
Water Industry Act 1991 247
Water Resources Act 1991 250
Access to Neighbouring Land Act 1992 252
Carriage of Goods by Sea Act 1992 257

Further and Higher Education Act 1992 260
Social Security Administration Act 1992 261
Social Security Contributions and Benefits Act 1992 265
Timeshare Act 1992 266
Trade Union and Labour Relations (Consolidation) Act 1992 267
Clean Air Act 1993 281
Leasehold Reform, Housing and Urban Development Act 1993 282
Noise and Statutory Nuisance Act 1993 282
Pension Schemes Act 1993 283
Railways Act 1993 285
Criminal Justice and Public Order Act 1994 286
Drug Trafficking Act 1994 289
Intelligence Services Act 1994 289
Trade Marks Act 1994 289
Value Added Tax Act 1994 290
Vehicle Excise and Registration Act 1994 296
Agricultural Tenancies Act 1995 297
Criminal Injuries Compensation Act 1995 298
Jobseekers Act 1995 300
Landlord and Tenant (Covenants) Act 1995 300
Merchant Shipping Act 1995 305
Pensions Act 1995 308
Arbitration Act 1996 309
Broadcasting Act 1996 310
Damages Act 1996 311
Defamation Act 1996 314
Education Act 1996 323
Employment Rights Act 1996 330
Housing Act 1996 330
Housing Grants, Construction and Regeneration Act 1996 332
Noise Act 1996 334
Party Wall Etc. Act 1996 339
Police Act 1996 339
Civil Procedure Act 1997 340
Contract (Scotland) Act 1997 341
Finance Act 1997 341
Justices of the Peace Act 1997 348
Police Act 1997 348
Protection from Harassment Act 1997 353
Social Security (Recovery of Benefits) Act 1997 355

PART II PROPOSED STATUTES
(Draft) Contributory Negligence Bill 367
(Draft) Restitution (Mistakes of Law) Bill 368
(Draft) Contracts (Rights of Third Parties) Bill 369

PART III STATUTORY INSTRUMENTS
Employers' Liability (Compulsory Insurance) General Regulations 1971 373
Consumer Transactions (Restrictions on Statements) Order 1976 373
Transfer of Undertakings (Protection of Employment) Regulations 1981 375
Package Travel, Package Holidays and Package Tours Regulations 1992 375
Provision and Use of Work Equipment Regulations 1992 383
General Product Safety Regulations 1994 388

Contents

Unfair Terms in Consumer Contracts Regulations 1994 393
Public Supply Contracts Regulations 1995 397

PART IV   EC MATERIALS
Treaty establishing the European Economic Community (Treaty of Rome, 1957) 399
EEC Council Directive (25 July 1985) on Liability for Defective Products 400
EEC Council Directive (29 June 1992) on General Product Safety 405
EEC Council Directive (5 April 1993) on Unfair Terms in Consumer Contracts . 412
Annex 416

PART V   CODES
Principles of European Contract Law 418
Unidroit Principles for International Commercial Contracts 427
Draft Rules on Unjustified Enrichment 444

Index 452

PREFACE

As in previous editions, this book sets out to present the principal legislative contributions to the law of contract, tort and restitution, together with a selection of specific provisions from more specialist legislation which affects the general law on civil liability and reveals something of its wider context.

It has always been intended that this book should include the core materials to be consulted by students of Contract, Restitution and Tort, a selection of other materials in the area of civil liability, and a few related regulatory and public law provisions. Case law and statute do not exist in isolation, any more than the three main subjects of this book do. They are all part of a dynamic legal architecture, combining elements of old and new, beautiful and ugly, awkward and useful. A citizen may prefer an area of outstanding natural beauty to an industrial estate or a plainly functional new hospital, but the modern landscape cannot be accurately recorded without noting all three or their different contributions.

This edition contains material of relevance to those interested in all three areas covered by the book. In particular, the Finance Act 1997 makes a number of important changes within the law of Restitution and relevant to the swaps litigation. The Social Security (Recovery of Benefits) Act 1997 enacts provisions which are not only relevant to those interested in Torts and Restitution but concern the relationship between the two areas. The Contract (Scotland) Act 1997 only extends to Scotland but is also of interest in relation to the English law on extrinsic evidence and damages for breach of contracts of sale.

Though the area covered by this book is traditionally regarded as one governed by case law, it is noteworthy that legislative developments continue to justify annual editions, because of both innovations in and amendments to the law. Fortunately the burden consequent on the modification of the common law by Parliament has been eased this year by the timing of that body's partial reconstitution as a result of the recent General Election, so drawing a neat line between what has received the Royal Assent and what is still passing through the Legislature. It is interesting to reflect that, although it cannot be attributed with all the credit or blame, the perhaps inappropriately named Conservative Party was in power while the larger part of the materials in this book came into being. No doubt the new Labour government is unlikely to be outdone in providing new law for future editions.

As in previous editions, in most cases the material is reproduced in its complete, most recent form, all amendments being incorporated within square brackets; occasional omissions are indicated by three dots. Supplementary notes and details of amending provisions, easily available elsewhere, are generally omitted for reasons of space.

I continue to be grateful for suggestions as to possible revisions of this collection of materials.

Francis Rose
St Swithun's Day 1997

PREFACE TO THE FOURTH EDITION

The first edition of this book was the forerunner of Blackstone's series of statute books and the first collection of statutory materials on contract and tort published. The choice of an appropriate title for the collection was not simple. Despite the known flexibility of the most obvious collective name for both contract and tort (namely "common law"), *Common Law Statutes* did seem something of a contradiction in terms, so the collection began life as *Civil Liability Statutes*. The name did not survive, because it was not always readily apparent to those unfamiliar with this area of the law what it concerned. But it had its merits, because it drew attention away from the familiar categories contract and tort and focused attention on the theme of this area — rights and liabilities governed by the civil law, as opposed to public law — and the title of the book indicated that the source material was not to be found exclusively, or even in some areas primarily, in the cases.

Indeed, the modern law on civil liability increasingly demonstrates the interrelationship between statutes and the cases and the challenges this poses. Even at the relatively straightforward level of codification, there arises the issues how far the statute is to be read independently of the underlying case law (most famously commented upon in relation to Chalmers' Sale of Goods Act) or how far and how a provision codifying one particular aspect of a general common law area applies to other ramifications of the same general issue (currently a hot issue in English and Scottish courts in relation to material non-disclosure in insurance contracts and the scope of Chalmers' least well received codification, the Marine Insurance Act 1906). At least codification has the advantage (although the process raises its own disadvantages) of easing the accessibility of the law, something also achieved by consolidation of prior case law, a process which has prompted several changes in this edition.

Of course, the principal means by which legislation affects the law is by deliberately changing it, either by creating new law or by altering existing rules. Thus, a growing case law on exemption clauses was overridden (in the Unfair Contract Terms Act 1977) by act of Parliament, a procedure which will be required to implement further such reforms, in compliance with this year's EC directive on Unfair Terms in Consumer Contracts, the last addition to the present edition of this book. Such implementation of parliamentary supremacy does not operate to suppress the work of the judiciary; it commonly provokes it. It is the judges who, in interpreting legislation, must decide its effect. More dramatically, unless the draftsman has clearly provided for the consequences of, say, an invalidating statutory rule, it is for the courts to complete the legislative process when practical problems generated by the statutes arise for adjudication. This in turn can provoke further legislation. Thus, a current live issue, both in the highest courts throughout the Commonwealth and in the Law Commissions, is whether money paid under a mistake of law or related circumstances should be recoverable under existing common law rules or whether this requires legislation. The answer may lie with either Parliament or the courts. The judicial committee of the House of Lords avoided its clear resolution last year in *Woolwich Equitable Building Society* v *IRC (No. 2)* but dramatically asserted a power of prospective overruling, simultaneously denying and acknowledging its familiar function of cautious restatement and reform. The complementary and opposing roles of the judiciary and the legislature are often demonstrated in civil liability cases, and in a variety of ways. They need to be examined with reference not only to the cases but also to the relevant statutory material, the importance of which is highlighted by the Law Society's evolving plans to make specific study of statutes a more overt requirement of basic legal education. The purpose of this book continues to be to offer both the leading statutory sources and a varied selection of other statutory materials in an easily accessible form.

In one important aspect of civil liability, the above mentioned *Woolwich* case was eclipsed by the House of Lords' decision a year previously in *Lipkin Gorman* v *Karpnale Ltd*. Both cases represent English law's recognition of unjust enrichment, the underlying principle of the law of restitution. This is not a new area of law: indeed, its existence was acknowledged in the full title of the first edition of this book: *Civil Liability Statutes (Contract, Tort & Restitution)*. Its recognition was previously suppressed by the established categories of contract and tort and competition for space in traditional law school curriculums. Although overtly recognised by Parliament fourteen years previously (in the *Torts (Interference with Goods) Act 1977*), *Lipkin Gorman* gave the subject a prominence which has revolutionised practice and caused an explosion of activity in litigation and the literature. There are increasing statutory provisions (as revealed in some of the new additions to this book), many more cases, a growing number of books, a stream of articles and, with the emergence this year of the *Restitution Law Review*, its own law journal. None of these developments can be avoided by present and intending practitioners or by any serious teacher or student of the law. They are recognised in the expanded title of this edition and its provision of materials complementing the related areas of contract and tort.

Francis Rose
Bastille Day 1993

PREFACE TO THE FIRST EDITION

Amongst the first impressions acquired by a student new to English law is of the common law system as one constructed from the decisions of the judges and best represented by, indeed often spoken of as synonymous with, the law of contract and the law of tort. He or she also learns that legislation is one of the two most important sources of law, indeed that it overrides case law. But statutes are not uncommonly seen as aberrations, tinkering with what is essentially a case law system or establishing self-contained regimes, distinct from other areas within the same subject of study. Their hostility is manifest in areas where they have to be faced in strength, most prominently in land law, habitually studied after the foundation year, where their potential for impenetrability is made manifest.

If the discerning student should ever gain such a picture of English law, he will hopefully soon realise that, whatever glimmer of truth it may contain, it is at least superficial and misleading. The arrangement of the curriculum should not be permitted to obscure the fact that contract and tort, as is being increasingly stressed, with their overlapping and fluctuating boundaries, are but major categorisations together with others, in particular the law of restitution, of a broader subject of civil liability. Moreover, statutory contributions to this subject are at least as valid as, and in some areas increasingly more important than, those of judicial decisions. In part, this book recognises that and seeks to give some indication of the different ways in which statutes have helped to shape modern law. Some, though necessarily limited, account is also taken of the intending practitioner's need to realise that individual 'fact situations' prompt not only consideration of the law of civil liability but also of elements of property law, criminal law, commercial law, public law and so on.

One skill that all students and all lawyers must have is the ability to research. That requires not only finding the right books in the library, which in the case of statutory materials can be quickly achieved, but also of reading through those materials to find the relevant answers. Hopefully, the convenience of the present collection will encourage more extensive, even if only casual, reading of the statutory materials, particularly those that would otherwise be passed by, and, in doing so, enhance the student's appreciation of the legislative sources of the law as well as making it apparent that those sources need not be as intimidating or demanding as they are sometimes believed to be. This book attempts to concentrate on the core statutory provisions and examples of some of the principal legislative devices in this area. It does not attempt to be complete or definitive. Where a provision is not included or a question remains unanswered, the answer to a query is as in all cases: look it up elsewhere.

Since most, if not all, students with a substantial legal content in their courses will have to study both contract and tort, and will have at least some contact with the increasingly prominent and usually related law of restitution, this collection ranges over the three areas. Hopefully, it will facilitate their study jointly. Moreover, recognising the increasing practice of candidates' being permitted to take primary source materials into their examinations, it provides a more economical means of doing so than having to acquire the relevant main sources individually. Indeed, more material is provided than a candidate would normally wish to purchase, particularly for one subject alone, but, as with all such materials, the candidate will not benefit from either the basic materials or relevant additional materials unless they have been digested in advance. With that in mind, hardly any supplementary notes are included.

The principal aim in selecting from the much wider range of potential material available has been to provide as much substantive material as possible. In general, therefore, apart from the title of the statute, the marginal note providing the title of the relevant section, and the material parts of those sections that are included, the statutes are printed without preambles, headings, provisions as to commencement, extent and citation, or references to the previous law. Provisions are printed as amended, amendments being indicated in square brackets, but details of the amending provisions are omitted. The occasional excision of, for present purposes, unnecessary words from the provisions included is marked by three dots, without brackets. Specific provisions for Scotland and Northern Ireland are in most cases also omitted. For ease of consultation, the statutes are arranged chronologically, although alphabetically within a given year. Following the primary statutory material, the book also includes a small section of some of the more significant secondary legislation and the EC product liability directive.

Francis Rose
29 January 1987

PART I
STATUTES

LIMITATION ACT 1623
(21 Jac. I, c. 16)

5. After judgment for defendant, etc., in trespas quare clausum fregit, upon disclaimer of defendant, etc., plaintiff barred of his action.
And in all accions of trespas quare clausum fregit hereafter to be brought, wherein the defendant or defendants shall disclaime in his or their plea to make any title or claime to the land in which the trespasse is by the declaracion supposed to be done, and the trespas be by negligence, or involuntary, the defendant or defendants shalbe admitted to pleade a disclaymer, and that the trespas was by negligence, or involuntary, and a tender or offer of sufficient amends for such trespase before the accion brought, whereuppon or uppon some of them, the plaintiffe or plaintiffes shalbe enforced to joyne issue; and if the said issue be found for the defendant or defendants, or the plaintiffe or plaintiffes shalbe nonsuted, the plaintiffe or plaintiffes shalbe clearlie barred from the said accion or accions and all other suite concerning the same.

STATUTE OF FRAUDS 1677
(29 Chas. II, c. 3)

4. No action against executors, etc. upon a special promise, or upon any agreement, or contract for sale of lands, etc. unless agreement, etc. be in writing and signed.
No action shall be brought [...] whereby to charge the defendant upon any speciall promise to answere for the debt default or miscarriages of another person [...] unlesse the agreement upon which such action shall be brought or some memorandum or note thereof shall be in writeing and signed by the partie to be charged therewith or some other person thereunto by him lawfully authorised.

FIRES PREVENTION (METROPOLIS) ACT 1774
(14 Geo. III, c. 78)

86. No action to lie against a person where the fire accidentally begins.
And no action, suit or process whatever shall be had, maintained or prosecuted against any person in whose house, chamber, stable, barn or other building, or on whose estate any fire shall [...] accidentally begin, nor shall any recompence be made by such person for any damage suffered thereby, any law, usage or custom to the contrary notwithstanding; [...] provided that no contract or agreement made between landlord and tenant shall be hereby defeated or made void.

LIBEL ACT 1792
(32 Geo. III, c. 60)

1. On the trial of an indictment for a libel the jury may give a general verdict upon the whole matter put in issue, and shall not be required by the court to find the defendant guilty merely on proof of the publication, and of the sense ascribed to it in the information.

On every such trial the jury sworn to try the issue may give a general verdict of guilty or not guilty upon the whole matter put in issue upon such indictment or information, and shall not be required or directed by the court or judge before whom such indictment or information shall be tried to find the defendant or defendants guilty merely on the proof of the publication by such defendant or defendants of the paper charged to be a libel, and of the sense ascribed to the same in such indictment or information.

2. But the court shall give their opinion and directions on the matter in issue as in other criminal cases.

Provided always, that on every such trial the court or judge before whom such indictment or information shall be tried shall, according to their or his discretion, give their or his opinion and directions to the jury on the matter in issue between the King and the defendant or defendants, in like manner as in other criminal cases.

STATUTE OF FRAUDS AMENDMENT ACT 1828
(9 Geo. IV, c. 14)

6. Action not maintainable on representations of character, etc., unless they be in writing signed by the party chargeable.

No action shall be brought whereby to charge any person upon or by reason of any representation or assurance made or given concerning or relating to the character, conduct, credit, ability, trade, or dealings of any other person, to the intent or purpose that such other person may obtain credit, money, or goods upon, unless such representation or assurance be made in writing, signed by the party to be charged therewith.

PARLIAMENTARY PAPERS ACT 1840
(3 & 4 Vict., c. 9)

1. Proceedings, criminal or civil, against persons for publication of papers printed by order of Parliament, to be stayed upon delivery of a certificate and affidavit to the effect that such publication is by order of either House of Parliament.

It shall and may be lawful for any person or persons who now is or are, or hereafter shall be, a defendant or defendants in any civil or criminal proceeding commenced or prosecuted in any manner soever, for or on account or in respect of the publication of any such report, paper, votes, or proceedings by such person or persons, or by his, her, or their servant or servants, by or under the authority of either House of Parliament, to bring before the court in which such proceeding shall have been or shall be so commenced or prosecuted, or before any judge of the same (if one of the superior courts at Westminster), first giving twenty-four hours notice of his intention so to do to the prosecutor or plaintiff in such proceeding, a certificate under the hand of the lord high chancellor of Great Britain, or the lord keeper of the great seal, or of the speaker of the House of Lords, for the time being, or of the clerk of the Parliaments, or of the speaker of the House of Commons, or of the clerk of the same house, stating that the report, paper, votes, or proceedings, as the case may be, in respect whereof such civil or criminal proceeding shall have been commenced or prosecuted, was published by such person or persons, or by his, her, or their servant or servants, by order or under the authority of the House of Lords or of the House of Commons, as the case may be, together with an affidavit verifying such certificate; and such court or judge shall thereupon immediately stay such civil or criminal proceeding; and the same, and every writ or process issued therein, shall be and shall be deemed and taken to be finally put an end to, determined, and superseded by virtue of this Act.

2. Proceedings to be stayed when commenced in respect of a copy of an authenticated report, etc.

In case of any civil or criminal proceeding hereafter to be commenced or prosecuted for or on account or in respect of the publication of any copy of such report, paper, votes, or proceedings, it shall be lawful for the defendant or defendants at any stage of the proceedings to lay before the court or judge such report, paper, votes, or proceedings, and such copy, with an affidavit verifying such report, paper, votes, or proceedings, and the correctness of such copy, and the court or judge shall immediately stay such civil or criminal proceedings; and the same, and every writ or process issued therein, shall be and shall be deemed and taken to be finally put an end to, determined, and superseded by virtue of this Act.

3. In proceedings for printing any extract or abstract of a paper, it may be shewn that such extract was bona fide made.

It shall be lawful in any civil or criminal proceeding to be commenced or prosecuted for printing any extract from or abstract of such report, paper, votes, or proceedings, to give in evidence [...] such report, paper, votes, or proceedings, and to show that such extract or abstract was published bona fide and without malice; and if such shall be the opinion of the jury, a verdict of not guilty shall be entered for the defendant or defendants.

4. Act not to affect the privileges of Parliament.

Provided always, that nothing herein contained shall be deemed or taken, or held or construed, directly or indirectly, by implication or otherwise, to affect the privileges of Parliament in any manner whatsoever.

LIBEL ACT 1843
(6 & 7 Vict., c.96)

1. Offer of an apology admissible in evidence of mitigation of damages in action for defamation.

In any action for defamation it shall be lawful for the defendant (after notice in writing of his intention so to do, duly given to the plaintiff at the time of filing or delivering the plea in such action,) to give in evidence, in mitigation of damages, that he made or offered an apology to the plaintiff for such defamation before the commencement of the action, or as soon afterwards as he had an opportunity of doing so, in case the action shall have been commenced before there was an opportunity of making or offering such apology.

2. In an action against a newspaper for libel, the defendant may plead that it was inserted without malice and without neglect and may pay money into court as amends.

In an action for libel contained in any public newspaper or other periodical publication it shall be competent to the defendant to plead that such libel was inserted in such newspaper or other periodical publication without actual malice, and without gross negligence, and that before the commencement of the action, or at the earliest opportunity afterwards, he inserted in such newspaper or other periodical publication a full apology for the said libel, or, if the newspaper or periodical publication in which the said libel appeared should be ordinarily published at intervals exceeding one week, had offered to publish the said apology in any newspaper or periodical publication to be selected by the plaintiff in such action; [...] and to such plea to such action it shall be competent to the plaintiff to reply generally, denying the whole of such plea.

GAMING ACT 1845
(8 & 9 Vict., c. 109)

18. Wages not recoverable at law.
All contracts or agreements, whether by parole or in writing, by way of gaming or wagering, shall be null and void; and no suit shall be brought or maintained in any court of law and equity for recovering any sum of money or valuable thing alleged to have been won upon any wager, or which shall have been deposited in the hands of any person to abide the event on which any wager shall have been made: Provided always, that this enactment shall not be deemed to apply to any subscription or contribution, or agreement to subscribe or contribute, for or towards any plate, prize or sum of money to be awarded to the winner or winners of any lawful game, sport, pastime, or exercise.

LIBEL ACT 1845
(8 & 9 Vict., c. 75)

2. Defendant not to file such plea without paying money into court by way of amends.
It shall not be competent to any defendant in such action, whether in England or Ireland, to file any such plea, without at the same time making a payment of money into court by way of amends [...], but every such plea so filed without payment of money into court shall be deemed a nullity, and may be treated as such by the plaintiff in the action.

MERCANTILE LAW AMENDMENT ACT 1856
(19 & 20 Vict., c. 97)

3. Consideration for guarantee need not appear in writing.
No special promise to be made by any person [...] to answer for the debt, default, or miscarriage or another person, being in writing, and signed by the party to be charged therewith, or some other person by him thereunto lawfully authorised, shall be deemed invalid to support an action, suit, or other proceeding to charge the person by whom such promise shall have been made, by reason only that the consideration for such promise does not appear in writing, or by necessary inference from a written document.

5. A surety who discharges the liability to be entitled to assignment of all securities held by the creditor.
Every person who, being surety for the debt or duty of another, or being liable with another for any debt or duty, shall pay such debt or perform such duty, shall be entitled to have assigned to him, or to a trustee for him, every judgment, specialty, or other security which shall be held by the creditor in respect of such debt or duty, whether such judgment, specialty, or other security shall or shall not be deemed at law to have been satisfied by the payment of the debt or performance of the duty, and such person shall be entitled to stand in the place of the creditor, and to use all the remedies, and, if need be, and upon a proper indemnity, to use the name of the creditor, in any action or other proceeding, at law or in equity, in order to obtain from the principal debtor, or any co-surety, co-contractor, or co-debtor, as the case may be, indemnification for the

advances made and loss sustained by the person who shall have so paid such debt or performed such duty, and such payment or performance so made by such surety shall not be pleadable in bar of any such action or other proceeding by him: Provided always, that no co-surety, co-contractor, or co-debtor shall be entitled to recover from any other co-surety, co-contractor, or co-debtor, by the means aforesaid, more than the just proportion to which, as between those parties themselves, such last-mentioned person shall be justly liable.

OFFENCES AGAINST THE PERSON ACT 1861
(24 & 25 Vict., c. 100)

44. If the magistrates dismiss the complaint, they shall make out a certificate to that effect.
If the Justices, upon the Hearing of any [...] Case of Assault or Battery upon the Merits, where the Complaint was preferred by or on the Behalf of the Party aggrieved, [...] shall deem the Offence not to be proved, or shall find the Assault or Battery to have been justified, or so trifling as not to merit any Punishment, and shall accordingly dismiss the Complaint, they shall forthwith make out a Certificate under their Hands stating the Fact of such Dismissal, and shall deliver such Certificate to the Party against whom the Complaint was preferred.

45. Certificate or conviction shall be a bar to any other proceedings.
If any Person, against whom any such Complaint as [is mentioned in section 44 of this Act] shall have been preferred by or on the Behalf of the Party aggrieved, shall have obtained such Certificate, or, having been convicted, shall have paid the whole Amount adjudged to be paid, or shall have suffered the Imprisonment or Imprisonment with Hard Labour awarded, in every such Case he shall be released from all further or other Proceedings, Civil or Criminal, for the same Cause.

APPORTIONMENT ACT 1870
(33 & 34 Vict., c. 35)

2. Rents, &c. to accrue from day to day and be apportionable in respect of time.
From and after the passing of this Act all rents, annuities, dividends, and other periodical payments in the nature of income (whether reserved or made payable under an instrument in writing or otherwise) shall, like interest on money lent, be considered as accruing from day to day, and shall be apportionable in respect of time accordingly.

3. Apportioned part of rent, &c. to be payable when the next entire portion shall have become due.
The apportioned part of any such rent, annuity, dividend, or other payment shall be payable or recoverable in the case of a continuing rent, annuity, or other such payment when the entire portion of which such apportioned part shall form part shall become due and payable, and not before, and in the case of a rent, annuity, or other such payment determined by re-entry, death, or otherwise when the next entire portion of the same would have been payable if the same had not so determined, and not before.

5. Interpretation of terms.
In the construction of this Act—
The word "rents" includes rent service, rentcharge, and rent seck, and also tithes and all periodical payments or renderings in lieu of or in the nature of rent or tithe.
The word "annuities" includes salaries and pensions.

The word "dividends" includes (besides dividends strictly so called) all payments made by the name of dividend, bonus, or otherwise out of the revenue of trading or other public companies, divisible between all or any of the members of such respective companies, whether such payments shall be usually made or declared at any fixed times or otherwise; and all such divisible revenue shall, for the purposes of this Act, be deemed to have accrued by equal daily increment during and within the period for or in respect of which the payment of the same revenue shall be declared or expressed to be made, but the said word "dividend" does not include payments in the nature of a return or reimbursement of capital.

6. Act not to apply to policies of assurance.
Nothing in this Act contained shall render apportionable any annual sums made payable in policies of assurance of any description.

7. Nor where stipulation made to the contrary.
The provisions of this Act shall not extend to any case in which it is or shall be expressly stipulated that no apportionment shall take place.

LAW OF LIBEL AMENDMENT ACT 1888
(51 & 52 Vict., c. 64)

4. Newspaper reports of proceedings of public meetings and of certain bodies and persons privileged.
A fair and accurate report published in any newspaper of the proceedings of a public meeting, or (except where neither the public nor any newspaper reporter is admitted) of any meeting of a vestry, town council, school board, board of guardians, board or local authority formed or constituted under the provisions of any Act of Parliament, or of any committee appointed by any of the above-mentioned bodies, or of any meeting of any commissioners authorised to act by letters patent, Act of Parliament, warrant under the Royal Sign Manual, or other lawful warrant or authority, select committees of either House of Parliament, justices of the peace in quarter sessions assembled for administrative or deliberative purposes, and the publication at the request of any Government office or department, officer of state, commissioner of police, or chief constable of any notice or report issued by them for the information of the public, shall be privileged, unless it shall be proved that such report or publication was published or made maliciously: Provided that nothing in this section shall authorise the publication of any blasphemous or indecent matter: Provided also, that the protection intended to be afforded by this section shall not be available as a defence in any proceedings if it shall be proved that the defendant has been requested to insert in the newspaper in which the report or other publication complained of appeared a reasonable letter or statement by way of contradiction or explanation of such report or other publication, and has refused or neglected to insert the same: Provided further, that nothing in this section contained shall be deemed or construed to limit or abridge any privilege now by law existing, or to protect the publication of any matter not of public concern and the publication of which is not for the public benefit.

For the purposes of this section "public meeting" shall mean any meeting bona fide and lawfully held for a lawful purpose, and for the furtherance or discussion of any matter of public concern, whether the admission thereto be general or restricted.

FACTORS ACT 1889
(52 & 53 Vict., c. 45)

1. Definitions.
For the purposes of this Act—

(1) The expression "mercantile agent" shall mean a mercantile agent having in the customary course of his business as such agent authority either to sell goods or to consign goods for the purpose of sale, or to buy goods, or to raise money on the security of goods:

(2) A person shall be deemed to be in possession of goods or of the documents of title to goods, where the goods or documents are in the actual custody or are held by any other person subject to his control or for him or on his behalf:

(3) The expression "goods" shall include wares and merchandise:

(4) The expression "document of title" shall include any bill of lading, dock warrant, warehouse-keeper's certificate, and warrant or order for the delivery of goods, and any other document used in the ordinary course of business as proof of the possession or control of goods, or authorising or purporting to authorise, either by endorsement or by delivery, the possessor of the document to transfer or receive goods thereby represented:

(5) The expression "pledge" shall include any contract pledging, or giving a lien or security on, goods, whether in consideration of an original advance or of any further or continuing advance or of any pecuniary liability:

(6) The expression "person" shall include any body of persons corporate or unincorporate.

2. Powers of mercantile agent with respect to disposition of goods.

(1) Where a mercantile agent is, with the consent of the owner, in possession of goods or of the documents of title to goods, any sale, pledge, or other disposition of the goods, made by him when acting in the ordinary course of business of a mercantile agent, shall, subject to the provisions of this Act, be as valid as if he were expressly authorised by the owner of the goods to make the same; provided that the person taking under the disposition acts in good faith, and has not at the time of the disposition notice that the person making the disposition has not authority to make the same.

(2) Where a mercantile agent has, with the consent of the owner, been in possession of goods or of the documents of title to goods, any sale, pledge, or other disposition, which would have been valid if the consent had continued, shall be valid notwithstanding the determination of the consent; provided that the person taking under the disposition has not at the time thereof notice that the consent has been determined.

(3) Where a mercantile agent has obtained possession of any documents of title to goods by reason of his being or having been, with the consent of the owner, in possession of the goods represented thereby, or of any other documents of title to the goods, his possession of the first-mentioned documents shall, for the purposes of this Act, be deemed to be with the consent of the owner.

(4) For the purposes of this Act the consent of the owner shall be presumed in the absence of evidence to the contrary.

SLANDER OF WOMEN ACT 1891
(54 & 55 Vict., c. 51)

1. Amendment of law.
Words spoken and published which impute unchastity or adultery to any woman or girl shall not require special damage to render them actionable.

Provided always, that in any action for words spoken and made actionable by this Act, a plaintiff shall not recover more costs than damages, unless the judge shall certify that there was reasonable ground for bringing the action.

GAMING ACT 1892
(55 & 56 Vict., c. 9)

1. Promises to repay sums paid under contracts void by 8 & 9 Vict. c. 109 to be null and void.

Any promise, express or implied, to pay any person any sum of money paid by him under or in respect of any contract or agreement rendered null and void by the [Gaming Act 1845] or to pay any sum of money by way of commission, fee, reward, or otherwise in respect of any such contract, or of any services in relation thereto or in connexion therewith, shall be null and void, and no action shall be brought or maintained to recover any such sum of money.

MARINE INSURANCE ACT 1906
(6 Edw. VII, c. 41)

4. Avoidance of wagering or gaming contracts.

(1) Every contract of marine insurance by way of gaming or wagering is void.

(2) A contract of marine insurance is deemed to be a gaming or wagering contract—

   (a) where the assured has not an insurable interest as defined by this Act, and the contract is entered into with no expectation of acquiring such an interest; or

   (b) where the policy is made "interest or no interest", or "without further proof of interest than the policy itself", or "without benefit of salvage to the insurer", or subject to any other like term:

Provided that, where there is no possibility of salvage, a policy may be effected without benefit of salvage to the insurer.

17. Insurance is uberrimae fidei.

A contract of marine insurance is a contract based upon the utmost good faith, and, if the utmost good faith be not observed by either party, the contract may be avoided by the other party.

18. Disclosure by assured.

(1) Subject to the provisions of this section, the assured must disclose to the insurer, before the contract is concluded, every material circumstance which is known to the assured, and the assured is deemed to know every circumstance which, in the ordinary course of business, ought to be known by him. If the assured fails to make such disclosure, the insurer may avoid the contract.

(2) Every circumstance is material which would influence the judgment of a prudent insurer in fixing the premium, or determining whether he will take the risk.

(3) In the absence of inquiry the following circumstances need not be disclosed, namely:

   (a) any circumstance which diminishes the risk;

   (b) any circumstance which is known or presumed to be known to the insurer. The insurer is presumed to know matters of common notoriety or knowledge, and matters which an insurer in the ordinary course of his business, as such, ought to know;

   (c) any circumstance as to which information is waived by the insurer;

   (d) any circumstance which it is superfluous to disclose by reason of any express or implied warranty.

(4) Whether any particular circumstance, which is not disclosed, be material or not is, in each case, a question of fact.

20. Representations pending negotiation of contract.

(1) Every material representation made by the assured or his agent to the insurer during the negotiations for the contract, and before the contract is concluded, must be true. If it be untrue the insurer may avoid the contract.

(2) A representation is material which would influence the judgment of a prudent insurer in fixing the premium, or determining whether he will take the risk.

(3) A representation may be either a representation as to a matter of fact, or as to a matter of expectation or belief.

(4) A representation as to a matter of fact is true, if it be substantially correct, that is to say, if the difference between what is represented and what is actually correct would not be considered material by a prudent insurer.

(5) A representation as to a matter of expectation or belief is true if it be made in good faith.

(6) A representation may be withdrawn or corrected before the contract is concluded.

(7) Whether a particular representation be material or not is, in each case, a question of fact.

22. Contract must be embodied in policy.

Subject to the provisions of any statute, a contract of marine insurance is inadmissible in evidence unless it is embodied in a marine policy in accordance with this Act. The policy may be executed and issued either at the time when the contract is concluded, or afterwards.

30. Construction of terms in policy.

(1) A policy may be in the form in the First Schedule to this Act.

(2) Subject to the provisions of this Act, and unless the context of the policy otherwise requires, the terms and expressions mentioned in the First Schedule to this Act shall be construed as having the scope and meaning in that schedule assigned to them.

33. Nature of warranty.

(1) A warranty, in the following sections relating to warranties, means a promissory warranty, that is to say, a warranty by which the assured undertakes that some particular thing shall or shall not be done, or that some condition shall be fulfilled, or whereby he affirms or negatives the existence of a particular state of facts.

(2) A warranty may be express or implied.

(3) A warranty, as above defined, is a condition which must be exactly complied with, whether it be material to the risk or not. If it be not so complied with, then, subject to any express provision in the policy, the insurer is discharged from liability as from the date of the breach of warranty, but without prejudice to any liability incurred by him before that date.

34. When breach of warranty excused.

(1) Non-compliance with a warranty is excused when, by reason of a change of circumstances, the warranty ceases to be applicable to the circumstances of the contract, or when compliance with the warranty is rendered unlawful by any subsequent law.

(2) Where a warranty is broken, the assured cannot avail himself of the defence that the breach has been remedied, and the warranty complied with, before loss.

(3) A breach of warranty may be waived by the insurer.

35. Express warranties.

(1) An express warranty may be in any form of words from which the intention to warrant is to be inferred.

(2) An express warranty must be included in, or written upon, the policy, or must be contained in some document incorporated by reference into the policy.

(3) An express warranty does not exclude an implied warranty, unless it be inconsistent therewith.

48. Delay in voyage.

In the case of a voyage policy, the adventure insured must be prosecuted throughout its course with reasonable dispatch, and, if without lawful excuse it is not so prosecuted, the insurer is discharged from liability as from the time when the delay became unreasonable.

49. Excuses for deviation or delay.

(1) Deviation or delay in prosecuting the voyage contemplated by the policy is excused—
   (a) where authorised by any special term in the policy; or
   (b) where caused by circumstances beyond the control of the master and his employer; or
   (c) where reasonably necessary in order to comply with an express or implied warranty; or
   (d) where reasonably necessary for the safety of the ship or subject-matter insured; or
   (e) for the purpose of saving human life, or aiding a ship in distress where human life may be in danger; or
   (f) where reasonably necessary for the purpose of obtaining medical or surgical aid for any person on board the ship; or
   (g) where caused by the barratrous conduct of the master or crew, if barratry be one of the perils insured against.

(2) When the cause excusing the deviation or delay ceases to operate, the ship must resume her course, and prosecute her voyage, with reasonable dispatch.

82. Enforcement of return.

Where the premium or a proportionate part thereof is, by this Act, declared to be returnable,—
   (a) If already paid, it may be recovered by the assured from the insurer; and
   (b) If unpaid, it may be retained by the assured or his agent.

83. Return by agreement.

Where the policy contains a stipulation for the return of the premium, or a proportionate part thereof, on the happening of a certain event, and that event happens, the premium, or, as the case may be, the proportionate part thereof, is thereupon returnable to the assured.

84. Return for failure of consideration.

(1) Where the consideration for the payment of the premium totally fails, and there has been no fraud or illegality on the part of the assured or his agents, the premium is thereupon returnable to the assured.

(2) Where the consideration for the payment of the premium is apportionable and there is a total failure of any apportionable part of the consideration, a proportionate part of the premium is, under the like conditions, thereupon returnable to the assured.

(3) In particular—
   (a) Where the policy is void, or is avoided by the insurer as from the commencement of the risk, the premium is returnable, provided that there has been no fraud or illegality on the part of the assured; but if the risk is not apportionable, and has once attached, the premium is not returnable;
   (b) Where the subject-matter insured, or part thereof, has never been imperilled, the premium, or, as the case may be, a proportionate part thereof, is returnable:

Provided that where the subject-matter has been insured 'lost or not lost' and has arrived in safety at the time when the contract is concluded, the premium is not returnable unless, at such time, the insurer knew of the safe arrival.

(c) Where the assured has no insurable interest throughout the currency of the risk, the premium is returnable, provided that this rule does not apply to a policy effected by way of gaming or wagering;

(d) Where the assured has a defeasible interest which is terminated during the currency of the risk, the premium is not returnable;

(e) Where the assured has over-insured under an unvalued policy, a proportionate part of the premium is returnable;

(f) Subject to the foregoing provisions, where the assured has over-insured by double insurance, a proportionate part of the several premiums is returnable:

Provided that, if the policies are effected at different times, and any earlier policy has at any time borne the entire risk, or if a claim has been paid on the policy in respect of the full sum insured thereby, no premium is returnable in respect of that policy, and when the double insurance is effected knowingly by the assured no premium is returnable.

87. Implied obligations varied by agreement or usage.

(1) Where any right, duty, or liability would arise under a contract of marine insurance by implication of law, it may be negatived or varied by express agreement, or by usage, if the usage be such as to bind both parties to the contract.

LAW OF PROPERTY ACT 1925
(15 & 16 Geo. V, c. 20)

41. Stipulations not of the essence of a contract.

Stipulations in a contract, as to time or otherwise, which according to rules of equity are not deemed to be or to have become of the essence of the contract, are also construed and have effect at law in accordance with the same rules.

49. Applications to the court by vendor and purchaser.

(2) Where the court refuses to grant specific performance of a contract, or in any action for the return of a deposit, the court may, if it thinks fit, order the repayment of any deposit.

(3) This section applies to a contract for the sale or exchange of any interest in land.

56. Persons taking who are not parties and as to indentures.

(1) A person may take an immediate or other interest in land or other property, or the benefit of any condition, right of entry, covenant or agreement over or respecting land or other property, although he may not be named as a party to the conveyance or other instrument.

136. Legal assignments of things in action.

(1) Any absolute assignment by writing under the hand of the assignor (not purporting to be by way of charge only) of any debt or other legal thing in action, of which express notice in writing has been given to the debtor, trustee or other person from whom the assignor would have been entitled to claim such debt or thing in action, is effectual in law (subject to equities having priority over the right of the assignee) to pass and transfer from the date of such notice—

(a) the legal right to such debt or thing in action;
(b) all legal and other remedies for the same; and
(c) the power to give a good discharge for the same without the concurrence of the assignor:

Provided that, if the debtor, trustee or other person liable in respect of such debt or thing in action has notice—

(a) that the assignment is disputed by the assignor or any person claiming under him; or

(b) of any other opposing or conflicting claims to such debt or thing in action; he may, if he thinks fit, either call upon the persons making claim thereto to interplead concerning the same, or pay the debt or other thing in action into court under the provisions of the Trustee Act 1925.

(2) This section does not affect the provisions of the Policies of Assurance Act 1867.

146. Restrictions on and relief against forfeiture of leases and underleases.

(1) A right of re-entry or forfeiture under any proviso or stipulation in a lease for a breach of any covenant or condition in the lease shall not be enforceable, by action or otherwise, unless and until the lessor serves on the lessee a notice—
    (a) specifying the particular breach complained of; and
    (b) if the breach is capable of remedy, requiring the lessee to remedy the breach; and
    (c) in any case, requiring the lessee to make compensation in money for the breach; and the lessee fails, within a reasonable time thereafter, to remedy the breach, if it is capable of remedy, and to make reasonable compensation in money, to the satisfaction of the lessor, for the breach.

(2) Where a lessor is proceeding, by action or otherwise, to enforce such a right of re-entry or forfeiture, the lessee may, in the lessor's action, if any, or in any action brought by himself, apply to the court for relief; and the court may grant or refuse relief, as the court, having regard to the proceedings and conduct of the parties under the foregoing provisions of this section, and to all the other circumstances, thinks fit; and in case of relief may grant it on such terms, if any, as to costs, expenses, damages, compensation, penalty, or otherwise, including the granting of an injunction to restrain any like breach in the future, as the court, in the circumstances of each case, thinks fit.

(11) This section does not, save as otherwise mentioned, affect the law relating to re-entry or forfeiture or relief in case of non-payment of rent.

(12) This section has effect notwithstanding any stipulation to the contrary.

205. General definitions.

(1) In this Act unless the context otherwise requires, the following expressions have the meanings hereby assigned to them respectively, that is to say: . . .
    (xvii) "Notice" includes constructive notice;
    (xx) "Property" includes any thing in action, and any interest in real or personal property;

. . .

RESERVOIRS (SAFETY PROVISIONS) ACT 1930
(20 & 21 Geo. V, c. 51)

7. Liability for damage and injury.

Where damage or injury is caused by the escape of water from a reservoir constructed after the commencement of this Act under statutory powers granted after the passing of this Act, the fact that the reservoir was so constructed shall not exonerate the undertakers from any indictment, action or other proceedings to which they would otherwise have been liable.

THIRD PARTIES (RIGHTS AGAINST INSURERS) ACT 1930
(20 & 21 Geo. V, c. 25)

1. Rights of third parties against insurers on bankruptcy, etc., of the insured.

(1) Where under any contract of insurance a person (hereinafter referred to as the insured) is insured against liabilities to third parties which he may incur, then

(a) in the event of the insured becoming bankrupt or making a composition or arrangement with his creditors; or

(b) in the case of the insured being a company, in the event of a winding-up order [or an administration order] being made, or a resolution for a voluntary winding-up being passed, with respect to the company, or of a receiver or manager of the company's business or undertaking being duly appointed, or of possession being taken, by or on behalf of the holders of any debentures secured by a floating charge, of any property comprised in or subject to that charge [or of a voluntary arrangement proposed for the purposes of Part I of the Insolvency Act 1986 being approved under that Part];

if, either before or after that event, any such liability as aforesaid is incurred by the insured, his rights against the insurer under the contract in respect of the liability shall, notwithstanding anything in any Act or rule of law to the contrary, be transferred to and vest in the third party to whom the liability was so incurred.

(2) Where [the estate of any person falls to be administered in accordance with an order under section 421 of the Insolvency Act 1986], then, if any debt provable in bankruptcy is owing by the deceased in respect of a liability against which he was insured under a contract of insurance as being a liability to a third party, the deceased debtor's rights against the insurer under the contract in respect of that liability shall, notwithstanding anything in [any such order], be transferred to and vest in the person to whom the debt is owing.

(3) In so far as any contract of insurance made after the commencement of this Act in respect of any liability of the insured to third parties purports, whether directly or indirectly, to avoid the contract or to alter the rights of the parties thereunder upon the happening to the insured of the events specified in paragraph (a) or paragraph (b) of subsection (1) of this section or upon the [estate of any person falling to be administered in accordance with an order under section 421 of the Insolvency Act 1986], the contract shall be of no effect.

(4) Upon a transfer under subsection (1) or subsection (2) of this section, the insurer shall, subject to the provisions of section three of this Act, be under the same liability to the third party as he would have been under to the insured, but—

(a) if the liability of the insurer to the insured exceeds the liability of the insured to the third party, nothing in this Act shall affect the rights of the insured against the insurer in respect of the excess; and

(b) if the liability of the insurer to the insured is less than the liability of the insured to the third party, nothing in this Act shall affect the rights of the third party against the insured in respect of the balance.

(5) For the purposes of this Act, the expression "liabilities to third parties", in relation to a person insured under any contract of insurance, shall not include any liability of that person in the capacity of insurer under some other contract of insurance.

(6) This Act shall not apply—

(a) where a company is wound up voluntarily merely for the purposes of reconstruction or of amalgamation with another company; or

(b) to any case to which subsections (1) and (2) of section seven of the Workmen's Compensation Act 1925 applies.

2. Duty to give necessary information to third parties.

(1) In the event of any person becoming bankrupt or making a composition or arrangement with his creditors, or in the event of [the estate of any person falling to be administered in accordance with an order under section 421 of the Insolvency Act 1986], or in the event of a winding-up order [or an administration order] being made, or a resolution for a voluntary winding-up being passed, with respect to any company or of a receiver or manager of the company's business or undertaking being duly appointed or of possession being taken by or on behalf of the holders of any debentures secured by

a floating charge of any property comprised in or subject to the charge it shall be the duty of the bankrupt, debtor, personal representative of the deceased debtor or company, and, as the case may be, of the trustee in bankruptcy, trustee, liquidator, [administrator], receiver, or manager, or person in possession of the property to give at the request of any person claiming that the bankrupt, debtor, deceased debtor, or company is under a liability to him such information as may be reasonably required by him for the purpose of ascertaining whether any rights have been transferred to and vested in him by this Act and for the purpose of enforcing such rights, if any, and any contract of insurance, in so far as it purports, whether directly or indirectly, to avoid the contract or to alter the rights of the parties thereunder upon the giving of any such information in the events aforesaid or otherwise to prohibit or prevent the giving thereof in the said events shall be of no effect.

[(1A) The reference in subsection (1) of this section to a trustee includes a reference to the supervisor of a voluntary arrangement proposed for the purposes of, and approved under, Part I or Part VIII of the Insolvency Act 1986.]

(2) If the information given to any person in pursuance of subsection (1) of this section discloses reasonable ground for supposing that there have or may have been transferred to him under this Act rights against any particular insurer, that insurer shall be subject to the same duty as is imposed by the said subsection on the persons therein mentioned.

(3) The duty to give information imposed by this section shall include a duty to allow all contracts of insurance, receipts for premiums, and other relevant documents in the possession or power of the person on whom the duty is so imposed to be inspected and copies thereof to be taken.

3. Settlement between insurers and insured persons.
Where the insured has become bankrupt or where in the case of the insured being a company, a winding-up order [or an administration order] has been made or a resolution for a voluntary winding-up has been passed, with respect to the company, no agreement made between the insurer and the insured after liability has been incurred to a third party and after the commencement of the bankruptcy or winding-up [or the day of the administration order], as the case may be, nor any waiver, assignment, or other disposition made by, or payment made to the insured after the commencement [or day] aforesaid shall be effective to defeat or affect the rights transferred to the third party under this Act, but those rights shall be the same as if no such agreement, waiver, assignment, disposition or payment had been made.

LAW REFORM (MISCELLANEOUS PROVISIONS) ACT 1934
(24 & 25 Geo. V, c. 41)

1. Effect of death on certain causes of action.

(1) Subject to the provisions of this section, on the death of any person after the commencement of this Act all causes of action subsisting against or vested in him shall survive against, or, as the case may be, for the benefit of, his estate. Provided that this subsection shall not apply to causes of action for defamation [...]

[(1A) The right of a person to claim under section 1A of the Fatal Accidents Act 1976 (bereavement) shall not survive for the benefit of his estate on his death.]

(2) Where a cause of action survives as aforesaid for the benefit of the estate of a deceased person, the damages recoverable for the benefit of the estate of that person:—
 [(a) shall not include—
  (i) any exemplary damages;
  (ii) any damages for loss of income in respect of any period after that person's death;]

(b) [...]

(c) where the death of that person has been caused by the act or omission which gives rise to the cause of action, shall be calculated without reference to any loss or gain to his estate consequent on his death, except that a sum in respect of funeral expenses may be included.

(4) Where damage has been suffered by reason of any act or omission in respect of which a cause of action would have subsisted against any person if that person had not died before or at the same time as the damage was suffered, there shall be deemed, for the purposes of this Act, to have been subsisting against him before his death such cause of action in respect of that act or omission as would have subsisted if he had died after the damage was suffered.

(5) The rights conferred by this Act for the benefit of the estates of deceased persons shall be in addition to and not in derogation of any rights conferred on the dependants of deceased persons by [the Fatal Accidents Act 1976 . . .] and so much of this Act as relates to causes of action against the estates of deceased persons shall apply in relation to causes of action under the said Act as it applies in relation to other causes of action not expressly excepted from the operation of subsection (1) of this section.

(6) In the event of the insolvency of an estate against which proceedings are maintainable by virtue of this section, any liability in respect of the cause of action in respect of which the proceedings are maintainable shall be deemed to be a debt provable in the administration of the estate, notwithstanding that it is a demand in the nature of unliquidated damages arising otherwise than by a contract, promise or breach of trust.

LAW REFORM (MARRIED WOMEN AND TORTFEASORS) ACT 1935
(25 & 26 Geo. V, c. 30)

3. Abolition of husband's liability for wife's torts and ante-nuptial contracts, debts and obligations.

Subject to the provisions of this Part of this Act, the husband of a married woman shall not, by reason only of his being her husband, be liable—

(a) in respect of any tort committed by her whether before or after the marriage, or in respect of any contract entered into, or debt or obligation incurred, by her before the marriage; or

(b) to be sued, or made a party to any legal proceeding brought, in respect of any such tort, contract, debt, or obligation.

4. Savings.

(2) For the avoidance of doubt it is hereby declared that nothing in this Part of this Act—

(a) renders the husband of a married woman liable in respect of any contract entered into, or debt or obligation incurred, by her after the marriage in respect of which he would not have been liable if this Act had not been passed;

(b) exempts the husband of a married woman from liability in respect of any contract entered into, or debt or obligation (not being a debt or obligation arising out of a commission of a tort) incurred, by her after the marriage in respect of which he would have been liable if this Act had not been passed;

(c) prevents a husband and wife from acquiring, holding, and disposing of, any property jointly or as tenants in common, or from rendering themselves, or being rendered, jointly liable in respect of any tort, contract, debt or obligation, and of suing and being sued either in tort or in contract or otherwise, in like manner as if they were not married;

(d) prevents the exercise of any joint power given to a husband and wife.

LAW REFORM (FRUSTRATED CONTRACTS) ACT 1943
(6 & 7 Geo. VI, c. 40)

1. Adjustment of rights and liabilities of parties to frustrated contracts.

(1) Where a contract governed by English law has become impossible of performance or been otherwise frustrated, and the parties thereto have for that reason been discharged from the further performance of the contract, the following provisions of this section shall, subject to the provisions of section two of this Act, have effect in relation thereto.

(2) All sums paid or payable to any party in pursuance of the contract before the time when the parties were so discharged (in this Act referred to as "the time of discharge") shall, in the case of sums so paid, be recoverable from him as money received by him for the use of the party by whom the sums were paid, and, in the case of sums so payable, cease to be so payable:

Provided that, if the party to whom the sums were so paid or payable incurred expenses before the time of discharge in, or for the purpose of, the performance of the contract, the court may, if it considers it just to do so having regard to all the circumstances of the case, allow him to retain or, as the case may be, recover the whole or any part of the sums so paid or payable, not being an amount in excess of the expenses so incurred.

(3) Where any party to the contract has, by reason of anything done by any other party thereto in, or for the purpose of, the performance of the contract, obtained a valuable benefit (other than a payment of money to which the last foregoing subsection applies) before the time of discharge there shall be recoverable from him by the said other party such sum (if any), not exceeding the value of the said benefit to the party obtaining it, as the court considers just, having regard to all the circumstances of the case and, in particular,—

    (a) the amount of any expenses incurred before the time of discharge by the benefited party in, or for the purpose of, the performance of the contract, including any sums paid or payable by him to any other party in pursuance of the contract and retained or recoverable by that party under the last foregoing subsection, and

    (b) the effect, in relation to the said benefit, of the circumstances giving rise to the frustration of the contract.

(4) In estimating, for the purposes of the foregoing provisions of this section, the amount of any expenses incurred by any party to the contract, the court may, without prejudice to the generality of the said provisions, include such sum as appears to be reasonable in respect of overhead expenses and in respect of any work or services performed personally by the said party.

(5) In considering whether any sum ought to be recovered or retained under the foregoing provisions of this section by any party to the contract, the court shall not take into account any sums which have, by reason of the circumstances giving rise to the frustration of the contract, become payable to that party under any contract of insurance unless there was an obligation to insure imposed by an express term of the frustrated contract or by or under any enactment.

(6) Where any person has assumed obligations under the contract in consideration of the conferring of a benefit by any other party to the contract upon any other person, whether a party to the contract or not, the court may, if in all the circumstances of the case it considers it just to do so, treat for the purposes of subsection (3) of this section any benefit so conferred as a benefit obtained by the person who has assumed the obligations as aforesaid.

2. Provision as to application of this Act.

(1) This Act shall apply to contracts, whether made before or after the commencement of this Act, as respects which the time of discharge is on or after the first day of

July, nineteen hundred and forty-three, but not to contracts as respects which the time of discharge is before the said date.

(2) This Act shall apply to contracts to which the Crown is a party in like manner as to contracts between subjects.

(3) Where any contract to which this Act applies contains any provision which, upon the true construction of the contract, is intended to have effect in the event of circumstances arising which operate, or would but for the said provision operate, to frustrate the contract, or is intended to have effect whether such circumstances arise or not, the court shall give effect to the said provision and shall only give effect to the foregoing section of this Act to such extent, if any, as appears to the court to be consistent with the said provision.

(4) Where it appears to the court that a part of any contract to which this Act applies can properly be severed from the remainder of the contract, being a part wholly performed before the time of discharge, or so performed except for the payment in respect of that part of the contract of sums which are or can be ascertained under the contract, the court shall treat that part of the contract as if it were a separate contract and had not been frustrated and shall treat the foregoing section of this Act as only applicable to the remainder of that contract.

(5) This Act shall not apply—

(a) to any charterparty, except a time charterparty or a charterparty by way of demise, or to any contract (other than a charterparty) for the carriage of goods by sea; or

(b) to any contract of insurance, save as is provided by subsection (5) of the foregoing section; or

(c) to any contract to which [section 7 of the Sale of Goods Act 1979] (which avoids contracts for the sale of specific goods which perish before the risk has passed to the buyer) applies, or to any other contract for the sale, or for the sale and delivery, of specific goods, where the contract is frustrated by reason of the fact that the goods have perished.

3. Short title and interpretation.

(1) This Act may be cited as the Law Reform (Frustrated Contracts) Act, 1943.

(2) In this Act the expression "court" means, in relation to any matter, the court or arbitrator by or before whom the matter falls to be determined.

LAW REFORM (CONTRIBUTORY NEGLIGENCE) ACT 1945
(8 & 9 Geo. VI, c. 28)

1. Apportionment of liability in case of contributory negligence.

(1) Where any person suffers damage as the result partly of his own fault and partly of the fault of any other person or persons, a claim in respect of that damage shall not be defeated by reason of the fault of the person suffering the damage, but the damages recoverable in respect thereof shall be reduced to such extent as the court thinks just and equitable having regard to the claimant's share in the responsibility of the damage: Provided that—

(a) this subsection shall not operate to defeat any defence arising under a contract;

(b) where any contract or enactment providing for the limitation of liability is applicable to the claim, the amount of damages recoverable by the claimant by virtue of this subsection shall not exceed the maximum limit so applicable.

(2) Where damages are recoverable by any person by virtue of the foregoing subsection subject to such reduction as is therein mentioned, the court shall find and record the total damages which would have been recoverable if the claimant had not been at fault.

(5) Where, in any case to which subsection (1) of this section applies, one of the persons at fault avoids liability to any other such person or his personal representative by pleading the Limitation Act, 1939, or any other enactment limiting the time within which proceedings may be taken, he shall not be entitled to recover any damages [...] from that other person or representative by virtue of the said subsection.

(6) Where any case to which subsection (1) of this section applies is tried with a jury, the jury shall determine the total damages which would have been recoverable if the claimant had not been at fault and the extent to which those damages are to be reduced.

4. Interpretation.

The following expressions have the meanings hereby respectively assigned to them, that is to say—

"court" means, in relation to any claim, the court or arbitrator by or before whom the claim falls to be determined;

"damage" includes loss of life and personal injury; [...]

"fault" means negligence, breach of statutory duty or other act or omission which gives rise to liability in tort or would, apart from this Act, give rise to the defence of contributory negligence.

CROWN PROCEEDINGS ACT 1947
(10 & 11 Geo. VI, c. 44)

2. Liability of the Crown in tort.

(1) Subject to the provisions of this Act, the Crown shall be subject to all those liabilities in tort to which, if it were a private person of full age and capacity, it would be subject—

(a) in respect of torts committed by its servants or agents;

(b) in respect of any breach of those duties which a person owes to his servants or agents at common law by reason of being their employer; and

(c) in respect of any breach of the duties attaching at common law to the ownership, occupation, possession or control of property:

Provided that no proceedings shall lie against the Crown by virtue of paragraph (a) of this subsection in respect of any act or omission of a servant or agent of the Crown unless the act or omission would apart from the provisions of this Act have given rise to a cause of action in tort against that servant or agent or his estate.

(2) Where the Crown is bound by a statutory duty which is binding also upon persons other than the Crown and its officers, then, subject to the provisions of this Act, the Crown shall, in respect of a failure to comply with that duty, be subject to all those liabilities in tort (if any) to which it would be so subject if it were a private person of full age and capacity.

10. Provisions relating to the armed forces.

(1) Nothing done or omitted to be done by a member of the armed forces of the Crown while on duty as such shall subject either him or the Crown to liability in tort for causing the death of another person, or for causing personal injury to another person, in so far as the death or personal injury is due to anything suffered by that other person while he is a member of the armed forces of the Crown if—

(a) at the time when that thing is suffered by that other person, he is either on duty as a member of the armed forces of the Crown or is, though not on duty as such, on any land, premises, ship, aircraft or vehicle for the time being used for the purposes of the armed forces of the Crown; and

(b) the [Secretary of State] certifies that his suffering that thing has been or will be treated as attributable to service for the purposes of entitlement to an award under the

Royal Warrant, Order in Council or Order of His Majesty relating to the disablement or death of members of the force of which he is a member:

Provided that this subsection shall not exempt a member of the said forces from liability in tort in any case in which the court is satisfied that the act or omission was not connected with the execution of his duties as a member of those forces.

(2) No proceedings in tort shall lie against the Crown for death or personal injury due to anything suffered by a member of the armed forces of the Crown if—

(a) that thing is suffered by him in consequence of the nature or condition of any such land, premises, ship, aircraft or vehicle as aforesaid, or in consequence of the nature or condition of any equipment or supplies used for the purposes of those forces; and

(b) the [Secretary of State] certifies as mentioned in the preceding subsection;

nor shall any act or omission of an officer of the Crown subject him to liability in tort for death or personal injury, in so far as the death or personal injury is due to anything suffered by a member of the armed forces of the Crown being a thing as to which the conditions aforesaid are satisfied.

(3) [...] a Secretary of State, if satisfied that it is the fact—

(a) that a person was or was not on any particular occasion on duty as a member of the armed forces of the Crown; or

(b) that at any particular time any land, premises, ship, aircraft, vehicle, equipment or supplies was or was not, or were or were not, used for the purposes of the said forces;

may issue a certificate certifying that to be the fact; and any such certificate shall, for the purposes of this section, be conclusive as to the fact which it certifies.

LAW REFORM (PERSONAL INJURIES) ACT 1948
(11 & 12 Geo. VI, c. 41)

1. Common employment.

(1) It shall not be a defence to an employer who is sued in respect of personal injuries caused by the negligence of a person employed by him, that that person was at the time the injuries were caused in common employment with the person injured.

(3) Any provision contained in a contract of service or apprenticeship, or in an agreement collateral thereto, (including a contract or agreement entered into before the commencement of this Act) shall be void in so far as it would have the effect of excluding or limiting any liability of the employer in respect of personal injuries caused to the person employed or apprenticed by the negligence of persons in common employment with him.

2. Measure of damges.

(4) In an action for damages for personal injuries (including any such action arising out of a contract), there shall be disregarded, in determining the reasonableness of any expenses, the possibility of avoiding those expenses or part of them by taking advantage of facilities available under the National Health Service Act, 1977, or the National Health Service (Scotland) Act, 1978, or of any corresponding facilities in Northern Ireland.

3. Definition of "personal injury".

In this Act the expression "personal injury" includes any disease and any impairment of a person's physical or mental condition, and the expression "injured" shall be construed accordingly.

NATIONAL PARKS AND ACCESS TO THE COUNTRYSIDE ACT 1949
(12, 13 & 14 Geo. VI, c. 97)

60. Rights of public where access agreement or order in force.

(1) Subject to the following provisions of this Part of this Act, where an access agreement or order is in force as respects any land a person who enters upon land comprised in the agreement or order for the purpose of open-air recreation without breaking or damaging any wall, fence, hedge or gate, or who is on such land for that purpose after having so entered thereon, shall not be treated as a trespasser on that land or incur any other liability by reason only of so entering or being on the land:

Provided that this subsection shall not apply to land which for the time being is excepted land as hereinafter defined.

(2) Nothing in the provisions of the last foregoing subsection shall entitle a person to enter or be on any land, or to do anything thereon, in contravention of any prohibition contained in or having effect under any enactment.

(3) An access agreement or order may specify or provide for imposing restrictions subject to which persons may enter or be upon land by virtue of subsection (1) of this section, including in particular, but without prejudice to the generality of this subsection, restrictions excluding the land or any part thereof at particular times from the operation of the said subsection (1); and that subsection shall not apply to any person entering or being on the land in contravention of any such restriction or failing to comply therewith while he is on the land.

66. Effect of access agreement or order on rights and liabilities of owners.

(1) A person interested in any land comprised in an access agreement or order, not being excepted land, shall not carry out any work thereon whereby the area to which the public are able to have access by virtue of the agreement or order is substantially reduced:

Provided that nothing in this subsection shall affect the doing of anything whereby any land becomes expected land.

(2) The operation of subsection (1) of section sixty of this Act in relation to any land shall not increase the liability, under any enactment not contained in this Act or under any rule of law, of a person interested in that land or adjoining land in respect of the state thereof or of things done or omitted thereon.

ARBITRATION ACT 1950
(1950, c. 27)

[13A. **Want of prosecution.**

(1) Unless a contrary intention is expressed in the arbitration agreement, the arbitrator or umpire shall have power to make an award dismissing any claim in a dispute referred to him if it appears to him that the conditions mentioned in subsection (2) are satisfied.

(2) The conditions are—
    (a) that there has been inordinate and inexcusable delay on the part of the claimant in pursuing the claim; and
    (b) that the delay—
        (i) will give rise to a substantial risk that it is not possible to have a fair resolution of the issues in that claim; or
        (ii) has caused, or is likely to cause or to have caused, serious prejudice to the respondent.]

RESERVE AND AUXILIARY FORCES (PROTECTION OF CIVIL INTERESTS) ACT 1951
(14 & 15 Geo. VI, c. 65)

13. Effect of failure to observe restrictions under Part I.

(2) In any action for damages for conversion or other proceedings which lie by virtue of any such omission, failure or contravention, the court may take account of the conduct of the defendant with a view, if the court thinks fit, to awarding exemplary damages in respect of the wrong sustained by the plaintiff.

DEFAMATION ACT 1952
(15 & 16 Geo. VI & 1 Eliz. II, c. 66)

2. Slander affecting official, professional or business reputation.

In an action for slander in respect of words calculated to disparage the plaintiff in an office, profession, calling, trade or business held or carried on by him at the time of the publication, it shall not be necessary to allege or prove special damage, whether or not the words are spoken of the plaintiff in the way of his office, profession, calling, trade or business.

3. Slander of title, etc.

(1) In an action for slander of title, slander of goods or other malicious falsehood, it shall not be necessary to allege or prove special damage—
    (a) if the words upon which the action is founded are calculated to cause pecuniary damage to the plaintiff and are published in writing or other permanent form; or
    (b) if the said words are calculated to cause pecuniary damage to the plaintiff in respect of any office, profession, calling, trade or business held or carried on by him at the time of the publication.

(2) Section one of this Act shall apply for the purposes of this section as it applies for the purposes of the law of libel and slander.

5. Justification.

In an action for libel or slander in respect of words containing two or more distinct charges against the plaintiff, a defence of justification shall not fail by reason only that the truth of every charge is not proved if the words not proved to be true do not materially injure the plaintiff's reputation having regard to the truth of the remaining charges.

6. Fair comment.

In an action for libel or slander in respect of words consisting partly of allegations of fact and partly of expression of opinion, a defence of fair comment shall not fail by reason only that the truth of every allegation or fact is not proved if the expression of opinion is fair comment having regard to such of the facts alleged or referred to in the words complained of as are proved.

9. Extension of certain defences to broadcasting.

(1) Section three of the Parliamentary Papers Act, 1840 (which confers protection in respect of proceedings for printing extracts from or abstracts of parliamentary papers) shall have effect as if the reference to printing included a reference to broadcasting by means of wireless telegraphy.

10. Limitation on privilege at elections.

A defamatory statement published by or on behalf of a candidate in any election to local government authority or to Parliament shall not be deemed to be published on a privileged occasion on the ground that it is material to a question in issue in the election, whether or not the person by whom it is published is qualified to vote at the election.

11. Agreements for indemnity.
An agreement for indemnifying any person against civil liability for libel in respect of the publication of any matter shall not be unlawful unless at the time of the publication that person knows that the matter is defamatory, and does not reasonably believe that there is a good defence to any action brought upon it.

12. Evidence of other damages recovered by plaintiff.
In any action for libel or slander the defendant may give evidence in mitigation of damages that the plaintiff has recovered damages, or has brought actions for damages, for libel or slander in respect of the publication of words to the same effect as the words on which the action is founded, or has received or agreed to receive compensation in respect of any such publication.

13. Consolidation of actions for slander etc.
Section five of the Law of Libel Amendment Act 1888 (which provides for the consolidation, on the application of the defendants, of two or more actions for libel by the same plaintiff) shall apply to actions for slander of title, slander of goods or other malicious falsehood as it applies to actions for libel; and references in that section to the same, or substantially the same, libel shall be construed accordingly.

16. Interpretation.
(1) Any reference in this Act to words shall be construed as including a reference to pictures, visual images, gestures and other methods of signifying meaning.

17. Proceedings affected and savings.
(2) Nothing in this Act affects the law relating to criminal libel.

OCCUPIERS' LIABILITY ACT 1957
(5 & 6 Eliz. II, c. 31)

1. Preliminary.
(1) The rules enacted by the two next following sections shall have effect, in place of the rules of the common law, to regulate the duty which an occupier of premises owes to his visitors in respect of dangers due to the state of the premises or to things done or omitted to be done on them.

(2) The rules so enacted shall regulate the nature of the duty imposed by law in consequence of a person's occupation or control of premises and of any invitation or permission he gives (or is to be treated as giving) to another to enter or use the premises, but they shall not alter the rules of the common law as to the persons on whom a duty is so imposed or to whom it is owed; and accordingly for the purpose of the rules so enacted the persons who are to be treated as an occupier and as his visitors are the same (subject to subsection (4) of this section) as the persons who would at common law be treated as an occupier and as his invitees or licensees.

(3) The rules so enacted in relation to an occupier of premises and his visitors shall also apply, in like manner and to the like extent as the principles applicable at common law to an occupier of premises and his invitees or licensees would apply, to regulate—

(a) the obligations of a person occupying or having control over any fixed or moveable structure, including any vessel, vehicle or aircraft; and

(b) the obligations of a person occupying or having control over any premises or structure in respect of damage to property, including the property of persons who are not themselves his visitors.

(4) A person entering any premises in exercise of rights conferred by virtue of an access agreement or order under the National Parks and Access to the Countryside Act, 1949, is not, for the purposes of this Act, a visitor of the occupier of those premises.

2. Extent of occupier's ordinary duty.

(1) An occupier of premises owes the same duty, the "common duty of care", to all his visitors, except in so far as he is free to and does extend, restrict, modify or exclude his duty to any visitor or visitors by agreement or otherwise.

(2) The common duty of care is a duty to take such care as in all the circumstances of the case is reasonable to see that the visitor will be reasonably safe in using the premises for the purposes for which he is invited or permitted by the occupier to be there.

(3) The circumstances relevant for the present purposes include the degree of care, and of want of care, which would ordinarily be looked for in such a visitor, so that (for example) in proper cases—

(a) an occupier must be prepared for children to be less careful than adults; and

(b) an occupier may expect that a person, in the exercise of his calling, will appreciate and guard against any special risks ordinarily incident to it, so far as the occupier leaves him free to do so.

(4) In determining whether the occupier of premises has discharged the common duty of care to a visitor, regard is to be had to all the circumstances, so that (for example)—

(a) where damage is caused to a visitor by a danger of which he had been warned by the occupier, the warning is not to be treated without more as absolving the occupier from liability, unless in all the circumstances it was enough to enable the visitor to be reasonably safe; and

(b) where damage is caused to a visitor by a danger due to the faulty execution of any work of construction, maintenance or repair by an independent contractor employed by the occupier, the occupier is not to be treated without more as answerable for the danger if in all the circumstances he had acted reasonably in entrusting the work to an independent contractor and had taken such steps (if any) as he reasonably ought in order to satisfy himself that the contractor was competent and that the work had been properly done.

(5) The common duty of care does not impose on an occupier any obligation to a visitor in respect of risks willingly accepted as his by the visitor (the question whether a risk was so accepted to be decided on the same principles as in other cases in which one person owes a duty of care to another).

(6) For the purposes of this section, persons who enter premises for any purpose in the exercise of a right conferred by law are to be treated as permitted by the occupier to be there for that purpose, whether they in fact have his permission or not.

3. Effect of contract on occupier's liability to third party.

(1) Where an occupier of premises is bound by contract to permit persons who are strangers to the contract to enter or use the premises, the duty of care which he owes to them as his visitors cannot be restricted or excluded by that contract, but (subject to any provision of the contract to the contrary) shall include the duty to perform his obligations under the contract, whether undertaken for their protection or not, in so far as those obligations go beyond the obligations otherwise involved in that duty.

(2) A contract shall not by virtue of this section have the effect, unless it expressly so provides, of making an occupier who has taken all reasonable care answerable to strangers to the contract for dangers due to the faulty execution of any work of construction, maintenance or repair or other like operation by persons other than himself, his servants and persons acting under his direction and control.

(3) In this section, "stranger to the contract" means a person not for the time being entitled to the benefit of the contract as a party to it or as the successor by assignment or otherwise of a party to it, and accordingly includes a party to the contract who has ceased to be so entitled.

(4) Where by the terms or conditions governing any tenancy (including a statutory tenancy which does not in law amount to a tenancy) either the landlord or the tenant is bound, though not by contract, to permit persons to enter or use premises of which he is the occupier, this section shall apply as if the tenancy were a contract between the landlord and the tenant.

(5) This section, in so far as it prevents the common duty of care from being restricted or excluded, applies to contracts entered into and tenancies created before the commencement of this Act, as well as to those entered into or created after its commencement; but, in so far as it enlarges the duty owed by an occupier beyond the common duty of care, it shall have effect only in relation to obligations which are undertaken after the commencement or which are renewed by agreement (whether express or implied) after that commencement.

5. Implied term in contracts.

(1) Where persons enter or use, or bring or send goods to, any premises in exercise of a right conferred by contract with a person occupying or having control of the premises, the duty he owes them in respect of dangers due to the state of the premises or to things done or omitted to be done by them, in so far as the duty depends on a term to be implied in the contract by reason of its conferring that right, shall be the common duty of care.

(2) The foregoing subsection shall apply to fixed and moveable structures as it applies to premises.

(3) This section does not affect the obligations imposed on a person by or by virtue of any contract for the hire of, or for the carriage for reward of persons or goods in, any vehicle, vessel, aircraft or other means of transport, or by virtue of any contract of bailment.

(4) This section does not apply to contracts entered into before the commencement of this Act.

PUBLIC BODIES (ADMISSION TO MEETINGS) ACT 1960
(8 & 9 Eliz. II, c. 67)

1. Admission to public meetings of local authorities and other bodies.

(5) Where a meeting of a body is required by this Act to be open to the public during the proceedings or any part of them, and there is supplied to a member of the public attending the meeting, or in pursuance of paragraph (b) of subsection (4) above there is supplied for the benefit of a newspaper, any such copy of the agenda as is mentioned in that paragraph, with or without further statements or particulars for the purpose of indicating the nature of any item included in the agenda, the publication thereby of any defamatory matter contained in the agenda or in the further statements or particulars shall be privileged, unless the publication is proved to be made with malice.

LAW REFORM (HUSBAND AND WIFE) ACT 1962
(10 & 11 Eliz. II, c. 48)

1. Actions in tort between husband and wife.

(1) Subject to the provisions of this section, each of the parties to a marriage shall have the like right of action in tort against the other as if they were not married.

(2) Where an action in tort is brought by one of the parties to a marriage against the other during the subsistence of the marriage, the court may stay the action if it appears—

(a) that no substantial benefit would accrue to either party from the continuation of the proceedings; or

(b) that the question or questions in issue could more conveniently be disposed of on an application made under section seventeen of the Married Women's Property Act 1882 (determination of questions between husband and wife as to the title to or possession of property);

and without prejudice to paragraph (b) of this subsection the court may, in such an action, either exercise any power which could be exercised on an application under that said section seventeen, or give such directions as it thinks fit for the disposal under that section of any question arising in the proceedings.

PLANT VARIETIES AND SEEDS ACT 1964
(1964, c. 14)

17. Civil liabilities of sellers of seeds.

(1) If and so far as seeds regulations provide that a statutory statement shall constitute a statutory warranty for the purposes of this section, the statutory statement, when received by the purchaser, shall, notwithstanding any contract or notice to the contrary, have effect as a written warranty by the seller that the particulars contained in the statutory statement are correct.

(2) If and so far as seeds regulations apply this subsection to the particulars in a statutory statement and prescribe limits of variation in relation to those particulars, those particulars shall, for the purposes of any legal proceedings on a contract for the sale of the seeds to which the statutory statement relates, be deemed to be true except so far as there is a mis-statement in the statutory particulars which exceeds the limits of variation so prescribed.

(3) If and so far as seeds regulations apply this subsection to the particulars in a statutory statement, the particulars in the statutory statement shall, for the purposes of any legal proceedings on a contract for the sale of the seeds to which the statutory statement relates, be deemed to be true unless it is made to appear on a test carried out at an official testing station, and made on a sample taken in the manner, and within the period, prescribed by seeds regulations, that the particulars were untrue.

(5) A contravention of seeds regulations shall not effect the validity of a contract for the sale of seeds, or the right to enforce such a contract.

NUCLEAR INSTALLATIONS ACT 1965
(1965, c. 57)

7. Duty of licensee of licensed site.

(1) Where a nuclear site licence has been granted in respect of any site, it shall be the duty of the licensee to secure that—

(a) no such occurrence involving nuclear matter as is mentioned in subsection (2) of this section causes injury to any person or damage to any property of any person other than the licensee, being injury or damage arising out of or resulting from the radioactive properties, or a combination of those and any toxic, explosive or other hazardous properties, of that nuclear matter; and

(b) no ionising radiations emitted during the period of the licensee's responsibility—

(i) from anything caused or suffered by the licensee to be on the site which is not nuclear matter; or

(ii) from any waste discharged (in whatever form) on or from the site,

cause injury to any person or damage to any property of any person other than the licensee.

(2) The occurrences referred to in subsection (1)(a) of this section are—

(a) any occurrence on the licensed site during the period of the licensee's responsibility, being an occurrence involving nuclear matter;

(b) any occurrence elsewhere than on the licensed site involving nuclear matter which is not excepted matter and which at the time of the occurrence—

    (i) is in the course of carriage on behalf of the licensee as licensee of that site; or

    (ii) is in the course of carriage to that site with the agreement of the licensee from a place outside the relevant territories; and

    (iii) in either case, is not on any other relevant site in the United Kingdom;

(c) any occurrence elsewhere than on the licensed site involving nuclear matter which is not excepted matter and which—

    (i) having been on the licensed site at any time during the period of the licensee's responsibility; or

    (ii) having been in the course of carriage on behalf of the licensee as licensee of that site,

has not subsequently been on any relevant site, or in the course of any relevant carriage, or (except in the course of relevant carriage) within the territorial limits of a country which is not a relevant territory.

(3) In determining the liability by virtue of subsection (1) of this section in respect of any occurrence of the licensee of a licensed site, any property which at the time of the occurrence is on that site, being—

(a) a nuclear installation; or

(b) other property which is on that site—

    (i) for the purpose of use in connection with the operation, or the cessation of the operation, by the licensee of a nuclear installation which is or has been on that site; or

    (ii) for the purpose of the construction of a nuclear installation on that site,

shall, notwithstanding that it is the property of some other person, be deemed to be the property of the licensee.

9. Duty of Crown in respect of certain sites.

If a government department uses any site for any purpose which, if section 1 of this Act applied to the Crown, would require the authority of a nuclear site licence in respect of that site, section 7 of this Act shall apply in like manner as if—

(a) the Crown were the licensee under a nuclear site licence in respect of that site; and

(b) any reference to the period of the licensee's responsibility were a reference to any period during which the department occupies this site.

12. Right to compensation by virtue of ss. 7 to 10.

(1) Where any injury or damage has been caused in breach of a duty imposed by section 7, 8, 9 or 10 of this Act—

(a) subject to sections 13(1), (3) and (4), 15 and 17(1) of this Act, compensation in respect of that injury or damage shall be payable in accordance with section 16 of this Act wherever the injury or damage was incurred;

(b) subject to subsections (3) and (4) of this section and to section 21(2) of this Act, no other liability shall be incurred by any person in respect of that injury or damage.

(2) Subject to subsection (3) of this section, any injury or damage which, though not caused in breach of such a duty as aforesaid, is not reasonably separable from injury or damage so caused shall be deemed for the purposes of subsection (1) of this section to have been so caused.

(3) Where any injury or damage is caused partly in breach of such a duty as aforesaid and partly by an emission of ionising radiations which does not constitute such a breach, subsection (2) of this section shall not affect any liability of any person in respect of that

emission apart from this Act, but a claimant shall not be entitled to recover compensation in respect of the same injury or damage both under this Act and otherwise than under this Act.

13. Exclusion, extension or reduction of compensation in certain cases.

(1) Subject to subsections (2) and (5) of this section, compensation shall not be payable under this Act in respect of injury or damage caused by a breach of a duty imposed by section 7, 8, 9 or 10 thereof if the injury or damage—

(a) was caused by such an occurrence as is mentioned in section 7(2)(b) or (c) or 10(2)(b) of this Act which is shown to have taken place wholly within the territorial limits of one, and one only, of the relevant territories other than the United Kingdom; or

(b) was incurred within the territorial limits of a country which is not a relevant territory.

(2) In the case of a breach of a duty imposed by section 7, 8 or 9 of this Act, subsection (1)(b) of this section shall not apply to injury or damage incurred by, or by persons or property on, a ship or aircraft registered in the United Kingdom.

(4) The duty imposed by section 7, 8, 9, 10 or 11 of this Act—

(a) shall not impose any liability on the person subject to that duty with respect to injury or damage caused by an occurrence which constitutes a breach of that duty if the occurrence, or the causing thereby of the injury or damage, is attributable to hostile action in the course of any armed conflict, including any armed conflict within the United Kingdom; but

(b) shall impose such a liability where the occurrence, or the causing thereby of the injury or damage, is attributable to a natural disaster, notwithstanding that the disaster is of such an exceptional character that it could not reasonably have been foreseen.

(6) The amount of compensation payable to or in respect of any person under this Act in respect of any injury or damage caused in breach of a duty imposed by section 7, 8, 9 or 10 of this Act may be reduced by reason of the fault of that person if, but only if, and to the extent that, the causing of that injury or damage is attributable to any act of that person committed with the intention of causing harm to any person or property or with reckless disregard for the consequences of his act.

15. Time for bringing claims under ss. 7 to 11.

(1) Subject to subsection (2) of this section and to section 16(3) of this Act, but notwithstanding anything in any other enactment, a claim by virtue of any of sections 7 to 11 of this Act may be made at any time before, but shall not be entertained if made at any time after, the expiration of thirty years from the relevant date, that is to say, the date of the occurrence which gave rise to the claim or, where that occurrence was a continuing one, or was one of a succession of occurrences all attributable to a particular happening on a particular relevant site or to the carrying out from time to time on a particular relevant site of a particular operation, the date of the last event in the course of that occurrence or succession of occurrences to which the claim relates.

(2) Notwithstanding anything in subsection (1) of this section, a claim in respect of injury or damage caused by an occurrence involving nuclear matter stolen from, or lost, jettisoned or abandoned by, the person whose breach of a duty imposed by section 7, 8, 9 or 10 of this Act gave rise to the claim shall not be entertained if the occurrence takes place after the expiration of the period of twenty years beginning with the day when the nuclear matter in question was so stolen, lost, jettisoned or abandoned.

16. Satisfaction of claims by virtue of ss. 7 to 10.

(1) The liability of any person to pay compensation under this Act by virtue of a duty imposed on that person by section 7, 8 or 9 thereof shall not require him to make

in respect of any one occurrence constituting a breach of that duty payments by way of such compensation exceeding in the aggregate, apart from payments in respect of interest or costs, [£20 million or, in the case of the licensees of such sites as may be prescribed, £5 million.]

[(1A) The Secretary of State may be with the approval of the Treasury by order increase or further increase either or both of the amounts specified in subsection (1) of this section; but an order under this subsection shall not affect liability in respect of any occurrence before (or beginning before) the order comes into force.]

(3) Any claim by virtue of a duty imposed on any person by section 7, 8, 9 or 10 of this Act—

(a) to the extent to which, by virtue of subsection (1) or (2) of this section, though duly established, it is not or would not be payable by that person; or

(b) which is made after the expiration of the relevant period; or

(c) which, being such a claim as is mentioned in section 15(2) of this Act, is made after the expiration of the period of twenty years so mentioned; or

(d) which is a claim the full satisfaction of which out of funds otherwise required to be, or to be made, available for the purpose is prevented by section 21(1) of this Act, shall be made to the appropriate authority, that is to say—

(i) in the case of a claim by virtue of the said section 8, the Minister of Technology;

(ii) in the case of a claim by virtue of the said section 9 (other than a claim in connection with a site used by a department of the Government of Northern Ireland), the Minister in charge of the government department concerned;

(iii) in any other case, the Minister,

and, if established to the satisfaction of the appropriate authority, and to the extent to which it cannot be satisfied out of sums made available for the purpose under section 18 of this Act or by means of a relevant foreign contribution, shall be satisfied by the appropriate authority to such extent and out of funds provided by such means as Parliament may determine.

(4) Where in pursuance of subsection (3) of this section a claim has been made to the appropriate authority, any question affecting the establishment of the claim or as to the amount of any compensation in satisfaction of the claim may, if the authority thinks fit, be referred for decision to the appropriate court, that is to say, to whichever of the High Court, the Court of Session and the High Court of Justice in Northern Ireland would, but for the provisions of this section, have had jurisdiction in accordance with section 17(1) and (2) of this Act to determine the claim; and the claimant may appeal to that court from any decision of the authority on any such question which is not so referred; and on any such reference or appeal—

(a) the authority shall be entitled to appear and be heard; and

(b) notwithstanding anything in any Act, the decision of the court shall be final.

(5) In this section, the expression "the relevant period" means the period of ten years beginning with the relevant date within the meaning of section 15(1) of this Act.

18. General cover for compensation by virtue of ss. 7 to 10.

(1) In the case of any occurrence in respect of which one or more persons incur liability by virtue of section 7, 8, 9 or 10 of this Act or by virtue of any relevant foreign law made for purposes corresponding to those of any of those sections, but subject to subsections (2) [to (4B)] of this section and to sections 17(3)(b) and 21(1) of this Act, there shall be made available out of moneys provided by Parliament such sums as, when aggregated—

(a) with any funds required by, or by any relevant foreign law made for purposes corresponding to those of, section 19(1) of this Act to be available for the purpose of satisfying claims in respect of that occurrence against any licensee or relevant foreign operator; and

(b) in the case of a claim by virtue of any such foreign law, with any relevant foreign contributions towards the satisfaction of claims in respect of that occurrence, may be necessary to ensure that all claims in respect of that occurrence made within the relevant period and duly established, excluding, but without prejudice to, any claim in respect of interest or costs, are satisfied up to [the aggregate amount specified in subsection (1A) of this section; and

(c) in the case of an occurrence in respect of which the Authority incurs liability, with any amounts payable under a contract of insurance or other arrangements for satisfying claims in respect of that occurrence against the Authority,]

[(1A) The aggregate amount referred to in subsection (1) of this section is the equivalent in sterling of 300 million special drawing rights on —

(a) the day (or first day) of the occurrence in question, or

(b) if the Secretary of State certifies that another day has been fixed in relation to the occurrence in accordance with an international agreement, that other day.]

[*Subsection (1B) provides for subsection (1A) similarly to s. 16(1A)'s provision for s. 16(1).*]

19. Special cover for licensee's liability.

(1) Subject to section 3(5) of this Act and to subsection (3) of this section, where a nuclear site licence has been granted in respect of any site, the licensee shall make such provision (either by insurance or by some other means) as the Minister may with the consent of the Treasury approve for sufficient funds to be available at all times to ensure that any claims which have been or may be duly established against the licensee as licensee of that site by virtue of section 7 of this Act or any relevant foreign law made for purposes corresponding to those of section 10 of this Act (excluding, but without prejudice to, any claim in respect of interest or costs) are satisfied up to [the required amount] in respect of each severally of the following periods, that is to say—

(a) the current cover period, if any;

(b) any cover period which ended less than ten years before the time in question;

(c) any earlier cover period in respect of which a claim remains to be disposed of, being a claim made—

(i) within the relevant period within the meaning of section 16 of this Act; and

(ii) in the case of a claim such as is mentioned in section 15(2) of this Act, also within the period of twenty years so mentioned;

and for the purposes of this section the cover period in respect of which any claim is to be treated as being made shall be that in which the beginning of the relevant period aforesaid fell.

[(1A) In this section "the required amount", in relation to the provision to be made by a licensee in respect of a cover period, means an aggregate amount equal to the amount applicable under section 16(1) of this Act to the licensee, as licensee of the site in question, in respect of an occurrence within that period.]

CRIMINAL LAW ACT 1967
(1967, c. 58)

3. Use of force in making arrest, etc.

(1) A person may use such force as is reasonable in the circumstances in the prevention of crime, or in effecting or assisting in the lawful arrest of offenders or suspected offenders or of persons unlawfully at large.

14. Civil rights in respect of maintenance and champerty.

(1) No person shall, under the law of England and Wales, be liable in tort for any conduct on account of its being maintenance or champerty as known to the common law, except in the case of a cause of action accruing before this section has effect.

(2) The abolition of criminal and civil liability under the law of England and Wales for maintenance and champerty shall not affect any rule of that law as to the cases in which a contract is to be treated as contrary to public policy or otherwise illegal.

MISREPRESENTATION ACT 1967
(1967, c. 7)

1. Removal of certain bars to rescission for innocent misrepresentation.
Where a person has entered into a contract after a misrepresentation has been made to him, and—
   (a) the misrepresentation has become a term of the contract; or
   (b) the contract has been performed;
or both, then, if otherwise he would be entitled to rescind the contract without alleging fraud, he shall be so entitled, subject to the provisions of this Act, notwithstanding the matters mentioned in paragraphs (a) and (b) of this section.

2. Damages for misrepresentation.
   (1) Where a person has entered into a contract after a misrepresentation has been made to him by another party thereto and as a result thereof he has suffered loss, then, if the person making the misrepresentation would be liable to damages in respect thereof had the misrepresentation been made fraudulently, that person shall be so liable notwithstanding that the misrepresentation was not made fraudulently, unless he proves that he had reasonable ground to believe and did believe up to the time the contract was made that the facts represented were true.
   (2) Where a person has entered into a contract after a misrepresentation has been made to him otherwise than fraudulently, and he would be entitled, by reason of the misrepresentation, to rescind the contract, then, if it is claimed, in any proceedings arising out of the contract, that the contract ought to be or has been rescinded, the court or arbitrator may declare the contract subsisting and award damages in lieu of rescission, if of opinion that it would be equitable to do so, having regard to the nature of the misrepresentation and the loss that would be caused by it if the contract were upheld, as well as to the loss that rescission would cause to the other party.
   (3) Damages may be awarded against a person under subsection (2) of this section whether or not he is liable to damages under subsection (1) thereof, but where he is so liable any award under the said subsection (2) shall be taken into account in assessing his liability under the said subsection (1).

3. Avoidance of provision excluding liability for misrepresentation.
[If a contract contains a term which would exclude or restrict—
   (a) any liability to which a party to a contract may be subject by reason of any misrepresentation made by him before the contract was made; or
   (b) any remedy available to another party to the contract by reason of such a misrepresentation,
that term shall be of no effect except in so far as it satisfies the requirement of reasonableness as stated in section 11(1) of the Unfair Contract Terms Act 1977; and it is for those claiming that the term satisfies that requirement to show that it does.]

4. Amendments of Sale of Goods Act 1893
...

5. Saving for past transactions.
Nothing in this Act shall apply in relation to any misrepresentation or contract of sale which is made before the commencement of this Act.

PARLIAMENTARY COMMISSIONER ACT 1967
(1967, c. 13)

10. Reports by Commissioner.

(5) For the purposes of the law of defamation, any such publication as is hereinafter mentioned shall be absolutely privileged, that is to say—

   (a) the publication of any matter by the Commissioner in making a report to either House of Parliament for the purposes of this Act;

   (b) the publication of any matter by a member of the House of Commons in communicating with the Commissioner or his officers for those purposes or by the Commissioner or his officers in communicating with such a member for those purposes;

   (c) the publication by such a member to the person by whom a complaint was made under this Act of a report or statement sent to the member in respect of the complaint in pursuance of subsection (1) of this section;

   (d) the publication by the Commissioner to such a person as is mentioned in subsection (2) of this section of a report sent to that person in pursuance of that subsection.

CIVIL EVIDENCE ACT 1968
(1968, c. 64)

11. Convictions as evidence in civil proceedings.

(1) In any civil proceedings the fact that a person has been convicted of an offence by or before any court in the United Kingdom or by a court-martial there or elsewhere shall (subject to subsection (3) below) be admissible in evidence for the purpose of proving where to do so is relevant to any issue in those proceedings, that he committed that offence, whether he was so convicted upon a plea of guilty or otherwise and whether or not he is a party to the civil proceedings; but no conviction other than a subsisting one shall be admissible in evidence by virtue of this section.

(2) In any civil proceedings in which by virtue of this section a person is proved to have been convicted of an offence by or before any court in the United Kingdom or by a court-martial there or elsewhere—

   (a) he shall be taken to have committed that offence unless the contrary is proved; and

   (b) without prejudice to the reception of any other admissible evidence for the purpose of identifying the facts on which the conviction was based, the contents of any documents which is admissible as evidence of the conviction, and the contents of the information, complaint, indictment or charge-sheet on which the person in question was convicted, shall be admissible in evidence for that purpose.

(3) Nothing in this section shall prejudice the operation of section 13 of this Act or any other enactment whereby a conviction or a finding of fact in any criminal proceedings is for the purposes of any other proceedings made conclusive evidence of any fact.

(4) Where in any civil proceedings the contents of any document are admissible in evidence by virtue of subsection (2) above, a copy of that document, or of the material part thereof, purporting to be certified or otherwise authenticated by or on behalf of the court or authority having custody of that document shall be admissible in evidence and shall be taken to be a true copy of that document or part unless the contrary is shown.

13. Conclusiveness of convictions for purposes of defamation actions.

(1) In an action for libel or slander in which the question whether [the plaintiff] did or did not commit a criminal offence is relevant to an issue arising in the action, proof

that at the time when that issue falls to be determined, [he] stands convicted of that offence shall be conclusive evidence that he committed that offence; and his conviction thereof shall be admissible in evidence accordingly.

(2) In any such action as aforesaid in which by virtue of this section [the plaintiff] is proved to have been convicted of an offence, the contents of any document which is admissible as evidence of the conviction, and the contents of the information, complaint, indictment or charge-sheet on which [he] was convicted, shall, without prejudice to the reception of any other admissible evidence for the purpose of identifying the facts on which the conviction was based, be admissible in evidence for the purpose of identifying those facts.

[(2A) In the case of an action for libel or slander in which there is more than one plaintiff—

(a) the references in subsections (1) and (2) above to the plaintiff shall be construed as references to any of the plaintiffs, and

(b) proof that any of the plaintiffs stands convicted of an offence shall be conclusive evidence that he committed that offence so far as that fact is relevant to any issue arising in relation to his cause of action or that of any other plaintiff.]

(3) For the purposes of this section a person shall be taken to stand convicted of an offence if but only if there subsists against him a conviction of that offence by or before a court in the United Kingdom or by a court-martial there or elsewhere.

(4) Subsections (4) to (6) of section 11 of this Act shall apply for the purposes of this section as they apply for the purposes of that section, but as if in the said subsection (4) the reference to subsection (2) were a reference to subsection (2) of this section.

THEATRES ACT 1968
(1968, c. 54)

4. Amendment of law of defamation.

(1) For the purposes of the law of libel and slander (including the law of criminal libel so far as it relates to the publication of defamatory matter) the publication of words in the course of a performance of a play shall, subject to section 7 of this Act, be treated as publication in permanent form.

(2) The foregoing subsection shall apply for the purposes of section 3 (slander of title, etc.) of the Defamation Act 1952 as it applies for the purposes of the law of libel and slander.

(3) In this section "words" includes pictures, visual images, gestures and other methods of signifying meaning.

7. Exceptions for performances given in certain circumstances.

(1) Nothing in sections 2 to 4 of this Act shall apply in relation to a performance of a play given on a domestic occasion in a private dwelling.

THEFT ACT 1968
(1968, c. 60)

28. Orders for restitution.

[(1) Where goods have been stolen, and either a person is convicted of any offence with reference to the theft (whether or not the stealing is the gist of his offence) or a person is convicted of any other offence but such an offence as aforesaid is taken into consideration in determining his sentence, the court by or before which the offender is convicted may on the conviction [(whether or not the passing of sentence is in other respects deferred)] exercise any of the following powers—

(a) the court may order anyone having possession or control of the goods to restore them to any person entitled to recover them from him; or

(b) on the application of a person entitled to recover from the person convicted any other goods directly or indirectly representing the first-mentioned goods (as being the proceeds of any disposal or realisation of the whole or part of them or of goods so representing them), the court may order those other goods to be delivered or transferred to the applicant; or

(c) the court may order that a sum not exceeding the value of the first-mentioned goods shall be paid, out of any money of the person convicted which was taken out of his possession on his apprehension, to any person who, if those goods were in the possession of the person convicted, would be entitled to recover them from him.

(2) Where under subsection (1) above the court has power on a person's conviction to make an order against him both under paragraph (b) and under paragraph (c) with reference to the stealing of the same goods, the court may make orders under both paragraphs provided that the person in whose favour the orders are made does not thereby recover more than the value of those goods.

(3) Where under subsection (1) above the court on a person's conviction makes an order under paragraph (a) for the restoration of any goods, and it appears to the court that the person convicted has sold the goods to a person acting in good faith, or has borrowed money on the security of them from a person so acting, the court may order that there shall be paid to the purchaser or lender, out of any money of the person convicted which was taken out of his possession on his apprehension, a sum not exceeding the amount paid for the purchase by the purchaser or, as the case may be, the amount owed to the lender in respect of the loan.]

(4) The court shall not exercise the powers conferred by this section unless in the opinion of the court the relevant facts sufficiently appear from evidence given at the trial or the available documents, together with admissions made by or on behalf of any person in connection with any proposed exercise of the powers; and for this purpose 'the available documents' means any written statements or admissions which were made for use, and would have been admissible, as evidence at the trial, [and such written statements, depositions and other documents as were tendered by or on behalf of the prosecutor at any committal proceedings].

(5) Any order under this section shall be treated as an order for the restitution of property within the meaning of [section 30 of the Criminal Appeal Act 1968 (which relates to the effect on such orders of appeals)].

(6) References in this section to stealing are to be construed in accordance with section 24(1) and (4) of this Act.

[(7) An order may be made under this section in respect of money owed by the Crown.]

TRADE DESCRIPTIONS ACT 1968
(1968, c. 29)

1. Prohibition of false trade descriptions.

(1) Any person who, in the course of a trade or business,—

(a) applies a false trade description to any goods; or

(b) supplies or offers to supply any goods to which a false trade description is applied;

shall, subject to the provisions of this Act, be guilty of an offence.

2. Trade description.

(1) A trade description is an indication, direct or indirect, and by whatever means given, of any of the following matters with respect to any goods or parts of goods, that is to say—

(a) quantity, size or gauge;
(b) method of manufacture, production, processing or re-conditioning;
(c) composition;
(d) fitness for purpose, strength, performance, behaviour or accuracy;
(e) any physical characteristics not included in the preceding paragraphs;
(f) testing by any person and results thereof;
(g) approval by any person or conformity with a type approved by any person;
(h) place or date of manufacture, production, processing or reconditioning;
(i) person by whom manufactured, produced, processed or reconditioned;
(j) other history, including previous ownership or use.

3. False trade description.
(1) A false trade description is a trade description which is false to a material degree.

(2) A trade description which, though not false, is misleading, that is to say, likely to be taken for such an indication of any of the matters specified in section 2 of this Act as would be false to a material degree, shall be deemed to be a false trade description.

(3) Anything which, though not a trade description, is likely to be taken for an indication of any of those matters and, as such an indication, would be false to a material degree, shall be deemed to be a false trade description.

(4) A false indication, or anything likely to be taken as an indication which would be false, that any goods comply with a standard specified or recognised by any person or implied by the approval of any person shall be deemed to be a false trade description, if there is no such person or no standard so specified, recognised or implied.

6. Offer to supply.
A person exposing goods for supply or having goods in his possession for supply shall be deemed to offer to supply them.

35. Saving for civil rights.
A contract for the supply of any goods shall not be void or unenforceable by reason only of a contravention of any provision of this Act.

EMPLOYERS' LIABILITY (COMPULSORY INSURANCE) ACT 1969
(1969, c. 57)

1. Insurance against liability for employees.
(1) Except as otherwise provided by this Act, every employer carrying on any business in Great Britain shall insure, and maintain insurance, under one or more approved policies with an authorised insurer or insurers against liability for bodily injury or disease sustained by his employees, and arising out of and in the course of their employment in Great Britain in that business, but except in so far as regulations otherwise provide not including injury or disease suffered or contracted outside Great Britain.

(2) Regulations may provide that the amount for which an employer is required by this Act to insure and maintain insurance shall, either generally or in such cases or classes of case as may be prescribed by the regulations, be limited in such manner as may be so prescribed.

2. Employees to be covered.
(1) For the purposes of this Act the term "employee" means an individual who has entered into or works under a contract of service or apprenticeship with an employer whether by way of manual labour, clerical work or otherwise, whether such contract is expressed or implied, oral or in writing.

(2) This Act shall not require an employer to insure —

(a) in respect of an employee of whom the employer is the husband, wife, father, mother, grandfather, grandmother, step-father, step-mother, son, daughter, grandson, granddaughter, stepson, stepdaughter, brother, sister, half-brother, half-sister; or

(b) except as otherwise provided by regulations, in respect of employees not ordinarily resident in Great Britain.

EMPLOYER'S LIABILITY (DEFECTIVE EQUIPMENT) ACT 1969
(1969, c. 37)

1. **Extension of employer's liability for defective equipment.**

(1) Where after the commencement of this Act—

(a) an employee suffers personal injury in the course of his employment in consequence of a defect in equipment provided by his employer for the purposes of the employer's business; and

(b) the defect is attributable wholly or partly to the fault of a third party (whether identified or not),

the injury shall be deemed to be also attributable to negligence on the part of the employer (whether or not he is liable in respect of the injury apart from this subsection), but without prejudice to the law relating to contributory negligence and to any remedy by way of contribution or in contract or otherwise which is available to the employer in respect of the injury.

(2) In so far as any agreement purports to exclude or limit any liability of an employer arising under subsection (1) of this section, the agreement shall be void.

(3) In this section—

"business" includes the activities carried on by any public body;

"employee" means a person who is employed by another person under a contract of service or apprenticeship and is so employed for the purposes of a business carried on by that other person, and "employer" shall be construed accordingly;

"equipment" includes any plant and machinery, vehicle, aircraft and clothing;

"fault" means negligence, breach of statutory duty or other act or omission which gives rise to liability in England and Wales or which is wrongful and gives rise to liability in damages in Scotland; and

"personal injury" includes loss of life, any impairment of a person's physical or mental condition and any disease.

(4) This section binds the Crown, and persons in the service of the Crown shall accordingly be treated for the purposes of this section as employees of the Crown if they would not be so treated apart from this subsection.

ADMINISTRATION OF JUSTICE ACT 1970
(1970, c. 31)

40. **Punishment for unlawful harassment of debtors.**

(1) A person commits an offence if, with the object of coercing another person to pay money claimed from the other as a debt due under a contract, he—

(a) harasses the other with demands for payment which, in respect of their frequency or the manner or occasion of making any such demand, or of any threat or publicity by which any demand is accompanied, are calculated to subject him or members of his family or household to alarm, distress or humiliation;

(b) falsely represents, in relation to the money claimed, that criminal proceedings lie for failure to pay it;

(c) falsely represents himself to be authorised in some official capacity to claim or enforce payment; or

(d) utters a document falsely represented by him to have some official character or purporting to have some official character which he knows it has not.

(2) A person may be guilty of an offence by virtue of subsection (1)(a) above if he concerts with others in the taking of such action as is described in that paragraph, notwithstanding that his own course of conduct does not by itself amount to harassment.

(3) Subsection (1)(a) above does not apply to anything done by a person which is reasonable (and otherwise permissible in law) for the purpose—

(a) of securing the discharge of an obligation due, or believed by him to be due, to himself or to persons for whom he acts, or protecting himself or them from future loss; or

(b) of the enforcement of any liability by legal process.

EQUAL PAY ACT 1970
(1970, c. 41)

1. Requirement of equal treatment for men and women in same employment.

[(1) If the terms of a contract under which a woman is employed at an establishment in Great Britain do not include (directly or by reference to a collective agreement or otherwise) an equality clause they shall be deemed to include one.

(2) An equality clause is a provision which relates to terms (whether concerned with pay or not) of a contract under which a woman is employed (the "woman's contract"), and has the effect that—

(a) where the woman is employed on like work with a man in the same employment—

(i) (apart from the equality clause) any term of the woman's contract is or becomes less favourable to the woman than a term of a similar kind in the contract under which that man is employed, that term of the woman's contract shall be treated as so modified as not to be less favourable, and

(ii) if (apart from the equality clause) at any time the woman's contract does not include a term corresponding to a term benefiting that man included in the contract under which he is employed, the woman's contract shall be treated as including such a term; ...]

[*Paragraphs (a), (b) and (c) contain similar provisions.*]

TAXES MANAGEMENT ACT 1970
(1970, c. 9)

[30. Recovery of overpayment of tax, etc.

(1) Where an amount of tax has been repaid to any person which ought not to have been repaid to him, that amount of tax may be assessed and recovered as if it were unpaid tax.

(1A) Subsection (1) above shall not apply where the amount of tax which has been repaid is assessable under section 29 of this Act.

(1B) Subsections (2) to (8) of section 29 of this Act shall apply in relation to an assessment under subsection (1) above as they apply in relation to an assessment under subsection (1) of that section; and subsection (4) of that section as so applied shall have effect as if the reference to the loss of tax were a reference to the repayment of the amount of tax which ought not to have been repaid.

(2) In any case where—

(a) a repayment of tax has been increased in accordance with section 824 or 825 of the principal Act or section 283 of the 1992 Act (supplements added to repayments of tax, etc.); and

(b) the whole or any part of that repayment has been paid to any person but ought not to have been paid to him; and

(c) that repayment ought not to have been increased either at all or to any extent;

then the amount of the repayment assessed under subsection (1) above may include an amount equal to the amount by which the repayment ought not to have been increased.

(2A) In any case where—

(a) interest has been paid under section [826 of the principal Act] on a repayment of tax, and

(b) the whole or any part of that repayment has been paid to any person but ought not to have been paid to him, and

(c) interest ought not to have been paid on that repayment, either at all or to any extent,

then the amount of the repayment assessed under subsection (1) above may include an amount equal to the interest that ought not to have been paid.

(3) In any case where—

(a) a payment, other than a repayment of tax to which subsection (2) above applies, is increased in accordance with section 824 or 825 of the principal Act or section 283 of the 1992 Act; and

(b) that payment ought not to have been increased either at all or to any extent;

then an amount equal to the amount by which the payment ought not to have been increased may be assessed and recovered as if it were unpaid income tax or corporation tax.

(3A) If, in a case not falling within subsection (2A) above,—

(a) interest has been paid under section 826 of the principal Act on a repayment of tax, and

(b) that interest ought not to have been paid, either at all or to any extent,

then an amount equal to the interest that ought not to have been paid may be assessed and recovered as if it were unpaid corporation tax.

(4) An assessment to income tax or corporation tax under this section shall be made under Case VI of Schedule D and an assessment to recover—

(a) an amount of corporation tax repaid to a company in respect of an accounting period, or

(b) an amount of income tax repaid to a company in respect of a payment received by the company in any accounting period, or

(c) interest on any such repayment of tax,

shall be treated as an assessment to corporation tax for the accounting period referred to in paragraph (a) or (b) above, as the case may be, and the sum assessed shall carry interest at the prescribed rate for the purposes of section 87A of this Act from the date when the payment being recovered was made until payment.

(4A) Where an assessment is made under this section to recover—

(a) corporation tax repaid to a company in respect of an accounting period, or

(b) income tax repaid to a company in respect of payments received by the company in an accounting period,

and more than one repayment of that tax has been made in respect of that period, any sum recovered in respect of income tax or corporation tax repaid shall as far as possible be treated as relating to a repayment of that tax made later rather than to a repayment made earlier.

(5) An assessment under this section shall not be out of time under section 34 of this Act if it is made before the end of whichever of the following ends the later, namely—

(a) the chargeable period following that in which the amount assessed was repaid or paid as the case may be, or

(b) where a return delivered by the person concerned, or an amendment of such a return, is enquired into by an officer of the Board, the period ending with the day on which, by virtue of section 28A(5) of this Act, the officer's enquiries are treated as completed.

(6) Subsection (5) above is without prejudice to section 36 of this Act.

(7) In this section any reference to an amount repaid or paid includes a reference to an amount allowed by way of set-off.]

33. Error or mistake.

(1) If any person who has paid tax charged under an assesment [(whether under section 9 or 11AA of this Act or otherwise)] alleges that the assessment was excessive by reason of some error or mistake in a return, he may by notice in writing at any time not later than

[(a) in the case of an assessment to income tax or capital gains tax, five years after the 31 January next following the year of assessment to which the return relates; and

(b) in the case of an assessment to corporation tax, six years after the end of the accounting period to which the return relates,]
make a claim to the Board for relief.

(2) On receiving the claim the Board shall inquire into the matter and shall subject to the provisions of this section give by way of repayment such relief [. . .] in respect of the error or mistake as is reasonable and just:

[(2A) No relief shall be given under this section in respect of—

(a) an error or mistake as to the basis on which the liability of the claimant ought to have been computed where the return was in fact made on the basis or in accordance with the practice generally prevailing at the time when it was made; or

(b) an error or mistake in a claim which is included in the return.]

(3) In determining the claim the Board shall have regard to all the relevant circumstances of the case, and in particular shall consider whether the granting of relief would result in the exclusion from charge to tax of any part of the profits of the claimant, and for this purpose the Board may take into consideration the liability of the claimant and assessment made on him in respect of chargeable periods other than that to which the claim relates.

(4) If any appeal is brought from the decision of the Board on the claim the Special Commissioners shall hear and determine the appeal in accordance with the principles to be followed by the Board in determining claims under this section; and neither the appellant nor the Board shall be entitled to [appeal under section 56A of this Act against the determination of the Special Commissioners except] on a point of law arising in connection with the computation of profits.

(5) In this section "profits"—
 (a) in relation to income tax, means income,
 (b) in relation to capital gains tax, means chargeable gains,
 (c) in relation to corporation tax, means profits as computed for the purposes of that tax.

[33A. Error or mistake in partnership statement.

(1) This section applies where, in the case of a trade, profession or business carried on by two or more persons in partnership, those persons allege that the tax charged by self-assessment of theirs under section 9 or 11AA of this Act was excessive by reason of some error or mistake in a partnership statement.

(2) One of those persons (the representative partner) may, not later than five years after the filing date, by notice in writing make a claim to the Board for relief.

(3) On receiving the claim the Board shall inquire into the matter and shall, subject to subsection (5) below, so amend the partnership statement so as to give such relief in respect of the error or mistake as is reasonable or just.

(4) Where a partnership statement is amended under subsection (3) above, the Board shall by notice to each of the relevant partners so amend their self-assessments under section 9 or 11AA of this Act as to give effect to the amendment of the partnership statement.

(5) No relief shall be given under this section in respect of an error or mistake as to the basis on which the liability of the partners ought to have been computed where the partnership statement was in fact made on the basis or in accordance with the practice generally prevailing at the time when it was made.

(6) In determining the claim the Board—
  (a) shall have regard to all the relevant circumstances of the case, and
  (b) in particular shall consider whether the granting of relief would result in the exclusion from charge to tax of any part of the profits of any of the partners;
and for the purposes of this subsection the Board may take into consideration the liability of the partners and their self-assessments in respect of chargeable periods other than that to which the claim relates.

(7) If any appeal is brought from the decision of the Board on the claim, the Special Commissioners shall hear and determine the appeal in accordance with the principles to be followed by the Board in determining claims under this section.

[(8) Subject to subsection (8A) below, the determination of the Special Commissioners of an appeal under subsection (6) above shall be final and conclusive (notwithstanding any provision having effect by virtue of section 56B of this Act).

(8A) Subsection (8) above does not apply in relation to a point of law arising in connection with the computation of profits.]

ANIMALS ACT 1971
(1971, c. 22)

1. New provisions as to strict liability for damage done by animals.

(1) The provisions of sections 2 to 5 of this Act replace—
  (a) the rules of the common law imposing a strict liability in tort for damage done by an animal on the ground that the animal is regarded as ferae naturae or that its vicious or mischievous propensities are known or presumed to be known;
  (b) subsections (1) and (2) of section 1 of the Dogs Act 1906 as amended by the Dogs (Amendment) Act 1928 (injury to cattle or poultry); and
  (c) the rules of the common law imposing a liability for cattle trespass.

(2) Expressions used in those sections shall be interpreted in accordance with the provisions of section 6 (as well as those of section 11) of this Act.

2. Liability for damage done by dangerous animals.

(1) Where any damage is caused by an animal which belongs to a dangerous species, any person who is a keeper of the animal is liable for the damage, except as otherwise provided by this Act.

(2) Where damage is caused by an animal which does not belong to a dangerous species, a keeper of the animal is liable for the damage, except as otherwise provided by this Act, if—
  (a) the damage is of a kind which the animal, unless restrained, was likely to cause or which, if caused by the animal, was likely to be severe; and
  (b) the likelihood of the damage or of its being severe was due to characteristics of the animal which are not normally found in animals of the same species or are not normally so found except at particular times or in particular circumstances; and

(c) those characteristics were known to that keeper or were at any time known to a person who at that time had charge of the animal as that keeper's servant or, where that keeper is the head of a household, were known to another keeper of the animal who is a member of that household and under the age of sixteen.

3. Liability for injury done by dogs to livestock.

Where a dog causes damage by killing or injuring livestock, any person who is a keeper of the dog is liable for the damage, except as otherwise provided by this Act.

4. Liability for damage and expenses due to trespassing livestock.

(1) Where livestock belonging to any person strays on to land in the ownership or occupation of another and—

(a) damage is done by the livestock to the land or to any property on it which is in the ownership or possession of the other person; or

(b) any expenses are reasonably incurred by that other person in keeping the livestock while it cannot be restored to the person to whom it belongs or while it is detained in pursuance of section 7 of this Act, or in ascertaining to whom it belongs;

the person to whom the livestock belongs is liable for the damage or expenses, except as otherwise provided by this Act.

(2) For the purposes of this section any livestock belongs to the person in whose possession it is.

5. Exceptions from liability under sections 2 to 4.

(1) A person is not liable under sections 2 to 4 of this Act for any damage which is due wholly to the fault of the person suffering it.

(2) A person is not liable under section 2 of this Act for any damage suffered by a person who has voluntarily accepted the risk thereof.

(3) A person is not liable under section 2 of this Act for any damage caused by an animal kept on any premises or structure to a person trespassing there, if it is proved either—

(a) that the animal was not kept there for the protection of persons or property; or

(b) (if the animal was kept there for the protection of persons or property) that keeping it there for that purpose was not unreasonable.

(4) A person is not liable under section 3 of this Act if the livestock was killed or injured on land on to which it had strayed and either the dog belonged to the occupier or its presence on the land was authorised by the occupier.

(5) A person is not liable under section 4 of this Act where the livestock strayed from a highway and its presence there was a lawful use of the highway.

(6) In determining whether any liability for damage under section 4 of this Act is excluded by subsection (1) of this section the damage shall not be treated as due to the fault of the person suffering it by reason only that he could have prevented it by fencing; but a person is not liable under that section where it is proved that the straying of the livestock on to the land would not have occurred but for a breach by any other person, being a person having an interest in the land, of a duty to fence.

6. Interpretation of certain expressions used in sections 2 to 5.

(1) The following provisions apply to the interpretation of sections 2 to 5 of this Act.

(2) A dangerous species is a species—

(a) which is not commonly domesticated in the British Islands; and

(b) whose fully grown animals normally have such characteristics that they are likely, unless restrained, to cause severe damage or that any damage they may cause is likely to be severe.

(3) Subject to subsection (4) of this section, a person is a keeper of an animal if—

(a) he owns the animal or has it in his possession; or

(b) he is the head of a household of which a member under the age of sixteen owns the animal or has it in his possession;

and if at any time an animal ceases to be owned by or to be in the possession of a person, any person who immediately before that time was a keeper thereof by virtue of the preceding provisions of this subsection continues to be a keeper of the animal until another person becomes a keeper thereof by virtue of those provisions.

(4) Where an animal is taken into and kept in possession for the purpose of preventing it from causing damage or of restoring it to its owner, a person is not a keeper of it by virtue only of that possession.

(5) Where a person employed as a servant by a keeper of an animal incurs a risk incidental to his employment he shall not be treated as accepting it voluntarily.

7. **Detention and sale of trespassing livestock.**

(1) The right to seize and detain any animal by way of distress damage feasant is hereby abolished.

(2) Where any livestock strays on to any land and is not then under the control of any person the occupier of the land may detain it, subject to subsection (3) of this section, unless ordered to return it by a court.

(3) Where any livestock is detained in pursuance of this section the right to detain it ceases—

(a) at the end of a period of forty-eight hours, unless within that period notice of the detention has been given to the officer in charge of a police station and also, if the person detaining the livestock knows to whom it belongs, to that person; or

(b) when such amount is tendered to the person detaining the livestock as is sufficient to satisfy any claim he may have under section 4 of this Act in respect of the livestock; or,

(c) if he has no such claim, when the livestock is claimed by a person entitled to its possession.

(4) Where livestock has been detained in pursuance of this section for a period of not less than fourteen days the person detaining it may sell it at a market or by public auction, unless proceedings are then pending for the return of the livestock or for any claim under section 4 of this Act in respect of it.

(5) Where any livestock is sold in the exercise of the right conferred by this section and the proceeds of the sale, less the costs thereof and any costs incurred in connection with it, exceed the amount of any claim under section 4 of this Act which the vendor had in respect of the livestock, the excess shall be recoverable from him by the person who would be entitled to the possession of the livestock but for the sale.

(6) A person detaining any livestock in pursuance of this section is liable for any damage caused to it by a failure to treat it with reasonable care and supply it with adequate food and water while it is so detained.

(7) References in this section to a claim under section 4 of this Act in respect of any livestock do not include any claim under that section for damage done by or expenses incurred in respect of the livestock before the straying in connection with which it is detained under this section.

8. **Duty to take care to prevent damage from animals straying on to the highway.**

(1) So much of the rules of the common law relating to liability for negligence as excludes or restricts the duty which a person might owe to others to take such care as is reasonable to see that damage is not caused by animals straying on to a highway is hereby abolished.

(2) Where damage is caused by animals straying from unfenced land to a highway a person who placed them on the land shall not be regarded as having committed a breach of the duty to take care by reason only of placing them there if—

(a) the land is common land, or is land situated in an area where fencing is not customary, or is a town or village green; and

(b) he had a right to place the animals on that land.

9. Killing of or injury to dogs worrying livestock.

(1) In any civil proceedings against a person (in this section referred to as the defendant) for killing or causing injury to a dog it shall be a defence to prove—

(a) that the defendant acted for the protection of any livestock and was a person entitled to act for the protection of that livestock; and

(b) that within forty-eight hours of the killing or injury notice thereof was given by the defendant to the officer in charge of a police station.

(2) For the purposes of this section a person is entitled to act for the protection of any livestock if, and only if—

(a) the livestock or the land on which it is belongs to him or to any person under whose express or implied authority he is acting; and

(b) the circumstances are not such that liability for killing or causing injury to the livestock would be excluded by section 5(4) of this Act.

(3) Subject to subsection (4) of this section, a person killing or causing injury to a dog shall be deemed for the purposes of this section to act for the protection of any livestock if, and only if, either—

(a) the dog is worrying or is about to worry the livestock and there are no other reasonable means of ending or preventing the worrying; or

(b) the dog has been worrying livestock, has not left the vicinity and is not under the control of any person and there are no practicable means of ascertaining to whom it belongs.

(4) For the purposes of this section the condition stated in either of the paragraphs of the preceding subsection shall be deemed to have been satisfied if the defendant believed that it was satisfied and had reasonable ground for that belief.

(5) For the purposes of this section—

(a) an animal belongs to any person if he owns it or has it in his possession; and

(b) land belongs to any person if he is the occupier thereof.

10. Application of certain enactments to liability under sections 2 to 4.

For the purposes of [the Fatal Accidents Act 1976], the Law Reform (Contributory Negligence) Act 1945 and [the Limitation Act 1980] any damage for which a person is liable under sections 2 to 4 of this Act shall be treated as due to his fault.

11. General interpretation.

In this Act—

"common land", and "town or village green" have the same meanings as in the Commons Regulation Act 1965;

"damage" includes the death of, or injury to, any person (including any disease and any impairment of physical or mental condition);

"fault" has the same meaning as in the Law Reform (Contributory Negligence) Act 1945;

"fencing" includes the construction of any obstacle designed to prevent animals from straying;

"livestock" means cattle, horses, asses, mules, hinnies, sheep, pigs, goats and poultry, and also deer not in the wild state and, in section 3 and 9 also, while in captivity, pheasants, partridges and grouse;

"poultry" means the domestic varieties of the following, that is to say, fowls, turkeys, geese, ducks, guinea-fowls, pigeons, peacocks and quails; and

"species" includes sub-species and variety.

12. Application to Crown.

(1) This Act binds the Crown, but nothing in this section shall authorise proceedings to be brought against Her Majesty in her private capacity.

(2) Section 38(3) of the Crown Proceedings Act 1947 (interpretation of references to Her Majesty in her private capacity) shall apply as if this section were contained in that Act.

CARRIAGE OF GOODS BY SEA ACT 1971
(1971, c. 19)

1. **Application of Hague Rules as amended.**
 (1) In this Act, "the Rules" means the International Convention for the unification of certain rules of law relating to bills of lading signed at Brussels on 25 August 1924, as amended by the Protocol signed at Brussels on 23 February 1968 [and by the Protocol signed at Brussels on 21 December 1979].
 (2) The provisions of the Rules, as set out in the Schedule to this Act, shall have the force of law.
 (3) Without prejudice to subsection (2) above, the said provisions shall have effect (and have the force of law) in relation to and in connection with the carriage of goods by sea in ships where the port of shipment is a port in the United Kingdom, whether or not the carriage is between ports in two different States within the meaning of Article X of the Rules.
 (4) Subject to subsection (6) below, nothing in this section shall be taken as applying anything in the Rules to any contract for the carriage of goods by sea, unless the contract expressly or by implication provides for the issue of a bill of lading or any similar document of title.
 (5) [...]
 (6) Without prejudice to Article X(c) of the Rules, the Rules shall have the force of law in relation to—
 (a) any bill of lading if the contract contained in or evidenced by it expressly provides that the Rules shall govern the contract, and
 (b) any receipt which is a non-negotiable document marked as such if the contract contained in or evidenced by it is a contract for the carriage of goods by sea which expressly provides that the Rules are to govern the contract as if the receipt were a bill of lading,
but subject, where paragraph (b) applies, to any necessary modifications and in particular with the omission in Article III of the Rules of the second sentence of paragraph 4 and of paragraph 7.
 (7) If and so far as the contract contained in or evidenced by a bill of lading or receipt within paragraph (a) or (b) of subsection (6) above applies to deck cargo or live animals, the Rules as given the force of law by that subsection shall have effect as if Article I(c) did not exclude deck cargo and live animals.
 In this subsection "deck cargo" means cargo which by the contract of carriage is stated as being carried on deck and is so carried.

2. **Contracting States, etc.**
 (1) If Her Majesty by Order in council certifies to the following effect, that is to say, that for the purposes of the Rules—
 (a) a State specified in the Order is a contracting State, or is a contracting State in respect of any place or territory so specified; or
 (b) any place or territory specified in the Order forms part of a State so specified (whether a contracting State or not),
the Order shall, except so far as it has been superseded by a subsequent Order, be conclusive evidence of the matters so certified.
 (2) An Order in Council under this section may be varied or revoked by a subsequent Order in Council.

3. Absolute warranty of seaworthiness not to be implied in contracts to which Rules apply.

There shall not be implied in any contract for the carriage of goods by sea to which the Rules apply by virtue of this Act any absolute undertaking by the carrier of the goods to provide a seaworthy ship.

4. Application of Act to British possessions, etc.

(1) Her Majesty may by Order in Council direct that this Act shall extend, subject to such exceptions, adaptations and modifications as may be specified in the Order, to all or any of the following territories, that is—

   (a) any colony (not being a colony for whose external relations a county other than the United Kingdom is responsible),

   (b) any country outside Her Majesty's dominions in which Her Majesty has jurisdiction in right of Her Majesty's Government of the United Kigndom.

(2) An Order in Council under this section may contain such transitional and other consequential and incidental provisions as appear to Her Majesty to be expedient, including provisions amending or repealing any legislation about the carriage of goods by sea forming part of the law of any of the territories mentioned in paragraphs (a) and (b) above.

(3) An Order in Council under this section may be varied or revoked by a subsequent Order in Council.

5. Extension of application of Rules to carriage from ports in British possessions, etc.

(1) Her Majesty may by Order in Council provide that section 1(3) of this Act shall have effect as if the reference therein to the United Kingdom included a reference to all or any of the following territories, that is—

   (a) the Isle of Man;

   (b) any of the Channel Islands specified in the Order;

   (c) any colony specified in the Order (not being a colony for whose external relations a country other than the United Kingdom is responsible);

   (d) any associated state (as defined by section 1(3) of the West Indies Act 1967) specified in the Order;

   (e) any country specified in the Order, being a country outside Her Majesty's dominions in which Her Majesty has jurisdiction in right of Her Majesty's Government of the United Kingdom.

(2) An Order in Council under this section may be varied or revoked by a subsequent Order in Council.

6. Supplemental.

(1) This Act may be cited as the Carriage of Goods by Sea Act 1971.

(2) It is hereby declared that this Act extends to Northern Ireland.

(3) The following enactments shall be repealed, that is—

   (a) the Carriage of Goods by Sea Act 1924,

   (b) section 12(4)(a) of the Nuclear Installations Act 1965,

and without prejudice to section 38(1) of the Interpretation Act 1889, the reference to the said Act of 1924 in section 1(1)(i)(ii) of the Hovercraft Act 1968 shall include a reference to this Act.

(4) It is hereby declared that for the purposes of Article VIII of the Rules [section 18 of the Merchant Shipping Act 1979 (which] entirely exempts shipowners and others in certain circumstances from liability for loss of, or damage to, goods) is a provision relating to limitation of liability.

(5) This Act shall come into force on such day as Her Majesty may by Order in Council appoint, and, for the purposes of the transition from the law

in force immediately before the day appointed under this subsection to the provisions of this Act, the Order appointing the day may provide that those provisions shall have effect subject to such transitional provisions as may be contained in the Order.

SCHEDULE
THE HAGUE RULES AS AMENDED BY THE BRUSSELS PROTOCOL 1968

Article I
In these Rules the following words are employed, with the meanings set out below—

(a) "Carrier" includes the owner or the charter who enters into a contract of carriage with a shipper.

(b) "Contract of carriage" applies only to contracts of carriage covered by a bill of lading or any similar document of title, in so far as such document relates to the carriage of goods by sea, including any bill of lading or any similar document as aforesaid issued under or pursuant to a charter party from the moment at which such bill of lading or similar document of title regulates the relations between a carrier and a holder of the same.

(c) "Goods" includes goods, wares, merchandise, and articles of every kind whatsoever except live animals and cargo which by the contract of carriage is stated as being carried on deck and is so carried.

(d) "Ship" means any vessel used for the carriage of goods by sea.

(e) "Carriage of goods" covers the period from the time when the goods are loaded on to the time they are discharged from the ship.

Article II
Subject to the provisions of Article VI, under every contract of carriage of goods by sea the carrier, in relation to the loading, handling, stowage, carriage, custody, care and discharge of such goods, shall be subject to the responsibilities and liabilities, and entitled to the rights and immunities hereinafter set forth.

Article III
(1) The carrier shall be bound before and at the beginning of the voyage to exercise due diligence to—

    (a) Make the ship seaworthy.

    (b) Properly man, equip and supply the ship.

    (c) Make the holds, refrigerating and cool chambers, and all other parts of the ship in which goods are carried, fit and safe for their reception, carriage and preservation.

(2) Subject to the provisions of Article IV, the carrier shall properly and carefully load, handle, stow, carry, keep, care for, and discharge the goods carried.

(3) After receiving the goods into his charge the carrier or the master or agent of the carrier shall, on demand of the shipper, issue to the shipper a bill of lading showing among other things—

    (a) The leading marks necessary for identification of the goods as the same are furnished in writing by the shipper before the loading of such goods starts, provided such marks are stamped or otherwise shown clearly upon the goods if uncovered, or on the cases or coverings in which such goods are contained, in such a manner as should ordinarily remain legible until the end of the voyage.

    (b) Either the number of packages or pieces, or the quantity, or weight, as the case may be, as furnished in writing by the shipper.

    (c) The apparent order and condition of the goods.

Provided that no carrier, master or agent of the carrier shall be bound to state or show in the bill of lading any marks, number, quantity, or weight which he has reasonable ground for suspecting not accurately to represent the goods actually received, or which he has had no reasonable means of checking.

(4) Such a bill of lading shall be prima facie evidence of the receipt by the carrier of the goods as therein described in accordance with paragraph 3(a), (b) and (c). However, proof to the contrary shall not be admissible when the bill of lading has been transferred to a third party acting in good faith.

(5) The shipper shall be deemed to have guaranteed to the carrier the accuracy at the time of shipment of the marks, number, quantity and weight, as furnished by him, and the shipper shall indemnify the carrier against all loss, damages and expenses arising or resulting from inaccuracies in such particulars. The right of the carrier to such indemnity shall in no way limit his responsibility and liability under the contract of carriage to any person other than the shipper.

(6) Unless notice of loss or damage and the general nature of such loss or damage be given in writing to the carrier or his agent at the port of discharge before or at the time of the removal of the goods into the custody of the person entitled to delivery thereof under the contract of carriage, or, if the loss or damage be not apparent, within three days, such removal shall be prima facie evidence of the delivery by the carrier of the goods as described in the bill of lading.

The notice in writing need not be given if the state of the goods has, at the time of their receipt, been the subject of joint survey or inspection.

Subject to paragraph 6*bis* the carrier and the ship shall in any event be discharged from all liability whatsoever in respect of the goods, unless suit is brought within one year of their delivery or of the date when they should have been delivered. This period may, however, be extended if the parties so agree after the cause of action has arisen.

In the case of any actual or apprehended loss or damage the carrier and the receiver shall give all reasonable facilities to each other for inspecting and tallying the goods.

(6*bis*) An action for indemnity against a third person may be brought even after the expiration of the year provided for in the preceding paragraph if brought within the time allowed by the law of the Court seized of the case. However, the time allowed shall be not less than three months, commencing from the day when the person bringing such action for indemnity has settled the claim or has been served with process in the action against himself.

(7) After the goods are loaded the bill of lading to be issued by the carrier, master, or agent of the carrier, to the shipper shall, if the shipper so demands, be a "shipped" bill of lading, provided that if the shipper shall have previously taken up any document of title to such goods, he shall surrender the same as against the issue of the "shipped" bill of lading, but at the option of the carrier such document of title may be noted at the port of shipment by the carrier, master, or agent with the name or names of the ship or ships upon which the goods have been shipped and the date or dates of shipment, and when so noted if it shows the particulars mentioned in paragraph 3 of Article III, shall for the purpose of this article be deemed to constitute a "shipped" bill of lading.

(8) Any clause, covenant, or agreement in a contract of carriage relieving the carrier or the ship from liability for loss or damage to, or in connection with, goods arising from negligence, fault, or failure in the duties and obligations provided in this article or lessening such liability otherwise than as provided in these Rules, shall be null and void and of no effect. A benefit of insurance in favour of the carrier or similar clause shall be deemed to be a clause relieving the carrier from liability.

Article IV

(1) Neither the carrier nor the ship shall be liable for loss or damage arising or resulting from unseaworthiness unless caused by want of due diligence on the part of the carrier to make the ship seaworthy, and to secure that the ship is properly manned, equipped and supplied, and to make the holds, refrigerating and cool chambers and all other parts of the ship in which goods are carried fit and safe for their reception, carriage and preservation in accordance with the provisions of paragraph 1 of Article III.

Whenever loss or damage has resulted from unseaworthiness the burden of proving the exercise of due diligence shall be on the carrier or other person claiming exemption under this article.

(2) Neither the carrier nor the ship shall be responsible for loss or damage arising or resulting from—

(a) Act, neglect, or default of the master, mariner, pilot, or the servants of the carrier in the navigation or in the management of the ship.
(b) Fire, unless caused by the actual fault or privity of the carrier.
(c) Perils, dangers and accidents of the sea or other navigable waters.
(d) Act of God.
(e) Act of war.
(f) Act of public enemies.
(g) Arrest or restraint of princes, rulers or people, or seizure under legal process.
(h) Quarantine restrictions.
(i) Act or omission of the shipper or owner of the goods, his agent or representative.
(j) Strikes or lockouts or stoppage or restraint of labour from whatever cause, whether partial or general.
(k) Riots and civil commotions.
(l) Saving or attempting to save life or property at sea.
(m) Wastage in bulk or weight or any other loss or damage arising from inherent defect, quality or vice of the goods.
(n) Insufficiency of packing.
(o) Insufficiency or inadequacy of marks.
(p) Latent defects not discoverable by due diligence.
(q) Any other cause arising without the actual fault or privity of the carrier, or without the fault or neglect of the agents or servants of the carrier, but the burden of proof shall be on the person claiming the benefit of this exception to show that neither the actual fault or privity of the carrier nor the fault or neglect of the agents or servants of the carrier contributed to the loss or damage.

(3) The shipper shall not be responsible for the loss or damage sustained by the carrier or the ship arising or resulting from any cause without the act, fault or neglect of the shipper, his agents or his servants.

(4) Any deviation in saving or attempting to save life or property at sea or any reasonable deviation shall not be deemed to be an infringement or breach of these Rules or of the contract of carriage, and the carrier shall not be liable for any loss or damage resulting therefrom.

(5)(a) Unless the nature and value of such goods have been declared by the shipper before shipment and inserted in the bill of lading, neither the carrier nor the ship shall in any event be or become liable for any loss or damage to or in connection with the goods in an amount exceeding [666.67 units of account] per package or unit or [2 units of account per kilogramme] of gross weight of the goods lost or damaged, whichever is the higher.

(b) The total amount recoverable shall be calculated by reference to the value of such goods at the place and time at which the goods are discharged from the ship in accordance with the contract or should have been so discharged.

The value of the goods shall be fixed according to the commodity exchange price, or, if there be no such price, according to the current market price, or, if there be no commodity exchange price or current market price, by reference to the normal value of goods of the same kind and quality.

(c) Where a container, pallet or similar article of transport is used to consolidate goods, the number of packages or units enumerated in the bill of lading as packed in such article of transport shall be deemed the number of packages or units for the purpose of this paragraph as far as these packages or units are concerned. Except as aforesaid such article of transport shall be considered the package or unit.

[(d) The unit of account mentioned in this Article is the special drawing right as defined by the International Monetary Fund. The amounts mentioned in sub-paragraph (a) of this paragraph shall be converted into national currency on the basis of the value of that currency on a date to be determined by the law of the court seized of the case.]

(e) Neither the carrier nor the ship shall be entitled to the benefit of the limitation of liability provided for in this paragraph if it is proved that the damage resulted from an act or omission of the carrier done with intent to cause damage, or recklessly and with knowledge that damage would probably result.

(f) The declaration mentioned in sub-paragraph (a) of this paragraph, if embodied in the bill of lading, shall be prima facie evidence, but shall not be binding or conclusive on the carrier.

(g) By agreement between the carrier, master or agent of the carrier and the shipper other maximum amounts than those mentioned in sub-paragraph (a) of this paragraph may be fixed, provided that no maximum amount so fixed shall be less than the appropriate maximum mentioned in that sub-paragraph.

(h) Neither the carrier nor the ship shall be responsible in any event for loss or damage to, or in connection with, goods if the nature or value thereof has been knowingly mis-stated by the shipper in the bill of lading.

(6) Goods of an inflammable, explosive or dangerous nature to the shipment whereof the carrier, master or agent of the carrier has not consented with knowledge of their nature and character, may at any time before discharge be landed at any place, or destroyed or rendered innocuous by the carrier without compensation and the shipper of such goods shall be liable for all damages and expenses directly or indirectly arising out of or resulting from such shipment. If any such goods shipped with such knowledge and consent shall become a danger to the ship or cargo, they may in like manner be landed at any place, or destroyed or rendered innocuous by the carrier without liability on the part of the carrier except to general average, if any.

Article IV bis

(1) The defences and limits of liability provided for in these Rules shall apply in any action against the carrier in respect of loss or damage to goods covered by a contract of carriage whether the action be founded in contract or in tort.

(2) If such an action is brought against a servant or agent of the carrier (such servant or agent not being an independent contractor), such servant or agent shall be entitled to avail himself of the defences and limits of liability which the carrier is entitled to invoke under these Rules.

(3) The aggregate of the amounts recoverable from the carrier, and such servants and agents, shall in no case exceed the limit provided for in these Rules.

(4) Nevertheless, a servant or agent of the carrier shall not be entitled to avail himself of the provisions of this article, if it is proved that the damage resulted from an act or omission of the servant or agent done with intent to cause damage or recklessly and with knowledge that damage would probably result.

Article V

A carrier shall be at liberty to surrender in whole or in part all or any of his rights and immunities or to increase any of his responsibilities and obligations under these Rules, provided such surrender or increase shall be embodied in the bill of lading issued to the shipper. The provisions of the Rules shall not be applicable to charter parties, but if bills of lading are issued in the case of a ship under a charter party they shall comply with the terms of these Rules. Nothing in these Rules shall be held to prevent the insertion in a bill of lading of any lawful provisions regarding general average.

Article VI
Notwithstanding the provisions of the preceding articles, a carrier, master or agent of the carrier and a shipper shall in regard to any particular goods be at liberty to enter into any agreement in any terms as to the responsibility and liability of the carrier for such goods, and as to the rights and immunities of the carrier in respect of such goods, or his obligation as to seaworthiness, so far as this stipulation is not contrary to public policy, or the care or diligence of his servants or agents in regard to the loading, handling, stowage, carriage, custody, care and discharge of the goods carried by sea, provided that in this case no bill of lading has been or shall be issued and that the terms agreed shall be embodied in a receipt which shall be a non-negotiable document and shall be marked as such.

Any agreement so entered into shall have full legal effect.

Provided that this article shall not apply to ordinary commercial shipments made in the ordinary course of trade, but only to other shipments where the character or condition of the property to be carried or the circumstances, terms and conditions under which the carriage is to be performed are such as reasonably to justify a special agreement.

Article VII
Nothing herein contained shall prevent a carrier or a shipper from entering into any agreement, stipulation, condition, reservation or exemption as to the responsibility and liability of the carrier or the ship for the loss or damage to, or in connection with, the custody and care and handling of goods prior to the loading on, and subsequent to the discharge from, the ship on which the goods are carried by sea.

Article VIII
The provisions of these Rules shall not affect the rights and obligations of the carrier under any statute for the time being in force relating to the limitation of the liability of owners of sea-going vessels.

Article IX
These rules shall not affect the provisions of any international Convention or national law governing liability for nuclear damage.

Article X
The provisions of these Rules shall apply to every bill of lading relating to the carriage of goods between ports in two different States if:
    (a) the bill of lading is issued in a contracting State,
or
    (b) the carriage is from a port in a contracting State,
or
    (c) the contract contained in or evidenced by the bill of lading provides that these Rules or legislation of any State giving effect to them are to govern the contract,
whatever may be the nationality of the ship, the carrier, the shipper, the consignee, or any other interested person.

[The last two paragraphs of this article are not reproduced. They require contracting States to apply the Rules to bills of lading mentioned in the article and authorise them to apply the Rules to other bills of lading.]

[Articles 11 to 16 of the international Convention for the unification of certain rules of law relating to bills of lading signed at Brussels on August 25 1974 are not reproduced. They deal with the coming into force of the Convention, procedure for ratification, accession and denunciation and the right to call for a fresh conference to consider amendments to the Rules contained in the Convention.]

MINERAL WORKINGS (OFFSHORE INSTALLATIONS) ACT 1971
(1971, c. 61)

6. Safety regulations.

(1) The Secretary of State may make regulations for the safety, health and welfare of persons on offshore installations in waters to which this Act applies, and generally, and whether or not by way of supplementing the preceding sections of this Act, for the safety of such installations and the prevention of accidents on or near them.

11. Civil liability for breach of statutory duty.

(1) This section has effect as respects—
    (a) a duty imposed on any person by any provision of this Act, or
    (b) a duty imposed on any person by any provision of regulations made under this Act which expressly applies the provisions of this section.

(2) Breach of any such duty shall be actionable so far, and only so far, as it causes personal injury, and references in section 1 of [the Fatal Accidents Act 1976], as it applies in England and Wales, and [in Article 3(1) of the Fatal Accidents (Northern Ireland) Order 1977], to a wrongful act, neglect or default shall include references to any breach of a duty which is so actionable.

(3) Subsection (2) above is without prejudice to any action which lies apart from the provisions of this Act.

(4) Neither section 9(3) of this Act, nor any defences afforded by regulations made in pursuance of section 7(2)(b) of this Act, shall afford a defence in any civil proceedings, whether brought by virtue of this section or not.

(7) In this section "personal injury" includes any disease and any impairment of a person's physical or mental condition and includes any fatal injury.

UNSOLICITED GOODS AND SERVICES ACT 1971
(1971, c. 30)

1. Rights of recipient of unsolicited goods.

(1) In the circumstances specified in the following subsection, a person who after the commencement of this Act receives unsolicited goods, may as between himself and the sender, use, deal with or dispose of them as if they were an unconditional gift to him, and any right of the sender to the goods shall be extinguished.

(2) The circumstances referred to in the preceding subsection are that the goods were sent to the recipient with a view to his acquiring them, that the recipient has no reasonable cause to believe that they were sent with a view to their being acquired for the purposes of a trade or business and has neither agreed to acquire nor agreed to return them, and either—
    (a) that during the period of six months beginning with the day on which the recipient received the goods the sender did not take possession of them and the recipient did not unreasonably refuse to permit the sender to do so; or
    (b) that not less than thirty days before the expiration of the period aforesaid the recipient gave notice to the sender in accordance with the following subsection, and that during the period of thirty days beginning with the day on which the notice was given the sender did not take possession of the goods and the recipient did not unreasonably refuse to permit the sender to do so.

(3) A notice in pursuance of the preceding subsection shall be in writing and shall—
    (a) state the recipient's name and address and, if possession of the goods in question may not be taken by the sender at this address, the address at which it may be so taken;

(b) contain a statement, however expressed, that the goods are unsolicited, and may be sent by post.

(4) In this section "sender", in relation to any goods, includes any person on whose behalf or with whose consent the goods are sent, and any other person claiming through or under the sender or any such person.

2. Demands and threats regarding payment.

(1) A person who, not having reasonable cause to believe there is a right to payment, in the course of any trade or business makes a demand for payment, or asserts a present or prospective right to payment, for what he knows are unsolicited goods sent (after the commencement of this Act) to another person with a view to his acquiring them, shall be guilty of an offence and on summary conviction shall be liable to a fine not exceeding £200.

(2) A person who, not having reasonable cause to believe there is a right to payment in the course of any trade or business and with a view to obtaining any payment for what he knows are unsolicited goods sent as aforesaid—

    (a) threatens to bring any legal proceedings; or

    (b) places or causes to be placed the name of any person on a list of defaulters or debtors or threatens to do so; or

    (c) invokes or causes to be invoked any other collection procedure or threatens to do so,

shall be guilty of an offence and shall be liable on summary conviction to a fine not exceeding £400.

3. Directory entries.

(1) A person shall not be liable to make any payment, and shall be entitled to recover the payment made by him, by way of charge for including or arranging for the inclusion in a directory of an entry relating to that person or his trade or business, unless there has been signed by him or on his behalf an order complying with this section or a note complying with this section of his agreement to the charge and, in the case of a note of agreement to the charge, before the note was signed, a copy of it was supplied, for retention by him, to him or to a person acting on his behalf.

(2) A person shall be guilty of an offence punishable on summary conviction with a fine not exceeding £400 if, in a case where a payment in respect of a charge would, in the absence of an order or note of agreement to the charge complying with this section, be recoverable from him in accordance with the terms of subsection (1) above, he demands payment, or asserts a present or prospective right to payment, of the charge or any part of it, without knowing or having reasonable cause to believe that the entry to which the charge relates was ordered in accordance with this section or a proper note of agreement has been duly signed.

(3) For the purposes of subsection (1) above, an order for an entry in a directory must be made by means of an order form or other stationery belonging to the person to whom, or to whose trade or business, the entry is to relate and bearing, in print, the name and address (or one or more of the addresses) of that person; and the note required by this section of a person's agreement to a charge must state the amount of the charge immediately above the place for signature, and—

    (a) must identify the directory or proposed directory, and give the following particulars of it—

        (i) the proposed date of publication of the directory or of the issue in which the entry is to be included and the name and address of the person producing it;

        (ii) if the directory or that issue is to be put on sale, the price at which it is to be offered for sale and the minimum number of copies which are to be available for sale;

        (iii) if the directory or that issue is to be distributed free of charge (whether or not it is also to be put on sale), the minimum number of copies which are to be so distributed; and

(b) must set out or give reasonable particulars of the entry in respect of which the charge would be payable.

(4) Nothing in this section shall apply to a payment due under a contract entered into before the commencement of this Act, or entered into by the acceptance of an offer made before that commencement.

[3A. Contents and form of notes of agreement, invoices and similar documents.

(1) For the purposes of this Act, the Secretary of State may make regulations as to the contents and form of notes of agreement, invoices and similar documents; and, without prejudice to the generality of the foregoing, any such regulations may—
- (a) require specified information to be included,
- (b) prescribe the manner in which specified information is to be included,
- (c) prescribe such other requirements (whether as to presentation, type, size, colour or disposition of lettering, quality or colour of paper or otherwise) as the Secretary of State may consider appropriate for securing that specified information is clearly brought to the attention of the recipient of any note of agreement, invoice or similar document.
- (d) make different provision for different classes or descriptions of notes of agreement, invoices and similar documents or for the same class or description in different circumstances,
- (e) contain such supplementary and incidental provisions as the Secretary of State may consider appropriate.

(2) Any reference in this section to a note of agreement includes any such copy as is mentioned in section 3(1) of this Act.

(3) Regulations under this section shall be made by statutory instrument and shall be subject to annulment in pursuance of a resolution of either House of Parliament.]

4. Unsolicited publications.

(1) A person shall be guilty of an offence if he sends or causes to be sent to another person any book, magazine or leaflet (or advertising material for any such publication) which he knows or ought reasonably to know is unsolicited and which describes or illustrates human sexual techniques.

(2) A person found guilty of an offence under this section shall be liable on summary conviction to a fine not exceeding £100 for a first offence and to a fine not exceeding £400 for any subsequent offence.

(3) A prosecution for an offence under this section shall not in England and Wales be instituted except by, or with the consent of, the Director of Public Prosecutions.

5. Offences by corporations.

(1) Where an offence under this Act which has been committed by a body corporate is proved to have been committed with the consent or connivance of, or to be attributable to any neglect on the part of, any director, manager, secretary, or other similar officer of the body corporate, or of any person who was purporting to act in any such capacity, he as well as the body corporate shall be guilty of that offence and shall be liable to be proceeded against and punished accordingly.

(2) Where the affairs of a body corporate are managed by its members, this section shall apply in relation to the acts or defaults of a member in connection with his functions of management as if he were a director of the body corporate.

6. Interpretation.

(1) In this Act, unless the context or subject matter otherwise requires,—

"acquire" includes hire;

"send" includes deliver, and "sender" shall be construed accordingly;

"unsolicited" means, in relation to goods sent to any person, that they are sent without any prior request made by him or on his behalf.

[(2) For the purposes of this Act any invoice or similar document stating the amount of any payment and not complying with the requirements of regulations under section 3A of this Act applicable thereto shall be regarded as asserting a right to the payment.]

DEFECTIVE PREMISES ACT 1972
(1972, c. 35)

1. Duty to build dwellings properly.

(1) A person taking on work for or in connection with the provision of a dwelling (whether the dwelling is provided by the erection or by the conversion or enlargement of a building) owes a duty—
  (a) if the dwelling is provided to the order of any person, to that person; and
  (b) without prejudice to paragraph (a) above, to every person who acquires an interest (whether legal or equitable) in the dwelling;
to see that the work which he takes on is done in a workmanlike or, as the case may be, professional manner, with proper materials and so that as regards that work the dwelling will be fit for habitation when completed.

(2) A person who takes on any such work for another on terms that he is to do it in accordance with instructions given by or on behalf of that other shall, to the extent to which he does it properly in accordance with those instructions, be treated for the purposes of this section as discharging the duty imposed on him by subsection (1) above except where he owes a duty to that other to warn him of any defects in the instructions and fails to discharge that duty.

(3) A person shall not be treated for the purposes of subsection (2) above as having given instructions for the doing of work merely because he has agreed to the work being done in a specified manner, with specified materials or to a specified design.

(4) A person who—
  (a) in the course of a business which consists of or includes providing or arranging for the provision of dwellings or installations in dwellings; or
  (b) in the exercise of a power of making such provision or arrangements conferred by or by virtue of any enactment;
arranges for another to take on work for or in connection with the provision of a dwelling shall be treated for the purposes of this section as included among the persons who have taken on the work.

(5) Any cause of action in respect of a breach of the duty imposed by this section shall be deemed, for the purposes of the Limitation Act 1939, the Law Reform (Limitation of Actions, etc.) Act 1954 and the Limitation Act 1963, to have accrued at the time when the dwelling was completed, but if after that time a person who has done work for or in connection with the provision of the dwelling does further work to rectify the work he has already done, any such cause of action in respect of that further work shall be deemed for those purposes to have accrued at the time when the further work was finished.

[*The references in s. 1(5) should now be read as to the Limitation Act 1980. See the Limitation Act, s. 40(2); the Interpretation Act 1978, s. 17(2).*]

2. Cases excluded from the remedy under section 1.

(1) Where—
  (a) in connection with the provision of a dwelling or its first sale or letting for habitation any rights in respect of defects in the state of the dwelling are conferred by an

approved scheme to which this section applies on a person having or acquiring an interest in the dwelling; and

(b) it is stated in a document of a type approved for the purposes of this section that the requirements as to design or construction imposed by or under the scheme have, or appear to have, been substantially complied with in relation to the dwelling;

no action shall be brought by any person having or acquiring an interest in the dwelling for breach of the duty imposed by section 1 above in relation to the dwelling.

(2) A scheme to which this section applies—

(a) may consist of any number of documents and any number of agreements or other transactions between any number of persons; but

(b) must confer, by virtue of agreements entered into with persons having or acquiring an interest in the dwellings to which the scheme applies, rights on such persons in respect of defects in the state of the dwellings.

(3) In this section "'approved" means approved by the Secretary of State, and the power of the Secretary of State to approve a scheme or document for the purposes of this section shall be exercisable by order, except that any requirements as to construction or design imposed under a scheme to which this section applies may be approved by him without making any order or, if he thinks fit, by order.

(4) The Secretary of State—

(a) may approve a scheme or document for the purposes of this section with or without limiting the duration of his approval; and

(b) may by order revoke or vary a previous order under this section or, without such an order, revoke or vary a previous approval under this section given otherwise than by order.

(5) The production of a document purporting to be a copy of an approval given by the Secretary of State otherwise than by order and certified by an officer of the Secretary of State to be a true copy of the approval shall be conclusive evidence of the approval, and without proof of the handwriting or official position of the person purporting to sign the certificate.

(6) The power to make an order under this section shall be exercisable by statutory instrument which shall be subject to annulment in pursuance of a resolution by either House of Parliament.

(7) Where an interest in a dwelling is compulsorily acquired—

(a) no action shall be brought by the acquiring authority for breach of the duty imposed by section 1 above in respect of the dwelling; and

(b) if any work for or in connection with the provision of the dwelling was done otherwise than in the course of a business by the person in occupation of the dwelling at the time of the compulsory acquisition, the acquiring authority and not that person shall be treated as the person who took on the work and accordingly as owing that duty.

3. Duty of care with respect to work done on premises not abated by disposal of premises.

(1) Where work of construction, repair, maintenance or demolition or any other work is done on or in relation to premises, any duty of care owed, because of the doing of the work, to persons who might reasonably be expected to be affected by defects in the state of the premises created by the doing of the work shall not be abated by the subsequent disposal of the premises by the person who owed the duty.

(2) This section does not apply—

(a) in the case of premises which are let, where the relevant tenancy of the premises commenced, or the relevant tenancy agreement of the premises was entered into, before the commencement of this Act;

(b) in the case of premises disposed of in any other way, when the disposal of the premises was completed, or a contract for their disposal was entered into, before the commencement of this Act; or

(c) in either case, where the relevant transaction disposing of the premises is entered into in pursuance of an enforceable option by which the consideration for the disposal was fixed before the commencement of this Act.

4. Landlord's duty of care in virtue of obligation or right to repair premises demised.

(1) Where premises are let under a tenancy which puts on the landlord an obligation to the tenant for the maintenance or repair of the premises the landlord owes to all persons who might reasonably be expected to be affected by defects in the state of the premises a duty to take such care as is reasonable in all the circumstances to see that they are reasonably safe from personal injury or from damage to their property caused by a relevant defect.

(2) The said duty is owed if the landlord knows (whether as the result of being notified by the tenant or otherwise) or if he ought in all the circumstances to have known of the relevant defect.

(3) In this section "relevant defect" means a defect in the state of the premises existing at or after the material time and arising from, or continuing because of, an act or omission by the landlord which constituted or would if he had had notice of the defect, have constituted a failure by him to carry out his obligation to the tenant for the maintenance or repair of the premises; and for the purposes of the foregoing provision "the material time" means—

(a) where the tenancy commenced before this Act, the commencement of this Act; and

(b) in all other cases, the earliest following times, that is to say—
   (i) the time when the tenancy commences;
   (ii) the time when the tenancy agreement is entered into;
   (iii) the time when possession is taken of the premises in contemplation of the letting.

(4) Where premises are let under a tenancy which expressly or impliedly gives the landlord the right to enter the premises to carry out any description of maintenance or repair of the premises, then, as from the time when he first is, or by notice or otherwise can put himself, in a position to exercise the right and so long as he is or can put himself in that position, he shall be treated for the purposes of subsections (1) to (3) above (but for no other purpose) as if he were under an obligation to the tenant for that description of maintenance or repair of the premises; but the landlord shall not owe the tenant any duty by virtue of this subsection in respect of any defect in the state of the premises arising from, or continuing because of, a failure to carry out an obligation expressly imposed on the tenant by the tenancy.

(5) For the purposes of this section obligations imposed or rights given by any enactment in virtue of a tenancy shall be treated as imposed or given by the tenancy.

(6) This section applies to a right of occupation given by contract or any enactment and not amounting to a tenancy as if the right were a tenancy, and "tenancy" and cognate expressions shall be construed accordingly.

5. Application to Crown.

This Act shall bind the Crown, but as regards the Crown's liability in tort shall not bind the Crown further than the Crown is made liable in tort by the Crown Proceedings Act 1947.

6. Supplemental.

(1) In this Act: "disposal", in relation to premises, includes a letting, and an assignment or surrender of a tenancy, of the premises and the creation by contract of any

other right to occupy the premises, and "dispose" shall be construed accordingly; "personal injury" includes any disease and any impairment of a person's physical or mental condition ...

(2) Any duty imposed by or enforceable by virtue of any provision of this Act is in addition to any duty a person may owe apart from that provision.

(3) Any term of an agreement which purports to exclude or restrict, or has the effect of excluding or restricting, the operation of any of the provisions of this Act, or any liability arising by virtue of any such provision, shall be void.

POWERS OF CRIMINAL COURTS ACT 1973
(1973, c. 62)

35. Compensation orders against convicted persons.

[(1) Subject to the provisions of this Part of this Act and to section 40 of the Magistrates' Courts Act 1980 (which imposes a monetary limit on the powers of a magistrates' court under this section), a court by or before which a person is convicted of an offence, instead of or in addition to dealing with him in any other way, may, on application or otherwise, make an order (in this Act referred to as "a compensation order") requiring him to pay compensation for any personal injury, loss or damage resulting from that offence or any other offence which is taken into consideration by the court in determining sentence [or to make payments for funeral expenses or bereavement in respect of a death resulting from any such offence, other than a death due to an accident arising out of the presence of a motor vehicle on a road; and a court shall give reasons, on passing sentence, if it does not make such an order in a case where this section empowers it to do so].

[(1A) Compensation under subsection (1) above shall be of such amount as the court considers appropriate having regard to any evidence and to any representations that are made by or on behalf of the accused or the prosecutor.]

(2) In the case of an offence under the Theft Act 1968, where the property in question is recovered, any damage to the property occurring while it was out of the owner's possession shall be treated for the purposes of subsection (1) above as having resulted from the offence, however and by whomsoever the damage was caused.

[(3) A compensation order may only be made in respect of injury, loss or damage (other than loss suffered by a person's dependants in consequence of his death) which was due to an accident arising out of the presence of a motor vehicle on a road, if—

(a) it is in respect of damage which is treated by subsection (2) above as resulting from an offence under the Theft Act 1968; or

(b) it is in respect of injury, loss or damage as respects which—

(i) the offender is uninsured in relation to the use of the vehicle; and

(ii) compensation is not payable under any arrangements to which the Secretary of State is a party;

and, where a compensation order is made in respect of injury, loss or damage due to such an accident, the amount to be paid may include an amount representing the whole or part of any loss of or reduction in preferential rates of insurance attributable to the accident.

(3A) A vehicle the use of which is exempted from insurance by section 144 of the Road Traffic Act 1972 is not uninsured for the purposes of subsection (3) above.

(3B) A compensation order in respect of funeral expenses may be made for the benefit of anyone who incurred the expenses.

(3C) A compensation order in respect of bereavement may only be made for the benefit of a person for whose benefit a claim for damages for bereavement could be made under section 1A of the Fatal Accidents Act 1976.

(3D) The amount of compensation in respect of bereavement shall not exceed the amount for the time being specified in section 1A(3) of the Fatal Accidents Act 1976.]

(4) In determining whether to make a compensation order against any person, and in determining the amount to be paid by any person under such an order, the court shall have regard to his means so far as they appear or are known to the court.

[(4A) Where the court considers:
    (a)   that it would be appropriate both to impose a fine and to make a compensation order; but
    (b)   that the offender has insufficient means to pay both an appropriate fine and appropriate compensation, the court shall give preference to compensation (though it may impose a fine as well).]

[**38. Effect of compensation order on subsequent award of damages in civil proceedings.**

(1) This section shall have effect where a compensation order [or a service compensation order or award] has been made in favour of any person in respect of any injury, loss or damage and a claim by him in civil proceedings for damages in respect the injury, loss or damage subsequently falls to be determined.

(2) The damages in the civil proceedings shall be assessed without regard to the order [or award]; but the plaintiff may only recover an amount equal to the aggregate of the following—
    (a)   any amount by which they exceed the compensation; and
    (b)   a sum equal to any portion of the compensation which he fails to recover,
and may not enforce the judgment, so far as it relates to a sum such as is mentioned in paragraph (b) above, without the leave of the court.]

SUPPLY OF GOODS (IMPLIED TERMS) ACT 1973
(1973, c. 13)

8. Implied terms as title.

[(1) In every hire-purchase agreement, other than one to which subsection (2) below applies, there is—
    (a)   an implied term on the part of the creditor that he will have a right to sell the goods at the time when the property is to pass; and
    (b)   an implied term that—
        (i)   the goods are free, and will remain free until the time when the property is to pass, from any charge or encumbrance not disclosed or known to the person to whom the goods are bailed or (in Scotland) hired before the agreement is made, and
        (ii)   that person will enjoy quiet possession of the goods except so far as it may be disturbed by any person entitled to the benefit of any charge or encumbrance so disclosed or known.

(2) In a hire-purchase agreement, in the case of which there appears from the agreement or is to be inferred from the circumstances of the agreement an intention that the creditor should transfer only such title as he or a third person may have, there is—
    (a)   an implied term that all charges or encumbrances known to the creditor and not known to the person to whom the goods are bailed or hired have been disclosed to that person before the agreement is made; and
    (b)   an implied term that neither—
        (i)   the creditor; nor
        (ii)   in a case where the parties to the agreement intend that any title which may be transferred shall be only such title as a third person may have, that person; nor
        (iii)   anyone claiming through or under the creditor or that third person otherwise than under a charge or encumbrance disclosed or known to the person to whom the goods are bailed or hired, before the agreement is made;

will disturb the quiet possession of the person to whom the goods are bailed or hired.]

[(3) As regards England and Wales and Northern Ireland, the term implied by subsection (1)(a) above is a condition and the terms implied by subsections (1)(b), (2)(a) and (2)(b) above are warranties.]

9. Bailing or hiring by description.

[(1) Where under a hire-purchase agreement goods are bailed or (in Scotland) hired by description, there is an implied term that the goods will correspond with the description, and if under the agreement the goods are bailed or hired by reference to a sample as well as a description, it is not sufficient that the bulk of the goods corresponds with the sample if the goods do not also correspond with the description.]

[(1A) As regards England and Wales and Northern Ireland, the term implied by subsection (1) above is a condition.]

[(2) Goods shall not be prevented from being bailed or hired by description by reason only that, being exposed for sale, bailment or hire, they are selected by the person to whom they are bailed or hired.]

10. Implied undertakings as to quality or fitness.

[(1) Except as provided by this section and section 11 below and subject to the provisions of any other enactment, including any enactment of the Parliament of Northern Ireland or the Northern Ireland Assembly, there is no implied term as to the quality or fitness for any particular purpose of goods bailed or (in Scotland) hired under a hire-purchase agreement.]

[(2) Where the creditor bails or hires goods under a hire purchase agreement in the course of a business, there is an implied term that the goods supplied under the agreement are of satisfactory quality.

(2A) For the purposes of this Act, goods are of satisfactory quality if they meet the standard that a reasonable person would regard as satisfactory, taking account of any description of the goods, the price (if relevant) and all the other relevant circumstances.

(2B) For the purposes of this Act, the quality of goods includes their state and condition and the following (among others) are in appropriate cases aspects of the quality of goods—

    (a) fitness for all the purposes for which goods of the kind in question are commonly supplied,

    (b) appearance and finish,

    (c) freedom from minor defects,

    (d) safety, and

    (e) durability.

(2C) The term implied by subsection (2) above does not extend to any matter making the quality of goods unsatisfactory—

    (a) which is specifically drawn to the attention of the person to whom the goods are bailed or hired before the agreement is made,

    (b) where that person examines the goods before the agreement is made, which that examination ought to reveal, or

    (c) where the goods are bailed or hired by reference to a sample, which would have been apparent on a reasonable examination of the sample.]

[(3) Where the creditor bails or hires goods under a hire-purchase agreement in the course of a business and the person to whom the goods are bailed or hired, expressly or by implication, makes known—

    (a) to the creditor in the course of negotiations conducted by the creditor in relation to the making of the hire-purchase agreement, or

    (b) to a credit-broker in the course of negotiations conducted by that broker in relation to goods sold by him to the creditor before forming the subject matter of the hire-purchase agreement, any particular purpose for which the goods are being bailed or hired, there is an implied term that the goods supplied under the agreement are reasonably fit for that purpose, whether or not that is a purpose for which such goods are commonly supplied, except where the circumstances show that the person to whom the goods are bailed or hired does not rely, or that it is unreasonable for him to rely, on the skill or judgment of the creditor or credit-broker.

(4) An implied term as to quality or fitness for a particular purpose may be annexed to a hire-purchase agreement by usage.

(5) The preceding provisions of this section apply to a hire-purchase agreement made by a person who in the course of a business is acting as agent for the creditor as they apply to an agreement made by the creditor in the course of a business, except where the creditor is not bailing or hiring in the course of a business and either the person to whom the goods are bailed or hired knows that fact or reasonable steps are taken to bring it to the notice of that person before the agreement is made.

(6) In subsection (3) above and this subsection—
(a) "credit-broker" means a person acting in the course of a business of credit brokerage;
(b) "credit brokerage" means the effecting of introductions of individuals desiring to obtain credit—
(i) to persons carrying on any business so far as it relates to the provision of credit, or
(ii) to other persons engaged in credit brokerage.]

[(7) As regards England and Wales and Northern Ireland, the terms implied by subsections (2) and (3) above are conditions.]

11. Samples.
[(1) Where under a hire-purchase agreement goods are bailed or (in Scotland) hired by reference to a sample, there is an implied term—
(a) that the bulk will correspond with the sample in quality; and
(b) that the person to whom the goods are bailed or hired will have a reasonable opportunity of comparing the bulk with the sample; and
(c) that the goods will be free from any defect, making their quality unsatisfactory, which would not be apparent on reasonable examination of the sample.]

[(2) As regards England and Wales and Northern Ireland, the term implied by subsection (1) above is a condition.]

[11A. Modification of remedies for breach of statutory condition in non-consumer cases.
(1) Where in the case of a hire purchase agreement—
(a) the person to whom goods are bailed would, apart from this subsection, have the right to reject them by reason of a breach on the part of the creditor of a term implied by section 9, 10 or 11(1)(a) or (c) above, but
(b) the breach is so slight that it would be unreasonable for him to reject them,
then, if the person to whom the goods are bailed does not deal as consumer, the breach is not to be treated as a breach of condition but may be treated as a breach of warranty.

(2) This section applies unless a contrary intention appears in, or is to be implied from, the agreement.

(3) It is for the creditor to show—
(a) that a breach fell within subsection (1)(b) above, and
(b) that the person to whom the goods were bailed did not deal as consumer.

(4) The references in this section to dealing as consumer are to be construed in accordance with Part I of the Unfair Contract Terms Act 1977.

(5) This section does not apply to Scotland.]

[12. Exclusion of implied terms and conditions.
(1) An express term does not negative a term implied by this Act unless inconsistent with it.]

[12A. Remedies for breach of hire-purchase agreement as respects Scotland.
...]

14. Special provisions as to conditional sale agreements.
[(1) Section 11(4) of the Sale of Goods Act 1979 (whereby in certain circumstances a breach of a condition in a contract of sale is treated only as a breach of warranty) shall not apply to [a conditional sale agreement where the buyer deals as consumer within Part I of the Unfair Contract Terms Act 1977 ...

(2) In England and Wales and Northern Ireland a breach of a condition (whether express or implied) to be fulfilled by the seller under any such agreement shall be treated as a breach of warranty, and not as grounds for rejecting the goods and treating the agreement as repudiated, if (but only if) it would have fallen to be so treated had the condition been contained or implied in a corresponding hire-purchase agreement as a condition to be fulfilled by the creditor.]

15. Supplementary.
[(1) In sections 8 to 14 above and this section—
"business" includes a profession and the activities of any government department (including a Northern Ireland department), [or local or public authority];
"buyer" and "seller" includes a person to whom rights and duties under a conditional sale agreement have passed by assignment or operation of law;
"conditional sale agreement" means an agreement for the sale of goods under which the purchase price or part of it is payable by instalments, and the property in the goods is to remain in the seller (notwithstanding that the buyer is to be in possession of the goods) until such conditions as to the payment of instalments or otherwise as may be specified in the agreement are fulfilled;
["consumer sale" has the same meaning as in section 55 of the Sale of Goods Act 1979 (as set out in paragraph 11 of Schedule 1 to that Act)];
"creditor" means the person by whom the goods are bailed or (in Scotland) hired under a hire-purchase agreement or the person to whom his rights and duties under the agreement have passed by assignment or operation of law; and
"hire-purchase agreement" means an agreement, other than conditional sale agreement, under which—
  (a) goods are bailed or (in Scotland) hired in return for periodical payments by the person to whom they are bailed or hired, and
  (b) the property in the goods will pass to that person if the terms of the agreement are complied with and one or more of the following occurs—
    (i) the exercise of an option to purchase by that person,
    (ii) the doing of any other specified act by any party to the agreement,
    (iii) the happening of any other specified event.

(3) In section 14(2) above "corresponding hire-purchase agreement" means, in relation to a conditional sale agreement, a hire-purchase agreement relating to the same goods as the conditional sale agreement and made between the same parties and at the same time and in the same circumstances and, as nearly as may be, in the same terms as the conditional sale agreement.

(4) Nothing in sections 8 to 13 above shall prejudice the operation of any other enactment including any enactment of the Parliament of Northern Ireland or the Northern Ireland Assembly or any rule of law whereby any term, other than one relating to quality or fitness, is to be implied in any hire-purchase agreement.]

CONSUMER CREDIT ACT 1974
(1974, c. 39)
PART IV

46. False or misleading advertisements.

(1) If an advertisement to which this Part applies conveys information which in a material respect is false or misleading the advertiser commits an offence.

(2) Information stating or implying an intention on the advertiser's part which he has not got is false.

PART V

55. Disclosure of information.

(1) Regulations may require specified information to be disclosed in the prescribed manner to the debtor or hirer before a regulated agreement is made.

(2) A regulated agreement is not properly executed unless regulations under subsection (1) were complied with before the making of the agreement.

56. Antecedent negotiations.

(1) In this Act "antecedent negotiations" means any negotiations with the debtor or hirer—
 (a) conducted by the creditor or owner in relation to the making of any regulated agreement, or
 (b) conducted by a credit-broker in relation to goods sold or proposed to be sold by the credit-broker to the creditor before forming the subject-matter of a debtor-creditor-supplier agreement within section 12(a), or
 (c) conducted by the supplier in relation to a transaction financed or proposed to be financed by a debtor-creditor-supplier agreement within section 12(b) or (c),
and "negotiator" means the person by whom negotiations are so conducted with the debtor or hirer.

(2) Negotiations with the debtor in a case falling within subsection (1)(b) or (c) shall be deemed to be conducted by the negotiator in the capacity of agent of the creditor as well as in his actual capacity.

(3) An agreement is void if, and to the extent that, it purports in relation to an actual or prospective regulated agreement—
 (a) to provide that a person acting as, or on behalf of, a negotiator is to be treated as the agent of the debtor or hirer, or
 (b) to relieve a person from liability for acts or omissions of any person acting as, or on behalf of, a negotiator.

(4) For the purposes of this Act, antecedent negotiations shall be taken to begin when the negotiator and the debtor or hirer first enter into communication (including communication by advertisement), and to include any representations made by the negotiator to the debtor or hirer and any other dealings between them.

57. Withdrawal from prospective agreement.

(1) The withdrawal of a party from a prospective regulated agreement shall operate to apply this Part to the agreement, any linked transaction and any other thing done in anticipation of the making of the agreement as it would apply if the agreement were made and then cancelled under section 69.

60. Form and content of agreements.

(1) The Secretary of State shall make regulations as to the form and content of documents embodying regulated agreements, and the regulations shall contain such provisions as appear to him appropriate with a view to ensuring that the debtor or hirer is made aware of—

(a) the rights and duties conferred or imposed on him by the agreement,
(b) the amount and rate of the total charge for credit (in the case of a consumer credit agreement),
(c) the protection and remedies available to him under this Act, and
(d) any other matters which, in the opinion of the Secretary of State, it is desirable for him to know about in connection with the agreement.

65. Consequences of improper execution.

(1) An improperly-executed regulated agreement is enforceable against the debtor or hirer on an order of the court only.

67. Cancellable agreements.

A regulated agreement may be cancelled by the debtor or hirer in accordance with this Part if the antecedent negotiations included oral representations made when in the presence of the debtor or hirer by an individual acting as, or on behalf of, the negotiator, unless—

(a) the agreement is secured on land, or is a restricted-use credit agreement to finance the purchase of land or is an agreement for a bridging loan in connection with the purchase of land, or

(b) the unexecuted agreement is signed by the debtor or hirer at premises at which any of the following is carrying on any business (whether on a permanent or temporary basis)—
  (i) the creditor or owner;
  (ii) any party to a linked transaction (other than the debtor or hirer or a relative of his);
  (iii) the negotiator in any antecedent negotiations.

68. Cooling-off period.

The debtor or hirer may serve notice of cancellation of a cancellable agreement between his signing of the unexecuted agreement and—

(a) the end of the fifth day following the day on which he received a copy under section 63(2) or a notice under section 64(1)(b), or

(b) if (by virtue of regulations made under section 64(4)) section 64(1)(b) does not apply, the end of the fourteenth day following the day on which he signed the unexecuted agreement.

69. Notice of cancellation.

(1) If within the period specified in section 68 the debtor or hirer under a cancellable agreement serves on—
(a) the creditor or owner, or
(b) the person specified in the notice under section 64(1), or
(c) a person who (whether by virtue of subsection (6) or otherwise) is the agent of the creditor or owner,
a notice (a "notice of cancellation') which, however expressed and whether or not conforming to the notice given under section 64(1), indicates the intention of the debtor or hirer to withdraw from the agreement, the notice shall operate—
  (i) to cancel the agreement, and any linked transaction, and
  (ii) to withdraw any offer by the debtor or hirer, or his relative, to enter into a linked transaction.

(4) Except as otherwise provided by or under this Act, an agreement or transaction cancelled under subsection (1) shall be treated as if it had never been entered into.

70. Cancellation: recovery of money paid by debtor or hirer.

(1) On the cancellation of a regulated agreement, and of any linked transaction,—

(a) any sum paid by the debtor or hirer, or his relative, under or in contemplation of the agreement or transaction, including any item in the total charge for credit, shall become repayable, and

(b) any sum, including any item in the total charge for credit, which but for the cancellation is, or would or might become, payable by the debtor or hirer, or his relative, under the agreement or transaction shall cease to be, or shall not become, so payable, and

(c) in the case of a debtor-creditor-supplier agreement falling within section 12(b), any sum paid on the debtor's behalf by the creditor to the supplier shall become repayable to the creditor.

(3) A sum repayable under subsection (1) is repayable by the person to whom it was originally paid, but in the case of a debtor-creditor-supplier agreement falling within section 12(b) the creditor and the supplier shall be under a joint and several liability to repay sums paid by the debtor, or his relative, under the agreement or under a linked transaction falling within section 19(1)(b) and accordingly, in such a case, the creditor shall be entitled, in accordance with rules of court, to have the supplier made a party to any proceedings brought against the creditor to recover any such sums.

(4) Subject to any agreement between them, the creditor shall be entitled to be indemnified by the supplier for loss suffered by the creditor in satisfying his liability under subsection (3), including costs reasonably incurred by him in defending proceedings instituted by the debtor.

71. Cancellation: repayment of credit.

(1) Notwithstanding the cancellation of a regulated consumer credit agreement, other than a debtor-creditor-supplier agreement for restricted-use credit, the agreement shall continue in force so far as it relates to repayment of credit and payment of interest.

PART VI

75. Liability of creditor for breaches by supplier.

(1) If the debtor under a debtor-creditor-supplier agreement falling within section 12(b) or (c) has, in relation to a transaction financed by the agreement, any claim against the supplier in respect of a misrepresentation or breach of contract, he shall have a like claim against the creditor, who, with the supplier, shall accordingly be jointly and severally liable to the debtor.

(2) Subject to any agreement between them, the creditor shall be entitled to be indemnified by the supplier for loss suffered by the creditor in satisfying his liability under subsection (1), including costs reasonably incurred by him in defending proceedings instituted by the debtor.

(3) Subsection (1) does not apply to a claim—

(a) under a non-commercial agreement, or

(b) so far as the claim relates to any single item to which the supplier has attached a cash price not exceeding £30 or more than £10,000.

(4) This section applies notwithstanding that the debtor, in entering into the transaction, exceeded the credit limit or otherwise contravened any term of the agreement.

(5) In an action brought against the creditor under subsection (1) he shall be entitled, in accordance with rules of court, to have the supplier made a party to the proceedings.

76. Duty to give notice before taking certain action.

(1) The creditor or owner is not entitled to enforce a term of a regulated agreement by—

(a) demanding earlier payment of any sum, or

(b) recovering possession of any goods or land, or

(c) treating any right conferred on the debtor or hirer by the agreement as terminated, restricted or deferred,

except by or after giving the debtor or hirer not less than seven days' notice of his intention to do so.

(2) Subsection (1) applies only where—
  (a) a period for the duration of the agreement is specified in the agreement, and
  (b) that period has not ended when the creditor or owner does an act mentioned in subsection (1),

but so applies notwithstanding that, under the agreement, any party is entitled to terminate it before the end of the period so specified.

(6) Subsection (1) does not apply to a right of enforcement arising by reason of any breach by the debtor or hirer of the regulated agreement.

PART VII

87. Need for default notice.

(1) Service of a notice on the debtor or hirer in accordance with section 88 (a "default notice') is necessary before the creditor or owner can become entitled, by reason of any breach by the debtor or hirer of a regulated agreement,—
  (a) to terminate the agreement, or
  (b) to demand earlier payment of any sum, or
  (c) to recover possession of any goods or land, or
  (d) to treat any right conferred on the debtor or hirer by the agreement as terminated, restricted or deferred, or
  (e) to enforce any security.

(2) Subsection (1) does not prevent the creditor from treating the right to draw upon any credit as restricted or deferred, and taking such steps as may be necessary to make the restriction or deferment effective.

(4) Regulations may provide that subsection (1) is not to apply to agreements described by the regulations.

88. Contents and effect of default notice.

(1) The default notice must be in the prescribed form and specify—
  (a) the nature of the alleged breach;
  (b) if the breach is capable of remedy, what action is required to remedy it and the date before which that action is to be taken;
  (c) if the breach is not capable of remedy, the sum (if any) required to be paid as compensation for the breach, and the date before which it is to be paid.

94. Right to complete payments ahead of time.

(1) The debtor under a regulated consumer credit agreement is entitled at any time, by notice to the creditor and the payment to the creditor of all amounts payable by the debtor to him under the agreement (less any rebate allowable under section 95), to discharge the debtor's indebtedness under the agreement.

96. Effect on linked transactions.

(1) Where for any reason the indebtedness of the debtor under a regulated consumer credit agreement is discharged before the time fixed by the agreement, he, and any relative of his, shall at the same time be discharged from any liability under a linked transaction, other than a debt which has already become payable.

99. Right to terminate hire-purchase etc., agreements.

(1) At any time before the final payment by the debtor under a regulated hire-purchase or regulated conditional sale agreement falls due, the debtor shall be entitled to terminate the agreement by giving notice to any person entitled or authorised to receive the sums payable under the agreement.

(2) Termination of an agreement under subsection (1) does not affect any liability under the agreement which has accrued before the termination.

(4) In the case of a conditional sale agreement relating to goods, where the property in the goods, having become vested in the debtor, is transferred to a person who does not become the debtor under the agreement, the debtor shall not thereafter be entitled to terminate the agreement under subsection (1).

100. Liability of debtor on termination of hire-purchase etc., agreement.

(1) Where a regulated hire-purchase or regulated conditional sale agreement is terminated under section 99 the debtor shall be liable, unless the agreement provides for a smaller payment, or does not provide for any payment, to pay to the creditor the amount (if any) by which one-half of the total price exceeds the aggregate of the sums paid and the sums due in respect of the total price immediately before the termination.

(3) If in any action the court is satisfied that a sum less than the amount specified in subsection (1) would be equal to the loss sustained by the creditor in consequence of the termination of the agreement by the debtor, the court may make an order for the payment of that sum in lieu of the amount specified in subsection (1).

PART VIII

113. Act not to be evaded by use of security.

(1) Where a security is provided in relation to an actual or prospective regulated agreement, the security shall not be enforced so as to benefit the creditor or owner, directly or indirectly, to an extent greater (whether as respects the amount of any payment or the time or manner of its being made) than would be the case if the security were not provided and any obligations of the debtor or hirer, or his relative, under or in relation to the agreement were carried out to the extent (if any) to which they would be enforced under this Act.

(2) In accordance with subsection (1), where a regulated agreement is enforceable on an order of the court or the Director only, any security provided in relation to the agreement is enforceable (so far as provided in relation to the agreement) where such an order has been made in relation to the agreement, but not otherwise.

(7) Where an indemnity [or guarantee] is given in a case where the debtor or hirer is a minor, or [an indemnity is given in a case where he] is otherwise not of full capacity, the reference in subsection (1) to the extent to which his obligations would be enforced shall be read in relation to the indemnity [or guarantee] as a reference to the extent to which [those obligations] would be enforced if he were of full capacity.

PART IX

127. Enforcement orders in cases of infringement.

(1) In the case of an application for an enforcement order under—

(a) section 65(1) (improperly executed agreements), ... the court shall dismiss the application if, but (subject to subsections (3) and (4)) only if, it considers it just to do so having regard to—

(i) prejudice caused to any person by the contravention in question, and the degree of culpability for it; and

(ii) the powers conferred on the court by subsection (2) and sections 135 and 136.

(2) If it appears to the court just to do so, it may in an enforcement order reduce or discharge any sum payable by the debtor or hirer, or any surety, so as to compensate him for prejudice suffered as a result of the contravention in question.

129. Time orders.

(1) If it appears to the court just to do so—

(a) on an application for an enforcement order; or

(b) on an application made by a debtor or hirer under this paragraph after service on him of—
    (i) a default notice, or
    (ii) a notice under section 76(1) or 98(1); or
(c) in an action brought by a creditor or owner to enforce a regulated agreement or any security, or recover possession of any goods or land to which a regulated agreement relates,
the court may make an order under this section (a "time order").

(2) A time order shall provide for one or both of the following, as the court considers just—
    (a) the payment by the debtor or hirer or any surety of any sum owed under a regulated agreement or a security by such instalments, payable at such times, as the court, having regard to the means of the debtor or hirer and any surety, considers reasonable;
    (b) the remedying by the debtor or hirer of any breach of a regulated agreement (other than non-payment of money) within such period as the court may specify.

132. Financial relief for hirer.

(1) Where the owner under a regulated consumer hire agreement recovers possession of goods to which the agreement relates otherwise than by action, the hirer may apply to the court for an order that—
    (a) the whole or part of any sum paid by the hirer to the owner in respect of the goods shall be repaid, and
    (b) the obligation to pay the whole or part of any sum owed by the hirer to the owner in respect of the goods shall cease,
and if it appears to the court just to do so, having regard to the extent of the enjoyment of the goods by the hirer, the court shall grant the application in full or in part.

137. Extortionate credit bargains.

(1) If the court finds a credit bargain extortionate it may reopen the credit agreement so as to do justice between the parties.

138. When bargains are extortionate.

(1) A credit bargain is extortionate if it—
    (a) requires the debtor or a relative of his to make payments (whether unconditionally, or on certain contingencies) which are grossly exorbitant, or
    (b) otherwise grossly contravenes ordinary principles of fair dealing.

(2) In determining whether a credit bargain is extortionate, regard shall be had to such evidence as is adduced concerning—
    (a) interest rates prevailing at the time it was made,
    (b) the factors mentioned in subsection (3) to (5), and
    (c) any other relevant considerations.

(3) Factors applicable under subsection (2) in relation to the debtor include—
    (a) his age, experience, business capacity and state of health; and
    (b) the degree to which, at the time of making the credit bargain, he was under financial pressure, and the nature of that pressure.

(4) Factors applicable under subsection (2) in relation to the creditor include—
    (a) the degree of risk accepted by him, having regard to the value of any security provided;
    (b) his relationship to the debtor; and
    (c) whether or not a colourable cash price was quoted for any goods or services included in the credit bargain.

(5) Factors applicable under subsection (2) in relation to a linked transaction include the question how far the transaction was reasonably required for the protection of debtor or creditor, or was in the interest of the debtor.

139. Reopening of extortionate agreements.

(2) In reopening the agreement, the court may, for the purpose of relieving the debtor or a surety from payment of any sum in excess of that fairly due and reasonable, by order—

(a) direct accounts to be taken, or (in Scotland) an accounting to be made, between any persons,

(b) set aside the whole or part of any obligation imposed on the debtor or a surety by the credit bargain or any related agreement,

(c) require the creditor to repay the whole or part of any sum paid under the credit bargain or any related agreement by the debtor or a surety, whether paid to the creditor or any other person,

(d) direct the return to the surety of any property provided for the purposes of the security, or

(e) alter the terms of the credit agreement or any security instrument.

(3) An order may be made under subsection (2) notwithstanding that its effect is to place a burden on the creditor in respect of an advantage unfairly enjoyed by another person who is a party to a linked transaction.

PART XI

162. Powers of entry and inspection.

(1) A duly authorised officer of an enforcement authority, at all reasonable hours and on production, if required, of his credentials, may—

(a) in order to ascertain whether a breach of any provision of or under this Act has been committed, inspect any goods and enter any premises (other than premises used only as a dwelling); ...

(c) if he has reasonable cause to believe that a breach of any provision of or under this Act has been committed, seize and detain any goods in order to ascertain (by testing or otherwise) whether such a breach has been committed;

(d) seize and detain any goods, books or documents which he has reason to believe may be required as evidence in proceedings for an offence under this Act;

(e) for the purpose of exercising his powers under this subsection to seize goods, books or documents, but only if and to the extent that it is reasonably necessary for securing that the provisions of this Act and of any regulations made under it are duly observed, require any person having authority to do so to break open any container and, if that person does not comply, break it open himself.

(2) An officer seizing goods, books or documents in exercise of his powers under this section shall not do so without informing the person he seizes them from.

(4) An officer entering premises by virtue of this section may take such other persons and equipment with him as he thinks necessary; and on leaving premises entered by virtue of a warrant under subsection (3) shall, if they are unoccupied or the occupier is temporarily absent, leave them as effectively secured against trespassers as he found them.

(6) A person who is not a duly authorised officer of an enforcement authority, but purports to act as such under this section, commits an offence.

163. Compensation for loss.

(1) Where, in exercising his powers under section 162, an officer of an enforcement authority seizes and detains goods and their owner suffers loss by reason of—

(a) that seizure, or

(b) the loss, damage or deterioration of the goods during detention,

then, unless the owner is convicted of an offence under this Act committed in relation to the goods, the authority shall compensate him for the loss so suffered.

165. Obstruction of authorised officers.

(1) Any person who—

(a) wilfully obstructs an officer of an enforcement authority acting in pursuance of this Act; or

(b) wilfully fails to comply with any requirement properly made to him by such an officer under section 162; or

(c) without reasonable cause fails to give such an officer (so acting) other assistance or information he may reasonably require in performing his functions under this Act,

commits an offence.

170. No further sanctions for breach of Act.

(1) A breach of any requirement made (otherwise than by any court) by or under this Act shall incur no civil or criminal sanction as being such a breach, except to the extent (if any) expressly provided by or under this Act.

173. Contracting-out forbidden.

(1) A term contained in a regulated agreement or linked transaction, or in any other agreement relating to an actual or prospective regulated agreement or linked transaction, is void if, and to the extent that, it is inconsistent with a provision for the protection of the debtor or hirer or his relative or any surety contained in this Act or in any regulation made under this Act.

(2) Where a provision specifies the duty or liability of the debtor or hirer or his relative or any surety in certain circumstances, a term is inconsistent with that provision if it purports to impose, directly or indirectly, an additional duty or liability on him in those circumstances.

(3) Notwithstanding subsection (1), a provision of this Act under which a thing may be done in relation to any person on an order of the court or the Director only shall not be taken to prevent its being done at any time with that person's consent given at that time, but the refusal of such consent shall not give rise to any liability.

175. Duty of persons deemed to be agents.

Where under this Act a person is deemed to receive a notice or payment as agent of the creditor or owner under a regulated agreement, he shall be deemed to be under a contractual duty to the creditor or owner to transmit the notice, or remit the payment, to him forthwith.

181. Power to alter monetary limits etc.

(1) The Secretary of State may by order made by statutory instrument amend, or further amend, any of the following provisions of this Act so as to reduce or increase a sum mentioned in that provision, namely, sections ... 75(3)(b) ...

189. Definitions.

(1) In this Act, unless the context otherwise requires—

"representation" includes any condition or warranty, and any other statement or undertaking, whether oral or in writing; ...

HEALTH AND SAFETY AT WORK ACT 1974
(1974, c. 37)

2. General duties of employers to their employees.

(1) It shall be the duty of every employer to ensure, so far as is reasonably practicable, the health, safety and welfare of work of all his employees.

3. General duties of employers and self-employed to persons other than their employees.

(1) It shall be the duty of every employer to conduct his undertaking in such a way as to ensure, so far as is reasonably practicable, that persons not in his employment who may be affected thereby are not thereby exposed to risks to their health or safety.

(2) It shall be the duty of every self-employed person to conduct his undertaking in such a way as to ensure, so far as is reasonably practicable, that he and other persons (not being his employees) who may be affected thereby are not thereby exposed to risks to their health or safety.

(3) In such cases as may be prescribed, it shall be the duty of every employer and every self-employed person, in the prescribed circumstances and in the prescribed manner, to give to persons (not being his employees) who may be affected by the way in which he conducts his undertaking the prescribed information about such aspects of the way in which he conducts his undertaking as might affect their health or safety.

4. General duties of persons concerned with premises to persons other than their employees.

(1) This section has effect for imposing on persons duties in relation to those who—

   (a) are not their employees; but

   (b) use non-domestic premises made available to them as a place of work or as a place where they may use plant or substances provided for their use there,

and applies to premises so made available and other non-domestic premises used in connection with them.

(2) It shall be the duty of each person who has, to any extent, control of premises to which this section applies or of the means of access thereto or egress therefrom or of any plant or substance in such premises to take such measures as it is reasonable for a person in his position to take to ensure, so far as is reasonably practicable, that the premises, all means of access thereto or egress therefrom available for use by persons using the premises, and any plant or substance in the premises or, as the case may be, provided for use there, is or are safe and without risks to health.

(3) Where a person has, by virtue of any contract or tenancy, an obligation of any extent in relation to—

   (a) the maintenance or repair of any premises to which this section applies or any means of access thereto or egress therefrom; or

   (b) the safety of or the absence of risks to health arising from plant or substances in any such premises;

that person shall be treated, for the purposes of subsection (2) above, as being a person who has control of the matters to which his obligation extends.

(4) Any reference in this section to a person having control of any premises or matter is a reference to a person having control of the premises or matter in connection with the carrying on by him of a trade, business or other undertaking (whether for profit or not).

10. Establishment of the Commission and the Executive.

(1) There shall be two bodies corporate to be called the Health and Safety Commission and the Health and Safety Executive ...

15. Health and safety regulations.

[(1) Subject to the provisions of section 50, the Secretary of State, the Minister of Agriculture, Fisheries and Food or the Secretary of State and the Minister acting jointly shall have power to make regulations under this section for any of the general purposes of this Part (and regulations so made are in this Part referred to as "health and safety regulations").]

(2) Without prejudice to the generality of the preceding subsection, health and safety regulations may for any of the general purposes of this Part make provision for any of the purposes mentioned in Schedule 3.

(3) Health and safety regulations—

(a) may repeal or modify any of the existing statutory provisions;

(b) may exclude or modify in relation to any specified class of case any of the provisions of sections 2 to 9 or any of the existing statutory provisions;

(c) may make a specified authority or class of authorities responsible, to such extent as may be specified, for the enforcement of any of the relevant statutory provisions.

(4) Health and safety regulations—

(a) may impose requirements by reference to the approval of the Commission or any other specified body or person;

(b) may provide for references in the regulations to any specified document to operate as references to that document as revised or re-issued from time to time.

(5) Health and safety regulations—

(a) may provide (either unconditionally or subject to conditions, and with or without limit of time) for exemptions from any requirement or prohibition imposed by or under any of the relevant statutory provisions;

(b) may enable exemptions from any requirement or prohibition imposed by or under any of the relevant statutory provisions to be granted (either unconditionally or subject to conditions, and with or without limit of time) by any specified person or by any person authorised in that behalf by a specified authority.

(6) Health and safety regulations—

(a) may specify the persons or classes of persons who, in the event of a contravention of a requirement or prohibition imposed by or under the regulations, are to be guilty of an offence, whether in addition to or to the exclusion of other persons or classes of persons;

(b) may provide for any specified defence to be available in proceedings for any offence under the relevant statutory provisions either generally or in specified circumstances;

(c) may exclude proceedings on indictment in relation to offences consisting of a contravention of a requirement or prohibition imposed by or under any of the existing statutory provisions, sections 2 to 9 or health and safety regulations;

(d) may restrict the punishments [(other than the maximum fine on conviction on indictment)] which can be imposed in respect of any such offence as is mentioned in paragraph (c) above.

(7) Without prejudice to section 35, health and safety regulations may make provision for enabling offences under any of the relevant statutory provisions to be treated as having been committed at any specified place for the purpose of bringing any such offence within the field of responsibility of any enforcing authority or conferring jurisdiction on any court to entertain proceedings for any such offence.

(8) Health and safety regulations may take the form of regulations applying to particular circumstances only or to a particular case only (for example, regulations applying to particular premises only).

(9) If an Order in Council is made under section 84(3) providing that this section shall apply to or in relation to persons, premises or work outside Great Britain then, notwithstanding the Order, health and safety regulations shall not apply to or in relation to aircraft in flight, vessels, hovercraft or offshore installations outside Great Britain or persons at work outside Great Britain in connection with submarine cables or submarine pipelines except in so far as the regulations expressly so provide.

(10) In this section "specified" means specified in health and safety regulations.

17. Use of approved codes of practice in criminal proceedings.
A failure on the part of any person to observe any provision of an approved code of practice shall not of itself render him liable to any civil or criminal proceedings; but where in any criminal proceedings a party is alleged to have committed an offence by reason of a contravention of any requirement or prohibition imposed by or under any such provision as is mentioned in section 16(1) being a provision for which there was an approved code of practice at the time of the alleged contravention, the following subsection shall have effect with respect to that code in relation to those proceedings.

47. Civil liability.
(1) Nothing in this Part shall be construed—
   (a) as conferring a right of action in any civil proceedings in respect of any failure to comply with any duty imposed by sections 2 to 7 or any contravention of section 8; or
   (b) as affecting the extent (if any) to which breach of a duty imposed by any of the existing statutory provisions is actionable; or
   (c) as affecting the operation of section 12 of the Nuclear Installations Act 1965 (right to compensation by virtue of certain provisions of that Act).
(2) Breach of a duty imposed by health and safety regulations [...] shall, so far as it causes damages, be actionable except in so far as the regulations provide otherwise.
(3) No provision made by virtue of section 15(6)(b) shall afford a defence in any civil proceedings, whether brought by virtue of subsection (2) above or not; but as regards any duty imposed as mentioned in subsection (2) above health and safety regulations [...] may provide for any defence specified in the regulations to be available in any action for breach of that duty.
(4) Subsections (1)(a) and (2) above are without prejudice to any right of action which exists apart from the provisions of this Act, and subsection (3) above is without prejudice to any defence which may be available apart from the provisions of the regulations there mentioned.
(5) Any term of an agreement which purports to exclude or restrict the operation of subsection (2) above, or any liability arising by virtue of that subsection, shall be void, except in so far as health and safety regulations [...] provide otherwise.
(6) In this section "damage" includes the death of, or injury to, any person (including any disease and any impairment of a person's physical or mental condition).

REHABILITATION OF OFFENDERS ACT 1974
(1974, c. 53)

4. Effect of rehabilitation.
(1) Subject to sections 7 and 8 below, a person who has become a rehabilitated person for the purposes of this Act in respect of a conviction shall be treated for all purposes in law as a person who has not committed or been charged with or prosecuted for or convicted of or sentenced for the offence or offences which were the subject of that conviction; and, notwithstanding the provisions of any other enactment or rule of law to the contrary, but subject as aforesaid—
   (a) no evidence shall be admissible in any proceedings before a judicial authority exercising its jurisdiction or functions in Great Britain to prove that any such person has committed or been charged with or prosecuted for or convicted of or sentenced for any offence which was the subject of a spent conviction; and
   (b) a person shall not, in any such proceedings, be asked, and, if asked, shall not be required to answer, any question relating to his past which cannot be answered without acknowledging or referring to a spent conviction or spent convictions or any circumstances ancillary thereto.

8. Defamation actions.
(1) This section applies to any action for libel or slander begun after the commencement of this Act by a rehabilitated person and founded upon the publication

of any matter imputing that the plaintiff has committed or been charged with or prosecuted for or convicted of or sentenced for an offence which was the subject of a spent conviction.

(2) Nothing in section 4(1) above shall affect an action to which this section applies where the publication complained of took place before the conviction in question became spent, and the following provisions of this section shall not apply in any such case.

(3) Subject to subsections (5) and (6) below, nothing in section 4(1) above shall prevent the defendant in an action to which this section applies from relying on any defence of justification or fair comment or of absolute or qualified privilege which is available to him, or restrict the matters he may establish in support of any such defence.

(4) Without prejudice to the generality of subsection (3) above, where in any such action malice is alleged against a defendant who is relying on a defence of qualified privilege, nothing in section 4(1) above shall restrict the matters he may establish in rebuttal of the allegation.

(5) A defendant in any such action shall not by virtue of subsection (3) above be entitled to rely upon the defence of justification if the publication is proved to have been made with malice.

(6) Subject to subsection (7) below a defendant in any such action shall not, by virtue of subsection (3) above, be entitled to rely on any matter or adduce or require any evidence for the purpose of establishing (whether under [section 14 of the Defamation Act 1996] or otherwise) the defence that the matter published constituted a fair and accurate report of judicial proceedings if it is proved that the publication contained a reference to evidence which was ruled to be inadmissible in the proceedings by virtue of section 4(1) above.

(7) Subsection (3) above shall apply without the qualifications imposed by subsection (6) above in relation to—

(a) any report of judicial proceedings contained in any bona fide series of law reports which does not form part of any other publication and consists solely of reports of proceedings in courts of law, and

(b) any report or account of judicial proceedings published for bona fide educational, scientific or professional purposes or given in the course of any lecture, class or discussion given or held for any of those purposes.

[(7A) Nothing in section 4(1) above shall restrict the evidence that may be adduced in mitigation of damages under section 13(2) of the Defamation Act 1996.]

SOLICITORS ACT 1974
(1974, c. 47)

37. Professional indemnity.

(1) The Council, with the concurrence of the Master of the Rolls, may make rules (in this Act referred to as "indemnity rules") concerning indemnity against loss arising from claims in respect of any description of civil liability incurred—

(a) by a solicitor or former solicitor in connection with his practice or with any trust of which he is or formerly was a trustee;

(b) by an employee or former employee of a solicitor or former solicitor in connection with that solicitor's practice or with any trust of which that solicitor or the employee is or formerly was a trustee.

(2) For the purpose of providing such indemnity, indemnity rules—

(a) may authorise or require the Society to establish and maintain a fund or funds;

(b) may authorise or require the Society to take out and maintain insurance with authorised insurers;

Solicitors Act 1974

(c) may require solicitors or any specified class of solicitors to take out and maintain insurance with authorised insurers.

[37A. Redress for inadequate professional services.
Schedule 1A shall have effect with respect to the provision by solicitors of services which are not of the quality which it is reasonable to expect of them.]

87. Interpretation.
(1) In this Act, except where the context otherwise requires,—
"the Council" means the Council of the Society...
"the Society" means the Law Society...
"the Tribunal" means the Solicitors Disciplinary Tribunal...

[SCHEDULE 1A
INADEQUATE PROFESSIONAL SERVICES

Circumstances in which Council's powers may be exercised

1.—(1) The Council may take any of the steps mentioned in paragraph 2 ("the steps") with respect to a solicitor where it appears to them that the professional services provided by him in connection with any matter in which he or his firm have been instructed by a client have, in any respect, not been of the quality which it is reasonable to expect of him as a solicitor.
   (2) The Council shall not take any of the steps unless they are satisfied that in all the circumstances of the case it is appropriate to do so.
   (3) In determining in any case whether it is appropriate to take any of the steps, the Council may—
   (a) have regard to the existence of any remedy which it is reasonable to expect to be available to the client in civil proceedings; and
   (b) where proceedings seeking any such remedy have not been begun by him, have regard to whether it is reasonable to expect him to begin them.

Directions which may be given

2.—(1) The steps are—
   (a) determining that the costs to which the solicitor is entitled in respect of his services ("the costs") are to be limited to such amount as may be specified in the determination and directing him to comply, or to secure compliance, with such one or more of the permitted requirements as appear to the Council to be necessary in order for effect to be given to their determination;
   (b) directing him to secure the rectification, at his expense or at that of his firm, of any such error, omission or other deficiency arising in connection with the matter in question as they may specify;
   (c) directing him to pay such compensation to the client as the Council sees fit to specify in the direction;
   (d) directing him to take, at his expense or at that of his firm, such other action in the interests of the client as they may specify.
   (2) The "permitted requirements" are—
   (a) that the whole or part of any amount already paid by or on behalf of the client in respect of the costs be refunded;
   (b) that the whole or part of the costs be remitted;
   (c) that the right to recover the costs be waived, whether wholly or to any specified extent.
   (3) The power of the Council to take any such steps is not confined to cases where the client may have a cause of action against the solicitor for negligence.

Compensation

3.—(1) The amount specified in a direction by virtue of paragraph 2(1)(c) shall not exceed £1,000.

(2) The Lord Chancellor may by order made by statutory instrument amend sub-paragraph (1) by substituting for the sum of £1,000 such other sum as he considers appropriate.

(3) Before making any such order the Lord Chancellor shall consult the Law Society.

Failure to comply with direction

5.—(1) If a solicitor fails to comply with a direction given under this Schedule, any person may make a complaint in respect of that failure to the Tribunal; but no other proceedings whatever shall be brought in respect of it.

(2) On the hearing of such a complaint the Tribunal may, if it thinks fit (and whether or not it makes any order under section 47(2)), direct that the direction be treated, for the purpose of enforcement, as if it were contained in an order made by the High Court.

Fees

6.—(1) The Council may, by regulations made with the concurrence of the Lord Chancellor and the Master of the Rolls, make provision for the payment, by any client with respect to whom the Council are asked to consider whether to take any of the steps, of such fee as may be prescribed.

(2) The regulations may provide for the exemption of such classes of client as may be prescribed.

(3) Where a client pays the prescribed fee it shall be repaid to him if the Council take any of the steps in the matter with respect to which the fee was paid.]

GUARD DOGS ACT 1975
(1975, c. 50)

1. Control of guard dogs.

(1) A person shall not use or permit the use of a guard dog at any premises unless a person ("the handler") who is capable of controlling the dog is present on the premises and the dog is under the control of the handler at all times while it is being so used except while it is secured so that it is not at liberty to go free about the premises.

(3) A person shall not use or permit the use of a guard dog at any premises unless a notice containing a warning that a guard dog is present is clearly exhibited at each entrance to the premises.

2. Restriction on keeping guard dogs without a licence.

(1) A person shall not keep a dog at guard dog kennels unless he holds a licence under section 3 of this Act in respect of the kennels.

(2) A person shall not use or permit the use at any premises of a guard dog if he knows or has reasonable cause to suspect that the dog (when not being used as a guard dog) is normally kept at guard dog kennels in breach of subsection (1) of this section.

5. Offences, penalties and civil liability.

(1) A person who contravenes section 1 or 2 of this Act shall be guilty of an offence and liable on summary conviction to a fine not exceeding £400.

(2) The provisions of this Act shall not be construed as—

  (a) conferring a right of action in any civil proceedings (other than proceedings for the recovery of a fine or any prescribed fee) in respect of any contravention of this

Act or of any regulations made under this Act or of any of the terms or conditions of a licence granted under section 3 of this Act; or

(b) derogating from any right of action or other remedy (whether civil or criminal) in proceedings instituted otherwise than by virtue of this Act.

PETROLEUM AND SUBMARINE PIPE-LINES ACT 1975
(1975, c. 74)

30. Civil liability for breach of statutory duty.

(1) Breach of a duty imposed on any person by a provision of regulations which are made in pursuance of this Part of this Act and which state that this subsection applies to such a breach shall be actionable so far, and only so far, as the breach causes personal injury; and references in section 1 of [the Fatal Accidents Act 1976], as it applies in England, Wales [and in Article 3(1) of the Fatal Accidents (Northern Ireland) Order 1977], to a wrongful act, neglect or default shall include references to any such breach which is so actionable.

(2) Nothing in the preceding subsection prejudices any action which lies apart from the provisions of that subsection.

(3) A defence to a charge which is available by virtue of section 32(3)(c) of this Act shall not be a defence in any civil proceedings which are brought either in pursuance of this section or otherwise.

(5) In subsection (1) of this section "personal injury" includes any disease, any impairment of a person's physical or mental condition and any fatal injury.

SEX DISCRIMINATION ACT 1975
(1975, c. 65)

1. Sex discrimination against women.

(1) A person discriminates against a woman in any circumstances relevant for the purposes of any provision of this Act if—

(a) on the ground of her sex he treats her less favourably than he treats or would treat a man, or

(b) he applies to her a requirement or condition which applies or would apply equally to a man but—

(i) which is such that the proportion of women who can comply with it is considerably smaller than the proportion of men who can comply with it, and

(ii) which he cannot show to be justifiable irrespective of the sex of the person to whom it is applied, and

(iii) which is to her detriment because she cannot comply with it.

(2) If a person treats or would treat a man differently according to the man's marital status, his treatment of a woman is for the purposes of subsection (1)(a) to be compared to his treatment of a man having the like marital status.

2. Sex discrimination against men.

(1) Section 1, and the provisions of Parts II and III relating to sex discrimination against women, are to be read as applying equally to the treatment of men, and for that purpose shall have effect with such modifications as are requisite.

(2) In the application of subsection (1) no account shall be taken of special treatment afforded to women in connection with pregnancy or childbirth.

29. Discrimination in provision of goods, facilities or services.

(1) It is unlawful for any person concerned with the provision (for payment or not) of goods, facilities or services to the public or a section of the public to discriminate against a woman who seeks to obtain or use those goods, facilities or services—

(a) by refusing or deliberately omitting to provide her with any of them, or

(b) by refusing or deliberately omitting to provide her with goods, facilities or services of the like quality, in the like manner and on the like terms as are normal in his case in relation to male members of the public or (where she belongs to a section of the public) to male members of that section.

41. Liability of employers and principals.

(1) Anything done by a person in the course of his employment shall be treated for the purposes of this Act as done by his employer as well as by him, whether or not it was done with the employer's knowledge or approval.

(2) Anything done by a person as agent for another person with the authority (whether express or implied, and whether precedent or subsequent) of that other person shall be treated for the purposes of this Act as done by that other person as well as by him.

(3) In proceedings brought under this Act against any person in respect of an act alleged to have been done by an employee of his it shall be a defence for that person to prove that he took such steps as were reasonably practicable to prevent the employee from doing that act, or from doing in the course of his employment acts of that description.

66. Claims under Part III [ss. 22-36].

(1) A claim by any person ("the claimant") that another person ("the respondent")—

(a) has committed an act of discrimination against the claimant which is unlawful by virtue of Part III, ... may be made the subject of civil proceedings in like manner as any other claim in tort or (in Scotland) in reparation for breach of statutory duty.

(3) As respects an unlawful act of discrimination falling within section 1(1)(b) [...] no award of damages shall be made if the respondent proves that the requirement or condition in question was not applied with the intention of treating the claimant unfavourably on the ground of his sex [...].

(4) For the avoidance of doubt it is hereby declared that damages in respect of an unlawful act of discrimination may include compensation for injury to feelings whether or not they include compensation under any other head.

71. Persistent discrimination.

(1) If, during the period of five years beginning on the date on which either of the following became final in the case of any person, namely,—

(a) a non-discrimination notice served on him,

(b) a finding by a court or tribunal under section 63 or 66, or section 2 of the Equal Pay Act 1970, that he has done an unlawful discriminatory act or an act in breach of a term modified or included by virtue of an equality clause,

it appears to the Commission that unless restrained he is likely to do one or more acts falling within paragraph (b), or contravening section 37, the Commission may apply to a county court for an injunction, or to the sheriff court for an order, restraining him from doing so; and the court, if satisfied that the application is well-founded, may grant the injunction or order in the terms applied for or in more limited terms.

77. Validity and revision of contracts.

(1) A term of a contract is void where—

(a) its inclusion renders the making of the contract unlawful by virtue of this Act, or

(b) it is included in furtherance of an act rendered unlawful by this Act, or

(c) it provides for the doing of an act which would be rendered unlawful by this Act.

(2) Subsection (1) does not apply to a term the inclusion of which constitutes or is in furtherance of, or provides for, unlawful discrimination against a party to the contract, but the term shall be unenforceable against that party.

(3) A term in a contract which purports to exclude or limit any provision of this Act or the Equal Pay Act 1970 is unenforceable by any person in whose favour the term would operate apart from this subsection.

(4) Subsection (3) does not apply—

(a) to a contract settling a complaint to which section 63(1) of this Act or section 2 of the Equal Pay Act 1970 applies where the contract is made with the assistance of a conciliation officer;

[(aa) to a contract settling a complaint to which section 63(1) of this Act or section 2 of the Equal Pay Act 1970 applies if the conditions regulating compromise contracts under this Act are satisfied in relation to the contract;]

(b) to a contract settling a claim to which section 66 applies.

[(4A) The conditions regulating compromise contracts under this Act are that—

(a) the contract must be in writing;

(b) the contract must relate to the particular complaint;

(c) the complainant must have received independent legal advice from a qualified lawyer as to the terms and effect of the proposed contract and in particular its effect on his ability to pursue his complaint before an industrial tribunal;

(d) there must be in force, when the adviser gives the advice, a policy of insurance covering the risk of a claim by the complainant in respect of loss arising in consequence of the advice;

(e) the contract must identify the adviser; and

(f) the contract must state that the conditions regulating compromise contracts under this Act are satisfied.]

(5) On the application of any person interested in a contract to which subsection (2) applies, a county court or sheriff court may make such order as it thinks just for removing or modifying any term made unenforceable by that subsection; but such an order shall not be made unless all persons affected have been given notice of the application (except where under rules of court notice may be dispensed with) and have been afforded an opportunity to make representations to the court.

(6) An order under subsection (5) may include provision as respects any period before the making of the order.

UNSOLICITED GOODS AND SERVICES (AMENDMENT) ACT 1975
(1975, c. 13)

2. Amendments consequential on section 1.

(1) In section 3(3) of the Act of 1971 for the words from "must state" to the end there shall be substituted the words "shall comply with the requirements of regulations under section 3A of this Act applicable thereto".

3. Provision for offence under section 3(2) of the Act of 1971 to be prosecuted on indictment.

(1) An offence under section 3(2) of the Act of 1971 may be prosecuted on indictment; and a person convicted on indictment of an offence under that section shall be liable to a fine.

(2) This section applies only to offences committed after the coming into operation of this section.

4. Short title, citation, commencement, transitional provisions and extent.

(2) Sections 1 and 3 of this Act and this section shall come into operation on the passing of this Act but any regulations made by virtue of the said section 1 shall not come

into operation before the date appointed by order under subsection (3) below for the coming into operation of section 2 of this Act.

(3) Section 2 of this Act shall come into operation on such date as the Secretary of State may by order made by statutory instrument appoint; and different dates may be appointed by order under this subsection for different provisions of that section.

CONGENITAL DISABILITIES (CIVIL LIABILITY) ACT 1976
(1976, c. 28)

1. Civil liability to child born disabled.

(1) If a child is born disabled as the result of such an occurrence before its birth as is mentioned in subsection (2) below, and a person (other than the child's own mother) is under this section answerable to the child in respect of the occurrence, the child's disabilities are to be regarded as damage resulting from the wrongful act of that person and actionable accordingly at the suit of the child.

(2) An occurrence to which this section applies is one which—
 (a) affected either parent of the child in his or her ability to have a normal, healthy child; or
 (b) affected the mother during her pregnancy, or affected her or the child in the course of its birth, so that the child is born with disabilities which would not otherwise have been present.

(3) Subject to the following subsections, a person (here referred to as "the defendant") is answerable to the child if he was liable in tort to the parent or would, if sued in due time, have been so; and it is no answer that there could not have been such liability because the parent suffered no actionable injury, if there was a breach of legal duty which, accompanied by injury, would have given rise to the liability.

(4) In the case of an occurrence preceding the time of conception, the defendant is not answerable to the child if at that time either or both of the parents knew the risk of their child being born disabled (that is to say, the particular risk created by the occurrence); but should it be the child's father who is the defendant, this subsection does not apply if he knew of the risk and the mother did not.

(5) The defendant is not answerable to the child, for anything he did or omitted to do when responsible in a professional capacity for treating or advising the parent, if he took reasonable care having due regard to then received professional opinion applicable to the particular class of case; but this does not mean that he is answerable only because he departed from received opinion.

(6) Liability to the child under this section may be treated as having been excluded or limited by contract made with the parent affected, to the same extent and subject to the same restrictions as liability in the parent's own case; and a contract term which could have been set up by the defendant in an action by the parent, so as to exclude or limit his liability to him or her, operates in the defendant's favour to the same, but no greater, extent in an action under this section by the child.

(7) If in the child's action under this section it is shown that the parent affected shared the responsibility for the child being born disabled, the damages are to be reduced to such extent as the court thinks just and equitable having regard to the extent of the parent's responsibility.

[1A. Extension of section 1 to cover infertility treatments.

(1) In any case where—
 (a) a child carried by a woman as the result of the placing in her or an embryo or of sperm and eggs or her artificial insemination is born disabled,
 (b) the disability results from an act or omission in the course of the selection, or the keeping or use outside the body, of the embryo carried by her or of the gametes used to bring about the creation of the embryo, and

(c) a person is under this section answerable to the child in respect of the act or omission,

the child's disabilities are to be regarded as damage resulting from the wrongful act of that person and actionable accordingly at the suit of the child.

(2) Subject to subsection (3) below and the applied provisions of section 1 of this Act, a person (here referred to as "the defendant") is answerable to the child if he was liable in tort to one or both of the parents (here referred to as "the parent or parents concerned") or would, if sued in due time, have been so; and it is no answer that there could not have been such liability because the parent or parents concerned suffered no actionable injury, if there was a breach of legal duty which, accompanied by injury, would have given rise to the liability.

(3) The defendant is not under this section answerable to the child if at the time the embryo, or the sperm and eggs, are placed in the woman or the time of her insemination (as the case may be) either or both of the parents knew the risk of their child being born disabled (that is to say, the particular risk created by the act or omission).

(4) Subsections (5) to (7) of section 1 of this Act apply for the purposes of this section as they apply for the purposes of that but as if references to the parent or the parent affected were references to the parent or parents concerned.]

2. Liability of woman driving while pregnant.

A woman driving a motor vehicle when she knows (or ought reasonably to know) herself to be pregnant is to be regarded as being under the same duty to take care for the safety of her unborn child as the law imposes on her with respect to the safety of other people; and if in consequence of her breach of that duty her child is born with disabilities which would not otherwise have been present, those disabilities are to be regarded as damage resulting from her wrongful act and actionable accordingly at the suit of the child.

3. Disabled birth due to radiation.

(1) Section 1 of this Act does not affect the operation of the Nuclear Installations Act 1965 as to liability for, and compensation in respect of, injury or damage caused by occurrences involving nuclear matter or the emission of ionising radiations.

(2) For the avoidance of doubt anything which—
   (a) affects a man in his ability to have a normal, healthy child; or
   (b) affects a woman in that ability, or so affects her when she is pregnant that her child is born with disabilities which would not otherwise have been present,
is an injury for the purposes of that Act.

(3) If a child is born disabled as the result of an injury to either of its parents caused in breach of a duty imposed by any of sections 7 to 11 of that Act (nuclear site licensees and others to secure that nuclear incidents do not cause injury to persons, etc.), the child's disabilities are to be regarded under the subsequent provisions of that Act (compensation and other matters) as injuries caused on the same occasion, and by the same breach of duty, as was the injury to the parent.

(4) As respects compensation to the child, section 13(6) of that Act (contributory fault of person injured by radiation) is to be applied as if the reference there to fault were to the fault of the parent.

(5) Compensation is not payable in the child's case if the injury to the parent preceded the time of the child's conception and at that time either or both of the parents knew the risk of their child being born disabled (that is to say, the particular risk created by the injury).

4. Interpretation and other supplementary provisions.

(1) References in this Act to a child being born disabled or with disabilities are to its being born with any deformity, disease or abnormality, including predisposition (whether or not susceptible or immediate prognosis) to physical or mental defect in the future.

(2) In this Act—
   (a) "born" means born alive (the moment of a child's birth being when it first has a life separate from its mother), and "birth" has a corresponding meaning; and
   (b) "motor vehicle" means a mechanically propelled vehicle intended or adapted for use on roads.
[and references to embryos shall be construed in accordance with section 1 of the Human Fertilisation and Embryology Act 1990].
(3) Liability to a child under section 1 [1A] or 2 of this Act is to be regarded—
   (a) as respects all its incidents and any matters arising or to arise out of it; and
   (b) subject to any contrary context or intention, for the purpose of construing references in enactments and documents to personal or bodily injuries and cognate matters,
as liability for personal injuries sustained by the child immediately after its birth.
(4) No damages shall be recoverable under [any] of those sections in respect of any loss of expectation of life, nor shall any such loss be taken into account in the compensation payable in respect of a child under the Nuclear Installations Act 1965 as extended by section 3, unless (in either case) the child lives for at least 48 hours.
[(4A) In any case where a child carried by a woman as the result of the placing in her of an embryo or of sperm and eggs or her artificial insemination is born disabled, any reference in section 1 of this Act to a parent includes a reference to a person who would be a parent but for sections 27 to 29 of the Human Fertilisation and Embryology Act 1990.]
(5) This Act applies in respect of births after (but not before) its passing, and in respect of any such birth it replaces any law in force before its passing, whereby a person could be liable to a child in respect of disabilities with which it might be born; but in section 1(3) of this Act the expression "liable in tort" does not include any reference to liability by virtue of this Act or to liability by virtue of any such law.

5. Crown application.
This Act binds the Crown.

DANGEROUS WILD ANIMALS ACT 1976
(1976, c. 38)

1. Licences.
(1) Subject to section 5 of this Act, no person shall keep any dangerous wild animal except under the authority of a licence granted in accordance with the provisions of this Act by a local authority.
(3) A local authority shall not grant a licence under this Act unless it is satisfied that—
   (a) it is not contrary to the public interest on the grounds of safety, nuisance or otherwise to grant the licence; ...
   (e) all reasonable precautions will be taken at all such times to prevent and control the spread of infectious diseases; ...

4. Power to seize and to dispose of animals without compensation.
(1) Where—
   (a) an animal is being kept contrary to section 1(1) of the Act, or
   (b) any condition of a licence under this Act is contravened or not complied with,
the local authority in whose area any animal concerned is for the time being may seize the animal, and either retain it in the authority's possession or destroy or otherwise dispose of it, and shall not be liable to pay compensation to any person in respect of the exercise of its powers under this subsection.

(2) A local authority which incurs any expenditure in exercising its powers under subsection (1)(a) of this section shall be entitled to recover the amount of the expenditure summarily as a civil debt from any person who was at the time of the seizure a keeper of the animal concerned.

(3) A local authority which incurs any expenditure in exercising its powers under subsection (1)(b) of this section shall be entitled to recover the amount of the expenditure summarily as a civil debt from the person to whom the licence concerned was granted.

FATAL ACCIDENTS ACT 1976
(1976, c. 30)

1. Right of action for wrongful act causing death.

[(1) If death is caused by any wrongful act, neglect or default which is such as would (if death had not ensued) have entitled the person injured to maintain an action and recover damages in respect thereof, the person who would have been liable if death had not ensued shall be liable to an action for damages, notwithstanding the death of the person injured.

(2) Subject to section 1A(2) below, every such action shall be for the benefit of the dependants of the person ("the deceased") whose death has been so caused.

(3) In this Act "dependant" means—
    (a) the wife or husband or former wife or husband of the deceased;
    (b) any person who—
        (i) was living with the deceased in the same household immediately before the date of the death; and
        (ii) had been living with the deceased in the same household for at least two years before that date; and
        (iii) was living during the whole of that period as the husband or wife of the deceased;
    (c) any parent or other ascendant of the deceased;
    (d) any person who was treated by the deceased as his parent;
    (e) any child or other descendant of the deceased;
    (f) any person (not being a child of the deceased) who, in the case of any marriage to which the deceased was at any time a party, was treated by the deceased as a child of the family in relation to that marriage;
    (g) any person who is, or is the issue of, a brother, sister, uncle or aunt of the deceased.

(4) The reference to the former wife or husband of the deceased in subsection (3)(a) above includes a reference to a person whose marriage to the deceased has been annulled or declared void as well as a person whose marriage to the deceased has been dissolved.

(5) In deducing any relationship for the purposes of subsection (3) above—
    (a) any relationship by affinity shall be treated as a relationship of consanguinity, any relationship of the half blood as a relationship of the whole blood, and the stepchild of any person as his child, and
    (b) an illegitimate person shall be treated as the legitimate child of his mother and reputed father.

(6) Any reference in this Act to injury includes any disease and any impairment of a person's physical or mental condition.]

[1A. Bereavement.

(1) An action under this Act may consist of or include a claim for damages for bereavement.

(2) A claim for damages for bereavement shall only be for the benefit—
  (a) of the wife or husband of the deceased; and
  (b) where the deceased was a minor who was never married—
    (i) of his parents, if he was legitimate; and
    (ii) of his mother, if he was illegitimate.
(3) Subject to subsection (5) below, the sum to be awarded as damages under this section shall be [£7,500].
(4) Where there is a claim for damages under this section for the benefit of both the parents of the deceased, the sum awarded shall be divided equally between them (subject to any deduction falling to be made in respect of costs not recovered from the defendant).
(5) The Lord Chancellor may by order made by statutory instrument, subject to annulment in pursuance of a resolution of either House of Parliament, amend this section by varying the sum for the time being specified in subsection (3) above.]

2. Persons entitled to bring the action.

[(1) The action shall be brought by and in the name of the executor or administrator of the deceased.
(2) If—
  (a) there is no executor or administrator of the deceased, or
  (b) no action is brought within six months after the death by and in the name of an executor or administrator of the deceased,
the action may be brought by and in the name of all or any of the persons for whose benefit an executor or administrator could have brought it.
(3) Not more than one action shall lie for and in respect of the same subject matter of complaint.
(4) The plaintiff in the action shall be required to deliver to the defendant or his solicitor full particulars of the persons for whom and on whose behalf the action is brought and of the nature of the claim in respect of which damages are sought to be recovered.]

3. Assessment of damages.

[(1) In the action such damages, other than damages for bereavement, may be awarded as are proportioned to the injury resulting from the death to the dependants respectively.
(2) After deducting the costs not recovered from the defendant any amount recovered otherwise than as damages for bereavement shall be divided among the dependants in such shares as may be directed.
(3) In an action under this Act where there fall to be assessed damages payable to a widow in respect of the death of her husband there shall not be taken into account the re-marriage of the widow or her prospects of re-marriage.
(4) In an action under this Act where there fall to be assessed damages payable to a person who is a dependant by virtue of section 1(3)(b) above in respect of the death of the person with whom the dependant was living as husband or wife there shall be taken into account (together with any other matter that appears to the court to be relevant to the action) the fact that the dependant had no enforceable right to financial support by the deceased as a result of their living together.
(5) If the dependants have incurred funeral expenses in respect of the deceased, damages may be awarded in respect of those expenses.
(6) Money paid into court in satisfaction of a cause of action under this Act may be in one sum without specifying any person's share.]

4. Assessment of damages; disregard of benefits.
[In assessing damages in respect of a person's death in an action under this Act, benefits which have accrued or will or may accrue to any person from his estate or otherwise as a result of his death shall be disregarded.]

5. Contributory negligence.
Where any person dies as the result partly of his own fault and partly of the fault of any other person or persons, and accordingly if an action were brought for the benefit of the estate under the Law Reform (Miscellaneous Provisions) Act 1934 the damages recoverable would be reduced under section 1(1) of the Law Reform (Contributory Negligence) Act 1945, any damages recoverable in an action [...] under this Act shall be reduced to a proportionate extent.

RACE RELATIONS ACT 1976
(1976, c. 74)

[*The following sections of this Act are similar to the corresponding provisions of the Sex Discrimination Act 1975 (ante) in brackets: RRA, ss. 1 (SDA, ss. 1, 2), 20 (SDA 29), 32 (SDA 41), 57 (SDA 66), 62 (SDA 71), 72 (SDA 77).*]

RESALE PRICES ACT 1976
(1976, c. 53)

1. Collective agreement by suppliers.
(1) It is unlawful for any two or more persons carrying on business in the United Kingdom as suppliers of any goods to make or carry out any agreement or arrangement by which they undertake—
   (a) to withhold supplies of goods for delivery in the United Kingdom from dealers (whether party to the agreement or arrangement or not) who resell or have resold goods in breach of any condition as to the price at which those goods may be resold;
   (b) to refuse to supply goods for delivery in the United Kingdom to such dealers except on terms and conditions which are less favourable than those applicable in the case of other dealers carrying on business in similar circumstances; or
   (c) to supply goods only to persons who undertake or have undertaken—
      (i) to withhold supplies of goods as described in paragraph (a) above; or
      (ii) to refuse to supply goods as described in paragraph (b) above.
(2) It is unlawful for any two or more such persons to make or carry out any agreement or arrangement authorising—
   (a) the recovery of penalties (however described) by or on behalf of the parties to the agreement or arrangement from dealers who resell or have resold goods in breach of any such condition as is described in paragraph (a) of subsection (1) above; or
   (b) the conduct of any domestic proceedings in connection therewith.

5. Exclusive dealing.
A contract for the sale of goods to which not more than two persons are party is not unlawful under this part of this Act by reason only of undertakings by the purchaser in relation to the goods sold and by the vendor in relation to other goods of the same description.

25. Contravention of and compliance with the Act.
(1) No criminal proceedings lie against any person on the ground that he has committed, or aided, abetted, counselled or procured the commission of, or conspired or attempted to commit, or incited others to commit, any contravention of sections 1 and 2 and sections 9 and 11 above.

(2) Without prejudice to the right of any person to bring civil proceedings by virtue of subsection (3) below, compliance with those sections shall be enforceable by civil proceedings on behalf of the Crown for an injunction or other appropriate relief.

(3) The obligation to comply with those sections is a duty owed to any person who may be affected by a contravention of them, and any breach of that duty is actionable accordingly (subject to the defences and other incidents applying to actions for breach of statutory duty).

PROTECTION FROM EVICTION ACT 1977
(1977, c. 43)

1. Unlawful eviction and harassment of occupier.

(1) In this section "residential occupier", in relation to any premises, means a person occupying the premises as a residence, whether under a contract or by virtue of any enactment or rule of law giving him the right to remain in occupation or restricting the right of any other person to recover possession of the premises.

(2) If any person unlawfully deprives the residential occupier of any premises of his occupation of the premises or any part thereof, or attempts to do so, he shall be guilty of an offence unless he proves that he believed, and had reasonable cause to believe, that the residential occupier had ceased to reside in the premises.

(3) If any person with intent to cause the residential occupier of any premises—
    (a) to give up the occupation of the premises or any part thereof; or
    (b) to refrain from exercising any right or pursuing any remedy in respect of the premises or part thereof;
does acts [likely] to interfere with the peace or comfort of the residential occupier or members of his household, or persistently withdraws or withholds services reasonably required for the occupation of the premises as a residence, he shall be guilty of an offence.

[(3A) Subject to subsection (3B) below, the landlord of a residential occupier or an agent of the landlord shall be guilty of an offence if—
    (a) he does acts likely to interfere with the peace or comfort of the residential occupier or members of his household, or
    (b) he persistently withdraws or withholds services reasonably required for the occupation of the premises in question as a residence,
and (in either case) he knows, or has reasonable cause to believe, that that conduct is likely to cause the residential occupier to give up the occupation of the whole or part of the premises or to refrain from exercising any right or pursuing any remedy in respect of the whole or part of the premises.

(3B) A person shall not be guilty of an offence under subsection (3A) above if he proves that he had reasonable grounds for doing the acts or withdrawing or withholding the services in question.]

(5) Nothing in this section shall be taken to prejudice any liability or remedy to which a person guilty of an offence thereunder may be subject in civil proceedings.

2. Restriction on re-entry without due process of law.

Where any premises are let as a dwelling on a lease which is subject to a right of re-entry or forfeiture it shall not be lawful to enforce that right otherwise than by proceedings in the court while any person is lawfully residing in the premises or part of them.

3. Prohibition of eviction without due process of law.

(1) Where any premises have been let as a dwelling under a tenancy which is not a statutorily protected tenancy and—
    (a) the tenancy (in this section referred to as the former tenancy) has come to an end, but

(b) the occupier continues to reside in the premises or part of them,

it shall not be lawful for the owner to enforce against the occupier, otherwise than by proceedings in the court, his right to recover possession of the premises.

(2) In this section "the occupier", in relation to any premises, means any person lawfully residing in the premises or part of them at the termination of the former tenancy.

TORTS (INTERFERENCE WITH GOODS) ACT 1977
(1977, c. 32)

1. Definition of "wrongful interference with goods".

In this Act "wrongful interference", or "wrongful interference with goods", means—
  (a) conversion of goods (also called trover),
  (b) trespass to goods,
  (c) negligence so far as it results in damage to goods or to an interest in goods,
  (d) subject to section 2, any other tort so far as it results in damage to goods or to an interest in goods.

[and references in this Act (however worded) to proceedings for wrongful interference or to a claim or right to claim for wrongful interference shall include references to proceedings by virtue of Part I of the Consumer Protection Act 1987 or Part II of the Consumer Protection (Northern Ireland) Order 1987 (product liability) in respect of any damage to goods or to an interest in goods or, as the case may be, to a claim or right to claim by virtue of that Part in respect of any such damage.]

2. Abolition of detinue.

(1) Detinue is abolished.

(2) An action lies in conversion for loss or destruction of goods which a bailee has allowed to happen in breach of his duty to his bailor (that is to say it lies in a case which is not otherwise conversion, but would have been detinue before detinue was abolished).

3. Forms of judgment where goods are detained.

(1) In proceedings for wrongful interference against a person who is in possession or in control of the goods relief may be given in accordance with this section, so far as appropriate.

(2) The relief is—
  (a) an order for delivery of the goods, and for payment of any consequential damages, or
  (b) an order for delivery of the goods, but giving the defendant the alternative of paying damages by reference to the value of the goods, together in either alternative with payment of any consequential damages, or
  (c) damages.

(3) Subject to rules of court—
  (a) relief shall be given under only one of paragraphs (a), (b) and (c) of subsection (2),
  (b) relief under paragraph (a) of subsection (2) is at the discretion of the court, and the claimant may choose between the others.

(4) If it is shown to the satisfaction of the court that an order under subsection (2)(a) had not been complied with, the court may—
  (a) revoke the order, or the relevant part of it, and
  (b) make an order for payment of damages by reference to the value of the goods.

(5) Where an order is made under subsection (2)(b) the defendant may satisfy the order by returning the goods at any time before execution of judgment, but without prejudice to liability to pay any consequential damages.

(6) An order for delivery of the goods under subsection (2)(a) or (b) may impose such conditions as may be determined by the court, or pursuant to rules of court, and in particular, where damages by reference to the value of the goods would not be the whole of the value of the goods, may require an allowance to be made by the claimant to reflect the difference.

For example, a bailor's action against the bailee may be one in which the measure of damages is not the full value of the goods, and then the court may order delivery of the goods, but require the bailor to pay the bailee a sum reflecting the difference.

(7) Where under subsection (1) or subsection (2) of section 6 an allowance is to be made in respect of an improvement of the goods, and an order is made under subsection (2)(a) or (b), the court may assess the allowance to be made in respect of the improvement, and by the order require, as a condition for delivery of the goods, that allowance to be made by the claimant.

(8) This section is without prejudice—
    (a) to the remedies afforded by section 133 of the Consumer Credit Act, or ...
    (c) to any jurisdiction to afford ancillary or incidental relief.

4. Interlocutory relief where goods are detained.

(1) In this section "proceedings" means proceedings for wrongful interference.

(2) On the application of any person in accordance with rules of court, the High Court shall, in such circumstances as may be specified in the rules, have power to make an order providing for the delivery up of any goods which are or may become the subject matter of subsequent proceedings in the court, or as to which any question may arise in proceedings.

(3) Delivery shall be, as the order may provide, to the claimant or to a person appointed by the court for the purpose, and shall be on such terms and conditions as may be specified in the order.

5. Extinction of title on satisfaction of claim for damages.

(1) Where damages for wrongful interference are, or would fall to be, assessed on the footing that the claimant is being compensated—
    (a) for the whole of his interest in the goods, or
    (b) for the whole of his interest in the goods subject to a reduction for contributory negligence,
payment of the assessed damages (under all heads), or as the case may be settlement of a claim for damages for the wrong (under all heads), extinguishes the claimant's title to that interest.

(2) In subsection (1) the reference to the settlement of the claim includes—
    (a) where the claim is made in court proceedings, and the defendant has paid a sum into court to meet the whole claim, the taking of that sum by the claimant, and
    (b) where the claim is made in court proceedings, and the proceedings are settled or compromised, the payment of what is due in accordance with the settlement or compromise, and
    (c) where the claim is made out of court and is settled or compromised, the payment of what is due in accordance with the settlement or compromise.

(3) It is hereby declared that subsection (1) does not apply where damages are assessed on the footing that the claimant is being compensated for the whole of his interest in the goods, but the damages paid are limited to some lesser amount by virtue of any enactment or rule of law.

(4) Where under section 7(3) the claimant accounts over to another person (the "third party") so as to compensate (under all heads) the third party for the whole of his interest in the goods, the third party's title to that interest is extinguished.

(5) This section has effect subject to any agreement varying the respective rights of the parties to the agreement, and where the claim is made in court proceedings has effect subject to any order of the court.

Torts (Interference with Goods) Act 1977

6. Allowance for improvement of the goods.

(1) If in proceedings for wrongful interference against a person (the "improver") who has improved the goods, it is shown that the improver acted in the mistaken but honest belief that he had a good title to them, an allowance shall be made for the extent to which, at the time as at which the goods fall to be valued in assessing damages, the value of the goods is attributable to the improvement.

(2) If, in proceedings for wrongful interference against a person ("the purchaser") who has purported to purchase the goods—
  (a) from the improver, or
  (b) where after such a purported sale the goods passed by a further purported sale on one or more occasions, on any such occasion,
it is shown that the purchaser acted in good faith, an allowance shall be made on the principle set out in subsection (1).

For example, where a person in good faith buys a stolen car from the improver and is sued in conversion by the true owner the damages may be reduced to reflect the improvement, but if the person who bought the stolen car from the improver sues the improver for failure of consideration, and the improver acted in good faith, subsection (3) below will ordinarily make a comparable reduction in the damages he recovers from the improver.

(3) If in a case within subsection (2) the person purporting to sell the goods acted in good faith, then in proceedings by the purchaser for recovery of the purchase price because of failure of consideration, or in any other proceedings founded on that failure of consideration, an allowance shall, where appropriate, be made on the principle set out in subsection (1).

(4) This section applies, with the necessary modifications, to a purported bailment or other disposition of goods as it applies to a purported sale of goods.

7. Double liability.

(1) In this section "double liability" means the double liability of the wrongdoer which can arise—
  (a) where one of two or more rights of action for wrongful interference is founded on a possessory title, or
  (b) where the measure of damages in an action for wrongful interference founded on a proprietary title is or includes the entire value of the goods, although the interest is one of two or more interests in the goods.

(2) In proceedings to which any two or more claimants are parties, the relief shall be such as to avoid double liability of the wrongdoer as between those claimants.

(3) On satisfaction, in whole or in part, of any claim for an amount exceeding that recoverable if subsection (2) applied, the claimant is liable to account over to the other person having a right to claim to such extent as will avoid double liability.

(4) Where, as the result of enforcement of a double liability, any claimant is unjustly enriched to an extent, he shall be liable to reimburse the wrongdoer to that extent.

For example, if a converter of goods pays damages first to a finder of the goods, and then to the true owner, the finder is unjustly enriched unless he accounts over to the true owner under subsection (3); and then the true owner is unjustly enriched and becomes liable to reimburse the converter of the goods.

8. Competing rights to the goods.

(1) The defendant in an action for wrongful interference shall be entitled to show, in accordance with rules of court, that a third party has a better right than the plaintiff as respects all or any part of the interest claimed by the plaintiff, or in right of which he sues, and any rule of law (sometimes called jus tertii) to the contrary is abolished.

(2) Rules of court relating to proceedings for wrongful interference may—
  (a) require the plaintiff to give particulars of his title,

(b) require the plaintiff to identify any person who, to his knowledge, has or claims any interest in the goods,

(c) authorise the defendant to apply for directions as to whether any person should be joined with a view to establishing whether he has a better right than the plaintiff, or has a claim as a result of which the defendant might be doubly liable,

(d) where a party fails to appear on an application within paragraph (c), or to comply with any direction given by the court on such an application, authorise the court to deprive him of any right of action against the defendant for the wrong either unconditionally, or subject to such terms or conditions as may be specified.

(3) Subsection (2) is without prejudice to any other power of making rules of court.

9. Concurrent actions.

(1) This section applies where goods are the subject of two or more claims for wrongful interference (whether or not the claims are founded on the same wrongful act, and whether or not any of the claims relates also to other goods).

(2) Where the goods are the subject of two or more claims under section 6 this section shall apply as if any claim under section 6(3) were a claim for wrongful interference.

(3) If proceedings have been brought in a county court on one of those claims, county court rules may waive, or allow a court to waive, any limit (financial or territorial) on the jurisdiction of county courts in [the County Courts Act 1984] or the County Courts Act [(Northern Ireland) Order 1980] so as to allow another of those claims to be brought in the same county court.

(4) If proceedings are brought on one of the claims in the High Court, and proceedings on any other are brought in a county court, whether prior to the High Court proceedings or not, the High Court may, on the application of the defendant, after notice has been given to the claimant in the county court proceedings—

(a) order that the county court proceedings be transferred to the High Court, and

(b) order security for costs or impose such other terms as the court thinks fit.

10. Co-owners.

(1) Co-ownership is no defence to an action founded on conversion or trespass to goods where the defendant without the authority of the other co-owner—

(a) destroys the goods, or disposes of the goods in a way giving a good title to the entire property in the goods, or otherwise does anything equivalent to the destruction of the other's interest in the goods, or

(b) purports to dispose of the goods in a way which would give a good title to the entire property in the goods if he was acting with the authority of all co-owners of the goods.

(2) Subsection (1) shall not affect the law concerning execution or enforcement of judgments, or concerning any form of distress.

(3) Subsection (1)(a) is by way of restatement of existing law so far as it relates to conversion.

11. Minor amendments.

(1) Contributory negligence is no defence in proceedings founded on conversion, or on intentional trespass to goods.

(2) Receipt of goods by way of pledge is conversion if the delivery of the goods is conversion.

(3) Denial of title is not of itself conversion.

12. Bailee's power of sale.

(1) This section applies to goods in the possession or under the control of a bailee where—

(a) the bailor is in breach of an obligation to take delivery of the goods or, if the terms of the bailment so provide, to give directions as to their delivery, or

(b) the bailee could impose such an obligation by giving notice to the bailor, but is unable to trace or communicate with the bailor, or

(c) the bailee can reasonably expect to be relieved of any duty to safeguard the goods on giving notice to the bailor, but is unable to trace or communicate with the bailor.

(2) In the cases of Part I of Schedule 1 to this Act a bailee may, for the purposes of subsection (1), impose an obligation on the bailor to take delivery of the goods, or as the case may be to give directions as to their delivery, and in those cases the said Part I sets out the method of notification.

(3) If the bailee—

(a) has in accordance with Part II of Schedule 1 to this Act given notice to the bailor of his intention to sell the goods under this subsection, or

(b) has failed to trace or communicate with the bailor with a view to giving him such a notice, after having taken reasonable steps for the purpose,

and is reasonably satisfied that the bailor owns the goods, he shall be entitled, as against the bailor, to sell the goods.

(4) Where subsection (3) applies but the bailor did not in fact own the goods, a sale under this section, or under section 13, shall not give a good title as against the owner, or as against a person claiming under the owner.

(5) A bailee exercising his powers under subsection (3) shall be liable to account to the bailor for the proceeds of sale, less any cost of sale, and—

(a) the account shall be taken on the footing that the bailee should have adopted the best method of sale reasonably available in the circumstances, and

(b) where subsection (3)(a) applies, any sum payable in respect of the goods by the bailor to the bailee which accrued due before the bailee gave notice of intention to sell the goods shall be deductible from the proceeds of sale.

(6) A sale duly made under this section gives a good title to the purchaser as against the bailor.

(7) In this section, section 13, and Schedule 1 to this Act,

(a) "bailor" and "bailee" include their respective successors in title, and

(b) references to what is payable, paid or due to the bailee in respect of the goods include references to what would be payable by the bailor to the bailee as a condition of delivery of the goods at the relevant time.

(8) This section, and Schedule 1 to this Act, have effect subject to the terms of the bailment.

(9) This section shall not apply where the goods were bailed before the commencement of this Act.

13. Sale authorised by the court.

(1) If a bailee of the goods to which section 12 applies satisfies the court that he is entitled to sell the goods under section 12, or that he would be so entitled if he had given any notice required in accordance with Schedule 1 to this Act, the court—

(a) may authorise the sale of the goods subject to such terms and conditions, if any, as may be specified in the order, and

(b) may authorise the bailee to deduct from the proceeds of sale any costs of sale and any amount due from the bailor to the bailee in respect of the goods, and

(c) may direct the payment into court of the net proceeds of sale, less any amount deducted under paragraph (b), to be held to the credit of the bailor.

(2) A decision of the court authorising a sale under this section shall, subject to any right of appeal, be conclusive, as against the bailor, of the bailee's entitlement to sell the goods, and gives a good title to the purchaser as against the bailor.

(3) In this section "the court" means the High Court or a county court, [and a county court shall have jurisdiction in the proceedings save that, in Northern Ireland, a

county court shall only have jurisdiction in proceedings if the value of the goods does not exceed the county court limit mentioned in Article 10(1) of the County Courts (Northern Ireland) Order 1980.]

14. Interpretation.
(1) In this Act, unless the context otherwise requires—
...
"goods" includes all chattels personal other than things in action and money. . . .

16. Extent and application to the Crown.
(3) This Act shall bind the Crown, but as regards the Crown's liability in tort shall not bind the Crown further than the Crown is made liable in tort by the Crown Proceedings Act 1947.

Section 12 SCHEDULES

SCHEDULE 1
UNCOLLECTED GOODS

PART I
POWER TO IMPOSE OBLIGATION TO COLLECT GOODS

1. (1) For the purposes of section 12(1) a bailee may, in the circumstances specified in this Part of this Schedule, by notice given to the bailor impose on him an obligation to take delivery of the goods.
   (2) The notice shall be in writing, and may be given either—
   (a) by delivering it to the bailor, or
   (b) by leaving it at his proper address, or
   (c) by post.
   (3) The notice shall—
   (a) specify the name and address of the bailee, and give sufficient particulars of the goods and the address or place where they are held, and
   (b) state that the goods are ready for delivery to the bailor, or where combined with a notice terminating the contract of bailment, will be ready for delivery when the contract is terminated, and
   (c) specify the amount, if any, which is payable by the bailor to the bailee in respect of the goods and which became due before the giving of the notice.
   (4) Where the notice is sent by post it may be combined with a notice under Part II of this Schedule if the notice is sent by post in a way complying with paragraph 6(4).
   (5) References in this Part of this Schedule to taking delivery of the goods include, where the terms of the bailment admit, references to giving directions as to their delivery.
   (6) This Part of this Schedule is without prejudice to the provisions of any contract requiring the bailor to take delivery of the goods.

Goods accepted for repair or other treatment

2. If a bailee has accepted goods for repair or other treatment on the terms (expressed or implied) that they will be re-delivered to the bailor when the repair or other treatment has been carried out, the notice may be given at any time after the repair or other treatment has been carried out.

Goods accepted for valuation or appraisal

3. If a bailee has accepted goods in order to value or appraise them, the notice may be given at any time after the bailee has carried out the valuation or appraisal.

Storage, warehousing, etc.

4. (1) If a bailee is in possession of goods which he has held as custodian, and his obligation as custodian has come to an end, the notice may be given at any time after the ending of the obligation, or may be combined with any notice terminating his obligation as custodian.

(2) This paragraph shall not apply to goods held by a person as mercantile agent, that is to say by a person having in the customary course of his business as a mercantile agent authority either to sell goods or to consign goods for the purpose of sale, or to buy goods, or to raise money on the security of goods.

Supplemental

5. Paragraphs 2, 3 and 4 apply whether or not the bailor has paid any amount due to the bailee in respect of the goods, and whether or not the bailment is for reward, or in the course of business, or gratuitous.

PART II
NOTICE OF INTENTION TO SELL GOODS

6. (1) A notice under section 12(3) shall—
   (a) specify the name and address of the bailee, and give sufficient particulars of the goods and the address or place where they are held, and
   (b) specify the date on or after which the bailee proposes to sell the goods, and
   (c) specify the amount, if any, which is payable by the bailor to the bailee in respect of the goods, and which became due before the giving of the notice.

(2) The period between giving of the notice and the date specified in the notice as that on or after which the bailee proposes to exercise the power of sale shall be such as will afford the bailor a reasonable opportunity of taking delivery of the goods.

(3) If any amount is payable in respect of the goods by the bailor to the bailee, and become due before giving of the notice, the said period shall be not less than three months.

(4) The notice shall be in writing and shall be sent by post in a registered letter, or by the recorded delivery service.

7. (1) The bailee shall not give a notice under section 12(3), or exercise his right to sell the goods pursuant to such a notice, at a time when he has notice that, because of a dispute concerning the goods, the bailor is questioning or refusing to pay all or any part of what the bailee claims to be due to him in respect of the goods.

(2) This paragraph shall be left out of account in determining under section 13(1) whether a bailee of goods is entitled to sell the goods under section 12, or would be so entitled if he had given any notice required in accordance with this Schedule.

UNFAIR CONTRACT TERMS ACT 1977
(1977, c. 50)

PART I

1. Scope of Part I.
(1) For the purposes of this Part of this Act, "negligence" means the breach—
   (a) of any obligation, arising from the express or implied terms of a contract, to take reasonable care or exercise reasonable skill in the performance of the contract;
   (b) of any common law duty to take reasonable care or exercise reasonable skill (but not any stricter duty);
   (c) of the common duty of care imposed by the Occupiers' Liability Act 1957 or the Occupier's Liability Act (Northern Ireland) 1957.

(2) This Part of this Act is subject to Part III; and in relation to contracts, the operation of sections 2 to 4 and 7 is subject to the exceptions made by Schedule I.

(3) In the case of both contract and tort, sections 2 to 7 apply (except where the contrary is stated in section 6(4)) only to business liability, that is liability for breach of obligations or duties arising—

(a) from things done or to be done by a person in the course of a business (whether his own business or another's); or

(b) from the occupation of premises used for business purposes of the occupier; and references to liability are to be read accordingly [but liability of an occupier of premises for breach of an obligation or duty towards a person obtaining access to the premises for recreational or educational purposes, being liability for loss or damage suffered by reason of the dangerous state of the premises, is not a business liability of the occupier unless granting that person such access for the purposes concerned falls within the business purposes of the occupier].

(4) In relation to any breach of duty or obligation, it is immaterial for any purpose of this Part of this Act whether the breach was inadvertent or intentional, or whether liability for it arises directly or vicariously.

2. Negligence liability.

(1) A person cannot by reference to any contract term or to a notice given to persons generally or to particular persons exclude or restrict his liability for death or personal injury resulting from negligence.

(2) In the case of other loss or damage, a person cannot so exclude or restrict his liability for negligence except in so far as the term or notice satisfies the requirement of reasonableness.

(3) Where a contract term or notice purports to exclude or restrict liability for negligence a person's agreement to or awareness of it is not of itself to be taken as indicating his voluntary acceptance of any risk.

3. Liability arising in contract.

(1) This section applies as between contracting parties where one of them deals as consumer or on the other's written standard terms of business.

(2) As against that party, the other cannot by reference to any contract term—

(a) when himself in breach of contract, exclude or restrict any liability of his in respect of the breach; or

(b) claim to be entitled—

(i) to render a contractual performance substantially different from that which was reasonably expected of him, or

(ii) in respect of the whole or any part of his contractual obligation, to render no performance at all,

except in so far as (in any of the cases mentioned above in this subsection) the contract term satisfies the requirement of reasonableness.

4. Unreasonable indemnity clauses.

(1) A person dealing as consumer cannot by reference to any contract term be made to indemnify another person (whether a party to the contract or not) in respect of liability that may be incurred by the other for negligence or breach of contract, except in so far as the contract term satisfies the requirement of reasonableness.

(2) This section applies whether the liability in question—

(a) is directly that of the person to be indemnified or is incurred by him vicariously;

(b) is to the person dealing as consumer or to someone else.

5. "Guarantee" of consumer goods.

(1) In the case of goods of a type ordinarily supplied for private use or consumption, where loss or damage—

(a) arises from the goods proving defective while in consumer use; and
(b) results from the negligence of a person concerned in the manufacture or distribution of the goods,
liability for the loss or damage cannot be excluded or restricted by reference to any contract term or notice contained in or operating by reference to a guarantee of the goods.

(2) For these purposes—
(a) goods are to be regarded as "in consumer use" when a person is using them, or has them in his possession for use, otherwise than exclusively for the purposes of a business; and
(b) anything in writing is a guarantee if it contains or purports to contain some promise or assurance (however worded or presented) that defects will be made good by complete or partial replacement, or by repair, monetary compensation or otherwise.

(3) This section does not apply as between the parties to a contract under or in pursuance of which possession or ownership of the goods passed.

6. Sale and hire-purchase.

(1) Liability for breach of the obligations arising from—
(a) [section 12 of the Sale of Goods Act 1979] (seller's implied undertakings as to title, etc.);
(b) section 8 of the Supply of Goods (Implied Terms) Act 1973 (the corresponding thing in relation to hire-purchase),
cannot be excluded or restricted by reference to any contract term.

(2) As against a person dealing as consumer, liability for breach of the obligations arising from—
(a) [section 13, 14 or 15 of the [1979] Act] (seller's implied undertakings as to conformity of goods with description or sample, or as to their quality or fitness for a particular purpose);
(b) section 9, 10 or 11 of the 1973 Act (the corresponding things in relation to hire-purchase),
cannot be excluded or restricted by reference to any contract term.

(3) As against a person dealing otherwise than as consumer, the liability specified in subsection (2) above can be excluded or restricted by reference to a contract term, but only in so far as the term satisfies the requirement of reasonableness.

(4) The liabilities referred to in this section are not only the business liabilities defined by section 1(3), but include those arising under any contract of sale of goods or hire-purchase agreement.

7. Miscellaneous contracts under which goods pass.

(1) Where the possession or ownership of goods passes under or in pursuance of a contract not governed by the law of sale of goods or hire-purchase, subsections (2) to (4) below apply as regards the effect (if any) to be given to contract terms excluding or restricting liability for breach of obligation arising by implication of law from the nature of the contract.

(2) As against a person dealing as consumer, liability in respect of the goods' correspondence with description or sample, or their quality or fitness for any particular purpose, cannot be excluded or restricted by reference to any such term.

(3) As against a person dealing otherwise than as consumer, that liability can be excluded or restricted by reference to such a term, but only in so far as the term satisfies the requirement of reasonableness.

[(3A) Liability for breach of the obligations arising under section 2 of the Supply of Goods and Services Act 1982 (implied terms about title etc. in certain contracts for the transfer of the property in goods) cannot be excluded or restricted by reference to any such term.]

(4) Liability in respect of—
   (a) the right to transfer ownership of the goods, or give possession; or
   (b) the assurance of quiet possession to a person taking goods in pursuance of the contract,
cannot [(in a case to which subsection (3A) above does not apply)] be excluded or restricted by reference to any such term except in so far as the term satisfies the requirement of reasonableness.
   (c) This section does not apply in the case of goods passing on a redemption of trading stamps within the Trading Stamps Act 1964 or the Trading Stamps Act (Northern Ireland) 1965.

9. Effect of breach.

(1) Where for reliance upon it a contract term has to satisfy the requirement of reasonableness, it may be found to do so and be given effect accordingly notwithstanding that the contract has been terminated either by breach or by a party electing to treat it as repudiated.

(2) Where on a breach the contract is nevertheless affirmed by a party entitled to treat it as repudiated, this does not of itself exclude the requirement of reasonableness in relation to any contract term.

10. Evasion by means of secondary contract.

A person is not bound by any contract term prejudicing or taking away rights of his which arise under, or in connection with the performance of, another contract, so far as those rights extend to the enforcement of another's liability which this Part of this Act prevents that other from excluding or restricting.

11. The "reasonableness" test.

(1) In relation to a contract term, the requirement of reasonableness for the purposes of this Part of this Act, section 3 of the Misrepresentation Act 1967 and section 3 of the Misrepresentation Act (Northern Ireland) 1967 is that the term shall have been a fair and reasonable one to be included having regard to the circumstances which were, or ought reasonably to have been, known to or in the contemplation of the parties when the contract was made.

(2) In determining for the purposes of section 6 or 7 above whether a contract term satisfies the requirement of reasonableness, regard shall be had in particular to the matters specified in Schedule 2 to this Act; but this subsection does not prevent the court or arbitrator from holding, in accordance with any rule of law, that a term which purports to exclude or restrict any relevant liability is not a term of the contract.

(3) In relation to a notice (not being a notice having contractual effect), the requirement of reasonableness under this Act is that it should be fair and reasonable to allow reliance on it, having regard to all the circumstances obtaining when the liability arose or (but for the notice) would have arisen.

(4) Where by reference to a contract term or notice a person seeks to restrict liability to a specified sum of money, and the question arises (under this or any other Act) whether the term or notice satisfies the requirement of reasonableness, regard shall be had in particular (but without prejudice to subsection (2) above in the case of contract terms) to—
   (a) the resources which he could expect to be available to him for the purpose of meeting the liability should it arise; and
   (b) how far it was open to him to cover himself by insurance.

(5) It is for those claiming that a contract term or notice satisfies the requirement of reasonableness to show that it does.

12. "Dealing as consumer".

(1) A party to a contract "deals as consumer" in relation to another party if—

(a) he neither makes the contract in the course of a business nor holds himself out as doing so; and
(b) the other party does make the contract in the course of a business; and
(c) in the case of a contract governed by the law of sale of goods or hire-purchase, or by section 7 of this Act, the goods passing under or in pursuance of the contract are of a type ordinarily supplied for private use or consumption.

(2) But on a sale by auction or by competitive tender the buyer is not in any circumstances to be regarded as dealing as consumer.

(3) Subject to this, it is for those claiming that a party does not deal as consumer to show that he does not.

13. Varieties of exemption clause.

(1) To the extent that this Part of this Act prevents the exclusion or restriction of any liability it also prevents—
(a) making the liability or its enforcement subject to restrictive or onerous conditions;
(b) excluding or restricting any right or remedy in respect of the liability, or subjecting a person to any prejudice in consequence of his pursuing any such right or remedy;
(c) excluding or restricting rules of evidence or procedure;
and (to that extent) sections 2 and 5 to 7 also prevent excluding or restricting liability by reference to terms and notices which exclude or restrict the relevant obligation or duty.

(2) But an agreement in writing to submit present or future differences to arbitration is not to be treated under this Part of this Act as excluding or restricting any liability.

14. Interpretation of Part I.

In this Part of the Act—
"business" includes a profession and the activities of any government department or local or public authority;
"goods" has the same meaning as in [the Sale of Goods Act 1979];
"hire-purchase agreement" has the same meaning as in the Consumer Credit Act 1974;
"negligence" has the meaning given by section 1(1);
"notice" includes an announcement, whether or not in writing, and any other communication or pretended communication; and
"personal injury" includes any disease and any impairment of physical or mental condition.

PART III

26. International supply contracts.

(1) The limits imposed by this Act on the extent to which a person may exclude or restrict liability by reference to a contract term do not apply to liability arising under such a contract as is described in subsection (3) below.

(2) The terms of such a contract are not subject to any requirement of reasonableness under section 3 or 4: and nothing in Part II of this Act shall require the incorporation of the terms of such a contract to be fair and reasonable for them to have effect.

(3) Subject to subsection (4), that description of contract is one whose characteristics are the following—
(a) either it is a contract of sale of goods or it is one under or in pursuance of which the possession or ownership of goods passes; and
(b) it is made by parties whose places of business (or, if they have none, habitual residences) are in the territories of different States (the Channel Islands and the Isle of Man being treated for this purpose as different States from the United Kingdom).

(4) A contract falls within subsection (3) above only if either—
  (a) the goods in question are, at the time of the conclusion of the contract, in the course of carriage, or will be carried, from the territory of one State to the territory of another; or
  (b) the acts constituting the offer and acceptance have been done in the territories of different States; or
  (c) the contract provides for the goods to be delivered to the territory of a State other than that within whose territory those acts were done.

27. Choice of law clauses.

(1) Where the [law applicable to] a contract is the law of any part of the United Kingdom only by choice of the parties (and apart from that choice would be the law of some country outside the United Kingdom) sections 2 to 7 and 16 to 21 of this Act do not operate as part [of the law applicable to the contract].

(2) This Act has effect notwithstanding any contract term which applies or purports to apply the law of some country outside the United Kingdom, where (either or both)—
  (a) the term appears to the court, or arbitrator or arbiter to have been imposed wholly or mainly for the purpose of enabling the party imposing it to evade the operation of this Act; or
  (b) in the making of the contract one of the parties dealt as consumer, and he was then habitually resident in the United Kingdom, and the essential steps necessary for the making of the contract were taken there, whether by him or by others on his behalf.

28. Temporary provision for sea carriage of passengers.

(1) This section applies to a contract for carriage by sea of a passenger or of a passenger and his luggage where the provisions of the Athens Convention (with or without modification) do not have, in relation to the contract, the force of law in the United Kingdom.

(2) In a case where—
  (a) the contract is not made in the United Kingdom, and
  (b) neither the place of departure nor the place of destination under it is in the United Kingdom,
a person is not precluded by this Act from excluding or restricting liability for loss or damage, being loss or damage for which the provisions of the Convention would, if they had the force of law in relation to the contract, impose liability on him.

(3) In any other case, a person is not precluded by this Act from excluding or restricting liability for that loss or damage—
  (a) in so far as the exclusion or restriction would have been effective in that case had the provisions of the Convention had the force of law in relation to the contract; or
  (b) in such circumstances and to such extent as may be prescribed, by reference to a prescribed term of the contract.

(4) For the purposes of subsection (3)(a), the values which shall be taken to be the official values in the United Kingdom of the amounts (expressed in gold francs) by reference to which liability under the provisions of the Convention is limited shall be such amounts in sterling as the Secretary of State may from time to time by order made by statutory instrument specify.

(5) In this section,—
  (a) the references to excluding or restricting liability include doing any of those things in relation to the liability which are mentioned in section 13 or section 25(3) and (5); and
  (b) "the Athens Convention" means the Athens Convention relating to the Carriage of Passengers and their Luggage by Sea, 1974; and
  (c) "prescribed" means prescribed by the Secretary of State by regulations made by statutory instrument;

and a statutory instrument containing the regulations shall be subject to annulment in pursuance of a resolution of either House of Parliament.

29. Saving for other relevant legislation.

(1) Nothing in this Act removes or restricts the effect of, or prevents reliance upon, any contractual provision which—

    (a) is authorised or required by the express terms or necessary implication of an enactment; or

    (b) being made with a view to compliance with an international agreement to which the United Kingdom is a party, does not operate more restrictively than is contemplated by the agreement.

(2) A contract term is to be taken—

    (a) for the purposes of Part I of this Act, as satisfying the requirement of reasonableness...

if it is incorporated or approved by, or incorporated pursuant to a decision or ruling of, a competent authority acting in the exercise of any statutory jurisdiction or function and is not a term in a contract to which the competent authority is itself a party.

(3) In this section—

"competent authority" means any court, arbitrator or arbiter, government department or public authority;

"enactment" means any legislation (including subordinate legislation) of the United Kingdom or Northern Ireland and any instrument having effect by virtue of such legislation; and

"statutory" means conferred by an enactment.

SCHEDULES

Section 1(2)   SCHEDULE 1

SCOPE OF SECTIONS 2 TO 4 AND 7

1. Sections 2 to 4 of this Act do not extend to—

    (a) any contract of insurance (including a contract to pay an annuity on human life);

    (b) any contract so far as it relates to the creation or transfer of an interest in land, or to the termination of such an interest, whether by extinction, merger, surrender, forfeiture or otherwise;

    (c) any contract so far as it relates to the creation or transfer of a right or interest in any patent, trade mark, copyright, registered design, technical or commercial information or other intellectual property, or relates to the termination of any such right or interest;

    (d) any contract so far as it relates—

        (i) to the formation or dissolution of a company (which means any body corporate or unincorporated association and includes a partnership), or

        (ii) to its constitution or the rights or obligations of its corporators or members;

    (e) any contract so far as it relates to the creation or transfer of securities or of any right or interest in securities.

2. Section 2(1) extends to—

    (a) any contract of marine salvage or towage;

    (b) any charterparty of a ship or hovercraft; and

    (c) any contract for the carriage of goods by ship or hovercraft;

but subject to this sections 2 to 4 and 7 do not extend to any such contract except in favour of a person dealing as consumer.

3. Where goods are carried by ship or hovercraft in pursuance of a contract which either—

(a) specifies that as the means of carriage over part of the journey to be covered, or
(b) makes no provision as to the means of carriage and does not exclude that means,

then sections 2(2), 3 and 4 do not, except in favour of a person dealing as consumer, extend to the contract as it operates for and in relation to the carriage of the goods by that means.

4. Section 2(1) and (2) do not extend to a contract of employment, except in favour of the employee.

5. Section 2(1) does not affect the validity of any discharge and indemnity given by a person, on or in connection with an award to him of compensation for pneumoconiosis attributable to employment in the coal industry, in respect of any further claim arising from his contracting that disease.

Sections 11 (2) and 24 (2) SCHEDULE 2

"GUIDELINES" FOR APPLICATION OF REASONABLENESS TEST

The matters to which regard is to be had in particular for the purposes of sections 6(3), 7(3) and (4), 20 and 21 are any of the following which appear to be relevant—

(a) the strength of the bargaining positions of the parties relative to each other, taking into account (among other things) alternative means by which the customer's requirements could have been met;

(b) Whether the customer received an inducement to agree to the term, or in accepting it had an opportunity of entering into a similar contract with other persons, but without having to accept a similar term;

(c) whether the customer knew or ought reasonably to have known of the existence and extent of the term (having regard, among other things, to any custom of the trade and any previous course of dealing between the parties);

(d) where the term excludes or restricts any relevant liability if some condition is not complied with, whether it was reasonable at the time of the contract to expect that compliance with that condition would be practicable;

(e) whether the goods were manufactured, processed or adapted to the special order of the customer.

CIVIL LIABILITY (CONTRIBUTION) ACT 1978
(1978, c. 47)

1. Entitlement to contribution.

(1) Subject to the following provisions of this section, any person liable in respect of any damage suffered by another person may recover contribution from any other person liable in respect of the same damage (whether jointly with him or otherwise).

(2) A person shall be entitled to recover contribution by virtue of subsection (1) above notwithstanding that he has ceased to be liable in respect of the damage in question since the time when the damage occurred, provided that he was so liable immediately before he made or was ordered or agreed to make the payment in respect of which the contribution is sought.

(3) A person shall be liable to make contribution by virtue of subsection (1) above notwithstanding that he has ceased to be liable in respect of the damage in question since the time when the damage occurred, unless he ceased to be liable by virtue of the expiry of a period of limitation or prescription which extinguished the right on which the claim against him in respect of the damage was based.

(4) A person who has made or agreed to make any payment in bona fide settlement or compromise of any claim made against him in respect of any damage (including a

Civil Liability (Contribution) Act 1978

payment into court which has been accepted) shall be entitled to recover contribution in accordance with this section without regard to whether or not he himself is or ever was liable in respect of the damage, provided, however, that he would have been liable assuming that the factual basis of the claim against him could be established.

(5) A judgment given in any action brought in any part of the United Kingdom by or on behalf of the person who suffered the damage in question against any person from whom contribution is sought under this section shall be conclusive in the proceedings for contribution as to any issue determined by that judgment in favour of the person from whom the contribution is sought.

(6) References in this section to a person's liability in respect of any damage are references to any such liability which has been or could be established in an action brought against him in England and Wales by or on behalf of the person who suffered the damage; but it is immaterial whether any issue arising in any such action was or would be determined (in accordance with the rules of private international law) by reference to the law of a country outside England and Wales.

2. **Assessment of contribution.**

(1) Subject to subsection (3) below, in any proceedings for contribution under section 1 above the amount of the contribution recoverable from any person shall be such as may be found by the court to be just and equitable having regard to the extent of that person's responsibility for the damage in question.

(2) Subject to subsection (3) below, the court shall have power in any such proceedings to exempt any person from liability to make contribution or to direct that the contribution to be recovered from any person shall amount to a complete indemnity.

(3) Where the amount of the damages which have or might have been awarded in respect of the damage in question in any action brought in England and Wales by or on behalf of the person who suffered it against the person from whom the contribution is sought was or would have been subject to—

    (a) any limit imposed by or under any enactment or by any agreement made before the damage occurred;

    (b) any reduction by virtue of section 1 of the Law Reform (Contributory Negligence) Act 1945 or section 5 of the Fatal Accidents Act 1976; or

    (c) any corresponding limit or reduction under the law of a country outside England and Wales;

the person from whom the contribution is sought shall not by virtue of any contribution awarded under section 1 above be required to pay in respect of the damage a greater amount than the amount of those damages as so limited or reduced.

3. **Proceedings against persons jointly liable for the same debt or damage.**

Judgment recovered against any person liable in respect of any debt or damage shall not be a bar to an action, or to the continuance of an action, against any other person who is (apart from any such bar) jointly liable with him in respect of the same debt or damage.

4. **Successive actions against persons liable (jointly or otherwise) for the same damage.**

If more than one action is brought in respect of any damage by or on behalf of the person by whom it was suffered against persons liable in respect of the damage (whether jointly or otherwise) the plaintiff shall not be entitled to costs in any of those actions, other than that in which judgment is first given, unless the court is of the opinion that there was reasonable ground for bringing the action.

5. **Application to the Crown.**

Without prejudice to section 4(1) of the Crown Proceedings Act 1947 (indemnity and contribution), this Act shall bind the Crown, but nothing in this Act shall be construed as in any way affecting Her Majesty in Her private capacity (including in right of Her Duchy of Lancaster) or the Duchy of Cornwall.

6. Interpretation.

(1) A person is liable in respect of any damage for the purposes of this Act if the person who suffered it (or anyone representing his estate or dependants) is entitled to recover compensation from him in respect of that damage (whatever the legal basis of his liability, whether tort, breach of contract, breach of trust or otherwise).

(2) References in this Act to an action brought by or on behalf of the person who suffered any damage include references to an action brought for the benefit of his estate or dependants.

(3) In this Act "dependants" has the same meaning as in the Fatal Accidents Act 1976.

(4) In this Act, except in section 1(5) above, "action" means an action brought in England and Wales.

7. Savings.

(3) The right to recover contribution in accordance with section 1 above supersedes any right, other than an express contractual right, to recover contribution (as distinct from indemnity) otherwise than under this Act in corresponding circumstances; but nothing in this Act shall affect—
    (a) any express or implied contractual or other right to indemnity; or
    (b) any express contractual provision regulating or excluding contribution;
which would be enforceable apart from this Act (or render enforceable any agreement for indemnity or contribution which would not be enforceable apart from this Act).

STATE IMMUNITY ACT 1978
(1978, c. 33)

1. General immunity from jurisdiction.

(1) A State is immune from the jurisdiction of the courts of the United Kingdom except as provided in the following provisions of this Part of this Act.

(2) A court shall give effect to the immunity conferred by this section even though the State does not appear in the proceedings in question.

3. Commercial transactions and contracts to be performed in United Kingdom.

(1) A State is not immune as respects proceedings relating to—
    (a) a commercial transaction entered into by the State; or
    (b) an obligation of the State which by virtue of a contract (whether a commercial transaction or not) falls to be performed wholly or partly in the United Kingdom.

(2) This section does not apply if the parties to the dispute are States or have otherwise agreed in writing; and subsection (1)(b) above does not apply if the contract (not being a commercial transaction) was made in the territory of the State concerned and the obligation in question is governed by its administrative law.

5. Personal injuries and damage to property.

A State is not immune as respects proceedings in respect of—
    (a) death or personal injury; or
    (b) damage to or loss of tangible property,
caused by an act or omission in the United Kingdom.

CUSTOMS AND EXCISE MANAGEMENT ACT 1979
(1979, c. 2)

[137A. Recovery of overpaid excise duty.

(1) Where a person pays to the Commissioners an amount by way of excise duty which is not due to them, the Commissioners are liable to repay that amount.

(2) The Commissioners shall not be required to make any such repayment unless a claim is made to them in such form, and supported by such documentary evidence, as may be prescribed by them by regulations; and regulations may make different provision for different cases.

(3) It is a defence to a claim for repayment that the repayment would unjustly enrich the claimant.]

[(4) The Commissioners shall not be liable, on a claim made under this section, to repay any amount paid to them more than three years before the making of the claim.]

[(5) Except as provided by this section the Commissioners are not liable to repay an amount paid to them by way of excise duty by reason of the fact that it was not duty due to them.]

PNEUMOCONIOSIS ETC. (WORKERS' COMPENSATION) ACT 1979
(1979, c. 41)

1. Lump sum payments.
(1) If, on a claim by a person who is disabled by a disease to which this Act applies, the Secretary of State is satisfied that the conditions of entitlement mentioned in section 2(1) below are fulfilled, he shall in accordance with this Act make to that person a payment of such amount as may be prescribed by regulations.

(2) If, on a claim by the dependant of a person who, immediately before he died, was disabled by a disease to which this Act applies, the Secretary of State is satisfied that the conditions of entitlement mentioned in section 2(2) below are fulfilled, he shall in accordance with this Act make to that dependant a payment of such amount as may be so prescribed.

(3) The diseases to which this Act applies are pneumoconiosis, byssinosis and diffuse mesothelioma.

(4) Regulations under this section may prescribe different amounts for different cases or classes of cases or for different circumstances.

2. Conditions of entitlement.
(1) In the case of a person who is disabled by a disease to which this Act applies, the conditions of entitlement are—
    (a) that disablement benefit is payable to him in respect of the disease;
    (b) that every relevant employer of his has ceased to carry on business; and
    (c) that he has not brought any action, or compromised any claim, for damages in repect of the disablement.

(2) In the case of the dependant of a person who, immediately before he died, was disabled by a disease to which this Act applies, the conditions of entitlement are—
    (a) that no payment under this Act has been made to the deceased in respect of the disease;
    (b) that death benefit is payable to or in respect of the dependant by reason of the deceased's death as a result of the disease, or that disablement benefit was payable to the deceased in respect of the disease immediately before he died;
    (c) that every relevant employer of the deceased has ceased to carry on business; and
    (d) that neither the deceased nor his personal representatives nor any relative of his has brought any action, or compromised any claim, for damages in respect of the disablement or death.

(4) For the purposes of this section any action which has been dismissed otherwise than on the merits (as for example for want of prosecution or under any enactment relating to the limitation of actions) shall be disregarded.

5. Reconsideration of determinations.

(1) Subject to subsection (2) below, the Secretary of State may reconsider a determination that a payment should not be made under this Act on the ground—

(a) that there has been a material change of circumstances since the determination was made; or

(b) that the determination was made in ignorance of, or was based on a mistake as to, some material fact;

and the Secretary of State may, on the ground set out in paragraph (b) above, reconsider a determination that such a payment should be made.

(4) If, whether fraudulently or otherwise, any person misrepresents or fails to disclose any material fact and in consequence of the misrepresentation or failure a payment is made under this Act, the person to whom the payment was made shall be liable to repay the amount of that payment to the Secretary of State unless he can show that the misrepresentation or failure occurred without his connivance or consent.

9. Financial provisions.

(1) There shall be paid out of moneys provided by Parliament—

(a) any expenditure incurred by the Secretary of State in making payments under this Act . . .

SALE OF GOODS ACT 1979
(1979, c. 54)

PART I
CONTRACTS TO WHICH ACT APPLIES

1. Contracts to which Act applies.

(1) This Act applies to contracts of sale of goods made on or after (but not to those made before) 1 January 1894.

(2) In relation to contracts made on certain dates, this Act applies subject to the modification of certain of its sections as mentioned in Schedule 1 below.

(3) Any such modification is indicated in the section concerned by a reference to Schedule 1 below.

(4) Accordingly, where a section does not contain such a reference, this Act applies in relation to the contract concerned without such modification of the section.

PART II
FORMATION OF THE CONTRACT

Contract of Sale

2. Contract of sale.

(1) A contract of sale of goods is a contract by which the seller transfers or agrees to transfer the property in goods to the buyer for a money consideration, called the price.

(2) There may be a contract of sale between one part owner and another.

(3) A contract of sale may be absolute or conditional.

(4) Where under a contract of sale the property in the goods is transferred from the seller to the buyer the contract is called a sale.

(5) Where under a contract of sale the transfer of the property in the goods is to take place at a future time or subject to some condition later to be fulfilled the contract is called an agreement to sell.

(6) An agreement to sell becomes a sale when the time elapses or the conditions are fulfilled subject to which the property in the goods is to be transferred.

Sale of Goods Act 1979

3. **Capacity to buy and sell.**
(1) Capacity to buy and sell is regulated by the general law concerning capacity to contract and to transfer and acquire property.
(2) Where necessaries are sold and delivered to a minor or to a person who by reason of mental incapacity or drunkenness is incompetent to contract, he must pay a reasonable price for them.
(3) In subsection (2) above "necessaries" means goods suitable to the condition in life of the minor or other person concerned and to his actual requirements at the time of the sale and delivery.
[*The words "to a minor or" in s. 3(2) and "minor or other" in s. 3(3) were repealed, for Scotland only, by the Age of Legal Capacity (Scotland) Act 1991, s. 10, Sched. 2.*]

4. **How contract of sale is made.**
(1) Subject to this and any other Act, a contract of sale may be made in writing (either with or without seal), or by word of mouth, or partly in writing and partly by word of mouth, or may be implied from the conduct of the parties.
(2) Nothing in this section affects the law relating to corporations.

5. **Existing or future goods.**
(1) The goods which form the subject of a contract of sale may be either existing goods, owned or possessed by the seller, or goods to be manufactured or acquired by him after the making of the contract of sale, in this Act called future goods.
(2) There may be a contract for the sale of goods the acquisition of which by the seller depends on a contingency which may or may not happen.
(3) Where by a contract of sale the seller purports to effect a present sale of future goods, the contract operates as an agreement to sell the goods.

6. **Goods which have perished.**
Where there is a contract for the sale of specific goods, and the goods without the knowledge of the seller have perished at the time when the contract is made, the contract is void.

7. **Goods perishing before sale but after agreement to sell.**
Where there is an agreement to sell specific goods and subsequently the goods, without any fault on the part of the seller or buyer, perish before the risk passes to the buyer, the agreement is avoided.

8. **Ascertainment of price.**
(1) The price in a contract of sale may be fixed by the contract, or may be left to be fixed in a manner agreed by the contract, or may be determined by the course of dealing between the parties.
(2) Where the price is not determined as mentioned in subsection (1) above the buyer must pay a reasonable price.
(3) What is a reasonable price is a question of fact dependent on the circumstances of each particular case.

9. **Agreement to sell at valuation.**
(1) Where there is an agreement to sell goods on the terms that the price is to be fixed by the valuation of a third party, and he cannot or does not make the valuation, the agreement is avoided; but if the goods or any part of them have been delivered to and appropriated by the buyer he must pay a reasonable price for them.
(2) Where the third party is prevented from making the valuation by the fault of the seller or buyer, the party not at fault may maintain an action for damages against the party at fault.

[*Implied terms etc.*]

10. Stipulations about time.

(1) Unless a different intention appears from the terms of the contract, stipulations as to time of payment are not of the essence of a contract of sale.

(2) Whether any other stipulation as to time is or is not of the essence of the contract depends on the terms of the contract.

(3) In a contract of sale "month" prima facie means calendar month.

11. When condition to be treated as warranty.

[(1) This section does not apply to Scotland.]

(2) Where a contract of sale is subject to a condition to be fulfilled by the seller, the buyer may waive the condition, or may elect to treat the breach of the condition as a breach of warranty and not as a ground for treating the contract as repudiated.

(3) Whether a stipulation in a contract of sale is a condition, the breach of which may give rise to a right to treat the contract as repudiated, or a warranty, the breach of which may give rise to a claim for damages but not to a right to reject the goods and treat the contract as repudiated, depends in each case on the construction of the contract; and a stipulation may be a condition, though called a warranty in the contract.

(4) [Subject to section 35A below] Where a contract of sale is not severable and the buyer has accepted the goods or part of them, the breach of a condition to be fulfilled by the seller can only be treated as a breach of warranty, and not as a ground for rejecting the goods and treating the contract as repudiated, unless there is an express or implied term of the contract to that effect.

(6) Nothing in this section affects a condition or warranty whose fulfilment is excused by law by reason of impossibility or otherwise.

(7) Paragraph 2 of Schedule 1 below applies in relation to a contract made before 22 April 1967 or (in the application of this Act to Northern Ireland) 28 July 1967.

12. Implied terms about title, etc.

(1) In a contract of sale, other than one to which subsection (3) below applies, there is an implied [term] on the part of the seller that in the case of a sale he has a right to sell the goods, and in the case of an agreement to sell he will have such a right at the time when the property is to pass.

(2) In a contract of sale, other than one to which subsection (3) below applies, there is also an implied [term] that—

(a) the goods are free, and will remain free until the time when the property is to pass, from any charge or encumbrance not disclosed or known to the buyer before the contract is made, and

(b) the buyer will enjoy quiet possession of the goods except so far as it may be disturbed by the owner or other person entitled to the benefit of any charge or encumbrance so disclosed or known.

(3) This subsection applies to a contract of sale in the case of which there appears from the contract or is to be inferred from its circumstances an intention that the seller should transfer only such title as he or a third person may have.

(4) In a contract to which subsection (3) above applies there is an implied [term] that all charges or encumbrances known to the seller and not known to the buyer have been disclosed to the buyer before the contract is made.

(5) In a contract to which subsection (3) above applies there is also an implied [term] that none of the following will disturb the buyer's quiet possession of the goods, namely—

(a) the seller;

(b) in a case where the parties to the contract intend that the seller should transfer only such title as a third person may have, that person;
(c) anyone claiming through or under the seller or that third person otherwise than under a charge or encumbrance disclosed or known to the buyer before the contract is made.

[(5A) As regards England and Wales and Northern Ireland, the term implied by subsection (1) above is a condition and the terms implied by subsections (2), (4) and (5) above are warranties.]

(6) Paragraph 3 of Schedule 1 below applies in relation to a contract made before 18 May 1973.

13. Sale by description.

(1) Where there is a contract for the sale of goods by description, there is an implied [term] that the goods will correspond with the description.

[(1A) As regards England and Wales and Northern Ireland, the term implied by subsection (1) above is a condition.]

(2) If the sale is by sample as well as by description it is not sufficient that the bulk of the goods corresponds with the sample if the goods do not also correspond with the description.

(3) A sale of goods is not prevented from being a sale by description by reason only that, being exposed for sale or hire, they are selected by the buyer.

(4) Paragraph 4 of Schedule 1 below applies in relation to a contract made before 18 May 1973.

14. Implied terms about quality or fitness.

(1) Except as provided by this section and section 15 below and subject to any other enactment, there is no implied [term] about the quality or fitness for any particular purpose of goods supplied under a contract of sale.

[(2) Where the seller sells goods in the course of a business, there is an implied term that the goods supplied under the contract are of satisfactory quality.

(2A) For the purposes of this Act, goods are of satisfactory quality if they meet the standard that a reasonable person would regard as satisfactory, taking account of any description of the goods, the price (if relevant) and all the other relevant circumstances.

(2B) For the purposes of this Act, the quality of goods includes their state and condition and the following (among others) are in appropriate cases aspects of the quality of goods—
(a) fitness for all the purposes for which goods of the kind in question are commonly supplied,
(b) appearance and finish,
(c) freedom from minor defects,
(d) safety, and
(e) durability.

(2C) The term implied by subsection (2) above does not extend to any matter making the quality of goods unsatisfactory—
(a) which is specifically drawn to the buyer's attention before the contract is made,
(b) where the buyer examines the goods before the contract is made, which that examination ought to reveal, or
(c) in the case of a contract for sale by sample, which would have been apparent on a reasonable examination of the sample.]

(3) Where the seller sells goods in the course of a business and the buyer, expressly or by implication, makes known—
(a) to the seller, or

(b) where the purchase price or part of it is payable by instalments and the goods were previously sold by a credit-broker to the seller, to that credit-broker,
any particular purpose for which the goods are being bought,
there is an implied [term] that the goods supplied under the contract are reasonably fit for that purpose, whether or not that is a purpose for which such goods are commonly supplied, except where the circumstances show that the buyer does not rely, or that it is unreasonable for him to rely, on the skill or judgment of the seller or credit-broker.

(4) An implied [term] about quality or fitness for a particular purpose may be annexed to a contract of sale by usage.

(5) The preceding provisions of this section apply to a sale by a person who in the course of a business is acting as agent for another as they apply to a sale by a principal in the course of a business, except where that other is not selling in the course of a business and either the buyer knows that fact or reasonable steps are taken to bring it to the notice of the buyer before the contract is made.

[(6) As regards England and Wales and Northern Ireland, the terms implied by subsections (2) and (3) above are conditions.]

(7) Paragraph 5 of Schedule 1 below applies in relation to a contract made on or after 18 May 1973 and before the appointed day, and paragraph 6 in relation to one made before 18 May 1973.

(8) In subsection (7) above and paragraph 5 of Schedule 1 below references to the appointed day are to the day appointed for the purposes of those provisions by an order of the Secretary of State made by statutory instrument.

Sale by sample

15. Sale by sample.

(1) A contract of sale is a contract for sale by sample where there is an express or implied term to that effect in the contract.

(2) In the case of a contract for sale by sample there is an implied [term]—
   (a) that the bulk will correspond with the sample in quality;
   [...]
   (c) that the goods will be free from any defect, making their quality unsatisfactory which would not be apparent on reasonable examination of the sample.

[(3) As regards England and Wales and Northern Ireland, the term implied by subsection (2) above is a condition.]

(4) Paragraph 7 of Schedule 1 below applies in relation to a contract made before 18 May 1973.

Miscellaneous

[15A. Modification of remedies for breach of condition in non-consumer cases.

(1) Where in the case of a contract of sale—
   (a) the buyer would, apart from this subsection, have the right to reject goods by reason of a breach on the part of the seller of a term implied by section 13, 14 or 15 above, but
   (b) the breach is so slight that it would be unreasonable for him to reject them,
then, if the buyer does not deal as consumer, the breach is not to be treated as a breach of condition but may be treated as a breach of warranty.

(2) This section applies unless a contrary intention appears in, or is to be implied from, the contract.

(3) It is for the seller to show that a breach fell within subsection (1)(b) above.

(4) This section does not apply to Scotland.]

Sale of Goods Act 1979

[15B. Remedies for breach of contract as respects Scotland.
(1) Where in a contract of sale the seller is in breach of any term of the contract (express or implied), the buyer shall be entitled—
    (a) to claim damages, and
    (b) if the breach is material, to reject any goods delivered under the contract and treat it as repudiated.
(2) Where a contract of sale is a consumer contract, then, for the purposes of subsection (1)(b) above, breach by the seller of any term (express or implied)—
    (a) as to the quality of the goods or their fitness for a purpose,
    (b) if the goods are, or are to be, sold by description, that the goods will correspond with the description,
    (c) if the goods are, or are to be, sold by reference to a sample, that the bulk will correspond with the sample in quality,
shall be deemed to be a material breach.
(3) This section applies to Scotland only.]

PART III
EFFECTS OF THE CONTRACT

Transfer of property as between seller and buyer

16. Goods must be ascertained.
[Subject to section (20A) below] Where there is a contract for the sale of unascertained goods no property in the goods is transferred to the buyer unless and until the goods are ascertained.

17. Property passes when intended to pass.
(1) Where there is a contract for the sale of specific or ascertained goods the property in them is transferred to the buyer at such time as the parties to the contract intend it to be transferred.
(2) For the purpose of ascertaining the intention of the parties regard shall be had to the terms of the contract, the conduct of the parties and the circumstances of the case.

18. Rules for ascertaining intention.
Unless a different intention appears, the following are rules for ascertaining the intention of the parties as to the time at which the property in the goods is to pass to the buyer.
Rule 1.—Where there is an unconditional contract for the sale of specific goods in a deliverable state the property in the goods passes to the buyer when the contract is made, and it is immaterial whether the time of payment or the time of delivery, or both, be postponed.
Rule 2.—Where there is a contract for the sale of specific goods and the seller is bound to do something to the goods for the purpose of putting them into a deliverable state, the property does not pass until the thing is done and the buyer has notice that it has been done.
Rule 3.—Where there is a contract for the sale of specific goods in a deliverable state but the seller is bound to weigh, measure, test, or do some other act or thing with reference to the goods for the purpose of ascertaining the price, the property does not pass until the act or thing is done and the buyer has notice that it has been done.
Rule 4.—When goods are delivered to the buyer on approval or on sale or return or other similar terms the property in the goods passes to the buyer—
    (a) when he signifies his approval or acceptance to the seller or does any other act adopting the transaction;
    (b) if he does not signify his approval or acceptance to the seller but retains the goods without giving notice of rejection, then, if a time has been fixed for the return

of the goods, on the expiration of that time, and, if no time has been fixed, on the expiration of a reasonable time.

Rule 5.—(1) Where there is a contract for the sale of unascertained or future goods by description, and goods of that description and in a deliverable state are unconditionally appropriated to the contract, either by the seller with the assent of the buyer or by the buyer with the assent of the seller, the property in the goods then passes to the buyer; and the assent may be express or implied, and may be given either before or after the appropriation is made.

(2) Where, in pursuance of the contract, the seller delivers the goods to the buyer or to a carrier or other bailee or custodier (whether named by the buyer or not) for the purpose of transmission to the buyer, and does not reserve the right of disposal, he is to be taken to have unconditionally appropriated the goods to the contract.

[(3) Where there is a contract for the sale of a specified quantity of unascertained goods in a deliverable state forming part of a bulk which is identified either in the contract or by subsequent agreement between the parties and the bulk is reduced to (or to less than) that quantity, then, if the buyer under that contract is the only buyer to whom goods are then due out of the bulk—

(a) the remaining goods are to be taken as appropriated to that contract at the time when the bulk is so reduced; and

(b) the property in those goods then passes to that buyer.

(4) Paragraph (3) above applies also (with the necessary modifications) where a bulk is reduced to (or to less than) the aggregate of the quantities due to a single buyer under separate contracts relating to that bulk and he is the only buyer to whom goods are then due out of that bulk.]

19. Reservation of right of disposal.

(1) Where there is a contract for the sale of specific goods or where goods are subsequently appropriated to the contract, the seller may, by the terms of the contract or appropriation, reserve the right of disposal of the goods until certain conditions are fulfilled; and in such a case, notwithstanding the delivery of the goods to the buyer, or to a carrier or other bailee or custodier for the purpose of transmission to the buyer, the property in the goods does not pass to the buyer until the conditions imposed by the seller are fulfilled.

(2) Where goods are shipped, and by the bill of lading the goods are deliverable to the order of the seller or his agent, the seller is prima facie to be taken to reserve the right of disposal.

(3) Where the seller of goods draws on the buyer for the price, and transmits the bill of exchange and bill of lading to the buyer together to secure acceptance or payment of the bill of exchange, the buyer is bound to return the bill of lading if he does not honour the bill of exchange, and if he wrongfully retains the bill of lading the property in the goods does not pass to him.

20. Risk prima facie passes with property.

(1) Unless otherwise agreed, the goods remain at the sellers's risk until the property in them is transferred to the buyer, but when the property in them is transferred to the buyer the goods are at the buyer's risk whether delivery has been made or not.

(2) But where delivery has been delayed through the fault of either buyer or seller the goods are at the risk of the party at fault as regards any loss which might not have occurred but for such fault.

(3) Nothing in this section affects the duties or liabilities of either seller or buyer as a bailee or custodier of the goods of the other party.

[20A. Undivided shares in goods forming part of a bulk.

(1) This section applies to a contract for the sale of a specified quantity of unascertained goods if the following conditions are met—

Sale of Goods Act 1979

    (a) the goods or some of them form part of a bulk which is identified either in the contract or by subsequent agreement between the parties; and
    (b) the buyer has paid the price for some or all of the goods which are the subject of the contract and which form part of the bulk.
    (2) Where this section applies, then (unless the parties agree otherwise), as soon as the conditions specified in paragraphs (a) and (b) of subsection (1) above are met or at such later time as the parties may agree—
        (a) property in an undivided share in the bulk is transferred to the buyer; and
        (b) the buyer becomes an owner in common of the bulk.
    (3) Subject to subsection (4) below, for the purposes of this section, the undivided share of a buyer in a bulk at any time shall be such share as the quantity of goods paid for and due to the buyer out of the bulk bears to the quantity of goods in the bulk at that time.
    (4) Where the aggregate of the undivided shares of buyers in a bulk determined under subsection (3) above would at any time exceed the whole of the bulk at that time, the undivided share in the bulk of each buyer shall be reduced proportionately so that the aggregate of the undivided shares is equal to the whole bulk.
    (5) Where a buyer has paid the price for only some of the goods due to him out of a bulk, any delivery to the buyer out of the bulk shall, for the purposes of this section, be ascribed in the first place to the goods in respect of which payment has been made.
    (6) For the purpose of this section payment of part of the price for any goods shall be treated as payment for a corresponding part of the goods.]

[20B. Deemed consent by co-owner to dealings in bulk goods.
    (1) A person who has become an owner in common of a bulk by virtue of section 20A above shall be deemed to have consented to—
        (a) any delivery of goods out of the bulk to any other owner in common of the bulk, being goods which are due to him under his contract;
        (b) any removal, dealing with, delivery or disposal of goods in the bulk by any other person who is an owner in common of the bulk in so far as the goods fall within that co-owner's undivided share in the bulk at the time of the removal, dealing, delivery or disposal.
    (2) No cause of action shall accrue to anyone against a person by reason of that person having acted in accordance with paragraph (a) or (b) of subsection (1) above in reliance on any consent deemed to have been given under that subsection.
    (3) Nothing in this section or section 20A above shall—
        (a) impose an obligation on a buyer of goods out of a bulk to compensate any other buyer of goods out of that bulk for any shortfall in the goods received by that other buyer;
        (b) affect any contractual arrangement between buyers of goods out of a bulk for adjustments between themselves; or
        (c) affect the rights of any buyer under his contract.]

Transfer of title

21. Sale by person not the owner.
    (1) Subject to this Act, where goods are sold by a person who is not their owner, and who does not sell them under the authority or with the consent of the owner, the buyer acquires no better title to the goods than the seller had, unless the owner of the goods is by his conduct precluded from denying the seller's authority to sell.
    (2) Nothing in this Act affects—
        (a) the provisions of the Factors Acts or any enactment enabling the apparent owner of goods to dispose of them as if he were their true owner;
        (b) the validity of any contract of sale under any special common law or statutory power of sale or under the order of a court of competent jurisdiction.

22. Market overt.

[...]

(2) This section does not apply to Scotland.

(3) Paragraph 8 of Schedule 1 below applies in relation to a contract under which goods were sold before 1 January 1968 or (in the application of this Act to Northern Ireland) 29 August 1967.

23. Sale under voidable title.

When the seller of goods has a voidable title to them, but his title has not been avoided at the time of the sale, the buyer acquires a good title to the goods, provided he buys them in good faith and without notice of the seller's defect of title.

24. Seller in possession after sale.

Where a person having sold goods continues or is in possession of the goods, or of the documents of title to the goods, the delivery or transfer by that person, or by a mercantile agent acting for him, of the goods or documents of title under any sale, pledge, or other disposition thereof, to any person receiving the same in good faith and without notice of the previous sale, has the same effect as if the person making the delivery or transfer were expressly authorised by the owner of the goods to make the same.

25. Buyer in possession after sale.

(1) Where a person having bought or agreed to buy goods obtains, with the consent of the seller, possession of the goods or the documents of title to the goods, the delivery or transfer by that person, or by a mercantile agent acting for him, of the goods or documents of title, under any sale, pledge, or other disposition thereof, to any person receiving the same in good faith and without notice of any lien or other right of the original seller in respect of the goods, has the same effect as if the person making the delivery or transfer were a mercantile agent in possession of the goods or documents of title with the consent of the owner.

(2) For the purposes of subsection (1) above—

   (a) the buyer under a conditional sale agreement is to be taken not to be a person who has bought or agreed to buy goods, and

   (b) "conditional sale agreement" means an agreement for the sale of goods which is a consumer credit agreement within the meaning of the Consumer Credit Act 1974 under which the purchase price or part of it is payable by instalments, and the property in the goods is to remain in the seller (notwithstanding that the buyer is to be in possession of the goods) until such conditions as to the payment of instalments or otherwise as may be specified in the agreement are fulfilled.

(3) Paragraph 9 of Schedule 1 below applies in relation to a contract under which a person buys or agrees to buy goods and which is made before the appointed day.

(4) In subsection (3) above and paragraph 9 of Schedule 1 below references to the appointed day are to the day appointed for the purposes of those provisions by an order of the Secretary of State made by statutory instrument.

26. Supplementary to sections 24 and 25.

In sections 24 and 25 above "mercantile agent" means a mercantile agent having in the customary course of his business as such agent authority either—

   (a) to sell goods, or
   (b) to consign goods for the purpose of sale, or
   (c) to buy goods, or
   (d) to raise money on the security of goods.

PART IV
PERFORMANCE OF THE CONTRACT

27. Duties of seller and buyer.
It is the duty of the seller to deliver the goods, and of the buyer to accept and pay for them, in accordance with the terms of the contract of sale.

28. Payment and delivery are concurrent conditions.
Unless otherwise agreed, delivery of the goods and payment of the price are concurrent conditions, that is to say, the seller must be ready and willing to give possession of the goods to the buyer in exchange for the price and the buyer must be ready and willing to pay the price in exchange for possession of the goods.

29. Rules about delivery.
(1) Whether it is for the buyer to take possession of the goods or for the seller to send them to the buyer is a question depending in each case on the contract, express or implied, between the parties.

(2) Apart from any such contract, express or implied, the place of delivery is the seller's place of business if he has one, and if not, his residence; except that, if the contract is for the sale of specific goods, which to the knowledge of the parties when the contract is made are in some other place, then that place is the place of delivery.

(3) Where under the contract of sale the seller is bound to send the goods to the buyer, but no time for sending them is fixed, the seller is bound to send them within a reasonable time.

(4) Where the goods at the time of sale are in the possession of a third person, there is no delivery by seller to buyer unless and until the third person acknowledges to the buyer that he holds the goods on his behalf; but nothing in this section affects the operation of the issue or transfer of any document of title to goods.

(5) Demand or tender of delivery may be treated as ineffectual unless made at a reasonable hour; and what is a reasonable hour is a question of fact.

(6) Unless otherwise agreed, the expenses of and incidental to putting the goods into a deliverable state must be borne by the seller.

30. Delivery of wrong quantity.
(1) Where the seller delivers to the buyer a quantity of goods less than he contracted to sell, the buyer may reject them, but if the buyer accepts the goods so delivered he must pay for them at the contract rate.

(2) Where the seller delivers to the buyer a quantity of goods larger than he contracted to sell, the buyer may accept the goods included in the contract and reject the rest, or he may reject the whole.

[(2A) A buyer who does not deal as consumer may not—
   (a) where the seller delivers a quantity of goods less than he contracted to sell, reject the goods under subsection (1) above, or
   (b) where the seller delivers a quantity of goods larger than he contracted to sell, reject the whole under subsection (2) above,
if the shortfall or, as the case may be, excess is so slight that it would be unreasonable for him to do so.

(2B) It is for the seller to show that a shortfall or excess fell within subsection (2A) above.

(2C) Subsections (2A) and (2B) above do not apply to Scotland.]

[(2D) Where the seller delivers a quantity of goods—
   (a) less than he contracted to sell, the buyer shall not be entitled to reject the goods under subsection (1) above,
   (b) larger than he contracted to sell, the buyer shall not be entitled to reject the whole under subsection (2) above,

unless the shortfall or excess is material.

(2E) Subsection (2D) above applies to Scotland only.]

(3) Where the seller delivers to the buyer a quantity of goods larger than he contracted to sell and the buyer accepts the whole of the goods so delivered he must pay for them at the contract rate.

(5) This section is subject to any usage of trade, special agreement, or course of dealing between the parties.

31. Instalment deliveries.

(1) Unless otherwise agreed, the buyer of goods is not bound to accept delivery of them by instalments.

(2) Where there is a contract for the sale of goods to be delivered by stated instalments, which are to be separately paid for, and the seller makes defective deliveries in respect of one or more instalments, or the buyer neglects or refuses to take delivery of or pay for one or more instalments, it is a question in each case depending on the terms of the contract and the circumstances of the case whether the breach of contract is a repudiation of the whole contract or whether it is a severable breach giving rise to a claim for compensation but not to a right to treat the whole contract as repudiated.

32. Delivery to carrier.

(1) Where, in pursuance of a contract of sale, the seller is authorised or required to send the goods to the buyer, delivery of the goods to a carrier (whether named by the buyer or not) for the purpose of transmission to the buyer is prima facie deemed to be delivery of the goods to the buyer.

(2) Unless otherwise authorised by the buyer, the seller must make such contact with the carrier on behalf of the buyer as may be reasonable having regard to the nature of the goods and the other circumstances of the case; and if the seller omits to do so, and the goods are lost or damaged in course of transit, the buyer may decline to treat the delivery to the carrier as a delivery to himself or may hold the seller responsible in damages.

(3) Unless otherwise agreed, where goods are sent by the seller to the buyer by a route involving sea transit, under circumstances in which it is usual to insure, the seller must give such notice to the buyer as may enable him to insure them during their sea transit, and if the seller fails to do so, the goods are at his risk during such sea transit.

33. Risk where goods are delivered at distant place.

Where the seller of goods agrees to deliver them at his own risk at a place other than that where they are when sold, the buyer must nevertheless (unless otherwise agreed) take any risk of deterioration in the goods necessarily incident to the course of transit.

34. Buyer's right of examining the goods.

Unless otherwise agreed, when the seller tenders delivery of goods to the buyer, he is bound on request to afford the buyer a reasonable opportunity of examining the goods for the purpose of ascertaining whether they are in conformity with the contract [and, in the case of a contract for sale by sample, of comparing the bulk with the sample].

35. Acceptance.

(1) The buyer is deemed to have accepted the goods [subject to subsection (2) below—

   (a) when he intimates to the seller that he has accepted them, or

   (b) when the goods have been delivered to him and he does any act in relation to them which is inconsistent with the ownership of the seller.

(2) Where goods are delivered to the buyer, and he has not previously examined them, he is not deemed to have accepted them under subsection (1) above until he has had a reasonable opportunity of examining them for the purpose—

(a) of ascertaining whether they are in conformity with the contract, and
(b) in the case of a contract for sale by sample, of comparing the bulk with the sample.

(3) Where the buyer deals as consumer or (in Scotland) the contract of sale is a consumer contract, the buyer cannot lose his right to rely on subsection (2) above by agreement, waiver or otherwise.

(4) The buyer is also deemed to have accepted the goods when after the lapse of a reasonable time he retains the goods without intimating to the seller that he has rejected them.

(5) The questions that are material in determining for the purposes of subsection (4) above whether a reasonable time has elapsed include whether the buyer has had a reasonable opportunity of examining the goods for the purpose mentioned in subsection (2) above.

(6) The buyer is not by virtue of this section deemed to have accepted the goods merely because—
(a) he asks for, or agrees to, their repair by or under an arrangement with the seller, or
(b) the goods are delivered to another under a sub-sale or other disposition.

(7) Where the contract is for the sale of goods making one or more commercial units, a buyer accepting any goods included in a unit is deemed to have accepted all the goods making the unit; and in this subsection "commercial unit" means a unit division of which would materially impair the value of the goods or the character of the unit.

(8)] Paragraph 10 of Schedule 1 below applies in relation to a contract made before 22 April 1967 or (in the application of this Act to Northern Ireland) 28 July 1967.

[35A. **Right of partial rejection.**
(1) If the buyer—
(a) has the right to reject the goods by reason of a breach on the part of the seller that affects some or all of them, but
(b) accepts some of the goods, including, where there are any goods unaffected by the breach, all such goods,
he does not by accepting them lose his right to reject the rest.

(2) In the case of a buyer having the right to reject an instalment of goods, subsection (1) above applies as if references to the goods were references to the goods comprised in the instalment.

(3) For the purposes of subsection (1) above, goods are affected by a breach if by reason of the breach they are not in conformity with the contract.

(4) This section applies unless a contrary intention appears in, or is to be implied from, the contract.]

36. **Buyer not bound to return rejected goods.**
Unless otherwise agreed, where goods are delivered to the buyer, and he refuses to accept them, having the right to do so, he is not bound to return them to the seller, but it is sufficient if he intimates to the seller that he refuses to accept them.

37. **Buyer's liability for not taking delivery of goods.**
(1) When the seller is ready and willing to deliver the goods, and requests the buyer to take delivery, and the buyer does not within a reasonable time after such request take delivery of the goods, he is liable to the seller for any loss occasioned by his neglect or refusal to take delivery, and also for a reasonable charge for the care and custody of the goods.

(2) Nothing in this section affects the rights of the seller where the neglect or refusal of the buyer to take delivery amounts to a repudiation of the contract.

PART V
RIGHTS OF UNPAID SELLER AGAINST THE GOODS

Preliminary

38. Unpaid seller defined.

(1) The seller of goods is an unpaid seller within the meaning of this Act—

(a) when the whole of the price has not been paid or tendered;

(b) when a bill of exchange or other negotiable instrument has been received as conditional payment, and the condition on which it was received has not been fulfilled by reason of the dishonour of the instrument or otherwise.

(2) In this Part of this Act "seller" includes any person who is in the position of a seller, as, for instance, an agent of the seller to whom the bill of lading has been indorsed, or a consignor or agent who has himself paid (or is directly responsible for) the price.

39. Unpaid seller's rights.

(1) Subject to this and any other Act, notwithstanding that the property in the goods may have passed to the buyer, the unpaid seller of goods, as such, has by implication of law—

(a) a lien on the goods or right to retain them for the price while he is in possession of them;

(b) in the case of the insolvency of the buyer, a right of stopping the goods in transit after he has parted with the possesion of them;

(c) a right of re-sale as limited by this Act.

(2) Where the property in goods has not passed to the buyer, the unpaid seller has (in addition to his other remedies) a right of withholding delivery similar to and coextensive with his rights of lien or retention and stoppage in transit where the property has passed to the buyer.

Unpaid seller's lien

41. Seller's lien.

(1) Subject to this Act, the unpaid seller of goods who is in possession of them is entitled to retain possession of them until payment or tender of the price in the following cases:—

(a) where the goods have been sold without any stipulation as to credit;

(b) where the goods have been sold on credit but the term of credit has expired;

(c) where the buyer becomes insolvent.

(2) The seller may exercise his lien or right of retention notwithstanding that he is in possession of the goods as agent or bailee or custodier for the buyer.

42. Part delivery.

Where an unpaid seller has made part delivery of the goods, he may exercise his lien or right of retention on the remainder, unless such part delivery has been made under such circumstances as to show an agreement to waive the lien or right of retention.

43. Termination of lien.

(1) The unpaid seller of goods loses his lien or right of retention in respect of them—

(a) when he delivers the goods to a carrier or other bailee or custodier for the purpose of transmission to the buyer without reserving the right of disposal of the goods;

(b) when the buyer or his agent lawfully obtains possession of the goods;

(c) by waiver of the lien or right of retention.

(2) An unpaid seller of goods who has a lien or right of retention in respect of them does not lose his lien or right of retention by reason only that he has obtained judgment or decree for the price of the goods.

Stoppage in transit

44. Right of stoppage in transit.
Subject to this Act, when the buyer of goods becomes insolvent the unpaid seller who has parted with the possession of the goods has the right of stopping them in transit, that is to say, he may resume possession of the goods as long as they are in course of transit, and may retain them until payment or tender of the price.

45. Duration of transit.
(1) Goods are deemed to be in course of transit from the time when they are delivered to a carrier or other bailee or custodier for the purpose of transmission to the buyer, until the buyer or his agent in that behalf takes delivery of them from the carrier or other bailee or custodier.

(2) If the buyer or his agent in that behalf obtains delivery of the goods before their arrival at the appointed destination, the transit is at an end.

(3) If, after the arrival of the goods at the appointed destination, the carrier or other bailee or custodier acknowledges to the buyer or his agent that he holds the goods on his behalf and continues in possession of them as bailee or custodier for the buyer or his agent, the transit is at an end, and it is immaterial that a further destination for the goods may have been indicated by the buyer.

(4) If the goods are rejected by the buyer, and the carrier or other bailee or custodier continues in possession of them, the transit is not deemed to be at an end, even if the seller has refused to receive them back.

(5) When goods are delivered to a ship chartered by the buyer it is a question depending on the circumstances of the particular case whether they are in the possession of the master as a carrier or as agent to the buyer.

(6) Where the carrier or other bailee or custodier wrongfully refuses to deliver the goods to the buyer or his agent in that behalf, the transit is deemed to be at an end.

(7) Where part delivery of the goods has been made to the buyer or his agent in that behalf, the remainder of the goods may be stopped in transit, unless such part delivery has been made under such circumstances as to show an agreement to give up possession of the whole of the goods.

46. How stoppage in transit is effected.
(1) The unpaid seller may exercise his right of stoppage in transit either by taking actual possession of the goods or by giving notice of his claim to the carrier or other bailee or custodier in whose possession the goods are.

(2) The notice may be given either to the person in actual possession of the goods or to his principal.

(3) If given to the principal, the notice is ineffective unless given at such time and under such circumstances that the principal, by the exercise of reasonable diligence, may communicate it to his servant or agent in time to prevent a delivery to the buyer.

(4) When notice of stoppage in transit is given by the seller to the carrier or other bailee or custodier in possession of the goods, he must re-deliver the goods to, or according to the directions of, the seller; and the expenses of the re-delivery must be borne by the seller.

Resale etc. by buyer

47. Effect of sub-sale etc. by buyer.
(1) Subject to this Act, the unpaid seller's right of lien or retention or stoppage in transit is not affected by any sale or other disposition of the goods which the buyer may have made, unless the seller has assented to it.

(2) Where a document of title to goods has been lawfully transferred to any person as buyer or owner of the goods, and that person transfers the document to a person who takes it in good faith and for valuable consideration, then—

(a) if the last-mentioned transfer was by way of sale the unpaid seller's right of lien or retention or stoppage in transit is defeated; and

(b) if the last-mentioned transfer was made by way of pledge or other disposition for value, the unpaid seller's right of lien or retention of stoppage in transit can only be exercised subject to the rights of the transferee.

Rescission: and re-sale by seller

48. Rescission: and re-sale by seller.

(1) Subject to this section, a contract of sale is not rescinded by the mere exercise by an unpaid seller of his right of lien or retention or stoppage in transit.

(2) Where an unpaid seller who has exercised his right of lien or retention or stoppage in transit re-sells the goods, the buyer acquires a good title to them as against the original buyer.

(3) Where the goods are of a perishable nature, or where the unpaid seller gives notice to the buyer of his intention to re-sell, and the buyer does not within a reasonable time pay or tender the price, the unpaid seller may re-sell the goods and recover from the original buyer damages for any loss occasioned by his breach of contract.

(4) Where the seller expressly reserves the right of re-sale in case the buyer should make default, and on the buyer making default re-sells the goods, the original contract of sale is rescinded but without prejudice to any claim the seller may have for damages.

PART VI
ACTIONS FOR BREACH OF THE CONTRACT

Seller's remedies

49. Action for price.

(1) Where, under a contract of sale, the property in the goods has passed to the buyer and he wrongfully neglects or refuses to pay for the goods according to the terms of the contract, the seller may maintain an action against him for the price of the goods.

50. Damages for non-acceptance.

(1) Where the buyer wrongfully neglects or refuses to accept and pay for the goods, the seller may maintain an action against him for damages for non-acceptance.

(2) The measure of damages is the estimated loss directly and naturally resulting, in the ordinary course of events, from the buyer's breach of contract.

(3) Where there is an available market for the goods in question the measure of damages is prima facie to be ascertained by the difference between the contract price and the market or current price at the time or times when the goods ought to have been accepted or (if no time was fixed for acceptance) at the time of the refusal to accept.

51. Damages for non-delivery.

(1) Where the seller wrongfully neglects or refuses to deliver the goods to the buyer, the buyer may maintain an action against the seller for damages for non-delivery.

(2) The measure of damages is the estimated loss directly and naturally resulting, in the ordinary course of events, from the seller's breach of contract.

(3) Where there is an available market for the goods in question the measure of damages is prima facie to be ascertained by the difference between the contract price and the market or current price of the goods at the time or times when they ought to have been delivered or (if no time was fixed) at the time of the refusal to deliver.

52. Specific performance.

(1) In any action for breach of contract to deliver specific or ascertained goods the court may, if it thinks fit, on the plaintiff's application, by its judgment or decree direct that the contract shall be performed specifically, without giving the defendant the option of retaining the goods on payment of damages.

(3) The judgment or decree may be unconditional, or on such terms and conditions as to damages, payment of the price and otherwise as seem just to the court.

53. Remedy for breach of warranty.

(1) Where there is a breach of warranty by the seller, or where the buyer elects (or is compelled) to treat any breach of a condition on the part of the seller as a breach of warranty, the buyer is not by reason only of such breach of warranty entitled to reject the goods; but he may—

    (a) set up against the seller the breach of warranty in diminution or extinction of the price, or

    (b) maintain an action against the seller for damages for the breach of warranty.

(2) The measure of damages for breach of warranty is the estimated loss directly and naturally resulting, in the ordinary course of events, from the breach of warranty.

(3) In the case of breach of warranty of quality such loss is prima facie the difference between the value of the goods at the time of delivery to the buyer and the value they would have had if they had fulfilled the warranty.

(4) The fact that the buyer has set up the breach of warranty in diminution or extinction of the price does not prevent him from maintaining an action for the same breach of warranty if he has suffered further damage.

[(5) This section does not apply to Scotland.]

[53A. Measure of damages as respects Scotland.

(1) The measure of damages for the seller's breach of contract is the estimated loss directly and naturally resulting, in the ordinary course of events, from the breach.

(2) Where the seller's breach consists of the delivery of goods which are not of the quality required by the contract and the buyer retains the goods, such loss as aforesaid is prima facie the difference between the value of the goods at the time of delivery to the buyer and the value they would have had if they had fulfilled the contract.

(3) This section applies to Scotland only.]

54. Interest, etc.

Nothing in this Act affects the right of the buyer or the seller to recover interest or special damages in any case where by law interest or special damages may be recoverable, or to recover money paid where the consideration for the payment of it has failed.

PART VII
SUPPLEMENTARY

55. Exclusion of implied terms.

(1) Where a right, duty or liability would arise under a contract of sale of goods by implication of law, it may (subject to the Unfair Contract Terms Act 1977) be negatived or varied by express agreement, or by the course of dealing between the parties, or by such usage as binds both parties to the contract.

(2) An express [term] does not negative a [term] implied by this Act unless inconsistent with it.

(3) Paragraph 11 of Schedule 1 below applies in relation to a contract made on or after 18 May 1973 and before 1 February 1978, and paragraph 12 in relation to one made before 18 May 1973.

56. Conflict of laws.

Paragraph 13 of Schedule 1 below applies in relation to a contract made on or after 18 May 1973 and before 1 February 1978, so as to make provision about conflict of laws in relation to such a contract.

57. Auction sales.

(1) Where goods are put up for sale by auction in lots, each lot is prima facie deemed to be the subject of a separate contract of sale.

(2) A sale by auction is complete when the auctioneer announces its completion by the fall of the hammer, or in other customary manner; and until the announcement is made any bidder may retract his bid.

(3) A sale by auction may be notified to be subject to a reserve or upset price, and a right to bid may also be reserved expressly by or on behalf of the seller.

(4) Where a sale by auction is not notified to be subject to a right to bid by or on behalf of the seller, it is not lawful for the seller to bid himself or to employ any person to bid at the sale, or for the auctioneer knowingly to take any bid from the seller or any such person.

(5) A sale contravening subsection (4) above may be treated as fraudulent by the buyer.

(6) Where, in respect of a sale by auction, a right to bid is expressly reserved (but not otherwise) the seller or any one person on his behalf may bid at the auction.

58. Payment into court in Scotland.

In Scotland where a buyer has elected to accept goods which he might have rejected, and to treat a breach of contract as only giving rise to a claim for damages, he may, in an action by the seller for the price, be required, in the discretion of the court before which the action depends, to consign or pay into court the price of the goods, or part of the price, or to give other reasonable security for its due payment.

59. Reasonable time a question of fact.

Where a reference is made in this Act to a reasonable time the question what is a reasonable time is a question of fact.

60. Rights etc. enforceable by action.

Where a right, duty or liability is declared by this Act, it may (unless otherwise provided by this Act) be enforced by action.

61. Interpretation.

(1) In this Act, unless the context or subject matter otherwise requires,—

"action" includes counterclaim and set-off, and in Scotland condescendence and claim and compensation;

["bulk" means a mass or collection of goods of the same kind which—
  (a) is contained in a defined space or area; and
  (b) is such that any goods in the bulk are interchangeable with any other goods therein of the same number or quantity;]

"business" includes a profession and the activities of any government department (including a Northern Ireland department) or local or public authority;

"buyer" means a person who buys or agrees to buy goods;

["consumer contract" has the same meaning as in section 25(1) of the Unfair Contract Terms Act 1977; and for the purposes of this Act the onus of proving that a contract is not to be regarded as a consumer contract shall lie on the seller]

"contract of sale" includes an agreement to sell as well as a sale;

"credit-broker" means a person acting in the course of a business of credit brokerage carried on by him, that is a business of effecting introductions of individuals desiring to obtain credit—
  (a) to persons carrying on any business so far as it relates to the provision of credit, or
  (b) to other persons engaged in credit brokerage;

"defendant" includes in Scotland defender, respondent, and claimant in a multiplepoinding;

"delivery" means voluntary transfer of possession from one person to another; [except that in relation to sections 20A and 20B above it includes such appropriation of goods to the contract as results in property in the goods being transferred to the buyer;]

"document of title to goods" has the same meaning as it has in the Factors Acts;
"Factors Acts" means the Factors Act 1889, the Factors (Scotland) Act 1890, and any enactment amending or substituted for the same;
"fault" means wrongful act or default;
"future goods" means goods to be manufactured or acquired by the seller after the making of the contract of sale;
"goods" includes all personal chattels other than things in action and money, and in Scotland all corporeal moveables except money; and in particular "goods" includes emblements, industrial growing crops, and things attached to or forming part of the land which are agreed to be severed before sale or under the contract of sale; [and includes an undivided share in goods;]
"plaintiff" includes pursuer, complainer, claimant in a multiplepoinding and defendant or defender counter-claiming;
"property" means the general property in goods, and not merely a special property;
"sale" includes a bargain and sale as well as a sale and delivery;
"seller" means a person who sells or agrees to sell goods;
"specific goods" means goods identified and agreed on at the time a contract of sale is made; [and includes an undivided share, specified as a fraction or percentage, of goods identified and agreed on as aforesaid]
"warranty" (as regards England and Wales and Northern Ireland) means an agreement with reference to goods which are the subject of a contract of sale, but collateral to the main purpose of such contract, the breach of which gives rise to a claim for damages, but not to a right to reject the goods and treat the contract as repudiated.

(3) A thing is deemed to be done in good faith within the meaning of this Act when it is in fact done honestly, whether it is done negligently or not.

(4) A person is deemed to be insolvent within the meaning of this Act if he has either ceased to pay his debts in the ordinary course of business or he cannot pay his debts as they become due, [...].

(5) Goods are in a deliverable state within the meaning of this Act when they are in such a state that the buyer would under the contract be bound to take delivery of them.

[(5A) References in this Act to dealing as consumer are to be construed in accordance with Part I of the Unfair Contract Terms Act 1977; and, for the purposes of this Act, it is for a seller claiming that the buyer does not deal as consumer to show that he does not.]

(6) As regards the definition of "business" in subsection (1) above, paragraph 14 of Schedule 1 below applies in relation to a contract made on or after 18 May 1973 and before 1 February 1978, and paragraph 15 in relation to one made before 18 May 1973.

62. Savings: rule of law etc.

(1) The rules in bankruptcy relating to contracts of sale apply to those contracts, notwithstanding anything in this Act.

(2) The rules of the common law, including the law merchant, except in so far as they are inconsistent with the provisions of this Act, and in particular the rules relating to the law of principal and agent and the effect of fraud, misrepresentation, duress or coercion, mistake, or other invalidating cause, apply to contracts for the sale of goods.

(3) Nothing in this Act or the Sale of Goods Act 1893 affects the enactments relating to bills of sale, or any enactment relating to the sale of goods which is not expressly repealed or amended by this Act or that.

(4) The provisions of this Act about contracts of sale do not apply to a transaction in the form of a contract of sale which is intended to operate by way of mortgage, pledge, charge, or other security.

(5) Nothing in this Act prejudices or affects the landlord's right of hypothec or sequestration for rent in Scotland.

63. Consequential amendments, repeals and savings.
...

64. Short title and commencement.
(1) This Act may be cited as the Sale of Goods Act 1979.
(2) This act comes into force on 1 January 1980.

VACCINE DAMAGE PAYMENTS ACT 1979
(1979, c. 17)

1. Payments to persons severely disabled by vaccination.
(1) If, on consideration of a claim, the Secretary of State is satisfied—
    (a) that a person is, or was immediately before his death, severely disabled as a result of vaccination against any of the diseases to which this Act applies; and
    (b) that the conditions of entitlement which are applicable in accordance with section 2 below are fulfilled,
he shall in accordance with this Act make a payment of [the relevant statutory sum] to or for the benefit of that person or to his personal representatives.

[(1A) In subsection (1) above "statutory sum" means [£30,000] or such other sum as is specified by the Secretary of State for the purposes of this Act by order made by statutory instrument with the consent of the Treasury; and the relevant statutory sum for the purposes of that subsection is the statutory sum at the time when a claim for payment is first made.]

(2) The diseases to which this Act applies are—
    (a) diphtheria,
    (b) tetanus,
    (c) whooping cough,
    (d) poliomyelitis,
    (e) measles,
    (f) rubella,
    (g) tuberculosis,
    (h) smallpox, and
    (i) any other disease which is specified by the Secretary of State for the purposes of this Act by order made by statutory instrument.

(3) Subject to section 2(3) below, this Act has effect with respect to a person who is severely disabled as a result of a vaccination given to his mother before he was born as if the vaccination had been given directly to him and, in such circumstances as may be prescribed by regulations under this Act, this Act has effect with respect to a person who is severely disabled as a result of contracting a disease through contact with a third person who was vaccinated against it as if the vaccination had been given to him and the disablement resulted from it.

2. Conditions of entitlement.
(1) Subject to the provisions of this section, the conditions of entitlement referred to in section 1(1)(b) above are—
(a) that the vaccination in question was carried out—
    (i) in the United Kingdom or the Isle of Man, and
    (ii) on or after 5 July 1948, and
    (iii) in the case of vaccination against smallpox, before 1st August 1971;
    (b) except in the case of vaccination against poliomyelitis or rubella, that the vaccination was carried out either at a time when the person to whom it was given was under the age of eighteen or at the time of an outbreak within the United Kingdom or the Isle of Man of the disease against which the vaccination was given; and

    (c) that the disabled person was over the age of two on the date when the claim was made or, if he died before that date, that he died after 9th May 1978 and was over the age of two when he died.

3. **Determination of claims.**
    (1) Any reference in this Act, other than section 7, to a claim is a reference to a claim for a payment under section 1(1) above which is made—
        (a) by or on behalf of the disabled person concerned or, as the case may be, by his personal representatives; and
        (b) in the manner prescribed by regulations under this Act; and
        (c) within the period of six years beginning on the latest of the following dates, namely, the date of the vaccination to which the claim relates, the date on which the disabled person attained the age of two and 9th May 1978 . . .

6. **Payments to or for the benefit of disabled persons.**
    (1) Where a payment under section 1(1) above falls to be made in respect of a disabled person who is over eighteen and capable of managing his own affairs, the payment shall be made to him.
    (2) Where such a payment falls to be made in respect of a disabled person who has died, the payment shall be made to his personal representatives.
    (3) Where such a payment falls to be made in respect of any other disabled person, the payment shall be made for his benefit by paying it to such trustees as the Secretary of State may appoint to be held by them upon such trusts or, in Scotland, for such purposes and upon such conditions as may be declared by the Secretary of State.
    (4) The making of a claim for, or the receipt of, a payment under section 1(1) above does not prejudice the right of any person to institute or carry on proceedings in respect of disablement suffered as a result of vaccination against any disease to which this Act applies; but in any civil proceedings brought in respect of disablement resulting from vaccination against such a disease, the court shall treat a payment made to or in repect of the disabled person concerned under section 1(1) above as paid on account of any damages which the court awards in respect of such disablement.

12. **Financial provisions.**
    (4) There shall be paid out of moneys provided by Parliament—
        (a) any expenditure incurred by the Secretary of State in making payments under section 1(1) above . . .

HIGHWAYS ACT 1980
(1980, c. 66)

41. **Duty to maintain highways maintainable at public expense.**
    (1) The authority who are for the time being the highway authority for a highway maintainable at the public expense are under a duty, subject to subsections (2) and (4) below, to maintain the highway.

58. **Special defence in action against a highway authority for damages for non-repair of highway.**
    (1) In an action against a highway authority in respect of damage resulting from their failure to maintain a highway maintainable at the public expense it is a defence (without prejudice to any other defence or the application of the law relating to contributory negligence) to prove that the authority had taken such care as in all the circumstances was reasonably required to secure that the part of the highway to which the action relates was not dangerous for traffic.

102. Provision of works for protecting highways against hazards of nature.
(1) The highway authority for a highway maintainable at the public expense may provide and maintain such barriers or other works as they consider necessary for the purpose of affording to the highway protection against snow, flood, landslide or other hazards of nature; and those works may be provided on the highway or on land which, or rights over which, has or have been acquired by the highway authority in the exercise of highway land acquisition powers for that purpose.

(3) A highway authority shall pay compensation to any person who suffers damage by reason of the execution by them under this section of any works on a highway.

165. Dangerous land adjoining street.
(1) If, in or on any land adjoining a street, there is an unfenced or inadequately fenced source of danger to persons using the street, the local authority in whose area the street is situated may, by notice to the owner or occupier of that land, require him within such time as may be specified in the notice to execute such works of repair, protection, removal or enclosure as will obviate the danger.

(3) Subject to any order made on appeal, if a person on whom a notice is served under this section fails to comply with the notice within the time specified in it, the authority by whom the notice was served may execute such works as are necessary to comply with the notice and may recover the expenses reasonably incurred by them in so doing from that person.

LIMITATION ACT 1980
(1980, c. 58)

PART I

1. Time limits under Part I subject to exclusion under Part II.
(1) This Part of this Act gives the ordinary time limits for bringing actions of the various classes mentioned in the following provisions of this Part.

(2) The ordinary time limits given in this Part of this Act are subject to extension or exclusion in accordance with the provisions of Part II of this Act.

2. Time limit for actions founded on tort.
An action founded on tort shall not be brought after the expiration of six years from the date on which the cause of action accrued.

3. Time limit in case of successive conversions and extinction of title of owner of converted goods.
(1) Where any cause of action in respect of the conversion of a chattel has accrued to any person and, before he recovers possession of the chattel, a further conversion takes place, no action shall be brought in respect of the further conversion after the expiration of six years from the accrual of the cause of action in respect of the original conversion.

(2) Where any such cause of action has accrued to any person and the period prescribed for bringing that action has expired and he has not during that period recovered possession of the chattel, the title of that person to the chattel shall be extinguished.

4. Special time limit in case of theft.
(1) The right of any person from whom a chattel is stolen to bring an action in respect of the theft shall not be subject to the time limits under sections 2 and 3(1) of this Act, but if his title to the chattel is extinguished under section 3(2) of this Act he may not bring an action in respect of a theft preceding the loss of his title, unless the theft

in question preceded the conversion from which time began to run for the purposes of section 3(2).

(2) Subsection (1) above shall apply to any conversion related to the theft of a chattel as it applies to the theft of a chattel; and, except as provided below, every conversion following the theft of a chattel before the person from whom it is stolen recovers possession of it shall be regarded for the purposes of this section as related to the theft. If anyone purchases the stolen chattel in good faith neither the purchase nor any conversion following it shall be regarded as related to the theft.

(3) Any cause of action accruing in respect of the theft or any conversion related to the theft of a chattel to any person from whom the chattel is stolen shall be disregarded for the purpose of applying section 3(1) or (2) of this Act to his case.

(4) Where in any action brought in respect of the conversion of a chattel it is proved that the chattel was stolen from the plaintiff or anyone through whom he claims it shall be presumed that any conversion following the theft is related to the theft unless the contrary is shown.

(5) In this section "theft" includes—
    (a)   any conduct outside England and Wales which would be theft if committed in England and Wales; and
    (b)   obtaining any chattel (in England and Wales or elsewhere) in the circumstances described in section 15(1) of the Theft Act 1968 (obtaining by deception) or by blackmail within the meaning of section 21 of that Act;
and references in this section to a chattel being "stolen" shall be construed accordingly.

[4A. Time limit for actions for defamation or malicious falsehood.
The time limit under section 2 of this Act shall not apply to an action for—
    (a)   libel or slander, or
    (b)   slander of title, slander of goods or other malicious falsehood,
but no such action shall be brought after the expiration of one year from the date on which the cause of action accrued.]

5. Time limit for actions founded on simple contract.
An action founded on simple contract shall not be brought after the expiration of six years from the date on which the cause of action accrued.

6. Special time limit for actions in respect of certain loans.
(1) Subject to subsection (3) below, section 5 of this Act shall not bar the right of action on a contract of loan to which this section applies.

(2) This section applies to any contract of loan which—
    (a)   does not provide for repayment of the debt on or before a fixed or determinable date; and
    (b)   does not effectively (whether or not it purports to do so) make the obligation to repay the debt conditional on a demand for repayment made by or on behalf of the creditor or on any other matter;
except where in connection with taking the loan the debtor enters into any collateral obligation to pay the amount of the debt or any part of it (as, for example, by delivering a promissory note as security for the debt) on terms which would exclude the application of this section to the contract of loan if they applied directly to repayment of the debt.

(3) Where a demand in writing for repayment of the debt under a contract of loan to which this section applies is made by or on behalf of the creditor (or, where there are joint creditors, by or on behalf of any one of them) section 5 of this Act shall thereupon apply as if the cause of action to recover the debt had accrued on the date on which the demand was made.

(4) In this section "promissory note" has the same meaning as in the Bills of Exchange Act 1882.

8. Time limit for actions on a specialty.

(1) An action upon a specialty shall not be brought after the expiration of twelve years from the date on which the cause of action accrued.

(2) Subsection (1) above shall not affect any action for which a shorter period of limitation is prescribed by any other provision of this Act.

9. Time limit for actions for sums recoverable by statute.

(1) An action to recover any sum recoverable by virtue of any enactment shall not be brought after the expiration of six years from the date on which the cause of action accrued.

(2) Subsection (1) above shall not affect any action to which section 10 of this Act applies.

10. Special time limit for claiming contribution.

(1) Where under section 1 of the Civil Liability (Contribution) Act 1978 any person becomes entitled to a right to recover contribution in respect of any damage from any other person, no action to recover contribution by virtue of that right shall be brought after the expiration of two years from the date on which that right accrued.

(2) For the purposes of this section the date on which a right to recover contribution in respect of any damage accrues to any person (referred to below in this section as "the relevant date") shall be ascertained as provided in subsections (3) and (4) below.

(3) If the person in question is held liable in respect of that damage—
   (a) by a judgment given in any civil proceedings; or
   (b) by an award made on any arbitration;
the relevant date shall be the date on which the judgment is given, or the date of the award (as the case may be).
For the purposes of this subsection no account shall be taken of any judgment or award given or made on appeal in so far as it varies the amount of damages awarded against the person in question.

(4) If, in any case not within subsection (3) above, the person in question makes or agrees to make any payment to one or more persons in compensation for that damage (whether he admits any liability in repect of the damage or not), the relevant date shall be the earliest date on which the amount to be paid by him is agreed between him (or his representative) and the person (or each of the persons, as the case may be) to whom the payment is to be made.

(5) An action to recover contribution shall be one to which sections 28, 32 and 35 of this Act apply, but otherwise Parts II and III of this Act (except sections 34, 37 and 38) shall not apply for the purposes of this section.

11. Special time limit for actions in respect of personal injuries.

(1) This section applies to any action for damages for negligence, nuisance or breach of duty (whether the duty exists by virtue of a contract or of provision made by or under a statute or independently of any contract or any such provision) where the damages claimed by the plaintiff for the negligence, nuisance or breach of duty consist of or include damages in respect of personal injuries to the plaintiff or any other person.

[(1A) This section does not apply to any action brought for damages under section 3 of the Protection from Harassment Act 1997.]

(3) An action to which this section applies shall not be brought after the expiration of the period applicable in accordance with subsection (4) or (5) below.

(4) Except where subsection (5) below applies, the period applicable is three years from—
   (a) the date on which the cause of action accrued; or
   (b) the date of knowledge (if later) of the person injured.

(5) If the injured person dies before the expiration of the period mentioned in subsection (4) above, the period applicable as respects the cause of action surviving for

the benefit of his estate by virtue of section 1 of the Law Reform (Miscellaneous Provisions) Act 1934 shall be three years from—
   (a)   the date of death; or
   (b)   the date of the personal representative's knowledge; whichever is the later.

[11A.   Actions in respect of defective products.
   (1)   This section shall apply to an action for damages by virtue of any provision of Part I of the Consumer Protection Act 1987.
   (2)   None of the time limits given in the preceding provisions of this Act shall apply to an action to which this section applies.
   (3)   An action to which this section applies shall not be brought after the expiration of the period of ten years from the relevant time, within the meaning of section 4 of the said Act of 1987; and this subsection shall operate to extinguish a right of action and shall do so whether or not that right of action had accrued, or time under the following provisions of this Act had begun to run, at the end of the said period of ten years.
   (4)   Subject to subsection (5) below, an action to which this section applies in which the damages claimed by the plaintiff consist of or include damages in respect of personal injuries to the plaintiff or any other person or loss of or damage to any property, shall not be brought after the expiration of the period of three years from whichever is the later of—
   (a)   the date on which the cause of action accrued; and
   (b)   the date of knowledge of the injured person or, in the case of loss of or damage to property, the date of knowledge of the plaintiff or (if earlier) of any person in whom his cause of action was previously vested.
   (5)   If in a case where the damages claimed by the plaintiff consist of or include damages in respect of personal injuries to the plaintiff or any other person the injured person died before the expiration of the period mentioned in subsection (4) above, the subsection shall have effect as respects the cause of action surviving for the benefit of his estate by virtue of section I of the Law Reform (Miscellaneous Provisions) Act 1934 as if for the reference to that period there were substituted a reference to the period of three years from whichever is the later of—
   (a)   the date of death; and
   (b)   the date of the personal representative's knowledge.
   (6)   For the purposes of this section "'personal representative" includes any person who is or has been a personal representative of the deceased, including an executor who has not proved the will (whether or not he has renounced probate) but not anyone appointed only as a special personal representative in relation to settled land; and regard shall be had to any knowledge acquired by any such person while a personal representative or previously.
   (7)   If there is more than one personal representative and their dates of knowledge are different, subsection (5)(b) above shall be read as referring to the earliest of those dates.
   (8)   Expressions used in this section or section 14 of this Act and in Part I of the Consumer Protection Act 1987 have the same meanings in this section or that section as in that Part; and section 1(1) of that Act (Part I to be construed as enacted for the purpose of complying with the product liability Directive) shall apply for the purpose of construing this section and the following provisions of this Act so far as they relate to an action by virtue of any provision of that Part as it applies for the purpose of construing that Part.]

12.   Special time limit for actions under Fatal Accidents legislation.
   (1)   An action under the Fatal Accidents Act 1976 shall not be brought if the death occurred when the person injured could no longer maintain an action and recover damages in respect of the injury (whether because of a time limit in this Act or in any other Act, or for any other reason).

Where any such action by the injured person would have been barred by the time limit in section 11 [or 11A] of this Act, no account shall be taken of the possibility of that time limit being overridden under section 33 of this Act.

(2) None of the time limits given in the preceding provisions of this Act shall apply to an action under the Fatal Accidents Act 1976, but no such action shall be brought after the expiration of three years from—
 (a) the date of death; or
 (b) the date of knowledge of the person for whose benefit the action is brought; whichever is the later.

(3) An action under the Fatal Accidents Act 1976 shall be one to which sections 28, 33 and 35 of this Act apply, and the application to any such action of the time limit under subsection (2) above shall be subject to section 39; but otherwise Parts II and III of this Act shall not apply to any such action.

13. Operation of time limit under section 12 in relation to different dependants.

(1) Where there is more than one person for whose benefit an action under the Fatal Accidents Act 1976 is brought, section 12(2)(b) of this Act shall be applied separately to each of them.

(2) Subject to subsection (3) below, if by virtue of subsection (1) above the action would be outside the time limit given by section 12(2) as regards one or more, but not all, of the persons for whose benefit it is brought, the court shall direct that any person as regards whom the action would be outside that limit shall be excluded from those for whom the action is brought.

(3) The court shall not give such a direction if it is shown that if the action were brought exclusively for the benefit of the person in question it would not be defeated by a defence of limitation (whether in consequence of section 28 of this Act or an agreement between the parties not to raise the defence, or otherwise).

14. Definition of date of knowledge for purposes of sections 11 and 12.

(1) [Subject to subsection (1A) below,] In sections 11 and 12 of this Act references to a person's date of knowledge are references to the date on which he first had knowledge of the following facts—
 (a) that the injury in question was significant; and
 (b) that the injury was attributable in whole or in part to the act or omission which is alleged to constitute negligence, nuisance or breach of duty; and
 (c) the identity of the defendant; and
 (d) if it is alleged that the act or omission was that of a person other than the defendant, the identity of that person and the additional facts supporting the bringing of an action against the defendant;
and knowledge that any acts or omissions did or did not, as a matter of law, involve negligence, nuisance or breach of duty is irrelevant.

[(1A) In section 11A of this Act and in section 12 of this Act so far as that section applies to an action by virtue of section 6(1)(a) of the Consumer Protection Act 1987 (death caused by defective product) references to a person's date of knowledge are references to the date on which he first had knowledge of the following facts—
 (a) such facts about the damage caused by the defect as would lead a reasonable person who had suffered such damage to consider it sufficiently serious to justify his instituting proceedings for damages against a defendant who did not dispute liability and was able to satisfy a judgment; and
 (b) that the damage was wholly or partly attributable to the facts and circumstances alleged to constitute the defect; and

(c) the identity of the defendant;
but, in determining the date on which a person first had such knowledge there shall be disregarded both the extent (if any) of that person's knowledge on any date of whether particular facts or circumstances would or would not, as a matter of law, constitute a defect and, in a case relating to loss of or damage to property, any knowledge which that person had on a date on which he had no right of action by virtue of Part of I of that Act in respect of the loss or damage.]

(2) For the purposes of this section an injury is significant if the person whose date of knowledge is in question would reasonably have considered it sufficiently serious to justify his instituting proceedings for damages against a defendant who did not dispute liability and was able to satisfy a judgment.

(3) For the purposes of this section a person's knowledge includes knowledge which he might reasonably have been expected to acquire—

(a) from facts observable or ascertainable by him; or

(b) from facts ascertainable by him with the help of medical or other appropriate expert advice which it is reasonable for him to seek;
but a person shall not be fixed under this subsection with knowledge of a fact ascertainable only with the help of expert advice so long as he has taken all reasonable steps to obtain (and, where appropriate, to act on) that advice.

[14A. Special time limit for negligence actions where facts relevant to cause of action are not known at date of accrual.

(1) This section applies to any action for damages for negligence, other than one to which section 11 of this Act applies, where the starting date for reckoning the period of limitation under subsection (4)(b) below falls after the date on which the cause of action accrued.

(2) Section 2 of this Act shall not apply to an action to which this section applies.

(3) An action to which this section applies shall not be brought after the expiration of the period applicable in accordance with subsection (4) below.

(4) That period is either—

(a) six years from the date on which the cause of action accrued; or

(b) three years from the starting date as defined by subsection (5) below, if that period expires later than the period mentioned in paragraph (a) above.

(5) For the purposes of this section, the starting date for reckoning the period of limitation under subsection (4)(b) above is the earliest date on which the plaintiff or any person in whom the cause of action was vested before him first had both the knowledge required for bringing an action for damages in respect of the relevant damage and a right to bring such an action.

(6) In subsection (5) above "the knowledge required for bringing an action for damages in respect of the relevant damage" means knowledge both—

(a) of the material facts about the damage in respect of which damages are claimed; and

(b) of the other facts relevant to the current action mentioned in subsection (8) below.

(7) For the purposes of subsection (6)(a) above, the material facts about the damage are such facts about the damage as would lead a reasonable person who had suffered such damage to consider it sufficiently serious to justify his instituting proceedings for damages against a defendant who did not dispute liability and was able to satisfy a judgment.

(8) The other facts referred to in subsection (6)(b) above are—

(a) that the damage was attributable in whole or in part to the act or omission which is alleged to constitute negligence; and

(b) the identity of the defendant; and

(c) if it is alleged that the act or omission was that of a person other than the defendant, the identity of that person and the additional facts supporting the bringing of an action against the defendant.

(9) Knowledge that any acts or omissions did or did not, as a matter of law, involve negligence is irrelevant for the purposes of subsection (5) above.

(10) For the purposes of this section a person's knowledge includes knowledge which he might reasonably have been expected to acquire—

(a) from facts observable or ascertainable by him; or

(b) from facts ascertainable by him with the help of appropriate expert advice which it is reasonable for him to seek;

but a person shall not be taken by virtue of this subsection to have knowledge of a fact ascertainable only with the help of expert advice so long as he has taken all reasonable steps to obtain (and, where appropriate, to act on) that advice.]

[14B. Overriding time limit for negligence actions not involving personal injuries.

(1) An action for damages for negligence, other than one to which section 11 of this Act applies, shall not be brought after the expiration of fifteen years from the date (or, if more than one, from the last of the dates) on which there occurred any act or omission—

(a) which is alleged to constitute negligence; and

(b) to which the damage in respect of which damages are claimed is alleged to be attributable (in whole or in part).

(2) This section bars the right of action in a case to which subsection (1) above applies notwithstanding that—

(a) the cause of action has not yet accrued; or

(b) where section 14A of this Act applies to the action, the date which is for the purposes of that section the starting date for reckoning the period mentioned in subsection (4)(b) of that section has not yet occurred;

before the end of the period of limitation prescribed by this section.]

15. Time limit for actions to recover land.

(1) No action shall be brought by any person to recover any land after the expiration of twelve years from the date on which the right of action accrued to him or, if it first accrued to some person through whom he claims, to that person.

(2) Subject to the following provisions of this section, where—

(a) the estate or interest claimed was an estate or interest in reversion or remainder or any other future estate or interest and the right of action to recover the land accrued on the date on which the estate or interest fell into possession by the determination of the preceding estate or interest; and

(b) the person entitled to the preceding estate or interest (not being a term of years absolute) was not in possession of the land on that date;

no action shall be brought by the person entitled to the succeeding estate or interest after the expiration of twelve years from the date on which the right of action accrued to the person entitled to the preceding estate or interest or six years from the date on which the right of action accrued to the person entitled to the succeeding estate or interest, whichever period last expires.

(3) Subsection (2) above shall not apply to any estate or interest which falls into possession on the determination of an entailed interest and which might have been barred by the person entitled to the entailed interest.

(4) No person shall bring an action to recover any estate or interest in land under an assurance taking effect after the right of action to recover the land had accrued to the person by whom the assurance was made or some person through whom he claimed or some person entitled to a preceding estate or interest, unless the action is brought within

the period during which the person by whom the assurance was made could have brought such an action.

(5) Where any person is entitled to any estate or interest in land in possession and, while so entitled, is also entitled to any future estate or interest in that land, and his right to recover the estate or interest in possession is barred under this Act, no action shall be brought by that person, or by any person claiming through him, in respect of the future estate or interest, unless in the meantime possession of the land has been recovered by a person entitled to an intermediate estate or interest.

(6) Part I of Schedule 1 to this Act contains provisions for determining the date of accrual of rights of action to recover land in the cases there mentioned.

(7) Part II of that Schedule contains provisions modifying the provisions of this section in their application to actions brought by, or by a person claiming through, the Crown or any spiritual or eleemosynary corporation sole.

16. Time limit for redemption actions.

When a mortgagee of land has been in possession of any of the mortgaged land for a period of twelve years, no action to redeem the land of which the mortgagee has been so in possession shall be brought after the end of that period by the mortgagor or any person claiming through him.

17. Extinction of title to land after expiration of time limit.

Subject to—
 (a) section 18 of this Act; and
 (b) section 75 of the Land Registration Act 1925;
at the expiration of the period prescribed by this Act for any person to bring an action to recover land (including a redemption action) the title of that person to the land shall be extinguished.

18. Settled land and land held on trust.

(1) Subject to section 21(1) and (2) of this Act, the provisions of this Act shall apply to equitable interests in land, [. . .] as they apply to legal estates.

Accordingly a right of action to recover the land shall, for the purposes of this Act but not otherwise, be treated as accruing to a person entitled in possession to such an equitable interest in the like manner and circumstances, and on the same date, as it would accrue if his interest were a legal estate in the land (and any relevant provision of Part I of Schedule 1 to this Act shall apply in any such case accordingly).

(2) Where the period prescribed by this Act has expired for the briging of an action to recover land by a tenant for life or a statutory owner of settled land—
 (a) his legal estate shall not be extinguished if and so long as the right of action to recover the land of any person entitled to a beneficial interest in the land either has not accrued or has not been barred by this Act; and
 (b) the legal estate shall accordingly remain vested in the tenant for life or statutory owner and shall devolve in accordance with the Settled Land Act 1925;
but if and when every such right of action has been barred by this Act, his legal estate shall be extinguished.

(3) Where any land is held upon trust [. . .] and the period prescribed by this Act has expired for the bringing of an action to recover the land by the trustees, the estate of the trustees shall not be extinguished if and so long as the right of action to recover the land of any person entitled to a beneficial interest in the land [. . .] either has not accrued or has not been barred by this Act; but if and when every such right of action has been so barred the estate of the trustees shall be extinguished.

(4) Where—
 (a) any settled land is vested in a statutory owner; or
 (b) any land is held upon trust [. . .];

an action to recover the land may be brought by the statutory owner or trustees on behalf of any person entitled to a beneficial interest in possession in the land [. . .] whose right of action has not been barred by this Act, notwithstanding that the right of action of the statutory owner or trustees would apart from this provision have been barred by this Act.

19. Time limit for actions to recover rent.
No action shall be brought, or distress made, to recover arrears of rent, or damages in respect of arrears of rent, after the expiration of six years from the date on which the arrears became due.

20. Time limit for actions to recover money secured by a mortgage or charge or to recover proceeds of the sale of land.
(1) No action shall be brought to recover—
 (a) any principal sum of money secured by a mortgage or other charge on property (whether real or personal); or
 (b) proceeds of the sale of land;
after the expiration of twelve years from the date on which the right to receive the money accrued.

(2) No foreclosure action in respect of mortgaged personal property shall be brought after the expiration of twelve years from the date on which the right to foreclose accrued.

But if the mortgagee was in possession of the mortgaged property after that date, the right to foreclose on the property which was in his possession shall not be treated as having accrued for the purposes of this subsection until the date on which his possession discontinued.

(3) The right to receive any principal sum of money secured by a mortgage or other charge and the right to foreclose on the property subject to the mortgage or charge shall not be treated as accruing so long as that property comprises any future interest or any life insurance policy which has not matured or been determined.

(4) Nothing in this section shall apply to a foreclosure action in respect of mortgaged land, but the provisions of this Act relating to actions to recover land shall apply to such an action.

(5) Subject to subsections (6) and (7) below, no action to recover arrears of interest payable in respect of any sum of money secured by a mortgage or other charge or payable in respect of proceeds of the sale of land, or to recover damages in respect of such arrears shall be brought after the expiration of six years from the date on which the interest became due.

(6) Where—
 (a) a prior mortgagee or other incumbrancer has been in possession of the property charged; and
 (b) an action is brought within one year of the discontinuance of that possession by the subsequent incumbrancer;
the subsequent incumbrancer may recover by that action all the arrears of interest which fell due during the period of possession by the prior incumbrancer or damages in respect of those arrears, notwithstanding that the period exceeded six years.

(7) Where—
 (a) the property subject to the mortgage or charge comprises any future interest or life insurance policy; and
 (b) it is a term of the mortgage or charge that arrears of interest shall be treated as part of the principal sum of money secured by the mortgage or charge;
interest shall not be treated as becoming due before the right to recover the principal sum of money has accrued or is treated as having accrued.

21. Time limit for actions in respect of trust property.

(1) No period of limitation prescribed by this Act shall apply to an action by a beneficiary under a trust, being an action—

    (a) in respect of any fraud or fraudulent breach of trust to which the trustee was a party or privy; or

    (b) to recover from the trustee trust property or the proceeds of trust property in the possession of the trustee, or previously received by the trustee and converted to his use.

(2) Where a trustee who is also a beneficiary under the trust receives or retains trust property or its proceeds as his share on a distribution of trust property under the trust, his liability in any action brought by virtue of subsection (1)(b) above to recover that property or its proceeds after the expiration of the period of limitation prescribed by this Act for bringing an action to recover trust property shall be limited to the excess over his proper share.

This subsection only applies if the trustee acted honestly and reasonably in making the distribution.

(3) Subject to the preceding provisions of this section, an action by a beneficiary to recover trust property or in respect of any breach of trust, not being an action for which a period of limitation is prescribed by any other provision of this Act, shall not be brought after the expiration of six years from the date on which the right of action accrued.

For the purposes of this subsection, the right of action shall not be treated as having accrued to any beneficiary entitled to a future interest in the trust property until the interest fell into possession.

(4) No beneficiary as against whom there would be a good defence under this Act shall derive any greater or other benefit from a judgment or order obtained by any other beneficiary than he could have obtained if he had brought the action and this Act had been pleaded in defence.

22. Time limit for actions claiming personal estate of a deceased person.

Subject to section 21(1) and (2) of this Act—

    (a) no action in respect of any claim to the personal estate of a deceased person or to any share or interest in any such estate (whether under a will or on intestacy) shall be brought after the expiration of twelve years from the date on which the right to receive the share or interest accrued; and

    (b) no action to recover arrears of interest in respect of any legacy, or damages in respect of such arrears, shall be brought after the expiration of six years from the date on which the interest became due.

23. Time limit in respect of actions for an account.

An action for an account shall not be brought after the expiration of any time limit under this Act which is applicable to the claim which is the basis of the duty to account.

24. Time limit for actions to enforce judgments.

(1) An action shall not be brought upon any judgment after the expiration of six years from the date on which the judgment became enforceable.

(2) No arrears of interest in respect of any judgment debt shall be recovered after the expiration of six years from the date on which the interest became due.

26. Administration to date back to death.

For the purposes of the provisions of this Act relating to actions for the recovery of land and advowsons an administrator of the estate of a deceased person shall be treated as claiming as if there had been no interval of time between the death of the deceased person and the grant of the letters of administration.

PART II

28. Extension of limitation period in case of disability.

(1) Subject to the following provisions of this section, if on the date when any right of action accrued for which a period of limitation is prescribed by this Act, the person to whom it accrued was under a disability, the action may be brought at any time before the expiration of six years from the date when he ceased to be under a disability or died (whichever first occurred) notwithstanding that the period of limitation has expired.

(2) This section shall not affect any case where the right of action first accrued to some person (not under a disability) through whom the person under a disability claims.

(3) When a right of action which has accrued to a person under a disability accrues, on the death of that person while still under a disability, to another person under a disability, no further extension of time shall be allowed by reason of the disability of the second person.

[(4A) If the action is one to which section 4A of this Act applies, subsection (1) above shall have effect—

(a) in the case of an action for libel or slander, as if for the words from "at any time" to "occurred)" there were substituted the words "by him at any time before the expiration of one year from the date on which he ceased to be under a disability"; and

(b) in the case of an action for slander of title, slander of goods or other malicious falsehood, as if for the words "six years" there were substituted the words "one year".]

(5) If the action is one to which section 10 of this Act applies, subsection (1) above shall have effect as if for the words "six years" there were substituted the words "two years".

(6) If the action is one to which section 11 or 12(2) of this Act applies, subsection (1) above shall have effect as if for the words "six years" there were substituted the words "three years".

[(7) If the action is one to which section 11A of this Act applies or one by virtue of section 6(1)(a) of the Consumer Protection Act 1987 (death caused by defective product), subsection (1) above—

(a) shall not apply to the time limit prescribed by subsection (3) of the said section 11A or to that time limit as applied by virtue of section 12(1) of this Act; and

(b) in relation to any other time limit prescribed by this Act shall have effect as if for the words "six years" there were substituted the words "three years".]

[28A. Extension for cases where the limitation period is the period under section 14A(4)(b).

(1) Subject to subsection (2) below, if in the case of any action for which a period of limitation is prescribed by section 14A of this Act—

(a) the period applicable in accordance with subsection (4) of that section is the period mentioned in paragraph (b) of that subsection;

(b) on the date which is for the purposes of that section the starting date for reckoning that period the person by reference to whose knowledge that date fell to be determined under subsection (5) of that section was under a disability; and

(c) section 28 of this Act does not apply to the action;

the action may be brought at any time before the expiration of three years from the date when he ceased to be under a disability or died (whichever first occurred) notwithstanding that the period mentioned above has expired.

(2) An action may not be brought by virtue of subsection (1) above after the end of the period of limitation prescribed by section 14B of this Act.]

29. Fresh accrual of action on acknowledgment or part payment.

(5) Subject to subsection (6) below, where any right of action has accrued to recover—

(a)　any debt or other liquidated pecuniary claim; or
(b)　any claim to the personal estate of a deceased person or to any share or interest in any such estate;
and the person liable or accountable for the claim acknowledges the claim or makes any payment in respect of it the right shall be treated as having accrued on and not before the date of the acknowledgment or payment.

(6)　A payment of a part of the rent or interest due at any time shall not extend the period for claiming the remainder then due, but any payment of interest shall be treated as a payment in respect of the principal debt.

(7)　Subject to subsection (6) above, a current period of limitation may be repeatedly extended under this section by further acknowledgments or payments, but a right of action, once barred by this Act shall not be revived by any subsequent acknowledgment or payment.

30. Formal provisions as to acknowledgments and part payments.

(1)　To be effective for the purposes of section 29 of this Act, an acknowledgment must be in writing and signed by the person making it.

(2)　For the purposes of section 29, any acknowledgment or payment—
(a)　may be made by the agent of the person by whom it is required to be made under that section; and
(b)　shall be made to the person, or to an agent of the person, whose title or claim is being acknowledged or, as the case may be, in respect of whose claim the payment is being made.

31. Effect of acknowledgment or part payment on persons other than the maker or recipient.

(6)　An acknowledgment of any debt or other liquidated pecuniary claim shall bind the acknowledgor and his successors but not any other person.

(7)　A payment made in respect of any debt or other liquidated pecuniary claim shall bind all persons liable in respect of the debt or claim.

(8)　An acknowledgment by one of several personal representatives of any claim to the personal estate of a deceased person or to any share or interest in any such estate, or a payment by one of several personal representatives in respect of any such claim, shall bind the estate of the deceased person.

(9)　In this section "successor", in relation to any mortgagee or person liable in respect of any debt or claim, means his personal representatives and any other person on whom the rights under the mortgage or, as the case may be, the liability in respect of the debt or claim devolve (whether on death or bankruptcy or the disposition of property or the determination of a limited estate or interest in settled property or otherwise).

32. Postponement of limitation period in case of fraud, concealment or mistake.

(1)　Subject to [subsections (3) and (4A)] below, where in the case of any action for which a period of limitation is prescribed by this Act, either—
(a)　the action is based upon the fraud of the defendant; or
(b)　any fact relevant to the plaintiff's right of action has been deliberately concealed from him by the defendant; or
(c)　the action is for relief from the consequences of a mistake;
the period of limitation shall not begin to run until the plaintiff has discovered the fraud, concealment or mistake (as the case may be) or could with reasonable diligence have discovered it.
References in this subsection to the defendant include references to the defendant's agent and to any person through whom the defendant claims and his agent.

(2) For the purposes of subsection (1) above, deliberate commission of a breach of duty in circumstances in which it is unlikely to be discovered for some time amounts to deliberate concealment of the facts involved in that breach of duty.

(3) Nothing in this section shall enable any action—
   (a) to recover, or recover the value of, any property; or
   (b) to enforce any charge against, or set aside any transaction affecting, any property;
to be brought against the purchaser of the property or any person claiming through him in any case where the property has been purchased for valuable consideration by an innocent third party since the fraud or concealment or (as the case may be) the transaction in which the mistake was made took place.

(4) A purchaser is an innocent third party for the purposes of this section—
   (a) in the case of fraud or concealment of any fact relevant to the plaintiff's right of action, if he was not a party to the fraud or (as the case may be) to the concealment of that fact and did not at the time of the purchase know or have reason to believe that the fraud or concealment had taken place; and
   (b) in the case of mistake, if he did not at the time of the purchase know or have reason to believe that the mistake had been made.

[(4A) Subsection (1) above shall not apply in relation to the time limit prescribed by section 11A(3) of this Act or in relation to that time limit as applied by virtue of section 12(1) of this Act.]

[(5) Sections 14A and 14B of this Act shall not apply to any action to which subsection (1)(b) above applies (and accordingly the period of limitation referred to in that subsection, in any case to which either of those sections would otherwise apply, is the period applicable under section 23 of this Act).]

[32A. Discretionary exclusion of time limit for actions for defamation or malicious falsehood.

(1) If it appears to the court that it would be equitable to allow an action to proceed having regard to the degree to which—
   (a) the operation of section 4A of this Act prejudices the plaintiff or any person whom he represents, and
   (b) any decision of the court under this subsection would prejudice the defendant or any person whom he represents,
the court may direct that that section shall not apply to the action or shall not apply to any specified cause of action to which the action relates.

(2) In acting under this section the court shall have regard to all the circumstances of the case and in particular to—
   (a) the length of, and the reasons for, the delay on the part of the plaintiff;
   (b) where the reason or one of the reasons for the delay was that all or any of the facts relevant to the cause of action did not become known to the plaintiff until after the end of the period mentioned in section 4A—
     (i) the date on which any such facts did become known to him, and
     (ii) the extent to which he acted promptly and reasonably once he knew whether or not the facts in question might be capable of giving rise to an action; and
   (c) the extent to which, having regard to the delay, relevant evidence is likely—
     (i) to be unavailable, or
     (ii) to be less cogent than if the action had been brought within the period mentioned in section 4A.

(3) In the case of an action for slander of title, slander of goods or other malicious falsehood brought by a personal representative—
   (a) the references in subsection (2) above to the plaintiff shall be construed as including the deceased person to whom the cause of action accrued and any previous personal representative of that person; and

Limitation Act 1980

(b) nothing in section 28(3) of this Act shall be construed as affecting the court's discretion under this section.

(4) In this section "the court" means the court in which the action has been brought.]

33. Discretionary exclusion of time limit for actions in respect of personal injuries or death.

(1) If it appears to the court that it would be equitable to allow an action to proceed having regard to the degree to which—

(a) the provisions of section 11 [or 11A] or 12 of this Act prejudice the plaintiff or any person whom he represents; and

(b) any decision of the court under this subsection would prejudice the defendant or any person whom he represents;

the court may direct that those provisions shall not apply to the action, or shall not apply to any specified cause of action to which the action relates.

[(1A) The court shall not under this section disapply—

(a) subsection (3) of section 11A; or

(b) where the damages claimed by the plaintiff are confined to damages for loss of or damage to any property, any other provision in its application to an action by virtue of Part I of the Consumer Protection Act 1987.]

(2) The court shall not under this section disapply section 12(1) except where the reason why the person injured could no longer maintain an action was because of the time limit in section 11 [or subsection (4) of section 11A].

If, for example, the person injured could at his death no longer maintain an action under the Fatal Accidents Act 1976 because of the time limit in Article 29 in Schedule 1 to the Carriage by Air Act 1961, the court has no power to direct that section 12(1) shall not apply.

(3) In acting under this section the court shall have regard to all the circumstances of the case and in particular to—

(a) the length of, and the reasons for, the delay on the part of the plaintiff;

(b) the extent to which, having regard to the delay, the evidence adduced or likely to be adduced by the plaintiff or the defendant is or is likely to be less cogent than if the action had been brought within the time allowed by section 11 [, by section 11A] or (as the case may be) by section 12;

(c) the conduct of the defendant after the cause of action arose, including the extent (if any) to which he responded to requests reasonably made by the plaintiff for information or inspection for the purpose of ascertaining facts which were or might be relevant to the plaintiff's cause of action against the defendant;

(d) the duration of any disability of the plaintiff arising after the date of the accrual of the cause of action;

(e) the extent to which the plaintiff acted promptly and reasonably once he knew whether or not the act or omission of the defendant, to which the injury was attributable, might be capable at that time of giving rise to an action for damages;

(f) the steps, if any, taken by the plaintiff to obtain medical, legal or other expert advice and the nature of any such advice he may have received.

(4) In a case where the person injured died when, because of section 11 [or subsection (4) of section 11A], he could no longer maintain an action and recover damages in respect of the injury, the court shall have regard in particular to the length of, and the reasons for, the delay on the part of the deceased.

(5) In a case under subsection (4) above, or any other case where the time limit, or one of the time limits, depends on the date of knowledge of a person other than the plaintiff, subsection (3) above shall have effect with appropriate modifications, and shall have effect in particular as if references to the plaintiff included references to any person whose date of knowledge is or was relevant in determining a time limit.

(6) A direction by the court disapplying the provisions of section 12(1) shall operate to disapply the provisions to the same effect in section 1(1) of the Fatal Accidents Act 1976.

(7) In this section "the court" means the court in which the action has been brought.

(8) References in this section to section 11 [or 11A] include references to that section as extended by any of the preceding provisions of this Part of this Act or by any provision of Part III of this Act.

35. New claims in pending actions; rules of court.

(1) For the purposes of this Act, any new claim made in the course of any action shall be deemed to be a separate action and to have been commenced—

    (a) in the case of a new claim made in or by way of third party proceedings, on the date on which those proceedings were commenced; and

    (b) in the case of any other new claim, on the same date as the original action.

(2) In this section a new claim means any claim by way of set-off or counterclaim, and any claim involving either—

    (a) the addition or substitution of a new cause of action; or

    (b) the addition or substitution of a new party;

and "third party proceedings" means any proceedings brought in the course of any action by any party to the action against a person not previously a party to the action, other than proceedings brought by joining any such person as defendant to any claim already made in the original action by the party bringing the proceedings.

(3) Except as provided by section 33 of this Act or by rules of court, neither the High Court nor any county court shall allow a new claim within subsection (1)(b) above, other than an original set-off or counterclaim, to be made in the course of any action after the expiry of any time limit under this Act which would affect a new action to enforce that claim.

For the purposes of this subsection, a claim is an original set-off or an original counterclaim if it is a claim made by way of set-off or (as the case may be) by way of counterclaim by a party who has not previously made any claim in the action.

(4) Rules of court may provide for allowing a new claim to which subsection (3) above applies to be made as there mentioned, but only if the conditions specified in subsection (5) below are satisfied, and subject to any further restrictions the rules may impose.

(5) The conditions referred to in subsection (4) above are the following—

    (a) in the case of a claim involving a new cause of action, if the new cause of action arises out of the same facts or substantially the same facts as are already in issue on any claim previously made in the original action; and

    (b) in the case of a claim involving a new party, if the addition or substitution of the new party is necessary for the determination of the original action.

(6) The addition or substitution of a new party shall not be regarded for the purposes of subsection (5)(b) above as necessary for the determination of the original action unless either—

    (a) the new party is substituted for a party whose name was given in any claim made in the original action in mistake for the new party's name; or

    (b) any claim already made in the original action cannot be maintained by or against an existing party unless the new party is joined or substituted as plaintiff or defendant in that action.

(7) Subject to subsection (4) above, rules of court may provide for allowing a party to any action to claim relief in a new capacity in respect of a new cause of action notwithstanding that he had no title to make that claim at the date of the commencement of the action.

This subsection shall not be taken as prejudicing the power of rules of court to provide for allowing a party to claim relief in a new capacity without adding or substituting a new cause of action.

(8) Subsections (3) to (7) above shall apply in relation to a new claim made in the course of third party proceedings as if those proceedings were the original action, and subject to such other modifications as may be prescribed by rules of court in any case or class of case.

PART III

36. Equitable jurisdiction and remedies.

(1) The following time limits under this Act, that is to say—
 (a) the time limit under section 2 for actions founded on tort;
 [(aa) the time limit under section 4A for actions for libel or slander;]
 (b) the time limit under section 5 for actions founded on simple contract;
 (c) the time limit under section 7 for actions to enforce awards where the submission is not by an instrument under seal;
 (d) the time limit under section 8 for actions on a specialty;
 (e) the time limit under section 9 for actions to recover a sum recoverable by virtue of any enactment; and
 (f) the time limit under section 24 for actions to enforce a judgment;
shall not apply to any claim for specific performance of a contract or for an injunction or for other equitable relief, except in so far as any such time limit may be applied by the court by analogy in like manner as the corresponding time limit under any enactment repealed by the Limitation Act 1939 was applied before 1st July 1940.

(2) Nothing in this Act shall affect any equitable jurisdiction to refuse relief on the ground of acquiescence or otherwise.

37. Application to the Crown and the Duke of Cornwall.

(1) Except as otherwise expressly provided in this Act, and without prejudice to section 39, this Act shall apply to proceedings by or against the Crown in like manner as it applies to proceedings between subjects.

38. Interpretation.

(1) In this Act, unless the context otherwise requires— ...
"personal injuries" includes any disease and any impairment of a person's physical or mental condition, and "injury" and cognate expressions shall be construed accordingly;

(2) For the purposes of this Act a person shall be treated as under a disability while he is an infant, or of unsound mind.

(3) For the purposes of subsection (2) above a person is of unsound mind if he is a person who, by reason of mental disorder within the meaning of the [Mental Health Act 1983], is incapable of managing and administering his property and affairs.

(4) Without prejudice to the generality of subsection (3) above, a person shall be conclusively presumed for the purposes of subsection (2) above to be of unsound mind—
 (a) while he is liable to be detained or subject to guardianship under [the Mental Health Act 1983 (otherwise than by virtue of section 35 or 89)]; ...

39. Saving for other limitation enactments.

This Act shall not apply to any action or arbitration for which a period of limitation is prescribed by or under any other enactment (whether passed before or after the passing of this Act) or to any action or arbitration to which the Crown is a party and for which, if it were between subjects, a period of limitation would be prescribed by or under any such other enactment.

BRITISH TELECOMMUNICATIONS ACT 1981
(1981, c. 38)

23. Exclusion of certain liabilities in tort in relation to telecommunications.
(1) No proceedings in tort shall lie against the Corporation in respect of any loss or damage suffered by any person by reason of—
  (a) failure to provide, or delay in providing, a telecommunication service, apparatus associated therewith or a service ancillary thereto;
  (b) failure, interruption, suspension or restriction of a telecommunication service or a service ancillary thereto or delay of, or fault in, communication by means of a telecommunication service; or
  (c) error in, or omission from, a directory for use in connection with a telecommunication service.

CONTEMPT OF COURT ACT 1981
(1981, c. 49)

4. Contemporary reports of proceedings.
(3) For the purposes of subsection (1) of this section [...] a report of proceedings shall be treated as published contemporaneously—
  (a) in the case of a report of which publication is postponed pursuant to an order under subsection (2) of this section, if published as soon as practicable after that order expires;
  (b) in the case of a report of [an application for dismissal under section 6 of the Magistrates' Courts Act 1980] of which publication is permitted by virtue only of [subsection (5) or (7) of section 8A of that Act], if published as soon as practicable after publication is so permitted.

SUPREME COURT ACT 1981
(1981, c. 54)

32. Orders for interim payment.
(1) As regards proceedings pending in the High Court, provision may be made by rules of court for enabling the court, in such circumstances as may be prescribed, to make an order requiring a party to the proceedings to make an interim payment of such amount as may be specified in the order, with provision for the payment to be made to such other party to the proceedings as may be so specified or, if the order so provides, by paying it into court.
(2) Any rules of court which make provision in accordance with subsection (1) may include provision for enabling a party to any proceedings who, in pursuance of such an order, has made an interim payment to recover the whole or part of the amount of the payment in such circumstances, and from such other party to the proceedings, as may be determined in accordance with the rules.
(3) Any rules made by virtue of this section may include such incidental, supplementary and consequential provisions as the rule-making authority may consider necessary or expedient.
(4) Nothing in this section shall be construed as affecting the exercise of any power relating to costs, including any power to make rules of court relating to costs.
(5) In this section "interim payment", in relation to a party to any proceedings, means a payment on account of any damages, debt or other sum (excluding any costs) which that party may be held liable to pay to or for the benefit of another party to the proceedings if a final judgment or order of the court in the proceedings is given or made in favour of that other party.

Supreme Court Act 1981

[32A. Orders for provisional damages for personal injuries.

(1) This section applies to an action for damages for personal injuries in which there is proved or admitted to be a chance that at some definite or indefinite time in the future the injured person will, as a result of the act or omission which gave rise to the cause of action, develop some serious disease or suffer some serious deterioration in his physical or mental condition.

(2) Subject to subsection (4) below, as regards any action for damages to which this section applies in which a judgment is given in the High Court, provision may be made by rules of court for enabling the court, in such circumstances as may be prescribed, to award the injured person—

    (a) damages assessed on the assumption that the injured person will not develop the disease or suffer the deterioration in his condition; and

    (b) further damages at a future date if he develops the disease or suffers the deterioration.

(3) Any rules made by virtue of this section may include such incidental, supplementary and consequential provisions as the rule-making authority may consider necessary or expedient.

(4) Nothing in this section shall be construed—

    (a) as affecting the exercise of any power relating to costs, including any power to make rules of court relating to costs; or

    (b) as prejudicing any duty of the court under any enactment or rule of law to reduce or limit the total damages which would have been recoverable apart from any such duty.]

35. Provisions supplementary to ss. 33 and 34.

(5) In sections [32A,] 33 and 34 and this section— ...
"personal injuries" includes any disease and any impairment of a person's physical or mental condition.

[35A. Powers of High Court to award interest on debts and damages.

(1) Subject to rules of court, in proceedings (whenever instituted) before the High Court for the recovery of a debt or damages there may be included in any sum for which judgment is given simple interest, at such rate as the court thinks fit or as rules of court may provide, on all or any part of the debt or damages in respect of which judgment is given, or payment is made before judgment, for all or any part of the period between the date when the cause of action arose and—

    (a) in the case of any sum paid before judgment, the date of the payment; and

    (b) in the case of the sum for which judgment is given, the date of the judgment.

(2) In relation to a judgment given for damages for personal injuries or death which exceed £200 subsection (1) shall have effect—

    (a) with the substitution of "shall be included" for "may be included'; and

    (b) with the addition of "unless the court is satisfied that there are special reasons to the contrary" after "given", where first occurring.

(3) Subject to rules of court, where—

    (a) there are proceedings (whenever instituted) before the High Court for the recovery of a debt; and

    (b) the defendant pays the whole debt to the plaintiff (otherwise than in pursuance of a judgment in the proceedings),

the defendant shall be liable to pay the plaintiff simple interest at such rate as the court thinks fit or as rules of court may provide on all or any part of the debt for all or any part of the period between the date when the cause of action arose and the date of the payment.

(4) Interest in respect of a debt shall not be awarded under this section for a period during which, for whatever reason, interest on the debt already runs.

(5) Without prejudice to the generality of section 84, rules of court may provide for a rate of interest by reference to the rate specified in section 17 of the Judgments Act 1838 as that section has effect from time to time or by reference to a rate for which any other enactment provides.

(6) Interest under this section may be calculated at different rates in respect of different periods.

(7) In this section "plaintiff" means the person seeking the debt or damages and "defendant" means the person from whom the plaintiff seeks the debt or damages and "personal injuries" includes any disease and any impairment of a person's physical or mental condition.]

37. Powers of High Court with respect to injunctions and receivers.

(1) The High Court may by order (whether interlocutory or final) grant an injunction or appoint a receiver in all cases in which it appears to the court to be just and convenient to do so.

49. Concurrent administration of law and equity.

(1) Subject to the provisions of this or any other Act, every court exercising jurisdiction in England and Wales in any civil cause or matter shall continue to administer law and equity on the basis that, wherever there is any conflict or variance between the rules of equity and the rules of the common law with reference to the same matter, the rules of equity shall prevail.

50. Power to award damages as well as, or in substitution for, injunction or specific performance.

Where the Court of Appeal or the High Court has jurisdiction to entertain an application for an injunction or specific performance, it may award damages in addition to, or in substitution for, an injunction or specific performance.

69. Trial by jury.

(1) Where, on the application of any party to an action to be tried in the Queen's Bench Division, the court is satisfied that there is in issue—

  (a) a charge of fraud against that party; or
  (b) a claim in respect of libel, slander, malicious prosecution or false imprisonment; or
  (c) any question or issue of a kind prescribed for the purposes of this paragraph,

the action shall be tried with a jury, unless the court is of opinion that the trial requires any prolonged examination of documents or accounts or any scientific or local investigation which cannot conveniently be made with a jury.

ADMINISTRATION OF JUSTICE ACT 1982
(1982, c. 53)

1. Abolition of right to damages for loss of expectation of life.

(1) In an action under the law of England and Wales or the law of Northern Ireland for damages for personal injuries—

  (a) no damages shall be recoverable in respect of any loss of expectation of life caused to the injured person by the injuries; but
  (b) if the injured person's expectation of life has been reduced by the injuries, the court, in assessing damages in respect of pain and suffering caused by the injuries, shall take account of any suffering caused or likely to be caused to him by awareness that his expectation of life has been so reduced.

(2) The reference in subsection (1)(a) above to damages in respect of loss of expectation of life does not include damages in respect of loss of income.

2. **Abolition of actions for loss of services, etc.**
No person shall be liable in tort under the law of England and Wales or the law of Northern Ireland—
 (a) to a husband on the ground only of having deprived him of the services or society of his wife;
 (b) to a parent (or person standing in the place of a parent) on the ground only of his having deprived him of the services of a child; or
 (c) on the ground only—
  (i) of having deprived another of the services of his menial servant;
  (ii) of having deprived another of the services of his female servant by raping or seducing her; or
  (iii) of enticement of a servant or harbouring a servant.

5. **Maintenance at public expense to be taken into account in assessment of damages.**
In an action under the law of England and Wales or the law of Northern Ireland for damages for personal injuries (including any such action arising out of a contract) any saving to the injured person which is attributable to his maintenance wholly or partly at public expense in a hospital, nursing home or other institution shall be set off against any income lost by him as a result of his injuries.

CIVIL AVIATION ACT 1982
(1982, c. 16)

76. **Liability of aircraft in respect of trespass, nuisance and surface damage.**
(1) No action shall lie in respect of trespass or in respect of nuisance, by reason only of the flight of an aircraft over any property at a height above the ground which, having regard to wind, weather and all the circumstances of the case is reasonable, or the ordinary incidents of such flight, so long as the provisions of any Air Navigation Order and of any orders under section 62 above have been duly complied with and there has been no breach of section 81 below.

(2) Subject to subsection (3) below, where material loss or damage is caused to any person or property on land or water by, or by a person in, or an article, animal or person falling from, an aircraft while in flight, taking off or landing, then unless the loss or damage was caused or contributed to by the negligence of the person by whom it was suffered, damages in respect of the loss or damage shall be recoverable without proof of negligence or intention or other cause of action, as if the loss or damage had been caused by the wilful act, neglect, or default of the owner of the aircraft.

(3) Where material loss or damage is caused as aforesaid in circumstances in which—
 (a) damages are recoverable in respect of the said loss or damage by virtue only of subsection (2) above, and
 (b) a legal liability is created in some person other than the owner to pay damages in respect of the said loss or damage,
the owner shall be entitled to be indemnified by that other person against any claim in respect of the said loss or damage.

77. **Nuisance caused by aircraft on aerodromes.**
(1) An Air Navigation Order may provide for regulating the conditions under which noise and vibration may be caused by aircraft on aerodromes and may provide that subsection (2) below shall apply to any aerodrome as respects which provision as to noise and vibration caused by aircraft is so made.

(2) No action shall lie in respect of nuisance by reason only of the noise and vibration caused by aircraft on an aerodrome to which this subsection applies by virtue

of an Air Navigation Order, as long as the provisions of any such Order are duly complied with.

FORFEITURE ACT 1982
(1982, c. 34)

1. The "forfeiture rule".

(1) In this Act, the "forfeiture rule" means the rule of public policy which in certain circumstances precludes a person who has unlawfully killed another from acquiring a benefit in consequence of the killing....

2. Power to modify the rule.

(1) Where a court determines that the forfeiture rule has precluded a person (in this section referred to as "the offender") who has unlawfully killed another from acquiring any interest in property mentioned in subsection (4) below, the court may make an order under this section modifying the effect of that rule.

(2) The court shall not make an order under this section modifying the effect of the forfeiture rule in any case unless it is satisfied that, having regard to the conduct of the offender and of the deceased and to such other circumstances as appear to the court to be material, the justice of the case requires the effect of the rule to be so modified in that case.

(3) In any case where a person stands convicted of an offence of which unlawful killing is an element, the court shall not make an order under this section modifying the effect of the forfeiture rule in that case unless proceedings for the purpose are brought before the expiry of the period of three months beginning with his conviction.

(4) The interests in property referred to in subsection (1) above are—

(a) any beneficial interest in property which (apart from the forfeiture rule) the offender would have acquired—

(i) under the deceased's will (including, as respects Scotland, any writing having testamentary effect) or the law relating to intestacy or by way of ius relicti, ius relictae or legitim;

(ii) on the nomination of the deceased in accordance with the provisions of any enactment;

(iii) as a donatio mortis causa made by the deceased; or

(iv) under a special destination (whether relating to heritable or moveable property); or

(b) any beneficial interest in property which (apart from the forfeiture rule) the offender would have acquired in consequence of the death of the deceased, being property which, before the death, was held on trust for any person.

(5) An order under this section may modify the effect of the forfeiture rule in respect of any interest in property to which the determination referred to in subsection (1) above relates and may do so in either or both of the following ways, that is—

(a) where there is more than one such interest, by excluding the application of the rule in respect of any (but not all) of those interests; and

(b) in the case of any such interest in property, by excluding the application of the rule in respect of part of the property.

(6) On the making of an order under this section, the forfeiture rule shall have effect for all purposes (including purposes relating to anything done before the order is made) subject to the modifications made by the order....

5. Exclusion of murderers.

Nothing in this Act or in any order made under section 2 or referred to in section 3(1) of this Act shall affect the application of the forfeiture rule in the case of a person who stands convicted of murder.

INSURANCE COMPANIES ACT 1982
(1982, c. 50)

2. Restriction on carrying on insurance business.

(1) Subject to the following provisions of this section, no person shall carry on any insurance business in the United Kingdom unless authorised to do so under section 3 or 4 below.

SUPPLY OF GOODS AND SERVICES ACT 1982
(1982, c. 29)

PART I
SUPPLY OF GOODS

Contracts for the transfer of property in goods

1. The contracts concerned.

(1) In this Act [in its application to England and Wales and Northern Ireland] "contract for the transfer of goods" means a contract under which one person transfers or agrees to transfer to another the property in goods, other than an excepted contract.

(2) For the purposes of this section an excepted contract means any of the following:—
    (a) a contract of sale of goods;
    (b) a hire-purchase agreement;
    (c) a contract under which the property in goods is (or is to be) transferred in exchange for trading stamps on their redemption;
    (d) a transfer or agreement to transfer which is made by deed and for which there is no consideration other than the presumed consideration imported by the deed;
    (e) a contract intended to operate by way of mortgage, pledge, charge or other security.

(3) For the purposes of this Act [in its application to England and Wales and Northern Ireland] a contract is a contract for the transfer of goods whether or not services are also provided or to be provided under the contract, and (subject to subsection (2) above) whatever is the nature of the consideration for the transfer or agreement to transfer.

2. Implied terms about title, etc.

(1) In a contract for the transfer of goods, other than one to which subsection (3) below applies, there is an implied condition on the part of the transferor that in the case of a transfer of the property in the goods he has a right to transfer the property and in the case of an agreement to transfer the property in the goods he will have such a right at the time when the property is to be transferred.

(2) In a contract for the transfer of goods, other than one to which subsection (3) below applies, there is also an implied warranty that—
    (a) the goods are free, and will remain free until the time when the property is to be transferred, from any charge or encumbrance not disclosed or known to the transferee before the contract is made, and
    (b) the transferee will enjoy quiet possession of the goods except so far as it may be disturbed by the owner or other person entitled to the benefit of any charge or encumbrance so disclosed or known.

(3) This subsection applies to a contract for the transfer of goods in the case of which there appears from the contract or is to be inferred from its circumstances an intention that the transferor should transfer only such title as he or a third person may have.

(4) In a contract to which subsection (3) above applies there is an implied warranty that all charges or encumbrances known to the transferor and not known to the transferee have been disclosed to the transferee before the contract is made.

(5) In a contract to which subsection (3) above applies there is also an implied warranty that none of the following will disturb the transferee's quiet possession of the goods, namely—

(a) the transferor;
(b) in a case where the parties to the contract intend that the transferor should transfer only such title as a third person may have, that person;
(c) anyone claiming through or under the transferor or that third person otherwise than under a charge or encumbrance disclosed or known to the transferee before the contract is made.

3. Implied terms where transfer is by description.

(1) This section applies where, under a contract for the transfer of goods, the transferor transfers or agrees to transfer the property in the goods by description.

(2) In such case there is an implied condition that the goods will correspond with the description.

(3) If the transferor transfers or agrees to transfer the property in the goods by sample as well as by description it is not sufficient that the bulk of the goods corresponds with the sample if the goods do not also correspond with the description.

(4) A contract is not prevented from falling within subsection (1) above by reason only that, being exposed for supply, the goods are selected by the transferee.

4. Implied terms about quality or fitness.

(1) Except as provided by this section and section 5 below and subject to the provision of any other enactment, there is no implied condition or warranty about the quality or fitness for any particular purpose of goods supplied under a contract for the transfer of goods.

[(2) Where, under such a contract, the transferor transfers the property in goods in the course of a business, there is an implied condition that the goods supplied under the contract are of satisfactory quality.

(2A) For the purposes of this section and section 5 below, goods are of satisfactory quality if they meet the standard that a reasonable person would regard as satisfactory, taking account of any description of the goods, the price (if relevant) and all the other relevant circumstances.]

[(3) The condition implied by subsection (2) above does not extend to any matter making the quality of goods unsatisfactory—

(a) which is specifically drawn to the transferee's attention before the contract is made,
(b) where the transferee examines the goods before the contract is made, which that examination ought to reveal, or
(c) where the property in the goods is transferred by reference to a sample, which would have been apparent on a reasonable examination of the sample.]

(4) Subsection (5) below applies where, under a contract for the transfer of goods, the transferor transfers the property in goods in the course of a business and the transferee, expressly or by implication, makes known—

(a) to the transferor, or
(b) where the consideration or part of the consideration for the transfer is a sum payable by instalments and the goods were previously sold by a credit-broker to the transferor, to that credit-broker,

any particular purpose for which the goods are being acquired.

(5) In that case there is (subject to subsection (6) below) an implied condition that the goods supplied under the contract are reasonably fit for that purpose, whether or not that is a purpose for which such goods are commonly supplied.

Supply of Goods and Services Act 1982

(6) Subsection (5) above does not apply where the circumstances show that the transferee does not rely, or that it is unreasonable for him to rely, on the skill or judgment of the transferor or credit-broker.

(7) An implied condition or warranty about quality or fitness for a particular purpose may be annexed by usage to a contract for the transfer of goods.

(8) The preceding provisions of this section apply to a transfer by a person who in the course of a business is acting as agent for another as they apply to a transfer by a principal in the course of a business, except where that other is not transferring in the course of a business and either the transferee knows that fact or reasonable steps are taken to bring it to the transferee's notice before the contract concerned is made.

5. Implied terms where transfer is by sample.

(1) This section applies where, under a contract for the transfer of goods, the transferor transfers or agrees to transfer the property in the goods by reference to a sample.

(2) In such a case there is an implied condition—
    (a) that the bulk will correspond with the sample in quality; and
    (b) that the transferee will have a reasonable opportunity of comparing the bulk with the sample; and
    (c) that the goods will be free from any defect, [making their quality unsatisfactory], which would not be apparent on reasonable examination of the sample.

(4) For the purposes of this section a transferor transfers or agrees to transfer the property in goods by reference to a sample where there is an express or implied term to that effect in the contract concerned.

[5A. Modification of remedies for breach of statutory condition in non-consumer cases.

(1) Where in the case of a contract for the transfer of goods—
    (a) the transferee would, apart from this subsection, have the right to treat the contract as repudiated by reason of a breach on the part of the transferor of a term implied by section 3, 4 or 5(2)(a) or (c) above, but
    (b) the breach is so slight that it would be unreasonable for him to do so,
then, if the transferee does not deal as consumer, the breach is not to be treated as a breach of condition but may be treated as a breach of warranty.

(2) This section applies unless a contrary intention appears in, or is to be implied from, the contract.

(3) It is for the transferor to show that a breach fell within subsection (1)(b) above.]

Contracts for the hire of goods

6. The contracts concerned.

(1) In this Act [in its application to England and Wales and Northern Ireland] a "contract for the hire of goods" means a contract under which one person bails or agrees to bail goods to another by way of hire, other than an excepted contract.

(2) For the purposes of this section an excepted contract means any of the following:—
    (a) a hire-purchase agreement;
    (b) a contract under which goods are (or are to be) bailed in exchange for trading stamps on their redemption.

(3) For the purposes of this Act [in its application to England and Wales and Northern Ireland] a contract is a contract for the hire of goods whether or not services are also provided or to be provided under the contract, and (subject to subsection (2) above) whatever is the nature of the consideration for the bailment or agreement to bail by way of hire.

7. Implied terms about right to transfer possession, etc.

(1) In a contract for the hire of goods there is an implied condition on the part of the bailor that in the case of a bailment he has a right to transfer possession of the goods by way of hire for the period of the bailment and in the case of an agreement to bail he will have such a right at the time of the bailment.

(2) In a contract for the hire of goods there is also an implied warranty that the bailee will enjoy quiet possession of the goods for the period of the bailment except so far as the possession may be disturbed by the owner or other person entitled to the benefit of any charge or encumbrance disclosed or known to the bailee before the contract is made.

(3) The preceding provisions of this section do not affect the right of the bailor to repossess the goods under an express or implied term of the contract.

8. Implied terms where hire is by description.

(1) This section applies where, under a contract for the hire of goods, the bailor bails or agrees to bail the goods by description.

(2) In such a case there is an implied condition that the goods will correspond with the description.

(3) If under the contract the bailor bails or agrees to bail the goods by reference to a sample as well as a description it is not sufficient that the bulk of the goods corresponds with the sample if the goods do not also correspond with the description.

(4) A contract is not prevented from falling within subsection (1) above by reason only that, being exposed for supply, the goods are selected by the bailee.

9. Implied terms about quality or fitness.

(1) Except as provided by this section and section 10 below and subject to the provisions of any other enactment, there is no implied condition or warranty about the quality or fitness for any particular purpose of goods bailed under a contract for the hire of goods.

[(2) Where, under such a contract, the bailor bails goods in the course of a business, there is an implied condition that the goods supplied under the contract are of satisfactory quality.]

[(2A) For the purposes of this section and section 10 below, goods are of satisfactory quality if they meet the standard that a reasonable person would regard as satisfactory, taking account of any description of the goods, the consideration for the bailment (if relevant) and all the other relevant circumstances.]

[(3) The condition implied by subsection (2) above does not extend to any matter making the quality of goods unsatisfactory—

(a) which is specifically drawn to the bailee's attention before the contract is made,

(b) where the bailee examines the goods before the contract is made, which that examination ought to reveal, or

(c) where the goods are bailed by reference to a sample, which would have been apparent on a reasonable examination of the sample.]

(4) Subsection (5) below applies where, under a contract for the hire of goods, the bailor bails goods in the course of a business and the bailee, expressly or by implication, makes known—

(a) to the bailor in the course of negotiations conducted by him in relation to the making of the contract, or

(b) to a credit-broker in the course of negotiations conducted by that broker in relation to goods sold by him to the bailor before forming the subject matter of the contract, any particular purpose for which the goods are being bailed.

(5) In that case there is (subject to subsection (6) below) an implied condition that the goods supplied under the contract are reasonably fit for that purpose,

whether or not that is a purpose for which such goods are commonly supplied.

(6) Subsection (5) above does not apply where the circumstances show that the bailee does not rely, or that it is unreasonable for him to rely, on the skill or judgment of the bailor or credit-broker.

(7) An implied condition or warranty about quality or fitness for a particular purpose may be annexed by usage to a contract for the hire of goods.

(8) The preceding provisions of this section apply to a bailment by a person who in the course of a business is acting as agent for another as they apply to a bailment by a principal in the course of a business, except where that other is not bailing in the course of a business and either the bailee knows that fact or reasonable steps are taken to bring it to the bailee's notice before the contract concerned is made.

10. Implied terms where hire is by sample.

(1) This section applies where, under a contract for the hire of goods, the bailor bails or agrees to bail the goods by reference to a sample.

(2) In such a case there is an implied condition—

   (a) that the bulk will correspond with the sample in quality; and

   (b) that the bailee will have a reasonable opportunity of comparing the bulk with the sample; and

   (c) that the goods will be free from any defect, [making their quality unsatisfactory], which would not be apparent on reasonable examination of the sample.

(4) For the purposes of this section a bailor bails or agrees to bail goods by reference to a sample where there is an express or implied term to that effect in the contract concerned.

[10A. Modification of remedies for breach of statutory condition in non-consumer cases.

(1) Where in the case of a contract for the hire of goods—

   (a) the bailee would, apart from this subsection, have the right to treat the contract as repudiated by reason of a breach on the part of the bailor of a term implied by section 8, 9 or 10(2)(a) or (c) above, but

   (b) the breach is so slight that it would be unreasonable for him to do so,

then, if the bailee does not deal as consumer, the breach is not to be treated as a breach of condition but may be treated as a breach of warranty.

(2) This section applies unless a contrary intention appears in, or is to be implied from, the contract.

(3) It is for the bailor to show that a breach fell within subsection (1)(b) above.]

Exclusion of implied terms, etc.

11. Exclusion of implied terms, etc.

(1) Where a right, duty or liability would arise under a contract for the transfer of goods or a contract for the hire of goods by implication of law, it may (subject to subsection (2) below and the 1977 Act) be negatived or varied by express agreement, or by the course of dealing between the parties, or by such usage as binds both parties to the contract.

(2) An express condition or warranty does not negative a condition or warranty implied by the preceding provisions of this Act unless inconsistent with it.

(3) Nothing in the preceding provisions of this Act prejudices the operation of any other enactment or any rule of law whereby any condition or warranty (other than one relating to quality or fitness) is to be implied in a contract for the transfer of goods or a contract for the hire of goods.

[PART IA
SUPPLY OF GOODS AS RESPECTS SCOTLAND
...]

PART II
SUPPLY OF SERVICES

12. The contracts concerned.

(1) In this Act a "contract for the supply of a service" means, subject to subsection (2) below, a contract under which a person ("the supplier") agrees to carry out a service.

(2) For the purposes of this Act, a contract of service or apprenticeship is not a contract for the supply of a service.

(3) Subject to subsection (2) above, a contract is a contract for the supply of a service for the purposes of this Act whether or not goods are also—
    (a) transferred or to be transferred, or
    (b) bailed or to be bailed by way of hire,
under the contract, and whatever is the nature of the consideration for which the service is to be carried out.

(4) The Secretary of State may by order provide that one or more of sections 13 to 15 below shall not apply to services of a description specified in the order, and such an order may make different provision for different circumstances.

(5) The power to make an order under subsection (4) above shall be exercisable by statutory instrument subject to annulment in pursuance of a resolution of either House of Parliament.

13. Implied term about care and skill.

In a contract for the supply of a service where the supplier is acting in the course of a business, there is an implied term that the supplier will carry out the service with reasonable care and skill.

14. Implied term about time of performance.

(1) Where, under a contract for the supply of a service by a supplier acting in the course of a business, the time for the service to be carried out is not fixed by the contract, left to be fixed in a manner agreed by the contract or determined by the course of dealing between the parties, there is an implied term that the supplier will carry out the service within a reasonable time.

(2) What is a reasonable time is a question of fact.

15. Implied term about consideration.

(1) Where, under a contract for the supply of a service, the consideration for the service is not determined by the contract, left to be determined in a manner agreed by the contract or determined by the course of dealing between the parties, there is an implied term that the party contracting with the supplier will pay a reasonable charge.

(2) What is a reasonable charge is a question of fact.

16. Exclusion of implied terms, etc.

(1) Where a right, duty or liability would arise under a contract for the supply of a service by virtue of this Part of this Act, it may (subject to subsection (2) below and the 1977 Act) be negatived or varied by express agreement, or by the course of dealing between the parties, or by such usage as binds both parties to the contract.

(2) An express term does not negative a term implied by this Part of this Act unless inconsistent with it.

(3) Nothing in this Part of this Act prejudices—
    (a) any rule of law which imposes on the supplier a duty stricter than that imposed by section 13 or 14 above; or

(b) subject to paragraph (a) above, any rule of law whereby any term not inconsistent with this Part of this Act is to be implied in a contract for the supply of a service.

(4) This Part of this Act has effect subject to any other enactment which defines or restricts the rights, duties or liabilities arising in connection with a service of any description.

PART III
SUPPLEMENTARY

18. Interpretation: general.

(1) In the preceding provisions of this Act and this section—

"bailee", in relation to a contract for the hire of goods means (depending on the context) a person to whom the goods are bailed under the contract, or a person to whom they are to be so bailed, or a person to whom the rights under the contract of either of those persons have passed;

"bailor", in relation to a contract for the hire of goods, means (depending on the context) a person who bails the goods under the contract, or a person who agrees to do so, or a person to whom the duties under the contract of either of those persons have passed;

"business" includes a profession and the activities of any government department or local or public authority;

"credit-broker" means a person acting in the course of a business of credit brokerage carried on by him;

"credit brokerage" means the effecting of introductions—

    (a) of individuals desiring to obtain credit to persons carrying on any business so far as it relates to the provision of credit; or

    (b) of individuals desiring to obtain goods on hire to persons carrying on a business which comprises or relates to the bailment [or as regards Scotland the hire] of goods under a contract for the hire of goods; or

    (c) of individuals desiring to obtain credit, or to obtain goods on hire, to other credit-brokers;

"enactment" means any legislation (including subordinate legislation) of the United Kingdom or Northern Ireland;

"goods" [includes all personal chattels, other than things in action and money, and as regards Scotland all corporeal moveables; and in particular "goods" includes] emblements, industrial growing crops, and things attached to or forming part of the land which are agreed to be severed before the transfer [bailment or hire] concerned or under the contract concerned];

"hire-purchase agreement" has the same meaning as in the 1974 Act;

"property", in relation to goods, means the general property in them and not merely a special property;

"redemption", in relation to trading stamps, has the same meaning as in the Trading Stamps Act 1964 or, as respects Northern Ireland, the Trading Stamps Act (Northern Ireland) 1965;

"trading stamps" has the same meaning as in the said Act of 1964 or, as respects Northern Ireland, the said Act of 1965;

"transferee", in relation to a contract for the transfer of goods, means (depending on the context) a person to whom the property in the goods is transferred under the contract, or a person to whom the property is to be so transferred, or a person to whom the rights under the contract of either of those persons have passed;

"transferor", in relation to a contract for the transfer of goods, means (depending on the context) a person who transfers the property in the goods under the contract, or a person who agrees to do so, or a person to whom the duties under the contract of either of those persons have passed.

(2) In subsection (1) above, in the definitions of bailee, bailor, transferee and transferor, a reference to rights or duties passing is to their passing by assignment, [assignation] operation of law or otherwise.

[(3) For the purposes of this Act, the quality of goods includes their state and condition and the following (among others) are in appropriate cases aspects of the quality of goods—

(a) fitness for all the purposes for which goods of the kind in question are commonly supplied,
(b) appearance and finish,
(c) freedom from minor defects,
(d) safety, and
(e) durability.

(4) References to this Act to dealing as consumer are to be construed in accordance with Part I of the Unfair Contract Terms Act 1977; and, for the purposes of this Act, it is for the transferor or bailor claiming that the transferee or bailee does not deal as consumer to show that he does not.]

19. Interpretation: references to Acts.

In this Act—

"the 1973 Act" means the Supply of Goods (Implied Terms) Act 1973;
"the 1974 Act" means the Consumer Credit Act 1974;
"the 1977 Act" means the Unfair Contract Terms Act 1977; and
"the 1979 Act" means the Sale of Goods Act 1979.

20. Citation, transitional provisions, commencement and extent.

(1) This Act may be cited as the Supply of Goods and Services Act 1982.
...

INTERNATIONAL TRANSPORT CONVENTIONS ACT 1983
(1983, c. 14)

1. Convention to have the force of law.

(1) The Convention concerning International Carriage by Rail signed on behalf of the United Kingdom on 9th May 1980 shall have the force of law in the United Kingdom.

3. Fatal accidents.

(1) Where by virtue of the Convention any person has a right of action in respect of the death of a passenger by reason of his being a person whom the passenger was under a legal duty to maintain—

(a) subject to subsection (2) below, no action in respect of the passenger's death shall be brought for the benefit of that person under the Fatal Accidents Act 1976; but
(b) nothing in section 2(3) of that Act (not more than one action in respect of the same subject-matter of complaint) shall prevent an action being brought under that Act for the benefit of any other person.

(2) Nothing in subsection (1)(a) above affects the right of any person to claim damages for bereavement under section 1A of the said Act of 1976.

(3) Section 4 of the said Act of 1976 (exclusion of certain benefits in assessment of damages) shall apply in relation to an action brought by any person under the Convention as it applies in relation to an action under that Act.

(4) Where separate proceedings are brought under the Convention and under the said Act of 1976 in respect of the death of a passenger, a court, in awarding damages under that Act, shall take into account any damages awarded in the proceedings brought under the Convention and shall have jurisdiction to make any part of its award conditional on the result of those proceedings.

MENTAL HEALTH ACT 1983
(1983, c. 20)

95. General functions of the judge with respect to property and affairs of patient.

(1) The judge may, with respect to the property and affairs of a patient, do or secure the doing of all such things as appear necessary or expedient—
    (a) for the maintenance or other benefit of the patient,
    (b) for the maintenance or other benefit of members of the patient's family,
    (c) for making provision for other persons or purposes for whom or which the patient might be expected to provide if he were not mentally disordered, or
    (d) otherwise for administering the patient's affairs.

(2) In the exercise of the powers conferred by this section regard shall be had first of all to the requirements of the patient, and the rules of law which restricted the enforcement by a creditor of rights against property under the control of the judge in lunacy shall apply to property under the control of the judge; but, subject to the foregoing provisions of this subsection, the judge shall, in administering a patient's affairs, have regard to the interests of creditors and also to the desirability of making provision for obligations of the patient notwithstanding that they may not be legally enforceable.

139. Protection for acts done in pursuance of this Act.

(1) No person shall be liable, whether on the ground of want of jurisdiction or on any other ground, to any civil or criminal proceedings to which he would have been liable apart from this section in respect of any act purporting to be done in pursuance of this Act or any regulations or rules made under this Act, or in, or in pursuance of anything done in, the discharge of functions conferred by any other enactment on the authority having jurisdiction under Part VII of this Act, unless the act was done in bad faith or without reasonable care.

(2) No civil proceedings shall be brought against any person in any court in respect of any such act without the leave of the High Court; and no criminal proceedings shall be brought against any person in any court in respect of any such act except by or with the consent of the Director of Public Prosecutions.

BUILDING ACT 1984
(1984, c. 55)

1. Power to make building regulations.

(1) The Secretary of State may, for any of the purposes of—
    (a) securing the health, safety, welfare and convenience of persons in or about buildings and of others who may be affected by buildings or matters connected with buildings,
    (b) furthering the conservation of fuel and power, and
    (c) preventing waste, undue consumption, misuse or contamination of water,
make regulations with respect to the design and construction of buildings and the provision of services, fittings and equipment in or in connection with buildings.

38. Civil liability.

(1) Subject to this section—
    (a) breach of a duty imposed by building regulations, so far as it causes damage, is actionable, except in so far as the regulations provide otherwise, and
    (b) as regards such a duty, building regulations may provide for a prescribed defence to be available in an action for breach of that duty brought by virtue of this subsection.

(2) Subsection (1) above, and any defence provided for in regulations made by virtue of it, do not apply in the case of a breach of such a duty in connection with a building erected before the date on which that subsection comes into force unless the regulations imposing the duty apply to or in connection with the building by virtue of section 2(2) above or paragraph 8 of Schedule 1 to this Act.

(3) This section does not affect the extent (if any) to which breach of—

(a) a duty imposed by or arising in connection with this Part of this Act or any other enactment relating to building regulations, or

(b) a duty imposed by building regulations in a case to which subsection (1) above does not apply,

is actionable, or prejudice a right of action that exists apart from the enactments relating to building regulations.

(4) In this section, "damage" includes the death of, or injury to, any person (including any disease and any impairment of a person's physical or mental condition).

DATA PROTECTION ACT 1984
(1984, c. 35)

22. Compensation for inaccuracy.

(1) An individual who is the subject of personal data held by a data user and who suffers damage by reason of the inaccuracy of the data shall be entitled to compensation from the data user for that damage and for any distress which the individual has suffered by reason of the inaccuracy....

(3) In proceedings brought against any person by virtue of this section it shall be a defence to prove that he had taken such care as in all the circumstances was reasonably required to ensure the accuracy of the data at the material time.

(4) Data are inaccurate for the purposes of this section if incorrect or misleading as to any matter of fact.

INHERITANCE TAX ACT 1984
(1984, c. 51)

241. Overpayments.

(1) If it is proved to the satisfaction of the Board that too much tax has been paid on the value transferred by a chargeable transfer or on so much of that value as is attributable to any property, the Board shall repay the excess unless the claim for repayment was made more than six years after the date on which the payment or last payment of the tax was made.

(2) References in this section to tax include references to interest on tax.

OCCUPIERS' LIABILITY ACT 1984
(1984, c. 3)

1. Duty of occupier to persons other than his visitors.

(1) The rules enacted by this section shall have effect, in place of the rules of the common law, to determine—

(a) whether any duty is owed by a person as occupier of premises to persons other than his visitors in respect of any risk of their suffering injury on the premises by reason of any danger due to the state of the premises or to things done or omitted to be done on them; and

(b) if so, what that duty is.

(2) For the purposes of this section, the persons who are to be treated respectively as an occupier of any premises (which, for those purposes, include any fixed or movable structure) and as his visitors are—

(a) any person who owes in relation to the premises the duty referred to in section 2 of the Occupiers' Liability Act 1957 (the common duty of care), and
(b) those who are his visitors for the purposes of that duty.
(3) An occupier of premises owes a duty to another (not being his visitor) in respect of any such risk as is referred to in subsection (1) above if—
(a) he is aware of the danger or has reasonable grounds to believe that it exists;
(b) he knows or has reasonable grounds to believe that the other is in the vicinity of the danger concerned or that he may come into the vicinity of the danger (in either case, whether the other has lawful authority for being in that vicinity or not); and
(c) the risk is one against which, in all the circumstances of the case, he may reasonably be expected to offer the other some protection.
(4) Where, by virtue of this section, an occupier of premises owes a duty to another in respect of such a risk, the duty is to take such care as is reasonable in all the circumstances of the case to see that he does not suffer injury on the premises by reason of the danger concerned.
(5) Any duty owed by virtue of this section in respect of a risk may, in an appropriate case, be discharged by taking such steps as are reasonable in all the circumstances of the case to give warning of the danger concerned or to discourage persons from incurring the risk.
(6) No duty is owed by virtue of this section to any person in respect of risks willingly accepted as his by that person (the question whether a risk was so accepted to be decided on the same principles as in other cases in which one person owes a duty of care to another).
(7) No duty is owed by virtue of this section to persons using the highway, and this section does not affect any duty owed to such persons.
(8) Where a person owes a duty by virtue of this section, he does not, by reason of any breach of the duty, incur any liability in respect of any loss of or damage to property.
(9) In this section—
"highway" means any part of a highway other than a ferry or waterway;
"injury" means anything resulting in death or personal injury, including any disease and any impairment of physical or mental condition; and
"movable structure" includes any vessel, vehicle or aircraft.

3. Application to Crown.

Section 1 of this Act shall bind the Crown, but as regards the Crown's liability in tort shall not bind the Crown further than the Crown is made liable in tort by the Crown Proceedings Act 1947.

POLICE AND CRIMINAL EVIDENCE ACT 1984
(1984, c. 60)

17. Entry for purpose of arrest etc.

(1) Subject to the following provisions of this section, and without prejudice to any other enactment, a constable may enter and search any premises for the purpose—
(a) of executing—
(i) a warrant of arrest issued in connection with or arising out of criminal proceedings; or
(ii) a warrant of commitment issued under section 76 of the Magistrates' Courts Act 1980;
(b) of arresting a person for an arrestable offence; ...
(e) of saving life or limb or preventing serious damage to property.
(4) The power of search conferred by this section is only a power to search to the extent that is reasonably required for the purpose for which the power of entry is exercised.

(5) Subject to subsection (6) below, all the rules of common law under which a constable has power to enter premises without a warrant are hereby abolished.

(6) Nothing in subsection (5) above affects any power of entry to deal with or prevent a breach of the peace.

19. General power of seizure etc.

(1) The powers conferred by subsections (2), (3) and (4) below are exercisable by a constable who is lawfully on any premises.

(2) The constable may seize anything which is on the premises if he has reasonable grounds for believing—
   (a) that it has been obtained in consequence of the commission of an offence; and
   (b) that it is necessary to seize it in order to prevent it being concealed, lost, damaged, altered or destroyed.

22. Retention.

(1) Subject to subsection (4) below, anything which has been seized by a constable or taken away by a constable following a requirement made by virtue of section 19 or 20 above may be retained so long as is necessary in all the circumstances.

(3) Nothing seized on the ground that it may be used—
   (a) to cause physical injury to any person;
   (b) to damage property;
   (c) to interfere with evidence; or
   (d) to assist in escape from police detention or lawful custody,
may be retained when the person from whom it was seized is no longer in police detention or the custody of a court or is in the custody of a court but has been released on bail.

24. Arrest without warrant for arrestable offences.

(4) Any person may arrest without a warrant—
   (a) anyone who is in the act of committing an arrestable offence;
   (b) anyone whom he has reasonable grounds for suspecting to be committing such an offence.

(5) Where an arrestable offence has been committed, any person may arrest without a warrant—
   (a) anyone who is guilty of the offence;
   (b) anyone whom he has reasonable grounds for suspecting to be guilty of it.

(6) Where a constable has reasonable grounds for suspecting that an arrestable offence has been committed, he may arrest without a warrant anyone whom he has reasonable grounds for suspecting to be guilty of the offence.

(7) A constable may arrest without a warrant—
   (a) anyone who is about to commit an arrestable offence;
   (b) anyone whom he has reasonable grounds for suspecting to be about to commit an arrestable offence.

25. General arrest conditions.

(1) Where a constable has reasonable grounds for suspecting that any offence which is not an arrestable offence has been committed or attempted, or is being committed or attempted, he may arrest the relevant person if it appears to him that service of a summons is impracticable or inappropriate because any of the general arrest conditions is satisfied.

32. Search upon arrest.

(1) A constable may search an arrested person, in any case where the person to be searched has been arrested at a place other than a police station, if the constable has reasonable grounds for believing that the arrested person may present a danger to himself or others.

34. Limitations on police detention.

(1) A person arrested for an offence shall not be kept in police detention except in accordance with the provisions of this Part of this Act.

(2) Subject to subsection (3) below, if at any time a custody officer—
  (a) becomes aware, in relation to any person in police detention, that the grounds for the detention of that person have ceased to apply; and
  (b) is not aware of any other grounds on which the continued detention of that person could be justified under the provisions of this Part of this Act,
it shall be the duty of the custody officer, subject to subsection (4) below, to order his immediate release from custody.

55. Intimate searches.

(2) An officer may not authorise an intimate search of a person for anything unless he has reasonable grounds for believing that it cannot be found without his being intimately searched.

62. Intimate samples.

(1) An intimate sample may be taken from a person in police detention only—
  (a) if a police officer of at least the rank of superintendent authorises it to be taken; and
  (b) if the appropriate consent is given.

[(1A) An intimate sample may be taken from a person who is not in police detention but from whom, in the course of the investigation of an offence, two or more intimate samples suitable for the same means of analysis have been taken which have proved insufficient—
  (a) if a police officer of at least the rank of superintendent authorises it to be taken; and
  (b) if the appropriate consent is given.]

65. Part V — supplementary.

In this Part of this Act— ...
"intimate sample" means a sample of blood, semen or any other tissue fluid, urine, saliva or pubic hair, or a swab taken from a person's body [orifices]; ...

TELECOMMUNICATIONS ACT 1984
(1984, c. 12)

[27F. Disputes about discrimination etc. in fixing charges.

(1) Any dispute, of a kind to which this section applies, between—
  (a) a person ("the customer") who is, or wishes to be, provided with any relevant service by a designated operator, and
  (b) that designated operator,
may be referred to the Director by either party.

(2) This section applies to any dispute as to whether the designated operator—
  (a) has exercised undue discrimination against the customer in respect of charges applied, or to be applied, in connection with the provision of the service in question;
  (b) has shown undue preference to any other person in respect of such charges, to the detriment of the customer; or
  (c) has applied, or proposes to apply, any charge in connection with the provision of the service in question to the customer which is neither specified in, nor determined in accordance with a method specified in, a notice required by a condition of a kind mentioned in section 8(1)(e) above.

(3) Where a dispute is referred to him under this section, the Director, or an arbitrator (or in Scotland an arbiter) appointed by him, shall determine whether the customer's allegation is well founded and, if it is, make such order as he considers appropriate.

(5) No act or omission of a designated operator which is permitted by any condition—
  (a) relating to any of the matters referred to in section 8(1)(d) above, and
  (b) included in the licence granted to him under section 7 above,
shall be taken to constitute undue discrimination or undue preference for the purposes of this section.

106. General interpretation.
(1) In this Act, under the content otherwise requires— ...
"the Director" means the Director General of Telecommunications ...

ADMINISTRATION OF JUSTICE ACT 1985
(1985, c. 61)

PART II

12. Establishment of the Council.
(1) For the purposes of this Part there shall be a body to be known as the Council for Licensed Conveyancers.

21. Professional indemnity and compensation.
(1) The Council shall make rules for indemnifying licensed conveyancers and former licensed conveyancers against losses arising from claims in respect of any description of civil liability incurred by them, or by employees or associates or former employees or associates of theirs, in connection with their practices as licensed conveyancers.

(2) The Council shall also make rules for the making of grants or other payments for the purpose of relieving or mitigating losses suffered by persons in consequence of—
  (a) negligence or fraud or other dishonesty on the part of licensed conveyancers, or of employees or associates of theirs, in connection with their practices (or purported practices) as licensed conveyancers; or
  (b) failure on the part of licensed conveyancers to account for money received by them in connection with their practices (or purported practices) as licensed conveyancers.

BUSINESS NAMES ACT 1985
(1985, c. 7)

4. Disclosure required of persons using business names.
...

5. Civil remedies for breach of s. 4.
(1) Any legal proceedings brought by a person to whom this Act applies to enforce a right arising out of a contract made in the course of a business in respect of which he was, at the time the contract was made, in breach of subsection (1) or (2) of section 4 shall be dismissed if the defendant (or, in Scotland, the defender) to the proceedings shows—
  (a) that he has a claim against the plaintiff (pursuer) arising out of that contract which he has been unable to pursue by reason of the latter's breach of section 4(1) or (2), or
  (b) that he has suffered some financial loss in connection with the contract by reason of the plaintiff's (pursuer's) breach of section 4(1) or (2),
unless the court before which the proceedings are brought is satisfied that it is just and equitable to permit the proceedings to continue.

(2) This section is without prejudice to the right of any person to enforce such rights as he may have against another person in any proceedings brought by that person.

COMPANIES ACT 1985
(1985, c. 6)

[3A. Statement of company's objects: general commercial company.
Where the company's memorandum states that the object of the company is to carry on business as a general commercial company—
    (a) the object of the company is to carry on any trade or business whatsoever, and
    (b) the company has power to do all such things as are incidental or conducive to the carrying on of any trade or business by it.]

14. Effect of memorandum and articles.
(1) Subject to the provisions of this Act, the memorandum and articles, when registered, bind the company and its members to the same extent as if they respectively had been signed and sealed by each member, and contained covenants on the part of each member to observe all the provisions of the memorandum and of the articles.

[35. A company's capacity not limited by its memorandum.
(1) The validity of an act done by a company shall not be called into question on the ground of lack of capacity by reason of anything in the company's memorandum.
(2) A member of a company may bring proceedings to restrain the doing of an act which but for subsection (1) would be beyond the company's capacity; but no such proceedings shall lie in respect of an act to be done in fulfilment of a legal obligation arising from a previous act of the company.
(3) It remains the duty of the directors to observe any limitations on their powers flowing from the company's memorandum; and action by the directors which but for subsection (1) would be beyond the company's capacity may only be ratified by the company by special resolution.
A resolution ratifying such action shall not affect any liability incurred by the directors or any other person; relief from any such liability must be agreed to separately by special resolution.]

[35A. Power of directors to bind the company.
(1) In favour of a person dealing with a company in good faith, the power of the board of directors to bind the company, or authorise others to do so, shall be deemed to be free of any limitation under the company's constitution.
(2) For this purpose—
    (a) a person "deals with" a company if he is a party to any transaction or other act to which the company is a party;
    (b) a person shall not be regarded as acting in bad faith by reason only of his knowing that an act is beyond the powers of the directors under the company's constitution; and
    (c) a person shall be presumed to have acted in good faith unless the contrary is proved.
(3) The references above to limitations on the directors' powers under the company's constitution include limitations deriving—
    (a) from a resolution of the company in general meeting or a meeting of any class of shareholders, or
    (b) from any agreement between the members of the company or of any class of shareholders.
(4) Subsection (1) does not affect any right of a member of the company to bring proceedings to restrain the doing of an act which is beyond the powers of the directors; but no such proceedings shall lie in respect of an act to be done in fulfilment of a legal obligation arising from a previous act of the company.
(5) Nor does that subsection affect any liability incurred by the directors, or any other person, by reason of the directors' exceeding their powers.]

[35B. No duty to enquire as to capacity of company or authority of directors.
A party to a transaction with a company is not bound to enquire as to whether it is permitted by the company's memorandum or as to any limitation on the powers of the board of directors to bind the company or authorise others to do so.]

[36. Company contracts: England and Wales.
Under the law of England and Wales a contract may be made—
  (a) by a company, by writing under its common seal, or
  (b) on behalf of a company, by any person acting under its authority, express or implied;
and any formalities required by law in the case of a contract made by an individual also apply, unless a contrary intention appears, to a contract made by or on behalf of a company.]

[36A. Execution of documents: England and Wales.
(1) Under the law of England and Wales the following provisions have effect with respect to the execution of documents by a company.
(2) A document is executed by a company by the affixing of its common seal.
(3) A company need not have a common seal, however, and the following subsections apply whether it does or not.
(4) A document signed by a director and the secretary of a company, or by two directors of a company, and expressed (in whatever form of words) to be executed by the company has the same effect as if executed under the common seal of the company.
(5) A document executed by a company which makes it clear on its face that it is intended by the person or persons making it to be a deed has effect, upon delivery, as a deed; and it shall be presumed, unless a contrary intention is proved, to be delivered upon its being so executed.
(6) In favour of a purchaser a document shall be deemed to have been duly executed by a company if it purports to be signed by a director and the secretary of the company, or by two directors of the company, and, where it makes it clear on its face that it is intended by the person or persons making it to be a deed, to have been delivered upon its being executed.
A "purchaser" means a purchaser in good faith for valuable consideration and includes a lessee, mortgagee or other person who for valuable consideration acquires an interest in property.]

[36C. Pre-incorporation contracts, deeds and obligations.
(1) A contract which purports to be made by or on behalf of a company at a time when the company has not been formed has effect, subject to any agreement to the contrary, as one made with the person purporting to act for the company or as agent for it, and he is personally liable on the contract accordingly.
(2) Subsection (1) applies—
  (a) to the making of a deed under the law of England and Wales . . .]

[111A. Right to damages, &c. not affected.
A person is not debarred from obtaining damages or other compensation from a company by reason only of his holding or having held shares in the company or any right to apply or subscribe for shares or to be included in the company's register in respect of shares.]

[322A. Invalidity of certain transactions involving directors, etc.
(1) This section applies where a company enters into a transaction to which the parties include—
  (a) a director of the company or of its holding company, or
  (b) a person connected with such a director or a company with whom such a director is associated,

Housing Act 1985

and the board of directors, in connection with the transaction, exceed any limitation on their powers under the company's constitution.

(2) The transaction is voidable at the instance of the company.

(3) Whether or not it is avoided, any such party to the transaction as is mentioned in subsection (1)(a) or (b), and any director of the company who authorised the transaction, is liable—

    (a) to account to the company for any gain which he has made directly or indirectly by the transaction, and

    (b) to indemnify the company for any loss or damage resulting from the transaction.

(4) Nothing in the above provisions shall be construed as excluding the operation of any other enactment of rule of law by virtue of which the transaction may be called in question or any liability to the company may arise.

(5) The transaction ceases to be voidable if—

    (a) restitution of any money or other asset which was the subject-matter of the transaction is no longer possible, or

    (b) the company is indemnified for any loss or damage resulting from the transaction, or

    (c) rights acquired bona fide for value and without actual notice of the directors' exceeding their powers by a person who is not party to the transaction would be affected by the avoidance, or

    (d) the transaction is ratified by the company in general meeting, by ordinary or special resolution or otherwise as the case may require.

(6) A person other than a director of the company is not liable under subsection (3) if he shows that at the time the transaction was entered into he did not know that the directors were exceeding their powers.

(7) This section does not affect the operation of section 35A in relation to any party to the transaction not within subsection (1)(a) or (b).

But where a transaction is voidable by virtue of this section and valid by virtue of that section in favour of such a person, the court may, on the application of that person or of the company, make such order affirming, severing or setting aside the transaction, on such terms, as appear to the court to be just.]

HOUSING ACT 1985
(1985, c. 68)

118. The right to buy.

(1) A secure tenant has the right to buy, that is to say, the right, in the circumstances and subject to the conditions and exceptions stated in the following provisions of this Part—

    (a) if the dwelling-house is a house and the landlord owns the freehold, to acquire the freehold of the dwelling-house;

    (b) if the landlord does not own the freehold or if the dwelling-house is a flat (whether or not the landlord owns the freehold), to be granted a lease of the dwelling-house.

164. Secretary of State's general power to intervene.

(5) While a notice under this section is in force the Secretary of State may do all such things as appear to him necessary or expedient to enable secure tenants of the landlord or landlords to which the notice was given to exercise the right to buy, the right to a mortgage and the right to be granted a shared ownership lease; and he is not bound to take the steps which the landlord would have been bound to take under this Part.

179. Provisions restricting right to buy etc. of no effect.
(1) A provision of a lease held by the landlord or a superior landlord, or of an agreement (whenever made), is void in so far as it purports to prohibit or restrict—
   (a) the grant of a lease in pursuance of the right to buy or the [right to acquire on rent to mortgage terms], or
   (b) the subsequent disposal (whether by way of assignment, sub-lease or otherwise) of a lease so granted,
or to authorise a forfeiture, or impose on the landlord or superior landlord a penalty or disability, in the event of such a grant or disposal.

LANDLORD AND TENANT ACT 1985
(1985, c. 70)

8. Implied terms as to fitness for human habitation.
(1) In a contract to which this section applies for the letting of a house for human habitation there is implied, notwithstanding any stipulation to the contrary—
   (a) a condition that the house is fit for human habitation at the commencement of the tenancy, and
   (b) an undertaking that the house will be kept by the landlord fit for human habitation during the tenancy.
(2) The landlord, or a person authorised by him in writing, may at reasonable times of the day, on giving 24 hours' notice in writing to the tenant or occupier, enter premises to which this section applies for the purpose of viewing their state and condition.

SURROGACY ARRANGEMENTS ACT 1985
(1985, c. 49)

1. Meaning of "surrogate mother", "surrogacy arrangement" and other terms.
(2) "Surrogate mother" means a woman who carries a child in pursuance of an arrangement—
   (a) made before she began to carry the child, and
   (b) made with a view to any child carried in pursuance of it being handed over to, and [parental responsibility being met] (so far as practicable) by, another person or other persons.
(3) An arrangement is a surrogacy arrangement if, were a woman to whom the arrangement relates to carry a child in pursuance of it, she would be a surrogate mother.
(9) This Act applies to arrangements whether or not they are lawful [...].

[1A. Surrogacy arrangements unenforceable.
No surrogacy arrangement is enforceable by or against any of the persons making it.]

2. Negotiating surrogacy arrangements on a commercial basis, etc.
(1) No person shall on a commercial basis do any of the following acts in the United Kingdom, that is—
   (a) initiate or take part in any negotiations with a view to the making of a surrogacy arrangement,
   (b) offer or agree to negotiate the making of a surrogacy arrangement, or
   (c) compile any information with a view to its use in making, or negotiating the making of, surrogacy arrangements;
and no person shall in the United Kingdom knowingly cause another to do any of those acts on a commercial basis.

AGRICULTURAL HOLDINGS ACT 1986
(1986, c. 5)

24. Restriction of landlord's remedies for breach of contract of tenancy.
Notwithstanding any provision in a contract of tenancy of an agricultural holding making the tenant liable to pay a higher rent or other liquidated damages in the event of a breach or non-fulfilment of a term or condition of the contract, the landlord shall not be entitled to recover in consequence of any such breach or non-fulfilment, by distress or otherwise, any sum in excess of the damage actually suffered by him in consequence of the breach or non-fulfilment.

BUILDING SOCIETIES ACT 1986
(1986, c. 53)

[**66A. Transactions with directors and persons connected with them.**
(1) This section applies where a building society enters into a transaction the parties to which include—
  (a) a director of the society; or
  (b) a person connected with such a director,
and the board of directors, in connection with the transaction, exceed any limitation on their powers by reason of anything included in the society's constitution, that is to say, its memorandum and rules.
  (2) The transaction is voidable at the instance of the society.
  (3) Whether or not it is avoided, any such party to the transaction as is mentioned in subsection (1)(a) or (b) above, and any director of the society who authorised the transaction, is liable—
  (a) to account to the society for any gain which he has made directly or indirectly by the transaction, and
  (b) to indemnify the society for any loss or damage resulting from the transaction.
  (4) Nothing in the above provisions shall be construed as excluding the operation of any other enactment or rule of law by the virtue of which the transaction may be called in question or any liability to the society may arise.
  (5) The transaction ceases to be voidable if—
  (a) restitution of any money or other asset which was the subject-matter of the transaction is no longer possible, or
  (b) the society is indemnified for any loss or damage resulting from the transaction, or
  (c) rights acquired bona fide for value and without actual notice of the directors' exceeding their powers by a person who is not party to the transaction would be affected by the avoidance, or
  (d) the transaction is ratified by the society in general meeting, by ordinary or special resolution or otherwise as the case may require.
  (6) A person other than a director of the society is not liable under subsection (3) above if he shows that at the time the transaction was entered into he did not know that the directors were exceeding their powers.
  (7) This section does not affect the operation of subparagraph (1) of paragraph 17 of Schedule 2 in relation to any party to the transaction not within subsection (1)(a) or (b) above.
  But where a transaction is voidable by virtue of this section and valid by virtue of that sub-paragraph in favour of such a person, the court may, on the application of that person or of the society, make such order affirming, severing or setting aside the transaction, on such terms, as appear to the court to be just.]

FINANCIAL SERVICES ACT 1986
(1986, c.60)

PART I

3. Persons entitled to carry on investment business.
No person shall carry on, or purport to carry on, investment business in the United Kingdom unless he is an authorised person under Chapter III or an exempted person under Chapter IV of this Part of this Act.

6. Injunctions and restitution orders.
(1) If on the application of the Secretary of State the court is satisfied—
    (a) that there is a reasonable likelihood that a person will contravene section 3 above; or
    (b) that any person has contravened that section and that there is a reasonable likelihood that the contravention will continue or be repeated,
the court may grant an injunction restraining the contravention ...
(2) If, on the application of the Secretary of State, the court is satisfied that a person has entered into any transaction in contravention of section 3 above the court may order that person and any other person who appears to the court to have been knowingly concerned in the contravention to take such steps as the court may direct for restoring the parties to the position in which they were before the transaction was entered into.
(3) The court may, on the application of the Secretary of State, make an order under subsection (4) below ... if satisfied that a person has been carrying on investment business in contravention of section 3 above and—
    (a) that profits have accrued to that person as a result of carrying on that business; or
    (b) that one or more investors have suffered loss or been otherwise adversely affected as a result of his contravention of section 47 or 56 below or failure to act substantially in accordance with any of the rules or regulations made under Chapter V of this Part of this Act.
(4) The court may under this subsection order the person concerned to pay into court, or appoint a receiver to recover from him, such sum as appears to the court to be just having regard—
    (a) in a case within paragraph (a) of subsection (3) above, to the profits appearing to the court to have accrued;
    (b) in a case within paragraph (b) of that subsection, to the extent of the loss or other adverse effect; or
    (c) in a case within both paragraphs (a) and (b) of that subsection, to the profits and to the extent of the loss or other adverse effect.

61. Injunctions and restitution orders.
...

62. Actions for damages.
(1) Without prejudice to section 61 above, a contravention of—
    (a) any rules or regulations made under this Chapter;
    (b) any conditions imposed under section 50 above;
    (c) any requirements imposed by an order under section 58(3) above;
    (d) the duty imposed by section 59(6) above,
shall be actionable at the suit of a person who suffers loss as a result of the contravention subject to the defences and other incidents applying to actions for breach of statutory duty.

[62A. Restriction of right of action.

(1) No action in respect of a contravention to which section 62 above applies shall lie at the suit of a person other than a private investor, except in such circumstances as may be specified by regulations made by the Secretary of State.]

63. Gaming contracts.

No contract entered into by an authorised person in the course of carrying on investment business shall be void or unenforceable by reason of—

    (a) section 18 of the Gaming Act 1845, section 1 of the Gaming Act 1892 . . .

132. Insurance contracts effected in contravention of s. 2 of Insurance Companies Act 1982.

(1) Subject to subsection (3) below, a contract of insurance (not being an agreement to which section 5(1) above applies) which is entered into by a person in the course of carrying on insurance business in contravention of section 2 of the Insurance Companies Act 1982 shall be unenforceable against the other party; and that party shall be entitled to recover any money or other property paid or transferred by him under the contract, together with compensation for any loss sustained by him as a result of having parted with it.

(2) The compensation recoverable under subsection (1) above shall be such as the parties may agree or as a court may, on the application of either party, determine.

(3) A court may allow a contract to which subsection (1) above applies to be enforced or money or property paid or transferred under it to be retained if it is satisfied—

    (a) that the person carrying on insurance business reasonably believed that his entering into the contract did not constitute a contravention of section 2 of the said Act of 1982;

    (b) that it is just and equitable for the contract to be enforced or, as the case may be, for the money or property paid or transferred under it to be retained.

(4) Where a person elects not to perform a contract which by virtue of this section is unenforceable against him or by virtue of this section recovers money or property paid or transferred under a contract he shall not be entitled to any benefits under the contract and shall repay any money and return any other property received by him under the contract.

(5) Where any property transferred under a contract to which this section applies has passed to a third party the references to that property in this section shall be construed as references to its value at the time of its transfer under the contract.

(6) A contravention of section 2 of the said Act of 1982 shall not make a contract of insurance illegal or invalid to any greater extent than is provided in this section; and a contravention of that section in respect of a contract of insurance shall not affect the validity of any re-insurance contract entered into in respect of that contract.

150. Compensation for false or misleading particulars.

(1) Subject to section 151 below, the person or persons responsible for any listing particulars or supplementary listing particulars shall be liable to pay compensation to any person who has acquired any of the securities in question and suffered loss in respect of them as a result of any untrue or misleading statement in the particulars or the omission from them of any matter required to be included by section 146 or 147 above.

(2) Where listing rules require listing particulars to include information as to any particular matter on the basis that the particulars must include a statement either as to that matter or, if such is the case, that there is no such matter, the omission from the particulars of the information shall be treated for the purposes of subsection (1) above as a statement that there is no such matter.

(3) Subject to section 151 below, a person who fails to comply with section 147 above shall be liable to pay compensation to any person who has acquired any of the securities in question and suffered loss in respect of them as a result of the failure.

(4) This section does not affect any liability which any person may incur apart from this section.

(5) References in this section to the acquisition by any person of securities include references to his contracting to acquire them or an interest in them.

(6) No person shall by reason of being a promoter of a company or otherwise incur any liability for failing to disclose any information which he would not be required to disclose in listing particulars in respect of a company's securities if he were responsible for those particulars or, if he is responsible for them, which he is entitled to omit by virtue of section 148 above.

[The reference above to a person incurring liability includes a reference to any other person being entitled as against that person to be granted any civil remedy or to rescind or repudiate any agreement.]

151. Exemption from liability to pay compensation.
...

154. Advertisements etc. in connection with listing applications.

(1) Where listing particulars are or are to be published in connection with an application for the listing of any securities no advertisement or other informaiton of a kind specified by listing rules shall be issued in the United Kingdom unless the contents of the advertisement or other information have been submitted to the competent authority and that authority has either—

    (a)   approved those contents; or

    (b)   authorised the issue of the advertisement or information without such approval.

(3) Subject to subsection (4) below, a person other than an authorised person, who contravenes this section shall be guilty of an offence ...

(4) A person who in the ordinary course of a business other than investment business issues an advertisement or other information to the order of another person shall not be guilty of an offence under this section if he proves that he believed on reasonable grounds that the advertisement or information had been approved or its issue authorised by the competent authority.

(5) Where information has been approved, or its issue has been authorised, under this section neither the person issuing it nor any person responsible for, or for any part of, the listing particulars shall incur any civil liability by reason of any statement in or omission from the information if that information and the listing particulars, taken together, would not be likely to mislead persons of the kind likely to consider the acquisition of the securities in question.

[The reference to a person incurring civil liability includes a reference to any other person being entitled as against that person to be granted any civil remedy or to rescind or repudiate any agreement.]

162. Form and content of prospectus.

(1) A prospectus shall contain such information and comply with such other requirements as may be prescribed by rules made by the Secretary of State for the purposes of this section.

163. General duty of disclosure in prospectus.

(1) In addition to the information required to be included in a prospectus by virtue of rules applying to it by virtue of section 162 above a prospectus shall contain all such information as investors and their professional advisers would reasonably require, and reasonably expect to find there, for the purpose of making an informed assessment of—

(a) the assets and liabilities, financial position, profits and losses, and prospects of the issuer of the securities; and

(b) the rights attaching to those securities.

166. Compensation for false or misleading prospectus.

(1) Subject to section 167 below, the person or persons responsible for a prospectus or supplementary prospectus shall be liable to pay compensation to any person who has acquired the securities to which the prospectus relates and suffered loss in respect of them as a result of any untrue or misleading statement in the prospectus or the omission from it of any matter required to be included by section 163 or 164 above.

INSOLVENCY ACT 1986
(1986, c. 45)

238. Transactions at an undervalue (England and Wales).

(1) This section applies in the case of a company where—
  (a) an administration order is made in relation to the company, or
  (b) the company goes into liquidation;
and "the office-holder" means the administrator or the liquidator, as the case may be.

(2) Where the company has at a relevant time (defined in section 240) entered into a transaction with any person at an undervalue, the office-holder may apply to the court for an order under this section.

(3) Subject as follows, the court shall, on such an application, make such order as it thinks fit for restoring the position to what it would have been if the company had not entered into that transaction.

(4) For the purposes of this section and section 241, a company enters into a transaction with a person at an undervalue if—
  (a) the company makes a gift to that person or otherwise enters into a transaction with that person on terms that provide for the company to receive no consideration, or
  (b) the company enters into a transaction with that person for a consideration the value of which, in money or money's worth, is significantly less than the value, in money or money's worth, of the consideration provided by the company.

(5) The court shall not make an order under this section in respect of a transaction at an undervalue if it is satisfied—
  (a) that the company which entered into the transaction did so in good faith and for the purpose of carrying on its business, and
  (b) that at the time it did so there were reasonable grounds for believing that the transaction would benefit the company.

LATENT DAMAGE ACT 1986
(1986, c. 37)

1. Time limits for negligence actions in respect of latent damage not involving personal injuries.

The following sections shall be inserted in the Limitation Act 1980 (referred to below in this Act as the 1980 Act) . . .

2. Provisions consequential on section 1.

. . .

3. Accrual of cause of action to successive owners in respect of latent damage to property.

(1) Subject to the following provisions of this section, where—

(a) a cause of action ("the original cause of action") has accrued to any person in respect of any negligence to which damage to any property in which he has an interest is attributable (in whole or in part); and

(b) another person acquires an interest in that property after the date on which the original cause of action accrued but before the material facts about the damage have become known to any person who, at the time when he first has knowledge of those facts, has any interest in the property;

a fresh cause of action in respect of that negligence shall accrue to that other person on the date on which he acquires his interest in the property.

(2) A cause of action accruing to any person by virtue of subsection (1) above—

(a) shall be treated as if based on breach of a duty of care at common law owed to the person to whom it accrues; and

(b) shall be treated for the purposes of section 14A of the 1980 Act (special time limit for negligence actions where facts relevant to cause of action are not known at date of accrual) as having accrued on the date on which the original cause of action accrued.

(3) Section 28 of the 1980 Act (extension of limitation period in case of disability) shall not apply in relation to any such cause of action.

(4) Subsection (1) above shall not apply in any case where the person acquiring an interest in the damaged property is either—

(a) a person in whom the original cause of action vests by operation of law; or

(b) a person in whom the interest in that property vests by virtue of any order made by a court under section 538 of the Companies Act 1985 (vesting of company property in liquidator).

[The Companies Act 1985, s. 538 has now been replaced by the Insolvency Act 1986, s. 145.]

(5) For the purposes of subsection (1)(b) above, the material facts about the damage are such facts about the damage as would lead a reasonable person who has an interest in the damaged property at the time when those facts become known to him to consider it sufficiently serious to justify his instituting proceedings for damages against a defendant who did not dispute liability and was able to satisfy a judgment.

(6) For the purposes of this section a person's knowledge includes knowledge which he might reasonably have been expected to acquire—

(a) from facts observable or ascertainable by him; or

(b) from facts ascertained by him with the help of appropriate expert advice which it is reasonable for him to seek;

but a person shall not be taken by virtue of this subsection to have knowledge of a fact ascertainable by him only with the help of expert advice so long as he has taken all reasonable steps to obtain (and, where appropriate, to act on) that advice.

(7) This section shall bind the Crown, but as regards the Crown's liability in tort shall not bind the Crown further than the Crown is made liable in tort by the Crown Proceedings Act 1947.

4. Transitional provisions.

(1) Nothing in section 1 or 2 of this Act shall—

(a) enable any action to be brought which was barred by the 1980 Act or (as the case may be) by the Limitation Act 1939 before this Act comes into force; or

(b) affect any action commenced before this Act comes into force.

(2) Subject to subsection (1) above, sections 1 and 2 of this Act shall have effect in relation to causes of action accruing before, as well as in relation to causes of action accruing after, this Act comes into force.

(3) Section 3 of this Act shall only apply in cases where an interest in damaged property is acquired after this Act comes into force but shall so apply, subject to subsection (4) below, irrespective of whether the original cause of action accrued before or after this Act comes into force.

(4) Where—
  (a) a person acquires an interest in damaged property in circumstances to which section 3 would apart from this subsection apply; but
  (b) the original cause of action accrued more than six years before this Act comes into force;
a cause of action shall not accrue to that person by virtue of subsection (1) of that section unless section 32(1)(b) of the 1980 Act (postponement of limitation period in case of deliberate concealment of relevant facts) would apply to any action founded on the original cause of action.

BANKING ACT 1987
(1987, c. 22)

3. Restriction on acceptance of deposits.

(1) Subject to section 4 below, no person shall in the United Kingdom accept a deposit in the course of carrying on (whether there or elsewhere) a business which for the purposes of this Act is a deposit-taking business unless that person is an institution for the time being authorised by the Bank under the following provisions of this Part of this Act.

(2) Any persons who contravenes this section shall be guilty of an offence...

(3) The fact that a deposit has been taken in contravention of this section shall not affect any civil liability arising in respect of the deposit or the money deposited.

CONSUMER PROTECTION ACT 1987
(1987, c. 43)

PART I
PRODUCT LIABILITY

1. Purpose and construction of Part I.

(1) This Part shall have effect for the purpose of making such provision as is necessary in order to comply with the product liability Directive and shall be construed accordingly.

(2) In this Part, except in so far as the context otherwise requires—
"agricultural produce" means any produce of the soil, of stock-farming or of fisheries;
"dependant" and "relative" have the same meaning as they have in, respectively, the Fatal Accidents Act 1976 and the Damages (Scotland) Act 1976;
"producer", in relation to a product, means—
  (a) the person who manufactured it;
  (b) in the case of a substance which has not been manufactured but has been won or abstracted, the person who won or abstracted it;
  (c) in the case of a product which has not been manufactured, won or abstracted but essential characteristics of which are attributable to an industrial or other process having been carried out (for example, in relation to agricultural produce), the person who carried out that process;
"product" means any goods or electricity and (subject to subsection (3) below) includes a product which is comprised in another product, whether by virtue of being a component part or raw material or otherwise; and

"the product liability Directive" means the Directive of the Council of the European Communities, dated 25th July 1985, (No. 85/374/EEC) on the approximation of the laws, regulations and administrative provisions of the member States concerning liability for defective products.

(3) For the purposes of this Part a person who supplies any product in which products are comprised, whether by virtue of being component parts or raw materials or otherwise, shall not be treated by reason only of his supply of that product as supplying any of the products so comprised.

2. Liability for defective products.

(1) Subject to the following provisions of this Part, where any damage is caused wholly or partly by a defect in a product, every person to whom subsection (2) below applies shall be liable for the damage.

(2) This subsection applies to—
  (a) the producer of the product;
  (b) any person who, by putting his name on the product or using a trade mark or other distinguishing mark in relation to the product, has held himself out to be the producer of the product;
  (c) any person who has imported the product into a member State from a place outside the member States in order, in the course of any business of his, to supply it to another.

(3) Subject as aforesaid, where any damage is caused wholly or partly by a defect in a product, any person who supplied the product (whether to the person who suffered the damage, to the producer of any product in which the product in question is comprised or to any other person) shall be liable for the damage if—
  (a) the person who suffered the damage requests the supplier to identify one or more of the persons (whether still in existence or not) to whom subsection (2) above applies in relation to the product;
  (b) that request is made within a reasonable period after the damage occurs and at a time when it is not reasonably practicable for the person making the request to identify all those persons; and
  (c) the supplier fails, within a reasonable period after receiving the request, either to comply with the request or to identify the person who supplied the product to him.

(4) Neither subsection (2) nor subsection (3) above shall apply to a person in respect of any defect in any game or agricultural produce if the only supply of the game or produce by that person to another was at a time when it had not undergone an industrial process.

(5) Where two or more persons are liable by virtue of this Part for the same damage, their liability shall be joint and several.

(6) This section shall be without prejudice to any liability arising otherwise than by virtue of this Part.

3. Meaning of "defect".

(1) Subject to the following provisions of this section, there is a defect in a product for the purposes of this Part if the safety of the product is not such as persons generally are entitled to expect; and for those purposes "safety", in relation to a product, shall include safety with respect to products comprised in that product and safety in the context of risks of damage to property, as well as in the context of risks of death or personal injury.

(2) In determining for the purposes of subsection (1) above what persons generally are entitled to expect in relation to a product all the circumstances shall be taken into account, including—
  (a) the manner in which, and purposes for which, the product has been marketed, its get-up, the use of any mark in relation to the product and any instructions for, or

Consumer Protection Act 1987

warnings with respect to, doing or refraining from doing anything with or in relation to the product;

    (b) what might reasonably be expected to be done with or in relation to the product; and

    (c) the time when the product was supplied by its producer to another;

and nothing in this section shall require a defect to be inferred from the fact alone that the safety of a product which is supplied after that time is greater than the safety of the product in question.

4. Defences.

(1) In any civil proceedings by virtue of this Part against any person ("the person proceeded against") in respect of a defect in a product it shall be a defence for him to show—

    (a) that the defect is attributable to compliance with any requirement imposed by or under any enactment or with any Community obligation; or

    (b) that the person proceeded against did not at any time supply the product to another; or

    (c) that the following conditions are satisfied, that is to say—

        (i) that the only supply of the product to another by the person proceeded against was otherwise than in the course of a business of that person's; and

        (ii) that section 2(2) above does not apply to that person or applies to him by virtue only of things done otherwise than with a view to profit; or

    (d) that the defect did not exist in the product at the relevant time; or

    (e) that the state of scientific and technical knowledge at the relevant time was not such that a producer of products of the same description as the product in question might be expected to have discovered the defect if it had existed in his products while they were under his control; or

    (f) that the defect—

        (i) constituted a defect in a product ("the subsequent product") in which the product in question had been comprised; and

        (ii) was wholly attributable to the design of the subsequent product or to compliance by the producer of the product in question with instructions given by the producer of the subsequent product.

(2) In this section "the relevant time", in relation to electricity, means the time at which it was generated, being a time before it was transmitted or distributed, and in relation to any other product, means—

    (a) if the person proceeded against is a person to whom subsection (2) of section 2 above applies in relation to the product, the time when he supplied the product to another;

    (b) if that subsection does not apply to that person in relation to the product, the time when the product was last supplied by a person to whom that subsection does apply in relation to the product.

5. Damage giving rise to liability.

(1) Subject to the following provisions of this section, in this Part "damage" means death or personal injury or any loss of or damage to any property (including land).

(2) A person shall not be liable under section 2 above in respect of any defect in a product for the loss of or any damage to the product itself or for the loss of or any damage to the whole or any part of any product which has been supplied with the product in question comprised in it.

(3) A person shall not be liable under section 2 above for any loss of or damage to any property which, at the time it is lost or damaged, is not—

    (a) of a description of property ordinarily intended for private use, occupation or consumption; and

(b) intended by the person suffering the loss or damage mainly for his own private use, occupation or consumption.

(4) No damages shall be awarded to any person by virtue of this Part in respect of any loss of or damage to any property if the amount which would fall to be so awarded to that person, apart from this subsection and any liability for interest, does not exceed £275.

(5) In determining for the purposes of this Part who has suffered any loss of or damage to property and when any such loss or damage occurred, the loss or damage shall be regarded as having occurred at the earliest time at which a person with an interest in the property had knowledge of the material facts about the loss or damage.

(6) For the purposes of subsection (5) above the material facts about any loss of or damage to any property are such facts about the loss or damage as would lead a reasonable person with an interest in the property to consider the loss or damage sufficiently serious to justify his instituting proceedings for damages against a defendant who did not dispute liability and was able to satisfy a judgment.

(7) For the purposes of subsection (5) above a person's knowledge includes knowledge which he might reasonably have been expected to acquire—
    (a) from facts observable or ascertainable by him; or
    (b) from facts ascertainable by him with the help of appropriate expert advice which it is reasonable for him to seek;
but a person shall not be taken by virtue of this subsection to have knowledge of a fact ascertainable by him only with the help of expert advice unless he has failed to take all reasonable steps to obtain (and, where appropriate, to act on) that advice.

6. Application of certain enactments etc.

(1) Any damage for which a person is liable under section 2 above shall be deemed to have been caused—
    (a) for the purposes of the Fatal Accidents Act 1976, by that person's wrongful act, neglect or default; ...

(2) Where—
    (a) a person's death is caused wholly or partly by a defect in a product, or a person dies after suffering damage which has been so caused;
    (b) a request such as mentioned in paragraph (a) of subsection (3) of section 2 above is made to a supplier of the product by that person's personal representatives or, in the case of a person whose death is caused wholly or partly by the defect, by any dependant or relative of that person; and
    (c) the conditions specified in paragraphs (b) and (c) of that subsection are satisfied in relation to that request,
this Part shall have effect for the purposes of the Law Reform (Miscellaneous Provisions) Act 1934, the Fatal Accidents Act 1976 and the Damages (Scotland) Act 1976 as if liability of the supplier to that person under that subsection did not depend on that person having requested the supplier to identify certain persons or on the said conditions having been satisfied in relation to a request made by that person.

(3) Section 1 of the Congenital Disabilities (Civil Liability) Act 1976 shall have effect for the purposes of this Part as if—
    (a) a person were answerable to a child in respect of an occurrence caused wholly or partly by a defect in a product if he is or has been liable under section 2 above in respect of any effect of the occurrence on a parent of the child, or would be so liable if the occurrence caused a parent of the child to suffer damage;
    (b) the provisions of this Part relating to liability under section 2 above applied in relation to liability by virtue of paragraph (a) above under the said section 1; and
    (c) subsection (6) of the said section 1 (exclusion of liability) were omitted.

(4) Where any damage is caused partly by a defect in a product and partly by the fault of the person suffering the damage, the Law Reform (Contributory Negligence) Act 1945 and section 5 of the Fatal Accidents Act 1976 (contributory negligence) shall have effect as if the defect were the fault of every person liable by virtue of this Part for the damage caused by the defect.

(5) In subsection (4) above "fault" has the same meaning as in the said Act of 1945.

(6) Schedule 1 to this Act shall have effect for the purpose of amending the Limitation Act 1980 and the Prescription and Limitation (Scotland) Act 1973 in their application in relation to the bringing of actions by virtue of this Part.

(7) It is hereby declared that liability by virtue of this Part is to be treated as liability in tort for the purposes of any enactment conferring jurisdiction on any court with respect to any matter.

(8) Nothing in this Part shall prejudice the operation of section 12 of the Nuclear Installations Act 1965 (rights to compensation for certain breaches of duties confined to rights under that Act).

7. Prohibition on exclusions from liability.

The liability of a person by virtue of this Part to a person who has suffered damage caused wholly or partly by a defect in a product, or to a dependant or relative of such a person, shall not be limited or excluded by any contract term, by any notice or by any other provision.

8. Power to modify Part I.

(1) Her Majesty may by Order in Council make such modifications of this Part and of any other enactment (including an enactment contained in the following Parts of this Act, or in an Act passed after this Act) as appear to Her Majesty in Council to be necessary or expedient in consequence of any modification of the product liability Directive which is made at any time after the passing of this Act.

9. Application of Part I to Crown.

(1) Subject to subsection (2) below, this Part shall bind the Crown.

(2) The Crown shall not, as regards the Crown's liability by virtue of this Part, be bound by this Part further than the Crown is made liable in tort or in reparation under the Crown Proceedings Act 1947, as that Act has effect from time to time.

PART II
CONSUMER SAFETY

10. The general safety requirement.

(1) A person shall be guilty of an offence if he—
    (a) supplies any consumer goods which fail to comply with the general safety requirement;
    (b) offers or agrees to supply any such goods; or
    (c) exposes or possesses any such goods for supply.

(2) For the purposes of this section consumer goods fail to comply with the general safety requirement if they are not reasonably safe having regard to all the circumstances, including—
    (a) the manner in which, and purposes for which, the goods are being or would be marketed, the get-up of the goods, the use of any mark in relation to the goods and any instructions or warnings which are given or would be given with respect to the keeping, use or consumption of the goods;
    (b) any standards of safety published by any person either for goods of a description which applies to the goods in question or for matters relating to goods of that description; and

(c) the existence of any means by which it would have been reasonable (taking into account the cost, likelihood and extent of any improvement) for the goods to have been made safer.

(3) For the purposes of this section consumer goods shall not be regarded as failing to comply with the general safety requirement in respect of—

(a) anything which is shown to be attributable to compliance with any requirement imposed by or under any enactment or with any Community obligation;

(b) any failure to do more in relation to any matter than is required by—

(i) any safety regulations imposing requirements with respect to the matter;

(iii) any provision of any enactment or subordinate legislation imposing such requirements with respect to that matter as are designated for the purposes of this subsection by any such regulations.

(4) In any proceedings against any person for an offence under this section in respect of any goods it shall be a defence for that person to show—

(a) that he reasonably believed that the goods would not be used or consumed in the United Kingdom; or

(b) that the following conditions are satisfied, that is to say—

(i) that he supplied the goods, offered or agreed to supply them or, as the case may be, exposed or possessed them for supply in the course of carrying on a retail business; and

(ii) that, at the time he supplied the goods or offered or agreed to supply them or exposed or possessed them for supply, he neither knew nor had reasonable grounds for believing that the goods failed to comply with the general safety requirement; or

(c) that the terms on which he supplied the goods or agreed or offered to supply them or, in the case of goods which he exposed or possessed for supply, the terms on which he intended to supply them—

(i) indicated that the goods were not supplied or to be supplied as new goods; and

(ii) provided for, or contemplated, the acquisition of an interest in the goods by the persons supplied or to be supplied.

(5) For the purposes of subsection (4)(b) above goods are supplied in the course of carrying on a retail business if—

(a) whether or not they are themselves acquired for a person's private use or consumption, they are supplied in the course of carrying on a business of making a supply of consumer goods available to persons who generally acquire them for private use or consumption; and

(b) the descriptions of goods the supply of which is made available in the course of that business do not, to a significant extent, include manufactured or imported goods which have not previously been supplied in the United Kingdom.

(6) A person guilty of an offence under this section shall be liable on summary conviction to imprisonment for a term not exceeding six months or to a fine not exceeding level 5 on the standard scale or to both.

(7) In this section "consumer goods" means any goods which are ordinarily intended for private use or consumption, not being—

(a) growing crops or things comprised in land by virtue of being attached to it;

(b) water, food, feeding stuff or fertiliser;

(c) gas which is, is to be or has been supplied by a person authorised to supply it by or under [section 7A of the Gas Act 1986 (licensing of gas suppliers and gas shippers) or paragraph 5 of Schedule 2A to that Act (supply to very large customers an exception to prohibition on unlicensed activities)];

(d) aircraft (other than hang-gliders) or motor vehicles;

(e) controlled drugs or licensed medicinal products;

(f) tobacco.

Consumer Protection Act 1987

11. Safety regulations.

(1) The Secretary of State may by regulations under this section ('safety regulations") make such provision as he considers appropriate for the purposes of section 10(3) above and for the purpose of securing—

    (a) that goods to which this section applies are safe;

    (b) that goods to which this section applies which are unsafe, or would be unsafe in the hands of persons of a particular description, are not made available to persons generally or, as the case may be, to persons of that description; and

    (c) that appropriate information is, and inappropriate information is not, provided in relation to goods to which this section applies.

(2) Without prejudice to the generality of subsection (1) above, safety regulations may contain provision—

    (a) with respect to the composition or contents, design, construction, finish or packing of goods to which this section applies, with respect to standards for such goods and with respect to other matters relating to such goods;

    (b) with respects to the giving, refusal, alteration or cancellation of approvals of such goods, of descriptions of such goods or of standards for such goods;

    (c) with respect to the conditions that may be attached to any approval given under the regulations;

    (d) for requiring such fees as may be determined by or under the regulations to be paid on the giving or alteration of any approval under the regulations and on the making of an application for such an approval or alteration;

    (e) with respect to appeals against refusals, alterations and cancellations of approvals given under the regulations and against the conditions contained in such approvals;

    (f) for requiring goods to which this section applies to be approved under the regulations or to conform to the requirements of the regulations or to descriptions or standards specified in or approved by or under the regulations;

    (g) with respect to the testing or inspection of goods to which this section applies (including provision for determining the standards to be applied in carrying out any test or inspection);

    (h) with respect to the ways of dealing with goods of which some or all do not satisfy a test required by or under the regulations or a standard connected with a procedure so required;

    (i) for requiring a mark, warning or instruction or any other information relating to goods to be put on or to accompany the goods or to be used or provided in some other manner in relation to the goods, and for securing that inappropriate information is not given in relation to goods either by means of misleading marks or otherwise;

    (j) for prohibiting persons from supplying, or from offering to supply, agreeing to supply, exposing for supply or possessing for supply, goods to which this section applies and component parts and raw materials for such goods;

    (k) for requiring information to be given to any such person as may be determined by or under the regulations for the purpose of enabling that person to exercise any function conferred on him by the regulations.

(3) Without prejudice as aforesaid, safety regulations may contain provision—

    (a) for requiring persons on whom functions are conferred by or under section 27 below to have regard, in exercising their functions so far as relating to any provision of safety regulations, to matters specified in a direction issued by the Secretary of State with respect to that provision;

    (b) for securing that a person shall not be guilty of an offence under section 12 below unless it is shown that the goods in question do not conform to a particular standard;

(c) for securing that proceedings for such an offence are not brought in England and Wales except by or with the consent of the Secretary of State or the Director of Public Prosecutions;

...

(e) for enabling a magistrates' court in England and Wales or Northern Ireland to try an information or, in Northern Ireland, a complaint in respect of such an offence if the information was laid or the complaint made within twelve months from the time when the offence was committed;

...

(g) for determining the persons by whom, and the manner in which, anything required to be done by or under the regulations is to be done.

(4) Safety regulations shall not provide for any contravention of the regulations to be an offence.

(5) Where the Secretary of State proposes to make safety regulations it shall be his duty before he makes them—

(a) to consult such organisations as appear to him to be representative of interests substantially affected by the proposal;

(b) to consult such other persons as he considers appropriate; and

(c) in the case of proposed regulations relating to goods suitable for use at work, to consult the Health and Safety Commission in relation to the application of the proposed regulations to Great Britain;

but the preceding provisions of this subsection shall not apply in the case of regulations which provide for the regulations to cease to have effect at the end of a period of not more than twelve months beginning with the day on which they come into force and which contain a statement that it appears to the Secretary of State that the need to protect the public requires that the regulations should be made without delay.

(6) The power to make safety regulations shall be exercisable by statutory instrument subject to annulment in pursuance of a resolution of either House of Parliament and shall include power—

(a) to make different provision for different cases; and

(b) to make such supplemental, consequential and transitional provision as the Secretary of State considers appropriate.

(7) This section applies to any goods other than—

(a) growing crops and things comprised in land by virtue of being attached to it;

(b) water, food, feeding stuff and fertiliser;

(c) gas which is, is to be or has been supplied by a person authorised to supply it by or under [section 7A of the Gas Act 1986 (licensing of gas suppliers and gas shippers) or paragraph 5 of Schedule 2A to that Act (supply to very large customers an exception to prohibition on unlicensed activities)];

(d) controlled drugs and licensed medicinal products.

12. Offences against the safety regulations.

(1) Where safety regulations prohibit a person from supplying or offering or agreeing to supply any goods or from exposing or possessing any goods for supply, that person shall be guilty of an offence if he contravenes the prohibition.

(2) Where safety regulations require a person who makes or processes any goods in the course of carrying on a business—

(a) to carry out a particular test or use a particular procedure in connection with the making or processing of the goods with a view to ascertaining whether the goods satisfy any requirements of such regulations; or

(b) to deal or not to deal in a particular way with a quantity of the goods of which the whole or part does not satisfy such a test or does not satisfy standards connected with such a procedure, that person shall be guilty of an offence if he does not comply with the requirement.

(3) If a person contravenes a provision of safety regulations which prohibits or requires the provision, by means of a mark or otherwise, of information of a particular kind in relation to goods, he shall be guilty of an offence.

(4) Where safety regulations require any person to give information to another for the purpose of enabling that other to exercise any function, that person shall be guilty of an offence if—
   (a) he fails without reasonable cause to comply with the requirement; or
   (b) in giving the information which is required of him—
      (i) he makes any statement which he knows is false in a material particular; or
      (ii) he recklessly makes any statement which is false in a material particular.

(5) A person guilty of an offence under this section shall be liable on summary conviction to imprisonment for a term not exceeding six months or to a fine not exceeding level 5 on the standard scale or to both.

13. Prohibition notices and notices to warn.

(1) The Secretary of State may—
   (a) serve on any person a notice ("a prohibition notice") prohibiting that person, except with the consent of the Secretary of State, from supplying, or from offering to supply, agreeing to supply, exposing for supply or possessing for supply, any relevant goods which the Secretary of State considers are unsafe and which are described in the notice;
   (b) serve on any person a notice ("a notice to warn") requiring that person at his own expense to publish, in a form and manner and on occasions specified in the notice, a warning about any relevant goods which the Secretary of State considers are unsafe, which that person supplies or has supplied and which are described in the notice.

(2) Schedule 2 to this Act shall have effect with respect to prohibition notices and notices to warn; and the Secretary of State may by regulations make provision specifying the manner in which information is to be given to any person under that Schedule.

(3) A consent given by the Secretary of State for the purposes of a prohibition notice may impose such conditions on the doing of anything for which the consent is required as the Secretary of State considers appropriate.

(4) A person who contravenes a prohibition notice or a notice to warn shall be guilty of an offence and liable on summary conviction to imprisonment for a term not exceeding six months or to a fine not exceeding level 5 on the standard scale or to both.

(5) The power to make regulations under subsection (2) above shall be exercisable by statutory instrument subject to annulment in pursuance of a resolution of either House of Parliament and shall include power—
   (a) to make different provision for different cases; and
   (b) to make such supplemental, consequential and transitional provision as the Secretary of State considers appropriate.

(6) In this section "relevant goods" means—
   (a) in relation to a prohibition notice, any goods to which section 11 above applies; and
   (b) in relation to a notice to warn, any goods to which that section applies or any growing crops or things comprised in land by virtue of being attached to it.

14. Suspension notices.

(1) Where an enforcement authority has reasonable grounds for suspecting that any safety provision has been contravened in relation to any goods, the authority may serve a notice ("a suspension notice") prohibiting the person on whom it is served, for such period ending not more than six months after the date of the notice as is specified therein, from doing any of the following things without the consent of the authority, that is to say, supplying the goods, offering to supply them, agreeing to supply them or exposing them for supply.

(2) A suspension notice served by an enforcement authority in respect of any goods shall—

(a) describe the goods in a manner sufficient to identify them;

(b) set out the grounds on which the authority suspects that a safety provision has been contravened in relation to the goods; and

(c) state that, and the manner in which, the person on whom the notice is served may appeal against the notice under section 15 below.

(3) A suspension notice served by an enforcement authority for the purpose of prohibiting a person for any period from doing the things mentioned in subsection (1) above in relation to any goods may also require that person to keep the authority informed of the whereabouts throughout that period of any of those goods in which he has an interest.

(4) Where a suspension notice has been served on any person in respect of any goods, no further such notice shall be served on that person in respect of the same goods unless—

(a) proceedings against that person for an offence in respect of a contravention in relation to the goods of a safety provision (not being an offence under this section); or

(b) proceedings for the forfeiture of the goods under section 16 or 17 below,

are pending at the end of the period specified in the first-mentioned notice.

(5) A consent given by an enforcement authority for the purposes of subsection (1) above may impose such conditions on the doing of anything for which the consent is required as the authority considers appropriate.

(6) Any person who contravenes a suspension notice shall be guilty of an offence and liable on summary conviction to imprisonment for a term not exceeding six months or to a fine not exceeding level 5 on the standard scale or to both.

(7) Where an enforcement authority serves a suspension notice in respect of any goods, the authority shall be liable to pay compensation to any person having an interest in the goods in respect of any loss or damage caused by reason of the service of the notice if—

(a) there has been no contravention in relation to the goods of any safety provision; and

(b) the exercise of the power is not attributable to any neglect or default by that person.

(8) Any disputed question as to the right to or the amount of any compensation payable under this section shall be determined by arbitration . . .

15. Appeals against suspension notices.

(1) Any person having an interest in any goods in respect of which a suspension notice is for the time being in force may apply for an order setting aside the notice.

(2) An application under this section may be made—

(a) to any magistrates' court in which proceedings have been brought in England and Wales or Northern Ireland—

(i) for an offence in respect of a contravention in relation to the goods of any safety provision; or

(ii) for the forfeiture of the goods under section 16 below;

(b) where no such proceedings have been so brought, by way of complaint to a magistrates' court; . . .

(3) On an application under this section to a magistrates' court in England and Wales or Northern Ireland the court shall make an order setting aside the suspension notice only if the court is satisfied that there has been no contravention in relation to the goods of any safety provision.

(4) On an application under this section to the sheriff he shall make an order setting aside the suspension notice only if he is satisfied that at the date of making the order—

(a) proceedings for an offence in respect of a contravention in relation to the goods of any safety provision; or

(b) proceedings for the forfeiture of the goods under section 17 below,

have not been brought or, having been brought, have been concluded.

(5) Any person aggrieved by an order made under this section by a magistrates' court in England and Wales or Northern Ireland, or by a decision of such a court not to make such an order, may appeal against that order or decision—

    (a) in England and Wales, to the Crown Court;

    (b) in Northern Ireland, to the county court;

and an order so made may contain such provision as appears to the court to be appropriate for delaying the coming into force of the order pending the making and determination of any appeal (including any application under section 111 of the Magistrates' Courts Act 1980 or Article 146 of the Magistrates' Courts (Northern Ireland) Order 1981 (statement of case)).

16. Forfeiture: England and Wales and Northern Ireland.

(1) An enforcement authority in England and Wales or Northern Ireland may apply under this section for an order for the forfeiture of any goods on the grounds that there has been a contravention in relation to the goods of a safety provision.

(2) An application under this section may be made—

    (a) where proceedings have been brought in a magistrates' court for an offence in respect of a contravention in relation to some or all of the goods of any safety provision, to that court;

    (b) where an application with respect to some or all of the goods has been made to a magistrates' court under section 15 above or section 33 below, to that court; and

    (c) where no application for the forfeiture of the goods has been made under paragraph (a) or (b) above, by way of complaint to a magistrates' court.

(3) On an application under this section the court shall make an order for the forfeiture of any goods only if it is satisfied that there has been a contravention in relation to the goods of a safety provision.

(4) For the avoidance of doubt it is declared that a court may infer for the purposes of this section that there has been a contravention in relation to any goods of a safety provision if it is satisfied that any such provision has been contravened in relation to goods which are representative of those goods (whether by reason of being of the same design or part of the same consignment or batch or otherwise).

(5) Any person aggrieved by an order made under this section by a magistrates' court, or by a decision of such a court not to make such an order, may appeal against that order or decision—

    (a) in England and Wales, to the Crown Court;

    (b) in Northern Ireland, to the county court;

and an order so made may contain such provision as appears to the court to be appropriate for delaying the coming into force of the order pending the making and determination of any appeal (including any application under section 111 of the Magistrates' Courts Act 1980 or Article 146 of the Magistrates' Courts (Northern Ireland) Order 1981 (statement of case)).

(6) Subject to subsection (7) below, where any goods are forfeited under this section they shall be destroyed in accordance with such directions as the court may give.

(7) On making an order under this section a magistrates' court may, if it considers it appropriate to do so, direct that the goods to which the order relates shall (instead of being destroyed) be released, to such person as the court may specify, on condition that that person—

    (a) does not supply those goods to any person otherwise than as mentioned in section 46(7)(a) or (b) below; and

(b) complies with any order to pay costs or expenses (including any order under section 35 below) which has been made against that person in the proceedings for the order for forfeiture.

18. Power to obtain information.

(1) If the Secretary of State considers that, for the purpose of deciding whether—

    (a) to make, vary or revoke any safety regulations; or

    (b) to serve, vary or revoke a prohibition notice; or

    (c) to serve or revoke a notice to warn,

he requires information which another person is likely to be able to furnish, the Secretary of State may serve on the other person a notice under this section.

(2) A notice served on any person under this section may require that person—

    (a) to furnish to the Secretary of State, within a period specified in the notice, such information as is so specified;

    (b) to produce such records as are specified in the notice at a time and place so specified and to permit a person appointed by the Secretary of State for the purpose to take copies of the records at that time and place.

(3) A person shall be guilty of an offence if he—

    (a) fails, without reasonable cause, to comply with a notice served on him under this section; or

    (b) in purporting to comply with a requirement which by virtue of paragraph (a) of subsection (2) above is contained in such a notice—

        (i) furnishes information which he knows is false in a material particular; or

        (ii) recklessly furnishes information which is false in a material particular.

(4) A person guilty of an offence under subsection (3) above shall—

    (a) in the case of an offence under paragraph (a) of that subsection, be liable on summary conviction to a fine not exceeding level 5 on the standard scale; and

    (b) in the case of an offence under paragraph (b) of that subsection be liable—

        (i) on conviction on indictment, to a fine;

        (ii) on summary conviction, to a fine not exceeding the statutory maximum.

19. Interpretation of Part II.

(1) In this Part—

"controlled drug" means a controlled drug within the meaning of the Misuse of Drugs Act 1971;

"feeding stuff" and "fertiliser" have the same meanings as in Part IV of the Agriculture Act 1970;

"food" does not include anything containing tobacco but, subject to that, has the same meaning as in the [Food Safety Act 1990] or, in relation to Northern Ireland, the same meaning as in the Food and Drugs Act (Northern Ireland) 1958;

"licensed medicinal product" means—

    (a) any medicinal product within the meaning of the Medicines Act 1968 in respect of which a product licence within the meaning of that Act is for the time being in force;

or

    (b) any other article or substance in respect of which any such licence is for the time being in force in pursuance of an order under section 104 or 105 of that Act (application of Act to other articles and substances);

"safe", in relation to any goods, means such that there is no risk, or no risk apart from one reduced to a minimum, that any of the following will (whether immediately or after a definite or indefinite period) cause the death of, or any personal injury to, any person whatsoever, that is to say—

    (a) the goods;

(b) the keeping, use or consumption of the goods;
(c) the assembly of any of the goods which are, or are to be, supplied unassembled;
(d) any emission or leakage from the goods or, as a result of the keeping, use or consumption of the goods, from anything else; or
(e) reliance on the accuracy of any measurement, calculation or other reading made by or by means of the goods,

and "safer" and "unsafe" shall be construed accordingly;

"tobacco" includes any tobacco produce within the meaning of the Tobacco Products Duty Act 1979 and any article or substance containing tobacco and intended for oral or nasal use.

(2) In the definition of "safe" in subsection (1) above, references to the keeping, use or consumption of any goods are references to—
(a) the keeping, use or consumption of the goods by the persons by whom, and in all or any of the ways or circumstances in which, they might reasonably be expected to be kept, used or consumed; and
(b) the keeping, use or consumption of the goods either alone or in conjunction with other goods in conjunction with which they might reasonably be expected to be kept, used or consumed.

PART III
MISLEADING PRICE INDICATIONS

20. Offence of giving misleading indication.

(1) Subject to the following provisions of this Part, a person shall be guilty of an offence if, in the course of any business of his, he gives (by any means whatever) to any consumers an indication which is misleading as to the price at which any goods, services, accommodation or facilities are available (whether generally or from particular persons).

(2) Subject as aforesaid, a person shall be guilty of an offence if—
(a) in the course of any business of his, he has given an indication to any consumers which, after it was given, has become misleading as mentioned in subsection (1) above; and
(b) some or all of those consumers might reasonably be expected to rely on the indication at a time after it has become misleading; and
(c) he fails to take all such steps as are reasonable to prevent those consumers from relying on the indication.

(3) For the purposes of this section it shall be immaterial—
(a) whether the person who gives or gave the indication is or was acting on his own behalf or on behalf of another;
(b) whether or not that person is the person, or included among the persons, from whom the goods, services, accommodation or facilities are available; and
(c) whether the indication is or has become misleading in relation to all the consumers to whom it is or was given or only in relation to some of them.

(4) A person guilty of an offence under subsection (1) or (2) above shall be liable—
(a) on conviction on indictment, to a fine;
(b) on summary conviction, to a fine not exceeding the statutory maximum.

(5) No prosecution for an offence under subsection (1) or (2) above shall be brought after whichever is the earlier of the following, that is to say—
(a) the end of the period of three years beginning with the day on which the offence was committed; and
(b) the end of the period of one year beginning with the day on which the person bringing the prosecution discovered that the offence had been committed.

(6) In this Part—

"consumer"—
  (a) in relation to any goods, means any person who might wish to be supplied with the goods for his own private use or consumption;
  (b) in relation to any services or facilities, means any person who might wish to be provided with the services or facilities otherwise than for the purposes of any business of his; and
  (c) in relation to any accommodation, means any person who might wish to occupy the accommodation otherwise than for the purposes of any business of his;
"price", in relation to any goods, services, accommodation or facilities, means—
  (a) the aggregate of the sums required to be paid by a consumer for or otherwise in respect of the supply of the goods or the provision of the services, accommodation or facilities;
  (b) except in section 21 below, any method which will be or has been applied for the purpose of determining that aggregate.

21. Meaning of "misleading".

(1) For the purposes of section 20 above an indication given to any consumers is misleading as to a price if what is conveyed by the indication, or what those consumers might reasonably be expected to infer from the indication or any omission from it, includes any of the following, that is to say—
  (a) that the price is less than in fact it is;
  (b) that the applicability of the price does not depend on facts or circumstances on which its applicability does in fact depend;
  (c) that the price covers matters in respect of which an additional charge is in fact made;
  (d) that a person who in fact has no such expectation—
    (i)   expects the price to be increased or reduced (whether or not at a particular time or by a particular amount); or
    (ii) expects the price, or the price as increased or reduced, to be maintained (whether or not for a particular period); or
  (e) that the facts or circumstances by reference to which the consumers might reasonably be expected to judge the validity of any relevant comparison made or implied by the indication are not what in fact they are.

(2) For the purposes of section 20 above, an indication given to any consumers is misleading as to a method of determining a price if what is conveyed by the indication, or what those consumers might reasonably be expected to infer from the indication or any omission from it, includes any of the following, that is to say—
  (a) that the method is not what in fact it is;
  (b) that the applicability of the method does not depend on facts or circumstances on which its applicability does in fact depend;
  (c) that the method takes into account matters in respect of which an additional charge will in fact be made;
  (d) that a person who in fact has no such expectation—
    (i)   expects the method to be altered (whether or not at a particular time or in a particular respect); or
    (ii) expects the method, or that method as altered, to remain unaltered (whether or not for a particular period); or
  (e) that the facts or circumstances by reference to which the consumers might reasonably be expected to judge the validity of any relevant comparison made or implied by the indication are not what in fact they are.

(3) For the purposes of subsections (1)(e) and (2)(e) above a comparison is a relevant comparison in relation to a price or method of determining a price if it is made

between that price or that method, or any price which has been or may be determined by that method, and—

(a) any price or value which is stated or implied to be, to have been or to be likely to be attributed or attributable to the goods, services, accommodation or facilities in question or to any other goods, services, accommodation or facilities; or

(b) any method, or other method, which is stated or implied to be, to have been or to be likely to be applied or applicable for the determination of the price or value of the goods, services, accommodation or facilities in question or of the price or value of any other goods, services, accommodation or facilities.

22. Application to provision of services and facilities.

(1) Subject to the following provisions of this section, references in this Part to services or facilities are references to any services or facilities whatever including, in particular—

(a) the provision of credit or of banking or insurance services and the provision of facilities incidental to the provision of such services;

(b) the purchase or sale of foreign currency;

(c) the supply of electricity;

(d) the provision of a place, other than on a highway, for the parking of a motor vehicle;

(e) the making or arrangements for a person to put or keep a caravan on any land other than arrangements by virtue of which that person may occupy the caravan as his only or main residence.

(2) References in this Part to services shall not include references to services provided to an employer under a contract of employment.

(3) References in this Part to services or facilities shall not include references to services or facilities which are provided by an authorised person or appointed representative in the course of the carrying on of an investment business.

(4) In relation to a service consisting in the purchase or sale of foreign currency, references in this Part to the method by which the price of the service is determined shall include references to the rate of exchange.

(5) In this section—

"appointed representative", "authorised person" and "investment business" have the same meanings as in the Financial Services Act 1986;

"caravan" has the same meaning as in the Caravan Sites and Control of Development Act 1960;

"contract of employment" and "employer" have the same meanings as in [the Employment Rights Act 1996];

"credit" has the same meaning as in the Consumer Credit Act 1974.

23. Application to provision of accommodation etc.

(1) Subject to subsection (2) below, references in this Part to accommodation or facilities being available shall not include references to accommodation or facilities being available to be provided by means of the creation or disposal of an interest in land except where—

(a) the person who is to create or dispose of the interest will do so in the course of any business of his; and

(b) the interest to be created or disposed of is a relevant interest in a new dwelling and is to be created or disposed of for the purpose of enabling that dwelling to be occupied as a residence, or one of the residences, of the person acquiring the interest.

(2) Subsection (1) above shall not prevent the application of any provision of this Part in relation to—

(a) the supply of any goods as part of the same transaction as any creation or disposal of an interest in land; or

(b) the provision of any services or facilities for the purposes of, or in connection with, any transaction for the creation or disposal of such an interest.

(3) In this section—

"new dwelling" means any building or part of a building in Great Britain which—

(a) has been constructed or adapted to be occupied as a residence; and

(b) has not previously been so occupied or has been so occupied only with other premises or as more than one residence,

and includes any yard, garden, out-houses or appurtenances which belong to that building or part or are to be enjoyed with it;

"relevant interest"—

(a) in relation to a new dwelling in England and Wales, means the freehold estate in the dwelling or a leasehold interest in the dwelling for a term of years absolute of more than twenty-one years, not being a term of which twenty-one years or less remains unexpired;

...

24. Defences.

(1) In any proceedings against a person for an offence under subsection (1) or (2) of section 2 above in respect of any indication it shall be a defence for that person to show that his acts or omissions were authorised for the purposes of this subsection by regulations made under section 26 below.

(2) In proceedings against a person for an offence under subsection (1) or (2) of section 20 above in respect of an indication published in a book, newspaper, magazine [or film or in a programme included in a programme service (within the meaning of the Broadcasting Act 1990),] it shall be a defence for that person to show that the indication was not contained in an advertisement.

(3) In proceedings against a person for an offence under subsection (1) or (2) of section 20 above in respect of an indication published in an advertisement it shall be a defence for that person to show that—

(a) he is a person who carries on a business of publishing or arranging for the publication of advertisements;

(b) he received the advertisement for publication in the ordinary course of that business; and

(c) at the time of publication he did not know and had no grounds for suspecting that the publication would involve the commission of the offence.

(4) In any proceedings against a person for an offence under subsection (1) of section 20 above in respect of any indication, it shall be a defence for that person to show that—

(a) the indication did not relate to the availability from him of any goods, services, accommodation or facilities;

(b) a price had been recommended to every person from whom the goods, services, accommodation or facilities were indicated as being available;

(c) the indication related to that price and was misleading as to that price only by reason of a failure by any person to follow the recommendation; and

(d) it was reasonable for the person who gave the indication to assume that the recommendation was for the most part being followed.

(5) The provisions of this section are without prejudice to the provisions of section 39 below.

(6) In this section—

"advertisement" includes a catalogue, a circular and a price list; ...

25. Code of practice.

(1) The Secretary of State may, after consulting the Director General of Fair Trading and such other persons as the Secretary of State considers it appropriate to

consult, by order approve any code of practice issued (whether by the Secretary of State or another person) for the purpose of—
 (a) giving practical guidance with respect to any of the requirements of section 20 above; and
 (b) Promoting what appear to the Secretary of State to be desirable practices as to the circumstances and manner in which any person gives an indication as to the price at which any goods, services, accommodation or facilities are available or indicates any other matter in respect of which any such indication may be misleading.
 (2) A contravention of a code of practice approved under this section shall not of itself give rise to any criminal or civil liability, but in any proceedings against any person for an offence under section 20(1) or (2) above—
 (a) any contravention by that person of such a code may be relied on in relation to any matter for the purpose of establishing that that person committed the offence or of negativing any defence;
 (b) compliance by that person with such a code may be relied on in relation to any matter for the purpose of showing that the commission of the offence by that person has not been established or that that person has a defence.
 (3) Where the Secretary of State approves a code of practice under this section he may, after such consultation as is mentioned in subsection (1) above, at any time by order—
 (a) approve any modification of the code; or
 (b) withdraw his approval;
and references in subsection (2) above to a code of practice approved under this section shall be construed accordingly.
 (4) The power to make an order under this section shall be exercisable by statutory instrument subject to annulment in pursuance of a resolution of either House of Parliament.

26. Power to make regulations.
 (1) The Secretary of State may, after consulting the Director General of Fair Trading and such other persons as the Secretary of State considers it appropriate to consult, by regulations make provision—
 (a) for the purpose of regulating the circumstances and manner in which any person—
  (i) gives any indication as to the price at which any goods, services, accommodation or facilities will be or are available or have been supplied or provided; or
  (ii) indicates any other matter in respect of which any such indication may be misleading;
 (b) for the purpose of facilitating the enforcement of the provisions of section 20 above or of any regulations made under this section.
 (2) The Secretary of State shall not make regulations by virtue of subsection (1)(a) above except in relation to—
 (a) indications given by persons in the course of business; and
 (b) such indications given otherwise than in the course of business as—
  (i) are given by or on behalf of persons by whom accommodation is provided to others by means of leases or licences; and
  (ii) relate to goods, services or facilities supplied or provided to those others in connection with the provision of the accommodation.
 (3) Without prejudice to the generality of subsection (1) above, regulations under this section may—
 (a) prohibit an indication as to a price from referring to such matters as may be prescribed by the regulations;

(b) require an indication as to a price or other matter to be accompanied or supplemented by such explanation or such additional information as may be prescribed by the regulations;

(c) require information or explanations with respect to a price or other matter to be given to an officer of an enforcement authority and to authorise such an officer to require such information or explanations to be given;

(d) require any information or explanation provided for the purposes of any regulations made by virtue of paragraph (b) or (c) above to be accurate;

(e) prohibit the inclusion in indications as to a price or other matter of statements that the indications are not to be relied upon;

(f) provide that expressions used in any indication as to a price or other matter shall be construed in a particular way for the purposes of this Part;

(g) provide that a contravention of any provision of the regulations shall constitute a criminal offence punishable—

(i) on conviction on indictment, by a fine;

(ii) on summary conviction, by a fine not exceeding the statutory maximum;

(h) apply any provision of this Act which relates to a criminal offence to an offence created by virtue of paragraph (g) above.

(4) The power to make regulations under this section shall be exercisable by statutory instrument...

PART IV
ENFORCEMENT OF PARTS II AND III

27. Enforcement.

(1) Subject to the following provisions of this section—

(a) it shall be the duty of every weights and measures authority in Great Britain to enforce within their area the safety provisions and the provisions made by or under Part III of this Act; and

(b) it shall be the duty of every district council in Northern Ireland to enforce within their area the safety provisions.

(2) The Secretary of State may by regulations—

(a) wholly or partly transfer any duty imposed by subsection (1) above on a weights and measures authority or a district council in Northern Ireland to such other person who has agreed to the transfer as is specified in the regulations;

(b) relieve such an authority or council of any such duty so far as it is exercisable in relation to such goods as may be described in the regulations.

(3) The power to make regulations under subsection (2) above shall be exercisable by statutory instrument...

28. Test purchases.

(1) An enforcement authority shall have power, for the purpose of ascertaining whether any safety provision or any provision made by or under Part III of this Act has been contravened in relation to any goods, services, accommodation or facilities—

(a) to make, or to authorise an officer of the authority to make, any purchase of any goods; or

(b) to secure, or to authorise an officer of the authority to secure, the provision of any services, accommodation or facilities.

(2) Where—

(a) any goods purchased under this section by or on behalf of an enforcement authority are submitted to a test; and

(b) the test leads to—

(i) the bringing of proceedings for an offence in respect of a contravention in relation to the goods of any safety provision or of any provision made by or under Part III of this Act or for the forfeiture of the goods under section 16 or 17 above; or

(ii) the serving of a suspension notice in respect of any goods; and

(c) the authority is requested to do so and it is practicable for the authority to comply with the request,

the authority shall allow the person from whom the goods were purchased or any person who is a party to the proceedings or has an interest in any goods to which the notice relates to have the goods tested.

(3) The Secretary of State may by regulations provide that any test of goods purchased under this section by or on behalf of an enforcement authority shall—

(a) be carried out at the expense of the authority in a manner and by a person prescribed by or determined under the regulations; or

(b) be carried out either as mentioned in paragraph (a) above or by the authority in a manner prescribed by the regulations.

(4) The power to make regulations under subsection (3) above shall be exercisable by statutory instrument...

(5) Nothing in this section shall authorise the acquisition by or on behalf of an enforcement authority of any interest in land.

29. Powers of search etc.

(1) Subject to the following provisions of this Part, a duly authorised officer of an enforcement authority may at any reasonable hour and on production, if required, of his credentials exercise any of the powers conferred by the following provisions of this section.

(2) The officer may, for the purpose of ascertaining whether there has been any contravention of any safety provision or of any provision made by or under Part III of this Act, inspect any goods and enter any premises other than premises occupied only as a person's residence.

(3) The officer may, for the purpose of ascertaining whether there has been any contravention of any safety provision, examine any procedure (including any arrangements for carrying out a test) connected with the production of any goods.

(4) If the officer has reasonable grounds for suspecting that any goods are manufactured or imported goods which have not been supplied in the United Kingdom since they were manufactured or imported he may—

(a) for the purpose of ascertaining whether there has been any contravention of any safety provision in relation to the goods, require any person carrying on a business, or employed in connection with the business, to produce any records relating to the business;

(b) for the purpose of ascertaining (by testing or otherwise) whether there has been any such contravention, seize and detain the goods;

(c) take copies of, or of any entry in, any records produced by virtue of paragraph (a) above.

(5) If the officer has reasonable grounds for suspecting that there has been a contravention in relation to any goods of any safety provision or of any provision made by or under Part III of this Act, he may—

(a) for the purpose of ascertaining whether there has been any such contravention, require any person carrying on a business, or employed in connection with a business, to produce any records relating to the business;

(b) for the purpose of ascertaining (by testing or otherwise) whether there has been any such contravention, seize and detain the goods;

(c) take copies of, or of any entry in, any records produced by virtue of paragraph (a) above.

(6) The officer may seize and detain—

(a) any goods or records which he has reasonable grounds for believing may be required as evidence in proceedings for an offence in respect of a contravention of any safety provision or of any provision made by or under Part III of this Act.

(b) any goods which he has reasonable grounds for suspecting may be liable to be forfeited under section 16 or 17 above.

(7) If and to the extent that it is reasonably necessary to do so to prevent a contravention of any safety provision or of any provision made by or under Part III of this Act, the officer may, for the purpose of exercising his power under subsection (4), (5) or (6) above to seize any goods or records—

(a) require any person having authority to do so to open any container or to open any vending machine; and

(b) himself open or break open any such container or machine where a requirement made under paragraph (a) above in relation to the container or machine has not been complied with.

30. Provisions supplemental to s. 29.

(1) An officer seizing any goods or records under section 29 above shall inform the following persons that the goods or records have been so seized, that is to say—

(a) the person from whom they are seized; and

(b) in the case of imported goods seized on any premises under the control of the Commissioners of Customs and Excise, the importer of those goods (within the meaning of the Customs and Excise Management Act 1979).

(2) If a justice of the peace—

(a) is satisfied by any written information on oath that there are reasonable grounds for believing either—

(i) that any goods or records which any officer has power to inspect under section 29 above are on any premises and that their inspection is likely to disclose evidence that there has been a contravention of any safety provision or of any provision made by or under part III of this Act; or

(ii) that such a contravention has taken place, is taking place or is about to take place on any premises; and

(b) is also satisfied by any such information either—

(i) that admission to the premises has been or is likely to be refused and that notice of intention to apply for a warrant under this subsection has been given to the occupier; or

(ii) that an application for admission, or the giving of such a notice, would defeat the object of the entry or that the premises are unoccupied or that the occupier is temporarily absent and it might defeat the object of the entry to await his return,

the justice may by warrant under his hand, which shall continue in force for a period of one month, authorise any officer of an enforcement authority to enter the premises, if need be by force.

(3) An officer entering any premises by virtue of section 29 above or a warrant under subsection (2) above may take with him such other persons and such equipment as may appear to him necessary.

(4) On leaving any premises which a person is authorised to enter by a warrant under subsection (2) above, that person shall, if the premises are unoccupied or the occupier is temporarily absent, leave the premises as effectively secured against trespassers as he found them.

(5) If any person who is not an officer of an enforcement authority purports to act as such under section 29 above or this section he shall be guilty of an offence and liable on summary conviction to a fine not exceeding level 5 on the standard scale.

(6) Where any goods seized by an officer under section 29 above are submitted to a test, the officer shall inform the persons mentioned in subsection (1) above of the result of the test and, if—

(a) proceedings are brought for an offence in respect of a contravention in relation to the goods of any safety provision or of any provision made by or under Part III of this

Consumer Protection Act 1987   187

Act or for the forfeiture of the goods under section 16 or 17 above, or a suspension notice is served in respect of any goods; and

(b) the officer is requested to do so and it is practicable to comply with the request, the officer shall allow any person who is a party to the proceedings or, as the case may be, has an interest in the goods to which the notice relates to have the goods tested.

(7) The Secretary of State may by regulations provide that any test of goods seized under section 29 above by an officer of an enforcement authority shall—

(a) be carried out at the expense of the authority in a manner and by a person prescribed by or determined under the regulations; or

(b) be carried out either as mentioned in paragraph (a) above or by the authority in a manner prescribed by the regulations.

(8) The power to make regulations under subsection (7) above shall be exercisable by statutory instrument...

31. Power of customs officer to detain goods.

(1) A customs officer may, for the purpose of facilitating the exercise by an enforcement authority or officer of such an authority of any functions conferred on the authority or officer by or under Part II of this Act, or by or under this Part in its application for the purposes of the safety provisions, seize any imported goods and detain them for not more than two working days.

(2) Anything seized and detained under this section shall be dealt with during the period of its detention in such manner as the Commissioners of Customs and Excise may direct.

32. Obstruction of authorised officer.

(1) Any person who—

(a) intentionally obstructs any officer of an enforcement authority who is acting in pursuance of any provision of this Part or any customs officer who is so acting; or

(b) intentionally fails to comply with any requirement made of him by any officer of any enforcement authority under any provision of this Part; or

(c) without reasonable cause fails to give any officer of an enforcement authority who is so acting any other assistance or information which the officer may reasonably require of him for the purposes of the exercise of the officer's functions under any provision of this Part,

shall be guilty of an offence and liable on summary conviction to a fine not exceeding level 5 on the standard scale.

(2) A person shall be guilty of an offence if, in giving any information which is required of him by virtue of subsection (1)(c) above—

(a) he makes any statement which he knows is false in a material particular; or

(b) he recklessly makes a statement which is false in a material particular.

(3) A person guilty of an offence under subsection (2) above shall be liable—

(a) on conviction on indictment, to a fine;

(b) on summary conviction, to a fine not exceeding the statutory maximum.

33. Appeals against detention of goods.

(1) Any person having an interest in any goods which are for the time being detained under any provision of this Part by an enforcement authority or by an officer of such an authority may apply for an order requiring the goods to be released to him or to another person.

(2) An application under this section may be made—

(a) to any magistrates' court in which proceedings have been brought in England and Wales or Northern Ireland—

(i) for an offence in respect of a contravention in relation to the goods of any safety provision or of any provision made by or under Part III of this Act; or

(ii) for the forfeiture of the goods under section 16 above;

(b) where no such proceedings have been so brought, by way of complaint to a magistrates' court ...

(3) On an application under this section to a magistrates' court ..., an order requiring goods to be released shall be made only if the court ... is satisfied—

(a) that proceedings—

(i) for an offence in respect of a contravention in relation to the goods of any safety provision or of any provision made by or under Part III of this Act; or

(ii) for the forfeiture of the goods under section 16 or 17 above,

have not been brought or, having been brought, have been concluded without the goods being forfeited; and

(b) where no such proceedings have been brought, that more than six months have elapsed since the goods were seized.

(4) Any person aggrieved by an order made under this section by a magistrates' court in England and Wales or Northern Ireland, or by a decision of such a court not to make such an order, may appeal against that order or decision—

(a) in England and Wales, to the Crown Court;

(b) in Northern Ireland, to the county court;

and an order so made may contain such provision as appears to the court to be appropriate for delaying the coming into force of the order pending the making and determination of any appeal (including any application under section 111 of the Magistrates' Courts Act 1980 or Article 146 of the Magistrates' Courts (Northern Ireland) Order 1981 (statement of case)).

34. Compensation for seizure and detention.

(1) Where an officer of an enforcement authority exercises any power under section 29 above to seize and detain goods, the enforcement authority shall be liable to pay compensation to any person having an interest in the goods in respect of any loss or damage caused by reason of the exercise of the power if—

(a) there has been no contravention in relation to the goods of any safety provision or of any provision made by or under Part III of this Act; and

(b) the exercise of the power is not attributable to any neglect or default by that person.

(2) Any disputed question as to the right to or the amount of any compensation payable under this section shall be determined by arbitration ...

35. Recovery of expenses of enforcement.

(1) This section shall apply where a court—

(a) convicts a person of an offence in respect of a contravention in relation to any goods of any safety provision or of any provision made by or under Part III of this Act; or

(b) makes an order under section 16 or 17 above for the forfeiture of any goods.

(2) The court may (in addition to any other order it may make as to costs or expenses) order the person convicted or, as the case may be, any person having an interest in the goods to reimburse an enforcement authority for an expenditure which has been or may be incurred by that authority—

(a) in connection with any seizure or detention of the goods by or on behalf of the authority; or

(b) in connection with any compliance by the authority with directions given by the court for the purposes of any order for the forfeiture of the goods.

PART V
MISCELLANEOUS AND SUPPLEMENTAL

37. Power of Commissioners of Customs and Excise to disclose information.

(1) If they think it appropriate to do so for the purpose of facilitating the exercise by any person to whom subsection (2) below applies of any functions conferred on that

Consumer Protection Act 1987

person by or under Part II of this Act, or by or under Part IV of this Act in its application for the purposes of the safety provisions, the Commissioners of Customs and Excise may authorise the disclosure to that person of any information obtained for the purposes of the exercise by the Commissioners of their functions in relation to imported goods.

(2) This subsection applies to an enforcement authority and to any officer of an enforcement authority.

(3) A disclosure of information made to any person under subsection (1) above shall be made in such manner as may be directed by the Commissioners of Customs and Excise and may be made through such person acting on behalf of that person as may be so directed.

(4) Information may be disclosed to a person under subsection (1) above whether or not the disclosure of the information has been requested by or on behalf of that person.

38. Restrictions on disclosure of information.

(1) Subject to the following provisions of this section, a person shall be guilty of an offence if he discloses any information—

    (a) which was obtained by him in consequence of its being given to any person in compliance with any requirement imposed by safety regulations or regulations under section 26 above;

    (b) which consists in a secret manufacturing process or a trade secret and was obtained by him in consequence of the inclusion of the information—

        (i) in written or oral representations made for the purposes of Part I or II of Schedule 2 to this Act; or

        (ii) in a statement of a witness in connection with any such oral representations;

    (c) which was obtained by him in consequence of the exercise by the Secretary of State of the power conferred by section 18 above;

    (d) which was obtained by him in consequence of the exercise by any person of any power conferred by Part IV of this Act; or

    (e) which was disclosed to or through him under section 37 above.

(2) Subsection (1) above shall not apply to a disclosure of information if the information is publicised information or the disclosure is made—

    (a) for the purpose of facilitating the exercise of a relevant person's functions under this Act or any enactment or subordinate legislation mentioned in subsection (3) below;

    (b) for the purposes of compliance with a Community obligation; or

    (c) in connection with the investigation of any criminal offence or for the purposes of any civil or criminal proceedings.

(3) The enactments and subordinate legislation referred to in subsection (2)(a) above are—

    (a) the Trade Descriptions Act 1968;

    (b) Parts II and III and section 125 of the Fair Trading Act 1973;

    (c) the relevant statutory provisions within the meaning of Part I of the Health and Safety at Work etc. Act 1974 or within the meaning of the Health and Safety at Work (Northern Ireland) Order 1978;

    (d) the Consumer Credit Act 1974;

    (e) The Restrictive Trade Practices Act 1976;

    (f) the Resale Prices Act 1976;

    (g) the Estate Agents Act 1979;

    (h) the Competition Act 1980;

    (i) the Telecommunications Act 1984;

    (j) the Airports Act 1986;

(k) The Gas Act 1986;

(l) any subordinate legislation made (whether before or after the passing of this Act) for the purpose of securing compliance with the Directive of the Council of the European Communities, dated 10th September 1984 (No. 84/450/EEC) on the approximation of the laws, regulations and administrative provisions of the member States concerning misleading advertising.

[(m) the Electricity Act 1989.]

[(n) the Electricity (Northern Ireland) Order 1992]

[(o) the Railways Act 1993]

(4) In subsection (2)(a) above the reference to a person's functions shall include a reference to any function of making, amending or revoking any regulations or order.

(5) A person guilty of an offence under this section shall be liable—

(a) on summary conviction, to a fine not exceeding the statutory maximum;

(b) on conviction on indictment, to imprisonment for a term not exceeding two years or to a fine or to both.

(6) In this section—

"publicised information" means any information which has been disclosed in any civil or criminal proceedings or is or has been required to be contained in a warning published in pursuance of a notice to warn; and

"relevant person" means any of the following, that is to say—

(a) a Minister of the Crown, Government department or Northern Ireland department;

(b) the Monopolies and Mergers Commission, the Director General of Fair Trading, the Director General of Telecommunications or the Director General of Gas Supply [or the Director General of Electricity Supply or the Director General of Electricity Supply for Northern Ireland or the Rail Regulator];

(c) the Civil Aviation Authority;

(d) any weights and measures authority, any district council in Northern Ireland or any person on whom functions are conferred by regulations under section 27(2) above;

(e) any person who is an enforcing authority for the purposes of Part I of the Health and Safety at Work etc. Act 1974 or for the purposes of Part II of the Health and Safety at Work (Northern Ireland) Order 1978.

39. Defence of due diligence.

(1) Subject to the following provisions of this section, in proceedings against any person for an offence to which this section applies it shall be a defence for that person to show that he took all reasonable steps and exercised all due diligence to avoid committing the offence.

(2) Where in any proceedings against any person for such an offence the defence provided by subsection (1) above involves an allegation that the commission of the offence was due—

(a) to the act or default of another; or

(b) to reliance on information given by another,

that person shall not, without the leave of the court, be entitled to rely on the defence unless, not less than seven clear days before the hearing of the proceedings, he has served a notice under subsection (3) below on the person bringing the proceedings.

(3) A notice under this subsection shall give such information identifying or assisting in the identification of the person who committed the act or default or gave the information as is in the possession of the person serving the notice at the time he serves it.

(4) It is hereby declared that a person shall not be entitled to rely on the defence provided by subsection (1) above by reason of his reliance on information supplied by

another, unless he shows that it was reasonable in all the circumstances for him to have relied on the information, having regard in particular—
    (a) to the steps which he took, and those which might reasonably have been taken, for the purpose of verifying the information; and
    (b) to whether he had any reason to disbelieve the information.
  (5) This section shall apply to an offence under section 10, 12(1), (2) or (3), 13(4), 14(6) or 20(1) above.

40. Liability of persons other than principal offender.

(1) Where the commission by any person of an offence to which section 39 above applies is due to an act or default committed by some other person in the course of any business of his, the other person shall be guilty of the offence and may be proceeded against and punished by virtue of this subsection whether or not proceedings are taken against the first mentioned person.

(2) Where a body corporate is guilty of an offence under this Act (including where it is so guilty by virtue of subsection (1) above) in respect of any act or default which is shown to have been committed with the consent or connivance of, or to be attributable to any neglect on the part of, any director, manager, secretary or other similar office of the body corporate or any person who was purporting to act in any such capacity he, as well as the body corporate, shall be guilty of that offence and shall be liable to be proceeded against and punished accordingly.

(3) Where the affairs of a body corporate are managed by its members, subsection (2) above shall apply in relation to the acts and defaults of a member in connection with his functions of management as if he were a director of the body corporate.

41. Civil proceedings.

(1) An obligation imposed by safety regulations shall be a duty owed to any person who may be affected by a contravention of the obligation and, subject to any provision to the contrary in the regulations and to the defences and other incidents applying to actions for breach of statutory duty, a contravention of any such obligation shall be actionable accordingly.

(2) This Act shall not be construed as conferring any other right of action in civil proceedings, apart from the right conferred by virtue of Part I of this Act, in respect of any loss or damage suffered in consequence of a contravention of a safety provision or of a provision made by or under Part III of this Act.

(3) Subject to any provision to the contrary in the agreement itself, an agreement shall not be void or unenforceable by reason only of a contravention of a safety provision or of a provision made by or under Part III of this Act.

(4) Liability by virtue of subsection (1) above shall not be limited or excluded by any contract term, by any notice or (subject to the power contained in subsection (1) above to limit or exclude it in safety regulations) by any other provision.

(5) Nothing in subsection (1) above shall prejudice the operation of section 12 of the Nuclear Installations Act 1965 (rights to compensation for certain breaches of duties confined to rights under that Act).

(6) In this section "damage" includes personal injury and death.

42. Reports etc.

(1) It shall be the duty of the Secretary of State at least once in every five years to lay before each House of Parliament a report on the exercise during the period to which the report relates of the functions which under Part II of this Act, or under Part IV of this Act in its application for the purposes of the safety provisions, are exercisable by the Secretary of State, weights and measures authorities, district councils in Northern Ireland and persons on whom functions are conferred by regulations made under section 27(2) above.

(2) The Secretary of State may from time to time prepare and lay before each House of Parliament such other reports on the exercise of those functions as he considers appropriate.

(3) Every weights and measures authority, every district council in Northern Ireland and every person on whom functions are conferred by regulations under subsection (2) of section 27 above shall, whenever the Secretary of State so directs, make a report to the Secretary of State on the exercise of the functions exercisable by the authority or council under that section or by that person by virtue of any such regulations.

45. Interpretation.

(1) In this Act, except in so far as the context otherwise requires—

"aircraft" includes gliders, balloons and hovercraft;

"business" includes a trade or profession and the activities of a professional or trade association or of a local authority or other public authority;

"conditional sale agreement", "credit—sale agreement" and "hire-purchase agreement" have the same meanings as in the Consumer Credit Act 1974 but as if in the definitions in that Act "goods" had the same meaning as in this Act;

"contravention" includes a failure to comply and cognate expressions shall be construed accordingly;

"enforcement authority" means the Secretary of State, any other Minister of the Crown in charge of a Government department, any such department and any authority, council or other person on whom functions under this Act are conferred by or under section 27 above;

"gas" has the same meaning as in Part I of the Gas Act 1986;

"goods" includes substances, growing crops and things comprised in land by virtue of being attached to it and any ship, aircraft or vehicle;

"information" includes accounts, estimates and returns;

"magistrates' court" in relation to Northern Ireland, means a court of summary jurisdiction;

"modifications" includes additions, alterations and omissions, and cognate expressions shall be construed accordingly;

"motor vehicle" has the same meaning as in [the Road Traffic Act 1988];

"notice" means a notice in writing;

"notice to warn" means a notice under section 13(1)(b) above;

"officer", in relation to an enforcement authority, means a person authorised in writing to assist the authority in carrying out its functions under or for the purposes of the enforcement of any of the safety provisions or of any of the provisions made by or under Part III of this Act;

"personal injury" includes any disease and any other impairment of a person's physical or mental condition;

"premises" includes any place and any ship, aircraft or vehicle;

"prohibition notice" means a notice under section 13(1)(a) above;

"records" includes any books or documents and any records in non-documentary form;

"safety provision" means the general safety requirement in section 10 above or any provision of safety regulations, a prohibition notice or a suspension notice;

"safety regulations" means regulations under section 11 above;

"ship" includes any boat and any other description of vessel used in navigation;

"subordinate legislation" has the same meaning as in the Interpretation Act 1978;

"substance" means any natural or artificial substance, whether in solid, liquid or gaseous form or in the form of a vapour, and includes substances that are comprised in or mixed with other goods;

"supply" and cognate expressions shall be construed in accordance with section 46 below;

"suspension notice" means a notice under section 14 above.

(2) Except in so far as the context otherwise requires, references in this Act to a contravention of a safety provision shall, in relation to any goods, include references to anything which would constitute such a contravention if the goods were supplied to any person.

(3) References in this Act to any goods in relation to which any safety provision has been or may have been contravened shall include references to any goods which it is not reasonably practicable to separate from any such goods.

46. Meaning of "supply".

(1) Subject to the following provisions of this section, references in this Act to supplying goods shall be construed as references to doing any of the following, whether as principal or agent, that is to say—

    (a) selling, hiring out or lending the goods;
    (b) entering into a hire-purchase agreement to furnish the goods;
    (c) the performance of any contract for work and materials to furnish the goods;
    (d) providing the goods in exchange for any consideration (including trading stamps) other than money;
    (e) providing the goods in or in connection with the performance of any statutory function; or
    (f) giving the goods as a prize or otherwise making a gift of the goods;
and, in relation to gas or water, those references shall be construed as including references to providing the service by which the gas or water is made available for use.

(2) For the purpose of any reference in this Act to supplying goods, where a person ('the ostensible supplier') supplies goods to another person ('the customer') under a hire-purchase agreement, conditional sale agreement or credit-sale agreement or under an agreement for the hiring of goods (other than a hire-purchase agreement) and the ostensible supplier—

    (a) carries on the business of financing the provision of goods for others by means of such agreements; and
    (b) in the course of that business acquired his interest in the goods supplied to the customer as a means of financing the provision of them for the customer by a further person ('the effective supplier'),
the effective supplier and not the ostensible supplier shall be treated as supplying the goods to the customer.

(3) Subject to subsection (4) below, the performance of any contract by the erection of any building or structure on any land or by the carrying out of any other building works shall be treated for the purposes of this Act as a supply of goods in so far as, but only in so far as, it involves the provision of any goods to any person by means of their incorporation into the building, structure or works.

(4) Except for the purposes of, and in relation to, notices to warn or any provision made by or under Part III of this Act, references in this Act to supplying goods shall not include references to supplying goods comprised in land where the supply is effected by the creation or disposal of an interest in the land.

(5) Except in Part I of this Act references in this Act to a person's supplying goods shall be confined to references to that person's supplying goods in the course of a business of his, but for the purposes of this subsection it shall be immaterial whether the business is a business of dealing in the goods.

(6) For the purposes of subsection (5) above goods shall not be treated as supplied in the course of a business if they are supplied, in pursuance of an obligation arising under or in connection with the insurance of the goods, to the person with whom they were insured.

(7) Except for the purposes of, and in relation to, prohibition notices or suspension notices, references in Parts II to IV of this Act to supplying goods shall not include—

(a) references to supplying goods where the person supplied carries on a business of buying goods of the same description as those goods and repairing or reconditioning them;

(b) references to supplying goods by a sale of articles as scrap (that is to say, for the value of materials included in the articles rather than for the value of the articles themselves).

(8) Where any goods have at any time been supplied by being hired out or lent to any person, neither a continuation or renewal of the hire or loan (whether on the same or different terms) nor any transaction for the transfer after that time of any interest in the goods to the person to whom they were hired or lent shall be treated for the purposes of this Act as a further supply of the goods to that person.

(9) A ship, aircraft or motor vehicle shall not be treated for the purposes of this Act as supplied to any person by reason only that services consisting in the carriage of goods or passengers in that ship, aircraft or vehicle, or in its use for any other purpose, are provided to that person in pursuance of an agreement relating to the use of the ship, aircraft or vehicle for a particular period or for particular voyages, flights or journeys.

Section 13.   SCHEDULE 2
PROHIBITION NOTICES AND NOTICES TO WARN

PART I
PROHIBITION NOTICES

1. A prohibition notice in respect of any goods shall—
   (a) state that the Secretary of State considers that the goods are unsafe;
   (b) set out the reasons why the Secretary of State considers that the goods are unsafe;
   (c) specify the day on which the notice is to come into force; and
   (d) state that the trader may at any time make representations in writing to the Secretary of State for the purpose of establishing that the goods are safe.

2.—(1) If representations in writing about a prohibition notice are made by the trader to the Secretary of State, it shall be the duty of the Secretary of State to consider whether to revoke the notice and—
   (a) if he decides to revoke it, to do so;
   (b) in any other case, to appoint a person to consider those representations, any further representations made (whether in writing or orally) by the trader about the notice and the statements of any witnesses examined under this Part of this Schedule.

(2) Where the Secretary of State has appointed a person to consider representations about a prohibition notice, he shall serve a notification on the trader which—
   (a) states that the trader may make oral representations to the appointed person for the purpose of establishing that the goods to which the notice relates are safe; and
   (b) specifies the place and time at which the oral representations may be made.

(3) The time specified in a notification served under sub-paragraph (2) above shall not be before the end of the period of twenty-one days beginning with the day on which the notification is served, unless the trader otherwise agrees.

(4) A person on whom a notification has been served for the purposes of sub-paragraph (2)(b) above or his representative may, at the place and time specified in the notification—
   (a) make oral representations to the appointed person for the purpose of establishing that the goods in question are safe; and
   (b) call and examine witnesses in connection with the representations.

4.—(1) Where a person is appointed to consider representations about a prohibition notice, it shall be his duty to consider—
   (a) any written representations made by the trader about the notice, other than those in respect of which a notification is served under paragraph 3(2)(a) above;

(b) any oral representations made under paragraph 2(4) or 3(4) above; and

(c) any statements made by witnesses in connection with the oral representations, and, after considering any matters under this paragraph, to make a report (including recommendations) to the Secretary of State about the matters considered by him and the notice.

(2) It shall be the duty of the Secretary of State to consider any report made to him under sub-paragraph (1) above and, after considering the report, to inform the trader of his decision with respect to the prohibition notice to which the report relates

5.—(1) The Secretary of State may revoke or vary a prohibition notice by serving on the trader a notification stating that the notice is revoked or, as the case may be, is varied as specified in the notification.

(2) The Secretary of State shall not vary a prohibition notice so as to make the effect of the notice more restrictive for the trader.

(3) Without prejudice to the power conferred by section 13(2) of this Act, the service of a notification under sub-paragraph (1) above shall be sufficient to satisfy the requirement of paragraph 4(2) above that the trader shall be informed of the Secretary of State's decision.

PART II
NOTICES TO WARN

6.—(1) If the Secretary of State proposes to serve a notice to warn on any person in respect of any goods, the Secretary of State, before he serves the notice, shall serve on that person a notification which—

(a) contains a draft of the proposed notice;

(b) states that the Secretary of State proposes to serve a notice in the form of the draft on that person;

(c) states that the Secretary of State considers that the goods described in the draft are unsafe;

(d) sets out the reasons why the Secretary of State considers that those goods are unsafe; and

(e) states that that person may make representations to the Secretary of State for the purpose of establishing that the goods are safe if, before the end of the period of fourteen days beginning with the day on which the notification is served, he informs the Secretary of State—

(i) of his intention to make representations; and

(ii) whether the representations will be made only in writing or both in writing and orally.

(2) Where the Secretary of State has served a notification containing a draft of a proposed notice to warn on any person, he shall not serve a notice to warn on that person in respect of the goods to which the proposed notice relates unless—

(a) the period of fourteen days beginning with the day on which the notification was served expires without the Secretary of State being informed as mentioned in sub-paragraph (1)(e) above;

(b) the period of twenty-eight days beginning with that day expires without any written representations being made by that person to the Secretary of State about the proposed notice; or

(c) the Secretary of State has considered a report about the proposed notice by a person appointed under paragraph 7(1) below.

7.—(1) Where a person on whom a notification containing a draft of a proposed notice to warn has been served—

(a) informs the Secretary of State as mentioned in paragraph 6(1)(e) above before the end of the period of fourteen days beginning with the day on which the notification was served; and

(b) makes written representations to the Secretary of State about the proposed notice before the end of the period of twenty-eight days beginning with that day,
the Secretary of State shall appoint a person to consider those representations, any further representations made by that person about the draft notice and the statements of any witnesses examined under this Part of this Schedule.

(2) Where—

(a) the Secretary of State has appointed a person to consider representations about a proposed notice to warn; and

(b) the person whose representations are to be considered has informed the Secretary of State for the purposes of paragraph 6(1)(e) above that the representations he intends to make will include oral representations,

the Secretary of State shall inform the person intending to make the representations of the place and time at which oral representations may be made to the appointed person.

(3) Where a person on whom a notification containing a draft of a proposed notice to warn has been served is informed of a time for the purposes of sub-paragraph (2) above, that time shall not be—

(a) before the end of the period of twenty-eight days beginning with the day on which the notification was served; or

(b) before the end of the period of seven days beginning with the day on which that person is informed of the time.

(4) A person who has been informed of a place and time for the purposes of sub-paragraph (2) above or his representative may, at that place and time—

(a) make oral representations to the appointed person for the purpose of establishing that the goods to which the proposed notice relates are safe; and

(b) call and examine witnesses in connection with the representations.

8.—(1) Where a person is appointed to consider representations about a proposed notice to warn, it shall be his duty to consider—

(a) any written representations made by the person on whom it is proposed to serve the notice; and

(b) in a case where a place and a time has been appointed under paragraph 7(2) above for oral representations to be made by that person or his representative, any representations so made and any statements made by witnesses in connection with those representations,

and, after considering those matters, to make a report (including recommendations) to the Secretary of State about the matters considered by him and the proposal to serve the notice.

(2) It shall be the duty of the Secretary of State to consider any report made to him under sub-paragraph (1) above and, after considering the report, to inform the person on whom it was proposed that a notice to warn should be served of his decision with respect to the proposal.

(3) If at any time after serving a notification on a person under paragraph 6 above the Secretary of State decides not to serve on that person either the proposed notice to warn or that notice with modifications, the Secretary of State shall inform that person of the decision; and nothing done for the purposes of any of the preceding provisions of this Part of this Schedule before that person was so informed shall—

(a) entitle the Secretary of State subsequently to serve the proposed notice or that notice with modifications; or

(b) require the Secretary of State, or any person appointed to consider representations about the proposed notice, subsequently to do anything in respect of, or in consequence of, any such representations.

(4) Where a notification containing a draft of a proposed notice to warn is served on a person in respect of any goods, a notice to warn served on him in consequence of a

decision made under sub-paragraph (2) above shall either be in the form of the draft or shall be less onerous than the draft.

9. The Secretary of State may revoke a notice to warn by serving on the person on whom the notice was served a notification stating that the notice is revoked.

PART III
GENERAL

10.—(1) Where in a notification served on any person under this Schedule the Secretary of State has appointed a time for the making of oral representations or the examination of witnesses, he may, by giving that person such notification as the Secretary of State considers appropriate, change that time to a later time or appoint further times at which further representations may be made or the examination of witnesses may be continued; and paragraphs 2(4), 3(4) and 7(4) above shall have effect accordingly.

(2) For the purposes of this Schedule the Secretary of State may appoint a person (instead of the appointed person) to consider any representations or statements, if the person originally appointed, or last appointed under this sub-paragraph, to consider those representations or statements has died or appears to the Secretary of State to be otherwise unable to act.

11. In this Schedule—

"the appointed person" in relation to a prohibition notice or a proposal to serve a notice to warn, means the person for the time being appointed under this Schedule to consider representations about the notice or, as the case may be, about the proposed notice;

"notification" means a notification in writing;

"trader", in relation to a prohibition notice, means the person on whom the notice is or was served.

CROWN PROCEEDINGS (ARMED FORCES) ACT 1987
(1987, c. 25)

1. Repeal of s. 10 of the Crown Proceedings Act 1947.

Subject to section 2 below, section 10 of the Crown Proceedings Act 1947 (exclusions from liability in tort in cases involving the armed forces) shall cease to have effect except in relation to anything suffered by a person in consequence of an act or omission committed before the date on which this Act is passed.

2. Revival of s. 10.

(1) Subject to the following provisions of this section, the Secretary of State may, at any time after the coming into force of section 1 above, by order—

(a) revive the effect of section 10 of the Crown Proceedings Act 1947 either for all purposes or for such purposes as may be described in the order; or

(b) where that section has effect for the time being in pursuance of an order made by virtue of paragraph (a) above, provide for that section to cease to have effect either for all of the purposes for which it so has effect or for such of them as may be so described.

(2) The Secretary of State shall not make an order reviving the effect of the said section 10 for any purposes unless it appears to him necessary or expedient to do so—

(a) by reason of any imminent national danger or of any great emergency that has arisen; or

(b) for the purposes of any warlike operations in any part of the world outside the United Kingdom or of any other operations which are or are to be carried out in connection with the warlike activity of any persons in any such part of the world.

(3) Subject to subsection (4) below, an order under this section describing purposes for which the effect of the said section 10 is to be revived, or for which that section is to cease to have effect, may describe those purposes by reference to any matter whatever and may make different provision for different cases, circumstances or persons.

(4) Nothing in any order under this section shall revive the effect of the said section 10, or provide for that section to cease to have effect, in relation to anything suffered by a person in consequence of an act or omission committed before the date on which the order comes into force.

(5) The power to make an order under this section shall be exercisable by statutory instrument subject to annulment in pursuance of a resolution of either House of Parliament.

MINORS' CONTRACTS ACT 1987
(1987, c. 13)

2. Guarantees.
Where—
    (a) a guarantee is given in respect of an obligation of a party to a contract made after the commencement of this Act, and
    (b) the obligation is unenforceable against him (or he repudiates the contract) because he was a minor when the contract was made,
the guarantee shall not for that reason alone be unenforceable against the guarantor.

3. Restitution.
(1) Where—
    (a) a person ("the plaintiff") has after the commencement of this Act entered into a contract with another ("the defendant"), and
    (b) the contract is unenforceable against the defendant (or he repudiates it) because he was a minor when the contract was made,
the court may, if it is just and equitable to do so, require the defendant to transfer to the plaintiff any property acquired by the defendant under the contract, or any property representing it.

(2) Nothing in this section shall be taken to prejudice any other remedy available to the plaintiff.

PILOTAGE ACT 1987
(1987, c. 21)

16. Liability for ships under compulsory pilotage.
The fact that a ship is being navigated in an area and in circumstances in which pilotage is compulsory for it shall not affect any liability of the owner or master of the ship for any loss or damage caused by the ship or by the manner in which it is navigated.

22. Limitation of liability in respect of pilots.
(8) A competent harbour authority shall not be liable for any loss or damage caused by any act or omission of a pilot authorised by it under section 3 above by virtue only of that authorisation.

CRIMINAL JUSTICE ACT 1988
(1988, c. 33)

PART VI
CONFISCATION OF THE PROCEEDS OF AN OFFENCE

71. Confiscation orders.
[(1) Where an offender is convicted, in any proceedings before the Crown Court or a magistrates' court, of an offence of a relevant description, it shall be the duty of the court—

(a) if the prosecutor has given written notice to the court that he considers that it would be appropriate for the court to proceed under this section, or

(b) if the court considers, even though it has not been given such notice, that it would be appropriate for it so to proceed,

to act as follows before sentencing or otherwise dealing with the offender in respect of that offence or any other relevant criminal conduct.

(1A) The court shall first determine whether the offender has benefited from any relevant criminal conduct.

(1B) Subject to subsection (1C) below, if the court determines that the offender has benefited from any relevant criminal conduct, it shall then—

(a) determine in accordance with subsection (6) below the amount to be recovered in his case by virtue of this section, and

(b) make an order under this section ordering the offender to pay that amount.

(1C) If, in a case falling within subsection (1B) above, the court is satisfied that a victim of any relevant criminal conduct has instituted, or intends to institute, civil proceedings against the defendant in respect of loss, injury or damage sustained in connection with that conduct—

(a) the court shall have a power, instead of a duty, to make an order under this section;

(b) subsection (6) below shall not apply for determining the amount to be recovered in that case by virtue of this section; and

(c) where the court makes an order in exercise of that power, the sum required to be paid under that order shall be of such amount, not exceeding the amount which (but for paragraph (b) above) would apply by virtue of subsection (6) below, as the court thinks fit.]

(4) For the purposes of this Part of this Act a person benefits from an offence if he obtains property as a result of or in connection with its commission and his benefit is the value of the property so obtained.

(5) Where a person derives a pecuniary advantage as a result of or in connection with the commission of an offence, he is to be treated for the purposes of this Part of this Act as if he had obtained as a result of or in connection with the commission of the offence a sum of money equal to the value of the pecuniary advantage.

(6) The sum which an order made by a court under this section requires an offender to pay must be at least the minimum amount, but must not exceed—

(a) the benefit in respect of which it is made; or

(b) the amount appearing to the court to be the amount that might be realised at the time the order is made,

whichever is the less.

72. Making of confiscation orders.

(5) Where a court makes a confiscation order against a defendant in any proceedings, it shall be its duty, in respect of any offence of which he is convicted in those proceedings, to take account of the order before—

(a) imposing any fine on him;

(b) making any order involving any payment by him, other than an order under section 35 of the Powers of Criminal Courts Act 1973 (compensation orders); or

(c) making any order under—

(i) section 27 of the Misuse of Drugs Act 1971 (forfeiture orders); or

(ii) section 43 of the Powers of Criminal Courts Act 1973 (deprivation orders),

but subject to that shall leave the order out of account in determining the appropriate sentence or other manner of dealing with him.

(7) Where—

(a) a court makes both a confiscation order and an order for the payment of compensation under section 35 of the Powers of Criminal Courts Act 1973 against the same person in the same proceedings; and

(b) it appears to the court that he will not have sufficient means to satisfy both the orders in full,

it shall direct that so much of the compensation as will not in its opinion be recoverable because of the insufficiency of his means shall be paid out of any sums recovered under the confiscation order.

[**72AA. Confiscation relating to a course of criminal conduct.**

(1) This section applies in a case where an offender is convicted, in any proceedings before the Crown Court or a magistrates' court, of a qualifying offence which is an offence of a relevant description, if—

(a) the prosecutor gives written notice for the purposes of subsection (1)(a) of section 71 above;

(b) that notice contains a declaration that it is the prosecutor's opinion that the case is one in which it is appropriate for the provisions of this section to be applied; and

(c) the offender—

(i) is convicted in those proceedings of at least two qualifying offences (including the offence in question); or

(ii) has been convicted of a qualifying offence on at least one previous occasion during the relevant period.

(2) In this section "qualifying offence", in relation to proceedings before the Crown Court or a magistrates' court, means any offence in relation to which all the following conditions are satisfied, that is to say—

(a) it is an offence to which this part of this Act applies;

(b) it is an offence which was committed after the commencement of section 2 of the Proceeds of Crime Act 1995; and

(c) that court is satisfied that it is an offence from which the defendant has benefited.

(3) When proceeding under section 71 above in pursuance of the notice mentioned in subsection (1)(a) above, the court may, if it thinks fit, determine that (subject to subsection (5) below) the assumptions specified in subsection (4) below are to be made for the purpose—

(a) of determining whether the defendant has benefited from relevant criminal conduct; and

(b) if he has, of assessing the value of the defendant's benefit from such conduct.

(4) Those assumptions are

(a) that any property appearing to the court—

(i) to be held by the defendant at the date of conviction or at any time in the period between that date and the determination in question, or

(ii) to have been transferred to him at any time since the beginning of the relevant period,

was received by him, at the earliest time when he appears to the court to have held it, as a result of or in connection with the commission of offences to which this Part of this Act applies;

(b) that any expenditure of his since the beginning of the relevant period was met out of payments received by him as a result of or in connection with the commission of offences to which this Part of this Act applies; and

(c) that, for the purposes of valuing any benefit which he had or which he is assumed to have had at any time, he received the benefit free of any other interests in it.

(5) Where the court has determined that the assumptions specified in subsection (4) above are to be made in any case it shall not in that case make any such assumption in relation to any particular property or expenditure if—

(a) that assumption, so far as it relates to that property or expenditure, is shown to be incorrect in the defendant's case;

(b) that assumption, so far as it so relates, is shown to be correct in relation to an offence the defendant's benefit from which has been the subject of a previous confiscation order; or

(c) the court is satisfied that there would (for any other reason) be a serious risk of injustice in the defendant's case if the assumption were to be made in relation to that property or expenditure.

(6) Where the assumptions specified in subsection (4) above are made in any case, the offences from which, in accordance with those assumptions, the defendant is assumed to have benefited shall be treated as if they were comprised, for the purposes of this Part of this Act, in the conduct which is to be treated, in that case, as relevant criminal conduct in relation to the defendant.]

[**74B. Revision of assessment of proceeds of crime.**

(1) This section applies where in any case there has been a determination under subsection (1A) of section 71 above ("the original determination") that the defendant in that case had not benefited from any relevant criminal conduct.

(2) If the prosecutor has evidence—

(a) which was not considered by the court which made the original determination, but

(b) which the prosecutor believes would have led that court (if it had been considered) to determine that the defendant had benefited from relevant criminal conduct,

the prosecutor may apply to the relevant court for it to consider that evidence.

(3) If, having considered the evidence, the relevant court is satisfied that (if that evidence had been available to it) it would have determined that the defendant had benefited from relevant criminal conduct, that court—

(a) shall proceed, as if it were proceeding under section 71 above before sentencing or otherwise dealing with the defendant in respect of any relevant criminal conduct—

(i) to make a fresh determination of whether the defendant has benefited from any relevant criminal conduct; and

(ii) then to make such a determination as is mentioned in subsection (1B)(a) of that section; and

(b) subject to subsection (4) below, shall have a power, after making those determinations, to make an order requiring the payment of such sum as it thinks fit;

and an order under paragraph (b) above shall be deemed for all purposes to be a confiscation order.

(4) The court shall not, in exercise of the power conferred by paragraph (b) of subsection (3) above, make any order for the payment of a sum which is more than the amount determined in pursuance of paragraph (a)(ii) of that subsection.

(5) In making any determination under or for the purposes of subsection (3) above the relevant court may take into account, to the extent that they represent respects in which the defendant has benefited from any relevant criminal conduct, any payments or other rewards which were not received by him until after the making of the original determination.

(6) Where, in a case in which section 72AA above does not otherwise apply, an application under this section contains such a declaration as is mentioned in paragraph (b) of subsection (1) of that section, that section shall apply (subject to subsection (7) below) in the case of any determination on the application as if it were a determination in a case in which the requirements of paragraphs (a) and (b) of that subsection had been satisfied.

(7) For the purposes of any determination under or for the purposes of subsection (3) above to which section 72AA above applies, none of the assumptions specified in subsection (4) of that section shall be made in relation to any property unless it is property held by or transferred to the defendant before the time when he was sentenced or otherwise dealt with in the case in question.

(8) No application shall be entertained by the court under this section if it is made after the end of the period of six years beginning with the date of conviction.

(9) Section 72A above shall apply where the court is acting under this section as it applies where the court is acting under section 71 above.]

[74C. **Revision of assessment of amount to be recovered.**

(1) This section applies where, in the case of a person convicted of any offence, there has been a determination under this Part of this Act ("the current determination") of any sum required to be paid in his case under any confiscation order.

(2) Where the prosecutor is of the opinion that the value of any benefit to the defendant from any relevant criminal conduct was greater than the value at which that benefit was assessed by the court on the current determination, the prosecutor may apply to the relevant court for the evidence on which the prosecutor has formed his opinion to be considered by the court.

(3) If, having considered the evidence, the relevant court is satisfied that the value of the benefit from any relevant criminal conduct is greater than the value so assessed by the court (whether because its real value was higher at the time of the current determination than was thought or because the value of the benefit in question has subsequently increased), the relevant court—

(a) subject to subsection (4) below, shall make a fresh determination, as if it were proceeding under section 71 above before sentencing or otherwise dealing with the defendant in respect of any relevant criminal conduct, of the following amounts, that is to say—

(i) the amount by which the defendant has benefited from such conduct; and
(ii) the amount appearing to be the amount that might be realised at the time of the fresh determination;
and

(b) subject to subsection (5) below, shall have a power to increase, to such extent as it thinks just in all the circumstances of the case, the amount to be recovered by virtue of that section and to vary accordingly any confiscation order made by reference to the current determination.

(4) Where—

(a) the court is under a duty to make a fresh determination for the purposes of subsection (3)(a) above in any case, and

(b) that case is a case to which section 72AA above applies,

the court shall not have power, in determining any amounts for those purposes, to make any of the assumptions specified in subsection (4) of that section in relation to any property unless it is property held by or transferred to the defendant before the time when he was sentenced or otherwise dealt with in the case in question.

(5) The court shall not, in exercise of the power conferred by paragraph (b) of subsection (3) above, vary any order so as to make it an order requiring the payment of any sum which is more than the lesser of the two amounts determined in pursuance of paragraph (a) of that subsection.

(6) In making any determination under or for the purposes of subsection (3) above the relevant court may take into account, to the extent that they represent respects in which the defendant has benefited from any relevant criminal conduct, any payments or other rewards which were not received by him until after the making of the original determination.

Criminal Justice Act 1988

(7) Where the Crown Court varies a confiscation order under subsection (3) above, it shall substitute for the term of imprisonment or of detention fixed under subsection (2) of section 31 of the Powers of Criminal Courts Act 1973 in respect of the amount to be recovered under the order a longer term determined in accordance with that section (as it has effect by virtue of section 75 below) in respect of any greater amount substituted under subsection (3) above.

(8) Subsection (7) above shall apply only if the effect of the substitution is to increase the maximum period applicable in relation to the order under section 31(3A) of that Act of 1973.

(9) No application shall be entertained by a court under this section if it is made after the end of the period of six years beginning with the date of conviction.

(10) Section 72A above shall apply where the court is acting under this section as it applies where the court is acting under section 71 above.]

98. Disclosure of information subject to contractual restriction upon disclosure.

(1) Where a person discloses to a constable—
   (a) a suspicion or belief that any property—
      (i) has been obtained as a result of or in connection with the commission or an offence to which this Part of this Act applies; or
      (ii) derives from property so obtained; or
   (b) any matter on which such a suspicion or belief is based,
the disclosure shall not be treated as a breach of any restriction upon the disclosure of information imposed by contract.

PART XI

133. Compensation for miscarriages of justice.

(1) Subject to subsection (2) below, when a person has been convicted of a criminal offence and when subsequently his conviction has been reversed or he has been pardoned on the ground that a new or newly discovered fact shows beyond reasonable doubt that there has been a miscarriage of justice, the Secretary of State shall pay compensation for the miscarriage of justice to the person who has suffered punishment as a result of such conviction or, if he is dead, to his personal representatives, unless the non-disclosure of the unknown fact was wholly or partly attributable to the person convicted.

134. Torture.

(1) A public official or person acting in an official capacity, whatever his nationality, commits the offence of torture if in the United Kingdom or elsewhere he intentionally inflicts severe pain or suffering on another in the performance or purported performance of his official duties.

(2) A person not falling within subsection (1) above commits the offence of torture, whatever his nationality, if—
   (a) in the United Kingdom or elsewhere he intentionally inflicts severe pain or suffering on another at the instigation or with the consent or acquiescence—
      (i) of a public official; or
      (ii) of a person acting in an official capacity; and
   (b) the official or other person is performing or purporting to perform his official duties when he instigates the commission of the offence or consents to or acquiesces in it.

(3) It is immaterial whether the pain or suffering is physical or mental and whether it is caused by an act or an omission.

(4) It shall be a defence for a person charged with an offence under this section in respect of any conduct of his to prove that he had lawful authority, justification or excuse for that conduct.

HOUSING ACT 1988
(1988, c. 50)

16. Access for repairs.

It shall be an implied term of every assured tenancy that the tenant shall afford to the landlord access to the dwelling-house let on the tenancy and all reasonable facilities for executing therein any repairs which the landlord is entitled to execute.

27. Damages for unlawful eviction.

(1) This section applies if, at any time after 9th June 1988, a landlord (in this section referred to as "the landlord in default") or any person acting on behalf of the landlord in default unlawfully deprives the residential occupier of any premises of his occupation of the whole or part of the premises.

(2) This section also applies if, at any time after 9th June 1988, a landlord (in this section referred to as "the landlord in default") or any person acting on behalf of the landlord in default—

    (a) attempts unlawfully to deprive the residential occupier of any premises of his occupation of the whole or part of the premises, or

    (b) knowing or having reasonable cause to believe that the conduct is likely to cause the residential occupier of any premises—

        (i) to give up his occupation of the premises or any part thereof, or

        (ii) to refrain from exercising any right or pursuing any remedy in respect of the premises or any part thereof,

does acts likely to interfere with the peace or comfort of the residential occupier or members of his household, or persistently withdraws or withholds services reasonably required for the occupation of the premises as a residence,

and, as a result, the residential occupier gives up his occupation of the premises as a residence.

(3) Subject to the following provisions of this section, where this section applies, the landlord in default shall, by virtue of this section, be liable to pay to the former residential occupier, in respect of his loss of the right to occupy the premises in question as his residence, damages assessed on the basis set out in section 28 below.

(4) Any liability arising by virtue of subsection (3) above—

    (a) shall be in the nature of a liability in tort; and

    (b) subject to subsection (5) below, shall be in addition to any liability arising apart from this section (whether in tort, contract or otherwise).

(5) Nothing in this section affects the right of a residential occupier to enforce any liability which arises apart from this section in respect of his loss of the right to occupy premises as his residence; but damages shall not be awarded both in respect of such a liability and in respect of a liability arising by virtue of this section on account of the same loss.

(6) No liability shall arise by virtue of subsection (3) above if—

    (a) before the date on which proceedings to enforce the liability are finally disposed of, the former residential occupier is reinstated in the premises in question in such circumstances that he becomes again the residential occupier of them; or

    (b) at the request of the former residential occupier, a court makes an order (whether in the nature of an injunction or otherwise) as a result of which he is reinstated as mentioned in paragraph (a) above;

and, for the purposes of paragraph (a) above, proceedings to enforce a liability are finally disposed of on the earliest date by which the proceedings (including any proceedings on or in consequence of an appeal) have been determined and any time for appealing or further appealing has expired, except that if any appeal is abandoned, the proceedings shall be taken to be disposed of on the date of the abandonment.

(7) If, in proceedings to enforce a liability arising by virtue of subsection (3) above, it appears to the court—

(a) that, prior to the event which gave rise to the liability, the conduct of the former residential occupier or any person living with him in the premises concerned was such that it is reasonable to mitigate the damages for which the landlord in default would otherwise be liable, or

(b) that, before the proceedings were begun, the landlord in default offered to reinstate the former residential occupier in the premises in question and either it was unreasonable of the former residential occupier to refuse that offer or, if he had obtained alternative accommodation before the offer was made, it would have been unreasonable of him to refuse that offer if he had not obtained that accommodation,

the court may reduce the amount of damages which would otherwise be payable to such amount as it thinks appropriate.

(8) In proceedings to enforce a liability arising by virtue of subsection (3) above, it shall be a defence for the defendant to prove that he believed, and had reasonable cause to believe—

(a) that the residential occupier had ceased to reside in the premises in question at the time when he was deprived of occupation as mentioned in subsection (1) above or, as the case may be, when the attempt was made or the acts were done as a result of which he gave up his occupation of those premises; or

(b) that, where the liability would otherwise arise by virtue only of the doing of acts or the withdrawal or withholding of services, he had reasonable grounds for doing the acts or withdrawing or withholding the services in question.

28. The measure of damages.

(1) The basis for the assessment of damages referred to in section 27(3) above is the difference in value, determined as at the time immediately before the residential occupier ceased to occupy the premises in question as his residence, between—

(a) the value of the interest of the landlord in default determined on the assumption that the residential occupier continues to have the same right to occupy the premises as before that time; and

(b) the value of that interest determined on the assumption that the residential occupier has ceased to have that right.

(2) In relation to any premises, any reference in this section to the interest of the landlord in default is a reference to his interest in the building in which the premises in question are comprised (whether or not that building contains any other premises) together with its curtilage.

(3) For the purposes of the valuations referred to in subsection (1) above, it shall be assumed—

(a) that the landlord in default is selling his interest on the open market to a willing buyer;

(b) that neither the residential occupier nor any member of his family wishes to buy; and

(c) that it is unlawful to carry out any substantial development of any of the land in which the landlord's interest subsists or to demolish the whole or part of any building on that land.

INCOME AND CORPORATION TAXES ACT 1988
(1988, c. 1)

148. Payments on retirement or removal from office or employment.

(1) Subject to the provisions of this section and section 188, tax shall be charged under Schedule E in respect of any payment to which this section applies which is made

to the holder or past holder of any office or employment, or to his executors or administrators, whether made by the person under whom he holds or held the office or employment or by any other person.

(2) This section applies to any payment (not otherwise chargeable to tax) which is made, whether in pursuance of any legal obligation or not, either directly or indirectly in consideration or in consequence of, or otherwise in connection with, the termination of the holding of the office or employment or any change in its functions or emoluments, including any payment in commutation of annual or periodical payments (whether chargeable to tax or not) which would otherwise have been so made.

(3) For the purposes of this section and section 188, any payment made to the spouse or any relative or dependant of a person who holds or has held an office or employment, or made on behalf of or to the order of that person, shall be treated as made to that person, and any valuable consideration other than money shall be treated as a payment of money equal to the value of that consideration at the date when it is given.

[329AA. Personal injury damages in the form of periodical payments.
(1) Where—
    (a) an agreement is made settling a claim or action for damages for personal injury on terms whereby the damages are to consist wholly or partly of periodical payments; or
    (b) a court awarding damages for personal injury makes an order incorporating such terms,
the payments shall not for the purposes of income tax be regarded as the income of any of the persons mentioned in subsection (2) below and accordingly shall be paid without any deduction under section 348(1)(b) or 349(1).

(2) The persons referred to in subsection (1) above are—
    (a) the person ("A") entitled to the damages under the agreement or order;
    (b) any person who, whether in pursuance of the agreement or order or otherwise, receives the payments or any of them on behalf of A;
    (c) any trustee who, whether in pursuance of the agreement or order or otherwise, receives the payments or any of them on trust for the benefit of A under a trust under which A is during his lifetime the sole beneficiary.

(3) The periodical payments referred to in subsection (1) above, or any of them, may, if the agreement or order mentioned in that subsection or a subsequent agreement so provides, consist of payments under one or more annuities purchased or provided for, or for the benefit of, A by the person by whom the payments would otherwise fall to be made.

(4) Sums paid to, or for the benefit of, A by a trustee or trustees shall not be regarded as his income for the purposes of income tax if made out of payments which by virtue of this section are not to be regarded for those purposes as income of the trustee or trustees.

(5) In this section "personal injury" includes any disease and any impairment of a person's physical or mental condition.

(6) For the purposes of this section a claim or action for personal injury includes—
    (a) such a claim or action brought by virtue of the Law Reform (Miscellaneous Provisions) Act 1934;
    (b) such a claim or action brought by virtue of the Law Reform (Miscellaneous Provisions) Act (Northern Ireland) 1937;
    (c) such a claim or action brought by virtue of the Damages (Scotland) Act 1976;
    (d) a claim or action brought by virtue of the Fatal Accidents Act 1976;
    (e) a claim or action brought by virtue of the Fatal Accidents (Northern Ireland) Order 1977.

(7) In relation to such an order as is mentioned in paragraph (b) of subsection (1) above "damages" includes an interim payment which the court, by virtue of rules of

court in that behalf, orders the defendant to make to the plaintiff; and where, without such an order, the defendant agrees to make a payment on account of the damages that may be awarded against him in such an action as is mentioned in paragraph (a) of that subsection, that paragraph shall apply to the payment and the agreement as it applies to damages and to such an agreement as is there mentioned.

(8) In the application of subsection (7) above to Scotland for references to the plaintiff and the defendant there shall be substitued references to the pursuer and the defender.]

[329AB. **Compensation for personal injury under statutory or other schemes.**

(1) Section 329AA applies to annuity payments under an award of compensation made under the Criminal Injuries Compensation Scheme as it applies to payments of damages in that form under such an agreement or order as is mentioned in subsection (1) of that section.

(2) In subsection (1) above "the Criminal Injuries Compensation Scheme" means—

(a) the scheme established by arrangements made under the Criminal Injuries Compensation Act 1995; or

(b) arrangements made by the Secretary of State for compensation for criminal injuries and in operation before the commencement of that scheme.

(3) If it appears to the Treasury that any other scheme or arrangement, whether established by statute or otherwise, makes provision for the making of periodical payments by way of compensation for personal injury within the meaning of section 329AA, the Treasury may by order apply that section to those payments with such modifications as the Treasury consider necessary.]

824. **Repayment supplements: individuals and others.**

[(1) Subject to the following provisions of this section, a repayment made by the Board or an officer of the Board of any of the following, namely—

(a) an amount paid on account of income tax under section 59A of the Management Act;

(b) any income tax paid by or on behalf of an individual for a year of assessment;

(c) a surcharge imposed under section 59C of that Act; and

(d) a penalty incurred by an individual under any of the provisions of that Act,

shall be increased under this section by an amount (a "repayment supplement") equal to interest on the amount repaid at the rate applicable under section 178 of the Finance Act 1989 for the period (if any) between the relevant time and the date on which the order for the repayment is issued.]

(7) A repayment supplement shall not be payable under this section in respect of a repayment or payment made in consequence of an order or judgment of a court having power to allow interest on the repayment or payment, or in respect of a repayment of a post-war credit within the meaning of the Income Tax (Repayment of Post-War Credits) Act 1959.

(8) A repayment supplement paid to any person under this section or under section [283 of the 1992 Act] shall not be income of that person for any tax purposes.

825. **Repayment supplements: companies.**

(1) This section applies to the following payments made to a company in connection with any accounting period for which the company was resident in the United Kingdom ("the relevant accounting period"), that is to say—

(a) a repayment of corporation tax paid by the company for that accounting period (including advance corporation tax paid in respect of distributions made by the company in that accounting period . . .; or

(b) a repayment of income tax in respect of a payment received by the company in that accounting period on which the company bore income tax by deduction; or

(c) a payment of the whole or part of the tax credit comprised in any franked investment income received by the company in that accounting period.

(2) Subject to the following provisions of this section, where a payment... to which this section applies is made by the Board or an inspector after the end of the 12 months beginning with the material date, the payment shall be increased under this section by an amount (a "repayment supplement") equal to interest on the amount paid at the [rate applicable under section 178 of the Finance Act 1989] for each complete tax month contained in the period (if any) beginning with the relevant date and ending at the end of the tax month in which the order for the payment is issued.

(5) [...] the Treasury may by order from time to time increase or decrease the rate of interest by reference to which repayment supplements are calculated under subsection (2) above.

(6) A repayment supplement shall not be payable under this section in respect of a payment made in consequence of an order or judgment of a court having power to allow interest on the payment.

(7) A repayment supplement paid under this section shall be disregarded for all purposes of income tax and corporation tax.

826. Interest on tax overpaid.

(1) In any case where—
 (a) a repayment falls to be made of corporation tax paid by a company for an accounting period which ends after the appointed day; or
 [(aa) a repayment falls to be made under section 246N and 246Q of advance corporation tax paid by a company in respect of distributions made by it in such an accounting period; or]
 (b) a repayment of income tax falls to be made in respect of a payment received by a company in such an accounting period; or
 (c) a payment falls to be made to a company of the whole or part of the tax credit comprised in any franked investment income received by the company in such an accounting period,
then, from the material date until [the order for repayment or payment is issued], the repayment or payment shall carry interest at the [rate applicable under section 178 of the Finance Act 1989].

(5) Interest paid under this section shall be paid without any deduction of income tax and shall not be brought into account in computing any profits or income.

LANDLORD AND TENANT ACT 1988
(1988, c. 26)

1. Qualified duty to consent to assigning, underletting etc. of premises.

(1) This section applies in any case where—
 (a) a tenancy includes a covenant on the part of the tenant not to enter into one or more of the following transactions, that is—
   (i) assigning,
   (ii) underletting,
   (iii) charging, or
   (iv) parting with the possession of,
the premises comprised in the tenancy or any part of the premises without the consent of the landlord or some other person, but
 (b) the covenant is subject to the qualification that the consent is not to be unreasonably withheld (whether or not it is also subject to any other qualification).

(2) In this section and section 2 of this Act—
 (a) references to a proposed transaction are to any assignment, underletting, charging or parting with possession to which the convenant relates, and

(b) references to the person who may consent to such a transaction are to the person who under the covenant may consent to the tenant entering into the proposed transaction.

(3) Where there is served on the person who may consent to a proposed transaction a written application by the tenant for consent to the transaction, he owes a duty to the tenant within a reasonable time—
  (a) to give consent, except in a case where it is reasonable not to give consent,
  (b) to serve on the tenant written notice of his decision whether or not to give consent specifying in addition—
    (i) if the consent is given subject to conditions, the conditions,
    (ii) if the consent is withheld, the reasons for withholding it.

(4) Giving consent subject to any condition that is not a reasonable condition does not satisfy the duty under subsection (3)(a) above.

4. Breach of duty.
A claim that a person has broken any duty under this Act may be made the subject of civil proceedings in like manner as any other claim in tort for breach of statutory duty.

6. Application to Crown.
This Act binds the Crown; but as regards the Crown's liability in tort shall not bind the Crown further than the Crown is made liable in tort by the Crown Proceedings Act 1947.

MALICIOUS COMMUNICATIONS ACT 1988
(1988, c. 27)

1. Offence of sending letters etc. with intent to cause distress or anxiety.
(1) Any person who sends to another person—
  (a) a letter or other article which conveys—
    (i) a message which is indecent or grossly offensive;
    (ii) a threat; or
    (iii) information which is false and known or believed to be false by the sender; or
  (b) any other article which is, in whole or part, of an indecent or grossly offensive nature,
is guilty of an offence if his purpose, or one of his purposes, in sending it is that it should, so far as falling within paragraph (a) or (b) above, cause distress or anxiety to the recipient or to any other person to whom he intends that it or its contents or nature should be communicated.

(2) A person is not guilty of an offence by virtue of subsection (1)(a)(ii) above if he shows—
  (a) that the threat was used to reinforce a demand which he believed he had reasonable grounds for making; and
  (b) that he believed that the use of the threat was a proper means of reinforcing the demand.

(3) In this section references to sending include references to delivering and to causing to be sent or delivered and "sender" shall be construed accordingly.

(4) A person guilty of an offence under this section shall be liable on summary conviction to a fine not exceeding level 4 on the standard scale.

ROAD TRAFFIC ACT 1988
(1988, c. 52)

16. Wearing of protective headgear.
(1) The Secretary of State may make regulations requiring, subject to such exceptions as may be specified in the regulations, persons driving or riding (otherwise

than in side-cars) on motor cycles of any class specified in the regulations to wear protective headgear of such description as may be so specified.

(2) A requirement imposed by regulations under this section shall not apply to any follower of the Sikh religion while he is wearing a turban.

(3) Regulations under this section may make different provision in relation to different circumstances.

(4) A person who drives or rides on a motor cycle in contravention of regulations under this section is guilty of an offence...

38. The Highway Code.

(7) A failure on the part of a person to observe a provision of the Highway Code shall not of itself render that person liable to criminal proceedings of any kind but any such failure may in any proceedings (whether civil or criminal, and including proceedings for an offence under the Traffic Acts, the Public Passenger Vehicles Act 1981 or sections 18 to 23 of the Transport Act 1985) be relied upon by any party to the proceedings as tending to establish or negative any liability which is in question in those proceedings.

143. Users of motor vehicles to be insured or secured against third-party risks.

(1) Subject to the provisions of this Part of this Act—

(a) a person must not use a motor vehicle on a road unless there is in force in relation to the use of the vehicle by that person such a policy of insurance or such a security in respect of third party risks as complies with the requirements of this Part of this Act, and

(b) a person must not cause or permit any other person to use a motor vehicle on a road unless there is in force in relation to the use of the vehicle by that other person such a policy of insurance or such a security in respect of third party risks as complies with the requirements of this Part of this Act.

(2) If a person acts in contravention of subsection (1) above he is guilty of an offence.

(3) A person charged with using a motor vehicle in contravention of this section shall not be convicted if he proves—

(a) that the vehicle did not belong to him and was not in his possession under a contract of hiring or of loan,

(b) that he was using the vehicle in the course of his employment, and

(c) that he neither knew nor had reason to believe that there was not in force in relation to the vehicle such a policy of insurance or security as is mentioned in subsection (1) above.

(4) This Part of this Act does not apply to invalid carriages.

144. Exceptions from requirement of third-party insurance or security.

(1) Section 143 of this Act does not apply to a vehicle owned by a person who has deposited and keeps deposited with the Accountant General of the Supreme Court the sum of [£500,000], at a time when the vehicle is being driven under the owner's control.

[(1A) The Secretary of State may by order made by statutory instrument substitute a greater sum for the sum for the time being specified in subsection (1) above.]

(2) Section 143 does not apply—

(a) to a vehicle owned—

(i) by the council of a county or county district in England and Wales, the Common Council of the City of London, the council of a London borough, the Inner London Education Authority, or a joint authority (other than a police authority) established by Part IV of the Local Government Act 1985,

(ii) by a [council constituted under section 2 of the Local Government etc. (Scotland) Act 1994] in Scotland, or

Road Traffic Act 1988

(iii) by a joint board or committee in England or Wales, or joint committee in Scotland, which is so constituted as to include among its members representatives of any such council,
at a time when the vehicle is being driven under the owner's control,

(b) to a vehicle owned by a police authority or the Receiver for the Metropolitan Police district, at a time when it is being driven under the owner's control, or to a vehicle at a time when it is being driven for police purposes by or under the direction of a constable, or by a person employed by a police authority, or employed by the Receiver, or

(c) to a vehicle at a time when it is being driven on a journey to or from any place undertaken for salvage purposes pursuant to Part IX of the Merchant Shipping Act 1894,

(d) to the use of a vehicle for the purpose of its being provided in pursuance of a direction under section 166(2)(b) of the Army Act 1955 or under the corresponding provision of the Air Force Act 1955,

[(da) to a vehicle owned by a health service body, as defined in section 60(7) of the National Health Service and Community Care Act 1990, at a time when the vehicle is being driven under the owner's control,

(db) to an ambulance owned by a National Health Service trust established under Part I of the National Health Service and Community Care Act 1990 or the National Health Service (Scotland) Act 1978, at a time when a vehicle is being driven under the owner's control.]

(e) to a vehicle which is made available by the Secretary of State to any person, body or local authority in pursuance of section 23 or 26 of the National Health Service Act 1977 at a time when it is being used in accordance with the terms on which it is so made available.

145. Requirements in respect of policies of insurance.

(1) In order to comply with the requirements of this Part of this Act, a policy of insurance must satisfy the following conditions.

(2) The policy must be issued by an authorised insurer.

(3) Subject to subsection (4) below, the policy—

(a) must insure such person, persons or classes of persons as may be specified in the policy in respect of any liability which may be incurred by him or them in respect of the death of or bodily injury to any person or damage to property caused by, or arising out of, the use of the vehicle on a road in Great Britain, and

[(aa) must, in the case of a vehicle normally based in the territory of another member State, insure him or them in respect of any civil liability which may be incurred by him or them as a result of an event related to the use of the vehicle in Great Britain if,—

(i) according to the law of that territory, he or they would be required to be insured in respect of a civil liability which would arise under that law as a result of that event if the place where the vehicle was used when the event occurred were in that territory, and

(ii) the cover required by that law would be higher than that required by paragraph (a) above, and]

(b) must [, in the case of a vehicle normally based in Great Britain,] insure him or them in respect of any liability which may be incurred by him or them in respect of the use of the vehicle and of any trailer, whether or not coupled, in the territory other than Great Britain and Gibraltar of each of the member States of the Communities according to

[(i) the law on compulsory insurance against civil liability in respect of the use of vehicles of the State in whose territory the event giving rise to the liability occurred; or

(ii) if it would give higher cover, the law which would be applicable under this Part of this Act if the place where the vehicle was used when that event occurred were in Great Britain; and]

(c) must also insure him or them in respect of any liability which may be incurred by him or them under the provisions of this Part of this Act relating to payment for emergency treatment.

(4) The policy shall not, by virtue of subsection (3)(a) above, be required—

(a) to cover liability in respect of the death, arising out of and in the course of his employment, of a person in the employment of a person insured by the policy or of bodily injury sustained by such a person arising out of and in the course of his employment, or

(b) to provide insurance of more than £250,000 in respect of all such liabilities as may be incurred in respect of damage to property caused by, or arising out of, any one accident involving the vehicle, or

(c) to cover liability in respect of damage to the vehicle, or

(d) to cover liability in respect of damage to goods carried for hire or reward in or on the vehicle or in or on any trailer (whether or not coupled) drawn by the vehicle, or

(e) to cover any liability of a person in respect of damage to property in his custody or under his control, or

(f) to cover any contractual liability.

[(4A) In the case of a person—

(a) carried in or upon a vehicle, or

(b) entering or getting on to, or alighting from, a vehicle,

the provisions of paragraph (a) of subsection (4) above do not apply unless cover in respect of the liability referred to in that paragraph is in fact provided pursuant to a requirement of the Employers' Liability (Compulsory Insurance) Act 1969.]

148. Avoidance of certain exceptions to policies or securities.

(1) Where a certificate of insurance or certificate of security has been delivered under section 147 of this Act to the person by whom a policy has been effected or to whom a security has been given, so much of the policy or security as purports to restrict—

(a) the insurance of the persons insured by the policy, or

(b) the operation of the security,

(as the case may be) by reference to any of the matters mentioned in subsection (2) below shall, as respects such liabilities as are required to be covered by a policy under section 145 of this Act, be of no effect.

(2) Those matters are—

(a) the age or physical or mental condition of persons driving the vehicle,

(b) the condition of the vehicle,

(c) the number of persons that the vehicle carries,

(d) the weight or physical characteristics of the goods that the vehicle carries,

(e) the time at which or the areas within which the vehicle is used,

(f) the horsepower or cylinder capacity or value of the vehicle,

(g) the carrying on the vehicle of any particular apparatus, or

(h) the carrying on the vehicle of any particular means of identification other than any means of identification required to be carried by or under [the Vehicles Excise and Registration Act 1994].

(3) Nothing in subsection (1) above requires an insurer or the giver of a security to pay any sum in respect of the liability of any person otherwise than in or towards the discharge of that liability.

(4) Any sum paid by an insurer or the giver of a security in or towards the discharge of any liability of any person which is covered by the policy or security by virtue only of

Road Traffic Act 1988

subsection (1) above is recoverable by the insurer or giver of the security from that person.

(5) A condition in a policy or security issued or given for the purposes of this Part of this Act providing—

(a) that no liability shall arise under the policy or security, or

(b) that any liability so arising shall cease,

in the event of some specified thing being done or omitted to be done after the happening of the event giving rise to a claim under the policy or security, shall be of no effect in connection with such liabilities as are required to be covered by a policy under section 145 of this Act.

(6) Nothing in subsection (5) above shall be taken to render void any provision in a policy or security requiring the person insured or secured to pay to the insurer or the giver of the security any sums which the latter may have become liable to pay under the policy or security and which have been applied to the satisfaction of the claims of third parties.

(7) Notwithstanding anything in any enactment, a person issuing a policy of insurance under section 145 of this Act shall be liable to indemnify the persons or classes of persons specified in the policy in respect of any liability which the policy purports to cover in the case of those persons or classes of persons.

149. Avoidance of certain agreements as to liability towards passengers.

(1) This section applies where a person uses a motor vehicle in circumstances such that under section 143 of this Act there is required to be in force in relation to his use of it such a policy of insurance or such a security in respect of third-party risks as complies with the requirements of this Part of this Act.

(2) If any other person is carried in or upon the vehicle when the user is so using it, any antecedent agreement or understanding between them (whether intended to be legally binding or not) shall be of no effect so far as it purports or might be held—

(a) to negative or restrict any such liability of the user in respect of persons carried in or upon the vehicle as is required by section 145 of this Act to be covered by a policy of insurance, or

(b) to impose any conditions with respect to the enforcement of any such liability of the user.

(3) The fact that a person so carried has willingly accepted as his the risk of negligence on the part of the user shall not be treated as negativing any such liability of the user.

(4) For the purposes of this section—

(a) references to a person being carried in or upon a vehicle include references to a person entering or getting on to, or alighting from, the vehicle, and

(b) the reference to an antecedent agreement is to one made at any time before the liability arose.

151. Duty of insurers of persons giving security to satisfy judgment against persons insured or secured against third-party risks.

(1) This section applies where, after a certificate of insurance or certificate of security has been delivered under section 147 of this Act to the person by whom a policy has been effected or to whom a security has been given, a judgment to which this subsection applies is obtained.

(2) Subsection (1) above applies to judgments relating to a liability with respect to any matter where liability with respect to that matter is required to be covered by a policy of insurance under section 145 of this Act and either—

(a) it is a liability covered by the terms of the policy or security to which the certificate relates, and the judgment is obtained against any person who is insured by the policy or whose liability is covered by the security, as the case may be, or

(b) it is a liability, other than an excluded liability, which would be so covered if the policy insured all persons or, as the case may be, the security covered the liability of all persons, and the judgment is obtained against any person other than one who is insured by the policy or, as the case may be, whose liability is covered by the security.

(3) In deciding for the purposes of subsection (2) above whether a liability is or would be covered by the terms of a policy or security, so much of the policy or security as purports to restrict, as the case may be, the insurance of the persons insured by the policy or the operation of the security by reference to the holding by the driver of the vehicle of a licence authorising him to drive it shall be treated as of no effect.

(4) In subsection (2)(b) above "excluded liability" means a liability in respect of the death of, or bodily injury to, or damage to the property of any person who, at the time of the use which gave rise to the liability, was allowing himself to be carried in or upon the vehicle and knew or had reason to believe that the vehicle had been stolen or unlawfully taken, not being a person who—

(a) did not know and had no reason to believe that the vehicle had been stolen or unlawfully taken until after the commencement of his journey, and

(b) could not reasonably have been expected to have alighted from the vehicle.

In this subsection the reference to a person being carried in or upon a vehicle includes a reference to a person entering or getting on to, or alighting from, the vehicle.

(5) Notwithstanding that the insurer may be entitled to avoid or cancel, or may have avoided or cancelled, the policy or security, he must, subject to the provisions of this section, pay to the persons entitled to the benefit of the judgment—

(a) as regards liability in respect of death or bodily injury, any sum payable under the judgment in respect of the liability, together with any sum which, by virtue of any enactment relating to interest on judgments, is payable in respect of interest on that sum,

(b) as regards liability in respect of damage to property, any sum required to be paid under subsection (6) below, and

(c) any amount payable in respect of costs.

(6) This subsection requires—

(a) where the total of any amounts paid, payable or likely to be payable under the policy or security in respect of damage to property caused by, or arising out of, the accident in question does not exceed £250,000, the payment of any sum payable under the judgment in respect of the liability, together with any sum which, by virtue of any enactment relating to interest on judgments, is payable in repect of interest on that sum,

(b) where that total exceeds £250,000, the payment of either—

(i) such proportion of any sum payable under the judgment in respect of the liability as £250,000 bears to that total, together with the same proportion of any sum which, by virtue of any enactment relating to interest on judgments, is payable in respect of interest on that sum, or

(ii) the difference between the total of any amounts already paid under the policy or security in respect of such damage and £250,000, together with such proportion of any sum which, by virtue of any enactment relating to interest on judgments, is payable in respect of interest on any sum payable under the judgment in respect of the liability as the difference bears to that sum,

whichever is the less, unless not less than £250,000 has already been paid under the policy or security in respect of such damage (in which case nothing is payable).

(7) Where an insurer becomes liable under this section to pay an amount in respect of a liability of a person who is insured by a policy or whose liability is covered by a security, he is entitled to recover from that person—

(a) that amount, in a case where he became liable to pay it by virtue only of subsection (3) above, or

(b) in a case where that amount exceeds the amount for which he would, apart from the provisions of this section, be liable under the policy or security in respect of that liability, the excess.

(8) Where an insurer becomes liable under this section to pay an amount in respect of a liability of a person who is not insured by a policy or whose liability is not covered by a security, he is entitled to recover the amount from that person or from any person who—

(a) is insured by the policy, or whose liability is covered by the security, by the terms of which the liability would be covered if the policy insured all persons or, as the case may be, the security covered the liability of all persons, and

(b) caused or permitted the use of the vehicle which gave rise to the liability.

(9) In this section—

(a) "insurer" includes a person giving a security,

(c) "liability covered by the terms of the policy or security" means a liability which is covered by the policy or security or which would be so covered but for the fact that the insurer is entitled to avoid or cancel, or has avoided or cancelled, the policy or security.

153. Bankruptcy, etc., of insured or secured persons not to affect claims by third parties.

(1) Where, after a certificate of insurance or certificate of security has been delivered under section 147 of this Act to the person by whom a policy has been effected or to whom a security as been given, any of the events mentioned in subsection (2) below happens, the happening of that event shall, notwithstanding anything in the Third Parties (Rights Against Insurers) Act 1930, not affect any such liability of that person as is required to be covered by a policy of insurance under section 145 of this Act.

(2) In the case of the person by whom the policy was effected or to whom the security was given, the events referred to in subsection (1) above are—

(a) that he becomes bankrupt or makes a composition or arrangement with his creditors or that his estate is sequestrated or he grants a trust deed for his creditors,

(b) that he dies and—

(i) his estate falls to be administered in accordance with an order under section 421 of the Insolvency Act 1986,

(ii) an award of sequestration of his estate is made, or

(iii) a judicial factor is appointed to administer his estate under section 11A of the Judicial Factors (Scotland) Act 1889,

(c) that if that person is a company—

(i) a winding-up order or an administration order is made with respect of the company,

(ii) a resolution for a voluntary winding-up is passed with respect to the company,

(iii) a receiver or manager of the company's business or undertaking is duly appointed, or

(iv) possession is taken, by or on behalf of the holders of any debentures secured by a floating charge, of any property comprised in or subject to the charge.

(3) Nothing in subsection (1) above affects any rights conferred by the Third Parties (Rights Against Insurers) Act 1930 on the person to whom the liability was incurred, being rights so conferred against the person by whom the policy was issued or the security was given.

157. Payment for hospital treatment of traffic casualties.

(1) Subject to subsection (2) below, where—

(a) a payment, other than a payment under section 158 of this Act, is made (whether or not with an admission of liability) in respect of the death of, or bodily injury to, any person arising out of the use of a motor vehicle on a road or in a place to which the public have a right of access, and

    (b)   the payment is made—

        (i)   by an authorised insurer, the payment being made under or in consequence of a policy issued under section 145 of this Act, or

        (ii)   by the owner of a vehicle in relation to the use of which a security under this Part of this Act is in force, or

        (iii)   by the owner of a vehicle who has made a deposit under this Part of this Act, and

    (c)   the person who has so died or been bodily injured has to the knowledge of the insurer or owner, as the case may be, received treatment at a hospital, whether as an in-patient or as an out-patient, in respect of the injury so arising,

the insurer or owner must pay the expenses reasonably incurred by the hospital in affording the treatment, after deducting from the expenses any moneys actually received in payment of a specific charge for the treatment, not being moneys received under any contributory scheme.

    (2)   The amount to be paid shall not exceed [£2,949.00] for each person treated as an in-patient or [£295.00] for each person treated as an out-patient.

    (3)   For the purposes of this section "expenses reasonably incurred" means—

    (a)   in relation to a person who receives treatment at a hospital as an in-patient, an amount for each day he is maintained in the hospital representing the average daily cost, for each in-patient, of the maintenance of the hospital and the staff of the hospital and the maintenance and treatment of the in-patients in the hospital, and

    (b)   in relation to a person who receives treatment at a hospital as an out-patient, reasonable expenses actually incurred.

158. Payment for emergency treatment of traffic casualties.

    (1)   Subsection (2) below applies where—

    (a)   medical or surgical treatment or examination is immediately required as a result of bodily injury (including fatal injury) to a person caused by, or arising out of, the use of a motor vehicle on a road, and

    (b)   the treatment or examination so required (in this Part of this Act referred to as "emergency treatment") is effected by a legally qualified medical practitioner.

    (2)   The person who was using the vehicle at the time of the event out of which the bodily injury arose must, on a claim being made in accordance with the provisions of section 159 of this Act, pay to the practitioner (or, where emergency treatment is effected by more than one practitioner, to the practitioner by whom it is first effected)—

    (a)   a fee of [£21.30] in respect of each person in whose case the emergency treatment is effected by him, and

    (b)   a sum, in respect of any distance in excess of two miles which he must cover in order—

        (i)   to proceed from the place from which he is summoned to the place where the emergency treatment is carried out by him, and

        (ii)   to return to the first mentioned place,

equal to [41 pence] for every complete mile and additional part of a mile of that distance.

    (3)   Where emergency treatment is first effected in a hospital, the provisions of subsections (1) and (2) above with respect to payment of a fee shall, so far as applicable, but subject (as regards the recipient of a payment) to the provisions of section 159 of this Act, have effect with the substitution of references to the hospital for references to a legally qualified medical practitioner.

(4) Liability incurred under this section by the person using a vehicle shall, where the event out of which it arose was caused by the wrongful act of another person, be treated for the purposes of any claim to recover damage by reason of that wrongful act as damage sustained by the person using the vehicle.

159. Supplementary provisions as to payments for treatment.

(2) A claim for a payment under section 158 of this Act may be made at the time when the emergency treatment is effected, by oral request to the person who was using the vehicle, and if not so made must be made by request in writing served on him within seven days from the day on which the emergency treatment was effected.

(4) A payment made under section 158 of this Act shall operate as a discharge, to the extent of the amount paid, of any liability of the person who was using the vehicle, or of any other person, to pay any sum in respect of the expenses of remuneration of the practitioner or hospital concerned of or for effecting the emergency treatment.

ROAD TRAFFIC (CONSEQUENTIAL PROVISIONS) ACT 1988
(1988, c. 54)

7. Saving for law of nuisance.
Nothing in the Road Traffic Acts authorises a person to use on a road a vehicle so constructed or used as to cause a public or private nuisance ... or affects the liability, whether under statute or common law, of the driver or owner so using a vehicle.

CHILDREN ACT 1989
(1989, c. 41)

2. Parental responsibility for children.

(9) A person who has parental responsibility for a child may not surrender or transfer any part of that responsibility to another but may arrange for some or all of it to be met by one or more persons acting on his behalf.

(10) The person with whom any such arrangement is made may himself be a person who already has parental responsibility for the child concerned.

(11) The making or any such arrangement shall not affect any liability of the person making it which may arise from any failure to meet any part of his parental responsibility for the child concerned.

COMPANIES ACT 1989
(1989, c. 40)

48. Exemption from liability for damages.

(1) Neither a recognised supervisory body, nor any of its officers or employees or members of its governing body, shall be liable in damages for anything done or omitted in the discharge or purported discharge of functions to which this subsection applies, unless the act or omission is shown to have been in bad faith.

(2) Subsection (1) applies to the functions of the body so far as relating to, or to matters arising out of—

    (a) such rules, practices, powers and arrangements of the body to which the requirements of Part II of Schedule 11 apply, or

    (b) the obligations with which paragraph 16 of that Schedule requires the body to comply,

    (c) any guidance issued by the body, or

    (d) the obligations to which the body is subject by virtue of this Part.

(3) Neither a body established by a delegation order nor any of its members, officers or employees, shall be liable in damages for anything done or omitted in the discharge or purported discharge of the functions exercisable by virtue of an order under section 46, unless the act or omission is shown to have been in bad faith.

ELECTRICITY ACT 1989
(1989, c. 29)

1. The Director General of Electricity Supply.

...

Consumer protection: standards of performance

39. Electricity supply: performance in individual cases.

(1) The Director may—
 (a) with the consent of the Secretary of State; [...]
 (b) after consultation with public electricity suppliers and with persons or bodies appearing to the Director to be representative of persons likely to be affected, [; and
 (c) after arranging for such research as the Director considers appropriate with a view of discovering the views of a representative sample of persons likely to be affected and considering the results,]
make regulations prescribing such standards of performance in connection with the provision by such suppliers of electricity supply services to tariff customers as, in his opinion, ought to be achieved in individual cases.

(3) If a public electricity supplier fails to meet a prescribed standard, he shall make to any person who is affected by the failure and is of a prescribed description such compensation as may be determined by or under the regulations.

(4) The making of compensation under this section in respect of any failure by a public electricity supplier to meet a prescribed standard shall not prejudice any other remedy which may be available in respect of the act or omission which constituted that failure.

EMPLOYMENT ACT 1989
(1989, c. 38)

11. Exemption of Sikhs from requirements as to wearing of safety helmets on construction sites.

(1) Any requirement to wear a safety helmet which (apart from this section) would, by virtue of any statutory provision or rule of law, be imposed on a Sikh who is on a construction site shall not apply to him at any time when he is wearing a turban.

(2) Accordingly, where—
 (a) a Sikh who is on a construction site is for the time being wearing a turban, and
 (b) (apart from this section) any associated requirement would, by virtue of any statutory provision or rule of law, be imposed—
  (i) on the Sikh, or
  (ii) on the other person,
in connection with the wearing by the Sikh of a safety helmet, that requirement shall not apply to the Sikh or (as the case may be) to that other person.

(4) It is hereby declared that, where a person does not comply with any requirement, being a requirement which for the time being does not apply to him by virtue of subsection (1) or (2)—
 (a) he shall not be liable in tort to any person in respect of any injury, loss or damage caused by his failure to comply with that requirement...

(5) If a Sikh who is on a construction site—

(a) does not comply with any requirement to wear a safety helmet, being a requirement which for the time being does not apply to him by virtue of subsection (1), and

(b) in consequence of any act or omission of some other person sustains any injury, loss or damage which is to any extent attributable to the fact that he is not wearing a safety helmet in compliance with the requirement,

that other person shall, if liable to the Sikh in tort (or, in Scotland, in an action for reparation), be so liable only to the extent that injury, loss or damage would have been sustained by the Sikh even if he had been wearing a safety helmet in compliance with the requirement.

(6) Where—

(a) the act or omission referred to in subsection (5) causes the death of the Sikh, and

(b) the Sikh would have sustained some injury (other than loss of life) in consequence of the act or omission even if he had been wearing a safety helmet in compliance with the requirement in question,

the amount of any damages which, by virtue of that subsection, are recoverable in tort (or, in Scotland, in an action for reparation) in respect of that injury shall not exceed the amount of any damages which would (apart from that subsection) be so recoverable in respect of the Sikh's death.

(7) In this section—

"injury" includes loss of life, any impairment of a person's physical or mental condition and any disease; ...

FINANCE ACT 1989
(1989, c. 26)

29. Recovery of overpaid excise duty and car tax.

(1) This section applies to proceedings for restitution of an amount paid to the Commissioners of Customs and Excise by way of excise duty or car tax.

(2) Proceedings to which this section applies shall not be dismissed by reason only of the fact that the amount was paid by reason of a mistake of law.

(3) In any proceedings to which this section applies it shall be a defence that repayment of an amount would unjustly enrich the claimant.

(4) This section shall have effect in relation to proceedings commenced on or after the day on which this Act is passed.

[*Section 29 shall cease to have effect so far as it relates to excise duty: Finance Act 1995, s. 20(3).*]

HUMAN ORGAN TRANSPLANTS ACT 1989
(1989, c. 31)

1. Prohibition of commercial dealings in human organs.

(1) A person is guilty of an offence if in Great Britain he—

(a) makes or receives any payment for the supply of, or for an offer to supply, an organ which has been or is to be removed from a dead or living person and is intended to be transplanted into another person whether in Great Britain or elsewhere;

(b) seeks to find a person willing to supply for payment such an organ as is mentioned in paragraph (a) above or offers to supply such an organ for payment;

(c) initiates or negotiates any arrangement involving the making of any payment for the supply of, or for an offer to supply, such an organ; or

(d) takes part in the management or control of a body of persons corporate or unincorporate whose activities consist of or include the initiation or negotiation of such arrangements.

LAW OF PROPERTY (MISCELLANEOUS PROVISIONS) ACT 1989
(1989, c. 34)

1. **Deeds and their execution.**

(1) Any rule of law which—
   (a) restricts the substances on which a deed may be written;
   (b) requires a seal for the valid execution of an instrument as a deed by an individual; or
   (c) requires authority by one person to another to deliver an instrument as a deed on his behalf to be given by deed,
is abolished.

(2) An instrument shall not be a deed unless—
   (a) it makes it clear on its face that it is intended to be a deed by the person making it or, as the case may be, by the parties to it (whether by describing itself as a deed or expressing itself to be executed or signed as a deed or otherwise); and
   (b) it is validly executed as a deed by that person or, as the case may be, one or more of those parties.

(3) An instrument is validly executed as a deed by an individual if, and only if—
   (a) it is signed—
      (i) by him in the presence of a witness who attests the signature; or
      (ii) at his direction and in his presence and the presence of two witnesses who each attest the signature; and
   (b) it is delivered as a deed by him or a person authorised to do so on his behalf.

(4) In subsections (2) and (3) above "sign", in relation to an instrument, includes making one's mark on the instrument and "signature" is to be construed accordingly.

(5) Where a solicitor [, duly certificated notary public] or licensed conveyancer, or an agent or employee of a solicitor [, duly certificated notary public] or licensed conveyancer, in the course of or in connection with a transaction involving the disposition or creation of an interest in land, purports to deliver an instrument as a deed on behalf of a party to the instrument, it shall be conclusively presumed in favour of a purchaser that he is authorised so to deliver the instrument.

(6) In subsection (5) above—
"disposition" and "purchaser" have the same meanings as in the Law of Property Act 1925
["duly certificated notary public" has the same meaning as it has in the Solicitors Act 1974 by virtue of section 87 of that Act;]; and
"interest in land" means any estate, interest or charge in or over land or in or over the proceeds of sale of land.

(7) Where an instrument under seal that constitutes a deed is required for the purposes of an Act passed before this section comes into force, this section shall have effect as to signing, sealing or delivery of an instrument by an individual in place of any provision of that Act as to signing, sealing or delivery.

(10) The references in this section to the execution of a deed by an individual do not include execution by a corporation sole and the reference in subsection (7) above to signing, sealing or delivery by an individual does not include signing, sealing or delivery by such a corporation.

(11) Nothing in this section applies in relation to instruments delivered as deeds before this section comes into force.

2. **Contracts for sale etc. of land to be made by signed writing.**

(1) A contract for the sale or other disposition of an interest in land can only be made in writing and only by incorporating all the terms which the parties have expressly agreed in one document or, where contracts are exchanged, in each.

(2) The terms may be incorporated in a document either by being set out in it or by reference to some other document.

(3) The document incorporating the terms or, where contracts are exchanged, one of the documents incorporating them (but not necessarily the same one) must be signed by or on behalf of each party to the contract.

(4) Where a contract for the sale or other disposition of an interest in land satisfies the conditions of this section by reason only of the rectification of one or more documents in pursuance of an order of a court, the contract shall come into being, or be deemed to have come into being, at such time as may be specified in the order.

(5) This section does not apply in relation to—
    (a) a contract to grant such a lease as is mentioned in section 54(2) of the Law of Property Act 1925 (short leases);
    (b) a contract made in the course of a public auction; or
    (c) a contract regulated under the Financial Services Act 1986;
and nothing in this section affects the creation or operation of resulting, implied or constructive trusts.

(6) In this section—
"disposition" has the same meaning as in the Law of Property Act 1925;
"interest in land" means any estate, interest or charge in or over land or in or over the proceeds of sale of land.

(7) Nothing in this section shall apply in relation to contracts made before this section comes into force.

(8) Section 40 of the Law of Property Act 1925 (which is superseded by this section) shall cease to have effect.

3. Abolition of rule in Bain v Fothergill.
The rule of law known as the rule in *Bain* v *Fothergill* is abolished in relation to contracts made after this section comes into force.

PREVENTION OF TERRORISM (TEMPORARY PROVISIONS) ACT 1989
(1989, c. 4)

PART III

12. Disclosure of information about terrorist funds.
(1) A person may notwithstanding any restriction on the disclosure of information imposed by [statute or otherwise] disclose to a constable a suspicion or belief that any money or other property is or is derived from terrorist funds or any matter on which such a suspicion or belief is based.

Section 13(8).   SCHEDULE 4
                       FORFEITURE ORDERS

Compensation

7.—(1) If proceedings are instituted against a person for an offence under Part III of this Act and either—
    (a) the proceedings do not result in his conviction for any such offence; or
    (b) where he is convicted of one or more such offences—
        (i) the conviction or convictions concerned are quashed; or
        (ii) he is pardoned by Her Majesty in respect of the conviction or convictions concerned,
the High Court may, on an application by a person who had an interest in any property which was subject to a forfeiture or restraint order made in or in relation to those

proceedings, order compensation to be paid to the applicant if, having regard to all the circumstances, it considers it appropriate to do so.

Protection of insolvency practitioners

33.—(1) In any case where—

(a) an insolvency practitioner seizes or disposes of any property in relation to which his functions are not exercisable because it is for the time being subject to a forfeiture or restraint order, and

(b) at the time of the seizure or disposal he believes and has reasonable grounds for believing that he is entitled (whether in pursuance of a court order or otherwise) to seize or dispose of that property,

he shall not be liable to any person in respect of any loss or damage resulting from the seizure or disposal except in so far as the loss or damage is caused by his negligence in so acting.

SECURITY SERVICE ACT 1989
(1989, c. 5)

1. The security service.

(1) There shall continue to be a Security Service (in this Act referred to as "the Service") under the authority of the Secretary of State.

3. Warrants.

(1) No entry on or interference with property shall be unlawful if it is authorised by a warrant issued by the Secretary of State under this section.

(2) The Secretary of State may on an application made by the Service issue a warrant under this section authorising the taking of such action as is specified in the warrant in respect of any property so specified if the Secretary of State—

(a) thinks it necessary for the action to be taken in order to obtain information which—

(i) is likely to be of substantial value in assisting the service to discharge any of its functions; and

(ii) cannot reasonably be obtained by other means; and

(b) is satisfied that satisfactory arrangements are in force under section 2(2)(a) above with respect to the disclosure of information obtained by virtue of this section and that the information obtained under the warrant will be subject to those arrangements.

ACCESS TO HEALTH RECORDS ACT 1990
(1990, c. 23)

3. Right of access to health records.

...

9. Avoidance of certain contractual terms.

Any term or condition of a contract shall be void in so far as it purports to require an individual to supply any other person with a copy of a health record, or of an extract from a health record, to which he has been given access under section 3(2) above.

BROADCASTING ACT 1990
(1990, c. 42)

166. Defamatory material.

(1) For the purposes of the law of libel and slander (including the law of criminal libel so far as it relates to the publication of defamatory matter) the publication of words

Contracts (Applicable Law) Act 1990

in the course of any programme included in a programme service shall be treated as publication in permanent form.

(2) Subsection (1) above shall apply for the purposes of section 3 of each of the Defamation Acts (slander of title etc.) as it applies for the purposes of the law of libel and slander.

...

(4) In this section "the Defamation Acts" means the Defamation Act 1952 and the Defamation Act (Northern Ireland) 1955.

201. Programme services.
...

Section 203(1)   SCHEDULE 20
MINOR AND CONSEQUENTIAL AMENDMENTS
PARLIAMENTARY PAPERS ACT 1840 (c. 9)

1. Section 3 (protection in respect of proceedings for printing extracts from or abstracts of parliamentary papers) shall have effect as if the reference to printing included a reference to including in a programme service.

CONTRACTS (APPLICABLE LAW) ACT 1990
(1990, c. 36)

1. Meaning of "the Conventions".
In this Act—
   (a) "the Rome Convention" means the Convention on the law applicable to contractual obligations opened for signature in Rome on 19th June 1980 and signed by the United Kingdom on December 7, 1981; ...

2. Conventions to have force of law.
(1) Subject to subsections (2) and (3) below, the Conventions shall have the force of law in the United Kingdom.

Section 2   SCHEDULE 1
TITLE I. SCOPE OF THE CONVENTION

Article 1. Scope of the Covention.
1. The rules of the Convention shall apply to contractual obligations in any situation involving a choice between the laws of different countries.

TITLE II. UNIFORM RULES

Article 3. Freedom of choice.
1. A contract shall be governed by the law chosen by the parties. The choice must be express or demonstrated with reasonable certainty by the terms of the contract or the circumstances of the case. By their choice the parties can select the law applicable to the whole or a part only of the contract.

3. The fact that the parties have chosen a foreign law, whether or not accompanied by the choice of a foreign tribunal, shall not, where all the other elements relevant to the situation at the time of the choice are connected with one country only, prejudice the application of rules of the law of that country which cannot be derogated from by contract, hereinafter called "mandatory rules".

Article 5. Certain consumer contracts.
1. This Article applies to a contract the object of which is the supply of goods or services to a person ("the consumer") for a purpose which can be regarded as being outside his trade or profession, or a contract for the provision of credit for that object.

2. Notwithstanding the provisions of Article 3, a choice of law made by the parties shall not have the result of depriving the consumer of the protection afforded to him by the mandatory rules of the law of the country in which he has his habitual residence:
— if in that country the conclusion of the contract was preceded by a specific invitation addressed to him or by advertising, and he had taken in that country all the steps necessary on his part for the conclusion of the contract, or
— if the other party or his agent received the consumer's order in that country, or
— if the contract is for the sale of goods and the consumer travelled from that country to another country and there gave his order, provided that the consumer's journey was arranged by the seller for the purpose of inducing the consumer to buy.

3. Notwithstanding the provisions of Article 4, a contract to which this Article applies shall, in the absence of choice in accordance with Article 3, be governed by the law of the country in which the consumer has his habitual residence if it is entered into in the circumstances described in paragraph 2 of this Article.

4. This Article shall not apply to:
   (a) a contract of carriage;
   (b) a contract for the supply of services where the services are to be supplied to the consumer exclusively in a country other than that in which he has his habitual residence.

5. Notwithstanding the provisions of paragraph 4, this Article shall apply to a contract which, for an inclusive price, provides for a combination of travel and accommodation.

Article 11. Incapacity.
In a contract concluded between persons who are in the same country, a natural person who would have capacity under the law of that country may invoke his incapacity resulting from another law only if the other party to the contract was aware of this incapacity at the time of the conclusion of the contract or was not aware thereof as a result of negligence.

COURTS AND LEGAL SERVICES ACT 1990
(1990, c. 41)

34. The Authorised Conveyancing Practitioners Board.
...

44. Compensation scheme.
(1) The Board may, with the approval of the Lord Chancellor, make rules establishing a scheme for compensating persons who have suffered loss in consequence of dishonesty on the part of the authorised practitioners or their employees.

(2) The rules may, in particular—
   (a) provide for the establishment and functioning of an independent body (whether corporate or unincorporate) to administer the scheme and, subject to the rules, determine and regulate any matter relating to its operation;
   (b) establish a fund out of which compensation is to be paid;
   (c) provide for the levying of contributions from authorised practitioners and otherwise for financing the scheme and for the payment of contributions and other money into the fund;
   (d) specify the terms and conditions on which, and the extent to which, compensation is to be payable and any circumstances in which the right to compensation is to be excluded or modified; and
   (e) contain incidental and supplementary provisions.

Environmental Protection Act 1990

61. Right of barrister to enter into contract for the provision of his services.

(1) Any rule of law which prevents a barrister from entering into a contract for the provision of his services as a barrister is hereby abolished.

(2) Nothing in subsection (1) prevents the General Council of the Bar from making rules (however described) which prohibit barristers from entering into contracts or restrict their right to do so.

62. Immunity of advocates from actions in negligence and for breach of contract.

A person—
  (a) who is not a barrister; but
  (b) who lawfully provides any legal services in relation to any proceedings,
shall have the same immunity from liability for negligence in respect of his acts or omissions as he would have if he were a barrister lawfully providing those services.

(2) No act or omission on the part of any barrister or other person which is accorded immunity from liability for negligence shall give rise to an action for breach of any contract relating to the provision by him of the legal services in question.

69. Exemption from liability for damages etc.

(1) Neither the Lord Chancellor nor any of the designated judges shall be liable in damages for anything done or omitted in the discharge or purported discharge of any of their functions under this Part.

(2) For the purposes of the law of defamation, the publication by the Lord Chancellor, a designated judge or the Director of any advice or reasons given by or to him in the exercise of functions under this Part shall be absolutely privileged.

ENVIRONMENTAL PROTECTION ACT 1990
(1990, c. 43)

PART I
INTEGRATED POLLUTION CONTROL AND AIR POLLUTION CONTROL BY LOCAL AUTHORITIES

18. Power to deal with cause of imminent danger of serious harm.

(1) Where, in the case of any article or substance found by him on any premises which he has power to enter, an inspector has reasonable cause to believe that, in the circumstances in which he finds it, the article or substance is a cause of imminent danger of serious harm he may seize it and cause it to be rendered harmless (whether by destruction or otherwise).

PART II
WASTE ON LAND

33. Prohibition on unauthorised or harmful deposit, treatment or disposal etc. of waste.

...

34. Duty of care etc. as respects waste.

(1) Subject to subsection (2) below, it shall be the duty of any person who imports, produces, carries, keeps, treats or disposes of controlled waste or, as a broker, has control of such waste, to take all such measures applicable to him in that capacity as are reasonable in the circumstances—
  (a) to prevent any contravention by any other person of section 33 above;
  (b) to prevent the escape of the waste from his control or that of any other person; and
  (c) on the transfer of the waste, to secure—

(i) that the transfer is only to an authorised person or to a person for authorised transport purposes; and

(ii) that there is transferred such a written description of the waste as will enable other persons to avoid a contravention of that section and to comply with the duty under this subsection as respects the escape of waste.

(2) The duty imposed by subsection (1) above does not apply to an occupier of domestic property as respects the household waste produced on the property.

(6) Any person who fails to comply with the duty imposed by subsection (1) above or with any requirement imposed under subsection (5) above shall be liable—

(a) on summary conviction, to a fine not exceeding the statutory maximum; and

(b) on conviction on indictment, to a fine.

(7) The Secretary of State shall, after consultation with such persons or bodies as appear to him representative of the interests concerned, prepare and issue a code of practice for the purpose of providing to persons practical guidance on how to discharge the duty imposed on them by subsection (1) above.

70. Power to deal with cause of imminent danger of serious pollution etc.

(1) Where, in the case of any article or substance found by him on any premises which he has power to enter, an inspector has reasonable cause to believe that, in the circumstances in which he finds it, the article or substance is a cause of imminent danger of serious pollution of the environment or serious harm to human health, he may seize it and cause it to be rendered harmless (whether by destruction or otherwise).

73. Appeals and other provisions relating to legal proceedings and civil liability.

(6) Where any damage is caused by waste which has been deposited in or on land, any person who deposited it, or knowingly caused or knowingly permitted it to be deposited, in either case so as to commit an offence under section 33(1) or 63(2) above, is liable for the damage except where the damage—

(a) was due wholly to the fault of the person who suffered it; or

(b) was suffered by a person who voluntarily accepted the risk of the damage being caused;

but without prejudice to any liability arising otherwise than under this subsection.

(7) The matters which may be proved by way of defence under section 33(7) above may be proved also by way of defence to an action brought under subsection (6) above.

(8) In subsection (6) above—

"damage" includes the death of, or injury to, any person (including any disease and any impairment of physical or mental condition); and

"fault" has the same meaning as in the Law Reform (Contributory Negligence) Act 1945.

(9) For the purposes of the following enactments—

(a) the Fatal Accidents Act 1976;

(b) the Law Reform (Contributory Negligence) Act 1945; and

(c) the Limitation Act 1980;

and for the purposes of any action of damages in Scotland arising out of the death of, or personal injury to, any person, any damage for which a person is liable under subsection (6) above shall be treated as due to his fault.

[PART IIA
CONTAMINATED LAND

78A. Preliminary.

(2) "Contaminated land" is any land which appears to the local authority in whose area it is situated to be in such a condition, by reason of substances in, on or under the land, that—

Environmental Protection Act 1990

(a) significant harm is being caused or there is a significant possibility of such harm being caused; or

(b) pollution of controlled waters is being, or is likely to be, caused;

and, in determining whether any land appears to be such land, a local authority shall, subject to subsection (5) below, act in accordance with guidance issued by the Secretary of State in accordance with section 78YA below with respect to the manner in which that determination is to be made.

(3) A "special site" is any contaminated land—

(a) which has been designated as such a site by virtue of section 78C(7) or 78D(6) below; and

(b) whose designation as such has not been terminated by the appropriate Agency under section 78Q(4) below.

(4) "Harm" means harm to the health of living organisms or other interference with the ecological systems of which they form part and, in the case of man, includes harm to his property.

(5) The questions—

(a) what harm is to be regarded as "significant",

(b) whether the possibility of significant harm being caused is "significant",

(c) whether pollution of controlled waters is being, or is likely to be caused,

shall be determined in accordance with guidance issued for the purpose by the Secretary of State in accordance with section 78YA below.

(6) Without prejudice to the guidance that may be issued under subsection (5) above, guidance under paragraph (a) of that subsection may make provision for different degrees of importance to be assigned to, or for the disregard of,—

(a) different descriptions of living organisms or ecological systems;

(b) different descriptions of places; or

(c) different descriptions of harm to health or property, or other interference;

and guidance under paragraph (b) of that subsection may make provision for different degrees of possibility to be regarded as "significant" (or as not being "significant") in relation to different descriptions of significant harm.

(7) "Remediation" means—

(a) the doing of anything for the purpose of assessing the condition of—

(i) the contaminated land in question;

(ii) any controlled waters affected by that land; or

(iii) any land adjoining or adjacent to that land;

(b) the doing of any works, the carrying out of any operations or the taking of any steps in relation to any such land or waters for the purpose—

(i) of preventing or minimising, or remedying or mitigating the effects of, any significant harm, or any pollution of controlled waters, by reason of which the contaminated land is such land; or

(ii) of restoring the land or waters to their former state; or

(c) the making of subsequent inspections from time to time for the purpose of keeping under review the condition of the land or waters;

and cognate expressions shall be construed accordingly.

(8) Controlled waters are "affected by" contaminated land if (and only if) it appears to the enforcing authority that the contaminated land in question is, for the purposes of subsection (2) above, in such a condition, by reason of substances in, on or under the land, that pollution of those waters is being, or is likely to be caused.

(9) The following expressions have the meaning respectively assigned to them—

"the appropriate Agency" means—

(a) in relation to England and Wales, the Environment Agency;

(b) in relation to Scotland, the Scottish Environment Protection Agency;

"appropriate person" means any person who is an appropriate person, determined in accordance with section 78F below, to bear responsibility for any thing which is to be done by way of remediation in any particular case;

"charging notice" has the meaning given by section 78P(3)(b) below;

"controlled waters"—

    (a) in relation to England and Wales, has the same meaning as in Part III of the Water Resources Act 1991; and

    (b) in relation to Scotland, has the same meaning as in section 30A of the Control of Pollution Act 1974;

"creditor" has the same meaning as in the Conveyancing and Feudal Reform (Scotland) Act 1970;

"enforcing authority" means—

    (a) in relation to a special site, the appropriate Agency;

    (b) in relation to contaminated land other than a special site, the local authority in whose area the land is situated;

"heritable security" has the same meaning as in the Conveyancing and Feudal Reform (Scotland) Act 1970;

"local authority" in relation to England and Wales means—

    (a) any unitary authority;

    (b) any district council, so far as it is not a unitary authority;

    (c) the Common Council of the City of London and, as respects the Temples, the Sub-Treasurer of the Inner Temple and the Under-Treasurer of the Middle Temple respectively;

and in relation to Scotland means a council for an area constituted under section 2 of the Local Goverment etc. (Scotland) Act 1994;

"notice" means notice in writing;

"notification" means notification in writing;

"owner", in relation to any land in England and Wales, means a person (other than a mortgagee not in possession) who, whether in his own right or as trustee for any other person, is entitled to receive the rack rent of the land, or, where the land is not let at a rack rent, would be so entitled if it were so let;

"owner", in relation to any land in Scotland, means a person (other than a creditor in a heritable security not in possession of the security subjects) for the time being entitled to receive or who would, if the land were let, be entitled to receive, the rents of the land in connection with which the word is used and includes a trustee, factor, guardian or curator and in the case of public or municipal land includes the persons to whom the management of the land is entrusted;

"pollution of controlled waters" means the entry into controlled waters of any poisonous, noxious or polluting matter or any solid waste matter;

"prescribed" means prescribed by regulations;

"regulations" means regulations made by the Secretary of State;

"remediation declaration" has the meaning given by section 78H(6) below;

"remediation notice" has the meaning given by section 78E(1) below;

"remediation statement" has the meaning given by section 78H(7) below;

"required to be designated as a special site" shall be construed in accordance with section 78C(8) below;

"substance" means any natural or artificial substance, whether in solid or liquid form or in the form of a gas or vapour;

"unitary authority" means—

    (a) the council of a county, so far as it is the council of an area for which there are no district councils;

    (b) the council of any district comprised in an area for which there is no county council;

(c) the council of a London borough;
(d) the council of a county borough in Wales.]

[78B. Identification of contaminated land.

(1) Every local authority shall cause its area to be inspected from time to time for the purpose—
  (a) of identifying contaminated land; and
  (b) of enabling the authority to decide whether any such land is land which is required to be designated as a special site.

(2) In performing its functions under subsection (1) above a local authority shall act in accordance with any guidance issued for the purpose by the Secretary of State in accorance with section 78YA below.

(3) If a local authority identifies any contaminated land in its area, it shall give notice of that fact to—
  (a) the appropriate Agency;
  (b) the owner of the land;
  (c) any person who appears to the authority to be in occupation of the whole or any part of the land; and
  (d) each person who appears to the authority to be an appropriate person;
and any notice given under this subsection shall state by virtue of which of paragraphs (a) to (d) above it is given.

(4) If, at any time after a local authority has given any person a notice pursuant to subsection (3)(d) above in respect of any land, it appears to the enforcing authority that another person is an appropriate person, the enforcing authority shall give notice to that other person—
  (a) of the fact that the local authority has identified the land in question as contaminated land; and
  (b) that he appears to the enforcing authority to be an appropriate person.]

[78C. Identification and designation of special sites.

(1) If at any time it appears to a local authority that any contaminated land in its area might be land which is required to be designated as a special site, the authority—
  (a) shall decide whether or not the land is land which is required to be so designated; and
  (b) if the authority decides that the land is land which is required to be so designated, shall give notice of that decision to the relevant persons.

(2) For the purposes of this section, "the relevant persons" at any time in the case of any land are the persons who at that time fall within paragraphs (a) to (d) below, that is to say—
  (a) the appropriate Agency;
  (b) the owner of the land;
  (c) any person who appears to the local authority concerned to be in occupation of the whole or any part of the land; and
  (d) each person who appears to that authority to be an appropriate person.

(3) Before making a decision under paragraph (a) of subsection (1) above in any particular case, a local authority shall request the advice of the appropriate Agency, and in making its decision shall have regard to any advice given by that Agency in response to the request.

(4) If at any time the appropriate Agency considers that any contaminated land is land which is required to be designated as a special site, that Agency may give notice of that fact to the local authority in whose area the land is situated.

(5) Where notice under subsection (4) above is given to a local authority, the authority shall decide whether the land in question—
  (a) is land which is required to be designated as a special site or

(b) is not land which is required to be so designated,
and shall give notice of that decision to the relevant persons.

(10) Without prejudice to the generality of his power to prescribe any description of land for the purposes of subsection (8) above, the Secretary of State, in deciding whether to prescribe a particular description of contaminated land for those purposes, may, in particular, have regard to—

(a) whether land of the description in question appears to him to be land which is likely to be in such a condition, by reason of substances in, on or under the land that—
    (i) serious harm would or might be caused, or
    (ii) serious pollution of controlled waters would be, or would be likely to be, caused; or

(b) whether the appropriate Agency is likely to have expertise in dealing with the kind of significant harm, or pollution of controlled waters, by reason of which land of the description in question is contaminated land.]

[78D. Referral of special site decisions to the Secretary of State.

(1) In any case where—
(a) a local authority gives notice of a decision to the appropriate Agency pursuant to subsection (1)(b) or (5)(b) of section 78C above, but
(b) before the expiration of the period of twenty-one days beginning with the day on which that notice is so given, that Agency gives the local authority notice that it disagrees with the decision, together with a statement of its reasons for disagreeing,
the authority shall refer the decision to the Secretary of State and shall send to him a statement of its reasons for reaching the decision.

(3) Where a local authority refers a decision to the Secretary of State under subsection (1) above, it shall give notice of that fact to the relevant persons.

(4) Where a decision of a local authority is referred to the Secretary of State under subsection (1) above, he—
(a) may confirm or reverse the decision with respect to the whole or any part of the land to which it relates; and
(b) shall give notice of his decision on the referral—
    (i) to the relevant persons; and
    (ii) to the local authority.]

[78E. Duty of enforcing authority to require remediation of contaminated land etc.

(1) In any case where—
(a) any land has been designated as a special site by virtue of section 78C(7) or 78D(6) above, or
(b) a local authority has identified any contaminated land (other than a special site) in its area,
the enforcing authority shall, in accordance with such procedure as may be prescribed and subject to the following provisions of this Part, serve on each person who is an appropriate person a notice (in this Part referred to as a "remediation notice") specifying what that person is to do by way of remediation and the periods within which he is required to do each of the things so specified.

(2) Different remediation notices requiring the doing of different things by way of remediation may be served on different persons in consequence of the presence of different substances in, on or under any land or waters.

(3) Where two or more persons are appropriate persons in relation to any particular thing which is to be done by way of remediation, the remediation notice served on each of them shall state the proportion, determined under section 78F(7) below, of the cost of doing that thing which each of them respectively is liable to bear.

Environmental Protection Act 1990

(4) The only things by way of remediation which the enforcing authority may do, or require to be done, under or by virtue of this Part are things which it considers reasonable, having regard to—
(a) the cost which is likely to be involved; and
(b) the seriousness of the harm, or pollution of controlled waters, in question.
(5) In determining for any purpose of this Part—
(a) what is to be done (whether by an appropriate person, the enforcing authority or any other person) by way of remediation in any particular case,
(b) the standard to which any land is, or waters are, to be remediated pursuant to the notice, or
(c) what is, or is not, to be regarded as reasonable for the purposes of subsection (4) above,
the enforcing authority shall have regard to any guidance issued for the purposes by the Secretary of State.]

[**78F. Determination of the appropriate person to bear responsibility for remediation.**
(1) This section has effect for the purpose of determining who is the appropriate person to bear responsibility for any particular thing which the enforcing authority determines is to be done by way of remediation in any particular case.
(2) Subject to the following provisions of this section, any person, or any of the persons, who caused or knowingly permitted the substances, or any of the substances, by reason of which the contaminated land in question is such land to be in, on or under that land is an appropriate person.
(3) A person shall only be an appropriate person by virtue of subsection (2) above in relation to things which are to be done by way of remediation which are to any extent referable to substances which he caused or knowingly permitted to be present in, on or under the contaminated land in question.
(4) If no person has, after reasonable inquiry, been found who is by virtue of subsection (2) above an appropriate person to bear responsibility for the things which are to be done by way of remediation, the owner or occupier for the time being of the contaminated land in question is an appropriate person.
(5) If, in consequence of subsection (3) above, there are things which are to be done by way of remediation in relation to which no person has, after reasonable inquiry, been found who is an appropriate person by virtue of subsection (2) above, the owner or occupier for the time being of the contaminated land in question is an appropriate person in relation to those things.
(6) Where two or more persons would, apart from this subsection, be appropriate persons in relation to any particular thing which is to be done by way of remediation, the enforcing authority shall determine in accordance with guidance issued for the purpose by the Secretary of State whether any, and if so which, of them is to be treated as not being an appropriate person in relation to that thing.
(7) Where two or more persons are appropriate persons in relation to any particular thing which is to be done by way of remediation, they shall be liable to bear the cost of doing that thing in proportions determined by the enforcing authority in accordance with guidance issued for the purpose by the Secretary of State.
(8) Any guidance issued for the purposes of subsection (6) or (7) above shall be issued in accordance with section 78YA below.
(9) A person who has caused or knowingly permitted any substance ("substance A") to be in, on or under any land shall also be taken for the purposes of this section to have caused or knowingly permitted there to be in, on or under that land any substance which is there as a result of a chemical reaction or biological process affecting substance A.

(10) A thing which is to be done by way of remediation may be regarded for the purposes of this Part as referable to the presence of any substance notwithstanding that the thing in question would not have to be done—
    (a) in consequence only of the presence of that substance in any quantity; or
    (b) in consequence only of the quantity of that substance which any particular person caused, or knowingly permitted to be present.]

[78G. Grant of, and compensation for, rights of entry etc.
(1) A remediation notice may require an appropriate person to do things by way of remediation, notwithstanding that he is not entitled to do those things.
(2) Any person whose consent is required before any thing required by a remediation notice may be done shall grant, or join in granting, such rights in relation to any of the relevant land or waters as will enable the appropriate person to comply with any requirements imposed by the remediation notice.
(3) Before serving a remediation notice, the enforcing authority shall reasonably endeavour to consult every person who appears to the authority—
    (a) to be the owner or occupier of any of the relevant land or waters, and
    (b) to be a person who might be required by subsection (2) above to grant, or join in granting, any rights,
concerning the rights which that person may be so required to grant.
(4) Subsection (3) above shall not preclude the service of a remediation notice in any case where it appears to the enforcing authority that the contaminated land in question is in such a condition, by reason of substances in, on or under the land, that there is imminent danger of serious harm, or serious pollution of controlled waters, being caused.
(5) A person who grants, or joins in granting, any rights pursuant to subsection (2) above shall be entitled on making an application within such period as may be prescribed and in such manner as may be prescribed to such person as may be prescribed, to be paid by the appropriate person compensation of such amount as may be determined in such manner as may be prescribed.
(6) Without prejudice to the generality of the regulations that may be made by virtue of subsection (5) above, regulations by virtue of that subsection may make such provision in relation to compensation under this section as may be made by regulations by virtue of subsection (4) of section 35A above in relation to compensation under that section.
(7) In this section, "relevant land or waters" means—
    (a) the contaminated land in question;
    (b) any controlled waters affected by that land; or
    (c) any land adjoining or adjacent to the land or those waters.]

[78H. Restrictions and prohibitions on serving remediation notices.
...]

[78J. Restrictions on liability relating to the pollution of controlled waters.
(1) This section applies where any land is contaminated land by virtue of paragraph (b) of subsection (2) of section 78A above (whether or not the land is also contaminated land by virtue of paragraph (a) of that subsection).
(2) Where this section applies, no remediation notice given in consequence of the land in question being contaminated land shall require a person who is an appropriate person by virtue of section 78F(4) and (5) above to do anything by way of remediation to that or any other land, or any waters, which he could not have been required to do by such a notice had paragraph (b) of section 78A(2) above (and all other references to pollution of controlled waters) been omitted from this Part.
(3) If, in a case where this section applies, a person permits, has permitted, or might permit, water from an abandoned mine or part of a mine—

Environmental Protection Act 1990

    (a) to enter any controlled waters, or
    (b) to reach a place from which it is or, as the case may be, was likely, in the opinion of the enforcing authority, to enter such waters,
no remediation notice shall require him in consequence to do anything by way of remediation (whether to the contaminated land in question or to any other land or waters) which he could not have been required to do by such a notice had paragraph (b) of section 78A(2) above (and all other references to pollution of controlled waters) been omitted from this Part.

    (4) Subsection (3) above shall not apply to the owner or former operator of any mine or part of a mine if the mine or part in question became abandoned after 31st December 1999.
...]

[78K. Liability in respect of contaminating substances which escape to other land.
    (1) A person who has caused or knowingly permitted any substances to be in, on or under any land shall also be taken for the purposes of this Part to have caused or, as the case may be, knowingly permitted those substances to be in, on or under any other land to which they appear to have escaped.

    (2) Subsections (3) and (4) below apply in any case where it appears that any substances are or have been in, on or under any land (in this section referred to as "land") as a result of their escape, whether directly or indirectly, from other land in, on or under which a person caused or knowingly permitted them to be.

    (3) Where this subsection applies, no remediation notice shall require a person—
    (a) who is the owner or occupier of land A, and
    (b) who has not caused or knowingly permitted the substances in question to be in, on or under that land,
to do anything by way of remediation to any land or waters (other than land or waters of which he is the owner or occupier) in consequence of land A appearing to be in such a condition, by reason of the presence of those substances in, on or under it, that significant harm is being caused, or there is a significant possibility of such harm being caused, or that pollution of controlled waters is being, or is likely to be caused.

    (4) Where this subsection applies, no remediation notice shall require a person—
    (a) who is the owner or occupier of land A, and
    (b) who has not caused or knowingly permitted the substances in question to be in, on or under that land,
to do anything by way of remediation in consequence of any further land in, on or under which those substances or any of them appear to be or to have been present as a result of their escape from land ("land B") appearing to be in such a condition, by reason of the presence of those substances in, on or under it, that significant harm is being caused, or there is a significant possibility of such harm being caused, or that pollution of controlled waters is being, or is likely to be caused, unless he is also the owner or occupier of land B.

    (5) In any case where—
    (a) a person ("person A") has caused or knowingly permitted any substances to be in, on, or under any land,
    (b) another person ("person B") who has not caused or knowingly permitted those substances to be in, on or under that land becomes the owner or occupier of that land, and
    (c) the substances, or any of the substances, mentioned in paragraph (a) above appear to have escaped to other land,
no remediation notice shall require person B to do anything by way of remediation to that other land in consequence of the apparent acts or omissions of person A, except to the extent that person B caused or knowingly permitted the escape.

(6) Nothing in subsection (3), (4) or (5) above prevents the enforcing authority from doing anything by way of remediation under section 78N below which it could have done apart from that subsection, but the authoirty shall not be entitled under section 78P below to recover from any person any part of the cost incurred by the authority in doing by way of remediation anything which it is precluded by subsection (3), (4) or (5) above from requiring that person to do.

(7) in this section, "appear" means appear to the enforcing authority, and cognate expressions shall be construed accordingly.]

[78L. **Appeals against remediation notices.**

(1) A person on whom a remediation notice is served may, within the period of twenty-one days beginning with the day on which the notice is served, appeal against the notice—

(a) if it was served by a local authority, to a magistrates' court or, in Scotland, to the sheriff by way of summary application; or

(b) if it was served by the appropriate Agency, to the Secretary of State;

and in the following provisions of this section "the appellate authority" means the magistrates' court, the sheriff or the Secretary of State, as the case may be.

(2) On any appeal under subsection (1) above the appellate authority—

(a) shall quash the notice, if it is satisfied that there is a material defect in the notice; but

(b) subject to that, may confirm the remediation notice, with or without modification, or quash it.

...]

[78M. **Offences of not complying with a remediation notice.**

(1) If a person on whom an enforcing authority serves a remediation notice fails, without reasonable excuse, to comply with any of the requirements of the notice, he shall be guilty of an offence.

...]

[78N. **Powers of the enforcing authority to carry out remediation.**

(1) Where this section applies, the enforcing authority shall itself have power, in a case falling within paragraph (a) or (b) of section 78E(1) above, to do what is appropriate by way of remediation to the relevant land or waters.

...]

[78P. **Recovery of, and security for, the cost of remediation by the enforcing authority.**

(1) Where, by virtue of section 78N(3)(a), (c), (e) or (f) above, the enforcing authority does any particular thing by way of remediation, it shall be entitled, subject to sections 78J(7) and 78K(6) above, to recover the reasonable cost incurred in doing it from the appropriate person or, if there are two or more appropriate persons in relation to the thing in question, from those persons in proportions determined pursuant to section 78F(7) above.

(2) In deciding whether to recover the cost, and, if so, how much of the cost, which it is entitled to recover under subsection (1) above, the enforcing authority shall have regard—

(a) to any hardship which the recovery may cause to the person from whom the cost is recoverable; and

(b) to any guidance issued by the Secretary of State for the purposes of this subsection.

(3) Subsection (4) below shall apply in any case where—

(a) any cost is recoverable under subsection (1) above from a person—

(i) who is the owner of any premises which consist of or include the contaminated land in question; and

Environmental Protection Act 1990

(ii) who caused or knowingly permitted the substances, or any of the substances, by reason of which the land is contaminated and to be in, on or under the land; and

(b) the enforcing authority serves a notice under this subsection (in this Part referred to as a "charging notice") on that person.

(4) Where this subsection applies—

(a) the cost shall carry interest, at such reasonable rate as the enforcing authority may determine, from the date of service of the notice until the whole amount is paid; and

(b) subject to the following provisions of this section, the cost and accrued interest shall be a charge on the premises mentioned in subsection (3)(a)(i) above.

...

(12) Where any cost is a charge on premises under this section, the enforcing authority may by order declare the cost to be payable with interest by instalments within the specified period until the whole amount is paid.
...]

[78Q. Special sites
...]

[78R. Registers.
(1) Every enforcing authority shall maintain a register containing prescribed particulars of or relating to—

(a) remediation notices served by that authority;

(b) appeals against any such remediation notices;

(c) remediation statements or remediation declarations prepared and published under section 78H above;

(d) in relation to an enforcing authority in England and Wales, appeals against charging notices served by that authority;

(e) notices under subsection (1)(b) or (5)(a) of section 78C above which have effect by virtue of subsection (7) of that section as the designation of any land as a special site;

(f) notices under subsection (4)(b) or section 78D above which have effect by virtue of subsection (6) of that section as the designation of any land as a special site;

(g) notices given by or to the enforcing authority under section 78Q(4) above terminating the designation of any land as a special site;

(h) notifications given to that authority by persons—

(i) on whom a remediation notice has been served, or

(ii) who are or were required by virtue of section 78H(8)(a) above to prepare and publish a remediation statement,

of what they claim has been done by them by way of remediation;

(j) notifications given to that authority by owners or occupiers of land—

(i) in respect of which a remediation notice has been served, or

(ii) in respect of which a remediation statement has been prepared and published,

of what they claim has been done on the land in question by way of remediation;

(k) convictions for such offences under section 78M above as may be prescribed;

(l) such other matters relating to contaminated land as may be prescribed;

but that duty is subject to section 78S and 78T beow.]

[78S. Exclusion from registers of information affecting national security.
(1) No information shall be included in a register maintained under section 78R above if and so long as, in the opinion of the Secretary of State, the inclusion in the register of that information, or information of that description, would be contrary to the interests of national security.]

[78T. Exclusion from registers of certain confidential information.

(1) No information relating to the affairs of any individual or business shall be included in a register maintained under section 78R above, without the consent of that individual or the person for the time being carrying on that business, if and so long as the information—

(a) is, in relation to him, commercially confidential; and

(b) is not required to be included in the register in pursuance of directions under subsection (7) below:

but information is not commercially confidential for the purposes of this section unless it is determined under this section to be so by the enforcing authority or, on appeal, by the Secretary of State.

(8) Information excluded from a register shall be treated as ceasing to be commercially confidential for the purposes of this section at the expiry of the period of four years beginning with the date of the determination by virtue of which it was excluded; but the person who furnished it may apply to the authority for the information to remain excluded from the register on the ground that it is still commercially confidential and the authority shall determine whether or not that is the case.

(10) Information is, for the purposes of any determination under this section, commercially confidential, in relation to any individual or person, if its being contained in the register would prejudice to an unreasonable degree the commercial interests of that individual or person.

(11) For the purposes of subsection (10) above, there shall be disregarded any prejudice to the commercial interests of any individual or person so far as relating only to the value of the contaminated land in question or otherwise to the ownership or occupation of that land.]

[78YC. This Part and radioactivity.

Except as provided by regulations, nothing in this Part applies in relation to harm, or pollution of controlled waters, so far as attributable, to any radioactivity possessed by any substance; but regulations may—

(a) provide for prescribed provisions of this Part to have effect with such modifications as the Secretary of State considers appropriate for the purpose of dealing with harm, or pollution of controlled waters, so far as attributable to any radioactivity possessed by any substances; or

(b) make such modifications of the Radioactive Substances Act 1993 or any other Act as the Secretary of State considers appropriate.]

PART III
STATUTORY NUISANCES AND CLEAN AIR

79. Statutory nuisances and inspections therefor.

(1) [Subject to subsections (2) to (6A) below], the following matters constitute "statutory nuisances" for the purposes of this Part, that is to say—

(a) any premises in such a state as to be prejudicial to health or a nuisance;

(b) smoke emitted from premises so as to be prejudicial to health or a nuisance;

(c) fumes or gases emitted from premises so as to be prejudicial to health or a nuisance;

(d) any dust, steam, smell or other effluvia arising on industrial, trade or business premises and being prejudicial to health or a nuisance;

(e) any accumulation or deposit which is prejudicial to health or a nuisance;

(f) any animal kept in such a place or manner as to be prejudicial to health or a nuisance;

Environmental Protection Act 1990

(g) noise emitted from premises so as to be prejudicial to health or a nuisance;

[(ga) noise that is prejudicial to health or a nuisance and is emitted from or caused by a vehicle, machinery or equipment in a street;]

(h) any other matter declared by any enactment to be a statutory nuisance;

and it shall be the duty of every local authority to cause its area to be inspected from time to time to detect any statutory nuisances which ought to be dealt with under section 80 below [or sections 80 and 80A below] and, where a complaint of a statutory nuisance is made to it by a person living within its area, to take such steps as are reasonably practicable to investigate the complaint.

(3) Subsection (1)(b) above does not apply to—

(i) smoke emitted from a chimney of a private dwelling within a smoke control area,

(ii) dark smoke emitted from a chimney of a building or a chimney serving the furnace of a boiler or industrial plant attached to a building or for the time being fixed to or installed on any land,

(iii) smoke emitted from a railway locomotive steam engine, or

(iv) dark smoke emitted otherwise than as mentioned above from industrial or trade premises.

(4) Subsection (1)(c) above does not apply in relation to premises other than private dwellings.

(5) Subsection (1)(d) above does not apply to steam emitted from a railway locomotive engine.

(6) Subsection (1)(g) above does not apply to noise caused by aircraft other than model aircraft.

[(6A) Subsection (1)(ga) above does not apply to noise made—

(a) by traffic,

(b) by any naval, military or air force of the Crown or by a visiting force (as defined in subsection (2) above), or

(c) by a political demonstration or a demonstration supporting or opposing a cause or campaign.]

(7) In this Part—

["equipment" includes a musical instrument;]

"noise" includes vibration;

["person responsible"—

(a) in relation to a statutory nuisance, means the person to whose act, default or sufferance the nuisance is attributable;

(b) in relation to a vehicle, includes the person in whose name the vehicle is for the time being registered under the Vehicles Excise and Registration Act 1994 and any other person who is for the time being the driver of the vehicle;

(c) in relation to machinery or equipment, includes any person who is for the time being the operator of the machinery or equipment;]

"prejudicial to health" means injurious, or likely to cause injury, to health;

"premises" includes land and, subject to subsection (12) below, any vessel;

"private dwelling" means any building, or part of a building, used or intended to be used, as a dwelling;

"smoke" includes soot, ash, grit and gritty particles emitted in smoke;

["street" means a highway and any other road, footway, square or court that is for the time being open to the public;]

and any expressions used in this section and in the Clean Air Act 1956 or the Clean Air Act 1968 have the same meaning in this section as in that Act and section 34(2) of the Clean Air Act 1956 shall apply for the interpretation of the expression "dark smoke" and the operation of this Part in relation to it.

80. Summary proceedings for statutory nuisances.
(1) Where a local authority is satisfied that a statutory nuisance exists, or is likely to occur or recur, in the area of the authority, the local authority shall serve a notice ("an abatement notice") imposing all or any of the following requirements—

(a) requiring the abatement of the nuisance or prohibiting or restricting its occurrence or recurrence;

(b) requiring the execution of such works, and the taking of such other steps, as may be necessary for any of those purposes,

and the notice shall specify the time or times within which the requirements of the notice are to be complied with.

(2) [Subject to section 80A(1) below, the abatement notice] shall be served—

(a) except in a case falling within paragraph (b) or (c) below, on the person responsible for the nuisance;

(b) where the nuisance arises from any defect of a structural character, on the owner of the premises;

(c) where the person responsible for the nuisance cannot be found or the nuisance has not yet occurred, on the owner or occupier of the premises.

(3) [A person served with an abatement notice] may appeal against the notice to a magistrates' court within the period of twenty-one days beginning with the date on which he was served with the notice.

(4) If a person on whom an abatement notice is served, without reasonable excuse, contravenes or fails to comply with any requirement or prohibition imposed by the notice, he shall be guilty of an offence.

(5) Except in a case falling within subsection (6) below, a person who commits an offence under subsection (4) above shall be liable on summary conviction to a fine not exceeding level 5 on the standard scale together with a further fine of an amount equal to one-tenth of that level for each day on which the offence continues after the conviction.

(6) A person who commits an offence under subsection (4) above on industrial, trade or business premises shall be liable on summary conviction to a fine not exceeding £20,000.

(7) Subject to subsection (8) below, in any proceedings for an offence under subsection (4) above in respect of a statutory nuisance it shall be a defence to prove that the best practicable means were used to prevent, or to counteract the effects of, the nuisance.

(8) The defence under subsection (7) above is not available—

(a) in the case of a nuisance falling within paragraph (a), (d), (e), (f) or (g) of section 79(1) above except where the nuisance arises on industrial, trade or business premises;

[(aa) in the case of a nuisance falling within paragraph (ga) of section 79(1) above except where the noise is emitted from or caused by a vehicle, machinery or equipment being used for industrial, trade or business purposes;]

(b) in the case of a nuisance falling within paragraph (b) of section 79(1) above except where the smoke is emitted from a chimney; and

(c) in the case of a nuisance falling within paragraph (c) or (h) of section 79(1) above.

(9) In proceedings for an offence under subsection (4) above in respect of a statutory nuisance falling within paragraph (g) [or (ga)] of section 79(1) above where the offence consists in contravening requirements imposed by virtue of subsection (1)(a) above it shall be a defence to prove—

(a) that the alleged offence was covered by a notice served under section 60 or a consent given under section 61 or 65 of the Control of Pollution Act 1974 (construction sites, etc); or

(b) where the alleged offence was committed at a time when the premises were subject to a notice under section 66 of that Act (noise reduction notice), that the level of noise emitted from the premises at that time was not such as to a constitute a contravention of the notice under that section; or

(c) where the alleged offence was committed at a time when the premises were not subject to a notice under section 66 of that Act, and when a level fixed under section 67 of that Act (new buildings liable to abatement order) applied to the premises, that the level of noise emitted from the premises at that time did not exceed that level.

(10) Paragraphs (b) and (c) of subsection (9) above apply whether or not the relevant notice was subject to appeal at the time when the offence was alleged to have been committed.

82. Summary proceedings by person aggrieved by statutory nuisances.

(1) A magistrates' court may act under this section on a complaint made by any person on the ground that he is aggrieved by the existence of a statutory nuisance.

(2) If the magistrates' court is satisfied that the alleged nuisance exists, or that although abated it is likely to recur on the same premises [or, in the case of a nuisance within section 79(1)(ga) above, in the same street], the court shall make an order for either or both of the following purposes—

(a) requiring the defendant to abate the nuisance, within a time specified in the order, and to execute any work necessary for that purpose;

(b) prohibiting a recurrence of the nuisance, and requiring the defendant, within a time specified in the order, to execute any works necessary to prevent the recurrence, and may also impose on the defendant a fine not exceeding level 5 on the standard scale.

(3) If the magistrates' court is satisfied that the alleged nuisance exists and is such as, in the opinion of the court, to render premises unfit for human habitation, an order under subsection (2) above may prohibit the use of the premises for human habitation until the premises are, to the satisfaction of the court, rendered fit for that purpose.

(4) Proceedings for an order under subsection (2) above shall be brought—

(a) except in a case falling within [paragraph (b), (c) or (d) below], against the person responsible for the nuisance;

(b) where the nuisance arises from any defect of a structural character, against the owner of the premises;

(c) where the person responsible for the nuisance cannot be found, against the owner or occupier of the premises.

[(d) in the case of a statutory nuisance within section 79(1)(ga) above caused by noise emitted from or caused by an unattended vehicle or unattended machinery or equipment, against the person responsible for the vehicle, machinery or equipment.]

(5) [Subject to subsection (5A) below, where] more than one person is responsible for a statutory nuisance, subsections (1) to (4) above shall apply to each of those persons whether or not what any one of them is responsible for would by itself amount to a nuisance.

[(5A) In relation to a statutory nuisance within section 79(1)(ga) above for which more than one person is responsible (whether or not what any one of those persons is responsible for would by itself amount to such a nuisance), subsection (4)(a) above shall apply with the substitution of "each person responsible for the nuisance who can be found" for "the person responsible for the nuisance".

(5B) In relation to a statutory nuisance within section 79(1)(ga) above caused by noise emitted from or caused by an unattended vehicle or unattended machinery or equipment for which more than one person is responsible, subsection (4)(d) above shall apply with the substitution of "any person" for "the person".]

(6) Before instituting proceedings for an order under subsection (2) above against any person, the person aggrieved by the nuisance shall give to that person such notice in writing of his intention to bring the proceedings as is applicable to proceedings in respect of a nuisance of that description and the notice shall specify the matter complained of.

(7) The notice of the bringing of proceedings in respect of a statutory nuisance required by subsection (6) above which is applicable is—

(a) in the case of a nuisance falling within paragraph (g) [or (ga)] of section 79(1) above, not less than three days' notice; and

(b) in the case of a nuisance of any other description, not less than twenty-one days' notice;

but the Secretary of State may, by order, provide that this subsection shall have effect as if such period as is specified in the order were the minimum period of notice applicable to any description of statutory nuisance specified in the order.

(8) A person who, without reasonable excuse, contravenes any requirement or prohibition imposed by an order under subsection (2) above shall be guilty of an offence and liable on summary conviction to a fine not exceeding level 5 on the standard scale together with a further fine of an amount equal to one-tenth of that level for each day on which the offence continues after the conviction.

(9) Subject to subsection (1) below, in any proceedings for an offence under subsection (8) above in respect of a statutory nuisance it shall be a defence to prove that the best practicable means were used to prevent, or to counteract the effects of, the nuisance.

(10) The defence under subsection (9) above is not available—

(a) in the case of a nuisance falling within paragraph (a), (d), (e), (f) or (g) of section 79(1) above except where the nuisance arises on industrial, trade or business premises;

[(aa) in the case of a nuisance falling within paragraph (ga) of section 79(1) above except where the noise is emitted from or caused by a vehicle, machinery or equipment being used for industrial, trade or business purposes;]

(b) in the case of a nuisance falling within paragraph (b) of section 79(1) above except where the smoke is emitted from a chimney; and

(c) in the case of a nuisance falling within paragraph (c) or (h) or section 79(1) above; and

(d) in the case of a nuisance which is such as to render the premises unfit for human habitation.

(11) If a person is convicted of an offence under subsection (8) above, a magistrates' court may, after giving the local authority in whose area the nuisance has occurred an opportunity of being heard, direct the authority to do anything which the person convicted was required to do by the order to which the conviction relates.

(12) Where on the hearing of proceedings for an order under subsection (2) above it is proved that the alleged nuisance existed at the date of the making of the complaint, then, whether or not at the date of the hearing it still exists or is likely to recur, the court shall order the defendant (or defendants in such proportions as appears fair and reasonable) to pay to the person bringing the proceedings such amount as the court considers reasonably sufficient to compensate him for any expenses properly incurred by him in the proceedings.

(13) If it appears to the magistrates' court that neither the person responsible for the nuisance nor the owner or occupier of the premises [or (as the case may be) the person responsible for the vehicle, machinery or equipment] can be found the court may, after giving the local authority in whose area the nuisance has occurred an opportunity of being heard, direct the authority to do anything which the court would have ordered that person to do.

FOOD SAFETY ACT 1990
(1990, c. 16)

44. Protection of officers acting in good faith.
(1) An officer of a food authority is not personally liable in respect of any act done by him—
  (a) in the execution or purported execution of this Act; and
  (b) within the scope of his employment,
if he did that act in the honest belief that his duty under this Act required or entitled him to do it.

(2) Nothing in subsection (1) above shall be construed as relieving any food authority from any liability in respect of the acts of their officers.

(3) Where an action has been brought against an officer of a food authority in respect of an act done by him—
  (a) in the execution or purported execution of this Act; but
  (b) outside the scope of his employment,
the authority may indemnify him against the whole or a part of any damages which he has been ordered to pay or any costs which he may have incurred if they are satisfied that he honestly believed that the act complained of was within the scope of his employment.

HUMAN FERTILISATION AND EMBRYOLOGY ACT 1990
(1990, c. 37)

27. Meaning of "mother".
(1) The woman who is carrying or has carried a child as a result of the placing in her of an embryo or of sperm and eggs, and no other woman, is to be treated as the mother of the child.

28. Meaning of "father".
...

29. Effect of sections 27 and 28.
...

35. Disclosure in interests of justice: congenital disabilities, etc.
(1) Where for the purpose of instituting proceedings under section 1 of the Congenital Disabilities (Civil Liability) Act 1976 (civil liability to child born disabled) it is necessary to identify a person who would or might be the parent of a child but for sections 27 to 29 of this Act, the court may, on the application of the child, make an order requiring the Authority to disclose any information contained in the register kept in pursuance of section 31 of this Act identifying that person.

NATIONAL HEALTH SERVICE AND COMMUNITY CARE ACT 1990
(1990, c. 19)

4. NHS contracts.
(1) In this Act the expression "NHS contract" means an arrangement under which one health service body ("the acquirer") arranges for the provision to it by another health service body ("the provider") of goods or services which it reasonably requires for the purposes of its functions.

(3) Whether or not an arrangement which constitutes an NHS contract would, apart from this subsection, be a contract in law, it shall not be regarded for any purpose as giving rise to contractual rights or liabilities, but if any dispute arises with respect to such an arrangement, either party may refer the matter to the Secretary of State for determination under the following provisions of this section.

(4) If, in the course of negotiations intending to lead to an arrangement which will be an NHS contract, it appears to a health service body—

(a) that the terms proposed by another health service body are unfair by reason that the other is seeking to take advantage of its position as the only, or the only practicable, provider of the goods or services concerned or by reason of any other unequal bargaining position as between the prospective parties to the proposed arrangement, or

(b) that for any other reason arising out of the relative bargaining position of the prospective parties any of the terms of the proposed arrangement cannot be agreed,

that health service body may refer the terms of the proposed arrangement to the Secretary of State for determination under the following provisions of this section.

(5) Where a reference is made to the Secretary of State under subsection (3) or subsection (4) above, the Secretary of State may determine the matter himself or, if he considers it appropriate, appoint a person to consider and determine it in accordance with regulations.

(6) By his determination of a reference under subsection (4) above, the Secretary of State or, as the case may be, the person appointed under subsection (5) above may specify terms to be included in the proposed arrangement and may direct that it be proceeded with; and it shall be the duty of the prospective parties to the proposed arrangement to comply with any such directions.

(7) A determination of a reference under subsection (3) above may contain such directions (including directions as to payment) as the Secretary of State or, as the case may be, the person appointed under subsection (5) above considers appropriate to resolve the matter in dispute; and it shall be the duty of the parties to the NHS contract in question to comply with any such directions.

(8) Without prejudice to the generality of his powers on a reference under subsection (3) above, the Secretary of State or, as the case may be, the person appointed under subsection (5) above may by his determination in relation to an arrangement constituting an NHS contract vary the terms of the arrangement or bring it to an end; and where an arrangement is so varied or brought to an end—

(a) subject to paragraph (b) below, the variation or termination shall be treated as being effected by agreement between the parties; and

(b) the directions included in the determination by virtue of subsection (7) above may contain such provisions as the Secretary of State or, as the case may be, the person appointed under subsection (5) above considers appropriate in order satisfactorily to give effect to the variation or to bring the arrangement to an end.

TOWN AND COUNTRY PLANNING ACT 1990
(1990, c. 8)

336. Interpretation.

(7) In relation to the sale or acquisition of an interest in land—

(a) in a case where the interest is or was conveyed or assigned without a preliminary contract, references in this Act to a contract are references to the conveyance or assignment; and

(b) references to the making of a contract are references to the execution of it.

CHILD SUPPORT ACT 1991
(1991, c. 48)

9. Agreements about maintenance.

(1) In this section "maintenance agreement" means any agreement for the making, or for securing the making, of periodical payments by way of maintenance, or in Scotland aliment, to or for the benefit of any child.

(2) Nothing in this Act shall be taken to prevent any person from entering into a maintenance agreement.

(3) The existence of a maintenance agreement shall not prevent any party to the agreement, or any other person, from applying for a maintenance assessment with respect to any child to or for whose benefit periodical payments are to be made or secured under the agreement.

(4) Where any agreement contains a provision which purports to restrict the right of any person to apply for a maintenance assessment, that provision shall be void.

(5) Where section 8 would prevent any court from making a maintenance order in relation to a child and an absent parent of his, no court shall exercise any power that it has to vary any agreement so as—

(a) to insert a provision requiring that absent parent to make or secure the making of periodical payments by way of maintenance, or in Scotland aliment, to or for the benefit of that child; or

(b) to increase the amount payable under such a provision.

[41B. **Repayment of overpaid child support maintenance.**

(1) This section applies where it appears to the Secretary of State that an absent parent has made a payment by way of child support maintenance which amounts to an overpayment by him of that maintenance and that—

(a) it would not be possible for the absent parent to recover the amount of the overpayment by way of an adjustment of the amount payable under a maintenance assessment; or

(b) it would be inappropriate to rely on an adjustment of the amount payable under a maintenance assessment as the means of enabling the absent parent to recover the amount of the overpayment.

(2) The Secretary of State may make such payment to the absent parent by way of reimbursement, or partial reimbursement, of the overpayment as the Secretary of State considers appropriate.

(3) Where the Secretary of State has made a payment under this section he may, in such circumstances as may be prescribed, require the relevant person to pay to him the whole, or a specified proportion, of the amount of that payment.

(4) Any such requirement shall be imposed by giving the relevant person a written demand for the amount which the Secretary of State wishes to recover from him.

(5) Any sum which a person is required to pay to the Secretary of State under this section shall be recoverable from him by the Secretary of State as a debt due to the Crown.

(6) The Secretary of State may by regulations make provision in relation to any case in which—

(a) one or more overpayments of child support maintenance are being reimbursed to the Secretary of State by the relevant person; and

(b) child support maintenance has continued to be payable by the absent parent concerned to the person with care concerned, or again becomes so payable.

(7) For the purposes of this section any payments made by a person under a maintenance assessment which was not validly made shall be treated as overpayments of child support maintenance made by an absent parent.

(8) In this section "relevant person", in relation to an overpayment, means the person with care to whom the overpayment was made.

(9) Any sum recovered by the Secretary of State under this section shall be paid by him into the Consolidated Fund.]

COAL MINING SUBSIDENCE ACT 1991
(1991, c. 45)

PART II

2. Duty to take remedial action.

(1) Subject to and in accordance with the provisions of this Part, it shall be the duty of the British Coal Corporation ("the Corporation") to take in respect of subsidence damage to any property remedial action of one or more of the kinds mentioned in subsection (2) below.

(2) The kinds of remedial action referred to in subsection (1) above are—
   (a) the execution of remedial works in accordance with section 7 below;
   (b) the making of payments in accordance with section 8 or 9 below in respect of the cost of remedial works executed by some other person; and
   (c) the making of a payment in accordance with section 10 or 11 below in respect of the depreciation in the value of the damaged property.

(3) References in this Act, in relation to any subsidence damage, to the Corporation's remedial obligation are references to their obligation under subsection (1) above.

(4) Where emergency works are executed by any other person, the Corporation shall also be under a duty, subject to the provisions of this Part, to make a payment in accordance with section 12 below in respect of the cost of the works.

8. Discretionary payments in lieu.

(1) The Corporation may elect to make payments in respect of the cost of remedial works instead of executing such works themselves in any of the cases mentioned below in this section.

12. Payments in respect of emergency works.

(1) The payment required by section 2(4) above in respect of emergency works, that is to say, works urgently and reasonably required—
   (a) in order that the damaged property may continue to be used for the purposes for which it was used immediately before the damage became evident; or
   (b) in order to prevent the property being affected by further subsidence damage,
is a payment equal to the cost reasonably incurred by any person other than the Corporation in executing those works.

(2) The Corporation shall not be required to make any payment in respect of any emergency works executed by any other person in connection with any property—
   (a) unless that person—
      (i) has given to the Corporation as soon as was reasonably practicable in all the circumstances a notice containing adequate particulars of those works; and
      (ii) has afforded the Corporation reasonable facilities to inspect the property, so far as he was in a position to do so; or
   (b) if the emergency works are executed after the Corporation have elected under section 10 above to make a depreciation payment in respect of the damaged property.

(3) Any payment in respect of emergency works shall be made to the person or persons by whom the cost of executing the works in question is (or is to be) incurred; and, if there are two or more such persons, the payment shall be apportioned between them—
   (a) in such manner as may be determined by agreement; or
   (b) in default of agreement, in shares corresponding to their respective shares in the cost.

PART V
37. Avoidance of double claims.
(1) A person entitled to give a damage notice under Part II of this Act in respect of subsidence damage to any property shall not be entitled to proceed at the same time in respect of the same damage to that property with both—
 (a) such a notice; and
 (b) a claim against the Corporation or a licensee of the Corporation for damages or compensation arising apart from this Act;
but a person so entitled may, subject to subsection (2) below, elect which notice or claim he will proceed with for the time being.

LAND DRAINAGE ACT 1991
(1991, c. 59)

21. Enforcement of obligations to repair watercourses, bridges, etc.
(2) If any person—
 (a) if liable, by reason of any obligation to which this section applies, to do any work in relation to any watercourse, bridge or drainage work (whether by way of repair, maintenance or otherwise); and
 (b) fails to do the work,
the drainage board concerned may serve a notice on that person requiring him to do the necessary work with all reasonable and proper despatch.

(4) If any person fails, within seven days, to comply with a notice served on him under subsection (2) above by the drainage board concerned, the board may do all such things as are necessary for that purpose.

(5) Any expenses reasonably incurred, in the exercise of their powers under this section, by the drainage board concerned may be recovered from the person liable to repair.

24. Contraventions of prohibition on obstructions etc.
(1) If any obstruction is erected or raised or otherwise altered, or any culvert is erected or altered, in contravention of section 23 above, it shall constitute a nuisance in respect of which the drainage board concerned may serve upon such person as is specified in subsection (2) below a notice requiring him to abate the nuisance within a period to be specified in the notice.

(2) The person upon whom a notice may be served under subsection (1) above is—
 (a) in a case where the person by whom the obstruction has been erected or raised or otherwise altered has, at the time when the notice is served, power to remove the obstruction, that person; and
 (b) in any other case, any person having power to remove the obstruction.

(3) If any person acts in contravention of, or fails to comply with, any notice served under subsection (1) above he shall be guilty of an offence ...

(4) If any person acts in contravention of, or fails to comply with, any notice served under subsection (1) above, the drainage board concerned may, without prejudice to any proceedings under subsection (3) above—
 (a) take such action as may be necessary to remedy the effect of the contravention or failure; and
 (b) recover the expenses reasonably incurred by them in doing so from the person in default.

PROPERTY MISDESCRIPTIONS ACT 1991
(1991, c. 29)

1. Offence of property misdescription.
(1) Where a false or misleading statement about a prescribed matter is made in the course of an estate agency business or a property development business, otherwise than

in providing conveyancing services, the person by whom the business is carried on shall be guilty of an offence under this section.

(2) Where the making of the statement is due to the act or default of an employee the employee shall be guilty of an offence under this section; and the employee may be proceeded against and punished whether or not proceedings are also taken against his employer.

(4) No contract shall be void or unenforceable, and no right of action in civil proceedings in respect of any loss shall arise, by reason only of the commission of an offence under this section.

(5) For the purposes of this section—

(a) "false" means false to a material degree,

(b) a statement is misleading if (though not false) what a reasonable person may be expected to infer from it, or from any omission from it, is false,

(c) a statement may be made by pictures or any other method of signifying meaning as well as by words and, if made by words, may be made orally or in writing,

(d) a prescribed matter is any matter relating to land which is specified in an order made by the Secretary of State,

(e) a statement is made in the course of an estate agency business if (but only if) the making of the statement is a thing done as mentioned in subsection (1) of section 1 of the Estate Agents Act 1979 and that Act either applies to it or would apply to it but for subsection (2)(a) of that section (exception for things done in course of profession by practising solicitor or employee),

(f) a statement is made in the course of a property development business if (but only if) it is made—

(i) in the course of a business (including a business in which the person making the statement is employed) concerned wholly or substantially with the development of land, and

(ii) for the purpose of, or with a view to, disposing of an interest in land consisting of or including a building, or a part of a building, constructed or renovated in the course of the business, and

(g) "conveyancing services" means the preparation of any transfer, conveyance, writ, contract or other document in connection with the disposal or acquisition of an interest in land, and services ancillary to that, but does not include anything done as mentioned in section 1(1)(a) of the Estate Agents Act 1979.

(6) For the purposes of this section any reference in this section or section 1 of the Estate Agents Act 1979 to disposing of or acquiring an interest in land—

(a) in England and Wales and Northern Ireland shall be construed in accordance with section 2 of that Act...

2. Due diligence defence.

(1) In proceedings against a person for an offence under section 1 above it shall be a defence for him to show that he took all reasonable steps and exercised all due diligence to avoid committing the offence.

(2) A person shall not be entitled to rely on the defence provided by subsection (1) above by reason of his reliance on information given by another unless he shows that it was reasonable in all the circumstances for him to have relied on the information, having regard in particular—

(a) to the steps which he took, and those which might reasonably have been taken, for the purpose of verifying the information, and

(b) to whether he had any reason to disbelieve the information.

(3) Where in any proceedings against a person for an offence under section 1 above the defence provided by subsection (1) above involves an allegation that the commission of the offence was due—

(a) to the act or default of another, or
(b) to reliance on information given by another,
the person shall not, without the leave of the court, be entitled to rely on the defence unless he has served a notice under subsection (4) below on the person bringing the proceedings not less than seven clear days before the hearing of the proceedings or, in Scotland, the diet of trial.

(4) A notice under this subsection shall give such information identifying or assisting in the identification of the person who committed the act or default, or gave the information, as is in the possession of the person serving the notice at the time he serves it.

WATER INDUSTRY ACT 1991
(1991, c. 56)

1. The Director General of Water Services.
...

3. General environmental and recreational duties.
(5) Subject to obtaining the consent of any navigation authority, harbour authority or conservancy authority before doing anything which causes navigation which is subject to the control of that authority to be obstructed or otherwise interfered with, it shall be the duty of every company holding an appointment as a relevant undertaker to take such steps as are—
(a) reasonably practicable; and
(b) consistent with the purposes of the enactments relating to the functions of the undertaker in question,
for securing, so long as that company has rights to the use of water or land associated with water, that those rights are exercised so as to ensure that the water or land is made available for recreational purposes and is so made available in the best manner.

45. Duty to make connections with main.
(4) The duty imposed on a water undertaker by this section shall be owed to the person who served the notice by virtue of which the duty arises.

(5) Where a duty is owed by virtue of subsection (4) above to any person, any breach of that duty which causes that person to sustain loss or damage shall be actionable at the suit of that person; but, in any proceedings brought against a water undertaker in pursuance of this subsection, it shall be a defence for the undertaker to show that it took all reasonable steps and exercised all due diligence to avoid the breach.

(6) Where a water undertaker carries out any works which it is its duty under this section to carry out at another person's expense, the undertaker shall be entitled to recover from that person an amount equal to the expenses reasonably incurred by the undertaker in carrying out the works.

98. Duty to comply with sewer requisition.
(3) The duty of a sewerage undertaker under this section to provide a public sewer shall be owed to the person who requires the provision of the sewer or, as the case may be, to each of the persons who joins in doing so.

(4) Where a duty is owed by virtue of subsection (3) above to any person, any breach of that duty which causes that person to sustain loss or damage shall be actionable at the suit of that person; but, in any proceedings brought against a [sewerage] undertaker in pursuance of this subsection, it shall be a defence for the undertaker to show that it took all reasonable steps and exercised all due diligence to avoid the breach.

107. Right of sewerage undertaker to undertake the making of communications with public sewers.

(4) If any payment made to a sewerage undertaker under subsection (3) above exceeds the expenses reasonably incurred by it in the carrying out of the work in question, the excess shall be repaid by the undertaker; and, if and so far as those expenses are not covered by such a payment, the undertaker may recover the expenses, or the balance of them, from the person for whom the work was done.

[(4A) Any dispute between a sewerage undertaker and any other person as to—
    (a) whether the undertaker's estimate of the cost of works given under subsection (3)(b)(i) above is reasonable,
    (b) whether any requirement of security for the payment of the cost of works was reasonably made by the undertakers, or
    (c) whether any excess is repayable, or any expenses are recoverable, by the undertaker under subsection (4) above, or the amount of any such excess or expenses, may be referred to the Director for determination under section 30A above by either party to the dispute.]

118. Consent required for discharge of trade effluent into public sewer.

(1) Subject to the following provisions of this Chapter, the occupier of any trade premises in the area of a sewerage undertaker may discharge any trade effluent proceeding from those premises into the undertaker's public sewers if he does so with the undertaker's consent.

(2) Nothing in this Chapter shall authorise the discharge of any effluent into a public sewer otherwise than by means of a drain or sewer.

180. Compensation for damage caused by works etc.

Schedule 12 to this Act shall have effect for making provision for imposing obligations for the purpose of minimising the damage caused in the exercise of certain powers conferred on undertakers and for imposing obligations as to the payment of compensation.

181. Complaints with respect to the exercise of works powers on private land.

(4) If on a complaint under subsection (1) above with respect to the exercise of any powers by a relevant undertaker, the Director is satisfied that that undertaker—
    (a) has failed adequately to consult the complainant, before and in the course of exercising those powers, about the manner in which they are exercised; or
    (b) by acting unreasonably in the manner of its exercise of those powers, has caused the complainant to sustain loss or damage or to be subjected to inconvenience, the Director may direct the undertaker to pay to the complainant an amount, not exceeding £5,000, in respect of that failure, loss, damage or inconvenience.

(5) The Director shall not under subsection (4) above direct a relevant undertaker to pay any amount to a complainant in respect of any loss, damage or inconvenience for which compensation is recoverable under any other enactment except in so far as it appears to him appropriate to do so by reason of any failure of the amount of any such compensation to reflect the fact that it was not reasonable for the undertaker to cause the complainant to sustain the loss or damage or to be subjected to the inconvenience.

(6) The duties of a relevant undertaker by virtue of subsection (3)(a) above shall be enforceable under section 18 above by the Director.

(7) A person to whom any amount is required, in pursuance of a direction under subsection (4) above, to be paid by a relevant undertaker shall be entitled to recover that amount from that undertaker by virtue of this section.

209. Civil liability of undertakers for escapes of water etc.

(1) Where an escape of water, however caused, from a pipe vested in a water undertaker causes loss or damage, the undertaker shall be liable, except as otherwise provided in this section, for the loss or damage.

(2) A water undertaker shall not incur any liability under subsection (1) above if the escape was due wholly to the fault of the person who sustained the loss or damage or of any servant, agent or contractor of his.

(3) A water undertaker shall not incur any liability under subsection (1) above in respect of any loss or damage for which the undertaker would not be liable apart from that subsection and which is sustained—

    (a) by [the Environment Agency], a relevant undertaker or any statutory undertakers, within the meaning of section 336(1) of the Town and Country Planning Act 1990;

    (b) by any public gas supplier within the meaning of Part I of the Gas Act 1986 or the holder of a licence under section 6(1) of the Electricity Act 1989;

    (c) by any highway authority; or

    (d) by any person on whom a right to compensation is conferred by section 82 of the New Roads and Street Works Act 1991.

(4) The Law Reform (Contributory Negligence) Act 1945, the Fatal Accidents Act 1976 and the Limitation Act 1980 shall apply in relation to any loss or damage for which a water undertaker is liable under this section, but which is not due to the undertaker's fault, as if it were due to its fault.

(5) Nothing in subsection (1) above affects any entitlement which a water undertaker may have to recover contribution under the Civil Liability (Contribution) Act 1978; and for the purposes of that Act, any loss for which a water undertaker is liable under that subsection shall be treated as if it were damage.

(6) Where a water undertaker is liable under any enactment or agreement passed or made before April 1, 1982, to make any payment in respect of any loss or damage the undertaker shall not incur liability under subsection (1) above in respect of the same loss or damage.

(7) In this section "fault" has the same meaning as in the Law Reform (Contributory Negligence) Act 1945.

Sections 71 to 84 & 162 to 172   SCHEDULE 6

SUPPLEMENTAL PROVISIONS RELATING TO RIGHTS OF ENTRY

11.—(1) Where any person exercises any right or power to which this Part of this Schedule applies, it shall be the duty of the relevant authority to make full compensation to any person who has sustained loss or damage by reason of—

    (a) the exercise by the designated person of that right or power or of any power to take any person or equipment with him when entering the premises in relation to which the right or power is exercised; or

    (b) the performance of, or failure of the designated person to perform, the duty imposed by paragraph 10 above.

(2) Compensation shall not be payable by virtue of sub-paragraph (1) above in respect of any loss or damage if the loss or damage—

    (a) is attributable to the default of the person who sustained it; or

    (b) is loss or damage in respect of which compensation is payable by virtue of any other provision of this Act.

(3) Any dispute as to a person's entitlement to compensation under this paragraph or as to the amount of any such compensation, shall be referred to the arbitration of a single arbitrator appointed by agreement between the relevant authority and the person who claims to have sustained the loss or damage or, in default of agreement—

    (a) by the President of the Lands Tribunal where the relevant authority is the Secretary of State; and

    (b) by the Secretary of State, in any other case.

WATER RESOURCES ACT 1991
(1991, c. 57)

70. Civil liability under Chapter II.
Except in so far as this Act otherwise expressly provides and subject to the provisions of section 18 of the Interpretation Act 1978 (which relates to offences under two or more laws), the restrictions imposed by sections 24, 25 and 30 above shall not be construed as—

(a) conferring a right of action in any civil proceedings (other than proceedings for the recovery of a fine) in respect of any contravention of those restrictions;

(b) affecting any restriction imposed by or under any other enactment, whether contained in a public general Act or in a local or private Act; or

(c) derogating from any right of action or other remedy (whether civil or criminal) in proceedings instituted otherwise than under this Chapter.

100. Civil liability in respect of pollution and savings.
Except in so far as this Part expressly otherwise provides and subject to the provisions of section 18 of the Interpretation Act 1978 (which relates to offences under two or more laws), nothing in this Part—

(a) confers a right of action in any civil proceedings (other than proceedings for the recovery of a fine) in respect of any contravention of this Part or any subordinate legislation, consent or other instrument made, given or issued under this Part;

(b) derogates from any right of action or other remedy (whether civil or criminal) in proceedings instituted otherwise than under this Part; or

(c) affects any restriction imposed by or under any other enactment, whether public, local or private.

161. Anti-pollution works and operations.
(1) [Subject to subsections (1A) and (2) below,] where it appears to the Authority that any poisonous, noxious or polluting matter or any solid waste matter is likely to enter, or to be or to have been present in, any controlled waters, the Authority shall be entitled to carry out the following works and operations, that is to say—

(a) in a case where the matter appears likely to enter any controlled waters, works and operations for the purpose of preventing it from doing so; or

(b) in a case where the matter appears to be or to have been present in any controlled waters, works and operations for the purpose—

(i) of removing or disposing of the matter;

(ii) of remedying or mitigating any pollution caused by its presence in the waters; or

(iii) so far as it is reasonably practicable to do so, of restoring the waters, including any flora and fauna dependent on the aquatic environment of the waters, to their state immediately before the matter became present in the waters.

[(1A) Without prejudice to the power of the Agency to carry out investigations under subsection (1) above, the power conferred by that subsection to carry out works and operations shall only be exercisable in a case where—

(a) the Agency considers it necessary to carry out forthwith any works or operations falling within paragraph (a) or (b) of that subsection; or

(b) it appears to the Agency, after reasonable inquiry, that no person can be found on whom to serve a works notice under section 161A below.]

(2) Nothing in subsection (1) above shall entitle the Authority to impede or prevent the making of any discharge in pursuance of a consent given under Chapter II of Part III of this Act.

(3) Where the Authority carries out any such works or operations as are mentioned in subsection (1) above, it shall, subject to subsection (4) below, be entitled to

recover the expenses reasonably incurred in doing so from any person who, as the case may be—

(a) caused or knowingly permitted the matter in question to be present at the place from which it was likely, in the opinion of the Authority, to enter any controlled waters; or

(b) caused or knowingly permitted the matter in question to be present in any controlled waters.

(4) No such expenses shall be recoverable from a person for any works or operations in respect of water from an abandoned mine which that person permitted to reach such a place as is mentioned in subsection (3) above or to enter any controlled waters.

(5) Nothing in this section—

(a) derogates from any right of action or other remedy (whether civil or criminal) in proceedings instituted otherwise than under this section; or

(b) affects any restriction imposed by or under any other enactment, whether public, local or private.

[161A. **Notices requiring persons to carry out anti-pollution works and operations.**

(1) Subject to the following provisions of this section, where it appears to the Agency that any poisonous, noxious or polluting matter or any solid waste matter is likely to enter, or to be or to have been present in, any controlled waters, the Agency shall be entitled to serve a works notice on any person who, as the case may be,—

(a) caused or knowingly permitted the matter in question to be present at the place from which it is likely, in the opinion of the Agency, to enter any controlled waters; or

(b) caused or knowingly permitted the matter in question to be present in any controlled waters.

(2) For the purposes of this section, a "works notice" is a notice requiring the person on whom it is served to carry out such of the following works or operations as may be specified in the notice, that is to say—

(a) in a case where the matter in question appears likely to enter any controlled waters, works or operations for the purpose of preventing it from doing so; or

(b) in a case where the matter appears to be or to have been present in any controlled waters, works or operations for the purpose—

(i) of removing or disposing of the matter;

(ii) of remedying or mitigating any pollution caused by its presence in the waters; or

(iii) so far as it is reasonably practicable to do so, of restoring the waters, including any flora and fauna dependent on the aquatic environment of the waters, to their state immediately before the matter became present in the waters.

(3) A works notice—

(a) must specify the periods within which the person on whom it is served is required to do each of the things specified in the notice; and

(b) is without prejudice to the powers of the Agency by virtue of section 161(1A)(a) above.

(4) Before serving a works notice on any person, the Agency shall reasonably endeavour to consult that person concerning the works or operations which are to be specified in the notice.

(11) Where the Agency—

(a) carries out any such investigations as are mentioned in section 161(1) above, and

(b) serves a works notice on a person in connection with the matter to which the investigations relate, it shall (unless the notice is quashed or withdrawn) be entitled to recover the costs or expenses reasonably incurred in carrying out those investigations from that person.]

[161B. Grant of, and compensation for, rights of entry etc.
...]

[161D. Consequences of not complying with a works notice.
(1) If a person on whom the Agency serves a works notice fails to comply with any of the requirements of the notice, he shall be guilty of an offence.]

208. Civil liability of the Authority for escapes of water etc.
(1) Where an escape of water, however caused, from a pipe vested in the Authority causes loss or damage, the Authority shall be liable, except as otherwise provided in this section, for the loss or damage.

(2) The Authority shall not incur any liability under subsection (1) above if the escape was due wholly to the fault of the person who sustained the loss or damage or of any servant, agent or contractor of his.

(3) The Authority shall not incur any liability under subsection (1) above in respect of any loss or damage for which the Authority would not be liable apart from that subsection and which is sustained—

(a) by any water undertaker or sewerage undertaker or by any statutory undertakers, within the meaning of section 336(1) of the Town and Country Planning Act 1990;

(b) by any public gas supplier within the meaning of Part I of the Gas Act 1986 or the holder of a licence under section 6(1) of the Electricity Act 1989;

(c) by any highway authority; or

(d) by any person on whom a right to compensation is conferred by section 82 of the New Roads and Street Works Act 1991.

(4) The Law Reform (Contributory Negligence) Act 1945, the Fatal Accidents Act 1976 and the Limitation Act 1980 shall apply in relation to any loss or damage for which the Authority is liable under this section, but which is not due to the Authority's fault, as if it were due to its fault.

(5) Nothing in subsection (1) above affects any entitlement which the Authority may have to recover contribution under the Civil Liability (Contribution) Act 1978; and for the purposes of that Act, any loss for which the Authority is liable under that subsection shall be treated as if it were damage.

(6) Where the Authority is liable under any enactment or agreement passed or made before April 1, 1982, to make any payment in respect of any loss or damage the Authority shall not incur liability under subsection (1) above in respect of the same loss or damage.

(7) In this section "fault" has the same meaning as in the Law Reform (Contributory Negligence) Act 1945.

221. General interpretation.
(1) In this Act, except in so far as the context otherwise requires —...
"the Authority" means the National Rivers Authority ...

ACCESS TO NEIGHBOURING LAND ACT 1992
(1992, c. 23)

1. Access orders.
(1) A person—
  (a) who, for the purpose of carrying out works to any land (the "dominant land"), desires to enter upon any adjoining or adjacent land (the "servient land"), and

Access to Neighbouring Land Act 1992

(b) who needs, but does not have, the consent of some other person to that entry, may make an application to the court for an order under this section ("an access order") against that other person.

(2) On an application under this section, the court shall make an access order if, and only if, it is satisfied—

(a) that the works are reasonably necessary for the preservation of the whole or any part of the dominant land; and

(b) that they cannot be carried out, or would be substantially more difficult to carry out, without entry upon the servient land;

but this subsection is subject to subsection (3) below.

(3) The court shall not make an access order in any case where it is satisfied that, were it to make such an order—

(a) the respondent or any other person would suffer interference with, or disturbance of, his use or enjoyment of the servient land, or

(b) the respondent, or any other person (whether of full age or capacity or not) in occupation of the whole or any part of the servient land, would suffer hardship,

to such a degree by reason of the entry (notwithstanding any requirement of this Act or any term or condition that may be imposed under it) that it would be unreasonable to make the order.

(4) Where the court is satisfied on an application under this section that it is reasonably necessary to carry out any basic preservation works to the dominant land, those works shall be taken for the purposes of this Act to be reasonably necessary for the preservation of the land; and in this subsection "basic preservation works" means any of the following, that is to say—

(a) the maintenance, repair or renewal of any part of a building or other structure comprised in, or situate on, the dominant land;

(b) the clearance, repair or renewal of any drain, sewer, pipe or cable so comprised or situate;

(c) the treatment, cutting back, felling, removal or replacement of any hedge, tree, shrub or other growing thing which is so comprised and which is, or is in danger of becoming, damaged, diseased, dangerous, insecurely rooted or dead;

(d) the filling in, or clearance, of any ditch so comprised;

but this subsection is without prejudice to the generality of the works which may, apart from it, be regarded by the court as reasonably necessary for the preservation of any land.

(5) If the court considers it fair and reasonable in all the circumstances of the case, works may be regarded for the purposes of this Act as being reasonably necessary for the preservation of any land (or, for the purposes of subsection (4) above, as being basic preservation works which it is reasonably necessary to carry out to any land) notwithstanding that the works incidentally involve—

(a) the making of some alteration, adjustment or improvement to the land, or

(b) the demolition of the whole or any part of a building or structure comprised in or situate upon the land.

(6) Where any works are reasonably necessary for the preservation of the whole or any part of the dominant land, the doing to the dominant land of anything which is requisite for, incidental to, or consequential on, the carrying out of those works shall be treated for the purposes of this Act as the carrying out of works which are reasonably necessary for the preservation of that land; and references in this Act to works, or to the carrying out of works, shall be construed accordingly.

(7) Without prejudice to the generality of subsection (6) above, if it is reasonably necessary for a person to inspect the dominant land—

(a) for the purpose of ascertaining whether any works may be reasonably necessary for the preservation of the whole or any part of that land,

(b) for the purpose of making any map or plan, or ascertaining the course of any drain, sewer, pipe or cable, in preparation for, or otherwise in connection with, the carrying out of works which are so reasonably necessary, or

(c) otherwise in connection with the carrying out of any such works,

the making of such an inspection shall be taken for the purposes of this Act to be the carrying out to the dominant land of works which are reasonably necessary for the preservation of that land; and references in this Act to works, or to the carrying out of works, shall be construed accordingly.

2. Terms and conditions of access orders.

(1) An access order shall specify—

(a) the works to the dominant land that may be carried out by entering upon the servient land in pursuance of the order;

(b) the particular area of servient land that may be entered upon by virtue of the order for the purpose of carrying out those works to the dominant land; and

(c) the date on which, or the period during which, the land may be so entered upon;

and in the following provisions of this Act any reference to the servient land is a reference to the area specified in the order in pursuance of paragraph (b) above.

(2) An access order may impose upon the applicant or the respondent such terms and conditions as appear to the court to be reasonably necessary for the purpose of avoiding or restricting—

(a) any loss, damage, or injury which might otherwise be caused to the respondent or any other person by reason of the entry authorised by the order; or

(b) any inconvenience or loss of privacy that might otherwise be so caused to the respondent or any other person.

(3) Without prejudice to the generality of subsection (2) above, the terms and conditions which may be imposed under that subsection include provisions with respect to—

(a) the manner in which the specified works are to be carried out;

(b) the days on which, and the hours between which, the work involved may be executed;

(c) the persons who may undertake the carrying out of the specified works or enter upon the servient land under or by virtue of the order;

(d) the taking of any such precautions by the applicant as may be specified in the order.

(4) An access order may also impose terms and conditions—

(a) requiring the applicant to pay, or to secure that such person connected with him as may be specified in the order pays, compensation for—

(i) any loss, damage or injury, or

(ii) any substantial loss of privacy or other substantial inconvenience,

which will, or might, be caused to the respondent or any other person by reason of the entry authorised by the order;

(b) requiring the applicant to secure that he, or such person connected with him as may be specified in the order, is insured against any such risks as may be so specified;

(c) requiring such a record to be made of the condition of the servient land, or of such part of it as may be so specified, as the court may consider expedient with a view to facilitating the determination of any question that may arise concerning damage to that land.

(5) An access order may include provision requiring the applicant to pay the respondent such sum by way of consideration for the privilege of entering the servient land in pursuance of the order as appears to the court to be fair and reasonable having regard to all the circumstances of the case, including in particular—

(a) the likely financial advantage of the order to the applicant and any persons connected with him; and

(b) the degree of inconvenience likely to be caused to the respondent or any other person by the entry;

but no payment shall be ordered under this subsection if and to the extent that the works which the applicant desires to carry out by means of the entry are works to residential land.

(6) For the purposes of subsection (5)(a) above, the likely financial advantage of an access order to the applicant and any persons connected with him shall in all cases be taken to be a sum of money equal to the greater of the following amounts, that is to say—

(a) the amount (if any) by which so much of any likely increase in the value of any land—

(i) which consists of or includes the dominant land, and

(ii) which is owned or occupied by the same person as the dominant land,

as may reasonably be regarded as attributable to the carrying out of the specified works exceeds the likely cost of carrying out those works with the benefit of the access order; and

(b) the difference (if it would have been possible to carry out the specified works without entering upon the servient land) between—

(i) the likely cost of carrying out those works without entering upon the servient land; and

(ii) the likely cost of carrying them out with the benefit of the access order.

(7) For the purposes of subsection (5) above, "residential land" means so much of any land as consists of—

(a) a dwelling or part of a dwelling;

(b) a garden, yard, private garage or outbuilding which is used and enjoyed wholly or mainly with a dwelling; or

(c) in the case of a building which includes one or more dwellings, any part of the building which is used and enjoyed wholly or mainly with those dwellings or any of them.

(8) The persons who are to be regarded for the purposes of this section as "connected with" the applicant are—

(a) the owner of any estate or interest in, or right over, the whole or any part of the dominant land;

(b) the occupier of the whole or any part of the dominant land; and

(c) any person whom the applicant may authorise under section 3(7) below to exercise the power of entry conferred by the access order.

(9) The court may make provision—

(a) for the reimbursement by the applicant of any expenses reasonably incurred by the respondent in connection with the application which are not otherwise recoverable as costs;

(b) for the giving of security by the applicant for any sum that might become payable to the respondent or any other person by virtue of this section or section 3 below.

3. Effect of access order.

(1) An access order requires the respondent, so far as he has power to do so, to permit the applicant or any of his associates to do anything which the applicant or associate is authorised or required to do under or by virtue of the order or this section.

(2) Except as otherwise provided by or under this Act, an access order authorises the applicant or any of his associates, without the consent of the respondent,—

(a) to enter upon the servient land for the purpose of carrying out the specified works;

(b) to bring on to that land, leave there during the period permitted by the order and, before the end of that period, remove, such materials, plant and equipment as are reasonably necessary for the carrying out of those works; and

(c) to bring on to that land any waste arising from the carrying out of those works, if it is reasonably necessary to do so in the course of removing it from the dominant land; but nothing in this Act or in any access order shall authorise the applicant or any of his associates to leave anything in, on or over the servient land (otherwise than in discharge of their duty to make good that land) after their entry for the purpose of carrying out works to the dominant land ceases to be authorised under or by virtue of the order.

(3) An access order requires the applicant—

(a) to secure that any waste arising from the carrying out of the specified works is removed from the servient land forthwith;

(b) to secure that, before the entry ceases to be authorised under or by virtue of the order, the servient land is, so far as reasonably practicable, made good; and

(c) to indemnify the respondent against any damage which may be caused to the servient land or any goods by the applicant or any of his associates which would not have been so caused had the order not been made;

but this subsection is subject to subsections (4) and (5) below.

(4) In making an access order, the court may vary or exclude, in whole or in part,—

(a) any authorisation that would otherwise be conferred by subsection 2(b) or (c) above; or

(b) any requirement that would otherwise be imposed by subsection (3) above.

(5) Without prejudice to the generality of subsection (4) above, if the court is satisfied that it is reasonably necessary for any such waste as may arise from the carrying out of the specified works to be left on the servient land for some period before removal, the access order may, in place of subsection (3)(a) above, include provision—

(a) authorising the waste to be left on that land for such period as may be permitted by the order; and

(b) requiring the applicant to secure that the waste is removed before the end of that period.

(6) Where the applicant or any of his associates is authorised or required under or by virtue of an access order or this section to enter, or do any other thing, upon the servient land, he shall not (as respects that access order) be taken to be a trespasser from the beginning on account of his, or any other person's, subsequent conduct.

(7) For the purposes of this section, the applicant's "associates" are such number of persons (whether or not servants or agents of his) whom he may reasonably authorise under this subsection to exercise the power of entry conferred by the access order as may be reasonably necessary for carrying out the specified works.

4. Persons bound by access order, unidentified persons and bar on contracting out.

(1) In addition to the respondent, an access order shall, subject to the provisions of the Land Charges Act 1972 and the Land Registration Act 1925, be binding on—

(a) any of his successors in title to the servient land; and

(b) any person who has an estate or interest in, or right over, the whole or any part of the servient land which was created after the making of the order and who derives his title to that estate, interest or right under the respondent;

and references to the respondent shall be construed accordingly.

(2) If and to the extent that the court considers it just and equitable to allow him to do so, a person on whom an access order becomes binding by virtue of subsection (1)(a) or (b) above shall be entitled, as respects anything falling to be done after the order becomes binding on him, to enforce the order or any of its terms or conditions as if he were the respondent, and references to the respondent shall be construed accordingly.

(3) Rules of court may—
(a) provide a procedure which may be followed where the applicant does not know, and cannot reasonably ascertain, the name of any person whom he desires to make respondent to the application; and
(b) make provision enabling such an applicant to make such a person respondent by description instead of by name;
and in this subsection "applicant" includes a person who proposes to make an application for an access order.
(4) Any agreement, whenever made, shall be void if and to the extent that it would, apart from this subsection, prevent a person from applying for an access order or restrict his right to do so.

6. Variation of orders and damages for breach.
(1) Where an access order or an order under this subsection has been made, the court may, on the application of any party to the proceedings in which the order was made or of any other person on whom the order is binding—
(a) discharge or vary the order or any of its terms or conditions;
(b) suspend any of its terms or conditions; or
(c) revive any term or condition suspended under paragraph (b) above;
and in the application of subsections (1) and (2) of section 4 above in relation to an access order, any order under this subsection which relates to the access order shall be treated for the purposes of those subsections as included in the access order.
(2) If any person contravenes or fails to comply with any requirement, term or condition imposed upon him by or under this Act, the court may, without prejudice to any other remedy available, make an order for the payment of damages by him to any other person affected by the contravention or failure who makes an application for relief under this subsection.

CARRIAGE OF GOODS BY SEA ACT 1992
(1992, c. 50)

1. Shipping documents etc. to which Act applies.
(1) This Act applies to the following documents, that is to say—
(a) any bill of lading;
(b) any sea waybill; and
(c) any ship's delivery order.
(2) References in this Act to a bill of lading—
(a) do not include references to a document which is incapable of transfer either by indorsement or, as a bearer bill, by delivery without indorsement; but
(b) subject to that, do include references to a received for shipment bill of lading.
(3) References in this Act to a sea waybill are references to any document which is not a bill of lading but—
(a) is such a receipt for goods as contains or evidences a contract for the carriage of goods by sea; and
(b) identifies the person to whom delivery of the goods is to be made by the carrier in accordance with that contract.
(4) References in this Act to a ship's delivery order are references to any document which is neither a bill of lading nor a sea waybill but contains an undertaking which—
(a) is given under or for the purposes of a contract for the carriage by sea of the goods to which the document relates, or of goods which include those goods; and
(b) is an undertaking by the carrier to a person identified in the document to deliver the goods to which the document relates to that person.

(5) The Secretary of State may by regulations make provision for the application of this Act to cases where a telecommunication system or any other information technology is used for effecting transactions corresponding to—
    (a)   the issue of a document to which this Act applies;
    (b)   the indorsement, delivery or other transfer of such a document; or
    (c)   the doing of anything else in relation to such a document.

(6) Regulations under subsection (5) above may—
    (a)   make such modifications of the following provisions of this Act as the Secretary of State considers appropriate in connection with the application of this Act to any case mentioned in that subsection; and
    (b)   contain supplemental, incidental, consequential and transitional provision;
and the power to make regulations under that subsection shall be exercisable by statutory instrument subject to annulment in pursuance of a resolution of either House of Parliament.

2. Rights under shipping documents.

(1) Subject to the following provisions of this section, a person who becomes—
    (a)   the lawful holder of a bill of lading;
    (b)   the person who (without being an original party to the contract of carriage) is the person to whom delivery of the goods to which a sea waybill relates is to be made by the carrier in accordance with that contract; or
    (c)   the person to whom delivery of the goods to which a ship's delivery order relates is to be made in accordance with the undertaking contained in the order,
shall (by virtue of becoming the holder of the bill or, as the case may be, the person to whom delivery is to be made) have transferred to and vested in him all rights of suit under the contract of carriage as if he had been a party to that contract.

(2) Where, when a person becomes the lawful holder of a bill of lading, possession of the bill no longer gives a right (as against the carrier) to possession of the goods to which the bill relates, that person shall not have any rights transferred to him by virtue of subsection (1) above unless he becomes the holder of the bill—
    (a)   by virtue of a transaction effected in pursuance of any contractual or other arrangements made before the time when such a right to possession ceased to attach to possession of the bill; or
    (b)   as a result of the rejection to that person by another person of goods or documents delivered to the other person in pursuance of any such arrangements.

(3) The rights vested in any person by virtue of the operation of subsection (1) above in relation to a ship's delivery order—
    (a)   shall be so vested subject to the terms of the order; and
    (b)   where the goods to which the order relates form a part only of the goods to which the contract of carriage relates, shall be confined to rights in respect of the goods to which the order relates.

(4) Where, in the case of any document to which this Act applies—
    (a)   a person with any interest or right in or in relation to goods to which the document relates sustains loss or damage in consequence of a breach of the contract of carriage; but
    (b)   subsection (1) above operates in relation to that document so that rights of suit in respect of that breach are vested in another person,
the other person shall be entitled to exercise those rights for the benefit of the person who sustained the loss or damage to the same extent as they could have been exercised if they had been vested in the person for whose benefit they are exercised.

(5) Where rights are transferred by virtue of the operation of subsection (1) above in relation to any document, the transfer for which that subsection provides shall extinguish any entitlement to those rights which derives—

(a) where that document is a bill of lading, from a person's having been an original party to the contract of carriage; or

(b) in the case of any document to which this Act applies, from the previous operation of that subsection in relation to that document;

but the operation of that subsection shall be without prejudice to any rights which derive from a person's having been an original party to the contract contained in, or evidenced by, a sea waybill and, in relation to a ship's delivery order, shall be without prejudice to any rights deriving otherwise than from the previous operation of that subsection in relation to that order.

3. Liabilities under shipping documents.

(1) Where subsection (1) of section 2 of this Act operates in relation to any document to which this Act applies and the person in whom rights are vested by virtue of that subsection—

(a) takes or demands delivery from the carrier of any of the goods to which the document relates;

(b) makes a claim under the contract of carriage against the carrier in respect of any of those goods; or

(c) is a person who, at a time before those rights were vested in him, took or demanded delivery from the carrier of any of those goods,

that person shall (by virtue of taking or demanding delivery or making the claim or, in a case falling within paragraph (c) above, of having the rights vested in him) become subject to the same liabilities under that contract as if he had been a party to that contract.

(2) Where the goods to which a ship's delivery order relates form a part only of the goods to which the contract of carriage relates, the liabilities to which any person is subject by virtue of the operation of this section in relation to that order shall exclude liabilities in respect of any goods to which the order does not relate.

(3) This section, so far as it imposes liabilities under any contract on any person, shall be without prejudice to the liabilities under the contract of any person as an original party to the contract.

4. Representations in bills of lading.

A bill of lading which—

(a) represents goods to have been shipped on board a vessel or to have been received for shipment on board a vessel; and

(b) has been signed by the master of the vessel or by a person who was not the master but had the express, implied or apparent authority of the carrier to sign bills of lading,

shall, in favour of a person who has become the lawful holder of the bill, be conclusive evidence against the carrier of the shipment of the goods or, as the case may be, of their receipt for shipment.

5. Interpretation etc.

(1) In this Act—

"bill of lading", "sea waybill" and "ship's delivery order" shall be construed in accordance with section 1 above;

"the contract of carriage"—

(a) in relation to a bill of lading or sea waybill, means the contract contained in or evidenced by that bill or waybill; and

(b) in relation to a ship's delivery order, means the contract under or for the purposes of which the undertaking contained in the order is given;

"holder", in relation to a bill of lading, shall be construed in accordance with subsection (2) below;

"information technology" includes any computer or other technology by means of which information or other matter may be recorded or communicated without being reduced to documentary form; and

"telecommunication system" has the same meaning as in the Telecommunications Act 1984.

(2) References in this Act to the holder of a bill of lading are references to any of the following persons, that is to say—

(a) a person with possession of the bill who, by virtue of being the person identified in the bill, is the consignee of the goods to which the bill relates;

(b) a person with possession of the bill as a result of the completion, by delivery of the bill, of any indorsement of the bill or, in the case of a bearer bill, of any other transfer of the bill;

(c) a person with possession of the bill as a result of any transaction by virtue of which he would have become a holder falling within paragraph (a) or (b) above had not the transaction been effected at a time when possession of the bill no longer gave a right (as against the carrier) to possession of the goods to which the bill relates;

and a person shall be regarded for the purposes of this Act as having become the lawful holder of a bill of lading wherever he has become the holder of the bill in good faith.

(3) References in this Act to a person's being identified in a document include references to his being identified by a description which allows for the identity of the person in question to be varied, in accordance with the terms of the document, after its issue; and the reference in section 1(3)(b) of this Act to a document's identifying a person shall be construed accordingly.

(4) Without prejudice to sections 2(2) and 4 above, nothing in this Act shall preclude its operation in relation to a case where the goods to which a document relates—

(a) cease to exist after the issue of the document; or

(b) cannot be identified (whether because they are mixed with other goods or for any other reason);

and references in this Act to the goods to which a document relates shall be construed accordingly.

(5) The preceding provisions of this Act shall have effect without prejudice to the application, in relation to any case, of the rules (the Hague-Visby Rules) which for the time being have the force of law by virtue of section 1 of the Carriage of Goods by Sea Act 1971.

FURTHER AND HIGHER EDUCATION ACT 1992
(1992, c. 13)

41. Control of contracts.

(1) This section applies, subject to subsection (5) below, to any contract which, if a relevant institution were to become an institution within the further education sector, would or might on or after the operative date bind the governing body of the institution.

(2) Except with the appropriate consent, a local authority shall not after the passing of this Act enter into a contract to which this section applies.

(4) In relation to any contract the appropriate consent is—

(a) the consent of the existing governing body of the institution, and

(b) if (on the assumption in subsection (1) above) the contract will require the governing body of the institution to make payments on or after 1 April 1993 amounting in aggregate to £50,000 or more, the consent of the Secretary of State.

(5) This section does not apply to—

(a) a works contract (within the meaning of Part III of the Local Government, Planning and Land Act 1980) which is entered into in accordance with section 7 of that Act, or

(b) a works contract (within the meaning of Part I of the Local Government Act 1988) which is entered into in accordance with section 4 of that Act.

(8) A contract shall not be void by reason only that it has been entered into in contravention of this section and (subject to section 42 of this Act) a person entering into a contract with a local authority shall not be concerned to enquire whether any consent required by this section has been given or any conditions of such a consent have been complied with.

(9) Where there is an obligation under a contract to which this section applies to provide any benefit other than money, subsection (4)(b) above shall apply as if the obligation were to pay a sum of money corresponding to the value of the benefit to the recipient.

(10) This section does not apply to a contract to dispose of land or to grant or dispose of any interest in land.

42. Wrongful contracts.

(1) This section applies where a local authority have entered into a contract to which section 41 of this Act applies in contravention of that section.

(2) The Education Assets Board may by notice in writing served on the other party to the contract repudiate the contract at any time before it is performed.

(3) A repudiation under subsection (2) above shall have effect as if made by the local authority concerned.

49. Avoidance of certain contractual terms.

(1) This section applies to any contract made between the governing body of an institution within the further education sector and any person employed by them, not being a contract made in contemplation of the employee's pending dismissal by reason of redundancy.

(2) In so far as a contract to which this section applies provides that the employee—
(a) shall not be dismissed by reason of redundancy, or
(b) if he is so dismissed, shall be paid a sum in excess of the sum which the employer is liable to pay to him under [Part XI of the Employment Rights Act 1996], the contract shall be void and of no effect.

SOCIAL SECURITY ADMINISTRATION ACT 1992
(1992, c. 5)

[61A. **Contributions paid in error.**
(1) This section applies in the case of any individual if—
(a) the individual has paid amounts by way of primary Class 1 contributions which, because the individual was not an employed earner, were paid in error, and
(b) prescribed conditions are satisfied.
(2) Regulations may, where—
(a) this section applies in the case of any individual, and
(b) the Secretary of State is of the opinion that it is appropriate for the regulations to apply to the individual,
provide for entitlement to, and the amount of, additional pension to be determined as if the individual had been an employed earner and, accordingly, those contributions had been properly paid.
(4) Regulations may, where—
(a) this section applies in the case of any individual, and

(b) the Secretary of State is of the opinion that it is appropriate for regulations made by virtue of section 4(8) of the Social Security (Incapacity of Work) Act 1994 (provision during transition from invalidity benefit to incapacity benefit for incapacity benefit to include the additional pension element of invalidity pension) to have the following effect in the case of the individual,
provide for the regulations made by virtue of that section to have effect as if, in relation to the provisions in force before the commencement of that section with respect to that additional pension element, the individual had been an employed earner and, accordingly, the contributions had been properly paid.

(5) Where such provision made by regulations as is mentioned in subsection (2) or (4) above applies in repect of any individual, regulations under paragraph 8(1)(m) of Schedule 1 to this Act may not require the amounts paid by way of primary Class 1 contributions to be repaid.]

[74A. Payment of benefit where maintenance payments collected by Secretary of State.

(1) This section applies where—
    (a) a person ("the claimant") is entitled to a benefit to which this section applies;
    (b) the Secretary of State is collecting periodical payments of child or spousal maintenance made in respect of the claimant of a member of the claimant's family; and
    (c) the inclusion of any such periodical payment in the claimant's relevant income would, apart from this section, have the effect of reducing the amount of the benefit to which the claimant is entitled.

(2) The Secretary of State may, to such extent as he considers appropriate, treat any such periodical payment as not being relevant income for the purposes of calculating the amount of benefit to which the claimant is entitled.

(3) The Secretary of State may, to the extent that any periodical payment collected by him is treated as not being relevant income for those purposes, retain the whole or any part of that payment.

(4) Any sum retained by the Secretary of State under subsection (3) shall be paid by him into the Consolidated fund.

(5) In this section—
"child" means a person under the age of 16;
"child maintenance", "spousal maintenance" and "relevant income" have such meaning as may be prescribed;
"family" means—
    (a) a married or unmarried couple;
    (b) a married or unmarried couple and a member of the same household for whom one of them is, or both are, responsible and who is a child or a person of a prescribed description;
    (c) except in prescribed circumstances, a person who is not a member of a married or unmarried couple and a member of the same household for whom that person is responsible and who is a child or a person of a prescribed description;
"married couple" means a man and woman who are married to each other and are members of the same household; and
"unmarried couple" means a man and woman who are not married to each other but are living together as husband and wife otherwise than in prescribed circumstances.

(6) For the purposes of this section, the Secretary of State may by regulations make provision as to the circumstances in which—
    (a) persons are to be treated as being or not being members of the same household;
    (b) one person is to be treated as responsible or not responsible for another.

(7) The benefits to which this section applies are income support, an income-based jobseeker's allowance and such other benefits (if any) as may be prescribed.]

75. **Overpayment of housing benefit.**

(1) Except where regulations otherwise provide, any amount of housing benefit [determined in accordance with regulations to have been] paid in excess of entitlement may be recovered {in such manner as may be prescribed} either by the Secretary of State or by the authority which paid the benefit.

[*The words in square brackets have effect, and the words in squiggly brackets are repealed from the time appointed under the Social Security Administration (Fraud) Act 1997, s. 25.*]

(2) Regulations may require such an authority to recover such an amount in such circumstances as may be prescribed.

(3) An amount recoverable under this section is in all cases recoverable from the person to whom it was paid; but, in such circumstances as may be prescribed, it may also be recovered from such other person as may be prescribed.

(4) Any amount recoverable under this section may, without prejudice to any other method of recovery, be recovered by deduction from prescribed benefits.

[(5) Where an amount paid to a person on behalf of another person is recoverable under this section, subsection (3) and (4) above authorise its recovery from the person to whom it was paid by deduction—
    (a) from prescribed benefits to which he is entitled;
    (b) from prescribed benefits paid to him to discharge (in whole or in part) an obligation owed to him by the person on whose behalf the recoverable amount was paid; or
    (c) from prescribed benefits paid to him to discharge (in whole or in part) an obligation owed to him by any other person.

(6) Where an amount is recovered as mentioned in paragraph (b) of subsection (5) above, the obligation specified in that paragraph shall in prescribed circumstances be taken to be discharged by the amount of the deduction; and where an amount is recovered as mentioned in paragraph (c) of that subsection, the obligation specified in that paragraph shall in all cases be taken to be so discharged.

(7) Where any amount recoverable under this section is to be recovered otherwise than by deduction from prescribed benefits—
    (a) if the person from whom it is recoverable resides in England and Wales and the county court so orders, it is recoverable by execution issued from the county court or otherwise as if it were payable under an order of that court; and
    (b) if he resides in Scotland, it may be enforced in the same manner as an extract registered decree arbitral bearing a warrant for execution issued by the sheriff court of any sheriffdom in Scotland.]

76. **Excess benefits.**

(1) Regulations may make provision as to any case where a [billing authority] or a levying authority has allowed [council tax benefit] to a person and the amount allowed exceeds the amount to which he is entitled in respect of the benefit.

(2) [...] the regulations may provide that—
    (a) a sum equal to the excess shall be due from the person concerned to the authority (whatever the form the benefit takes);
    (b) any liability under any provision included under paragraph (a) above shall be met by such method mentioned in subsection (3) below as is prescribed as regards the case concerned, or by such combination of two or all three of the methods as is prescribed as regards the case concerned.

(3) The methods are—
    (a) payment by the person concerned;
    (b) addition to any amount in respect of [council tax];
    (c) deduction from prescribed benefits.

78. Recovery of social fund awards.

(1) A social fund award which is repayable shall be recoverable by the Secretary of State.

(2) Without prejudice to any other method of recovery, the Secretary of State may recover an award by deduction from prescribed benefits.

(3) The Secretary of State may recover an award—
  (a) from the person to or for the benefit of whom it was made;
  (b) where that person is a member of a married or unmarried couple, from the other member of the couple;
  (c) from a person who is liable to maintain the person by or on behalf of whom the application for the award was made or any person in relation to whose needs the award was made.

(4) Payments to meet funeral expenses may in all cases be recovered, as if they were funeral expenses, out of the estate of the deceased, and (subject to section 71 above) by no other means.

106. Recovery of expenditure on benefit from person liable for maintenance.

(1) Subject to the following provisions of this section, if income support is claimed by or in respect of a person whom another person is liable to maintain or paid to or in respect of such a person, the Secretary of State may make a complaint against the liable person to a magistrates' court for an order under this section.

(2) On the hearing of a complaint under this section the court shall have regard to all the circumstances and, in particular, to the income of the liable person, and may order him to pay such sum, weekly or otherwise, as it may consider appropriate, except that in a case falling within section 78(6)(c) above that sum shall not include any amount which is not attributable to income support (whether paid before or after the making of the order).

(3) In determining whether to order any payments to be made in respect of income support for any period before the complaint was made, or the amount of any such payments, the court shall disregard any amount by which the liable person's income exceeds the income which was his during that period.

(4) Any payments ordered to be made under this section shall be made—
  (a) to the Secretary of State in so far as they are attributable to any income support (whether paid before or after the making of the order);
  (b) to the person claiming income support or (if different) the dependant; or
  (c) to such other person as appears to the court expedient in the interests of the dependant.

119. Recovery of unpaid contributions on prosecution.

(1) Where—
  (a) a person has been convicted of an offence under section 114(1) above of failing to pay a contribution at or within the time prescribed for the purpose; and
  (b) the contribution remains unpaid at the date of the conviction,
he shall be liable to pay to the Secretary of State a sum equal to the amount which he failed to pay.

(2) Where—
  (a) a person is convicted of an offence—
    (i) under section 114(3)(b) above; or
    (ii) under section 13 of the Stamp Duties Management Act 1891 as applied by regulations made under paragraph 7(3) of Schedule 1 to the Contributions and Benefits Act; or
    (iii) of contravening or failing to comply with regulations; and
  (b) the evidence on which he is convicted shows that he, for the purposes of paying any contribution which he was liable or entitled to pay, has affixed to any contribution card any used contribution stamp; and

(c) the contribution (not being a Class 3 contribution) in respect of which the stamp was affixed remains unpaid at the date of the conviction,
he shall be liable to pay to the Secretary of State a sum equal to the amount of the contribution.

140C. Payment of subsidy.
(3) Where subsidy has been paid to an authority and it appears to the Secretary of State—
   (a) that subsidy has been overpaid; or
   (b) that there has been a breach of any condition specified in an order under this section, he may recover from the authority the whole or such part of the payment as he may determine.
Without prejudice to other methods of recovery, a sum recoverable under this subsection may be recovered by withholding or reducing subsidy.]

187. Certain benefit to be inalienable.
(1) Subject to the provisions of this Act, every assignment of or charge on—
   (a) benefit as defined in section 122 of the Contributions and Benefits Act;
   [(aa) a jobseeker's allowance;]
   (b) any income-related benefit; or
   (c) child benefit,
and every agreement to assign or charge such benefit shall be void; and, on the bankruptcy of a beneficiary, such benefit shall not pass to any trustee or other person acting on behalf of his creditors.

SOCIAL SECURITY CONTRIBUTIONS AND BENEFITS ACT 1992
(1992, c. 4)

94. Right to industrial injuries benefit.
(1) Industrial injuries benefit shall be payable where an employed earner suffers personal injury caused after 4 July 1948 by accident arising out of and in the course of his employment, being employed earner's employment.
(3) For the purposes of industrial injuries benefit an accident arising in the course of an employed earner's employment shall be taken, in the absence of evidence to the contrary, also to have arisen out of that employment.

97. Accidents in course of illegal employments.
(1) Subsection (2) below has effect in any case where—
   (a) a claim is made for industrial injuries benefit in respect of an accident, or of a prescribed disease or injury; or
   (b) an application is made under section 44 of the Administration Act for a declaration that an accident was an industrial accident, or for a corresponding declaration as to a prescribed disease or injury.
(2) The Secretary of State may direct that the relevant employment shall, in relation to that accident, disease or injury, be treated as having been employed earner's employment notwithstanding that by reason of a contravention of, or non-compliance with, some provision contained in or having effect under an enactment passed for the protection of employed persons or any class of employed persons, either—
   (a) the contract purporting to govern the employment was void; or
   (b) the employed person was not lawfully employed in the relevant employment at the time when, or in the place where, the accident happened or the disease or injury was contracted or received.
(3) In subsection (2) above "relevant employment" means—
   (a) in relation to an accident, the employment out of and in the course of which the accident arises; and

(b) in relation to a prescribed disease or injury, the employment to the nature of which the disease or injury is due.

98. Earner acting in breach of regulations, etc.
An accident shall be taken to arise out of and in the course of an employed earner's employment, notwithstanding that he is at the time of the accident acting in contravention of any statutory or other regulations applicable to his employment, or of any orders given by or on behalf of his employer, or that he is acting without instructions from his employer, if—
    (a) the accident would have been taken so to have arisen had the act not been done in contravention of any such regulations or orders, or without such instructions, as the case may be; and
    (b) the act is done for the purposes of and in connection with the employer's trade or business.

100. Accidents happening while meeting emergency.
An accident happening to an employed earner in or about any premises at which he is for the time being employed for the purposes of his employer's trade or business shall be taken to arise out of and in the course of his employment if it happens while he is taking steps, on an actual or supposed emergency at those premises, to rescue, succour or protect persons who are, or are thought to be or possibly to be, injured or imperilled, or to avert or minimise serious damage to property.

101. Accident caused by another's misconduct etc.
An accident happening after 19 December 1961 shall be treated for the purposes of industrial injuries benefit, where it would not apart from this section be so treated, as arising out of an employed earner's employment if—
    (a) the accident arises in the course of the employment; and
    (b) the accident either is caused—
        (i) by another person's misconduct, skylarking or negligence, or
        (ii) by steps taken in consequence of any such misconduct, skylarking or negligence, or
        (iii) by the behaviour or presence of an animal (including a bird, fish or insect), or is caused by or consists in the employed earner being struck by any object or by lightning; and
    (c) the employed earner did not directly or indirectly induce or contribute to the happening of the accident by his conduct outside the employment or by any act not incidental to the employment.

174. References to Acts.
In this Act—
"the Administration Act" means the Social Security Administration Act 1992;

TIMESHARE ACT 1992
(1992, c. 35)

7. Repayment of credit and interest.
(1) This section applies following—
    (a) the giving of notice of cancellation of a timeshare agreement in accordance with section 5 of this Act in a case where subsection (9) of that section applies, [...]
    (b) the giving of notice of cancellation of a timeshare credit agreement in accordance with section 6 of this Act [or
    (c) the cancellation of a timeshare credit agreement by virtue of section 6A of this Act.]

(2) If the offeree repays the whole or a portion of the credit—
   (a) before the expiry of one month following the giving of the notice [or the cancellation of the timeshare credit agreement by virtue of section 6A of this Act], or
   (b) in the case of a credit repayable by instalments, before the date on which the first instalment is due,
no interest shall be payable on the amount repaid.

(3) If the whole of a credit repayable by instalments is not repaid on or before the date specified in subsection (2)(b) above, the offeree shall not be liable to repay any of the credit except on receipt of a request in writing in such form as may be prescribed, signed by or on behalf of the offeror or (as the case may be) creditor, stating the amounts of the remaining instalments (recalculated by the offeror or creditor as nearly as may be in accordance with the agreement and without extending the repayment period), but excluding any sum other than principal and interest.

TRADE UNION AND LABOUR RELATIONS (CONSOLIDATION) ACT 1992
(1992, c. 52)

1. Meaning of "trade union".
In this Act a "trade union" means an organisation (whether temporary or permanent)—
   (a) which consists wholly or mainly of workers of one or more descriptions and whose principal purposes include the regulation of relations between workers of that description or those descriptions and employers or employers' associations; or ...

5. Meaning of "independent trade union".
In this Act an "independent trade union" means a trade union which—
   (a) is not under the domination or control of an employer or group of employers or of one or more employers' associations, and
   (b) is not liable to interference by an employer or any such group or association (arising out of the provision of financial or material support or by any other means whatsoever) tending towards such control;
and references to "independence", in relation to a trade union, shall be construed accordingly.

10. Quasi-corporate status of trade unions.
(1) A trade union is not a body corporate but—
   (a) it is capable of making contracts;
   (b) it is capable of suing and being sued in its own name, whether in proceedings relating to property or founded on contract or tort or any other cause of action; and
   (c) proceedings for an offence alleged to have been committed by it or on its behalf may be brought against it in its own name.

11. Exclusion of common law rules as to restraint of trade.
(1) The purposes of a trade union are not, by reason only that they are in restraint of trade, unlawful so as—
   (a) to make any member of the trade union liable to criminal proceedings for conspiracy or otherwise, or
   (b) to make any agreement or trust void or voidable.
(2) No rule of a trade union is unlawful or unenforceable by reason only that it is in restraint of trade.

15. Prohibition on use of funds to indemnify unlawful conduct.
(1) It is unlawful for property of a trade union to be applied in or towards—
   (a) the payment for an individual of a penalty which has been or may be imposed on him for an offence or for contempt of court,
   (b) the securing of any such payment, or

(c) the provision of anything for indemnifying an individual in respect of such a penalty.

(2) Where any property of a trade union is so applied for the benefit of an individual on whom a penalty has been or may be imposed, then—

(a) in the case of a payment, an amount equal to the payment is recoverable by the union from him, and

(b) in any other case, he is liable to account to the union for the value of the property applied.

(3) If a trade union fails to bring or continue proceedings which it is entitled to bring by virtue of subsection (2), a member of the union who claims that the failure is unreasonable may apply to the court on that ground for an order authorising him to bring or continue the proceedings on the union's behalf and at the union's expense.

(4) In this section "penalty", in relation to an offence, includes an order to pay compensation and an order for the forfeiture of any property; and references to the imposition of a penalty for an offence shall be construed accordingly.

(6) This section does not affect—

(a) any other enactment, any rule of law or any provision of the rules of a trade union which makes it unlawful for the property of a trade union to be applied in a particular way; or

(b) any other remedy available to a trade union, the trustees of its property or any of its members in respect of an unlawful application of the union's property.

16. Remedy against trustees for unlawful use of union property.

(1) A member of a trade union who claims that the trustees of the union's property—

(a) have so carried out their functions, or are proposing so to carry out their functions, as to cause or permit an unlawful application of the union's property ...

may apply to the court for an order under this section.

The court may in particular—

(a) require the trustees (if necessary, on behalf of the union) to take all such steps as may be specified in the order for protecting or recovering the property of the union;

...

20. Liability of trade union in certain proceedings in tort.

(1) Where proceedings in tort are brought against a trade union—

(a) on the ground that an act—

(i) induces another person to break a contract or interferes or induces another person to interfere with its performance, or

(ii) consists in threatening that a contract (whether one to which the union is a party or not) will be broken or its performance interfered with, or that the union will induce another person to break a contract or interfere with its performance, or

(b) in respect of an agreement or combination by two or more persons to do or to procure the doing of an act which, if it were done without any such agreement or combination, would be actionable in tort on such a ground,

then, for the purpose of determining in those proceedings whether the union is liable in respect of the act in question, that act shall be taken to have been done by the union if, but only if, it is to be taken to have been authorised or endorsed by the trade union in accordance with the following provisions.

(5) Where for the purposes of any proceedings an act is by virtue of this section taken to have been done by a trade union, nothing in this section shall affect the liability of any other person, in those or any other proceedings, in respect of that act.

(6) In proceedings arising out of an act which is by virtue of this section taken to have been done by a trade union, the power of the court to grant an injunction or

Trade Union and Labour Relations (Consolidation) Act 1992   269

interdict includes power to require the union to take such steps as the court considers appropriate for ensuring—
    (a) that there is no, or no further, inducement of persons to take part or to continue to take part in industrial action, and
    (b) that no person engages in any conduct after the granting of the injunction or interdict by virtue of having been induced before it was granted to take part or to continue to take part in industrial action.
    The provisions of subsections (2) to (4) above apply in relation to proceedings for failure to comply with any such injunction or interdict as they apply in relation to the original proceedings.

21. Repudiation by union of certain acts.
    (7) In this section "commercial contract" means any contract other than—
        (a) a contract of employment, or
        (b) any other contract under which a person agrees personally to do work or perform services for another.

22. Limit on damages awarded against trade unions in actions in tort.
    (1) This section applies to any proceedings in tort brought against a trade union, except—
        (a) proceedings for personal injury as a result of negligence, nuisance or breach of duty;
        (b) proceedings for breach of duty in connection with the ownership, occupation, possession, control or use of property;
        (c) proceedings brought by virtue of Part I of the Consumer Protection Act 1987 (product liability).
In any proceedings in tort to which this section applies the amount which may [be] awarded against the union by way of damages shall not exceed the following limit—

Number of members of union	*Maximum award of damages*
Less than 5,000	£10,000
5,000 or more but less than 25,000	£50,000
25,000 or more but less than 100,000	£125,000
100,000 or more	£250,000

    (3) The Secretary of State may by order amend subsection (2) so as to vary any of the sums specified . . .

113. Recovery of sums paid in case of fraud.
    (1) Where the Commissioner grants an application to a person who for the purposes of the application—
        (a) has made a statement which he knew to be false in a material particular, or
        (b) has recklessly made a statement which was false in a material particular,
he is entitled to recover from that person any sums paid by him to that person, or to any other person, by way of assistance.
    (2) This does not affect the power of the Commissioner to enter into any agreement he thinks fit as to the terms on which assistance is provided.

127. Corporate or quasi-corporate status of employers' associations.
    (1) An employers' association may be either a body corporate or an unincorporated association.
    (2) Where an employers' association is unincorporated—
        (a) it is capable of making contracts;
        (b) it is capable of suing and being sued in its own name, whether in proceedings relating to property or founded on contract or tort or any other cause of action; and

(c) proceedings for an offence alleged to have been committed by it or on its behalf may be brought against it in its own name.

128. Exclusion of common law rules as to restraint of trade.

(1) The purposes of an unincorporated employers' association and, so far as they relate to the regulation of relations between employers and workers or trade unions, the purposes of an employers' association which is a body corporate are not, by reason only that they are in restraint of trade, unlawful so as—

    (a) to make any member of the association liable to criminal proceedings for conspiracy or otherwise, or

    (b) to make any agreement or trust void or voidable.

(2) No rule of an unincorporated employers' association or, so far as it relates to the regulation of relations between employers and workers or trade unions, of an employers' association which is a body corporate, is unlawful or unenforceable by reason only that it is in restraint of trade.

137. Refusal of employment on grounds related to union membership.

(1) It is unlawful to refuse a person employment—

    (a) because he is, or is not, a member of a trade union, or

    (b) because he is unwilling to accept a requirement—

        (i) to take steps to become or cease to be, or to remain or not to become, a member of a trade union, or

        (ii) to make payments or suffer deductions in the event of his not being a member of a trade union.

(2) A person who is thus unlawfully refused employment has a right of complaint to an industrial tribunal.

138. Refusal of service of employment agency on grounds related to union membership.

(1) It is unlawful for an employment agency to refuse a person any of its services—

    (a) because he is, or is not, a member of a trade union, or

    (b) because he is unwilling to accept a requirement to take steps to become or cease to be, or to remain or not to become, a member of a trade union.

(2) A person who is thus unlawfully refused any service of an employment agency has a right of complaint to an industrial tribunal.

140. Remedies.

(1) Where the industrial tribunal finds that a complaint under section 137 or 138 is well-founded, it shall make a declaration to that effect and may make such of the following as it considers just and equitable—

    (a) an order requiring the respondent to pay compensation to the complainant of such amount as the tribunal may determine;

    (b) a recommendation that the respondent take within a specified period action appearing to the tribunal to be practicable for the purpose of obviating or reducing the adverse effect on the complainant of any conduct to which the complaint relates.

(2) Compensation shall be assessed on the same basis as damages for breach of statutory duty and may include compensation for injury to feelings.

(3) If the respondent fails without reasonable justification to comply with a recommendation to take action, the tribunal may increase its award of compensation or, if it has not made such an award, make one.

(4) The total amount of compensation shall not exceed the limit for the time being imposed by [section 124(1) of the Employment Rights Act 1996] (limit on compensation for unfair dismissal).

142. Awards against third parties.

(1) If in proceedings on a complaint under section 137 or 138 either the complainant or the respondent claims that the respondent was induced to act in the manner complained of by pressure which a trade union or other person exercised on him by calling, organising, procuring or financing a strike or other industrial action, or by threatening to do so, the complainant or the respondent may request the industrial tribunal to direct that the person who he claims exercised the pressure be joined or sisted as a party to the proceedings.

(3) Where a person has been so joined or sisted as a party to the proceedings and the tribunal—
- (a) finds that the complaint is well-founded,
- (b) makes an award of compensation, and
- (c) also finds that the claim in subsection (1) above is well-founded,

it may order that the compensation shall be paid by the person joined instead of by the respondent, or partly by that person and partly by the respondent, as the tribunal may consider just and equitable in the circumstances.

143. Interpretation and other supplementary provisions.

(4) The remedy of a person for conduct which is unlawful by virtue of section 137 or 138 is by way of a complaint to an industrial tribunal in accordance with this Part, and not otherwise.

No other legal liability arises by reason that conduct is unlawful by virtue of either of those sections.

144. Union membership requirement in contract for goods or services void.

A term or condition of a contract for the supply of goods or services is void in so far as it purports to require that the whole, or some part, of the work done for the purposes of the contract is done only by persons who are, or are not, members of trade unions or of a particular trade union.

145. Refusal to deal on union membership grounds prohibited.

(1) A person shall not refuse to deal with a supplier or prospective supplier of goods or services on union membership grounds.

"Refuse to deal" and "union membership grounds" shall be construed as follows.

(2) A person refuses to deal with a person if, where he maintains (in whatever form) a list of approved suppliers of goods or services, or of persons from whom tenders for the supply of goods or services may be invited, he fails to include the name of that person in that list.

He does so on union membership grounds if the grounds, or one of the grounds, for failing to include his name is that if that person were to enter into a contract with him for the supply of goods or services, work to be done for the purposes of the contract would, or would be likely to, be done by persons who were, or who were not, members of trade unions or of a particular trade union.

(3) A person refuses to deal with a person if, in relation to a proposed contract for the supply of goods or services—
- (a) he excludes that person from the group of persons from whom tenders for the supply of the goods or services are invited, or
- (b) he fails to permit that person to submit such a tender, or
- (c) he otherwise determines not to enter into a contract with that person for the supply of the goods or services.

He does so on union membership grounds if the ground, or one of the grounds, on which he does so is that if the proposed contract were entered into with that person, work to be done for the purposes of the contract would, or would be likely to, be done by persons who were, or who were not, members of trade unions or of a particular trade union.

(4) A person refuses to deal with a person if he terminates a contract with him for the supply of goods or services.

He does so on union membership grounds if the ground, or one of the grounds, on which he does so is that work done, or to be done, for the purposes of the contract has been, or is likely to be, done by persons who are or are not members of trade unions or of a particular trade union.

(5) The obligation to comply with this section is a duty owed to the person with whom there is a refusal to deal and to any other person who may be adversely affected by its contravention; and a breach of the duty is actionable accordingly (subject to the defences and other incidents applying to actions for breach of statutory duty).

152. Dismissal on grounds related to union membership or activities.

(1) For purposes of [Part X of the Employment Rights Act 1996] (unfair dismissal) the dismissal of an employee shall be regarded as unfair if the reason for it (or, if more than one, the principal reason) was that the employee—

    (a) was, or proposed to become, a member of an independent trade union, or

    (b) had taken part, or proposed to take part, in the activities of an independent trade union at an appropriate time, or

    (c) was not a member of any trade union, or of a particular trade union, or of one of a number of particular trade unions, or had refused, or proposed to refuse, to become or remain a member.

153. Selection for redundancy on grounds related to union membership or activities.

Where the reason or principal reason for the dismissal of an employee was that he was redundant, but it is shown—

    (a) that the circumstances constituting the redundancy applied equally to one or more other employees in the same undertaking who held positions similar to that held by him and who have not been dismissed by the employer, and

    (b) that the reason (or, if more than one, the principal reason) why he was selected for dismissal was one of those specified in section 152(1),

the dismissal shall be regarded as unfair for the purposes of [Part X of the Employment Rights Act 1996] (unfair dismissal).

155. Matters to be disregarded in assessing contributory fault.

(1) Where an industrial tribunal makes an award of compensation for unfair dismissal in a case where the dismissal is unfair by virtue of section 152 or 153, the tribunal shall disregard, in considering whether it would be just and equitable to reduce, or further reduce, the amount of any part of the award, any such conduct or action of the complainant as is specified below.

(2) Conduct or action of the complainant shall be disregarded in so far as it constitutes a breach or proposed breach of a requirement—

    (a) to be or become a member of any trade union or of a particular trade union or of one of a number of particular trade unions,

    (b) to cease to be, or refrain from becoming, a member of any trade union or of a particular trade union or of one of a number of particular trade unions, or

    (c) not to take part in the activities of any trade union or of a particular trade union or of one of a number of particular trade unions.

For the purposes of this subsection a requirement means a requirement imposed on the complainant by or under an arrangement or contract of employment or other agreement.

(3) Conduct or action of the complainant shall be disregarded in so far as it constitutes a refusal, or proposed refusal, to comply with a requirement of a kind mentioned in section 152(3)(a) (payments in lieu of membership) or an objection, or

proposed, objection, (however expressed) to the operation of a provision of a kind mentioned in section 152(3)(b) (deductions in lieu of membership).

156. Minimum basic award.

(1) Where a dismissal is unfair by virtue of section 152(1) or 153, the amount of the basic award of compensation, before any reduction is made under [section 122 of the Employment Rights Act 1996], shall be not less than £2,700.

(2) But where the dismissal is unfair by virtue of section 153, [subsection (2)] of that section (reduction for contributory fault) applies in relation to so much of the basic award as is payable because of subsection (1) above.

157. Special award of compensation.

(1) Where an industrial tribunal makes an award of compensation for unfair dismissal in a case where the dismissal is unfair by virtue of section 152(1) or 153, then, unless—

(a) the complainant does not request the tribunal to make an order for reinstatement or re-engagement, or

(b) the case falls within [section 121 of the Employment Rights Act 1996] (cases where employer takes requisite steps to renew employment or re-engage employee),

the award shall include a special award calculated in accordance with section 158.

(2) [section [sic] 117(3) of the Employment Rights Act 1996] (additional award of compensation in case of failure to comply with an order for reinstatement or re-engagement) does not apply in a case where the dismissal is unfair by virtue of section 152(1) or 153.

164. Order for continuation of contract of employment.

(1) An order under section 163 for the continuation of a contract of employment is an order that the contract of employment continue in force—

(a) for the purposes of pay or [any other benefit] derived from the employment, seniority, pension rights and other similar matters, and

(b) for the purpose of determining for any purpose the period for which the employee has been continuously employed,

from the date of its termination (whether before or after the making of the order) until the determination or settlement of the complaint.

(2) Where the tribunal makes such an order it shall specify in the order the amount which is to be paid by the employer to the employee by way of pay in respect of each normal pay period, or part of any such period, falling between the date of dismissal and the determination or settlement of the complaint.

(3) Subject as follows, the amount so specified shall be that which the employee could reasonably have been expected to earn during that period, or part, and shall be paid—

(a) in the case of payment for any such period falling wholly or partly after the making of the order, on the normal pay day for that period, and

(b) in the case of a payment for any past period, within such time as may be specified in the order.

(5) Any payment made to an employee by an employer under his contract of employment, or by way of damages for breach of that contract, in respect of a normal pay period or part of any such period shall go towards discharging the employer's liability in respect of that period under subsection (2); and conversely any payment under that subsection in respect of a period shall go towards discharging any liability of the employer under, or in respect of the breach of, the contract of employment in respect of that period.

166. Consequences of failure to comply with order.

(1) If on the application of an employee an industrial tribunal is satisfied that the employer has not complied with the terms of an order for the reinstatement

or re-engagement of the employee under section 163(4) or [(5)], the tribunal shall—
    (a) make an order for the continuation of the employee's contract of employment, and
    (b) order the employer to pay the employee such compensation as the tribunal considers just and equitable in all the circumstances having regard—
        (i) to the infringement of the employee's right to be reinstated or re-engaged in pursuance of the order, and
        (ii) to any loss suffered by the employee in consequence of the non-compliance.
(2) Section 164 applies to an order under subsection (1)(a) as in relation to an order under section 163.
(3) If on the application of an employee an industrial tribunal is satisfied that the employer has not complied with the terms of an order for the continuation of a contract of employment, the following provisions apply.
(4) If the non-compliance consists of a failure to pay an amount by way of pay specified in the order, the tribunal shall determine the amount owed by the employer on the date of the determination.
If on that date the tribunal also determines the employee's complaint that he has been unfairly dismissed, it shall specify that amount separately from any other sum awarded to the employee.
(5) In any other case, the tribunal shall order the employer to pay the employee such compensation as the tribunal considers just and equitable in all the circumstances having regard to any loss suffered by the employee in consequence of the non-compliance.

167. Interpretation and other supplementary provisions.
(1) [Part X of the Employment Rights Act 1996] (unfair dismissal) has effect subject to the provisions of sections 152 to 166 above.
(2) Those sections shall be construed as one with that Part; and in those sections—
"complaint of unfair dismissal" means a complaint under [section 111 of the Employment Rights Act 1996];
"award of compensation for unfair dismissal" means an award of compensation for unfair dismissal under [section 112(4) or 117(3)(a)] of that Act; and
"order for reinstatement or re-engagement" means an order for reinstatement or re-engagement under [section 113] of that Act.
(3) Nothing in those sections shall be construed as conferring a right to complain of unfair dismissal from employment of a description to which that Part does not otherwise apply.

178. Collective agreements and collective bargaining.
(1) In this Act "collective agreement" means any agreement or arrangement made by or on behalf of one or more trade unions and one or more employers or employers' associations and relating to one or more of the matters specified below; and "collective bargaining" means negotiations relating to or connected with one or more of those matters.
(2) The matters referred to above are—
    (a) terms and conditions of employment, or the physical conditions in which any workers are required to work;
    (b) engagement or non-engagement, or termination or suspension of employment or the duties of employment, of one or more workers;
    (c) allocation of work or the duties of employment between workers or groups of workers;
    (d) matters of discipline;

(e) a worker's membership or non-membership of a trade union;
(f) facilities for officials of trade unions; and
(g) machinery for negotiation or consultation, and other procedures, relating to any of the above matters, including the recognition by employers or employers' associations of the right of a trade union to represent workers in such negotiation or consultation or in the carrying out of such procedures.

179. Whether agreement intended to be a legally enforceable contract.

(1) A collective agreement shall be conclusively presumed not to have been intended by the parties to be a legally enforceable contract unless the agreement—
(a) is in writing, and
(b) contains a provision which (however expressed) states that the parties intend that the agreement shall be a legally enforceable contract.

(2) A collective agreement which does satisfy those conditions shall be conclusively presumed to have been intended by the parties to be a legally enforceable contract.

(3) If a collective agreement is in writing and contains a provision which (however expressed) states that the parties intend that one or more parts of the agreement specified in that provision, but not the whole of the agreement, shall be a legally enforceable contract, then—
(a) the specified part or parts shall be conclusively presumed to have been intended by the parties to be a legally enforceable contract, and
(b) the remainder of the agreement shall be conclusively presumed not to have been intended by the parties to be such a contract.

(4) A part of a collective agreement which by virtue of subsection (3)(b) is not a legally enforceable contract may be referred to for the purpose of interpreting a party of the agreement which is such a contract.

180. Effect of provisions restricting right to take industrial action.

(1) Any terms of a collective agreement which prohibit or restrict the right of workers to engage in a strike or other industrial action, or have the effect of prohibiting or restricting that right, shall not form part of any contract between a worker and the person for whom he works unless the following conditions are met.

(2) The conditions are that the collective agreement—
(a) is in writing,
(b) contains a provision expressly stating that those terms shall or may be incorporated in such a contract,
(c) is reasonably accessible at his place of work to the worker to whom it applies and is available for him to consult during working hours, and
(d) is one where each trade union which is a party to the agreement is an independent trade union;
and that the contract with the worker expressly or impliedly incorporates those terms in the contract.

(3) The above provisions have effect notwithstanding anything in section 179 and notwithstanding any provision to the contrary in any agreement (including a collective agreement or a contract with any worker).

186. Recognition requirement in contract for goods or services void.

A term or condition of a contract for the supply of goods or services is void in so far as it purports to require a party to the contract—
(a) to recognise one or more trade unions (whether or not named in the contract) for the purpose of negotiating on behalf of workers, or any class of worker, employed by him, or
(b) to negotiate or consult with, or with an official of, one or more trade unions (whether or not so named).

187. Refusal to deal on grounds of union exclusion prohibited.

(1) A person shall not refuse to deal with a supplier or prospective supplier of goods or services if the ground or one of the grounds for his action is that the person against whom it is taken does not, or is not likely to—

    (a) recognise one or more trade unions for the purpose of negotiating on behalf of workers, or any class of worker, employed by him, or

    (b) negotiate or consult with, or with an official of, one or more trade unions.

(2) A person refuses to deal with a person if—

    (a) where he maintains (in whatever form) a list of approved suppliers of goods or services, or of persons from whom tenders for the supply of goods or services may be invited, he fails to include the name of that person in that list; or

    (b) in relation to a proposed contract for the supply of goods or services—

        (i) he excludes that person from the group of persons from whom tenders for the supply of the goods or services are invited, or

        (ii) he fails to permit that person to submit such a tender; or

        [(iii)] he otherwise determines not to enter into a contract with that person for the supply of the goods or services. [or]

    [(c) he terminates a contract with that person for the supply of goods or services.]

(3) The obligation to comply with this section is a duty owed to the person with whom there is a refusal to deal and to any other person who may be adversely affected by its contravention; and a breach of the duty is actionable accordingly (subject to the defences and other incidents applying to actions for breach of statutory duty).

219. Protection from certain tort liabilities.

(1) An act done by a person in contemplation or furtherance of a trade dispute is not actionable in tort on the ground only—

    (a) that it induces another person to break a contract or interferes or induces another person to interfere with its performance, or

    (b) that it consists in his threatening that a contract (whether one to which he is a party or not) will be broken or its performance interfered with, or that he will induce another person to break a contract or interfere with its performance.

(2) An agreement or combination by two or more persons to do or procure the doing of an act in contemplation or furtherance of a trade dispute is not actionable in tort if the act is one which if done without any such agreement or combination would not be actionable in tort.

(3) Nothing in subsections (1) and (2) prevents an act done in the course of picketing from being actionable in tort unless it is done in the course of attendance declared lawful by section 220 (peaceful picketing).

(4) Subsections (1) and (2) have effect subject to sections 222 to 225 (action excluded from protection) [and to sections 226 (requirement of ballot before action by trade union) and 234A (requirement of notice to employer of industrial action); and in those sections "not protected" means excluded from the protection afforded by this section or, where the expression is used with reference to a particular person, excluded from that protection as respects that person.]

220. Peaceful picketing.

(1) It is lawful for a person in contemplation or furtherance of a trade dispute to attend—

    (a) at or near his own place of work, or

    (b) if he is an official of a trade union, at or near the place of work of a member of the union whom he is accompanying and whom he represents,

for the purpose only of peacefully obtaining or communicating information, or peacefully persuading any person to work or abstain from working.

222. Action to enforce trade union membership.

(1) An act is not protected if the reason, or one of the reasons, for which it is done is the fact or belief that a particular employer—

    (a) is employing, has employed or might employ a person who is not a member of a trade union, or

    (b) is failing, has failed or might fail to discriminate against such a person.

(2) For the purposes of subsection (1)(b) an employer discriminates against a person if, but only if, he ensures that his conduct in relation to—

    (a) persons, or persons of any description, employed by him, or who apply to be, or are, considered by him for employment, or

    (b) that provision of employment for such persons,

is different, in some or all cases, according to whether or not they are members of a trade union, and is more favourable to those who are.

(3) An act is not protected if it constitutes, or is one of a number of acts which together constitute, an inducement or attempted inducement of a person—

    (a) to incorporate in a contract to which that person is a party, or a proposed contract to which he intends to be a party, a term or condition which is or would be void by virtue of section 144 (union membership requirement in contract for goods or services), or

    (b) to contravene section 145 (refusal to deal with person on grounds relating to union membership).

224. Secondary action.

(1) An Act is not protected if one of the facts relied on for the purpose of establishing liability is that there has been secondary action which is not lawful picketing.

(2) There is secondary action in relation to a trade dispute when, and only when, a person—

    (a) induces another to break a contract of employment or interferes or induces another to interfere with its performance, or

    (b) threatens that a contract of employment under which he or another is employed will be broken or its performance interfered with, or that he will induce another to break a contract of employment or to interfere with its performance,

and the employer under the contract of employment is not the employer party to the dispute.

(3) Lawful picketing means acts done in the course of such attendance as is declared lawful by section 220 (peaceful picketing)—

    (a) by a worker employed (or, in the case of a worker not in employment, last employed) by the employer party to the dispute, or

    (b) by a trade union official whose attendance is lawful by virtue of subsection (1)(b) of that section.

(4) For the purposes of this section an employer shall not be treated as party to a dispute between another employer and workers of that employer; and where more than one employer is in dispute with his workers, the dispute between each employer and his workers shall be treated as a separate dispute.

In this subsection "worker" has the same meaning as in section 244 (meaning of "trade dispute").

(5) An act in contemplation or furtherance of a trade dispute which is primary action in relation to that dispute may not be relied on as secondary action in relation to another trade dispute.

Primary action means such action as is mentioned in paragraph (a) or (b) of subsection (2) where the employer under the contract of employment is the employer party to the dispute.

(6) In this section "contract of employment" includes any contract under which one person personally does work or performs services for another, and related expressions shall be construed accordingly.

225. Pressure to impose union recognition requirement.

(1) An act is not protected if it constitutes, or is one of a number of acts which together constitute, an inducement or attempted inducement of a person—

(a) to incorporate in a contract to which that person is a party, or a proposed contract to which he intends to be a party, a term or condition which is or would be void by virtue of section 186 (recognition requirement in contract for goods or services), or

(b) to contravene section 187 (refusal to deal with person on grounds of union exclusion).

(2) An act is not protected if—

(a) it interferes with the supply (whether or not under a contract) of goods or services, or can reasonably be expected to have that effect, and

(b) one of the facts relied upon for the purpose of establishing liability is that a person has—

(i) induced another to break a contract of employment or interfered or induced another to interfere with its performance, or

(ii) threatened that a contract of employment under which he or another is employed will be broken or its performance interfered with, or that he will induce another to break a contract of employment or to interfere with its performance, and

(c) the reason, or one of the reasons, for doing the act is the fact or belief that the supplier (not being the employer under the contract of employment mentioned in paragraph (b)) does not, or might not—

(i) recognise one or more trade unions for the purpose of negotiating on behalf of workers, or any class of worker, employed by him, or

(ii) negotiate or consult with, or with an official of, one or more trade unions.

226. Requirement of ballot before action by trade union.

(1) An act done by a trade union to induce a person to take part, or continue to take part, in industrial action—

[(a) is not protected unless the industrial action has the support of a ballot, and

(b) where section 226A falls to be complied with in relation to the person's employer, is not protected as respects the employer unless the trade union has complied with section 226A in relation to him.]

236. No compulsion to work.

No court shall, whether by way of—

(a) an order for specific performance or specific implement of a contract of employment, or

(b) an injunction or interdict restraining a breach or threatened breach of such a contract,

compel an employee to do any work or attend at any place for the doing of any work.

237. Dismissal of those taking part in unofficial industrial action.

(1) An employee has no right to complain of unfair dismissal if at the time of dismissal he was taking part in an unofficial strike or other unofficial industrial action.

(2) A strike or other industrial action is unofficial in relation to an employee unless—

(a) he is a member of a trade union and the action is authorised or endorsed by that union, or

(b) he is not a member of a trade union but there are among those taking part in the industrial action members of a trade union by which the action has been authorised or endorsed.

Provided that, a strike or other industrial action shall not be regarded as unofficial if none of those taking part in it are members of a trade union.

240. Breach of contract involving injury to persons or property.

(1) A person commits an offence who wilfully and maliciously breaks a contract of service or hiring, knowing or having reasonable cause to believe that the probable consequences of his so doing, either alone or in combination with others, will be—

    (a) to endanger human life or cause serious bodily injury, or

    (b) to expose valuable property, whether real or personal, to destruction or serious injury.

(2) Subsection (1) applies equally whether the offence is committed from malice conceived against the person endangered or injured or, as the case may be, the owner of the property destroyed or injured, or otherwise.

(4) This section does not apply to seamen.

241. Intimidation or annoyance by violence or otherwise.

(1) A person commits an offence who, with a view to compelling another person to abstain from doing or to do any act which that person has a legal right to do or abstain from doing, wrongfully and without legal authority—

    (a) uses violence to or intimidates that person or his wife or children, or injures his property,

    (b) persistently follows that person about from place to place,

    (c) hides any tools, clothes or other property owned or used by that person, or deprives him of or hinders him in the use thereof,

    (d) watches or besets the house or other place where that person resides, works, carries on business or happens to be, or the approach to any such house or place, or

    (e) follows that person with two or more other persons in a disorderly manner in or through any street or road.

(3) A constable may arrest without warrant anyone he reasonably suspects is committing an offence under this section.

244. Meaning of "trade dispute" in Part V [*ss. 219-246*]

(1) In this Part a "trade dispute" means a dispute between workers and their employer which relates wholly or mainly to one or more of the following—

    (a) terms and conditions of employment, or the physical conditions in which any workers are required to work;

    (b) engagement or non-engagement, or termination or suspension of employment or the duties of employment, of one or more workers;

    (c) allocation of work or the duties of employment between workers or groups of workers;

    (d) matters of discipline;

    (e) a worker's membership or non-membership of a trade union;

    (f) facilities for officials of trade unions; and

    (g) machinery for negotiation or consultation, and other procedures, relating to any of the above matters, including the recognition by employers or employers' associations of the right of a trade union to represent workers in such negotiation or consultation or in the carrying out of such procedures.

245. Crown employees and contracts.

Where a person holds any office or employment under the Crown on terms which do not constitute a contract of employment between that person and the Crown, those terms shall nevertheless be deemed to constitute such a contract for the purposes of—

    (a) the law relating to liability in tort of a person who commits an act which—

        (i) induces another person to break a contract, interferes with the performance of a contract or induces another person to interfere with its performance, or

(ii) consists in a threat that a contract will be broken or its performance interfered with, or that any person will be induced to break a contract or interfere with its performance, and

(b) the provisions of this or any other Act which refer (whether in relation to contracts generally or only in relation to contracts of employment) to such an act.

[266. The Commissioners.
(1) There
(a) shall continue to be an officer called the Commissioner for the Rights of Trade Union Members . . .]

273. Crown employment.
(1) The provisions of this Act have effect (except as mentioned below) in relation to Crown employment and persons in Crown employment as in relation to other employment and other workers or employees.

(5) Sections 137 to 143 (rights in relation to trade union membership: access to employment) apply in relation to Crown employment otherwise than under a contract only where the terms of employment correspond to those of a contract of employment.

274. Armed forces.
(1) Section 273 (application of Act to Crown employment) does not apply to service as a member of the naval, military or air forces of the Crown.

275. Exemption on grounds of national security.
(1) Section 273 (application of Act to Crown employment) does not apply to employment in respect of which there is in force a certificate issued by or on behalf of a Minister of the Crown certifying that employment of a description specified in the certificate, or the employment of a particular person so specified, is (or, at a time specified in the certificate, was) required to be excepted from that section for the purpose of safeguarding national security.

280. Police service.
(1) In this Act "employee" or "worker" does not include a person in police service; and the provisions of sections 137 and 138 (rights in relation to trade union membership: access to employment) do not apply in relation to police service.

288. Restriction on contracting out.
(1) Any provision in an agreement (whether a contract of employment or not) is void in so far as it purports—
 (a) to exclude or limit the operation of any provision of this Act, or
 (b) to preclude a person from bringing—
  (i) proceedings before an industrial tribunal or the Central Arbitration Committee under any provision of this Act, or
  (ii) an application to the Employment Appeal Tribunal under section 67 (remedy for infringement of right not to be unjustifiably disciplined) or section 176 (compensation for unreasonable exclusion or expulsion).

[(2A) Subsection (1) does not apply to an agreement to refrain from instituting or continuing any proceedings, other than excepted proceedings, specified in subsection 1(b) of that section before an industrial tribunal if the conditions regulating compromise agreements under this Act are satisfied in relation to the agreement.

(2B) The conditions regulating compromise agreements under this Act are that—
 (a) the agreement must be in writing;
 (b) the agreement must relate to the particular complaint;

(c) the complainant must have received independent legal advice from a qualified lawyer as to the terms and effect of the proposed agreement and in particular its effect on his ability to pursue his rights before an industrial tribunal;
(d) there must be in force, when the adviser gives the advice, a policy of insurance covering the risk of a claim by the complainant in respect of loss arising in consequence of the advice;
(e) the agreement must identify the adviser; and
(f) the agreement must state that the conditions regulating compromise agreements under this Act are satisfied.]

CLEAN AIR ACT 1993
(1993, c. 11)

1. Prohibition of dark smoke from chimneys.
(1) Dark smoke shall not be emitted from a chimney of any building, and if, on any day, dark smoke is so emitted, the occupier of the building shall be guilty of an offence.
(3) This section does not apply to emissions of smoke from any chimney, in such classes of case and subject to such limitations as may be prescribed in regulations made by the Secretary of State, lasting for not longer than such periods as may be specified.
(6) This section has effect subject to section 51 (duty to notify offences to occupier or other person liable).

34. Research and publicity.
(1) A local authority may—
(a) undertake, or contribute towards the cost of, investigation and research relevant to the problem of air pollution;
(b) arrange for the publication of information on that problem; ...
(2) In acting under subsection (1)(b), a local authority shall ensure that the material published is presented in such a way that no information relating to a trade secret is disclosed, except with the consent in writing of a person authorised to disclose it.
(3) Breach of a duty imposed by subsection (2) shall be actionable.
(4) In any civil or criminal proceedings (whether or not arising under this Act) brought against a local authority, or any member or officer of a local authority, on the grounds that any information has been published, it shall be a defence to show that it was published in compliance with subsections (1) and (2).

51. Duty to notify occupiers of premises.
(1) If, in the opinion of an authorised officer of the local authority—
(a) an offence is being or has been committed under section 1, 2 or 20 (prohibition of certain emissions of smoke); [...]
he shall, unless he has reason to believe that notice of it has already been given by or on behalf of the local authority, as soon as may be notify the appropriate person, and, if his notification is not in writing, shall before the end of the four days next following the day on which he became aware of the offence, confirm the notification in writing.
(2) For the purposes of subsection (1), the appropriate person to notify is the occupier of the premises, the person having possession of the boiler or plant, the owner of the railway locomotive engine or the owner or master or other officer or person in charge of the vessel concerned, as the case may be.
(3) In any proceedings for an offence under section 1, 2 or 20 it shall be a defence to prove that the provisions of subsection (1) have not been complied with in the case of the offence; and if no such notification as is required by that subsection has been given before the end of the four days next following the day of the offence, that subsection shall be taken not to have been complied with unless the contrary is proved.

LEASEHOLD REFORM, HOUSING AND URBAN DEVELOPMENT ACT 1993
(1993, c. 28)

158. The Agency.

(1) There shall be a body corporate to be known as the Urban Regeneration Agency ("the Agency") ...

163. Power to enter and survey land.

(1) Any person who is duly authorised in writing by the Agency may at any reasonable time enter any land for the purpose of surveying it, or estimating its value, in connection with—

    (a) any proposal to acquire that land or any other land; or

    (b) any claim for compensation in respect of any such acquisition.

168. Validity of transactions.

(1) A transaction between a person and the Agency shall not be invalidated by reason only of any failure by the Agency to observe its objects or the requirement in subsection (1) of section 160 that the Agency shall exercise the powers conferred by that subsection for the purpose of achieving its objects, and such a person shall not be concerned to see or enquire whether there has been any such failure.

NOISE AND STATUTORY NUISANCE ACT 1993
(1993, c. 40)

Section 9   SCHEDULE 3
                         AUDIBLE INTRUDER ALARMS

Requirements for operation of alarms

5.—(1) This paragraph is satisfied if—

    (a) the alarm complies with any prescribed requirements,

    (b) the police have been notified in writing of the names, addresses and telephone numbers of the current key-holders, and

    (c) the local authority has been informed of the address of the police station to which notification has been given under paragraph (b).

(2) Notification under sub-paragraph (1)(b) may be given to the police at any police station in the local authority's area.

Entry to premises

6.—(1) Where—

    (a) an intruder alarm installed on or in any premises is operating audibly more than one hour after it was activated, and

    (b) the audible operation of the alarm is such as to give persons living or working in the vicinity of the premises reasonable cause for annoyance,

an officer of the local authority who has been authorised (whether generally or specially) for that purpose may, on production (if so required) of his authority, enter the premises to turn off the alarm.

(2) An officer may not enter premises by force under this paragraph.

7.—(1) If, on an application made by an officer of the local authority who has been authorised (whether generally or specifically) for that purpose, a justice of the peace is satisfied—

    (a) that an intruder alarm installed on or in any premises is operating audibly more than one hour after it was activated,

(b) that the audible operation of the alarm is such as to give persons living or working in the vicinity of the premises reasonable cause for annoyance,

(c) where notification of any current key-holders has been given in accordance with paragraph 5(1)(b), that the officer has taken steps to obtain access to the premises with their assistance, and

(d) that the officer has been unable to obtain access to the premises without the use of force,

the justice may issue a warrant authorising the officer to enter the premises, if need be by force.

(2) Before applying for such a warrant, an officer shall leave a notice at the premises stating—

(a) that the audible operation of the alarm is such as to give persons living or working in the vicinity reasonable cause for annoyance, and

(b) that an application is to be made to a justice of the peace for a warrant authorising the officer to enter the premises and turn off the alarm.

(3) An officer shall not enter premises by virtue of this paragraph unless he is accompanied by a constable.

(4) A warrant under this paragraph shall continue in force until the alarm has been turned off and the officer has complied with paragraph 10.

8. An officer who enters premises by virtue of paragraph 6 or 7 may take with him such other persons and such equipment as may be necessary to turn off the alarm.

9. A person who enters premises by virtue of paragraph 6, 7 and 8 shall not cause more damage or disturbance than is necessary.

10. An officer who has entered premises by virtue of paragraph 6 or 7 which are unoccupied or from which the occupier is temporarily absent shall—

(a) after the alarm has been turned off, re-set it if reasonably practicable,

(b) leave a notice at the premises stating what action has been taken on the premises under this Schedule, and

(c) leave the premises, so far as reasonably practicable, as effectually secured against trespassers as he found them.

Recovery of expenses

11. Where any premises are entered by virtue of paragraph 6 or 7 in a case where the occupier of those premises has committed an offence under paragraph 2, 3 or 4, any expenses reasonably incurred by the local authority in connection with the entry, turning off the alarm or complying with paragraph 10 may be recovered by the authority from that occupier.

Protection from personal liability

12. Nothing done by, or by a member of, a local authority or by an officer of or another person authorised by a local authority shall, if done in good faith for the purposes of this Schedule, subject them or any of them personally to any action, liability, claim or demand whatsoever, other than any liability under section 19 or 20 of the Local Government Finance Act 1982 (powers of district auditor and court).

PENSION SCHEMES ACT 1993
(1993, c. 48)

61. Deduction of contributions equivalent premium from refund of scheme contributions.

(1) This section applies where—

[(a) an earner's service in contracted-out employment ceases or his employment ceases to be contracted-out employment, and]

(b) he (or, by virtue of a connection with him, any other person) is entitled to a refund of any payments made by or in respect of him towards the provision of benefits under the scheme by reference to which that employment was contracted-out; and

(c) a contributions equivalent premium falls to be paid by any person in respect of him.

(2) Where this section applies, then, subject to the following provisions of this section, the person by whom the premium falls to be paid shall be entitled on paying it to recover an amount equal to so much of the premium as is attributable to primary Class 1 contributions (and on paying any part of it to recover a proportionate part of that amount) from the person liable for the refund.

(3) The amount recoverable under this section shall not exceed the amount of the refund or so much of it as has not been made.

(6) Where the person liable for the premium is himself liable for the refund, he shall be entitled to retain out of the refund the amount which he could recover under this section from another person liable for the refund.

(7) The amount of the refund shall be reduced by the amount recovered or retained under this section; and provision shall be made by regulations for requiring the making of refunds to be delayed for the purpose of enabling any right of recovery or retainer conferred by this section to be exercised, notwithstanding anything in any enactment relating to the making of the refund.

(8) Where—

[(a) an earner's service in contracted-out employment ceases or his employment ceases to be contracted-out employment];

(b) he (or, by virtue of a connection with him, any other person) is entitled to a refund of any payments made by or in respect of him under the scheme by reference to which that employment was contracted-out in relation to any previous contracted-out employment of his, being payments towards the provision of benefits under that scheme;

(c) a contributions equivalent premium falls to be paid in respect of him; and

(d) the period taken into account in arriving at the amount mentioned in subsection (2) includes the period of the previous contracted-out employment,

then the person liable for that premium shall have the like right of recovery from that refund (so far as the premium is not recoverable or retainable out of a refund in respect of a later employment) as a person has under this section where the refund relates to service in the employment on the [cessation] of which the premium falls to be paid (and subsection (7) shall apply accordingly).

62. No recovery of state scheme premiums from earners etc.

(1) Notwithstanding any contract to the contrary, a person shall not be entitled—

(a) to recover any part of a state scheme premium from any earner in respect of whom it is payable; or

(b) except in accordance with section 61, to recover or retain any part of such a premium out of any money payable to or for the benefit of the earner or any other person.

127. Transfer to Secretary of State of rights and remedies.

(1) Where in pursuance of section 124 the Secretary of State makes any payment into the resources of an occupational pension scheme or a personal pension scheme in respect of any contributions to the scheme, any rights and remedies in respect of those contributions belonging to the persons competent to act in respect of the scheme shall, on the making of the payment, become rights and remedies of the Secretary of State.

RAILWAYS ACT 1993
(1993, c. 43)

1. The Rail Regulator and the Director of Passenger Rail Franchising.
...

50. Exclusion of liability for breach of statutory duty.
(1) The obligations of the Franchising Director, imposed by or under any provision of this Part—
  (a) to comply with any closure conditions,
  (b) to secure compliance with any closure conditions,
  (c) to secure the provision of any services, or
  (d) to secure the operation of any additional railway asset,
shall not give rise to any form of duty or liability enforceable by civil proceedings for breach of statutory duty.

93. Assignment of employees to particular parts of undertakings.
(1) Schemes may be made—
  (a) assigning such qualifying employees, or qualifying employees of such a class or description, as may be specified in the scheme to such part of their employer's undertaking as may be so specified;
  (b) modifying the terms and conditions of employment of those employees; and
  (c) providing for the payment of compensation to any of those employees by his employer in respect of an overall detriment incurred by the employee in consequence of any modifications made by the scheme to his terms and conditions of employment.

(4) Where a scheme modifies the terms and conditions of employment of any person, the person's terms and conditions of employment after the modification takes effect must overall, and taking account of the amount or value of any compensation payable to him by virtue of subsection (1)(c) above in respect of any such detriment as is there mentioned, be no less favourable to him than his terms and conditions of employment before the modification takes effect.

122. Statutory authority as a defence to actions in nuisance etc.
(1) Subject to the following provisions of this section—
  (a) any person shall have authority—
    (i) to use, or to cause or permit any agent or independent contractor of his to use, rolling stock on any track, or
    (ii) to use, or to cause or permit any agent or independent contractor of his to use, any land comprised in a network, station or light maintenance depot for or in connection with the provision of network services, station services in light maintenance services, and
  (b) any person who is the owner or occupier of any land shall have authority to authorise, consent to or acquiesce in—
    (i) the use by another of rolling stock on any track comprised in that land, or
    (ii) the use by another of that land for or in connection with the provision of network services, station services or light maintenance services,
if and so long as the qualifying conditions are satisfied in the particular case.

(3) The authority conferred by this section is conferred only for the purpose of providing a defence of statutory authority—
  (a) in England and Wales—
    (i) in any proceedings, whether civil or criminal, in nuisance; or
    (ii) in any civil proceedings, other than proceedings for breach of statutory duty, in respect of the escape of things from land;

(4) Nothing in this section shall be construed as excluding a defence of statutory authority otherwise available under or by virtue of any enactment.

151. General interpretation.

(6) Nothing in this Act affects the operation of the Transfer of Undertakings (Protection of Employment) Regulations 1981, in their application in relation to the transfer of an undertaking, or part of an undertaking, within the meaning of those Regulations.

CRIMINAL JUSTICE AND PUBLIC ORDER ACT 1994
(1994, c. 33)

60. Powers to stop and search in anticipation of violence.

(1) Where a police officer of or above the rank of superintendent reasonably believes that—

    (a) incidents involving serious violence may take place in any locality in his area, and

    (b) it is expedient to do so to prevent their occurrence,

he may give an authorisation that the powers to stop and search persons and vehicles conferred by this section shall be exercisable at any place within that locality for a period not exceeding twenty four hours.

(5) A constable may, in the exercise of those powers, stop any person or vehicle and make any search he thinks fit whether or not he has any grounds for suspecting that the person or vehicle is carrying weapons or articles of that kind.

(6) If in the course of a search under this section a constable discovers a dangerous instrument or an article which he has reasonable grounds for suspecting to be an offensive weapon, he may seize it.

61. Power to remove trespassers on land.

(1) If the senior police officer present at the scene reasonably believes that two or more persons are trespassing on land and are present there with the common purpose of residing there for any period, that reasonable steps have been taken by or on behalf of the occupier to ask them to leave and—

    (a) that any of those persons has caused damage to the land or to property on the land or used threatening, abusive or insulting words or behaviour towards the occupier, a member of his family or an employee or agent of his, or

    (b) that those persons have between them six or more vehicles on the land,

he may direct those persons, or any of them, to leave the land and to remove any vehicles or other property they have with them on the land.

(2) Where the persons in question are reasonably believed by the senior police officer to be persons who were not originally trespassers but have become trespassers on the land, the officer must reasonably believe that the other conditions specified in subsection (1) are satisfied after those persons became trespassers before he can exercise the power conferred by that subsection.

(4) If a person knowing that a direction under subsection (1) above has been given which applies to him—

    (a) fails to leave the land as soon as reasonably practicable, or

    (b) having left again enters the land as a trespasser within the period of three months beginning with the day on which the direction was given, he commits an offence

...

62. Supplementary powers of seizure.

(1) If a direction has been given under section 61 and a constable reasonably suspects that any person to whom the direction applies has, without reasonable excuse—

    (a) failed to remove any vehicle on the land which appears to the constable to belong to him or to be in his possession or under his control; or

(b) entered the land as a trespasser with a vehicle within the period of three months beginning with the day on which the direction was given,
the constable may seize and remove that vehicle.

63. Powers to remove persons attending or preparing for a rave.

(1) This section applies to a gathering on land in the open air of 100 or more persons (whether or not trespassers) at which amplified music is played during the night (with or without intermissions) and is such as, by reason of its loudness and duration and the time at which it is played, is likely to cause serious distress to the inhabitants of the locality; and for this purpose—

(a) such a gathering continues during intermissions in the music and where the gathering extends over several days, throughout the period during which amplified music is played at night (with or without intermissions); and

(b) "music" includes sounds wholly or predominantly characterised by the emission of a succession of repetitive beats.

(2) If, as respects any land in the open air, a police officer of at least the rank of superintendent reasonably believes that—

(a) two or more persons are making preparations for the holding there of a gathering to which this section applies,

(b) ten or more persons are waiting for such a gathering to begin there, or

(c) ten or more persons are attending such a gathering which is in progress,

he may give a direction that those persons and any other persons who come to prepare or wait for or to attend the gathering are to leave the land and remove any vehicles or other property which they have with them on the land.

(6) If a person knowing that a direction has been given which applies to him—

(a) fails to leave the land as soon as reasonably practicable, or

(b) having left again enters the land within the period of 7 days beginning with the day on which the direction was given,

he commits an offence . . .

64. Supplementary powers of entry and seizure.

(4) If a direction has been given under section 63 and a constable reasonably suspects that any person to whom the direction applies has, without reasonable excuse—

(a) failed to remove any vehicle or sound equipment on the land which appears to the constable to belong to him or to be in his possession or under his control; or

(b) entered the land as a trespasser with a vehicle or sound equipment within the period of 7 days beginning with the day on which the direction was given,

the constable may seize and remove that vehicle or sound equipment.

65. Raves: power to stop persons from proceeding.

(1) If a constable in uniform reasonably believes that a person is on his way to a gathering to which section 63 applies in relation to which a direction under section 63(2) is in force, he may, subject to subsections (2) and (3) below—

(a) stop that person, and

(b) direct him not to proceed in the direction of the gathering.

(2) The power conferred by subsection (1) above may only be exercised at a place within 5 miles of the boundary of the site of the gathering.

66. Power of court to forfeit sound equipment.

(1) Where a person is convicted of an offence under section 63 in relation to a gathering to which that section applies and the court is satisfied that any sound equipment which has been seized from him under section 64(4), or which was in his possession or under his control at the relevant time, has been used at the gathering the court may make an order for forfeiture under this subsection in respect of that property.

(2) The court may make an order under subsection (1) above whether or not it also deals with the offender in respect of the offence in any other way and without regard to any restrictions on forfeiture in any enactment.

(3) In considering whether to make an order under subsection (1) above in respect of any property a court shall have regard—

(a) to the value of the property; and

(b) to the likely financial and other effects on the offender of the making of the order (taken together with any other order that the court contemplates making).

(4) An order under subsection (1) above shall operate to deprive the offender of his rights, if any, in the property to which it relates, and the property shall (if not already in their possession) be taken into the possession of the police.

(5) Except in a case to which subsection (6) below applies, where any property has been forfeited under subsection (1) above, a magistrates' court may, on application by a claimant of the property, other than the offender from whom it was forfeited under subsection (1) above, make an order for delivery of the property to the applicant if it appears to the court that he is the owner of the property.

(7) No application shall be made under subsection (5), or by virtue of subsection (6), above by any claimant of the property after the expiration of 6 months from the date on which an order under subsection (1) above was made in respect of the property.

(8) No such application shall succeed unless the claimant satisfies the court either that he had not consented to the offender having possession of the property or that he did not know, and had no reason to suspect, that the property was likely to be used at a gathering to which section 63 applies.

68. Offence of aggravated trespass.

(1) A person commits the offence of aggravated trespass if he trespasses on land in the open air and, in relation to any lawful activity which persons are engaging in or are about to engage in on that or adjoining land in the open air, does there anything which is intended by him to have the effect—

(a) of intimidating those persons or any of them so as to deter them or any of them from engaging in that activity,

(b) of obstructing that activity, or

(c) of disrupting that activity.

(2) Activity on any occasion on the part of a person or persons on land is "lawful" for the purposes of this section if he or they may engage in the activity on the land on that occasion without committing an offence or trespassing on the land.

69. Powers to remove persons committing or participating in aggravated trespass.

(1) If the senior police officer present at the scene reasonably believes—

(a) that a person is committing, has committed or intends to commit the offence of aggravated trespass on land in the open air; or

(b) that two or more persons are trespassing on land in the open air and are present there with the common purpose of intimidating persons so as to deter them from engaging in a lawful activity or of obstructing or disrupting a lawful activity,

he may direct that person or (as the case may be) those persons (or any of them) to leave the land.

(2) A direction under subsection (1) above, if not communicated to the persons referred to in subsection (1) by the police officer giving the direction, may be communicated to them by any constable at the scene.

(3) If a person knowing that a direction under subsection (1) above has been given which applies to him—

(a) fails to leave the land as soon as practicable, or

(b) having left again enters the land as a trespasser within the period of three months beginning with the day on which the direction was given, he commits an offence.

DRUG TRAFFICKING ACT 1994
(1994, c. 37)

[2. **External confiscation orders.**

(1) An order made by a court in a designated country for the purpose of recovering payments or other rewards received in connection with drug trafficking or their value is referred to in this Act as an 'external confiscation order'.

(2) In subsection (1) above the reference to an order includes any order, decree, direction or judgment, or any part thereof, however described.]

INTELLIGENCE SERVICES ACT 1994
(1994, c. 13)

5. **Warrants: general.**

(1) No entry on or interference with property or with wireless telegraphy shall be unlawful if it is authorised by a warrant issued by the Secretary of State under this section.

TRADE MARKS ACT 1994
(1994, c. 26)

16. **Order for delivery up of infringing goods, material or articles.**

(1) The proprietor of a registered trade mark may apply to the court for an order for the delivery up to him, or such other person as the court may direct, of any infringing goods, material or articles which a person has in his possession, custody or control in the course of a business.

19. **Order as to disposal of infringing goods, material or articles.**

(1) Where infringing goods, material or articles have been delivered up in pursuance of an order under section 16, an application may be made to the court—

    (a) for an order that they be destroyed or forfeited to such person as the court may think fit, or

    (b) for a decision that no such order should be made.

(2) In considering what order (if any) should be made, the court shall consider whether other remedies available in an action for infringement of the registered trade mark would be adequate to compensate the proprietor and any licensee and protect their interests.

(3) Provision shall be made by rules of court as to the service of notice on persons having an interest in the goods, material or articles, and any such person is entitled—

    (a) to appear in proceedings for an order under this section, whether or not he was served with notice, and

    (b) to appeal against any order made, whether or not he appeared;

and an order shall not take effect until the end of the period within which notice of an appeal may be given or, if before the end of that period notice of appeal is duly given, until the final determination or abandonment of the proceedings on the appeal.

(4) Where there is more than one person interested in the goods, material or articles, the court shall make such order as it thinks just.

VALUE ADDED TAX ACT 1994
(1994, c. 23)

78. Interest in certain cases of official error.

(1) Where, due to an error on the part of the Commissioners, a person has—

(a) accounted to them for an amount by way of output tax which was not output tax due from him and which they are in consequence liable to repay to him, or

(b) failed to claim credit under section 25 for an amount for which he was entitled so to claim credit and which they are in consequence liable to pay to him, or

(c) (otherwise than in a case falling within paragraph (a) or (b) above) paid to them by way of VAT an amount that was not VAT due and which they are in consequence liable to repay to him, or

(d) suffered delay in receiving payment of an amount due to him from them in connection with VAT,

then, if and to the extent that they would not be liable to do so apart from this section, they shall pay interest to him on that amount for the applicable period, but subject to the following provisions of this section.

[(1A) In subsection (1) above—

(a) references to an amount which the Commissioners are liable in consequence of any matter to pay or repay to any person are references, where a claim for the payment or repayment has to be made, to only so much of that amount as is the subject of a claim that the Commissioners are required to satisfy or have satisfied; and

(b) the amounts referred to in paragraph (d) do not include any amount payable under this section.]

(2) Nothing in subsection (1) above requires the Commissioners to pay interest—

(a) on any amount which falls to be increased by a supplement under section 79; or

(b) where an amount is increased under that section, on so much of the increased amount as represents the supplement.

(3) Interest under this section shall be payable at such rates as may from time to time be prescribed by order made by the Treasury; and any such order—

(a) may prescribe different rates for different purposes; and

(b) shall apply to interest for periods beginning on or after the date on which the order is expressed to come into force, whether or not interest runs from before that date; and the first such order may prescribe, for cases where interest runs from before the date on which that order is expressed to come into force, rates for periods ending before that date.

(4) The "applicable period" in a case falling within subsection (1)(a) or (b) above is the period—

(a) beginning with the appropriate commencement date, and

(b) ending with the date on which the Commissioners authorise payment of the amount on which the interest is payable.

(5) In subsection (4) above, the "appropriate commencement date"—

(a) in a case where an amount would have been due from the person by way of VAT in connection with the relevant return, had his input tax and output tax been as stated in that return, means the date on which the Commissioners received payment of that amount; and

(b) in a case where no such payment would have been due from him in connection with the return, means the date on which the Commissioners would, apart from the error, have authorised payment of the amount on which the interest is payable; and in this subsection "the relevant return" means the return in which the person accounted for, or (as the case may be) ought to have claimed credit for, the amount on which the interest is payable.

(6) The "applicable period" in a case falling within subsection (1)(c) above is the period—
(a) beginning with the date on which the payment is received by the Commissioners, and
(b) ending with the date on which they authorise payment of the amount on which the interest is payable.

(7) The "applicable period" in a case falling within subsection (1)(d) above is the period—
(a) beginning with the date on which, apart from the error, the Commissioners might reasonably have been expected to authorise payment of the amount on which the interest is payable, and
(b) ending with the date on which they in fact authorise payment of that amount.

[(8) In determining in accordance with subsection (4), (6) or (7) above the applicable period for the purposes of subsection (1) above, there shall be left out of account any period by which the Commissioners' authorisation of the payment of interest is delayed by the conduct of the person who claims the interest.

(8A) The reference in subsection (8) above to a period by which the Commissioners' authorisation of the payment of interest is delayed by the conduct of the person who claims it includes, in particular, any period which is referable to—
(a) any unreasonable delay in the making of the claim for interest or in the making of any claim for the payment or repayment of the amount on which interest is claimed;
(b) any failure by that person or a person acting on his behalf or under his influence to provide the Commissioners—
(i) at or before the time of the making of a claim, or
(ii) subsequently in response to a request for information by the Commissioners,
with all the information required by them to enable the existence and amount of the claimant's entitlement to a payment or repayment, and to interest on that payment or repayment, to be determined; and
(c) the making, as part of or in association with either—
(i) the claim for interest, or
(ii) any claim for the payment or repayment of the amount on which interest is claimed,
of a claim to anything to which the claimant was not entitled.

(9) In determining for the purposes of subsection (8A) above whether any period of delay is referable to a failure by any person to provide information in response to a request by the Commissioners, there shall be taken to be so referable, except so far as may be prescribed, any period which—
(a) begins with the date on which the Commissioners require that person to provide information which they reasonably consider relevant to the matter to be determined; and
(b) ends with the earliest date on which it would be reasonable for the Commissioners to conclude—
(i) that they have received a complete answer to their request for information;
(ii) that they have received all that they need in answer to that request; or
(iii) that it is unnecessary for them to be provided with any information in answer to that request.]

(10) The Commissioners shall only be liable to pay interest under this section on a claim made in writing for that purpose.

[(11) A claim under the section shall not be made more than three years after the end of the applicable period to which it relates.]

(12) In this section—

[(a) references to the authorisation by the Commissioners of the payment of any amount include references to the discharge by way of set-off (whether under section 81(3) or otherwise) of the Commissioners' liability to pay that amount; and]

(b) any reference to a return is a reference to a return required to be made in accordance with paragraph 2 of Schedule 11.

[**78A. Assessment for interest overpayments.**

(1) Where—

(a) any amount has been paid to any person by way of interest under section 78, but

(b) that person was not entitled to that amount under that section.

the Commissioners may, to the best of their judgment, assess the amount so paid to which that person was not entitled and notify it to him.

(2) An assessment made under subsection (1) above shall not be made more than two years after the time when evidence of facts sufficient in the opinion of the Commissioners to justify the making of the assessment comes to the knowledge of the Commissioners.

(3) Where an amount has been assessed and notified to any person under subsection (1) above, that amount shall be deemed (subject to the provisions of this Act as to appeals) to be an amount of VAT due from him and may be recovered accordingly.]

79. Repayment supplement in respect of certain delayed payments or refunds.

(1) In any case where—

(a) a person is entitled to a VAT credit, or

(b) a body which is registered and to which section 33 applies is entitled to a refund under that section,

and the conditions mentioned in subsection (2) below are satisfied, the amount which, apart from the section, would be due by way of that payment or refund shall be increased by the addition of a supplement equal to 5 per cent of that amount or £50, whichever is the greater.

(2) The said conditions are—

(a) that the requisite return or claim is received by the Commissioners not later than the last day on which it is required to be furnished or made, and

(b) that a written instruction directing the making of the payment or refund is not issued by the Commissioners within the period of 30 days beginning on the date of the receipt by the Commissioners of that return or claim, and

(c) that the amount shown on that return or claim as due by way of payment or refund does not exceed the payment or refund which was in fact due by more than 5 per cent of that payment or refund or £250, whichever is the greater.

(3) Regulations may provide that, in computing the period of 30 days referred to in subsection (2)(b) above, there shall be left out of account periods determined in accordance with the regulations and referable to—

(a) the raising and answering of any reasonable inquiry relating to the requisite return or claim,

(b) the correction by the Commissioners of any errors or omissions in that return or claim, and

(c) in the case of a payment, the following matters, namely—

(i) any such continuing failure to submit returns as is referred to in section 25(5), and

(ii) compliance with any such condition as is referred to in paragraph 4(1) of Schedule 11.

(4) In determining for the purposes of regulations under subsection (3) above whether any period is referable to the raising and answering of such an inquiry as is mentioned in that subsection, there shall be taken to be so referable any period which—

(a) begins with the date on which the Commissioners first consider it necessary to make such an inquiry, and

(b) ends with the date on which the Commissioners—

(i) satisfy themselves that they have received a complete answer to the inquiry, or

(ii) determine not to make the inquiry or, if they have made it, not to pursue it further,

but excluding so much of that period as may be prescribed; and it is immaterial whether any inquiry is in fact made or whether it is or might have been made of the person or body making the requisite return or claim or of an authorised person or of some other person.

(5) Except for the purpose of determining the amount of the supplement—

(a) a supplement paid to any person under subsection (1)(a) above shall be treated as an amount due to him by way of credit under section 25(3), and

(b) a supplement paid to any body under subsection (1)(b) above shall be treated as an amount due to it by way of refund under section 33.

(6) In this section "requisite return or claim" means—

(a) in relation to a payment, the return for the prescribed accounting period concerned which is required to be furnished in accordance with regulations under this Act, and

(b) in relation to a refund, the claim for that refund which is required to be made in accordance with the Commissioners' determination under section 33.

(7) If the Treasury by order so direct, any period specified in the order shall be disregarded for the purpose of calculating the period of 30 days referred to in subsection (2)(b) above.

80. Recovery of overpaid VAT.

(1) Where a person has (whether before or after the commencement of this Act) paid an amount to the Commissioners by way of VAT which was not VAT due to them, they shall be liable to repay the amount to him.

(2) The Commissioners shall only be liable to repay an amount under this section on a claim being made for the purpose.

(3) It shall be a defence, in relation to a claim under this section, that repayment of an amount would unjustly enrich the claimant.

[(3A) Subsection (3B) below applies for the purposes of subsection (3) above where—

(a) there is an amount paid by way of VAT which (apart from subsection (3) above) would fall to be repaid under this section to any person ("the taxpayer"), and

(b) the whole or a part of the cost of the payment of that amount to the Commissioners has, for practical purposes, been borne by a person other than the taxpayer.

(3B) Where, in a case to which this subsection applies, loss or damage has been or may be incurred by the taxpayer as a result of mistaken assumptions made in his case about the operation of any VAT provisions, that loss or damage shall be disregarded, except to the extent of the quantified amount, in the making of any determination—

(a) of whether or to what extent the repayment of an amount to the taxpayer would enrich him; or

(b) of whether or to what extent any enrichment of the taxpayer would be unjust.

(3C) In subsection (3B) above—

"the quantified amount" means the amount (if any) which is shown by the taxpayer to constitute the amount that would appropriately compensate him for loss or damage shown by him to have resulted, for any business carried on by him, from the making of the mistaken assumptions; and

"VAT provisions" means the provisions of—

(a) any enactment, subordinate legislation or Community legislation (whether or not still in force) which relates to VAT or to any matter connected with VAT; or

(b) any notice published by the Commissioners under or for the purposes of any such enactment or subordinate legislation.]

[(4) The Commissioners shall not be liable, on a claim made under this section, to repay any amount paid to them more than three years before the making of the claim.]

[(4A) Where—

(a) any amount has been paid, at any time on or after 18th July 1996, to any person by way of a repayment under this section, and

(b) the amount paid exceeded the Commissioners' repayment liability to that person at that time,

the Commissioners may, to the best of their judgment, assess the excess paid to that person and notify it to him.

(4B) For the purposes of subsection (4A) above the Commissioners' repayment liability to a person at any time is—

(a) in a case where any provision affecting the amount which they were liable to repay to that person at that time is subsequently deemed to have been in force at that time, the amount which the Commissioners are to be treated, in accordance with that provision, as having been liable at that time to repay to that person; and

(b) in any other case, the amount which they were liable at that time to repay to that person.

(4C) Subsections (2) to (8) of section 78A apply in the case of an assessment under subsection (4A) above as they apply in the case of an assessment under section 78A(1).]

(6) A claim under this section shall be made in such form and manner and shall be supported by such documentary evidence as the Commissioners prescribe by regulations; and regulations under this subsection may make different provision for different cases.

(7) Except as provided by this section, the Commissioners shall not be liable to repay an amount paid to them by way of VAT by virtue of the fact that it was not VAT due to them.

[80A. **Arrangements for reimbursing customers.**

(1) The Commissioners may by regulations make provision for reimbursement arrangements made by any person to be disregarded for the purposes of section 80(3) except where the arrangements—

(a) contain such provision as may be required by the regulations; and

(b) are supported by such undertakings to comply with the provisions of the arrangements as may be required by the regulations to be given to the Commissioners.

(2) In this section "reimbursement arrangements" means any arrangements for the purposes of a claim under section 80 which—

(a) are made by any person for the purpose of securing that he is not unjustly enriched by the repayment of any amount in pursuance of the claim; and

(b) provide for the reimbursement of persons who have for practical purposes borne the whole or any part of the cost of the original payment of that amount to the Commissioners.

(3) Without prejudice to the generality of subsection (1) above, the provision that may be required by regulations under this section to be contained in reimbursement arrangements includes—

(a) provision requiring a reimbursement for which the arrangements provide to be made within such period after the repayment to which it relates as may be specified in the regulations;

Value Added Tax Act 1994 295

(b) provision for the repayment of amounts to the Commissioners where those amounts are not reimbursed in accordance with the arrangements;

(c) provision requiring interest paid by the Commissioners on any amount repaid by them to be treated in the same way as that amount for the purposes of any requirement under the arrangements to make reimbursement or to repay the Commissioners;

(d) provision requiring such records relating to the carrying out of the arrangements as may be described in the regulations to be kept and produced to the Commissioners, or to an officer of theirs.

(4) Regulations under this section may impose obligations on such persons as may be specified in the regulations—

(a) to make the repayments to the Commissioners that they are required to make in pursuance of any provisions contained in any reimbursement arrangements by virtue of subsection (3)(b) or (c) above;

(b) to comply with any requirements contained in any such arrangements by virtue of subsection (3)(d) above.

(5) Regulations under this section may make provision for the form and manner in which, and the times at which, undertakings are to be given to the Commissioners in accordance with the regulations; and any such provision may allow for those matters to be determined by the Commissioners in accordance with the regulations.

(6) Regulations under this section may—

(a) contain any such incidental, supplementary, consequential or transitional provision as appears to the Commissioners to be necessary or expedient; and

(b) make different provision for different circumstances.

(7) Regulations under this section may have effect (irrespective of when the claim for repayment was made) for the purposes of the making of any repayment by the Commissioners after the time when the regulations are made; and, accordingly, such regulations may apply to arrangements made before that time.]

[80B. Assessment of amounts due under section 80A arrangements.

[(1) Where any person is liable to pay any amount to the Commissioners in pursuance of an obligation imposed by virtue of section 80A(4)(a), the Commissioners may, to the best of their judgment, assess the amount due from that person and notify it to him.

(2) Subsections (2) to (8) of section 78A apply in the case of an assessment under subsection (1) above as they apply in the case of an assessment under section 78A(1).]

81. Interest given by way of credit and set-off of credits.

(1) Any interest payable by the Commissioners (whether under an enactment or instrument or otherwise) to a person on a sum due to him under or by virtue of any provision of this Act shall be treated as an amount due by way of credit under section 25(3).

(2) Subsection (1) above shall be disregarded for the purpose of determining a person's entitlement to interest or the amount of interest to which he is entitled.

(3) Subject to subsection (1) above, in any case where—

(a) an amount is due from the Commissioners to any person under any provision of this Act, and

(b) that person is liable to pay a sum by way of VAT, penalty, interest or surcharge, the amount referred to in paragraph (a) above shall be set against the sum referred to in paragraph (b) above and, accordingly, to the extent of the set-off, the obligations of the Commissioners and the person concerned shall be discharged.

[(3A) Where—

(a) the Commissioners are liable to pay or repay any amount to any person under this Act,

(b) that amount falls to be paid or repaid in consequence of a mistake previously made about whether or to what extent amounts were payable under this Act to or by that person, and

(c) by reason of that mistake a liability of that person to pay a sum by way of VAT, penalty, interest or surcharge was not assessed, was not enforced or was not satisfied, any limitation on the time within which the Commissioners are entitled to take steps for recovering that sum shall be disregarded in determining whether that sum is required by subsection (3) above to be set against the amount mentioned in paragraph (a) above.]

(4) Subsection (3) above shall not apply in the case of any such amount as is mentioned in paragraph (a) of that subsection where that amount became due to the person in question—

(a) at a time when that person's estate was vested in any other person as that person's trustee in bankruptcy;

(b) at a time when that person's estate was vested in any other person as that person's interim trustee or permanent trustee;

(c) at a time, other than a time before the appointment of a liquidator, when that person was being wound up, either voluntarily or by the court;

(d) at a time when an administration order was in force in relation to that person;

(e) at a time when there was an administrative receiver of that person;

(f) at a time when—

(i) a voluntary arrangement approved in accordance with Part I or VIII of the Insolvency Act 1986, or Part II or Chapter II of Part VIII of the Insolvency (Northern Ireland) Order 1989, or

(ii) a deed of arrangement registered in accordance with the Deeds of Arrangement Act 1914 or Chapter I of Part VIII of that Order of 1989,

was in force in relation to that person; or

(g) at a time when that person's estate was vested in any other person as that person's trustee under a trust deed.

(5) In subsection (4) above—

(a) "administration order" means an administration order under Part II of the Insolvency Act 1986 or an administration order within the meaning of Article 5(1) of the Insolvency (Northern Ireland) Order 1989;

(b) "administrative receiver" means an administrative receiver within the meaning of section 251 of that Act of 1986 or Article 5(1) of that Order of 1989; and

(c) "trust deed" has the same meaning as in the Bankruptcy (Scotland) Act 1985.

89. Adjustments of contracts on changes in VAT.

(1) Where, after the making of a contract for the supply of goods/or services and before the goods or services are supplied, there is a change in the VAT charged on the supply, then, unless the contract otherwise provided, there shall be added to or deducted from the consideration for the supply an amount equal to the change.

VEHICLE EXCISE AND REGISTRATION ACT 1994
(1994, c. 22)

50. Time-limit for recovery of underpayments and overpayments.

No proceedings shall be brought—

(a) by the Secretary of State for the recovery of any underpayment of duty on a vehicle licence, or

(b) by any person for the recovery of any overpayment of duty on a vehicle licence taken out by him,

after the end of the period of twelve months beginning with the end of the period in respect of which the licence was taken out.

AGRICULTURAL TENANCIES ACT 1995
(1996, c. 8)

16. Tenant's right to compensation for tenant's improvement.

(1) The tenant under a farm business tenancy shall, subject to the provisions of this Part of this Act, be entitled on the termination of the tenancy, on quitting the holding, to obtain from his landlord compensation in respect of any tenant's improvement.

17. Consent of landlord as condition of compensation for tenant's improvement.

(1) A tenant shall not be entitled to compensation under section 16 of this Act in repect of any tenant's improvement unless the landlord has given his consent in writing to the provision of the tenant's improvement.

(3) Any such consent may be given either unconditionally or on condition that the tenant agrees to a specified variation in the terms of the tenancy.

(4) The variation referred to in subsection (3) above must be related to the tenant's improvement in question.

20. Amount of compensation for tenant's improvement not consisting of planning permission.

(1) The amount of compensation payable to the tenant under section 16 of this Act in respect of any tenant's improvement shall be an amount equal to the increase attributable to the improvement in the value of the holding at the termination of the tenancy as land comprised in a tenancy.

(2) Where the landlord and the tenant have entered into an agreement in writing whereby any benefit is given or allowed to the tenant in consideration of the provision of a tenant's improvement, the amount of compensation otherwise payable in respect of that improvement shall be reduced by the proportion which the value of the benefit bears to the amount of the total cost of providing the improvement.

(3) Where a grant has been or will be made to the tenant out of public money in respect of a tenant's improvement, the amount of compensation otherwise payable in respect of that improvement shall be reduced by the proportion which the amount of the grant bears to the amount of the total cost of providing the improvement.

(4) Where a physical improvement which has been completed or a change of use which has been effected is authorised by any planning permission granted on an application made by the tenant, section 18 of this Act does not prevent any value attributable to the fact that the physical improvement or change of use is so authorised from being taken into account under this section in determining the amount of compensation payable in respect of the physical improvement or in respect of any intangible advantage obtained as a result of the change of use.

(5) This section does not apply where the tenant's improvement consists of planning permission.

22. Settlement of claims for compensation.

(1) Any claim by the tenant under a farm business tenancy for compensation under section 16 of this Act shall, subject to the provisions of this section, be determined by arbitration under this section.

(2) No such claim for compensation shall be enforceable unless before the end of the period of two months beginning with the date of the termination of the tenancy the tenant has given notice in writing to his landlord of his intention to make the claim and of the nature of the claim.

26. Extent to which compensation recoverable under agreements.

(1) In any case for which apart from this section the provisions of this Part of this Act provide for compensation, a tenant shall be entitled to compensation in accordance

with those provisions and not otherwise, and shall be so entitled notwithstanding any agreement to the contrary.

(2) Nothing in the provisions of this Part of this Act, apart from this section, shall be construed as disentitling a tenant to compensation in any case for which those provisions do not provide for compensation.

CRIMINAL INJURIES COMPENSATION ACT 1995
(1995, c. 53)

1. The Criminal Injuries Compensation Scheme.

(1) The Secretary of State shall make arrangements for the payment of compensation to, or in respect of, persons who have sustained one or more criminal injuries.

(2) Any such arrangements shall include the making of a scheme providing, in particular, for—

    (a) the circumstances in which awards may be made; and

    (b) the categories of person to whom awards may be made.

(3) The scheme shall be known as the Criminal Injuries Compensation Scheme.

(4) In this Act—

"adjudicator" means a person appointed by the Secretary of State under section 5(1)(b);

"award" means an award of compensation made in accordance with the provisions of the Scheme;

"claim officer" means a person appointed by the Secretary of State under section 3(4)(b);

"compensation" means compensation payable under an award;

"criminal injury", "loss of earnings" and "special expenses" have such meaning as may be specified;

"the Scheme" means the Criminal Injuries Compensation Scheme;

"Scheme manager" means a person appointed by the Secretary of State to have overall responsibility for managing the provisions of the Scheme (other than those to which section 5(2) applies); and

"specified" means specified by the Scheme.

2. Basis on which compensation is to be calculated.

(1) The amount of compensation payable under an award shall be determined in accordance with the provisions of the Scheme.

(2) Provision shall be made for—

    (a) a standard amount of compensation, determined by reference to the nature of the injury;

    (b) in such cases as may be specified, an additional amount of compensation calculated with respect to loss of earnings;

    (c) in such cases as may be specified, an additional amount of compensation calculated with respect to special expenses; and

    (d) in cases of fatal injury, such additional amounts as may be specified or otherwise determined in accordance with the Scheme.

(3) Provision shall be made for the standard amount to be determined—

    (a) in accordance with a table ("the Tariff") prepared by the Secretary of State as part of the Scheme and such other provisions of the Scheme as may be relevant; or

    (b) where no provision is made in the Tariff with respect to the injury in question, in accordance with such provisions of the Scheme as may be relevant.

(4) The Tariff shall show, in respect of each description of injury mentioned in the Tariff, the standard amount of compensation payable in respect of that description of injury.

(5) An injury may be described in the Tariff in such a way, including by reference to the nature of the injury, its severity or the circumstances in which it was sustained, as the Secretary of State considers appropriate.

(6) The Secretary of State may at any time alter the Tariff—
 (a) by adding to the descriptions of injury mentioned there;
 (b) by removing a description of injury;
 (c) by increasing or reducing the amount shown as the standard amount of compensation payable in respect of a particular description of injury; or
 (d) in such other way as he considers appropriate.

(7) The Scheme may—
 (a) provide for amounts of compensation not to exceed such maximum amounts as may be specified;
 (b) include such transitional provision with respect to any alteration of its provisions relating to compensation as the Secretary of State considers appropriate.

3. Claims and awards.

(1) The Scheme may, in particular, include provision—
 (a) as to the circumstances in which an award may be withheld or the amount of compensation reduced;
 (b) for an award to be made subject to conditions;
 (c) for the whole or any part of any compensation to be repayable in specified circumstances;
 (d) for compensation to be held subject to trusts, in such cases as may be determined in accordance with the Scheme;
 (e) requiring claims under the Scheme to be made within such periods as may be specified by the Scheme; and
 (f) imposing other time limits.

(2) Where, in accordance with any provision of the Scheme, it falls to one person to satisfy another as to any matter, the standard of proof required shall be that applicable in civil proceedings.

(3) Where, in accordance with any provision of the Scheme made by virtue of subsection (1)(c), any amount falls to be repaid it shall be recoverable as a debt due to the Crown.

(4) The Scheme shall include provision for claims for compensation to be determined and awards and payments of compensation to be made—
 (a) if a Scheme manager has been appointed, by persons appointed for the purpose by the Scheme manager; but
 (b) otherwise by persons ("claims officers") appointed for the purpose by the Secretary of State.

(5) A claims officer—
 (a) shall be appointed on such terms and conditions as the Secretary of State considers appropriate; but
 (b) shall not be regarded as having been appointed to exercise functions of the Secretary of State or to act on his behalf.

(6) No decision taken by a claims officer shall be regarded as having been taken by, or on behalf of, the Secretary of State.

(7) If a Scheme manager has been appointed—
 (a) he shall not be regarded as exercising functions of the Secretary of State or as acting on his behalf; and
 (b) no decision taken by him or by any person appointed by him shall be regarded as having been taken by, or on behalf of, the Secretary of State.

7. Inalienability of awards.

(1) Every assignment (or, in Scotland, assignation) of, or charge on, an award and every agreement to assign or charge an award shall be void.

(2) On the bankruptcy of a person in whose favour an award is made (or, in Scotland, on the sequestration of such a person's estate), the award shall not pass to any trustee or other person acting on behalf of his creditors.

9. Financial provisions.

(1) The Secretary of State may pay such remuneration, allowances or gratuities to or in respect of claims officers and other persons appointed by him under this Act (other than adjudicators) as he considers appropriate.

(2) The Secretary of State may pay, or make such payments towards the provision of, such remuneration, pensions, allowances or gratuities to or in respect of adjudicators, as he considers appropriate.

(3) The Secretary of State may make such payments by way of compensation for loss of office to any adjudicator who is removed from office under section 5(7), as he considers appropriate.

(4) Sums required for the payment of compensation in accordance with the Scheme shall be provided by the Secretary of State out of money provided by Parliament.

(5) Where a Scheme manager has been appointed, the Secretary of State may make such payments to him, in respect of the discharge of his functions in relation to the Scheme, as the Secretary of State considers appropriate.

(6) Any expenses incurred by the Secretary of State under this Act shall be paid out of money provided by Parliament.

(7) Any sums received by the Secretary of State under any provision of the Scheme made by virtue of section 3(1)(c) shall be paid by him into the Consolidated Fund.

JOBSEEKERS ACT 1995
(1995, c. 18)

23. Recovery of sums in respect of maintenance.

(1) Regulations may make provision for the court to have power to make a recovery order against any person where an award of income-based jobseeker's allowance has been made to that person's spouse.

(2) In this section "recovery order" means an order requiring the person against whom it is made to make payments to the Secretary of State or to such other person or persons as the court may determine.

(3) Regulations under this section may make provision for the transfer by the Secretary of State of the right to receive payments under, and to exercise rights in relation to, a recovery order.

(4) Regulations made under this section may, in particular, include provision—

(a) as to the matters to which the court is, or is not, to have regard in determining any application under the regulations; and

(b) as to the enforcement of recovery orders.

LANDLORD AND TENANT (COVENANTS) ACT 1995
(1995, c. 30)

3. Transmission of benefit and burden of covenants.

(1) The benefit and burden of all landlord and tenant covenants of a tenancy—

(a) shall be annexed and incident to the whole, and to each and every part, of the premises demised by the tenancy and of the reversion in them, and

Landlord and Tenant (Covenants) Act 1995

(b) shall in accordance with this section pass on an assignment of the whole or any part of those premises or of the reversion in them.

(2) Where the assignment is by the tenant under the tenancy, then as from the assignment the assignee—

(a) becomes bound by the tenant covenants of the tenancy except to the extent that—

(i) immediately before the assignment they did not bind the assignor, or

(ii) they fall to be complied with in relation to any demised premises not comprised in the assignment; and

(b) becomes entitled to the benefit of the landlord covenants of the tenancy except to the extent that they fall to be complied with in relation to any such premises.

(3) Where the assignment is by the landlord under the tenancy, then as from the assignment the assignee—

(a) becomes bound by the landlord covenants of the tenancy except to the extent that—

(i) immediately before the assignment they did not bind the asignor, or

(ii) they fall to be complied with in relation to any demised premises not comprised in the assignment; and

(b) becomes entitled to the benefit of the tenant covenants of the tenancy except to the extent that they fall to be complied with in relation to any such premises.

(4) In determining for the purposes of subsection (2) or (3) whether any covenant bound the assignor immediately before the assignment, any waiver or release of the covenant (in whatever terms) is expressed to be personal to the assignor shall be disregarded.

(5) Any landlord or tenant covenant of a tenancy which is restrictive of the user of land shall, as well as being capable of enforcement against an assignee, be capable of being enforced against any other person who is the owner or occupier of any demised premises to which the covenant relates, even though there is no express provision in the tenancy to that effect.

(6) Nothing in this section shall operate—

(a) in the case of a covenant which (in whatever terms) is expressed to be personal to any person, to make the covenant enforceable by or (as the case may be) against any other person; or

(b) to make a covenant enforceable against any person if, apart from this section, it would not be enforceable against him by reason of its not having been registered under the Land Registration Act 1925 or the Land Charges Act 1972.

(7) To the extent that there remains in force any rule of law by virtue of which the burden of a covenant whose subject matter is not in existence at the time when it is made does not run with the land affected unless the covenantor covenants on behalf of himself and his assigns, that rule of law is hereby abolished in relation to tenancies.

4. Transmission of rights of re-entry.

The benefit of a landlord's right of a re-entry under a tenancy—

(a) shall be annexed and incident to the whole, and to each and every part, of the reversion in the premises demised by the tenancy, and

(b) shall pass on an assignment of the whole or any part of the reversion in those premises.

5. Tenant released from covenants on assignment of tenancy.

(1) This section applies where a tenant assigns premises demised to him under a tenancy.

(2) If the tenant assigns the whole of the premises demised to him, he—

(a) is released from the tenant covenants of the tenancy, and

(b) ceases to be entitled to the benefit of the landlord covenants of the tenancy, as from the assignment.

(3) If the tenant assigns part only of the premises demised to him, then as from the assignment he—

(a) is released from the tenant covenants of the tenancy, and

(b) ceases to be entitled to the benefit of the landlord covenants of the tenancy,

only to the extent that those covenants fall to be complied with in relation to that part of the demised premises.

(4) This section applies as mentioned in subsection (1) whether or not the tenant is tenant of the whole of the premises comprised in the tenancy.

6. Landlord may be released from covenants on assignment of reversion.

...

7. Former landlord may be released from covenants on assignment of reversion.

...

9. Apportionment of liability under covenants binding both assignor and assignee of tenancy or reversion.

(1) This section applies where—

(a) a tenant assigns part only of the premises demised to him by a tenancy;

(b) after the assignment both the tenant and his assignee are to be bound by a non-attributable tenant covenant of the tenancy; and

(c) the tenant and his assignee agree that as from the assignment liability under the covenant is to be apportioned between them in such manner as is specified in the agreement.

(2) This section also applies where—

(a) a landlord assigns the reversion in part only of the premises of which he is the landlord under a tenancy;

(b) after the assignment both the landlord and his assignee are to be bound by a non-attributable landlord covenant of the tenancy; and

(c) the landlord and his assignee agree that as from the assignment liability under the covenant is to be apportioned between them in such manner as is specified in the agreement.

(3) Any such agreement as is mentioned in subsection (1) or (2) may apportion liability in such a way that a party to the agreement is exonerated from all liability under a covenant.

(4) In any case falling within subsection (1) or (2) the parties to the agreement may apply for the apportionment to become binding on the appropriate person in accordance with section 10.

(5) In any such case the parties to the agreement may also apply for the apportionment to become binding on any person (other than the appropriate person) who is for the time being entitled to enforce the covenant in question; and section 10 shall apply in relation to such an application as it applies in relation to an application made with respect to the appropriate person.

(6) For the purposes of this section a covenant is, in relation to an assignment, a "non-attributable" covenant if it does not fall to be complied with in relation to any premises comprised in the assignment.

(7) In this section "the appropriate person" means either—

(a) the landlord of the entire premises referred to in subsection (1)(a) (or, if different parts of those premises are held under the tenancy by different landlords, each of those landlords), or

Landlord and Tenant (Covenants) Act 1995

(b) the tenant of the entire premises referred to in subsection (2)(a) (or, if different parts of those premises are held under the tenancy by different tenants, each of those tenants),
depending on whether the agreement in question falls within subsection (1) or subsection (2).

10. Procedure for making apportionment bind other party to lease.

(1) For the purposes of section 9 the parties to an agreement falling within subsection (1) or (2) of that section apply for an apportionment to become binding on the appropriate person if, either before or within the period of four weeks beginning with the date of the assignment in question, they serve on that person a notice informing him of—

(a) the proposed assignment or (as the case may be) the fact that the assignment has taken place;
(b) the prescribed particulars of the agreement; and
(c) their request that the apportionment should become binding on him.

(2) Where an application for an apportionment to become binding has been made in accordance with subsection (1), the apportionment becomes binding on the appropriate person if—

(a) he does not, within the period of four weeks beginning with the day on which the notice is served under subsection (1), serve on the parties to the agreement a notice in writing objecting to the apportionment becoming binding on him, or
(b) he does so serve such a notice but the court, on the application of the parties to the agreement, makes a declaration that it is reasonable for the apportionment to become binding on him, or
(c) he serves on the parties to the agreement a notice in writing consenting to the apportionment becoming binding on him and, if he has previously served a notice objecting thereto, stating that the notice is withdrawn.

(3) Where any apportionment becomes binding in accordance with this section, this shall be regarded as occurring at the time when the assignment in question takes place,

(4) In this section—
"the appropriate persons" has the same meaning as in section 9;
"the court" means a county court;
"prescribed" means prescribed by virtue of section 27.

11. Assignments in breach of covenant or by operation of law.

(1) This section provides for the operation of sections 5 to 10 in relation to assignments in breach of a covenant of a tenancy or assignments by operation of law ("excluded assignment").

(2) In the case of an excluded assignment subsection (2) or (3) of section 5—

(a) shall not have the effect mentioned in the subsection in relation to the tenant as from that assignment, but
(b) shall have that effect as from the next assignment (if any) of the premises asigned by him which is not an excluded assignment.

(3) In the case of an excluded assignment subsection (2) or (3) of section 6 or 7—

(a) shall not enable the landlord or former landlord to apply for such a release as is mentioned in that subsection as from that assignment, but
(b) shall apply on the next assignment (if any) of the reversion assigned by the landlord which is not an excluded assignment so as to enable the landlord or former landlord to apply for any such release as from that subsequent assignment.

...

13. Covenants binding two or more persons.

(1) Where in consequence of this Act two or more persons are bound by the same covenant, they are so bound both jointly and severally.

(2) Subject to section 24(2), where by virtue of this Act—

(a) two or more persons are bound jointly and severally by the same covenant, and

(b) any of the persons so bound is released from the covenant,

the release does not extend to any other of those persons.

(3) For the purpose of providing for contribution between persons who, by virtue of this Act, are bound jointly and severally by a covenant, the Civil Liability (Contribution) Act 1978 shall have effect as if—

(a) liability to a person under a covenant were liability in respect of damage suffered by that person;

(b) references to damage accordingly include a breach of a covenant of a tenancy; and

(c) section 7(2) of that Act were omitted.

23. Effects of becoming subject to liability under, or entitled to benefit of, covenant etc.

(1) Where as a result of an assignment a person becomes by virtue of this Act, bound by or entitled to the benefit of a covenant, he shall not by virtue of this Act have any liability or rights under the covenant in relation to any time falling before the assignment.

(2) Subsection (1) does not preclude any such rights being expressly assigned to the person in question.

(3) Where as a result of an assignment a person becomes, by virtue of this Act, entitled to a right of re-entry contained in a tenancy, that right shall be exercisable in relation to any breach of a covenant of the tenancy occurring before the assignment as in relation to one occurring thereafter, unless by reason of any waiver or release it was not so exercisable immediately before the assignment.

24. Effects of release from liability under, or loss of benefit of, covenant.

(1) Any release of a person from a covenant by virtue of this Act does not affect any liability of his arising from a breach of the covenant occurring before the release.

(2) Where—

(a) by virtue of this Act a tenant is released from a tenant covenant of a tenancy, and

(b) immediately before the release another person is bound by a covenant of the tenancy imposing any liability or penalty in the event of a failure to comply with that tenant covenant,

then, as from the release of the tenant, that other person is released from the covenant mentioned in paragraph (b) to the same extent as the tenant is released from that tenant covenant.

(3) Where a person bound by a landlord or tenant covenant of a tenancy—

(a) assigns the whole or part of his interest in the premises demised by the tenancy, but

(b) is not released by virtue of this Act from the covenant (with the result that subsection (1) does not apply),

the assignment does not affect any liability of his arising from a breach of the coveant occurring before the assignment.

(4) Where by virtue of this Act a person ceases to be entitled to the benefit of a covenant, this does not affect any rights of his arising from a breach of the covenant occurring before he ceases to be so entitled.

25. Agreement void if it restricts operation of the Act.

(1) Any agreement relating to a tenancy is void to the extent that—

(a) it would apart from this section have effect to exclude, modify or otherwise frustrate the operation of any provision of this Act, or

(b) it provides for—
  (i) the termination or surrender of the tenancy, or
  (ii) the imposition on the tenant of any penalty, disability or liability,
in the event of the operation of any provision of this Act, or
(c) it provides for any of the matters referred to in paragraph (b)(i) or (ii) and does so (whether expressly or otherwise) in connection with, or in consequence of, the operation of any provision of this Act.

(2) To the extent that an agreement relating to a tenancy constitutes a covenant (whether absolute or qualified) against the assignment, or parting with the possession, of the premises demised by the tenancy or any part of them—
  (a) the agreement is not void by virtue of subsection (1) by reason only of the fact that as such the covenant prohibits or restricts any such assignment or parting with possession; but
  (b) paragraph (a) above does not otherwise affect the operation of that subsection in relation to the agreement (and in particular does not preclude its application to the agreement to the extent that it purports to regulate the giving of, or the making of any application for, consent to any such assignment or parting with possession).

(3) In accordance with section 16(1) nothing in this section applies to any agreement to the extent that it is an authorised guarantee agreement; but (without prejudice to the generality of subsection (1) above) an agreement is void to the extent that it is one falling within section 16(4)(a) or (b).

(4) This section applies to an agreement relating to a tenancy whether or not the agreement is—
  (a) contained in the instrument creating the tenancy; or
  (b) made before the creation of the tenancy.

MERCHANT SHIPPING ACT 1995
(1995, c. 21)

39. Protection of certain rights and remedies.

(1) A seaman's lien, his remedies for the recovery of his wages, his right to wages in case of the wreck or loss of his ship, and any right he may have or obtain in the nature of salvage shall not be capable of being renounced by any agreement.

(2) Subsection (1) above does not affect such of the terms of any agreement made with the seamen belonging to a ship which, in accordance with the agreement, is to be employed on salvage service, as provide for the remuneration to be paid to them for salvage services rendered by that ship.

70. Civil liability for absence without leave.

(1) The following provisions of this section shall apply with respect to the liability of a seaman employed in a United Kingdom ship, to damages for being absent from his ship at a time when he is required, under his contract of employment to be on board.

(2) If he proves that his absence was due to an accident or mistake or some other cause beyond his control and that he took all reasonable precautions to avoid being absent has absence shall not be treated as a breach of contract.

(3) Where subsection (2) above does not apply, then—
  (a) if no special damages are claimed his liability shall be £10;
  (b) if special damages are claimed his liability shall not be more than £100.

92. Duty of ship to assist the other in case of collision.

In every case of collision between two ships, it shall be the duty of the master of each ship, if and so far as he can do so without danger to his own ship, crew and passengers (if any)—

(a) to render to the other ship, its master, crew and passengers (if any) such assistance as may be practicable, and may be necessary to save them from any danger caused by the collision, and to stay by the other ship until he has ascertained that it has no need of further assistance; and

(b) to give to the master of the other ship the name of his own ship and also the names of the ports from which it comes and to which it is bound.

(2) The duties imposed on the master of a ship by subsection (1) above apply to the masters of United Kingdom ships and to the masters of foreign ships when in United Kingdom waters.

(3) The failure of the master of a ship to comply with the provisions of this section shall not raise any presumption of law that the collision was caused by his wrongful act, neglect, or default.

(4) If the master fails without reasonable excuse to comply with this section, he shall—

(a) in the case of a failure to comply with subsection (1)(a) above, be liable—

(i) on summary conviction, to a fine not exceeding £50,000 or imprisonment for a term not exceeding six months or both;

(ii) on conviction on indictment, to a fine or imprisonment for a term not exceeding two years or both; and

(b) in the case of a failure to comply with subsection (1)(b) above, be liable—

(i) on summary coviction, to a fine not exceeding the statutory maximum;

(ii) on conviction on indictment, to a fine;

and in either case if he is a certified officer, an inquiry into his conduct may be held, and his certificate cancelled or suspended.

93. Duty to assist ships, etc. in distress.

(1) The master of a ship, on receiving at sea a signal of distress or information from any source that a ship or aircraft is in distress, shall proceed with all speed to the assistance of the persons in distress (informing them if possible that he is doing so) unless he is unable, or in the special circumstances of the case considers it unreasonable or unnecessary, to do so, or unless he is released from this duty under subsection (4) or (5) below.

185. Limitation of liability for maritime claims.

(1) The provisions of the Convention on Limitation of Liability for Maritime Claims 1976 as set out in Part I of Schedule 7 (in this section and Part II of that Schedule referred to as "the Convention") shall have the force of law in the United Kingdom.

231. Application of, and discharge of functions under, sections 232, 233, 234 and 235.

(1) Sections 232, 233, 234 and 235 apply in circumstances where a United Kingdom or foreign vessel is wrecked, stranded, or in distress at any place on or near the coasts of the United Kingdom or any tidal water within United Kingdom waters.

234. Power to pass over adjoining land.

(1) In circumstances where this section applies by virtue of section 231 in relation to any vessel, all persons may, subject to subsections (3) and (4) below, for the purpose of—

(a) rendering assistance to the vessel,

(b) saving the lives of shipwrecked persons, or

(c) saving the cargo or equipment of the vessel,

pass and repass over any adjoining land without being subject to interruption by the owner or occupier and deposit on the land any cargo or other article recovered from the vessel.

(2) The right of passage conferred by subsection (1) above is a right of passage with or without vehicles.

(3) No right of passage is conferred by subsection (1) above where there is some public road equally convenient.

(4) The rights conferred by subsection (1) above shall be so exercised as to do as little damage as possible.

(5) Any damage sustained by an owner or occupier of land in consequence of the exercise of the right conferred by this section shall be a charge on the vessel, cargo or articles in respect of or by which the damage is caused.

(6) Any amount payable in respect of such damage shall, in case of dispute, be determined and shall, in default of payment, be recoverable in the same manner as the amount of salvage is determined and recoverable under this Part.

(7) If the owner or occupier of any land—

(a) impedes or hinders any person in the exercise of the rights conferred by this section;

(b) impedes or hinders the deposit on the land of any cargo or other article recovered from the vessel; or

(c) prevents or attempts to prevent any cargo or other article recovered from the vessel from remaining deposited on the land for a reasonable time until it can be removed to a safe place of public deposit;

he shall be liable, on summary conviction, to a fine not exceeding level 3 on the standard scale.

Section 185 **SCHEDULE 7**

CONVENTION ON LIMITATION OF LIABILITY FOR MARITIME CLAIMS 1976

Art. 1. Persons entitled to limit liability.

1. Shipowners and salvors, as hereinafter defined, may limit their liability in accordance with the rules of this Convention for claims set out in Article 2.

4. If any claims set out in Article 2 are made against any person for whose act, neglect or default the shipowner or salvor is responsible, such person shall be entitled to avail himself of the limitation of liability provided for in this Convention.

Art. 2. Claims subject to limitation.

1. Subject to Articles 3 and 4 the following claims, whatever the basis of liability may be, shall be subject to limitation of liability:

(a) claims in respect of loss of life or personal injury or loss of or damage to property (including damage to harbour works, basins and waterways and aids to navigation), occurring on board or in direct connection with the operation of the ship or with salvage operations, and consequential loss resulting therefrom;

(b) claims in respect of loss resulting from delay in the carriage by sea of cargo, passengers, or their luggage;

(c) claims in respect of other loss resulting from infringement of rights other than contractual rights, occurring in direct connection with the operation of the ship or salvage operations;

(d) claims in respect of the raising, removal, destruction or the rendering harmless of a ship which is sunk, wrecked, stranded or abandoned, including anything that is or has been on board such ship;

(e) claims in respect of the removal, destruction or the rendering harmless of the cargo of the ship;

(f) claims of a person other than the person liable in respect of measures taken in order to avert or minimise loss for which the person liable may limit his liability in accordance with this Convention, and further loss caused by such measures.

Art. 11. Constitution of the Fund.
1. Any person alleged to be liable may constitute a fund with the Court or other competent authority in any State Party in which legal proceedings are instituted in respect of claims subject to limitation. The fund shall be constituted in the sum of such of the amounts set out in Articles 6 and 7 as are applicable to claims for which that person may be liable, together with interest thereon from the date of the occurrence giving rise to the liability until the date of the constitution of the fund. Any fund thus constituted shall be available only for the payment of claims in respect of which limitation of liability can be invoked.

Art. 13. Bar to other actions.
1. Where a limitation fund has been constituted in accordance with Article 11, any person having made a claim against the fund shall be barred from exercising any right in respect of such a claim against any other assets of a person by or on behalf of whom the fund has been constituted.

PENSIONS ACT 1995
(1995, c. 26)

1. The new authority.
(1) There shall be a body corporate called the Occupational Pensions Regulatory Authority (referred to in this Part as "the Authority").

14. Restitution.
(1) If, on the application of the Authority, the court is satisfied—
   (a) that a power to make a payment, or distribute any assets, to the employer, has been exercised in contravention of section 37, 76 or 77, or
   (b) that any act or omission of the trustees or managers of an occupational pension scheme was in contravention of section 40,
the court may order the employer and any other person who appears to the court to have been knowingly concerned in the contravention to take such steps as the court may direct for restoring the parties to the position in which they were before the payment or distribution was made, or the act or omission occurred.

48. "Blowing the whistle".
(1) If the auditor or actuary of any occupational pension scheme has reasonable cause to believe that—
   (a) any duty relevant to the administration of the scheme imposed by any enactment or rule of law on the trustees or managers, the employer, any professional adviser or any prescribed person acting in connection with the scheme has not been or is not being complied with, and
   (b) the failure to comply is likely to be of material significance in the exercise by the Authority of any of their functions,
he must immediately give a written report of the matter to the Authority.

(2) The auditor or actuary of any occupational pension scheme must, in any prescribed circumstances, immediately give a written report of any prescribed matter to the Authority.

(3) No duty to which the auditor or actuary of any occupational pension scheme is subject shall be regarded as contravened merely because of any information or opinion contained in a written report under this section.

(4) If in the case of any occupational pension scheme any professional adviser (other than the auditor or actuary), any trustee or manager or any person involved in the administration of the scheme has reasonable cause to believe as mentioned in paragraphs (a) and (b) of subsection (1), he may give a report of the matter to the Authority.

(5) In the case of any such scheme, no duty to which any such adviser, trustee or manager or other person is subject shall be regarded as contravened merely because of any information or opinion contained in a report under this section; but this subsection does not apply to any information disclosed in such a report by the legal adviser of an occupational pension scheme if he would be entitled to refuse to produce a document containing the information in any proceedings in any court on the grounds that it was the subject of legal professional privilege or, in Scotland, that it contained a confidential communication made by or to an advocate or solicitor in that capacity.

(8) If it appears to the Authority that an auditor or actuary has failed to comply with subsection (1) or (2), the Authority may by order disqualify him for being the auditor or, as the case may be, actuary of any occupational pension scheme specified in the order.

91. Inalienablity of occupational pension.

(1) Subject to subsection (5), where a person is entitled, or has an accrued right, to a pension under an occupational pension scheme—

(a) the entitlement or right cannot be assigned, commuted or surrendered,

(b) the entitlement or right cannot be charged or a lien exercised in respect of it, and

(c) no set-off can be exercised in respect of it,

and an agreement to effect any of those things is unenforceable.

ARBITRATION ACT 1996
(1996, c. 23)

8. Whether agreement discharged by death of a party

(1) Unless otherwise agreed by the parties, an arbitration agreement is not discharged by the death of a party and may be enforced by or against the personal representatives of that party

(2) Subsection (1) does not affect the operation of any enactment or rule of law by virtue of which a substantive right or obligation is extinguished by death.

29. Immunity of arbitrator.

(1) An arbitrator is not liable for anything done or omitted in the discharge or purported discharge of his functions as arbitrator unless the act or omission is shown to have been in bad faith.

40. General duty of parties.

(1) The parties shall do all things necessary for the proper and expeditious conduct of the arbitral proceedings.

41. Powers of tribunal in case of party's default.

(1) The parties are free to agree on the powers of the tribunal in case of a party's failure to do something necessary for the proper and expeditious conduct of the arbitration.

(2) Unless otherwise agreed by the parties, the following provisions apply.

(3) If the tribunal is satisfied that there has been inordinate and inexcusable delay on the part of the claimant in pursuing his claim and that the delay—

(a) gives rise, or is likely to give rise, to a substantial risk that it is not possible to have a fair resolution of the issues in that claim, or

(b) has caused, or is likely to cause, serious prejudice to the respondent, the tribunal may make an award dismissing the claim.

74. Immunity of arbitral institutions, &c.

(1) An arbitral or other institution or person designated or requested by the parties to appoint or nominate an arbitrator is not liable for anything done or omitted in the

discharge or purported discharge of that function unless the act or omission is shown to have been in bad faith.

(2) An arbitral or other institution or person by whom an arbitrator is appointed or nominated is not liable, by reason of having appointed or nominated him, for anything done or omitted by the arbitrator (or his employees or agents) in the discharge or purported discharge of his functions as arbitrator.

(3) The above provisions apply to an employee or agent of an arbitral or other institution or person as they apply to the institution or person himself.

87. Effectiveness of agreement to exclude court's jurisdiction.

(1) In the case of a domestic arbitration agreement any agreement to exclude the jurisdiction of the court under—
    (a)   section 45 (determination of preliminary point of law), or
    (b)   section 69 (challenging the award: appeal on point of law),
is not effective unless entered into after the commencement of the arbitral proceedings in which the question arises or the award is made.

89. Application of unfair terms regulations to consumer arbitration agreements.

(1) The following sections extend the application of the Unfair Terms in Consumer Contracts Regulations 1994 in relation to a term which constitutes an arbitration agreement.

For this purpose 'arbitration agreement" means an agreement to submit to arbitration present or future disputes or differences (whether or not contractual).

90. Regulations apply where consumer is a legal person.

The Regulations apply where the consumer is a legal person as they apply where the consumer is a natural person.

91. Arbitration agreement unfair where modest amount sought.

(1) A term which constitutes an arbitration agreement is unfair for the purposes of the Regulations so far as it relates to a claim for a pecuniary remedy which does not exceed the amount specified by order for the purposes of this section.

BROADCASTING ACT 1996
(1996, c. 55)

99. Contract for exclusive right to televise listed event to be void.

(1) Any contract entered into after the commencement of this section under which a television programme provider acquires rights to televise the whole or any part of a listed event live for reception in the United Kingdom, or in any area of the United Kingdom, shall be void so far as it purports, in relation to the whole or any part of the event or in relation to reception in the United Kingdom or any area of the United Kingdom, to grant those rights exclusively to any one television programme provider.

106. The Broadcasting Standards Commission.

(1) There shall be a commission, to be known as the Broadcasting Standards Commission (in this Part referred to as "the BSC").

107. Preparation by BSC of code relating to avoidance of unjust or unfair treatment or interference with privacy.

(1) It shall be the duty of the BSC to draw up, and from time to time review, a code giving guidance as to principles to be observed, and practices to be followed, in connection with the avoidance of—
    (a)   unjust or unfair treatment in programmes to which this section applies, or
    (b)   unwarranted infringement of privacy in, or in connection with the obtaining of material included in, such programmes.

121. Certain statements etc. protected by qualified privilege for purposes of defamation.

(1) For the purposes of the law relating to defamation—

(a) publication of any statement in the course of the consideration by the BSC of, and their adjudication on, a fairness complaint,

(b) publication by the BSC of directions under section 119(1) relating to a fairness complaint, or

(c) publication of a report of the BSC, so far as the report relates to fairness complaints,

is privileged unless the publication is shown to be made with malice.

(2) Nothing in subsection (1) shall be construed as limiting any privilege subsisting apart from that subsection.

DAMAGES ACT 1996
(1996, c. 48)

1. Assumed rate of return on investment of damages.

(1) In determining the return to be expected from the investment of a sum awarded as general damages for future pecuniary loss in an action for personal injury the court shall, subject to and in accordance with rules of court made for the purposes of this section, take into account such rate of return as may from time to time be prescribed by an order made by the Lord Chancellor.

(2) Subsection (1) above shall not however prevent the court taking a different rate of return into account if any party to the proceedings shows that it is more appropriate in the case in question.

(3) An order under subsection (1) above may prescribe different rates of return for different classes of case.

(4) Before making an order under subsection (1) above the Lord Chancellor shall consult the Government Actuary and the Treasury; and any order under that subsection shall be made by statutory instrument subject to annulment in pursuance of a resolution of either House of Parliament.

(5) In the application of this section to Scotland for references to general damages and to the Lord Chancellor there shall be substituted respectively references to damages and to the Secretary of State.

2. Consent orders for periodical payments.

(1) A court awarding damages in an action for personal injury may, with the consent of the parties, make an order under which the damages are wholly or partly to take the form of periodical payments.

(2) In this section "damages" includes an interim payment which the court, by virtue of rules of court in that behalf, orders the defendant to make to the plaintiff (or, in the application of this section to Scotland, the defender to make to the pursuer).

(3) This section is without prejudice to any powers exercisable apart from this section.

3. Provisional damages and fatal accident claims.

(1) This section applies where a person—

(a) is awarded provisional damages; and

(b) subsequently dies as a result of the act or omission which gave rise to the cause of action for which the damages were awarded.

(2) The award of the provisional damages shall not operate as a bar to an action in respect of that person's death under the Fatal Accidents Act 1976.

(3) Such part (if any) of—

(a) the provisional damages; and
(b) any further damages awarded to the person in question before his death,
as was intended to compensate him for pecuniary loss in a period which in the event falls after his death, shall be taken into account in assessing the amount of any loss of support suffered by the person or persons for whose benefit the action under the Fatal Accidents Act 1976 is brought.

(4) No award of further damages made in respect of that person after his death shall include any amount for loss of income in respect of any period after his death.

(5) In this section "provisional damages" means damages awarded by virtue of subsection (2)(a) of section 32A of the Supreme Court Act 1981 or section 51 of the County Courts Act 1984 and "further damages" means damages awarded by virtue of subsection (2)(b) of either of those sections.

(6) Subsection (2) above applies whether the award of provisional damages was before or after the coming into force of that subsection; and subsections (3) and (4) apply to any award of damages under the 1976 Act or, as the case may be, further damages after the coming into force of those subsections.

(7) In the application of this section to Northern Ireland—
(a) for references to the Fatal Accidents Act 1976 there shall be substituted references to the Fatal Accidents (Northern Ireland) Order 1977;
(b) for the reference to subsection (2)(a) and (b) of section 32A of the Supreme Court Act 1981 and section 51 of the County Courts Act 1984 there shall be substituted a reference to paragraph 10(2)(a) and (b) of Schedule 6 to the Administration of Justice Act 1982.

4. Enhanced protection for structured settlement annuitants.

(1) In relation to an annuity purchased for a person pursuant to a structured settlement from an authorised insurance company within the meaning of the Policyholders Protection Act 1975 (and in respect of which that person as annuitant is accordingly the policyholder for the purposes of that Act) sections 10 and 11 of that Act (protection in the event of liquidation of the insurer) shall have effect as if any reference to ninety per cent. of the amount of the liability, of any future benefit or of the value attributed to the policy were a reference to the full amount of the liability, benefit or value.

(2) Those sections shall also have effect as mentioned in subsection (1) above in relation to an annuity purchased from an authorised insurance company within the meaning of the 1975 Act pursuant to any order incorporating terms corresponding to those of a structured settlement which a court makes when awarding damages for personal injury.

(3) Those sections shall also have effect as mentioned in subsection (1) above in relation to an annuity purchased from or otherwise provided by an authorised insurance company within the meaning of the 1975 Act pursuant to terms corresponding to those of a structured settlement contained in an agreement made by—
(a) the Motor Insurer's Bureau; or
(b) a Domestic Regulations Insurer,
in respect of damages for personal injury which the Bureau or Insurer undertakes to pay in satisfaction of a claim or action against an uninsured driver.

(4) In subsection (3) above "the Motor Insurers' Bureau" means the company of that name incorporated on 14th June 1946 under the Companies Act 1929 and "a Domestic Regulations Insurer" has the meaning given in the Bureau's Domestic Regulations.

(5) This section applies if the liquidation of the authorised insurance company begins (within the meaning of the 1975 Act) after the coming into force of this section irrespective of when the annuity was purchased or provided.

5. Meaning of structured settlement.

(1) In section 4 above a "structured settlement" means an agreement settling a claim or action for damages for personal injury on terms whereby—

(a) the damages are to consist wholly or partly of periodical payments; and

(b) the person to whom the payments are to be made is to receive them as the annuitant under one or more annuities purchased for him by the person against whom the claim or action is brought or, if he is insured against the claim, by his insurer.

(2) The periodical payments may be for the life of the claimant, for a specified period or of a specified number or minimum number or include payments of more than one of those descriptions.

(3) The amounts of the periodical payments (which need not be at a uniform rate or payable at uniform intervals) may be—

(a) specified in the agreement, with or without provision for increases of specified amounts or percentages; or

(b) subject to adjustment in a specified manner so as to preserve their real value; or

(c) partly specified as mentioned in paragraph (a) above and partly subject to adjustment as mentioned in paragraph (b) above.

(4) The annuity or annuities must be such as to provide the annuitant with sums which as to amount and time of payment correspond to the periodical payments described in the agreement.

(5) Payments in respect of the annuity or annuities may be received on behalf of the annuitant by another person or received and held on trust for his benefit under a trust of which he is, during his lifetime, the sole beneficiary.

(6) The Lord Chancellor may by an order made by statutory instrument provide that there shall for the purposes of this section be treated as an insurer any body specified in the order, being a body which, though not an insurer, appears to him to fulfil corresponding functions in relation to damages for personal injury claimed or awarded against persons of any class or description, and the reference in subsection (1)(b) above to a person being insured against the claim and his insurer shall be construed accordingly.

(7) In the application of subsection (6) above to Scotland for the reference to the Lord Chancellor there shall be substituted a reference to the Secretary of State.

(8) Where—

(a) an agreement is made settling a claim or action for damages for personal injury on terms whereby the damages are to consist wholly or partly of periodical payments;

(b) the person against whom the claim or action is brought (or, if he is insured against the claim, his insurer) purchases one or more annuities; and

(c) a subsequent agreement is made under which the annuity is, or the annuities are, assigned in favour of the person entitled to the payments (so as to secure that from a future date he receives the payments as the annuitant under the annuity or annuities), then, for the purposes of section 4 above, the agreement settling the claim or action shall be treated as a structured settlement and any such annuity assigned in favour of that person shall be treated as an annuity purchased for him pursuant to the settlement.

6. Guarantees for public sector settlements.

(1) This section applies where—

(a) a claim or action for damages for personal injury is settled on terms corresponding to those of a structured settlement as defined in section 5 above except that the person to whom the payments are to be made is not to receive them as mentioned in subsection (1)(b) of that section; or

(b) a court awarding damages for personal injury makes an order incorporating such terms.

(2) If it appears to a Minister of the Crown that the payments are to be made by a body in relation to which he has, by virtue of this section, power to do so, he may guarantee the payments to be made under the agreement or order.

(3) The bodies in relation to which a Minister may give such a guarantee shall, subject to subsection (4) below, be such bodies as are designated in relation to the relevant government department by guidelines agreed upon between that department and the Treasury.

(4) A guarantee purporting to be given by a Minister under this section shall not be invalidated by any failure on his part to act in accordance with such guidelines as are mentioned in subsection (3) above.

(5) A guarantee under this section shall be given on such terms as the Minister concerned may determine but those terms shall in every case require the body in question to reimburse the Minister, with interest, for any sums paid by him in fulfilment of the guarantee.

(6) Any sums required by a Minister for fulfilling a guarantee under this section shall be defrayed out of money provided by Parliament and any sums received by him by way of reimbursement or interest shall be paid into the Consolidated Fund.

(7) A Minister who has given one or more guarantees under this section shall, as soon as possible after the end of each financial year, lay before each House of Parliament a statement showing what liabilities are outstanding in respect of the guarantees in that year, what sums have been paid in that year in fulfilment of the guarantees and what sums (including interest) have been recovered in that year in respect of the guarantees or are still owing.

(8) In this section "government department" means any department of Her Majesty's government in the United Kingdom and for the purposes of this section a government department is a relevant department in relation to a Minister if he has responsibilities in respect of that department.

(9) The Schedule to this act has effect for conferring corresponding powers on Northern Ireland departments.

7. Interpretation.

(1) Subject to subsection (2) below, in this Act "personal injury" includes any disease and any impairment of a person's physical or mental condition and references to a claim or action for personal injury include references to such a claim or action brought by virtue of the Law Reform (Miscellaneous Provisions) Act 1934 and to a claim or action brought by virtue of the Fatal Accidents Act 1976.

(2) In the application of this Act to Scotland "personal injury" has the meaning given by section 10(1) of the Damages (Scotland) Act 1976.

(3) In the application of subsection (1) above to Northern Ireland for the references to the Law Reform (Miscellaneous Provisions) Act 1934 and to the Fatal Accidents Act 1976 there shall be substituted respectively references to the Law Reform (Miscellaneous Provisions) Act (Northern Ireland) 1937 and the Fatal Accidents (Northern Ireland) Order 1977.

8. Short title, extent and commencement.

(2) Section 3 does not extend to Scotland but, subject to that, this Act extends to the whole of the United Kingdom.

DEFAMATION ACT 1996
(1996, c. 31)

Responsibility for publication

1. Responsibility for publication.

(1) In defamation proceedings a person has a defence if he shows that—

(a) he was not the author, editor or publisher of the statement complained of,
(b) he took reasonable care in relation to its publication, and
(c) he did not know, and had no reason to believe, that what he did caused or contributed to the publication of a defamatory statement.

(2) For this purpose "author", "editor" and "publisher" have the following meanings, which are further explained in subsection (3)—

"author" means the originator of the statement, but does not include a person who did not intend that his statement be published at all;

"editor" means a person having editorial or equivalent responsibility for the content of the statement or the decision to publish it; and

"publisher" means a commercial publisher, that is, a person whose business is issuing material to the public, or a section of the public, who issues material containing the statement in the course of that business.

(3) A person shall not be considered the author, editor or publisher of a statement if he is only involved—
(a) in printing, producing, distributing or selling printed material containing the statement;
(b) in processing, making copies of, distributing, exhibiting or selling a film or sound recording (as defined in Part I of the Copyright, Designs and Patents Act 1988) containing the statement;
(c) in processing, making copies of, distributing or selling any electronic medium in or on which the statement is recorded, or in operating or providing any equipment, system or service by means of which the statement is retrieved, copied, distributed or made available in electronic form;
(d) as the broadcaster of a live programme containing the statement in circumstances in which he has no effective control over the maker of the statement;
(e) as the operator of or provider of access to a communications system by means of which the statement is transmitted, or made available, by a person over whom he has no effective control.

In a case not within paragraphs (a) to (e) the court may have regard to those provisions by way of analogy in deciding whether a person is to be considered the author, editor or publisher of a statement.

(4) Employees or agents of an author, editor or publisher are in the same position as their employer or principal to the extent that they are responsible for the content of the statement or the decision to publish it.

(5) In determining for the purposes of this section whether a person took reasonable care, or had reason to believe that what he did caused or contributed to the publication of a defamatory statement, regard shall be had to—
(a) the extent of his responsibility for the content of the statement or the decision to publish it,
(b) the nature or circumstances of the publication, and
(c) the previous conduct or character of the author, editor or publisher.

(6) This section does not apply to any cause of action which arose before the section came into force.

Offer to make amends

2. Offer to make amends.

(1) A person who has published a statement alleged to be defamatory of another may offer to make amends under this section.

(2) The offer may be in relation to the statement generally or in relation to a specific defamatory meaning which the person making the offer accepts that the statement conveys ("a qualified offer").

(3) An offer to make amends—

(a) must be in writing,

(b) must be expressed to be an offer to make amends under section 2 of the Defamation Act 1996, and

(c) must state whether it is a qualified offer and, if so, set out the defamatory meaning in relation to which it is made.

(4) An offer to make amends under this section is an offer—

(a) to make a suitable correction of the statement complained of and a sufficient apology to the aggrieved party,

(b) to publish the correction and apology in a manner that is reasonable and practicable in the circumstances, and

(c) to pay the aggrieved party such compensation (if any), and such costs, as may be agreed or determined to be payable.

The fact that the offer is accompanied by an offer to take specific steps does not affect the fact that an offer to make amends under this section is an offer to do all the things mentioned in paragraphs (a) to (c).

(5) An offer to make amends under this section may not be made by a person after serving a defence in defamation proceedings brought against him by the aggrieved party in respect of the publication in question.

(6) An offer to make amends under this section may be withdrawan before it is accepted; and a renewal of an offer which has been withdrawn shall be treated as a new offer.

3. Accepting an offer to make amends.

(1) If an offer to make amends under section 2 is accepted by the aggrieved party, the following provisions apply.

(2) The party accepting the offer may not bring or continue defamation proceedings in respect of the publication concerned against the person making the offer, but he is entitled to enforce the offer to make amends, as follows.

(3) If the parties agree on the steps to be taken in fulfilment of the offer, the aggrieved party may apply to the court for an order that the other party fulfil his offer by taking the steps agreed.

(4) If the parties do not agree on the steps to be taken by way of correction, apology and publication, the party who made the offer may take such steps as he thinks appropriate, and may in particular—

(a) make the correction and apology by a statement in open court in terms approved by the court, and

(b) give an undertaking to the court as to the manner of their publication.

(5) If the parties do not agree on the amount to be paid by way of compensation, it shall be determined by the court on the same principles as damages in defamation proceedings.

The court shall take account of any steps taken in fulfilment of the offer and (so far as not agreed between the parties) of the suitability of the correction, the sufficiency of the apology and whether the manner of their publication was reasonable in the circumstances, and may reduce or increase the amount of compensation accordingly.

(6) If the parties do not agree on the amount to be paid by way of costs, it shall be determined by the court on the same principles as costs awarded in court proceedings.

(7) The acceptance of an offer by one person to make amends does not affect any cause of action against another person in respect of the same publication, subject as follows.

(8) In England and Wales or Northern Ireland, for the purposes of the Civil Liability (Contribution) Act 1978—

(a) the amount of compensation paid under the offer shall be treated as paid in bona fide settlement or compromise of the claim; and

(b) where another person is liable in respect of the same damage (whether jointly or otherwise), the person whose offer to make amends was accepted is not required to pay by virtue of any contribution under section 1 of that Act a greater amount than the amount of the compensation payable in pursuance of the offer.

(9) In Scotland—

(a) subsection (2) of section 3 of the Law Reform (Miscellaneous Provisions) (Scotland) Act 1940 (right of one joint wrongdoer as respects another to recover contribution towards damages) applies in relation to compensation paid under an offer to make amends as it applies in relation to damages in an action to which that section applies; and

(b) where another person is liable in respect of the same damage (whether jointly or otherwise), the person whose offer to make amends was accepted is not required to pay by virtue of any contribution under section 3(2) of that Act a greater amount than the amount of compensation payable in pursuance of the offer.

(10) Proceedings under this section shall be heard and determined without a jury.

4. Failure to accept offer to make amends.

(1) If an offer to make amends under section 2, duly made and not withdrawn, is not accepted by the aggrieved party, the following provisions apply.

(2) The fact that the offer was made is a defence (subject to subsection (3)) to defamation proceedings in respect of the publication in question by that party against the person making the offer.

A qualified offer is only a defence in respect of the meaning to which the offer related.

(3) There is no such defence if the person by whom the offer was made knew or had reason to believe that the statement complained of—

(a) referred to the aggrieved party or was likely to be understood as referring to him, and

(b) was both false and defamatory of that party;

but it shall be presumed until the contrary is shown that he did not know and had no reason to believe that was the case.

(4) The person who made the offer need not rely on it by way of defence, but if he does he may not rely on any other defence.

If the offer was a qualified offer, this applies only in respect of the meaning to which the offer related.

(5) The offer may be relied on in mitigation of damages whether or not it was relied on as a defence.

The meaning of a statement

7. Ruling on the meaning of a statement.

In defamation proceedings the court shall not be asked to rule whether a statement is arguably capable, as opposed to capable, of bearing a particular meaning or meanings attributed to it.

Summary disposal of claim

8. Summary disposal of claim.

(1) In defamation proceedings the court may dispose summarily of the plaintiff's claim in accordance with the following provisions.

(2) The court may dismiss the plaintiff's claim if it appears to the court that it has no realistic prospect of success and there is no reason why it should be tried.

(3) The court may give judgment for the plaintiff and grant him summary relief (see section 9) if it appears to the court that there is no defence to the claim which has a realistic prospect of success, and that there is no other reason why the claim should be tried.

Unless the plaintiff asks for summary relief, the court shall not act under this subsection unless it is satisfied that summary relief will adequately compensate him for the wrong he has suffered.

(4) In considering whether a claim should be tried the court shall have regard to—

(a) whether all the persons who are or might be defendants in repect of the publication complained of are before the court;

(b) whether summary disposal of the claim against another defendant would be inappropriate;

(c) the extent to which there is a conflict of evidence;

(d) the seriousness of the alleged wrong (as regards the content of the statement and the extent of publication); and

(e) whether it is justifiable in the circumstances to proceed to a full trial.

(5) Proceedings under this section shall be heard and determined without a jury.

9. Meaning of summary relief.

(1) For the purposes of section 8 (summary disposal of claim) "summary relief" means such of the following as may be appropriate—

(a) a declaration that the statement was false and defamatory of the plaintiff;

(b) an order that the defendant publish or cause to be published a suitable correction and apology;

(c) damages not exceeding £10,000 or such other amount as may be prescribed by order of the Lord Chancellor;

(d) an order restraining the defendant from publishing or further publishing the matter complained of.

(2) The content of any correction and apology, and the time, manner, form and place of publication, shall be for the parties to agree.

If they cannot agree on the content, the court may direct the defendant to publish or cause to be published a summary of the court's judgment agreed by the parties or settled by the court in accordance with rules of court.

If they cannot agree on the time, manner, form or place of publication, the court may direct the defendant to take such reasonable and practicable steps as the court considers appropriate.

(3) Any order under subsection (1)(c) shall be made by statutory instrument which shall be subject to annulment in pursuance of a resolution of either House of Parliament.

10. Summary disposal: rules of court.

(1) Provision may be made by rules of court as to the summary disposal of the plaintiff's claim in defamation proceedings.

(2) Without prejudice to the generality of that power, provision may be made—

(a) authorising a party to apply for summary disposal at any stage of the proceedings;

(b) authorising the court at any stage of the proceedings—

(i) to treat any application, pleading or other step in the proceedings as an application for summary disposal, or

(ii) to make an order for summary disposal without any such application;

(c) as to the time for serving pleadings or taking any other step in the proceedings in a case where there are proceedings for summary disposal;

(d) requiring the parties to identify any question of law or construction which the court is to be asked to determine in the proceedings;

(e) as to the nature of any hearing on the question of summary disposal, and in particular—

(i) authorising the court to order affidavits or witness statements to be prepared for use as evidence at the hearing, and

(ii) requiring the leave of the court for the calling of oral evidence, or the introduction of new evidence, at the hearing;

Defamation Act 1996

(f) authorising the court to require a defendant to elect, at or before the hearing, whether or not to make an offer to make amends under section 2.

Evidence concerning proceedings in Parliament

13. Evidence concerning proceedings in Parliament.

(1) Where the conduct of a person in or in relation to proceedings in Parliament is in issue in defamation proceedings, he may waive for the purposes of those proceedings, so far as concerns him, the protection of any enactment or rule of law which prevents proceedings in Parliament being impeached or questioned in any court or place out of Parliament.

(2) Where a person waives that protection—

(a) any such enactment or rule of law shall not apply to prevent evidence being given, questions being asked or statements, submissions, comments or findings being made about his conduct, and

(b) none of those things shall be regarded as infringing the privilege of either House of Parliament.

(3) The waiver by one person of that protection does not affect its operation in relation to another person who has not waived it.

(4) Nothing in this section affects any enactment or rule of law so far as it protects a person (including a person who has waived the protection referred to above) from legal liability for words spoken or things done in the course of, or for the purposes of or incidental to, any proceedings in Parliament.

(5) Without prejudice to the generality of subsection (4), that subsection applies to—

(a) the giving of evidence before either House or a committee;

(b) the presentation or submission of a document to either House or a committee;

(c) the preparation of a document for the purposes of or incidental to the transacting of any such business;

(d) the formulation, making or publication of a document, including a report, by or pursuant to an order of either House or a committee; and

(e) any communication with the Parliamentary Commissioner for Standards or any person having functions in connection with the registration of members' interests.

In this subsection "a committee" means a committee of either House or a joint committee of both Houses of Parliament.

Statutory privilege

14. Reports of court proceedings absolutely privileged.

(1) A fair and accurate report of proceedings in public before a court to which this section applies, if published contemporaneously with the proceedings, is absolutely privileged.

(2) A report of proceedings which by an order of the court, or as a consequence of any statutory provision, is required to be postponed shall be treated as published contemporaneously if it is published as soon as practicable after publication is permitted.

(3) This section applies to—

(a) any court in the United Kingdom,

(b) the European Court of Justice or any court attached to that court,

(c) the European Court of Human Rights, and

(d) any international criminal tribunal established by the Security Council of the United Nations or by an international agreement to which the United Kingdom is a party.

In paragraph (a) "court" includes any tribunal or body exercising the judicial power of the State.

15. Reports, &c. protected by qualified privilege.

(1) The publication of any report or other statement mentioned in Schedule 1 to this Act is privileged unless the publication is shown to be made with malice, subject as follows.

(2) In defamation proceedings in respect of the publication of a report or other statement mentioned in Part II of that Schedule, there is no defence under this section if the plaintiff shows that the defendant—

    (a) was requested by him to publish in a suitable manner a reasonable letter or statement by way of explanation or contradiction, and

    (b) refused or neglected to do so.

For this purpose "in a suitable manner" means in the same manner as the publication complained of or in a manner that is adequate and reasonable in the circumstances.

(3) This section does not apply to the publication to the public, or a section of the public, of matter which is not of public concern and the publication of which is not for the public benefit.

(4) Nothing in this section shall be construed—

    (a) as protecting the publication of matter the publication of which is prohibited by law, or

    (b) as limiting or abridging any privilege subsisting apart from this section.

Supplementary provisions

17. Interpretation.

(1) In this Act—

"publication" and "publish", in relation to a statement, have the meaning they have for the purposes of the law of defamation generally, but "publisher" is specially defined for the purposes of section 1;

"statement" means words, pictures, visual images, gestures or any other method of signifying meaning; and

"statutory provision" means—

    (a) a provision contained in an Act or in subordinate legislation within the meaning of the Interpretation Act 1978, or

    (b) a statutory provision within the meaning given by section 1(f) of the Interpretation Act (Northern Ireland) 1954.

20. Short title and saving.

(2) Nothing in this Act affects the law relating to criminal libel.

SCHEDULES

Section 15

SCHEDULE 1
QUALIFIED PRIVILEGE

PART I
STATEMENTS HAVING QUALIFIED PRIVILEGE WITHOUT EXPLANATION OR CONTRADICTION

1. A fair and accurate report of proceedings in public of a legislature anywhere in the world.

2. A fair and accurate report of proceedings in public before a court anywhere in the world.

3. A fair and accurate report of proceedings in public of a person appointed to hold a public inquiry by a government or legislature anywhere in the world.

4. A fair and accurate report of proceedings in public anywhere in the world of an international organisation or an international conference.

5. A fair and accurate copy of or extract from any register or other document required by law to be open to public inspection.

6. A notice or advertisement published by or on the authority of a court, or of a judge or officer of a court, anywhere in the world.

7. A fair and accurate copy of or extract from matter published by or on the authority of a government or legislature anywhere in the world.

8. A fair and accurate copy of or extract from matter published anywhere in the world by an international organisation or an international conference.

PART II
STATEMENTS PRIVILEGED SUBJECT TO EXPLANATION OR CONTRADICTION

9.—(1) A fair and accurate copy of or extract from a notice or other matter issued for the information of the public by or on behalf of—

(a) a legislature in any member State or the European Parliament;

(b) the government of any member State, or any authority performing governmental functions in any member State or part of a member State, or the European Commission;

(c) an international organisation or international conference.

(2) In this paragraph "governmental functions" includes police functions.

10. A fair and accurate copy of or extract from a document made available by a court in any member State or the European Court of Justice (or any court attached to that court), or by a judge or officer of any such court.

11.—(1) A fair and accurate report of proceedings at any public meeting or sitting in the United Kingdom of—

(a) a local authority or local authority committee;

(b) a justice or justices of the peace acting otherwise than as a court exercising judicial authority;

(c) a commission, tribunal, committee or person appointed for the purposes of any inquiry by any statutory provision, by Her Majesty or by a Minister of the Crown or a Northern Ireland Department;

(d) a person appointed by a local authority to hold a local inquiry in pursuance of any statutory provision;

(e) any other tribunal, board, committee or body constituted by or under, and exercising functions under, any statutory provision.

(2) In sub-paragraph (1)(a)—

"local authority" means—

(a) in relation to England and Wales, a principal council within the meaning of the Local Government Act 1972, any body falling within any paragraph of section 100J(1) of that Act or an authority or body to which the Public Bodies (Admission to Meetings) Act 1960 applies,

(b) in relation to Scotland, a council constituted under section 2 of the Local Government etc. (Scotland) Act 1994 or an authority or body to which the Public Bodies (Admission to Meetings) Act 1960 applies,

(c) in relation to Northern Ireland, any authority or body to which sections 23 to 27 of the Local Government Act (Northern Ireland) 1972 apply; and

"local authority committee" means any committee of a local authority or of local authorities, and includes—

(a) any committee or sub-committee in relation to which sections 100A to 100D of the Local Government Act 1972 apply by virtue of section 100E of that Act (whether or not also by virtue of section 100J of that Act), and

(b) any committee or sub-committee in relation to which sections 50A to 50D of the Local Government (Scotland) Act 1973 apply by virtue of section 50E of that Act.

(3) A fair and accurate report of any corresponding proceedings in any of the Channel Islands or the Isle of Man or in another member State.

12.—(1) A fair and accurate report of proceedings at any public meeting held in a member State.

(2) In this paragraph a "public meeting" means a meeting bona fide and lawfully held for a lawful purpose and for the furtherance or discussion of a matter of public concern, whether admission to the meeting is general or restricted.

13.—(1) A fair and accurate report of proceedings at a general meeting of a UK public company.

(2) A fair and accurate copy of or extract from any document circulated to members of a UK public company—

(a) by or with the authority of the board of directors of the company,

(b) by the auditors of the company, or

(c) by any member of the company in pursuance of a right conferred by any statutory provision.

(3) A fair and accurate copy or extract from any document circulated to members of a UK public company which relates to the appointment, resignation, retirement or dismissal of directors of the company.

(4) In this paragraph "UK public company" means—

(a) a public company within the meaning of section 1(3) of the Companies Act 1985 or Article 12(3) of the Companies (Northern Ireland) Order 1986, or

(b) a body corporate incorporated by or registered under any other statutory provision, or by Royal Charter, or formed in pursuance of letters patent.

(5) A fair and accurate report of proceedings at any corresponding meeting of, or copy of or extract from any corresponding document circulated to members of, a public company formed under the law of any of the Channel Islands or the Isle of Man or of another member State.

14. A fair and accurate report of any finding or decision of any of the following descriptions of association, formed in the United Kingdom or another member State, or of any committee or governing body of such an association—

(a) an association formed for the purpose of promoting or encouraging the exercise of or interest in any art, science, religion or learning, and empowered by its constitution to exercise control over or adjudicate on matters of interest or concern to the association, or the actions or conduct of any person subject to such control or adjudication;

(b) an association formed for the purpose of promoting or safeguarding the interests of any trade, business, industry or profession, or of the persons carrying on or engaged in any trade, business, industry or profession, and empowered by its constitution to exercise control over or adjudicate upon matters connected with that trade, business, industry or profession, or the actions or conduct of those persons;

(c) an association formed for the purpose of promoting or safeguarding the interests of a game, sport or pastime to the playing or exercise of which members of the public are invited or admitted, and empowered by its constitution to exercise control over or adjudicate upon persons connected with or taking part in the game, sport or pastime;

(d) an association formed for the purpose of promoting charitable objects or other objects beneficial to the community and empowered by its constitution to exercise control over or to adjudicate on matters of interest or concern to the association, or the actions or conduct of any person subject to such control or adjudication.

15.—(1) A fair and accurate report of, or copy of or extract from, any adjudication, report, statement or notice issued by a body, officer or other person designated for the purposes of this paragraph—

(a) for England and Wales or Northern Ireland, by order of the Lord Chancellor, and

(b) for Scotland, by order of the Secretary of State.

(2) An order under this paragraph shall be made by statutory instrument which shall be subject to annulment in pursuance of a resolution of either House of Parliament.

PART III
SUPPLEMENTARY PROVISIONS

16.—(1) In this Schedule—
"court" includes any tribunal or body exercising the judicial power of the State;
"international conference" means a conference attended by representatives of two or more governments;
"international organisation" means an organisation of which two or more governments are members, and includes any committee or other subordinate body of such an organisation; and
"legislature" includes a local legislature.

(2) References in this Schedule to a member State include any European dependent territory of a member State.

(3) In paragraphs 2 and 6 "court" includes—
  (a) the European Court of Justice (or any court attached to that court) and the Court of Auditors of the European Communities,
  (b) the European Court of Human Rights,
  (c) any international criminal tribunal established by the Security Council of the United Nations or by an international agreement to which the United Kingdom is a party, and
  (d) the International Court of Justice and any other judicial or arbitral tribunal deciding matters in dispute between States.

(4) In paragraphs 1, 3 and 7 "legislature" includes the European Parliament.

17.—(1) Provision may be made by order identifying—
  (a) for the purposes of paragraph 11, the corresponding proceedings referred to in sub-paragraph (3);
  (b) for the purposes of paragraph 13, the corresponding meetings and documents referred to in sub-paragraph (5).

(2) An order under this paragraph may be made—
  (a) for England and Wales or Northern Ireland, by the Lord Chancellor, and
  (b) for Scotland, by the Secretary of State.

(3) An order under this paragraph shall be made by statutory instrument which shall be subject to annulment in pursuance of a resolution of either House of Parliament.

EDUCATION ACT 1996
(1996, c. 56)

206. Control of contracts.

(1) Where the procedure for acquisition of grant-maintained status is pending in relation to any school, this section applies to any contract which, if the proposals for acquisition of grant-maintained status were implemented, would or might bind the governing body incorporated under Chapter II.

(2) Except with the appropriate consent, a local authority shall not enter into a contract to which this section applies.

(3) In the case of a contract entered into after the proposals have been approved by the Secretary of State, "the appropriate consent" is that of the new governing body.

(4) In relation to any other contract, "the appropriate consent" is—
  (a) the consent of the existing governing body, and
  (b) if (on the assumption set out in subsection (1)) the contract will require the governing body incorporated under Chapter II to make payments amounting in aggregate to £15,000 or more, the consent of the Secretary of State.

(5) Any consent for the purposes of this section may be given either in respect of a particular contract or in respect of contracts of any class or description and either unconditionally or subject to conditions.

(6) A contract shall not be void by reason only that it has been entered into in contravention of this section and (subject to section 207) a person entering into a contract with a local authority or governing body shall not be concerned to enquire whether any consent required by this section has been given or any conditions of such a consent have been complied with.

(7) Where there is an obligation under a contract to which this section applies to provide any benefit other than money, subsection (4)(b) shall apply as if the obligation were to pay a sum of money corresponding to the value of the benefit to the recipient.

(8) This section does not apply to—

    (a) a works contract (within the meaning of Part III of the Local Government, Planning and Land Act 1980) which is entered into in accordance with section 7 of that Act,

    (b) a works contract (within the meaning of Part I of the Local Government Act 1988) which is entered into in accordance with section 4 of that Act,

    (c) a contract to dispose of land (within the meaning of section 204) or to grant an option to acquire land or an interest in land, or

    (d) a contract of employment.

(9) The Secretary of State may by order substitute for the sum specified in subsection (4) (whether as originally enacted or as previously amended by an order under this subsection) such sum as may be specified in the order.

207. Wrongful contracts.

(1) This section applies where—

    (a) proposals for acquisition of grant-maintained status in respect of a school have been approved, and

    (b) a local authority have entered into a contract to which section 206 applies in contravention of that section.

(2) The Education Assets Board may by notice in writing served on the other party to the contract repudiate the contract at any time before it is performed.

(3) A repudiation under subsection (2) shall have effect—

    (a) where it is made after the date of implementation of the proposals, as if the local authority (and not the governing body) were party to the contract, and

    (b) as if the repudiation were made by the local authority.

256. Recovery from local funds of sums in respect of maintenance grant.

(1) Where the Secretary of State so determines, this section applies to a local education authority in respect of any financial year for which the determination is made; and the determination may apply this section in respect of all grant-maintained schools in the area of the authority or in respect of such grant-maintained schools in that area as may be ascertained by or in accordance with the determination.

(2) The Secretary of State shall, in respect of each financial year for which he makes a determination under subsection (1) in respect of a local education authority, give notice in writing to the authority of the terms of the determination.

(3) The Secretary of State may, in the case of a local education authority to which this section applies in respect of any financial year, recover from the authority sums in respect of the maintenance grant payable for that year to the governing bodies of any grant-maintained schools in respect of which the determination applies.

(4) Subject to subsection (5), sums recoverable by virtue of this section in respect of a school for any financial year—

    (a) shall be of such amounts, and

    (b) shall fall due on such date or dates,

Education Act 1996

as may be determined by the Secretary of State.

(5) The amount of any sum so recoverable shall be determined by reference to any amount—

(a) which has previously been determined under section 257 as the total amount recoverable in respect of the school and financial year in question, or

(b) (where no amount has previously been determined as mentioned in paragraph (a)) which is estimated by the Secretary of State as the amount which will initially be determined under section 257 as the total amount recoverable in respect of the school and financial year in question,

and which the Secretary of State considers it appropriate to adopt for the time being as a basis for determining the amounts of sums so recoverable.

(6) The Secretary of State may recover sums due to him under this section in either or both of the following ways—

(a) by requiring the local education authority to pay the whole or any part of any such sum at such time or times as he thinks fit, and

(b) by deducting, at such time or times as he thinks fit, the whole or any part of any such sum from any grant payable by him to the authority under any enactment (whenever passed) or from any amount payable by him to the authority under Part III of Schedule 8 to the Local Government Finance Act 1988 (redistributed non-domestic rates).

257. Determination of total amount recoverable under section 256.

(1) The total amount recoverable by virtue of section 256 in respect of a school for any financial year shall be such as may be determined (and from time to time revised) in accordance with regulations made by the Secretary of State ("recoupment regulations").

(2) Subject to any provision made by such regulations by virtue of subsection (3), recoupment regulations shall provide for the total amount so recoverable to be determined by reference to any amount determined under grant regulations as the amount of the maintenance grant payable in respect of the school and the financial year in question (as from time to time revised).

(3) Recoupment regulations may provide for reducing any amount which would otherwise fall to be determined under the regulations as the total amount recoverable from any local education authority by virtue of section 256 for a financial year by reference to any excess amounts recovered under that section in respect of any previous financial year.

(4) For the purposes of subsection (3) an excess amount is recovered under section 256 in respect of a financial year if the aggregate amount of the sums recovered under that section for that year from the local education authority—

(a) in respect of any school in respect of which sums are recoverable from the authority under that section, or

(b) (where there is more than one such school) in respect of both or all of those schools,

exceeds the total amount recoverable in accordance with recoupment regulations in respect of that school or (as the case may be) in respect of both or all of those schools for that year.

258. Provisions consequential on section 256.

(1) For the purposes of sections 492 and 493 (recoupment for provision for education of pupils belonging to, or having connection with, area of another authority), the provision for education made in any financial year in respect of a registered pupil at a grant-maintained school which is not made by the local education authority shall, if sums are recoverable under section 256 in respect of the school and that year from the authority, be taken to have been made by them.

(2) The reference in subsection (1) to provision for education includes a reference to provision of any benefits or services for which provision is made by or under this Act or any other enactment relating to education.

(3) The governing body of a grant-maintained school shall, if sums are recoverable under section 256 in respect of the school from a local education authority, provide the authority with such information relating to the registered pupils at the school as the authority may require for the purpose of claiming any amount in respect of such a pupil from another authority by virtue of regulations under section 492 or 493.

492. Recoupment: adjustment between local education authorities.

(1) Regulations may provide, in relation to cases where any provision for education to which this section applies is made by a local education authority in respect of a person who belongs to the area of another local education authority, for requiring or authorising the other authority to pay to the providing authority—

    (a) such amount as the authorities may agree, or

    (b) failing agreement, such amount as may be determined by or under the regulations.

(2) This section applies to primary education, secondary education and further education and to part-time education for those who have not attained the age of five.

(3) The regulations may provide for the amounts payable by one authority to another—

    (a) to reflect the whole or any part of the average costs incurred by local education authorities in the provision of education (whether in England and Wales as a whole or in any particular area or areas); and

    (b) to be based on figures for average costs determined by such body or bodies representing local education authorities, or on such other figures relating to costs so incurred, as the Secretary of State considers appropriate.

(4) The regulations may provide for the amounts so payable, in such cases as may be specified in or determined in accordance with the regulations, to be such amounts as may be determined by the Secretary of State....

(5) Any dispute between local education authorities as to whether one of them is entitled to be paid any amount by another under the regulations shall be determined by the Secretary of State....

493. Recoupment: cross-border provisions.

(1) Regulations may make provision requiring or authorising payments of amounts determined by or under the regulations to be made by one authority to another where—

    (a) the authority receiving the payment makes, in such cases or circumstances as may be specified in the regulations, provision for education in respect of a person having such connection with the area of the paying authority as may be so specified, and

    (b) one of the authorities is a local education authority and the other an education authority in Scotland.

494. Recoupment: excluded pupils.

(1) Subsection (2) applies where a pupil is permanently excluded from any school maintained by a local education authority or any grant-maintained school and, in the financial year in which the exclusion first takes effect—

    (a) he is subsequently provided with—

        (i) education at a school maintained by a local education authority,

        (ii) education provided by such an authority otherwise than at school, or

        (iii) education at a grant-maintained school, and

    (b) the person accountable for that education ("the new provider") is not the same as the person accountable for the education provided for him immediately before his exclusion ("the former provider").

Education Act 1996

(2) The former provider shall pay to the new provider an amount determined in accordance with regulations as the appropriate amount of funding to be transferred to the new provider in respect of that pupil for that financial year.

(3) Every local education authority shall, where any scheme made (or treated as made) by them as mentioned in section 101(1) does not make the provision required by subsection (4) below, exercise their powers to revise the scheme so that it makes such provision.

...

(6) Subject to subsection (7), for the purposes of this section—

(a) the local education authority are accountable for education provided at any school maintained by them or education provided by them otherwise than at school; and

(b) the governing body are accountable for education provided at a grant-maintained school.

(7) Where a pupil is permanently excluded from any school maintained by a local education authority or from any grant-maintained school and, in the financial year in which the exclusion first takes effect, the following events subsequently occur—

(a) he is first provided with education for which a different local education authority or, in the case of exclusion from a grant-maintained school, any local education authority are accountable ("the first new provider") and which is provided in a pupil referral unit or otherwise than at school, and

(b) at any time afterwards he is provided with education at a grant-maintained school or with education for which a local education authority other than the first new provider are accountable,

then, in relation to the education mentioned in paragraph (b), the first new provider is to be treated as accountable for the education provided for the pupil immediately before the exclusion first took effect.

(8) Any dispute as to whether any local education authority or governing body or a grant-maintained school are entitled to be paid any amount under this section by any other such authority or body shall be determined by the Secretary of State.

521. Examination of pupils for cleanliness.

(1) A local education authority may by directions in writing authorise a medical officer of theirs to have the persons and clothing of pupils in attendance at relevant schools examined whenever in his opinion such examinations are necessary in the interests of cleanliness.

(3) An examination under this section shall be made by a person authorised by the authority to make such examinations; and, if the examination is of a girl, it shall not be made by a man unless he is a registered medical practitioner.

522. Compulsory cleansing of a pupil.

(1) If, on an examination under section 521, the person or clothing of a pupil is found to be infested with vermin or in a foul condition, any officer of the local education authority may serve a notice on the pupil's parent requiring him to cause the pupil's person and clothing to be cleansed.

(2) The notice shall inform the parent that, unless within the period specified in the notice the pupil's person and clothing are cleansed to the satisfaction of such person as is specified in the notice, the cleansing will be carried out under arrangements made by the authority.

(3) The period so specified shall not be less than 24 hours from the service of the notice.

(4) If, on a report being made to him by the specified person at the end of the specified period, a medical officer of the authority is not satisfied that the pupil's person and clothing have been properly cleansed, he may by order direct that they shall be cleansed under arrangements made by the authority under section 523.

(a) a school maintained by a local education authority;
(b) a grant-maintained or grant-maintained special school; or
(c) a city technology college or city college for the technology of the arts.

(3) The conditions referred to in subsection (1) are as follows—

(a) the head teacher of the school must have previously determined, and have—
   (i) made generally known within the school, and
   (ii) taken steps to bring to the attention of the parent of every person who is for the time being a registered pupil there,
that the detention of pupils after the end of a school session is one of the measures that may be taken with a view to regulating the conduct of pupils;
(b) the detention must be imposed by the head teacher or by another teacher at the school specifically or generally authorised by him for the purpose;
(c) the detention must be reasonable in all the circumstances; and
(d) the pupil's parent must have been given at least 24 hours' notice in writing that the detention was due to take place.

(4) In determining for the purposes of subsection (3)(c) whether a pupil's detention is reasonable, the following matters in particular shall be taken into account—

(a) whether the detention constitutes a proportionate punishment in the circumstances of the case; and
(b) any special circumstances relevant to its imposition on the pupil which are known to the person imposing it (or of which he ought reasonably to be aware) including in particular—
   (i) the pupil's age,
   (ii) any special educational needs he may have,
   (iii) any religious requirements affecting him, and
   (iv) where arrangements have to be made for him to travel from the school to his home, whether suitable alternative arrangements can reasonably be made by his parent.]

EMPLOYMENT RIGHTS ACT 1996
(1996, c. 18)

15. Right not to have to make payments to employer.

(1) An employer shall not receive a payment from a worker employed by him unless—

(a) the payment is required or authorised to be made by virtue of a statutory provision or a relevant provision of the worker's contract, or
(b) the worker has previously signified in writing his agreement or consent to the making of the payment.

16. Excepted payments.

(1) Section 15 does not apply to a payment received from a worker by his employer where the purpose of the payment is the reimbursement of the employer in respect of—

(a) an overpayment of wages, or
(b) an overpayment in respect of expenses incurred by the worker in carrying out his employment,
made (for any reason) by the employer to the worker.

HOUSING ACT 1996
(1996, c. 52)

11. Covenant for repayment of discount on disposal.

(1) Where on a disposal of a house by a registered social landlord, in accordance with a consent given by the Corporation under section 9, a discount has been given to

the purchaser, and the consent does not provide otherwise, the conveyance, grant or assignment shall contain a covenant binding on the purchaser and his successors in title to the following effect.

(2) The covenant shall be to pay to the landlord on demand, if within a period of three years there is a relevant disposal which is not an exempted disposal (but if there is more than one such disposal then only on the first of them), an amount equal to the discount reduced by one-third for each complete year which has elapsed after the conveyance, grant or assignment and before the further disposal.

(3) The liability that may arise under the covenant is a charge on the house, taking effect as if it had been created by deed expressed to be by way of legal mortgage.

12. Priority of charge for repayment of discount.

...

152. Power to grant injunctions against anti-social behaviour.

(1) The High Court or a county court may, on an application by a local authority, grant an injunction prohibiting a person from—

(a) engaging in or threatening to engage in conduct causing or likely to cause a nuisance or annoyance to a person residing in, visiting or otherwise engaging in a lawful activity in residential premises to which this section applies or in the locality of such premises,

(b) using or threatening to use residential premises to which this section applies for immoral or illegal purposes, or

(c) entering residential premises to which this section applies or being found in the locality of any such premises.

(2) This section applies to residential premises of the following descriptions—

(a) dwelling-houses held under secure or introductory tenancies from the local authority;

(b) accommodation provided by that authority under Part VII of this Act or Part III of the Housing Act 1985 (homelessness).

(3) The court shall not grant an injunction under this section unless it is of the opinion that—

(a) the respondent has used or threatened to use violence against any person of a description mentioned in subsection (1)(a), and

(b) there is a significant risk of harm to that person or a person of a similar description if the injunction is not granted.

(4) An injunction under this section may—

(a) in the case of an injunction under subsection (1)(a) or (b), relate to particular acts or to conduct, or types of conduct, in general or to both, and

(b) in the case of an injunction under subsection (1)(c), relate to particular premises or a particular locality;

and may be made for a specified period or until varied or discharged.

(5) An injunction under this section may be varied or discharged by the court on an application by—

(a) the respondent, or

(b) the local authority which made the original application.

(6) The court may attach a power of arrest to one or more of the provisions of an injunction which it intends to grant under this section.

(7) The court may, in any case where it considers that it is just and convenient to do so, grant an injunction under this section, or vary such an injunction, even though the respondent has not been given such notice of the proceedings as would otherwise be required by rules of court.

If the court does so, it must afford the respondent an opportunity to make representations relating to the injunction or variation as soon as just and convenient at a hearing of which notice has been given to all the parties in accordance with rules of court.

153. Power of arrest for breach of other injunctions against anti-social behaviour.

(1) In the circumstances set out in this section, the High Court or a county court may attach a power of arrest to one or more of the provisions of an injunction which it intends to grant in relation to a breach or anticipated breach of the terms of a tenancy.

211. Protection of property of homeless persons and persons threatened with homelessness.

(1) This section applies where a local housing authority have reason to believe that—
    (a) there is danger of loss of, or damage to, any personal property of an applicant by reason of his inability to protect it or deal with it, and
    (b) no other suitable arrangements have been or are being made.

(2) If the authority have become subject to a duty towards the applicant under—
section 188 (interim duty to accommodate),
section 190, 193 or 195 (duties to persons found to be homeless or threatened with homelessness), or
section 200 (duties to applicant whose case is considered for referral or referred),
then, whether or not they are still subject to such a duty, they shall take reasonable steps to prevent the loss of the property or prevent or mitigate damage to it.

(3) If they have not become subject to such a duty, they may take any steps they consider reasonable for the purpose.

(4) The authority may decline to take action under this section except upon such conditions as they consider appropriate in the particular case, which may include conditions as to—
    (a) the making and recovery by the authority of reasonable charges for the action taken, or
    (b) the disposal by the authority, in such circumstances as may be specified, of property in relation to which they have taken action.

HOUSING GRANTS, CONSTRUCTION AND REGENERATION ACT 1996
(1996, c. 53)

43. Repayment where applicant not entitled to grant.

(1) This section applies where an application for a grant is approved but it subsequently appears to the local housing authority that the applicant (or, in the case of a joint application, any of the applicants) was not, at the time the application was approved, entitled to a grant of that description.

(2) Where this section applies—
    (a) in the case of a renovation grant, disabled facilities grant or HMO grant, no grant shall be paid or, as the case may be, no further instalments shall be paid, and
    (b) in the case of a common parts grant approved on a landlord's application, the local housing authority may refuse to pay the grant or any further instalment,
and the authority may demand that any grant which has been paid be repaid forthwith, together with interest from the date on which it was paid until repayment, at such reasonable rate as the authority may determine.

45. Condition for repayment on disposal: renovation grants.

(1) It is a condition of a renovation grant that if an owner of the premises to which the application relates makes a relevant disposal (other than an exempt disposal)—

(a) of the whole or part of the premises to which the application relates,
(b) after any instalment of grant has been paid, and
(c) before the certified date,
he shall repay to the local housing authority on demand the amount of grant that has been paid.

(2) It is a condition of a renovation grant that if an owner of the dwelling to which the application relates or, in the case of a conversion application, any dwelling provided by the relevant works, makes a relevant disposal (other than an exempt disposal)—
(a) of the whole or part of the dwelling,
(b) on or after the certified date, and
(c) before the end of the grant condition period,
he shall repay to the local housing authority on demand the amount of grant that has been paid.

In the case of a conversion application the grant shall be treated for this purpose as apportioned equally between the dwellings provided.

(3) A condition under this section is a local land charge and is binding on any person who is for the time being an owner of the premises concerned.

(4) Where the authority have the right to demand repayment of an amount as mentioned in subsection (1) or (2), they may—
(a) if the case falls within subsection (5), or
(b) in any other case, with the consent of the Secretary of State,
determine not to demand payment or to demand a lesser amount.

(5) The cases referred to in subsection (4)(a) are where the authority are satisfied that the owner of the dwelling—
(a) is elderly or infirm and is making the disposal with the intention—
   (i) of going to live in a hospital, hospice, sheltered housing, residential care home or similar institution as his only or main residence, or
   (ii) of moving to somewhere where care will be provided by any person; or
(b) is making the disposal with the intention of going to live with and care for an elderly or infirm member of his family or his partner's family.

(6) Any condition under this section shall cease to be in force with respect to any premises if there is a relevant disposal of the premises that is an exempt disposal, other than—
(a) a disposal within section 54(1)(a) (disposal to associates of person making disposal), or
(b) a disposal within section 54(1)(b) (vesting under will or on intestacy).

51. Conditions as to repayment in case of other compensation, etc.

(1) Where a local housing authority approve an application for a grant they may, with the consent of the Secretary of State, impose a condition requiring the applicant to take reasonable steps to pursue any relevant claim to which this section applies and to repay the grant, so far as appropriate, out of the proceeds of such a claim.

(2) The claims to which this section applies are—
(a) an insurance claim, or a legal claim against another person, in respect of damage to the premises to which the grant relates, or
(b) a legal claim for damages in which the cost of the works to premises to which the grant relates is part of the claim;
and a claim is a relevant claim to the extent that works to make good the damage mentioned in paragraph (a), or the cost of which is claimed as mentioned in paragraph (b), are works to which the grant relates.

(3) In the event of a breach of a condition under this section, the applicant shall on demand pay to the local housing authority the amount of the grant so far as relating to any such works, together with compound interest as from such date as may be

prescribed by or determined in accordance with the regulations, calculated at such reasonable rate as the authority may determine and with yearly rests.

(4) The local housing authority may determine not to make such a demand or to demand a lesser amount.

52. Power to impose other conditions with consent of Secretary of State.

(1) Where a local housing authority approve an application for a grant they may, with the consent of the Secretary of State, impose such conditions as they think fit—

(a) relating to things done or omitted before the certified date and requiring the repayment to the local housing authority on demand of any instalments of grant paid; or

(b) relating to things done or omitted on or after that date and requiring the payment to the local housing authority on demand of a sum equal to the amount of the grant paid;

and, in either case, that amount may be required to be paid together with compound interest on that amount as from the date of payment, calculated at such reasonable rate as the authority may determine and with yearly rests.

(2) A condition under this section is a local land charge and is binding on—

(a) any person who is for the time being an owner of the dwelling, house or building, and

(b) such other persons (if any) as the authority may, with the consent of the Secretary of State, specify.

...

(4) Where the authority have the right to demand repayment of an amount as mentioned in subsection (1), they may determine not to demand payment or to demand a lesser amount.

(5) Any conditions imposed under this section are in addition to the conditions provided for by sections 45 to 51.

55. Cessation of conditions on repayment of grant, etc.

(1) If at any time while a grant condition remains in force with respect to a dwelling, house or building—

(a) the owner of the dwelling, house or building to which the condition relates pays the amount of the grant to the local housing authority by whom the grant was made,

(b) a mortgagee of the interest of the owner in that dwelling, house or building being a mortgagee entitled to exercise a power of sale, makes such a payment,

(c) the local housing authority determine not to demand repayment on the breach of a grant condition, or

(d) the authority demand repayment in whole or in part on the breach of a grant condition and that demand is satisfied,

that grant condition and any other grant conditions shall cease to be in force with respect to that dwelling, house or building.

NOISE ACT 1996
(1996, c. 37)

1. Adoption of these provisions by local authorities.

(1) Sections 2 to 9 only apply to the area of a local authority if the authority have so resolved or an order made by the Secretary of State so provides.

2. Investigation of complaints of noise from a dwelling at night.

(1) A local authority must, if they receive a complaint of the kind mentioned in subsection (2), secure that an officer of the authority takes reasonable steps to investigate the complaint.

(2) The kind of complaint referred to is one made by any individual present in a dwelling during night hours (referred to in this Act as "the complaint's dwelling") that excessive noise is being emitted from another dwelling (referred to in this group of sections as "the offending dwelling").

(3) A complaint under subsection (2) may be made by any means.

(4) If an officer of the authority is satisfied, in consequence of an investigation under subsection (1), that—
    (a) noise is being emitted from the offending dwelling during night hours, and
    (b) the noise, if it were measured from within the complainant's dwelling, would or might exceed the permitted level,
he may serve a notice about the noise under section 3.

(5) For the purposes of subsection (4), it is for the officer of the authority dealing with the particular case—
    (a) to decide whether any noise, if it were measured from within the complainant's dwelling, would or might exceed the permitted level, and
    (b) for the purposes of that decision, to decide whether to assess the noise from within or outside the complainant's dwelling and whether or not to use any device for measuring the noise.

(6) In this group of sections, "night hours" means the period beginning with 11 p.m. and ending with the following 7 a.m.

(7) Where a local authority receive a complaint under subsection (2) and the offending dwelling is within the area of another local authority, the first local authority may act under this group of sections as if the offending dwelling were within their area, and accordingly may so act whether or not this group of sections applies to the area of the other local authority.

3. Warning notices.

(1) A notice under this section (referred to in this Act as "a warning notice") must—
    (a) state that an officer of the authority considers—
        (i) that noise is being emitted from the offending dwelling during night hours, and
        (ii) that the noise exceeds, or may exceed, the permitted level, as measured from within the complainant's dwelling, and
    (b) give warning that any person who is responsible for noise which is emitted from the dwelling, in the period specified in the notice, and exceeds the permitted level, as measured from within the complainant's dwelling, may be guilty of an offence.

...

(5) For the purposes of this group of sections, a person is responsible for noise emitted from a dwelling if he is a person to whose act, default or sufferance the emission of the noise is wholly or partly attributable.

4. Offence where noise exceeds permitted level after service of notice.

(1) If a warning notice has been served in respect of noise emitted from a dwelling, any person who is responsible for noise which—
    (a) is emitted from the dwelling in the period specified in the notice, and
    (b) exceeds the permitted level, as measured from within the complainant's dwelling,
is guilty of an offence.

(2) It is a defence for a person charged with an offence under this section to show that there was a reasonable excuse for the act, default or sufferance in question.

5. Permitted level of noise.

(1) For the purposes of this group of sections, the Secretary of State may by directions in writing determine the maximum level of noise (referred to in this group of

sections as "the permitted level") which may be emitted during night hours from any dwelling.

(2) The permitted level is to be a level applicable to noise as measured from within any other dwelling in the vicinity by an approved device used in accordance with any conditions subject to which the approval was given.

10. Powers of entry and seizure etc.

(1) The power conferred by subsection (2) may be exercised where an officer of a local authority has reason to believe that—

(a) a warning notice has been served in respect of noise emitted from a dwelling, and

(b) at any time in the period specified in the notice, noise emitted from the dwelling has exceeded the permitted level, as measured from within the complainant's dwelling.

(2) An officer of a local authority, or a person authorised by the authority for the purpose, may enter the dwelling from which the noise in question is being or has been emitted and may seize and remove any equipment which it appears to him is being or has been used in the emission of the noise.

(3) A person exercising the power conferred by subsection (2) must produce his authority, if he is required to do so.

(4) If it is shown to a justice of the peace on sworn information in writing that—

(a) a warning notice has been served in respect of noise emitted from a dwelling,

(b) at any time in the period specified in the notice, noise emitted from the dwelling has exceeded the permitted level, as measured from within the complainant's dwelling, and

(c) entry of an officer of the local authority, or of a person authorised by the authority for the purpose, to the dwelling has been refused, or such a refusal is apprehended, or a request by an officer of the authority, or of such a person, for admission would defeat the object of the entry,

the justice may by warrant under his hand authorise the local authority, by any of their officers or any person authorised by them for the purpose, to enter the premises, if need be by force.

(5) A person who enters any premises under subsection (2), or by virtue of a warrant issued under subsection (4), may take with him such other persons and such equipment as may be necessary; and if, when he leaves, the premises are unoccupied, must leave them as effectively secured against trespassers as he found them.

(6) A warrant issued under subsection (4) continues in force until the purpose for which the entry is required has been satisfied.

(7) The power of a local authority under section 81(3) of the Environmental Protection Act 1990 to abate any matter, where that matter is a statutory nuisance by virtue of section 79(1)(g) of that Act (noise emitted from premises so as to be prejudicial to health or a nuisance), includes power to seize and remove any equipment which it appears to the authority is being or has been used in the emission of the noise in question.

(8) A person who wilfully obstructs any person exercising any powers conferred under subsection (2) or by virtue of subsection (7) is liable, on summary conviction, to a fine not exceeding level 3 on the standard scale.

(9) The Schedule to this Act (which makes further provision in relation to anything seized and removed by virtue of this section) has effect.

12. Protection from personal liability.

(1) A member of a local authority or an officer or other person authorised by a local authority is not personally liable in respect of any act done by him or by the local authority or any such person if the act was done in good faith for the purpose of executing powers conferred by, or by virtue, of this Act.

SCHEDULE

Section 10 POWERS IN RELATION TO SEIZED EQUIPMENT

Introductory

1. In this Schedule—
    (a) a "noise offence" means—
        (i) in relation to equipment seized under section 10(2) of this Act, an offence under section 4 of this Act, and
        (ii) in relation to equipment seized under section 81(3) of the Environmental Protection Act 1990 (as extended by section 10(7) of this Act), an offence under section 80(4) of that Act in respect of a statutory nuisance falling within section 79(1)(g) of that Act,
    (b) "seized equipment" means equipment seized in the exercise of the power of seizure and removal conferred by section 10(2) of this Act or section 81(3) of the Environment Protection Act 1990 (as so extended),
    (c) "related equipment", in relation to any conviction of or proceedings for a noise offence, means seized equipment used or alleged to have been used in the commission of the offence,
    (d) "responsible local authority", in relation to seized equipment, means the local authority by or on whose behalf the equipment was seized.

Retention

2.—(1) Any seized equipment may be retained—
    (a) during the period of twenty-eight days beginning with the seizure, or
    (b) if it is related equipment in proceedings for a noise offence instituted within that period against any person, until—
        (i) he is sentenced or otherwise dealt with for the offence or acquitted of the offence, or
        (ii) the proceedings are discontinued.
    (2) Sub-paragraph (1) does not authorise the retention of seized equipment if—
    (a) a person has been given a fixed penalty notice under section 8 of this Act in respect of any noise,
    (b) the equipment was seized because of its use in the emission of the noise in respect of which the fixed penalty notice was given, and
    (c) that person has paid the fixed penalty before the end of the period allowed for its payment.

Forfeiture

3.—(1) Where a person is convicted of a noise offence the court may make an order ("a forfeiture order") for forfeiture of any related equipment.
    (2) The court may make a forfeiture order whether or not it also deals with the offender in respect of the offence in any other way and without regard to any restrictions on forfeiture in any equipment.
    (3) In considering whether to make a forfeiture order in respect of any equipment a court must have regard—
    (a) to the value of the equipment, and
    (b) to the likely financial and other effects on the offender of the making of the order (taken together with any other order that the court contemplates making).
    (4) A forfeiture order operates to deprive the offender of any rights in the equipment to which it relates.

Consequences of forfeiture

4.—(1) Where any equipment has been forfeited under paragraph 3, a magistrates' court may, on application by a claimant of the equipment (other than the person in whose case the forfeiture order was made) make an order for delivery of the equipment to the applicant if it appears to the court that he is the owner of the equipment.

(2) No application may be made under sub-paragraph (1) by any claimant of the equipment after the expiry of the period of six months beginning with the date on which a forfeiture order was made in respect of the equipment.

(3) Such an application cannot succeed unless the claimant satisfies the court—

(a) that he had not consented to the offender having possession of the equipment, or

(b) that he did not know, and had no reason to suspect, that the equipment was likely to be used in the commission of a noise offence.

(4) Where the responsible local authority is of the opinion that the person in whose case the forfeiture order was made is not the owner of the equipment, it must take reasonable steps to bring to the attention of persons who may be entitled to do so their right to make an application under sub-paragraph (1).

(5) An order under sub-paragraph (1) does not affect the right of any person to take, within the period of six months beginning with the date of the order, proceedings for the recovery of the equipment from the person in possession of it in pursuance of the order, but the right ceases on the expiry of that period.

(6) If on the expiry of the period of six months beginning with the date on which a forfeiture order was made in respect of the equipment no order has been made under sub-paragraph (1), the responsible local authority may dispose of the equipment.

Return etc. of seized equipment

5. If in proceedings for a noise offence no order for forfeiture of related equipment is made, the court (whether or not a person is convicted of the offence) may give such directions as to the return, retention or disposal of the equipment by the responsible local authority as it thinks fit.

6.—(1) Where in the case of any seized equipment no proceedings in which it is related equipment are begun within the period mentioned in paragraph 2(1)(a)—

(a) the responsible local authority must return the equipment to any person who—

(i) appears to them to be the owner of the equipment, and

(ii) makes a claim for the return of the equipment within the period mentioned in sub-paragraph (2), and

(b) if no such person makes such a claim within that period, the responsible local authority may dispose of the equipment.

(2) The period referred to in sub-paragraph (1)(a)(ii) is the period of six months beginning with the expiry of the period mentioned in paragraph 2(1)(a).

(3) The responsible local authority must take reasonable steps to bring to the attention of persons who may be entitled to do so their right to make such a claim.

(4) Subject to sub-paragraph (6), the responsible local authority is not required to return any seized equipment under sub-paragraph (1)(a) until the person making the claim has paid any such reasonable charges for the seizure, removal and retention of the equipment as the authority may demand.

(5) If—

(a) equipment is sold in pursuance of—

(i) paragraph 4(6),

(ii) directions under paragraph 5, or

(iii) this paragraph, and

(b) before the expiration of the period of one year beginning with the date on which the equipment is sold any person satisfies the responsible local authority that at the time of its sale he was the owner of the equipment,
the authority is to pay him any sum by which any proceeds of sale exceed any such reasonable charges for the seizure, removal or retention of the equipment as the authority may demand.

(6) The responsible local authority cannot demand charges from any person under sub-paragraph (4) or (5) who they are satisfied did not know, and had no reason to suspect, that the equipment was likely to be used in the emission of noise exceeding the level determined under section 5.

PARTY WALL ETC. ACT 1996
(1996, c. 40)

7. Compensation etc.

(1) A building owner shall not exercise any right conferred on him by this Act in such a manner or at such time as to cause unnecessary inconvenience to any adjoining owner or to any adjoining occupier.

(2) The building owner shall compensate any adjoining owner and any adjoining occupier for any loss or damage which may result to any of them by reason of any work executed in pursuance of this Act.

(3) Where a building owner in exercising any right conferred on him by this Act lays open any part of the adjoining land or building he shall at his own expense make and maintain so long as may be necessary a proper hoarding, shoring or fans or temporary construction for the protection of the adjoining land or building and the security of any adjoining occupier.

(4) Nothing in this Act shall authorise the building owner to place special foundations on land of an adjoining owner without his previous consent in writing.

8. Rights of entry.

(1) A building owner, his servants, agents and workmen may during usual working hours enter and remain on any land or premises for the purpose of executing any work in pursuance of this Act and may remove any furniture or fittings or take any other action necessary for that purpose.

(2) If the premises are closed, the building owner, his agents and workmen may, if accompanied by a constable or other police officer, break open any fences or doors in order to enter the premises.

(3) No land or premises may be entered by any person under subsection (1) unless the building owner serves on the owner and the occupier of the land or premises—

　　(a) in case of emergency, such notice of the intention to enter as may be reasonably practicable;

　　(b) in any other case, such notice of the intention to enter as complies with subsection (4).

(4) Notice complies with this subsection if it is served in a period of not less than fourteen days ending with the day of the proposed entry.

POLICE ACT 1996
(1996, c. 16)

88. Liability for wrongful acts of constables.

(1) The chief officer of police for a police area shall be liable in respect of torts committed by constables under his direction and control in the performance or purported performance of their functions in like manner as a master is liable in respect

of torts committed by his servants in the course of their employment, and accordingly shall in respect of any such tort be treated for all purposes as a joint tortfeasor.

(2) There shall be paid out of the police fund—

(a) any damages or costs awarded against the chief officer of police in any proceedings brought against him by virtue of this section and any costs incurred by him in any such procceedings so far as not recovered by him in the proceedings; and

(b) any sum required in connection with the settlement of any claim made against the chief officer of police by virtue of this section, if the settlement is approved by the police authority.

(3) Any proceedings in respect of a claim made by virtue of this section shall be brought against the chief officer of police for the time being or, in the case of a vacancy in that office, against the person for the time being performing the functions of the chief officer of police; and references in subsections (1) and (2) to the chief officer of police shall be construed accordingly.

(4) A police authority may, in such cases and to such extent as appear to it to be appropriate, pay out of the police fund—

(a) any damages or costs awarded against a person to whom this subsection applies in proceedings for a tort committed by that person,

(b) any costs incurred and not recovered by such a person in such proceedings, and

(c) any sum required in connection with the settlement of a claim that has or might have given rise to such proceedings.

CIVIL PROCEDURE ACT 1997
(1997, c. 12)

7. Power of courts to make orders for preserving evidence, etc.

(1) The court may make an order under this section for the purpose of securing, in the case of any existing or proposed proceedings in the court—

(a) the preservation of evidence which is or may be relevant, or

(b) the preservation of property which is or may be the subject-matter of the proceedings or as to which any question arises or may arise in the proceedings.

(2) A person who is, or appears to the court likely to be, a party to proceedings in the court may make an application for such an order.

(3) Such an order may direct any person to permit any person described in the order, or secure that any person so described is permitted—

(a) to enter premises in England and Wales, and

(b) while on the premises, to take in accordance with the terms of the order any of the following steps.

(4) Those steps are—

(a) to carry out a search for or inspection of anything described in the order, and

(b) to make or obtain a copy, photograph, sample or other record of anything so described.

(5) The order may also direct the person concerned—

(a) to provide any person described in the order, or secure that any person so described is provided, with any information or article described in the order, and

(b) to allow any person described in the order, or secure that any person so described is allowed, to retain for safe keeping anything described in the order.

(6) An order under this section is to have effect subject to such conditions as are specified in the order.

(7) This section does not affect any right of a person to refuse to do anything on the ground that to do so might tend to expose him or his spouse to proceedings for an offence or for the recovery of a penalty.

(8) In this section—
"court" means the High Court, and
"premises" includes any vehicle;
and an order under this section may describe anything generally, whether by reference to a class or otherwise.

CONTRACT (SCOTLAND) ACT 1997
(1997, c. 34)

1. Extrinsic evidence of additional contract term etc.

(1) Where a document appears (or two or more documents appear) to comprise all the express terms of a contract or unilateral voluntary obligation, it shall be presumed, unless the contrary is proved, that the document does (or the documents do) comprise all the express terms of the contract or unilateral voluntary obligation.

(2) Extrinsic oral or documentary evidence shall be admissible to prove, for the purposes of subsection (1) above, that the contract or unilateral voluntary obligation includes additional express terms (whether or not written terms).

(3) Notwithstanding the foregoing provisions of this section, where one of the terms in the document (or in the documents) is to the effect that the document does (or the documents do) comprise all the express terms of the contract or unilateral voluntary obligation, that term shall be conclusive in the matter.

(4) This section is without prejudice to any enactment which makes provision as respects the constitution, or formalities of execution, of a contract or unilateral voluntary obligation.

2. Supersession.

(1) Where a deed is executed in implement, or purportedly in implement, of a contract, an unimplemented, or otherwise unfulfilled, term of the contract shall not be taken to be superseded by virtue only of that execution or of the delivery and acceptance of the deed.

(2) Subsection (1) above is without prejudice to any agreement which the parties to a contract may reach (whether or not an agreement incorporated into the contract) as to supersession of the contract.

3. Damages for breach of contract of sale.

Any rule of law which precludes the buyer in a contract of sale of property from obtaining damages for breach of that contract by the seller unless the buyer rejects the property and rescinds the contract shall cease to have effect.

4. Short title, extent etc.

(4) This Act extends to Scotland only.

FINANCE ACT 1997
(1997, c. 16)

47. Repayments and assessment: time limits.

(2) Subject to subsection (3) and (4) below, subsection (1) above shall be deemed to have come into force on 18 July 1996 as a provision applying, for the purposes of the making of any repayment on or after that date, to all claims under section 80 of the Value Added Tax Act 1994, including claims made before that date and claims relating to payments made before that date

(3) Subsection (4) below applies as respects the making of any repayment on or after 18 July 1996 on a claim under section 80 of the Value Added Tax Act 1994 if—

(a) legal proceedings for questioning any decision ("the disputed decision") of the Commissioners, or of an officer of the Commissioners, were brought by any person at any time before that date,

(b) a determination has been or is made in those proceedings that the disputed decision was wrong or should be set aside,

(c) the claim is one made by that person at a time after the proceedings were brought (whether before or after the making of the determination), and

(d) the claim relates to—

(i) an amount paid by that person to the Commissioners on the basis of the disputed decision, or

(ii) an amount paid by that person to the Commissioners before the relevant date (including an amount paid before the making of the disputed decision) on grounds which, in all material respects, correspond to those on which that decision was made.

(4) Where this subsection applies in the case of any claim—

(a) subsection (4) of section 80 of the Value Added Tax Act 1994 (as inserted by this section) shall not apply, and shall be taken never to have applied, in relation to so much of that claim as relates to an amount falling within subsection (3)(d)(i) or (ii) above, but

(b) the Commissioners shall not be liable on that claim, and shall be taken never to have been liable on that claim, to repay any amount so falling which was paid to them more than three years before the proceedings mentioned in subsection (3)(a) above were brought.

(5) In subsection (3)(d) above—

(a) the reference to the relevant date is a reference to whichever is the earlier of 18 July 1996 and the date of the making of the determination in question; and

(b) the reference to an amount paid on the basis of a decision, or on any grounds, includes an amount so paid on terms (however expressed) which questioned the correctness of the decision or, as the case may be, of those grounds.

(8) Nothing contained in—

(a) any regulations under section 25(1) of, or paragraph 2 of Schedule 11 to, that Act relating to the correction of errors or the making of adjustments, or

(b) any requirement imposed under any such regulations,

shall be taken, in relation to any time on or after 18 July 1996, to have conferred an entitlement on any person to receive, by way of repayment, any amount to which he would not have had any entitlement on a claim under section 80 of that Act.

50. Overpayments, interest, assessments, etc.

(1) Schedule 5 to this Act (which makes provision in relation to excise duties, insurance premium tax and landfill tax which corresponds to that made for VAT by sections 44 to 48 above) shall have effect.

(2) Schedule 6 to this Act (which makes further provision for the assessment of amounts payable under enactments relating to excise duty) shall also have effect.

51. Enforcement by distress.

(1) The Commissioners may by regulations make provision—

(a) for authorising distress to be levied on the goods and chattels of any person refusing or neglecting to pay—

(i) any amount of relevant tax due from him, or

(ii) any amount recoverable as if it were relevant tax due from him;

(b) for the disposal of any goods or chattels on which distress is levied in pursuance of the regulations; and

(c) for the imposition and recovery of costs, charges, expenses and fees in connection with anything done under the regulations.

(2) The provision that may be contained in regulations under this section shall include, in particular—

(a) provision for the levying of distress, by any person authorised to do so under the regulations, on goods or chattels located at any place whatever (including on a public highway); and

(b) provision authorising distress to be levied at any such time of the day or night, and on any such day of the week, as may be specified or described in the regulations.

(3) Regulations under this section may—
   (a) make different provision for different cases, and
   (b) contain any such incidental, supplemental, consequential or transitional provision as the Commissioners think fit;
and the transitional provision that may be contained in regulations under this section shall include transitional provision in connection with the coming into force of the repeal by this Act or any other power by regulations to make provision for or in connection with the levying of distress.

(4) The power to make regulations under this section shall be exercisable by statutory instrument subject to annulment in pursuance of a resolution of the House of Commons.

(5) The following are relevant taxes for the purposes of this section, that is to say—
   (a) any duty of customs or excise, other than vehicle excise duty;
   (b) value added tax;
   (c) insurance premium tax;
   (d) landfill tax;
   (e) any agricultural levy of the European Community.

(6) In this section "the Commissioners" means the Commissioners of Customs and Excise.

Section 50   SCHEDULE 5

INDIRECT TAXES: OVERPAYMENTS ETC.

PART I
UNJUST ENRICHMENT

Application of Part I

1.—(1) This Part of this Schedule has effect for the purposes of the following provisions (which make it a defence to a claim for repayment that the repayment would unjustly enrich the claimant), namely—
   (a) section 137A(3) of the Customs and Excise Management Act 1979 (excise duties);
   (b) paragraph 8(3) of Schedule 7 to the Finance Act 1994 (insurance premium tax); and
   (c) paragraph 14(3) of Schedule 5 to the Finance Act 1996 (landfill tax).

(2) Those provisions are referred to in this Part of this Schedule as unjust enrichment provisions.

(3) In this Part of this Schedule—
"the Commissioners" means the Commissioners of Customs and Excise;
"relevant repayment provision" means—
   (a) section 137A of the Customs and Excise Management Act 1979 (recovery of overpaid excise duty);
   (b) paragraph 8 of Schedule 7 to the Finance Act 1994 (recovery of overpaid insurance premium tax); or
   (c) paragraph 14 of Schedule 5 to the Finance Act 1996 (recovery of overpaid landfill tax);
"relevant tax" means any duty of excise, insurance premium tax or landfill tax; and
"subordinate legislation" has the same meaning as in the Interpretation Act 1978.

Disregard of business losses

2.—(1) This paragraph applies where—

(a) there is an amount paid by way of relevant tax which (apart from an unjust enrichment provision) would fall to be repaid under a relevant repayment provision to any person ("the tax payer"), and

(b) the whole or a part of the cost of the payment of that amount to the Commissioners has, for practical purposes, been borne by a person other than the taxpayer.

(2) Where, in a case to which this paragraph applies, loss or damage has been or may be incurred by the taxpayer as a result of mistaken assumptions made in his case about the operation of any provisions relating to a relevant tax, that loss or damage shall be disregarded, except to the extent of the quantified amount, in the making of any determination—

(a) of whether or to what extent the repayment of an amount to the taxpayer would enrich him; or

(b) of whether or to what extent any enrichment of the taxpayer would be unjust.

(3) In sub-paragraph (2) above "the quantified amount" means the amount (if any) which is shown by the taxpayer to constitute the amount that would appropriately compensate him for loss or damage shown by him to have resulted, for any business carried on by him, from the making of the mistaken assumptions.

(4) The reference in sub-paragraph (2) above to provisions relating to a relevant tax is a reference to any provisions of—

(a) any enactment, subordinate legislation or Community legislation (whether or not still in force) which relates to that tax or to any matter connected with it; or

(b) any notice published by the Commissioners under or for the purposes of any such enactment or subordinate legislation.

(5) This paragraph has effect for the purposes of making any repayment on or after the day on which this Act is passed, even if the claim for that repayment was made before that day.

Reimbursement arrangements

3.—(1) The Commissioners may by regulations make provision for reimbursement arrangements made by any person to be disregarded for the purposes of any or all of the unjust enrichment provisions except where the arrangements—

(a) contain such provision as may be required by the regulations; and

(b) are supported by such undertakings to comply with the provisions of the arrangements as may be required by the regulations to be given to the Commissioners.

(2) In this paragraph "reimbursement arrangements" means any arrangements for the purposes of a claim under a relevant repayment provision which—

(a) are made by any person for the purpose of securing that he is not unjustly enriched by the repayment of any amount in pursuance of the claim; and

(b) provide for the reimbursement of persons who have for practical purposes borne the whole or any part of the cost of the original payment of that amount to the Commissioners.

(3) Without prejudice to the generality of sub-paragraph (1) above, the provision that may be required by regulations under this paragraph to be contained in reimbursement arrangements includes—

(a) provision requiring a reimbursement for which the arrangements provide to be made within such period after the repayment to which it relates as may be specified in the regulations;

(b) provision for the repayment of amounts to the Commissioners where those amounts are not reimbursed in accordance with the arrangements;

(c) provision requiring interest paid by the Commissioners on any amount repaid by them to be treated in the same way as that amount for the purposes of any requirement under the arrangements to make reimbursement or to repay the Commissioners;

(d) provision requiring such records relating to the carrying out of the arrangements as may be described in the regulations to be kept and produced to the Commissioners, or to an officer of theirs.

(4) Regulations under this paragraph may impose obligations on such persons as may be specified in the regulations—

(a) to make the repayments to the Commissioners that they are required to make in pursuance of any provisions contained in any reimbursement arrangements by virtue of sub-paragraph (3)(b) or (c) above;

(b) to comply with any requirements contained in any such arrangements by virtue of sub-paragraph (3)(d) above.

(5) Regulations under this paragraph may make provision for the form and manner in which, and the times at which, undertakings are to be given to the Commissioners in accordance with the regulations; and any such provision may allow for those matters to be determined by the Commissioners in accordance with the regulations.

(6) Regulations under this paragraph may—

(a) contain any such incidental, supplementary, consequential or transitional provision as appears to the Commissioners to be necessary or expedient; and

(b) make different provision for different circumstances.

(7) Regulations under this paragraph may have effect (irrespective of when the claim for repayment was made) for the purposes of the making of any repayment by the Commissioners after the time when the regulations are made; and, accordingly, such regulations may apply to arrangements made before that time.

(8) Regulations under this paragraph shall be made by statutory instrument subject to annulment in pursuance of a resolution of the House of Commons.

Contravention of requirement to repay Commissioners

4.—(1) Where any obligation is imposed by regulations made by virtue of paragraph 3(4) above, a contravention or failure to comply with that obligation shall, to the extent that it relates to amounts repaid under section 137A of the Customs and Excise Management Act 1979, attract a penalty under section 9 of the Finance Act 1994 (penalties in connection with excise duties).

(2) For the purposes of Schedule 7 to the Finance Act 1994 (insurance premium tax), a contravention of failure to comply with an obligation imposed by regulations made by virtue of paragraph 3(4) above shall be deemed, to the extent that it relates to amounts repaid under paragraph 8 of that Schedule (recovery of overpaid insurance premium tax), to be a failure to comply with a requirement falling within paragraph 17(1)(c) of that Schedule (breach of regulations).

(3) Paragraph 23 of Schedule 5 to the Finance Act 1996 (power to provide for penalty) shall have effect as if an obligation imposed by regulations made by virtue of paragraph 3(4) above were, to the extent that it relates to amounts repaid under paragraph 14 of this Schedule (recovery of overpaid landfill tax), a requirement imposed by regulations under Part III of that Act; and the provisions of that Schedule in relation to penalties under Part V of that Schedule shall have effect accordingly.

PART V
RECOVERY OF EXCESS PAYMENTS BY THE COMMISSIONERS

Assessment for excessive repayment

14.—(1) Where—

(a) any amount has been paid at any time to any person by way of a repayment under a relevant repayment provison, and

(b) the amount paid exceeded the amount which the Commissioners were liable at that time to repay to that person,

the Commissioners may, to the best of their judgment, assess the excess paid to that person and notify it to him.

(2) Where any person is liable to pay any amount to the Commissioners in pursuance of an obligation imposed by virtue of paragraph 3(4)(a) above, the Commissioners may, to the best of their judgment, assess the amount due from that person and notify it to him.

(3) In this paragraph "relevant repayment provision" means—

(a) section 137A of the Customs and Excise Management Act 1979 (recovery of overpaid excise duty);

(b) paragraph 8 of Schedule 7 to the Finance Act 1994 (recovery of overpaid insurance premium tax); or

(c) paragraph 14 of Schedule 5 to the Finance Act 1996 (recovery of overpaid landfill tax).

Assessment for overpayments of interest

15.—(1) Where—

(a) any amount has been paid to any person by way of interest under a relevant interest provision, but

(b) that person was not entitled to that amount under that provision,

the Commissioners may, to the best of their judgment, assess the amount so paid to which that person was not entitled and notify it to him.

(2) In this paragraph "relevant interest provision" means—

(a) paragraph 9 of Schedule 6 to the Finance Act 1994 (interest payable by the Commissioners on overpayments of air passenger duty);

(b) paragraph 22 of Schedule 7 to that Act (interest payable by the Commissioners on overpayments etc. of insurance premium tax); or

(c) paragraph 29 of Schedule 5 to the Finance Act 1996 (interest payable by the Commissioners on overpayments etc. of landfill tax).

Assessments under paragraphs 14 and 15

16.—(1) An assessment under paragraph 14 or 15 above shall not be made more than two years after the time when evidence of facts sufficient in the opinion of the Commissioners to justify the making of the assessment comes to the knowledge of the Commissioners.

(2) Where an amount has been assessed and notified to any person under paragraph 14 or 15 above, it shall be recoverable (subject to any provision having effect in accordance with paragraph 19 below) as if it were relevant tax due from him.

(3) Sub-paragraph (2) above does not have effect if, or to the extent that, the assessment in question has been withdrawn or reduced.

Interest on amounts assessed

17.—(1) Where an assessment is made under paragraph 14 or 15 above, the whole of the amount assessed shall carry interest at the rate applicable under section 197 of the Finance Act 1996 from the date on which the assessment is notified until payment.

(2) Where any person is liable to interest under sub-paragraph (1) above the Commissioners may assess the amount due by way of interest and notify it to him.

(3) Without prejudice to the power to make assessments under this paragraph for later periods, the interest to which an assessment under this paragraph may relate shall be confined to interest for a period of no more than two years ending with the time when the assessment under this paragraph is made.

(4) Interest under this paragraph shall be paid without any deduction of income tax.

(5) A notice of assessment under this paragraph shall specify a date, being not later than the date of the notice, to which the amount of interest is calculated; and, if the interest continues to accrue after that date, a further assessment or assessments may be made under this paragraph in respect of amounts which so accrue.

(6) If, within such period as may be notified by the Commissioners to the person liable for interest under sub-paragraph (1) above, the amount referred to in that sub-paragraph is paid, it shall be treated for the purposes of that sub-paragraph as paid on the date specified as mentioned in sub-paragraph (5) above.

(7) Where an amount has been assessed and notified to any person under this paragraph it shall be recoverable as if it were relevant tax due from him.

(8) Sub-paragraph (7) above does not have effect if, or to the extent that, the assessment in question has been withdrawn or reduced.

Supplementary assessments

18. If it appears to the Commissioners that the amount which ought to have been assessed in an assessment under paragraph 14, 15 or 17 above exceeds the amount which was so assessed, then—
 (a) under the same paragraph as that assessment was made, and
 (b) on or before the last day on which that assessment could have been made,
the Commissioners may make a supplementary assessment of the amount of the excess and shall notify the person concerned accordingly.

Interpretation of Part V

20.—(1) In this Part of this Schedule "the Commissioners" means the Commissioners of Customs and Excise.

(2) In this Part of this Schedule "relevant tax", in relation to any assessment, means—
 (a) a duty of excise if the assessment relates to—
  (i) a repayment of an amount paid by way of such a duty,
  (ii) an overpayment of interest under paragraph 9 of Schedule 6 to the Finance Act 1994, or
  (iii) interest on an amount specified in an assessment in relation to which the relevant tax is a duty of excise;
 (b) insurance premium tax if the assessment relates to—
  (i) a repayment of an amount paid by way of such tax,
  (ii) an overpayment of interest under paragraph 22 of Schedule 7 to the Finance Act 1994, or
  (iii) interest on an amount specified in an assessment in relation to which the relevant tax is insurance premium tax;
and
 (c) landfill tax if the assessment relates to—
  (i) a repayment of an amount paid by way of such tax,
  (ii) an overpayment of interest under paragraph 29 of Schedule 5 to the Finance Act 1996, or
  (iii) interest on an amount specified in an assessment in relation to which the relevant tax is landfill tax.

(3) For the purposes of this Part of this Schedule notification to a personal representative, trustee in bankruptcy, interim or permanent trustee, receiver, liquidator or person otherwise acting in a representative capacity in relation to another shall be treated as notification to the person in relation to whom he so acts.

JUSTICES OF THE PEACE ACT 1997
(1997, c. 25)

51. Immunity for acts within jurisdiction.
No action shall lie against any justice of the peace or justices' clerk in respect of any act or omission of his—
    (a) in the execution of his duty—
        (i) as such a justice; or
        (ii) as such a clerk exercising, by virtue of any statutory provision, any of the functions of a single justice; and
    (b) with respect to any matter within his jurisdiction.

52. Immunity for certain acts beyond jurisdiction.
An action shall lie against any justice of the peace or justices' clerk in respect of any act or omission of his—
    (a) in the purported execution of his duty—
        (i) as such a justice; or
        (ii) as such a clerk exercising, by virtue of any statutory provision, any of the functions of a single justice; but
    (b) with respect to a matter which is not within his jurisdiction,
if, but only if, it is proved that he acted in bad faith.

POLICE ACT 1997
(1997, c. 50)

PART I
THE NATIONAL CRIMINAL INTELLIGENCE SERVICE

1. The Service Authority for the National Criminal Intelligence Service.
(1) There shall be a body corporate to be known as the Service Authority for the National Criminal Intelligence Service (in this Part referred to as "the NCIS Service Authority").

42. Liability for wrongful acts of constables etc.
(1) The Director General of NCIS shall be liable in respect of torts committed by constables under his direction and control in the performance or purported performance of their functions in like manner as a master is liable in respect of torts committed by his servants in the course of their employment, and accordingly shall in respect of any such tort be treated for all purposes as a joint tortfeasor.
(2) There shall be paid out of the NCIS service fund—
    (a) any damages or costs awarded against the Director General in any proceedings brought against him by virtue of this section and any costs incurred by him in any such proceedings so far as not recovered by him in the proceedings, and
    (b) any sum required in connection with the settlement of any claim made against the Director General by virtue of this section, if the settlement is approved by the NCIS Service Authority.
(3) Any proceedings in respect of a claim made by virtue of this section shall be brought against the Director General of NCIS for the time being or, in the case of a vacancy in that office, against the person for the time being performing the functions of the Director General; and references in this section to the Director General shall be construed accordingly.
(4) The NCIS Service Authority may, in such cases and to such extent as appear to it to be appropriate, pay out of the NCIS service fund—

(a) any damages or costs awarded against a person to whom this subsection applies in proceedings for a tort committed by that person,
(b) any costs incurred and not recovered by such a person in such proceedings, and
(c) any sum required in connection with the settlement of a claim that has or might have given rise to such proceedings.
(5) Subsection (4) applies to a person who is—
(a) a member of NCIS, or
(b) a constable for the time being required to serve with NCIS by virtue of section 23.

86. Liability for wrongful acts of constables etc.

(1) The Director General of the National Crime Squad shall be liable in respect of torts committed by constables under his direction and control in the performance or purported performance of their functions in like manner as a master is liable in respect of torts committed by his servants in the course of their employment, and accordingly shall in respect of any such tort be treated for all purposes as a joint tortfeasor.
(2) There shall be paid out of the NCS service fund—
(a) any damages or costs awarded against the Director General in any proceedings brought against him by virtue of this section and any costs incurred by him in any such proceedings so far as not recovered by him in the proceedings, and
(b) any sum required in connection with the settlement of any claim made against the Director General by virtue of this section, if the settlement is approved by the NCS Service Authority.
(3) Any proceedings in respect of a claim made by virtue of this section shall be brought against the Director General of the National Crime Squad for the time being or, in the case of a vacancy in that office, against the person for the time being performing the functions of the Director General; and references in subsections (1) and (2) to the Director General shall be construed accordingly.
(4) The NCS Service Authority may, in such cases and to such extent as appear to it to be appropriate, pay out of the NCS service fund—
(a) any damages or costs awarded against a person to whom this subsection applies in proceedings for a tort committed by that person,
(b) any costs incurred and not recovered by such a person in such proceedings, and
(c) any sum required in connection with the settlement of a claim that has or might have given rise to such proceedings.
(5) Subsection (4) applies to a person who is—
(a) a member of the National Crime Squad, or
(b) a constable for the time being required to serve with the National Crime Squad by virtue of section 23 above or section 24 or 98 of the Police Act 1996.

PART III
AUTHORISATION OF ACTION IN RESPECT OF PROPERTY

92. Effect of authorisation under Part III.

No entry on or interference with property or with wireless telegraphy shall be unlawful if it is authorised by an authorisation having effect under this Part.

93. Authorisations to interfere with property etc.

(1) Where subsection (2) applies, an authorising officer may authorise—
(a) the taking of such action, in respect of such property in the relevant area, as he may specify, or
(b) the taking of such action in the relevant area as he may specify, in respect of wireless telegraphy.

(2) This subsection applies where the authorising officer believes—

(a) that it is necessary for the action specified to be taken on the ground that it is likely to be of substantial value in the prevention or detection or serious crime, and

(b) that what the action seeks to achieve cannot reasonably be achieved by other means.

(3) An authorising officer shall not give an authorisation under this section except on an application made—

(a) if the authorising officer is within subsection (5)(a) to (e), by a member of his police force,

(b) if the authorising officer is within subsection (5)(f), by a member of the National Criminal Intelligence Service,

(c) if the authorising officer is within subsection (5)(g), by a member of the National Crime Squad, or

(d) if the authorising officer is within subsection (5)(h), by a customs officer.

(4) For the purposes of subsection (2), conduct which constitutes one or more offences shall be regarded as serious crime if, and only if,—

(a) it involves the use of violence, results in substantial financial gain or is conduct by a large number of persons in pursuit of a common purpose, or

(b) the offence or one of the offences is an offence for which a person who has attained the age of twenty-one and has no previous convictions could reasonably be expected to be sentenced to imprisonment for a term of three years or more,

and, where the authorising officer is within subsection (5)(h), it relates to an assigned matter within the meaning of section 1(1) of the Customs and Excise Management Act 1979.

(5) In this section "authorising officer" means—

(a) the chief constable of a police force maintained under section 2 of the Police Act 1996 (maintenance of police forces for areas in England and Wales except London);

(b) the Commissioner, or an Assistant Commissioner, of Police of the Metropolis;

(c) the Commissioner of Police for the City of London;

(d) the chief constable of a police force maintained under or by virtue of section 1 of the Police (Scotland) Act 1967 (maintenance of police forces for areas in Scotland);

(e) the Chief Constable or a Deputy Chief Constable of the Royal Ulster Constabulary;

(f) the Director General of the National Criminal Intelligence Service;

(g) the Director General of the National Crime Squad; or

(h) the customs officer designated by the Commissioners of Customs and Excise for the purposes of this paragraph.

(6) In this section "relevant area"—

(a) in relation to a person within paragraph (a), (b) or (c) of subsection (5), means the area in England and Wales for which his police force is maintained;

(b) in relation to a person within paragraph (d) of that subsection means the area in Scotland for which his police force is maintained;

(c) in relation to a person within paragraph (e) of that subsection, means Northern Ireland;

(d) in relation to the Director General of the National Criminal Intelligence Service, means the United Kingdom;

(e) in relation to the Director General of the National Crime Squad, means England and Wales; and

(f) in relation to the customs officer designated for the purposes of paragraph (h) of that subsection, means the United Kingdom,

and in each case includes the adjacent United Kingdom waters.

(7) The powers conferred by, or by virtue of, this section are additional to any other powers which a person has as a constable either at common law or under or by virtue of any other enactment and are not to be taken to affect any of those other powers.

94. Authorisations given in absence of authorising officer.
...

95. Authorisations: form and duration etc.
(1) An authorisation shall be in writing, except that in an urgent case an authorisation (other than one given by virtue of section 94) may be given orally.

(2) An authorisation shall, unless renewed under subsection (3), cease to have effect—

(a) if given orally or by virtue of section 94, at the end of the period of 72 hours beginning with the time when it took effect;

(b) in any other case, at the end of the period of three months beginning with the day on which it took effect.

(3) If at any time before an authorisation would cease to have effect the authorising officer who gave the authorisation, or in whose absence it was given, considers it necessary for the authorisation to continue to have effect for the purpose for which it was issued, he may, in writing, renew it for a period of three months beginning with the day on which it would cease to have effect.

(4) A person shall cancel an authorisation given by him if satisfied that the action authorised by it is no longer necessary.

(5) An authorising officer shall cancel an authorisation given in his absence if satisfied that the action authorised by it is no longer necessary ...

96. Notification of authorisations etc.
(1) Where a person gives, renews or cancels an authorisation, he shall, as soon as is reasonably practicable and in accordance with arrangements made by the Chief Commissioner, give notice in writing that he has done so to a Commission appointed under section 91(1)(b).

(2) Subject to subsection (3), a notice under this section shall specify such matters as the Secretary of State may by order prescribe.

(3) A notice under this section of the giving or renewal of an authorisation shall specify—

(a) whether section 97 applies to the authorisation or renewal, and

(b) where that section does not apply by virtue of subsection (3) of that section, the grounds on which the case is believed to be one of urgency.

(4) Where a notice is given to a Commissioner under this section, he shall, as soon as is reasonably practicable, scrutinise the notice.

(5) An order under subsection (2) shall be made by statutory instrument.

(6) A statutory instrument which contains an order under subsection (2) shall not be made unless a draft has been laid before, and approved by a resolution of, each House of Parliament.

97. Authorisations requiring approval.
(1) An authorisation to which this section applies shall not take effect until—

(a) it has been approved in accordance with this section by a Commissioner appointed under section 91(1)(b), and

(b) the person who gave the authorisation has been notified under subsection (4).

(2) Subject to subsection (3), this section applies to an authorisation if, at the time it is given, the person who gives it believes—

(a) that any of the property specified in the authorisation—

(i) is used wholly or mainly as a dwelling or as a bedroom in a hotel, or

(ii) constitutes office premises, or

(b) that the action authorised by it is likely to result in any person acquiring knowledge of—
 (i) matters subject to legal privilege,
 (ii) confidential personal information, or
 (iii) confidential journalistic material.

(3) This section does not apply to an authorisation where the person who gives it believes that the case is one of urgency.

(4) Where a Commissioner receives a notice under section 96 which specifies that this section applies to the authorisation, he shall as soon as is reasonably practicable—
 (a) decide whether to approve the authorisation or refuse approval, and
 (b) give written notice of his decision to the person who gave the authorisation.

(5) A Commissioner shall approve an authorisation if, and only if, he is satisfied that there are reasonable grounds for believing the matters specified in section 93(2).

(6) Where a Commissioner refuses to approve an authorisation, he shall, as soon as is reasonably practicable, make a report of his findings to the authorising officer who gave it or in whose absence it was given (and paragraph 7 of Schedule 7 shall apply for the purposes of this subsection as it applies for the purposes of that Schedule).

(7) This section shall apply in relation to a renewal of an authorisation as it applies in relation to an authorisation (the references in subsection (2)(a) and (b) to the authorisation being construed as references to the authorisation renewed).

98. Matters subject to legal privilege.
...

99. Confidential personal information.

(1) In section 97 "confidential personal information" means—
 (a) personal information which a person has acquired or created in the course of any trade, business, profession or other occupation or for the purposes of any paid or unpaid office, and which he holds in confidence, and
 (b) communications as a result of which personal information—
  (i) is acquired or created as mentioned in paragraph (a), and
  (ii) is held in confidence.

(2) For the purposes of this section "personal information" means information concerning an individual (whether living or dead) who can be identified from it and relating—
 (a) to his physical or mental health, or
 (b) to spiritual counselling or assistance given or to be given to him.

(3) A person holds information in confidence for the purposes of this section if he holds it subject—
 (a) to an express or implied undertaking to hold it in confidence, or
 (b) to a restriction on disclosure or an obligation of secrecy contained in any enactment (including an enactment contained in an Act passed after this Act).

100. Confidential journalistic material.

(1) In section 97 "confidential journalistic material" means—
 (a) material acquired or created for the purposes of journalism which—
  (i) is in the possession of persons who acquired or created it for those purposes,
  (ii) is held subject to an undertaking, restriction or obligation of the kind mentioned in section 99(3), and
  (iii) has been continuously held (by one or more persons) subject to such an undertaking, restriction or obligation since it was first acquired or created for the purposes of journalism, and

(b) communications as a result of which information is acquired for the purposes of journalism and held as mentioned in paragraph (a)(ii).

(2) For the purpose of subsection (1), a person who receives material, or acquires information, from someone who intends that the recipient shall use it for the purposes of journalism is to be taken to have acquired it for those purposes.

101. Code of practice.

(1) The Secretary of State shall issue a code of practice in connection with the performance of functions under this Part by persons other than Commissioners appointed under section 91.

...

(9) A failure on the part of any person to comply with any provision of a code of practice issued under this section shall not of itself render him liable to any criminal or civil proceedings.

(10) A code issued under this section shall be admissible in evidence in criminal and civil proceedings; and if any provision of such a code appears to the court or tribunal conducting the proceedings to be relevant to any question arising in the proceedings it shall be taken into account in determining that question.

Section 102(4)   SCHEDULE 7
INVESTIGATION OF COMPLAINTS BY COMMISSIONERS ETC.

5.—(1) Where the Commissioner gives a complainant notice that a determination in his favour has been made on the complaint, he may (whether or not he has exercised, or intends to exercise, any of the powers under section 103) direct the authorising officer who gave the authorisation, or in whose absence it was given, to pay the complainant such sum by way of compensation as may be specified in the direction.

PROTECTION FROM HARASSMENT ACT 1997
(1997, c. 40)

1. Prohibition of harassment.

(1) A person must not pursue a course of conduct—
   (a) which amounts to harassment of another, and
   (b) which he knows or ought to know amounts to harassment of the other.

(2) For the purposes of this section, the person whose course of conduct is in question ought to know that it amounts to harassment of another if a reasonable person in possession of the same information would think the course of conduct amounted to harassment of the other.

(3) Subsection (1) does not apply to a course of conduct if the person who pursued it shows—
   (a) that it was pursued for the purpose of presenting or detecting crime,
   (b) that it was pursued under any enactment or rule of law or to comply with any condition or requirement imposed by any person under any enactment, or
   (c) that in the particular circumstances the pursuit of the course of conduct was reasonable.

2. Offence of harassment.

(1) A person who pursues a course of conduct in breach of section 1 is guilty of an offence.

3. Civil remedy.

(1) An actual or apprehended breach of section 1 may be the subject of a claim in civil proceedings by the person who is or may be the victim of the course of conduct in question.

(2) On such a claim, damages may be awarded for (among other things) any anxiety caused by the harassment and any financial loss resulting from the harassment.

(3) Where—

(a) in such proceedings the High Court or a county court grants an injunction for the purpose of restraining the defendant from pursuing any conduct which amounts to harassment, and

(b) the plaintiff considers that the defendant has done anything which he is prohibited from doing by the injunction,

the plaintiff may apply for the issue of a warrant for the arrest of the defendant.

...

(5) The judge or district judge to whom an application under subsection (3) is made may only issue a warrant if—

(a) the application is substantiated on oath, and

(b) the judge or district judge has reasonable grounds for believing that the defendant has done anything which he is prohibited from doing by the injunction.

(6) Where—

(a) the High Court or a county court grants an injunction for the purpose mentioned in subsection (3)(a), and

(b) without reasonable excuse the defendant does anything which he is prohibited from doing by the injunction,

he is guilty of an offence.

4. Putting people in fear of violence.

(1) A person whose course of conduct causes another to fear, on at least two occasions, that violence will be used against him is guilty of an offence if he knows or ought to know that his course of conduct will cause the other so to fear on each of those occasions.

(2) For the purposes of this section, the person whose course of conduct is in question ought to know that it will cause another to fear that violence will be used against him on any occasion if a reasonable person in possession of the same information would think the course of conduct would cause the other so to fear on that occasion.

(3) It is a defence for a person charged with an offence under this section to show that—

(a) his course of conduct was pursued for the purpose of preventing or detecting crime,

(b) his course of conduct was pursued under any enactment or rule of law or to comply with any condition or requirement imposed by any person under any enactment, or

(c) the pursuit of his course of conduct was reasonable for the protection of himself or another or for the protection of his or another's property.

5. Restraining orders.

(1) A court sentencing or otherwise dealing with a person ("the defendant") convicted of an offence under section 2 or 4 may (as well as sentencing him or dealing with him in any other way) make an order under this section.

(2) The order may, for the purpose of protecting the victim of the offence, or any other person mentioned in the order, from further conduct which—

(a) amounts to harassment, or

(b) will cause a fear of violence,

prohibit the defendant from doing anything described in the order.

...

(5) If without reasonable excuse the defendant does anything which he is prohibited from doing by an order under this section, he is guilty of an offence.

7. Interpretation of this group of sections.
(1) This section applies for the interpretation of sections 1 to 5.
(2) References to harassing a person include alarming the person or causing the person distress.
(3) A "course of conduct" must involve conduct on at least two occasions.
(4) "Conduct" includes speech.

12. National security, etc.
(1) If the Secretary of State certifies that in his opinion anything done by a specified person on a specified occasion related to—
   (a) national security,
   (b) the economic well-being of the United Kingdom, or
   (c) the prevention or detection of serious crime,
and was done on behalf of the Crown, the certificate is conclusive evidence that this Act does not apply to any conduct of that person on that occasion.

SOCIAL SECURITY (RECOVERY OF BENEFITS) ACT 1997
(1997, c. 27)

1. Cases in which this Act applies.
(1) This Act applies in cases where—
   (a) a person makes a payment (whether on his own behalf or not) to or in respect of any other person in consequence of any accident, injury or disease suffered by the other, and
   (b) any listed benefits have been, or are likely to be, paid to or for the other during the relevant period in respect of the accident, injury or disease.
(2) The reference above to a payment in consequence of any accident, injury or disease is to a payment made—
   (a) by or on behalf of a person who is, or is alleged to be, liable to any extent in respect of the accident, injury or disease, or
   (b) in pursuance of a compensation scheme for motor accidents;
but does not include a payment mentioned in Part I of Schedule 1.
(3) Subsection (1)(a) applies to a payment made—
   (a) voluntarily, or in pursuance of a court order or an agreement, or otherwise, and
   (b) in the United Kingdom or elsewhere.
(4) In a case where this Act applies—
   (a) the "injured person" is the person who suffered the accident, injury or disease,
   (b) the "compensation payment" is the payment within subsection (1)(a), and
   (c) "recoverable benefit" is any listed benefit which has been or is likely to be paid as mentioned in subsection (1)(b).

2. Compensation payments to which this Act applies.
This Act applies in relation to compensation payments made on or after the day on which this section comes into force, unless they are made in pursuance of a court order or agreement made before that day.

3. "The relevant period".
(1) In relation to a person ("the claimant") who has suffered any accident, injury or disease, "the relevant period" has the meaning given by the following subsections.
(2) Subject to subsection (4), if it is a case of accident or injury, the relevant period is the period of five years immediately following the day on which the accident or injury in question occurred.

(3) Subject to subsection (4), if it is a case of disease, the relevant period is the period of five years beginning with the date on which the claimant first claims a listed benefit in consequence of the disease.

(4) If at any time before the end of the period referred to in subsection (2) or (3)—

(a) a person makes a compensation payment in final discharge of any claim made by or in respect of the claimant and arising out of the accident, injury or disease, or

(b) an agreement is made under which an earlier compensation payment is treated as having been made in final discharge of any such claim,

the relevant period ends at that time.

4. Applications for certificates of recoverable benefits.

(1) Before a person ("the compensator") makes a compensation payment he must apply to the Secretary of State for a certificate of recoverable benefits.

...

5. Information contained in certificates.

(1) A certificate of recoverable benefits must specify, for each recoverable benefit—

(a) the amount which has been or is likely to have been paid on or before a specified date, and

(b) if the benefit is paid or likely to be paid after the specified date, the rate and period for which, and the intervals at which, it is or is likely to be so paid.

(2) In a case where the relevant period has ended before the day on which the Secretary of State receives the application for the certificate, the date specified in the certificate for the purposes of subsection (1) must be the day on which the relevant period ended.

(3) In any other case, the date specified for those purposes must not be earlier than the day on which the Secretary of State received the application.

(4) The Secretary of State may estimate, in such manner as he thinks fit, any of the amounts, rates or periods specified in the certificate.

(5) Where the Secretary of State issues a certificate of recoverable benefits, he must provide the information contained in the certificate to—

(a) the person who appears to him to be the injured person, or

(b) any person who he thinks will receive a compensation payment in respect of the injured person.

(6) A person to whom a certificate of recoverable benefits is issued or who is provided with information under subsection (5) is entitled to particulars of the manner in which any amount, rate or period specified in the certificate has been determined, if he applies to the Secretary of State for those particulars.

6. Liability to pay Secretary of State amount of benefits.

(1) A person who makes a compensation payment in any case is liable to pay to the Secretary of State an amount equal to the total amount of the recoverable benefits.

(2) The liability referred to in subsection (1) arises immediately before the compensation payment or, if there is more than one, the first of them is made.

(3) No amount becomes payable under this section before the end of the period of 14 days following the day on which the liability arises.

(4) Subject to subsection (3), an amount becomes payable under this section at the end of the period of 14 days beginning with the day on which a certificate of recoverable benefits is first issued showing that the amount of recoverable benefit to which it relates has been or is likely to have been paid before a specified date.

7. Recovery of payments due under section 6.

(1) This section applies where a person has made a compensation payment but—

(a) has not applied for a certificate of recoverable benefits, or

(b) has not made a payment to the Secretary of State under section 6 before the end of the period allowed under that section.

(2) The Secretary of State may—

(a) issue the person who made the compensation payment with a certificate of recoverable benefits, if none has been issued, or

(b) issue him with a copy of the certificate of recoverable benefits or (if more than one has been issued) the most recent one,

and (in either case) issue him with a demand that payment of any amount due under section 6 be made immediately.

(3) The Secretary of State may, in accordance with subsections (4) and (5), recover the amount for which a demand for payment is made under subsection (2) from the person who made the compensation payment.

(4) If the person who made the compensation payment resides or carries on business in England and Wales and a county court so orders, any amount recoverable under subsection (3) is recoverable by execution issued from the county court or otherwise as if it were payable under an order of that court.

(5) If the person who made the payment resides or carries on business in Scotland, any amount recoverable under subsection (3) may be enforced in like manner as an extract registered decree arbitral bearing a warrant for execution issued by the sheriff court of any sheriffdom in Scotland.

(6) A document bearing a certificate which—

(a) is signed by a person authorised to do so by the Secretary of State, and

(b) states that the document, apart from the certificate, is a record of the amount recoverable under subsection (3),

is conclusive evidence that that amount is so recoverable.

(7) A certificate under subsection (6) purporting to be signed by a person authorised to do so by the Secretary of State is to be treated as so signed unless the contrary is proved.

8. Reduction of compensation payment.

(1) This section applies in a case where, in relation to any head of compensation listed in column 1 of Schedule 2—

(a) any of the compensation payment is attributable to the head, and

(b) any recoverable benefit is shown against that head in column 2 of the Schedule.

(2) In such a case, any claim of a person to receive the compensation payment is to be treated for all purposes as discharged if—

(a) he is paid the amount (if any) of the compensation payment calculated in accordance with this section, and

(b) if the amount of the compensation payment so calculated is nil, he is given a statement saying so by the person who (apart from this section) would have paid the gross amount of the compensation payment.

(3) For each head of compensation listed in column 1 of the Schedule for which paragraphs (a) and (b) of subsection (1) are met, so much of the gross amount of the compensation payment as is attributable to that head is to be reduced (to nil, if necessary) by deducting the amount of the recoverable benefit or, as the case may be, the aggregate amount of the recoverable benefits shown against it.

(4) Subsection (3) is to have effect as if a requirement to reduce a payment by deducting an amount which exceeds the payment were a requirement to reduce that payment to nil.

(5) The amount of the compensation payment calculated in accordance with this section is—

(a) the gross amount of the compensation payment,

less

(b) the sum of the reductions made under subsection (3),
(and, accordingly, the amount may be nil).

9. Section 8: supplementary.

(1) A person who makes a compensation payment calculated in accordance with section 8 must inform the person to whom the payment is made—
   (a) that the payment has been so calculated, and
   (b) of the date for payment by reference to which the calculation has been made.

(2) If the amount of a compensation payment calculated in accordance with section 8 is nil, a person giving a statement saying so is to be treated for the purposes of this Act as making a payment within section 1(1)(a) on the day on which he gives the statement.

(3) Where a person—
   (a) makes a compensation payment calculated in accordance with section 8, and
   (b) if the amount of the compensation payment so calculated is nil, gives a statement saying so,
he is to be treated, for the purpose of determining any rights and liabilities in respect of contribution or indemnity, as having paid the gross amount of the compensation payment.

(4) For the purposes of this Act—
   (a) the gross amount of the compensation payment is the amount of the compensation payment apart from section 8, and
   (b) the amount of any recoverable benefit is the amount determined in accordance with the certificate of recoverable benefits.

10. Review of certificates of recoverable benefits.

(1) The Secretary of Satte may review any certificate of recoverable benefits if he is satisfied—
   (a) that it was issued in ignorance of, or was based on a mistake as to, a material fact, or
   (b) that a mistake (whether in computation or otherwise) has occurred in its preparation.

(2) On a review under this section the Secretary of State may either—
   (a) confirm the certificate, or
   (b) (subject to subsection (3)) issue a fresh certificate containing such variations as he considers appropriate.

(3) The Secretary of State may not vary the certificate so as to increase the total amount of the recoverable benefits unless it appears to him that the variation is required as a result of the person who applied for the certificate supplying him with incorrect or insufficient information.

11. Appeals against certificates of recoverable benefits.

(1) An appeal against a certificate of recoverable benefits may be made on the ground—
   (a) that any amount, rate or period specified in the certificate is incorrect, or
   (b) that listed benefits which have been, or are likely to be, paid otherwise than in respect of the accident, injury or disease in question have been brought into account.

(2) An appeal under this section may be made by—
   (a) the person who applied for the certificate of recoverable benefits, or
   (b) (in a case where the amount of the compensation payment has been calculated under section 8) the injured person or other person to whom the payment is made.

(3) No appeal may be made under this section until—
   (a) the claim giving rise to the compensation payment has been finally disposed of, and
   (b) the liability under section 6 has been discharged.

Social Security (Recovery of Benefits) Act 1997

(4) For the purposes of subsection (3)(a), if an award of damages in respect of a claim has been made under or by virtue of—
  (a) section 32A(2)(a) of the Supreme Court Act 1981,
  (b) section 12(2)(a) of the Administration of Justice Act 1982, or
  (c) section 51(2)(a) of the County Courts Act 1984,
(orders for provisional damages in personal injury cases), the claim is to be treated as having been finally disposed of.

(5) Regulations may make provision—
  (a) as to the manner in which, and the time within which, appeals under this section may be made,
  (b) as to the procedure to be followed where such an appeal is made, and
  (c) for the purpose of enabling any such appeal to be treated as an application for review under section 10.

(6) Regulations under subsection (5)(c) may (among other things) provide that the circumstances in which a review may be carried out are not to be restricted to those specified in section 10(1).

12. Reference of questions to medical appeal tribunal.

(1) The Secretary of State must refer to a medical appeal tribunal any question mentioned in subsection (2) arising for determination on an appeal under section 11.

(2) The questions are any concerning—
  (a) any amount, rate or period specified in the certificate of recoverable benefits, or
  (b) whether listed benefits which have been, or are likely to be, paid otherwise than in respect of the accident, injury or disease in question have been brought into account.

(3) In determining any question referred to it under subsection (1), the tribunal must take into account any decision of a court relating to the same, or any similar, issue arising in connection with the accident, injury or disease in question.

(4) On a reference under subsection (1) a medical appeal tribunal may either—
  (a) confirm the amounts, rates and periods specified in the certificate of recoverable benefits, or
  (b) specify any variations which are to be made on the issue of a fresh certificate under subsection (5).

(5) When the Secretary of State has received the decisions of the tribunal on the questions referred to it under subsection (1), he must in accordance with those decisions either—
  (a) confirm the certificate against which the appeal was brought, or
  (b) issue a fresh certificate.

(6) Regulations may make provision—
  (a) as to the manner in which, and the time within which, a reference under subsection (1) is to be made, and
  (b) as to the procedure to be followed where such a reference is made.

(7) Regulations under subsection (6)(b) may (among other things) provide for the non-disclosure of medical advice or medical evidence given or submitted following a reference under subsection (1).

(8) In this section "medical appeal tribunal" means a medical appeal tribunal constituted under section 50 of the Social Security Administration Act 1992.

13. Appeal to Social Security Commissioner.

(1) An appeal may be made to a Commissioner against any decision of a medical appeal tribunal under section 12 on the ground that the decision was erroneous in point of law.

(2) An appeal under this section may be made by—

(a) the Secretary of State,
(b) the person who applied for the certificate of recoverable benefits, or
(c) (in a case where the amount of the compensation payment has been calculated in accordance with section 8) the injured person or other person to whom the payment is made.

14. Reviews and appeals: supplementary.

(1) This section applies in cases where a fresh certificate of recoverable benefits is issued as a result of a review under section 10 or an appeal under section 11.

(2) If—
(a) a person has made one or more payments to the Secretary of State under section 6, and
(b) in consequence of the review or appeal, it appears that the total amount paid is more than the amount that ought to have been paid,
regulations may provide for the Secretary of State to pay the difference to that person, or to the person to whom the compensation payment is made, or partly to one and partly to the other.

(3) If—
(a) a person has made one or more payments to the Secretary of State under section 6, and
(b) in consequence of the review or appeal, it appears that the total amount paid is less than the amount that ought to have been paid,
regulations may provide for that person to pay the difference to the Secretary of State.

(4) Regulations under this section may provide—
(a) for the re-calculation in accordance with section 8 of the amount of any compensation payment,
(b) for giving credit for amounts already paid, and
(c) for the payment by any person of any balance or the recovery from any person of any excess,
and may provide for any matter by modifying this Act.

15. Court orders.

(1) This section applies where a court makes an order for a compensation payment to be made in any case, unless the order is made with the consent of the injured person and the person by whom the payment is to be made.

(2) The court must, in the case of each head of compensation listed in column 1 of Schedule 2 to which any of the compensation payment is attributable, specify in the order the amount of the compensation payment which is attributable to that head.

16. Payments into court.

(1) Regulations may make provision (including provision modifying this Act) for any case in which a payment into court is made.

(2) The regulations may (among other things) provide—
(a) for the making of a payment into court to be treated in prescribed circumstances as the making of a compensation payment,
(b) for application for, and issue of, certificates of recoverable benefits, and
(c) for the relevant period to be treated as ending on a date determined in accordance with the regulations.

(3) Rules of court may make provision governing practice and procedure in such cases.

(4) This section does not extend to Scotland.

17. Benefits irrelevant to assessment of damages.

In assessing damages in respect of any accident, injury or disease, the amount of any listed benefits paid or likely to be paid is to be disregarded.

18. Lump sum and periodical payments.

(1) Regulations may make provision (including provision modifying this Act) for any case in which two or more compensation payments in the form of lump sums are made by the same person to or in respect of the injured person in consequence of the same accident, injury or disease.

(2) The regulations may (among other things) provide—
    (a) for the re-calculation in accordance with section 8 of the amount of any compensation payment,
    (b) for giving credit for amounts already paid, and
    (c) for the payment by any person of any balance or the recovery from any person of any excess.

(3) For the purposes of subsection (2), the regulations may provide for the gross amounts of the compensation payments to be aggregated and for—
    (a) the aggregate amount to be taken to be the gross amount of the compensation payment for the purposes of section 8,
    (b) so much of the aggregate amount as is attributable to a head of compensation listed in column 1 of Schedule 2 to be taken to be the part of the gross amount which is attributable to that head;
and for the amount of any recoverable benefit shown against any head in column 2 of that Schedule to be taken to be the amount determined in accordance with the most recent certificate of recoverable benefits.

(4) Regulations may make provision (including provision modifying this Act) for any case in which, in final settlement of the injured person's claim, an agreement is entered into for the making of—
    (a) periodical compensation payments (whether of an income or capital nature), or
    (b) periodical compensation payments and lump sum compensation payments.

(5) Regulations made by virtue of subsection (4) may (among other things) provide—
    (a) for the relevant period to be treated as ending at a prescribed time,
    (b) for the person who is to make the payments under the agreement to be treated for the purposes of this Act as if he had made a single compensation payment on a prescribed date.

(6) A periodical payment may be a compensation payment for the purposes of this section even though it is a small payment (as defined in Part II of Schedule 1).

19. Payments by more than one person.

(1) Regulations may make provision (including provision modifying this Act) for any case in which two or more persons ("the compensators") make compensation payments to or in respect of the same injured person in consequence of the same accident, injury or disease.

(2) In such a case, the sum of the liabilities of the compensators under section 6 is not to exceed the total amount of the recoverable benefits, and the regulations may provide for determining the respective liabilities under that section of each of the compensators.

(3) The regulations may (among other things) provide in the case of each compensator—
    (a) for determining or re-determining the part of the recoverable benefits which may be taken into account in his case,
    (b) for calculating or re-calculating in accordance with section 8 the amount of any compensation payment,
    (c) for giving credit for amounts already paid, and
    (d) for the payment by any person of any balance or the recovery from any person of any excess.

20. Amounts overpaid under section 6.

(1) Regulations may make provision (including provision modifying this Act) for cases where a person has paid to the Secretary of State under section 6 any amount ("the amount of the overpayment") which he was not liable to pay.

(2) The regulations may provide—

(a) for the Secretary of State to pay the amount of the overpayment to that person, or to the person to whom the compensation payment is made, or partly to one and partly to the other, or

(b) for the receipt by the Secretary of State of the amount of the overpayment to be treated as the recovery of that amount.

(3) Regulations made by virtue of subsection (2)(b) are to have effect in spite of anything in section 71 of the Social Security Administration Act 1992 (overpayments—general).

(4) The regulations may also (among other things) provide—

(a) for the re-calculation in accordance with section 8 of the amount of any compensation payment,

(b) for giving credit for amounts already paid, and

(c) for the payment by any person of any balance or the recovery from any person of any excess.

(5) This section does not apply in a case where section 14 applies.

21. Compensation payments to be disregarded.

(1) If, when a compensation payment is made, the first and second conditions are met, the payment is to be disregarded for the purposes of sections 6 and 8.

(2) The first condition is that the person making the payment—

(a) has made an application for a certificate of recoverable benefits which complies with subsection (3), and

(b) has in his possession a written acknowledgement of the receipt of his application.

(3) An application complies with this subsection if it—

(a) accurately states the prescribed particulars relating to the injured person and the accident, injury or disease in question, and

(b) specifies the name and address of the person to whom the certificate is to be sent.

(4) The second condition is that the Secretary of State has not sent the certificate to the person, at the address, specified in the application, before the end of the period allowed under section 4.

(5) In any case where—

(a) by virtue of subsection (1), a compensation payment is disregarded for the purposes of sections 6 and 8, but

(b) the person who made the compensation payment nevertheless makes a payment to the Secretary of State for which (but for subsection (1)) he would be liable under section 6,

subsection (1) is to cease to apply in relation to the compensation payment.

(6) If, in the opinion of the Secretary of State, circumstances have arisen which adversely affect normal methods of communication—

(a) he may by order provide that subsection (1) is not to apply during a specified period not exceeding three months, and

(b) he may continue any such order in force for further periods not exceeding three months at a time.

22. Liability of insurers.

(1) If a compensation payment is made in a case where—

(a) a person is liable to any extent in respect of the accident, injury or disease, and

(b) the liability is covered to any extent by a policy of insurance,
the policy is also to be treated as covering any liability of that person under section 6.

(2) Liability imposed on the insurer by subsection (1) cannot be excluded or restricted.

(3) For that purpose excluding or restricting liability includes—
   (a) making the liability or its enforcement subject to restrictive or onerous conditions,
   (b) excluding or restricting any right or remedy in respect of the liability, or subjecting a person to any prejudice in consequence of his pursuing any such right or remedy, or
   (c) excluding or restricting rules of evidence or procedure.

(4) Regulations may in prescribed cases limit the amount of the liability imposed on the insurer by subsection (1).

(5) This section applies to policies of insurance issued before (as well as those issued after) its coming into force.

(6) References in this section to policies of insurance and their issue include references to contracts of insurance and their making.

23. Provision of information.

(1) Where compensation is sought in respect of any accident, injury or disease suffered by any person ("the injured person"), the following persons must give the Secretary of State the prescribed information about the injured person—
   (a) anyone who is, or is alleged to be, liable in respect of the accident, injury or disease, and
   (b) anyone acting on behalf of such a person.

(2) A person who receives or claims a listed benefit which is or is likely to be paid in respect of an accident, injury or disease suffered by him, must give the Secretary of State the prescribed information about the accident, injury or disease.

(3) Where a person who has received a listed benefit dies, the duty in subsection (2) is imposed on his personal representative.

(4) Any person who makes a payment (whether on his own behalf or not)—
   (a) in consequence of, or
   (b) which is referable to any costs (in Scotland, expenses) incurred by reason of,
any accident, injury or disease, or any damage to property, must, if the Secretary of State requests him in writing to do so, give the Secretary of State such particulars relating to the size and composition of the payment as are specified in the request.

(5) The employer of a person who suffers or has suffered an accident, injury or disease, and anyone who has been the employer of such a person at any time during the relevant period, must give the Secretary of State the prescribed information about the payment of statutory sick pay in respect of that person.

(6) In subsection (5) "employer" has the same meaning as it has in Part XI of the Social Security Contributions and Benefits Act 1992.

(7) A person who is required to give information under this section must do so in the prescribed manner, at the prescribed place and within the prescribed time.

(8) Section 1 does not apply in relation to this section.

24. Power to amend Schedule 2.

(1) The Secretary of State may by regulations amend Schedule 2.

(2) A statutory instrument which contains such regulations shall not be made unless a draft of the instrument has been laid before and approved by resolution of each House of Parliament.

28. The Crown.

This Act applies to the Crown.

29. General interpretation.

In this Act—

"benefit" means any benefit under the Social Security Contributions and Benefits Act 1992, a jobseeker's allowance or mobility allowance,

"compensation scheme for motor accidents" means any scheme or arrangement under which funds are available for the payment of compensation in respect of motor accidents caused, or alleged to have been caused, by uninsured or unidentified persons,

"listed benefit" means a benefit listed in column 2 of Schedule 2,

"payment" means payment in money or money's worth, and related expressions are to be interpreted accordingly,

"prescribed" means prescribed by regulations, and

"regulations" means regulations made by the Secretary of State.

30. Regulations and orders.

(1) Any power under this Act to make regulations or an order is exercisable by statutory instrument.

(2) A statutory instrument containing regulations or an order under this Act (other than regulations under section 24 or an order under section 34) shall be subject to annulment in pursuance of a resolution of either House of Parliament.

(3) Regulations under section 20, under section 24 amending the list of benefits in column 2 of Schedule 2 or under paragraph 9 of Schedule 1 may not be made without the consent of the Treasury.

(4) Subsections (4), (5), (6) and (9) of section 189 of the Social Security Administration Act 1992 (regulations and orders — general) apply for the purposes of this Act as they apply for the purposes of that.

31. Financial arrangements.

(1) There are to be paid out of the National Insurance Fund any expenses of the Secretary of State in making payments under section 14 or 20 to the extent that he estimates that those payments relate to sums paid out of that Fund.

(2) There are to be paid out of money provided by Parliament—

   (a) any expenses of the Secretary of State in making payments under section 14 or 20 to the extent that he estimates that those payments relate to sums paid out of the Consolidated Fund, and

   (b) (subject to subsection (1)) any other expenses of the Secretary of State incurred in consequence of this Act.

(3) Any sums paid to the Secretary of State under section 6 or 14 are to be paid—

   (a) into the Consolidated Fund, to the extent that the Secretary of State estimates that the sums relate to payments out of money provided by Parliament, and

   (b) into the National Insurance Fund, to the extent that he estimates that they relate to payments out of that Fund.

32. Power to make transitional, consequential etc. provisions.

(1) Regulations may make such transitional and consequential provisions, and such savings, as the Secretary of State considers necessary or expedient in preparation for, in connection with, or in consequence of—

   (a) the coming into force of any provision of this Act, or

   (b) the operation of any enactment repealed or amended by a provision of this Act during any period when the repeal or amendment is not wholly in force.

(2) Regulations under this section may (among other things) provide—

(a) for compensation payments in relation to which, by virtue of section 2, this Act does not apply to be treated as payments in relation to which this Act applies,

(b) for compensation payments in relation to which, by virtue of section 2, this Act applies to be treated as payments in relation to which this Act does not apply, and

(c) for the modification of any enactment contained in this Act or referred to in subsection (1)(b) in its application to any compensation payment.

SCHEDULES

Section 1

SCHEDULE 1

COMPENSATION PAYMENTS
PART I
EXEMPTED PAYMENTS

1. Any small payment (defined in Part II of this Schedule).

2. Any payment made to or for the injured person under section 35 of the Powers of Criminal Courts Act 1973 or section 249 of the Criminal Procedure (Scotland) Act 1995 (compensation orders against convicted persons).

3. Any payment made in the exercise of a discretion out of property held subject to a trust in a case where no more than 50 per cent. by value of the capital contributed to the trust was directly or indirectly provided by persons who are, or are alleged to be, liable in respect of—
    (a) the accident, injury or disease suffered by the injured person, or
    (b) the same or any connected accident, injury or disease suffered by another.

4. Any payment made out of property held for the purposes of any prescribed trust (whether the payment also falls within paragraph 3 or not).

5. Any payment made to the injured person by an insurance company within the meaning of the Insurance Companies Act 1982 under the terms of any contract of insurance entered into between the injured person and the company before—
    (a) the date on which the injured person first claims a listed benefit in consequence of the disease in question, or
    (b) the occurrence of the accident or injury in question.

6. Any redundancy payment falling to be taken into account in the assessment of damages in respect of an accident, injury or disease.

7. So much of any payment as is referable to costs.

8. Any prescribed payment.

PART II
POWER TO DISREGARD SMALL PAYMENTS

9.—(1) Regulations may make provision for compensation payments to be disregarded for the purposes of sections 6 and 8 in prescribed cases where the amount of the compensation payment, or the aggregate amount of two or more connected compensation payments, does not exceed the prescribed sum.

(2) A compensation payment disregarded by virtue of this paragraph is referred to in paragraph 1 as a "small payment".

(3) For the purposes of this paragraph—
    (a) two or more compensation payments are "connected" if each is made to or in respect of the same injured person and in respect of the same accident, injury or disease, and
    (b) any reference to a compensation payment is a reference to a payment which would be such a payment apart from paragraph 1.

Section 8 SCHEDULE 2

CALCULATION OF COMPENSATION PAYMENT

(1) Head of compensation	(2) Benefit
1. Compensation for earnings lost during the the relevant period	Disability working allowance Disablement pension payable under section 103 of the 1992 Act Incapacity benefit Income support Invalidity pension and allowance Jobseeker's allowance Reduced earnings allowance Severe disablement allowance Sickness benefit Statutory sick pay Unemployability supplement Unemployment benefit
2. Compensation for cost of care incurred during the relevant period	Attendance allowance Care component of disability living allowance Disablement pension increase payable under section 104 or 105 of the 1992 Act
3. Compensation for loss of mobility during the relevant period	Mobility allowance Mobility component of disability living allowance

Notes

1.—(1) References to incapacity benefit, invalidity pension and allowance, severe disablement allowance, sickness benefit and unemployment benefit also include any income support paid with each of those benefits on the same instrument of payment or paid concurrently with each of those benefits by means of an instrument for benefit payment.

(2) For the purpose of this Note, income support includes personal expenses addition, special transitional additions and transitional addition as defined in the Income Support (Transitional) Regulations 1987.

2. Any reference to statutory sick pay—

    (a) includes only 80 per cent. of payments made between 6 April 1991 and 5 April 1994, and

    (b) does not include payments made on or after 6 April 1994.

3. In this Schedule "the 1992 Act" means the Social Security Contributions and Benefits Act 1992.

PART II
PROPOSED STATUTES

(DRAFT) CONTRIBUTORY NEGLIGENCE BILL
(Law Com. No. 219)

A Bill to provide for reducing the damages recoverable for breach of a contractual duty to take reasonable care or exercise reasonable skill in cases where the claimant's failure to take reasonable care has contributed to the damage suffered by him. [1993]

1. Contributory negligence in claims for breach of contract.

(1) Where by virtue of an express or implied term of a contract a party is under a duty to take reasonable care or exercise reasonable skill or both in the performance of the contract and the party to whom that duty is owed suffers damage as the result—

 (a) partly of a breach of that duty; and
 (b) partly of his own failure to take reasonable care for the protection of himself or his interests,

the damages recoverable by that party on a claim in respect of the damage shall be reduced to such extent as the court thinks just and equitable having regard to the claimant's share in the responsibility for the damage.

(2) Subsection (1) above does not apply if the parties have agreed (in whatever terms and whether expressly or by implication) that the damages for breach of the contract are not to be reduced as there mentioned, for example by specifying a sum payable in the event of breach and constituting liquidated damages.

(3) Where subsection (1) above applies the court, in deciding whether and, if so, to what extent the damages recoverable by the claimant are to be reduced—

 (a) shall disregard anything done or omitted by him before the contract was entered into; but
 (b) shall have regard to the nature of the contract and the mutual obligations of the parties,

and in other respects shall apply the like principles as those applicable under section 1(1) of the Law Reform (Contributory Negligence) Act 1945.

(4) Where the damages recoverable by any person are reduced by virtue of subsection (1) above the court shall find and record what the damages would have been without the reduction.

(5) In subsection (1) above references to the party by or to whom the duty under the contract is owed include references to any person subject to, or entitled to the performance of, that duty by virtue of assignment or otherwise.

(6) In this section "the court" means, in relation to any claim, the court or arbitrator by whom the claim falls to be determined and "damage" includes loss of life and personal injury.

2. Consequential amendments.

(1) In section 4(3) of the Crown Proceedings Act 1947 (Crown bound by Law Reform (Contributory Negligence) Act 1945) after "1945" there shall be inserted "and the Contributory Negligence Act 1993".

(2) In section 5 of the Fatal Accidents Act 1976 (reduction of damages under that Act if Law Reform (Contributory Negligence) Act 1945 would have reduced the damages recoverable in an action brought for the benefit of the deceased's estate) there shall be added at the end "and likewise if the damages in an action so brought would be reduced under section 1(1) of the Contributory Negligence Act 1993".

(3) In section 2(3)(b) of the Civil Liability (Contribution) Act 1978 (limit on liability of contributor) after "the Law Reform (Contributory Negligence) Act 1945" there shall be inserted ", the Contributory Negligence Act 1993".

3. Short title, commencement, saving and extent.

(1) This Act may be cited as the Contributory Negligence Act 1993.

(2) This Act comes into force at the end of the period of two months beginning with the day on which it is passed.

(3) This Act does not apply to any contract entered into before the coming into force of this Act.

(4) This Act does not extend to Scotland or Northern Ireland.

(DRAFT) RESTITUTION (MISTAKES OF LAW) BILL
(Law Com. No. 227)

An Act to make provision in relation to claims made in any proceedings for restitution in respect of acts done under mistake. [1994]

1. Claims to which Act applies.

(1) In this Act "mistake claim" means a claim made in any proceedings for restitution of a sum in respect of an act done under mistake.

(2) In this Act "act" includes anything which may found a claim for restitution, that is to say, the making of a payment, the conferring of a non-pecuniary benefit or the doing of work.

2. Abrogation of mistake of law rule.

The classification of a mistake as a mistake of law or as a mistake of fact shall not of itself be material to the determination of a mistake claim; and no such claim shall be denied on the ground that the alleged mistake is a mistake of law.

3. Effect on mistake claim of judicial change in the law.

(1) An act done in accordance with a settled view of the law shall not be regarded as founding a mistake claim by reason only that a subsequent decision of a court or tribunal departs from that view.

(2) A view of the law may be regarded for the purposes of this section as having been settled at any time notwithstanding that it was not held unanimously or had not been the subject of a decision by a court or tribunal.

4. Savings.

(1) This Act does not affect any mistake claim (whenever made) in respect of an act done before the date on which this Act comes into force.

(2) Without prejudice to the generality of subsection (1), nothing in this Act shall be taken to affect any question as to the existence or operation before that date of any

rule whereby a mistake claim would be denied by reason of the alleged mistake being a mistake of law.

(3) An enactment which has the effect of excluding or restricting the right to bring a mistake claim in any particular circumstances shall have the same effect on any right to bring a mistake claim in those circumstances that may arise by virtue of section 2.

(4) In subsection (3) "enactment" includes an enactment comprised in subordinate legislation within the meaning of the Interpretation Act 1978.

5. Short title, commencement and extent.

(1) This Act may be cited as the Restitution (Mistakes of Law) Act 1994.

(2) This Act shall come into force on such day as the Lord Chancellor may appoint by order made by statutory instrument.

(3) This Act extends to England and Wales only.

(DRAFT) CONTRACTS (RIGHTS OF THIRD PARTIES) BILL
(Law Com. No. 242)

An Act to make provision for the enforcement of a contract in certain circumstances by a person who is not a party to the contract; and for connected purposes. [1996]

1. Right of third party to enforce contract.

(1) Subject to the provisions of this Act, a person who is not a party to a contract (in this Act referred to as a third party) may in his own right enforce the contract if—

    (a) the contract contains an express term to that effect; or

    (b) subject to subsection (2) below, the contract purports to confer a benefit on the third party.

(2) Subsection (1)(b) above does not apply if on a proper construction of the contract it appears that the parties did not intend the contract to be enforceable by the third party.

(3) The third party must be expressly identified in the contract by name, as a member of a class or as answering a particular description but need not be in existence when the contract is entered into.

(4) For the purpose of exercising the rights conferred on him by this section there shall be available to the third party all such remedies as would have been available to him in an action for breach of the contract if he had been a party to it, and the rules relating to damages, injunctions, specific performance and other relief shall apply accordingly.

(5) Where the contract excludes or limits the third party's liability in relation to any matter references in this Act to his enforcing it shall be construed as references to his availing himself of the exclusion or limitation.

(6) In this Act "the promisor" means the party to the contract against whom it is enforceable by the third party by virtue of this section and "the promisee" means the party to the contract by whom it is enforceable against the promisor.

2. Variation and cancellation of contract.

(1) Subject to the provisions of this section, where a contract is enforceable by a third party by virtue of section 1 above the parties to the contract may not without his consent vary or cancel the contract if—

    (a) the third party has communicated his assent to the contract to the promisor;

    (b) the promisor is aware that the third party has relied on the contract; or

    (c) the promisor can reasonably be expected to have foreseen that the third party would rely on the contract and the third party has in fact relied on it.

(2) The assent referred to in subsection (1)(a) above—

    (a) may be by words or conduct; and

    (b) if sent to the promisor by post or other means, shall not be regarded as communicated to the promisor until received by him.

(3) A contract which is enforceable by a third party by virtue of section 1 above may expressly provide—
   (a) that it shall be capable of cancellation or variation without the consent of the third party; or
   (b) that his consent is to be required in circumstances specified in the contract instead of those specified in subsection (1) above.
(4) Where by virtue of the foregoing provisions of this section the consent of a third party is required for the cancellation or variation of a contract the court may, on the application of the parties to the contract, dispense with that consent if satisfied—
   (a) that the third party's consent cannot be obtained because his whereabouts cannot reasonably be ascertained; or
   (b) that he is mentally incapable of giving his consent.
(5) The court may, on the application of the parties to a contract, dispense with any consent to a variation or cancellation of the contract that may be required by virtue of subsection (1)(c) above if satisfied that it cannot reasonably be ascertained whether or not the third party has in fact relied on the contract.
(6) Where the court dispenses with a third party's consent it may impose such conditions as it thinks fit, including a condition requiring the payment of compensation to the third party.
(7) The jurisdiction conferred by subsection (4) to (6) above shall be exercisable both by the High Court and a county court.

3. Defences etc. available to promisor.

(1) Subsections (2) to (5) below apply where in reliance on section 1 above proceedings for the enforcement of a contract are brought by a third party.
(2) The promisor shall have available to him by way of defence or set-off any matter that—
   (a) arises from or in connection with the contract; and
   (b) would have been available to him by way of defence or set-off in proceedings for the enforcement of the contract if those proceedings had been brought by the promisee.
(3) Subsection (2) above is subject to any express term of the contract as to the matters that are not to be available to the promisor by way of defence or set-off, and is without prejudice to any express term of the contract which makes available to the promisor by way of defence or set-off any other matter which would have been so available in proceedings for the enforcement of the contract had they been brought by the promisee.
(4) The promisor shall also have available to him—
   (a) by way of defence or set-off any matter, and
   (b) by way of counterclaim any matter not arising from the contract,
that would have been available to him by way of defence or set-off or, as the case may be, by way of counterclaim against the third party if the third party had been a party to the contract.
(5) Subsection (4) above is subject to any express term of the contract as to the matters that are not to be available to the promisor by way of defence, set-off or counterclaim.
(6) Where in any proceedings brought against him a third party seeks in reliance on section 1 above to enforce a contract (including, in particular, a contract purporting to exclude or limit any liability of his), he may not do so to the extent that he could not have done so (whether by reason of any particular circumstances relating to him or otherwise) if he had been a party to the contract.

4. Enforcement of contract by promisee.

Section 1 above is without prejudice to any right of the promisee to enforce the contract.

5. **Protection of promisor from double liability.**
Where by virtue of section 1 above a contract is enforceable by a third party, and the promisee has recovered from the promisor a sum in respect of—
   (a) the third party's loss in respect of the contract, or
   (b) the expense to the promisee of making good to the third party the default of the promisor,
then, in any proceedings brought by virtue of that section by the third party, the court shall reduce any award to the third party to such extent as it thinks appropriate to take account of the sum recovered by the promisee.

6. **Supplementary provisions relating to third party.**
   (1) Section 1 above is without prejudice to any right or remedy of a third party which exists or is available apart from this Act.
   (2) Section 1 above confers no rights on a third party in the case of—
      (a) a contract for the carriage of goods by sea, except that a third party may by virtue of that section avail himself of an exclusion or limitation of liability in such a contract;
      (b) a contract for the carriage of goods by rail or road, or for the carriage of cargo by air, which is subject to the rules of the appropriate international transport convention, except that a third party may by virtue of that section avail himself of an exclusion or limitation of liability in such a contract;
      (c) a contract contained in a bill of exchange, promissory note or other negotiable instrument;
      (d) an agreement to submit to arbitration present or future disputes; or
      (e) an agreement as to the court, or courts, which are to have jurisdiction to settle present or future disputes or are not to have such jurisdiction.
   (3) For the purposes of subsection (2) above—
      (a) "contract for the carriage of goods by sea" means a contract of carriage—
         (i) which is contained in or evidenced by a bill of lading or sea waybill to which the Carriage of Goods by Sea Act 1992 applies; or
         (ii) under, or for the purposes of, which there is given an undertaking which is contained in a ship's delivery order to which that Act applies;
      (b) "the appropriate international transport convention"—
         (i) in relation to a contract for the carriage of goods by rail, means the Convention which has force of law in the United Kingdom by virtue of section 1 of the International Transport Conventions Act 1983;
         (ii) in relation to a contract for the carriage of goods by road, means the Convention which has force of law in the United Kingdom by virtue of section 1 of the Carriage of Goods by Road Act 1965; and
         (iii) in relation to a contract for the carriage of cargo by air, means the Convention which has force of law in the United Kingdom by virtue of section 1 of the Carriage by Air Act 1961 or the Convention which has such force by virtue of section 1 of the Carriage by Air (Supplementary Provisions) Act 1962 (or either of the amended Conventions set out in Part B of Schedule 2 to the Carriage by Air Acts (Application of Provisions) Order 1967).
   (4) Section 2(2) of the Unfair Contract Terms Act 1977 (restriction on exclusion etc. of liability for negligence) shall not apply where the negligence consists of the breach of an obligation arising from the terms of a contract and the person seeking to enforce them is a third party acting by virtue of section 1 above.
   (5) In sections 5 and 8 of the Limitation Act 1980 the references to an action founded on a simple contract and an action upon a specialty shall repectively include references to an action brought by virtue of section 1 above relating to a simple contract and an action brought by virtue of that section relating to a specialty.

(6) A third party shall not by virtue of section 1(4) or 3(4) or (6) above be treated, for the purposes of any other Act (or any instrument made under any Act), as a party to the contract.

7. Enforcement limited to particular provisions of contract.

(1) Section 1 above applies also where—

(a) the express term referred to in paragraph (a) of subsection (1) applies only to a particular provision of the contract; or

(b) it is only a particular provision of the contract that purports to confer a benefit as mentioned in paragraph (b) of that subsection.

(2) In any such case—

(a) references in this Act to the enforcement of the contract, or to a contract being enforceable, by a third party shall be construed as references to the enforcement of the particular provision in question, or to its being enforceable, by a third party; and

(b) the reference in section 3(2)(a) above to the contract shall be construed as a reference to the contract so far as relevant to that particular provision.

8. Joint promisee not providing consideration.

(1) Where the persons to whom a contractual promise is made include a person who does not provide consideration for the promise, that person shall not be treated as a third party for the purposes of this Act.

(2) Subsection (1) above is without prejudice to any right or remedy of such a person in relation to the contract which exists or is available apart from this Act.

9. Short title, commencement and extent.

(1) This Act may be cited as the Contracts (Rights of Third Parties) Act 1996.

(2) This Act comes into force at the end of the period of six months beginning with the day on which it is passed and does not apply in relation to contracts entered into before the end of that period.

(3) This Act extends to England and Wales only.

PART III
STATUTORY INSTRUMENTS

EMPLOYERS' LIABILITY (COMPULSORY INSURANCE) GENERAL REGULATIONS 1971
(SI 1971, No. 1117)

2. Prohibition of certain conditions in policies of insurance.

(1) Any condition in a policy of insurance issued or renewed in accordance with the requirements of the Act after the coming into operation of this Regulation which provides (in whatever terms) that no liability (either generally or in respect of a particular claim) shall arise under the policy, or that any such liability so arising shall cease—

(a) in the event of some specified thing being done or omitted to be done after the happening of the event giving rise to a claim under the policy;

(b) unless the policy holder takes reasonable care to protect his employees risk of bodily injury or disease in the course of their employment;

(c) unless the policy holder complies with the requirements of any enactment for the protection of employees against the risk of bodily injury or disease in the course of their employment; and

(d) unless the policy holder keeps specified records or provides the insurer with or makes available to him information therefrom,

is hereby prohibited for the purposes of the Act.

(2) Nothing in this Regulation shall be taken as prejudicing any provision in a policy requiring the policy holder to pay to the insurer any sums which the latter may have become liable to pay under the policy and which have been applied to the satisfaction of claims in respect of employees or any costs and expenses incurred in relation to such claims.

[3. Limit of amount of compulsory insurance.

(1) Subject to paragraph (2) below, the amount for which an employer is required by the Act to insure and maintain insurance shall be two million pounds in respect of claims relating to any one or more of his employees arising out of any one occurrence.]

CONSUMER TRANSACTIONS (RESTRICTIONS ON STATEMENTS) ORDER 1976
(SI 1976, No. 1813)

3. A person shall not, in the course of a business—

(a) display, at any place where consumer transactions are effected (whether wholly or partly), a notice containing a statement which purports to apply, in relation to consumer transactions effected there, a term which would—

[(i) be void by virtue of section 6 or 20 of the Unfair Contract Terms Act 1977]

(ii) be inconsistent with a warranty (in Scotland a stipulation) implied by section 4(1)(c) of the Trading Stamps Act 1964 or section 4(1)(c) of the Trading Stamps Act (Northern Ireland) 1965 both as amended by the Act of 1973,
if applied to some or all such consumer transactions;

(b) publish or cause to be published any advertisement which is intended to induce persons to enter into consumer transactions and which contains a statement purporting to apply in relation to such consumer transactions such a term as is mentioned in paragraph (a)(i) or (ii), being a term which would be void by virtue of, or as the case may be, inconsistent with, the provisions so mentioned if applied to some or all of those transactions;

(c) supply to a consumer pursuant to a consumer transaction goods bearing, or goods in a container bearing, a statement which is a term of that consumer transaction and which is void by virtue of, or inconsistent with, the said provisions, or if it were a term of that transaction, would be so void or inconsistent;

(d) furnish to a consumer in connection with the carrying out of a consumer transaction or to a person likely, as a consumer, to enter into such a transaction, a document which includes a statement which is a term of that transaction and is void or inconsistent as aforesaid, or, if it were a term of that transaction or were to become a term of a prospective transaction, would be so void or inconsistent.

4. A person shall not in the course of a business—

(i) supply to a consumer pursuant to a consumer transaction goods bearing, or goods in a container bearing, a statement about the rights that the consumer has against that person or about the obligations to the consumer accepted by that person in relation to the goods (whether legally enforceable or not), being rights or obligations that arise if the goods are defective or are not fit for a purpose or do not correspond with a description;

(ii) furnish to a consumer in connection with the carrying out of a consumer transaction or to a person likely, as a consumer, to enter into such a transaction with him or through his agency a document containing a statement about such rights and obligations, unless there is in close proximity to any such statement another statement which is clear and conspicuous and to the effect that the first mentioned statement does not or will not affect the statutory rights of a consumer.

5.—(1) This Article applies to goods which are supplied in the course of a business by one person ("the supplier") to another where, at the time of the supply, the goods were intended by the supplier to be, or might reasonably be expected by him to be, the subject of a subsequent consumer transaction.

(2) A supplier shall not—

(a) supply goods to which this Article applies if the goods bear, or are in a container bearing, a statement which sets all or describes or limits obligations (whether legally enforceable or not) accepted or to be accepted by him in relation to the goods, or

(b) furnish a document in relation to the goods which contains such a statement, unless there is in close proximity to any such statement another statement which is clear and conspicuous and to the effect that the first mentioned statement does not or will not affect the statutory rights of a consumer.

(3) A person does not contravene paragraph (2) above—

(i) in a case to which sub-paragraph (a) of that paragraph applies, unless the goods have become the subject of a consumer transaction;

(ii) in a case to which sub-paragraph (b) applies unless the document has been furnished to a consumer in relation to goods which were the subject of a consumer transaction, or to a person likely to become a consumer pursuant to such a transaction; or

(iii) by virtue of any statement if before the date on which this Article comes into operation the document containing, or the goods or container bearing, the statement has ceased to be in his possession.

TRANSFER OF UNDERTAKINGS (PROTECTION OF EMPLOYMENT) REGULATIONS 1981
(SI 1981, No. 1794)

5. Effect of relevant transfer on contracts of employment, etc.

(1) [Except where objection is made under paragraph (4A) below,] A relevant transfer shall not operate so as to terminate the contract of employment of any person employed by the transferor in the undertaking or part transferred but any such contract which would otherwise have been terminated by the transfer shall have effect after the transfer as if originally made between the person so employed and the transferee.

[(4A) Paragraphs (1) and (2) above shall not operate to transfer his contract of employment and the rights, powers, duties and liabilities under or in connection with it if the employee informs the transferor or the transferee that he objects to becoming employed by the transferee.

(4B) Where an employee so objects the transfer of the undertaking or part in which he is employed shall operate so as to terminate his contract of employment with the transferor but he shall not be treated, for any purpose, as having been dismissed by the transferor.]

PACKAGE TRAVEL, PACKAGE HOLIDAYS AND PACKAGE TOURS REGULATIONS 1992
(SI 1992, No. 3288)

2. Interpretation.

(1) In these Regulations—
"brochure" means any brochure in which packages are offered for sale;
"contract" means the agreement linking the consumer to the organiser or to the retailer, or to both, as the case may be;
"the Directive" means Council Directive 90/314/EEC on package travel, package holidays and package tours;
"offer" includes an invitation to treat whether by means of advertising or otherwise, and cognate expressions shall be construed accordingly;
"organiser" means the person who, otherwise than occasionally, organises packages and sells or offers them for sale, whether directly or through a retailer;
"the other party to the contract" means the party, other than the consumer, to the contract, that is, the organiser or the retailer, or both, as the case may be;
"package" means the pre-arranged combination of at least two of the following components when sold or offered for sale at an inclusive price and when the service covers a period of more than twenty-four hours or includes overnight accommodation—

    (a) transport;
    (b) accommodation;
    (c) other tourist services not ancillary to transport or accommodation and accounting for a significant proportion of the package,
and
    (i) the submission of separate accounts for different components shall not cause the arrangements to be other than a package;
    (ii) the fact that a combination is arranged at the request of the consumer and in accordance with his specific instructions (whether modified or not) shall not of itself cause it to be treated as other than pre-arranged;

and

"retailer" means the person who sells or offers for sale the package put together by the organiser.

(2) In the definition of "contract" in paragraph (1) above, "consumer" means the person who takes or agrees to take the package ("the principal contractor") and elsewhere in these Regulations "consumer" means, as the context requires, the principal contractor, any person on whose behalf the principal contractor agrees to purchase the package ("the other beneficiaries") or any person to whom the principal contractor or any of the other beneficiaries transfers the package ("the transferee").

3. Application of Regulations.

(1) These Regulations apply to packages sold or offered for sale in the territory of the United Kingdom.

4. Descriptive matter relating to packages must not be misleading.

(1) No organiser or retailer shall supply to a consumer any descriptive matter concerning a package, the price of a package or any other conditions applying to the contract which contains any misleading information.

(2) If an organiser or retailer is in breach of paragraph (1) he shall be liable to compensate the consumer for any loss which the consumer suffers in consequence.

5. Requirements as to brochures.

(1) Subject to paragraph (4) below, no organiser shall make available a brochure to a possible consumer unless it indicates in a legible, comprehensive and accurate manner the price and adequate information about the matters specified in Schedule 1 to these Regulations in respect of the packages offered for sale in the brochure to the extent that those matters are relevant to the packages so offered.

(2) Subject to paragraph (4) below, no retailer shall make available to a possible consumer a brochure which he knows or has reasonable cause to believe does not comply with the requirements of paragraph (1).

(3) An organiser who contravenes paragraph (1) of this regulation and a retailer who contravenes paragraph (2) thereof shall be guilty of an offence and liable—

    (a) on summary conviction, to a fine not exceeding level 5 on the standard scale; and

    (b) on conviction on indictment, to a fine.

(4) Where a brochure was first made available to consumers generally before 31 December 1992 no liability shall arise under this regulation in respect of an identical brochure being made available to a consumer at any time.

6. Circumstances in which particulars in brochure are to be binding.

(1) Subject to paragraphs (2) and (3) of this regulation, the particulars in the brochure (whether or not they are required by regulation 5(1) above to be included in the brochure) shall constitute implied warranties (or, as regards Scotland, implied terms) for the purposes of any contract to which the particulars relate.

(2) Paragraph (1) of this regulation does not apply—

    (a) in relation to information required to be included by virtue of paragraph 9 of Schedule 1 to these Regulations; or

    (b) where the brochure contains an express statement that changes may be made in the particulars contained in it before a contract is concluded and changes in the particulars so contained are clearly communicated to the consumer before a contract is concluded.

(3) Paragraph (1) of this regulation does not apply when the consumer and the other party to the contract agree after the contract has been made that the particulars in the brochure, or some of those particulars, should not form part of the contract.

7. Information to be provided before contract is concluded.

(1) Before a contract is concluded, the other party to the contract shall provide the intending consumer with the information specified in paragraph (2) below in writing or in some other appropriate form.

(2) The information referred to in paragraph (1) is—

    (a) general information about passport and visa requirements which apply to British Citizens who purchase the package in question, including information about the length of time it is likely to take to obtain the appropriate passports and visas;

    (b) information about health formalities required for the journey and the stay; and

    (c) the arrangements for security for the money paid over and (where applicable) for the repatriation of the consumer in the event of insolvency.

(3) If the intending consumer is not provided with the information required by paragraph (1) in accordance with that paragraph the other party to the contract shall be guilty of an offence and liable—

    (a) on summary conviction, to a fine not exceeding level 5 on the standard scale; and

    (b) on conviction on indictment, to a fine.

8. Information to be provided in good time.

(1) The other party to the contract shall in good time before the start of the journey provide the consumer with the information specified in paragraph (2) below in writing or in some other appropriate form.

(2) The information referred to in paragraph (1) is the following—

    (a) the times and places of intermediate stops and transport connections and particulars of the place to be occupied by the traveller (for example, cabin or berth on ship, sleeper compartment on train);

    (b) the name, address and telephone number—

        (i) of the representative of the other party to the contract in the locality where the consumer is to stay,

or, if there is no such representative,

        (ii) of an agency in that locality on whose assistance a consumer in difficulty would be able to call,

or, if there is no such representative or agency, a telephone number or other information which will enable the consumer to contact the other party to the contract during the stay; and

    (c) in the case of a journey or stay abroad by a child under the age of 16 on the day when the journey or stay is due to start, information enabling direct contact to be made with the child or the person responsible at the place where he is to stay; and

    (d) except where the consumer is required as a term of the contract to take out an insurance policy in order to cover the cost of cancellation by the consumer or the cost of assistance, including repatriation, in the event of accident or illness, information about an insurance policy which the consumer may, if he wishes, take out in respect of the risk of those costs being incurred.

(3) If the consumer is not provided with the information required by paragraph (1) in accordance with that paragraph the other party to the contract shall be guilty of an offence and liable—

    (a) on summary conviction, to a fine not exceeding level 5 on the standard scale; and

    (b) on conviction on indictment, to a fine.

9. Contents and form of contract.

(1) The other party to the contract shall ensure that—

    (a) depending on the nature of the package being purchased, the contract contains at least the elements specified in Schedule 2 to these Regulations;

(b) subject to paragraph (2) below, all the terms of the contract are set out in writing or such other form as is comprehensible and accessible to the consumer and are communicated to the consumer before the contract is made; and

(c) a written copy of these terms is supplied to the consumer.

(2) Paragraph (1)(b) above does not apply when the interval between the time when the consumer approaches the other party to the contract with a view to entering it is impracticable to comply with the sub-paragraph.

(3) It is an implied condition (or, as regards Scotland, an implied term) of the contract that the other party to the contract complies with the provisions of paragraph (1).

10. Transfer of bookings.

(1) In every contract there is an implied term that where the consumer is prevented from proceeding with the package the consumer may transfer his booking to a person who satisfies all the conditions applicable to the package, provided that the consumer gives reasonable notice to the other party to the contract of his intention to transfer before the date when departure is due to take place.

(2) Where a transfer is made in accordance with the implied term set out in paragraph (1) above, the transferor and the transferee shall be jointly and severally liable to the other party to the contract for payment of the price of the package (or, if part of the price has been paid, for payment of the balance) and for any additional costs arising from such transfer.

11. Price revision.

(1) Any term in a contract to the effect that the prices laid down in the contract may be revised shall be void and of no effect unless the contract provides for the possibility of upward or downward revision and satisfies the conditions laid down in paragraph (2) below.

(2) The conditions mentioned in paragraph (1) are that—

(a) the contract states precisely how the revised price is to be calculated;

(b) the contract provides that price revisions are to be made solely to allow for variations in—

(i) transportation costs, including the cost of fuel,

(ii) dues, taxes or fees chargeable for services such as landing taxes or embarkation or disembarkation fees at ports and airports, or

(iii) the exchange rates applied to the particular package; and

(3) Notwithstanding any terms of a contract,

(i) no price increase may be made in a specified period which may not be less than 30 days before the departure date stipulated; and

(ii) as against an individual consumer liable under the contract, no price increase may be made in respect of variations which would produce an increase of less than 2 per cent, or such greater percentage as the contract may specify ("non-eligible variations") and that the non-eligible variations shall be left out of account in the calculation.

12. Significant alterations to essential terms.

In every contract there are implied terms to the effect that—

(a) where the organiser is constrained before the departure to alter significantly an essential term of the contract, such as the price (so far as regulation 11 permits him to do so), he will notify the consumer as quickly as possible in order to enable him to take appropriate decisions and in particular to withdraw from the contract without penalty or to accept a rider to the contract specifying the alterations made and their impact on the price; and

(b) the consumer will inform the organiser or the retailer of his decision as soon as possible.

13. Withdrawal by consumer pursuant to regulation 12 and cancellation by organiser.

(1) The terms set out in paragraphs (2) and (3) below are implied in every contract and apply where the consumer withdraws from the contract pursuant to the term in it implied by virtue of regulation 12(a), or where the organiser, for any reason other than the fault of the consumer, cancels the package before the agreed date of departure.

(2) The consumer is entitled—

    (a) to take a substitute package of equivalent or superior quality if the other party to the contract is able to offer him such a substitute; or

    (b) to take a substitute package of lower quality if the other party to the contract is able to offer him one and to recover from the organiser the difference in price between the price of the package purchased and that of the substitute package; or

    (c) to have repaid to him as soon as possible all the monies paid by him under the contract.

(3) The consumer is entitled, if appropriate, to be compensated by the organiser for non-performance of the contract except where—

    (a) the package is cancelled because the number of persons who agree to take it is less than the minimum number required and the consumer is informed of the cancellation, in writing, within the period indicated in the description of the package; or

    (b) the package is cancelled by reason of unusual and unforeseeable circumstances beyond the control of the party by whom this exception is pleaded, the consequences of which could not have been avoided even if all due care had been exercised.

(4) Overbooking shall not be regarded as a circumstance falling within the provisions of sub-paragraph (b) of paragraph (3) above.

14. Significant proportion of services not provided.

(1) The terms set out in paragraphs (2) and (3) below are implied in every contract and apply where, after departure, a significant proportion of the services contracted for is not provided or the organiser becomes aware that he will be unable to procure a significant proportion of the services to be provided.

(2) The organiser will make suitable alternative arrangements, at no extra cost to the consumer, for the continuation of the package and will, where appropriate, compensate the consumer for the difference between the services to be supplied under the contract and those supplied.

(3) If it is impossible to make arrangements as described in paragraph (2), or these are not accepted by the consumer for good reasons, the organiser will, where appropriate, provide the consumer with equivalent transport back to the place of departure or to another place to which the consumer has agreed and will, where appropriate, compensate the consumer.

15. Liability of other party to the contract for proper performance of obligations under contract.

(1) The other party to the contract is liable to the consumer for the proper performance of the obligations under the contract, irrespective of whether such obligations are to be performed by that other party or by other suppliers of services but this shall not affect any remedy or right of action which that other party may have against those other suppliers of services.

(2) The other party to the contract is liable to the consumer for any damage caused to him by the failure to perform the contract or the improper performance of the contract unless the failure or the improper performance is due neither to any fault of that other party nor to that of another supplier of services, because—

(a) the failures which occur in the performance of the contract are attributable to the consumer;

(b) such failures are attributable to a third party unconnected with the provision of the services contracted for, and are unforeseeable or unavoidable; or

(c) such failures are due to—

  (i) unusual and unforeseeable circumstances beyond the control of the party by whom this exception is pleaded, the consequences of which could not have been avoided even if all due care had been exercised; or

  (ii) an event which the other party to the contract or the supplier of services, even with all due care, could not foresee or forestall.

(3) In the case of damage arising from the non-performance or improper performance of the services involved in the package, the contract may provide for compensation to be limited in accordance with the international conventions which govern such services.

(4) In the case of damage other than personal injury resulting from the non-performance or improper performance of the services involved in the package, the contract may include a term limiting the amount of compensation which will be paid to the consumer, provided that the limitation is not unreasonable.

(5) Without prejudice to paragraph (3) and paragraph (4) above, liability under paragraphs (1) and (2) above cannot be excluded by any contractual term.

(6) The terms set out in paragraphs (7) and (8) below are implied in every contract.

(7) In the circumstances described in paragraph (2)(b) and (c) of this regulation, the other party to the contract will give prompt assistance to a consumer in difficulty.

(8) If the consumer complains about a defect in the performance of the contract, the other party to the contract, or his local representative, if there is one, will make prompt efforts to find appropriate solutions.

(9) The contract must clearly and explicitly oblige the consumer to communicate at the earliest opportunity, in writing or any other appropriate form, to the supplier of the services concerned and to the other party to the contract any failure which he perceives at the place where the services concerned are supplied.

23. Enforcement.

Schedule 3 to these Regulations (which makes provision about the enforcement of regulations 5, 7, 8, 16 and 22 of these Regulations) shall have effect.

24. Due diligence defence.

(1) Subject to the following provisions of this regulation, in proceedings against any person for an offence under regulation 5, 7, 8, 16 or 22 of these Regulations, it shall be a defence for that person to show that he took all reasonable steps and exercised all due diligence to avoid committing the offence.

(2) Where in any proceedings against any person for such an offence the defence provided by paragraph (1) above involves an allegation that the commission of the offence was due—

(a) to the act or default of another; or

(b) to reliance on the information given by another,

that person shall not, without the leave of the court, be entitled to rely on the defence unless, not less than seven clear days before the hearing of the proceedings, or, in Scotland, the trial diet, he has served a notice under paragraph (3) below on the person bringing the proceedings.

(3) A notice under this paragraph shall give such information identifying or assisting in the identification of the person who committed the act or default or gave the information as is in the possession of the person serving the notice at the time he serves it.

(4) It is hereby declared that a person shall not be entitled to rely on the defence provided by paragraph (1) above by reason of his reliance on information supplied by another, unless he shows that it was reasonable in all the circumstances for him to have relied on the information, having regard in particular—
    (a) to the steps which he took, and those which might reasonably have been taken, for the purpose of verifying the information; and
    (b) to whether he had any reason to disbelieve the information.

25. Liability of persons other than principal offender.
(1) Where the commission by any person of an offence under regulations 5, 7, 8, 16 or 22 of these Regulations is due to an act or default committed by some other person in the course of any business of his, the other person shall be guilty of the offence and may be proceeded against and punished by virtue of this paragraph whether or not proceedings are taken against the first-mentioned person.
(2) Where a body corporate is guilty of an offence under any of the provisions mentioned in paragraph (1) above (including where it is so guilty by virtue of the said paragraph (1)) in respect of any act or default which is shown to have been committed with the consent or connivance of, or to be attributable to any neglect on the part of, any director, manager, secretary or other similar officer of the body corporate or any person who was purporting to act in any such capacity he, as well as the body corporate, shall be guilty of that offence and shall be liable to be proceeded against and punished accordingly.
(3) Where the affairs of a body corporate are managed by its members, paragraph (2) above shall apply in relation to the acts and defaults of a member in connection with his functions of management as if he were a director of the body corporate.
(5) On proceedings for an offence under regulation 5 by virtue of paragraph (1) above committed by the making available of a brochure it shall be a defence for the person charged to prove that he is a person whose business it is to publish or arrange for the publication of brochures and that he received the brochure for publication in the ordinary course of business and did not know and had no reason to suspect that its publication would amount to an offence under these Regulations.

26. Prosecution time limit.
(1) No proceedings for an offence under regulation 5, 7, 8, 16 or 22 of these Regulations or under paragraphs 5(3), 6 or 7 of Schedule 3 thereto shall be commenced after—
    (a) the end of the period of three years beginning within the date of the commission of the offence; or
    (b) the end of the period of one year beginning with the date of the discovery of the offence by the prosecutor,
whichever is the earlier.
(2) For the purposes of this regulation a certificate signed by or on behalf of the prosecutor and stating the date on which the offence was discovered by him shall be conclusive evidence of that fact; and a certificate stating that matter and purporting to be so signed shall be treated as so signed unless the contrary is proved.

27. Saving for civil consequences.
No contract shall be void or unenforceable, and no right of action in civil proceedings in respect of any loss shall arise, by reason only of the commission of an offence under regulations 5, 7, 8, 16 or 22 of these Regulations.

28. Terms implied in contract.
Where it is provided in these Regulations that a term (whether so described or whether described as a condition or warranty) is implied in the contract it is so implied irrespective of the law which governs the contract.

Regulation 5   **SCHEDULE 1**
INFORMATION TO BE INCLUDED (IN ADDITION TO THE PRICE) IN BROCHURES WHERE RELEVANT TO PACKAGES OFFERED

1. The destination and the means, characteristics and categories of transport used.
2. The type of accommodation, its location, category or degree of comfort and its main features and, where the accommodation is to be provided in a member State, its approval or tourist classification under the rules of that member State.
3. The meals which are included in the package.
4. The itinerary.
5. General information about passport and visa requirements which apply for British citizens and health formalities required for the journey and the stay.
6. Either the monetary amount or the percentage of the price which is to be paid on account and the timetable for payment of the balance.
7. Whether a minimum number of persons is required for the package to take place and, if so, the deadline for informing the consumer in the event of cancellation.
8. The arrangements (if any) which apply if consumers are delayed at the outward or homeward points of departure.
9. The arrangements for security for money paid over and for the repatriation of the consumer in the event of insolvency.

Regulation 9   **SCHEDULE 2**
ELEMENTS TO BE INCLUDED IN THE CONTRACT IF RELEVANT TO THE PARTICULAR PACKAGE

1. The travel destination(s) and, where periods of stay are involved, the relevant periods, with dates.
2. The means, characteristics and categories of transport to be used and the dates, times and points of departure and return.
3. Where the package includes accommodation, its location, its tourist category of degree of comfort, its main features and, where the accommodation is to be provided in a member State, its compliance with the rules of that member State.
4. The meals which are included in the package.
5. Whether a minimum number of persons is required for the package to take place and, if so, the deadline for informing the consumer in the event of cancellation.
6. The itinerary.
7. Visits, excursions or other services which are included in the total price agreed for the package.
8. The name and address of the organiser, the retailer and, where appropriate, the insurer.
9. The price of the package, if the price may be revised in accordance with the term which may be included in the contract under regulation 11, an indication of the possibility of such price revisions, and an indication of any dues, taxes or fees chargeable for certain services (landing, embarkation or disembarkation fees at ports and airports and tourist taxes) where such costs are not included in the package.
10. The payment schedule and method of payment.
11. Special requirements which the consumer has communicated to the organiser or retailer when making the booking and which both have accepted.
12. The periods within which the consumer must make any complaint about the failure to perform or the inadequate performance of the contract.

Regulation 23 SCHEDULE 3
ENFORCEMENT

1. **Enforcement authority.**
(1) Every local weights and measures authority in Great Britain shall be an enforcement authority for the purposes of regulations 5, 7, 8, 16 and 22 of these Regulations ("the relevant regulations"), and it shall be the duty of each such authority to enforce those provisions within their area.

2. **Prosecutions.**
(1) Where an enforcement authority in England or Wales proposes to institute proceedings for an offence under any of the relevant regulations, it shall as between the enforcement authority and the Director General of Fair Trading be the duty of the enforcement authority to give to the Director General of Fair Trading notice of the intended proceedings, together with a summary of the facts on which the charges are to be founded, and to postpone institution of the proceedings until either—
   (a) twenty-eight days have elapsed since the giving of that notice; or
   (b) the Director General of Fair Trading has notified the enforcement authority that he has received the notice and the summary of the facts.
(2) Nothing in paragraph 1 above shall authorise a local weights and measures authority to bring proceedings in Scotland for an offence.

PROVISION AND USE OF WORK EQUIPMENT REGULATIONS 1992
(SI 1992, No. 2932)

1. **Citation and commencement.**
(2) Subject to paragraph (3), these Regulations shall come into force on 1st January 1993.
(3) Regulations 11 to 24 and 27 and Schedule 2 in so far as they apply to work equipment first provided for use in the premises or undertaking before 1st January 1993 shall come into force on 1st January 1997.

2. **Interpretation.**
(1) In these Regulations, unless the context otherwise requires—
"use" in relation to work equipment means any activity involving work equipment and includes starting, stopping, programming, setting, transporting, repairing, modifying, maintaining, servicing and cleaning, and related expressions shall be construed accordingly;
"work equipment" means any machinery, appliance, apparatus or tool and any assembly of components which, in order to achieve a common end, are arranged and controlled so that they function as a whole.

5. **Suitability of work equipment.**
(1) Every employer shall ensure that work equipment is so constructed or adapted as to be suitable for the purpose for which it is used or provided.
(2) In selecting work equipment, every employer shall have regard to the working conditions and to the risks to the health and safety of persons which exist in the premises or undertaking in which that work equipment is to be used and any additional risk posed by the use of that work equipment.
(3) Every employer shall ensure that work equipment is used only for operations for which, and under conditions for which, it is suitable.
(4) In this regulation "suitable" means suitable in any respect which it is reasonably foreseeable will affect the health or safety of any person.

6. Maintenance.

(1) Every employer shall ensure that work equipment is maintained in an efficient state, in efficient working order and in good repair.

(2) Every employer shall ensure that where any machinery has a maintenance log, the log is kept up to date.

7. Specific risks.

(1) Where the use of work equipment is likely to involve a specific risk to health or safety, every employer shall ensure that—

    (a) the use of that work equipment is restricted to those persons given the task of using it; and

    (b) repairs, modifications, maintenance or servicing of that work equipment is restricted to those persons who have been specifically designated to perform operations of that description (whether or not also authorised to perform other operations).

(2) The employer shall ensure that the persons designated for the purposes of sub-paragraph (b) of paragraph (1) have received adequate training related to any operations in respect of which they have been so designated.

8. Information and instructions.

(1) Every employer shall ensure that all persons who use work equipment have available to them adequate health and safety information and, where appropriate, written instructions pertaining to the use of the work equipment.

(2) Every employer shall ensure that any of his employees who supervises or manages the use of work equipment has available to him adequate health and safety information and, where appropriate, written instructions pertaining to the use of the work equipment.

(3) Without prejudice to the generality of paragraphs (1) or (2), the information and instructions required by either of those paragraphs shall include information and, where appropriate, written instructions on—

    (a) the conditions in which and the methods by which the work equipment may be used;

    (b) foreseeable abnormal situations and the action to be taken if such a situation were to occur; and

    (c) any conclusions to be drawn from experience in using the work equipment.

(4) Information and instructions required by this regulation shall be readily comprehensible to those concerned.

9. Training.

(1) Every employer shall ensure that all persons who use work equipment have received adequate training for purposes of health and safety, including training in the methods which may be adopted when using the work equipment, any risks which such use may entail and precautions to be taken.

(2) Every employer shall ensure that any of his employees who supervises or manages the use of work equipment has received adequate training for purposes of health and safety, including training in the methods which may be adopted when using the work equipment, any risks which such use may entail and precautions to be taken.

10. Conformity with Community requirements.

(1) Every employer shall ensure that any item of work equipment provided for use in the premises or undertaking of the employer complies with any enactment (whether in an Act or instrument) which implements in Great Britain any of the relevant Community directives listed in Schedule 1 which is applicable to that item of work equipment.

(2) Where it is shown that an item of work equipment complies with an enactment (whether in an Act or instrument) to which it is subject by virtue of paragraph (1), the requirements of regulations 11 to 24 shall apply in respect of that item of work

Provision and Use of Work Equipment Regulations 1992

equipment only to the extent that the relevant Community directive implemented by that enactment is not applicable to that item of work equipment.

(3) This regulation applies to items of work equipment provided for use in the premises or undertaking of the employer for the first time after 31st December 1992.

11. Dangerous parts of machinery.

(1) Every employer shall ensure that measures are taken in accordance with paragraph (2) which are effective—

    (a) to prevent access to any dangerous part of machinery or to any rotating stock-bar, or

    (b) to stop the movement of any dangerous part of machinery or rotating stock-bar before any part of a person enters a danger zone.

(2) The measures required by paragraph (1) shall consist of—

    (a) the provision of fixed guards enclosing every dangerous part or rotating stock-bar where and to the extent that it is practicable to do so, but where or to the extent that it is not, then

    (b) the provision of other guards or protection devices where and to the extent that it is practicable to do so, but where or to the extent that it is not, then

    (c) the provision of jigs, holders, push-sticks or similar protection appliances used in conjunction with the machinery where and to the extent that it is practicable to do so, but where or to the extent that it is not, then

    (d) the provision of information, instruction, training and supervision.

(3) All guards and protection devices provided under sub-paragraphs (a) or (b) of paragraph (2) shall—

    (a) be suitable for the purpose for which they are provided;

    (b) be of good construction, sound material and adequate strength;

    (c) be maintained in an efficient state, in efficient working order and in good repair;

    (d) not give rise to any increased risk to health or safety;

    (e) not be easily bypassed or disabled;

    (f) be situated at sufficient distance from the danger zone;

    (g) not unduly restrict the view of the operating cycle of the machinery, where such a view is necessary;

    (h) be so constructed or adapted that they allow operations necessary to fit or replace parts and for maintenance work, restricting access so that it is allowed only to the area where the work is to be carried out and, if possible, without having to dismantle the guard or protection device.

(4) All protection appliances provided under sub-paragraph (c) of paragraph (2) shall comply with sub-paragraphs (a) to (d) and (g) of paragraph (3).

(5) In this regulation—

"danger zone" means any zone in or around machinery in which a person is exposed to a risk to health or safety from contact with a dangerous part of machinery or a rotating stock-bar;

"stock-bar" means any part of a stock-bar which projects beyond the head-stock of a lathe.

12. Protection against specified hazards.

(1) Every employer shall take measures to ensure that the exposure of a person using work equipment to any risk to his health or safety from any hazard specified in paragraph (3) is either prevented, or, where that is not reasonably practicable, adequately controlled.

(2) The measures required by paragraph (1) shall—

    (a) be measures other than the provision of personal protective equipment or of information, instruction, training and supervision, so far as is reasonably practicable; and

(b) include, where appropriate, measures to minimise the effects of the hazard as well as to reduce the likelihood of the hazard occurring.

(3) The hazards referred to in paragraph (1) are—
   (a) any article or substance falling or being ejected from work equipment;
   (b) rupture or disintegration of parts of work equipment;
   (c) work equipment catching fire or overheating;
   (d) the unintended or premature discharge of any article or of any gas, dust, liquid, vapour or other substance which, in each case, is produced, used or stored in the work equipment;
   (e) the unintended or premature explosion of the work equipment or any article or substance produced, used or stored in it.

(4) For the purposes of this regulation "adequate" means adequate having regard only to the nature of the hazard and the nature and degree of exposure to the risk, and "adequately" shall be construed accordingly.

(5) This regulation shall not apply where any of the following Regulations apply in respect of any risk to a person's health or safety for which such Regulations require measures to be taken to prevent or control such risk, namely—
   (a) the Control of Lead at Work Regulations 1980;
   (b) the Ionising Radiations Regulations 1985;
   (c) the Control of Asbestos at Work Regulations 1987;
   (d) the Control of Substances Hazardous to Health Regulations 1988;
   (e) the Noise at Work Regulations 1989;
   (f) the Construction (Head Protection) Regulations 1989.

13. High or very low temperature.
Every employer shall ensure that work equipment, parts of work equipment and any article or substance produced, used or stored in work equipment which, in each case, is at a high or very low temperature shall have protection where appropriate so as to prevent injury to any person by burn, scald or sear.

14. Controls for starting or making a significant change in operating conditions.
(1) Every employer shall ensure that, where appropriate, work equipment is provided with one or more controls for the purposes of—
   (a) starting the work equipment (including re-starting after a stoppage for any reason); or
   (b) controlling any change in the speed, pressure or other operating conditions of the work equipment where such conditions after the change result in risk to health and safety which is greater than or of a different nature from such risks before the change.

(2) Subject to paragraph (3), every employer shall ensure that where a control is required by paragraph (1), it shall not be possible to perform any operation mentioned in sub-paragraph (a) or (b) of that paragraph except by a deliberate action on such control.

(3) Paragraph (1) shall not apply to re-starting or changing operating conditions as a result of the normal operating cycle of an automatic device.

15. Stop controls.
(1) Every employer shall ensure that, where appropriate, work equipment is provided with one or more readily accessible controls the operation of which will bring the work equipment to a safe condition in a safe manner.

(2) Any control required by paragraph (1) shall bring the work equipment to a complete stop where necessary for reasons of health and safety.

(3) Any control required by paragraph (1) shall, if necessary for reasons of health and safety, switch off all sources of energy after stopping the functioning of the work equipment.

(4) Any control required by paragraph (1) shall operate in priority to any control which starts or changes the operating conditions of the work equipment.

16. Emergency stop controls.

(1) Every employer shall ensure that, where appropriate, work equipment is provided with one or more readily accessible emergency stop controls unless it is not necessary by reason of the nature of the hazards and the time taken for the work equipment to come to a complete stop as a result of the action of any control provided by virtue of regulation 15(1).

(2) Any control required by paragraph (1) shall operate in priority to any control required by regulation 15(1).

17. Controls.

(1) Every employer shall ensure that all controls for work equipment shall be clearly visible and identifiable, including by appropriate marking where necessary.

(2) Except where necessary, the employer shall ensure that no control for work equipment is in a position where any person operating the control is exposed to a risk to his health or safety.

(3) Every employer shall ensure where appropriate—

(a) that, so far as is reasonably practicable, the operator of any control is able to ensure from the position of that control that no person is in a place where he would be exposed to any risk to his health or safety as a result of the operation of that control, but where or to the extent that it is not reasonably practicable;

(b) that, so far as is reasonably practicable, systems of work are effective to ensure that, when work equipment is about to start, no person is in a place where he would be exposed to a risk to his health or safety as a result of the work equipment starting, but where neither of these is reasonably practicable;

(c) that an audible, visible or other suitable warning is given by virtue of regulation 24 whenever work equipment is about to start.

(4) Every employer shall take appropriate measures to ensure that any person who is in a place where he would be exposed to a risk to his health or safety as a result of the starting or stopping of work equipment has sufficient time and suitable means to avoid that risk.

18. Control systems.

(1) Every employer shall ensure, so far as is reasonably practicable, that all control systems of work equipment are safe.

(2) Without prejudice to the generality of paragraph (1), a control system shall not be safe unless—

(a) its operation does not create any increased risk to health or safety;

(b) it ensures, so far as is reasonably practicable, that any fault in or damage to any part of the control system or the loss of supply of any source of energy used by the work equipment cannot result in additional or increased risk to health or safety;

(c) it does not impede the operation of any control required by regulation 15 or 16.

19. Isolation from sources of energy.

(1) Every employer shall ensure that where appropriate work equipment is provided with suitable means to isolate it from all its sources of energy.

(2) Without prejudice to the generality of paragraph (1), the means mentioned in that paragraph shall not be suitable unless they are clearly identifiable and readily accessible.

(3) Every employer shall take appropriate measures to ensure that re-connection of any energy source to work equipment does not expose any person using the work equipment to any risk to his health or safety.

20. Stability.

Every employer shall ensure that work equipment or any part of work equipment is stabilised by clamping or otherwise where necessary for purposes of health or safety.

21. Lighting.

Every employer shall ensure that suitable and sufficient lighting, which takes account of the operations to be carried out, is provided at any place where a person uses work equipment.

22. Maintenance operations.

Every employer shall take appropriate measures to ensure that work equipment is so constructed or adapted that, so far as is reasonably practicable, maintenance operations which involve a risk to health or safety can be carried out while the work equipment is shut down or, in other cases—

(a) maintenance operations can be carried out without exposing the person carrying them out to a risk to his health or safety; or

(b) appropriate measures can be taken for the protection of any person carrying out maintenance operations which involve a risk to his health or safety.

23. Markings.

Every employer shall ensure that work equipment is marked in a clearly visible manner with any marking appropriate for reasons of health and safety.

24. Warnings.

(1) Every employer shall ensure that work equipment incorporates any warnings or warning devices which are appropriate for reasons of health and safety.

(2) Without prejudice to the generality of paragraph (1), warnings given by warning devices on work equipment shall not be appropriate unless they are unambiguous, easily perceived and easily understood.

GENERAL PRODUCT SAFETY REGULATIONS 1994
(SI 1994, No. 2328)

1. Citation and commencement.

[(1)] These Regulations may be cited as the General Safety Regulations 1994 and shall come into force on 3rd October 1994.

[(2) Nothing in these Regulations applies to a medicinal product for human use to which the Medicines for Human Use (Marketing Authorisations Etc.) Regulations 1994 apply.]

2. Interpretation.

(1) In these Regulations—

"the 1968 Act" means the Medicines Act 1968;

"the 1987 Act" means the Consumer Protection Act 1987;

"the 1990 Act" means the Food Safety Act 1990;

"commercial activity" includes a business and a trade;

"consumer" means a consumer acting otherwise than in the course of a commercial activity;

"dangerous product" means any product other than a safe product;

"distributor" means any professional in the supply chain whose activity does not affect the safety properties of a product;

"enforcement authority" means the Secretary of State, any other Minister of the Crown in charge of a Government Department, any such department and any authority, council and other person on whom functions under these Regulations are imposed by or under regulation 11;

"general safety requirement" means the requirement in regulation 7;

"the GPS Directive" means Council Directive 92/59/EEC on general product safety;
"the 1991 Order" means the Food Safety (Northern Ireland) Order 1991;
"producer" means

(a) the manufacturer of the product, when he is established in the Community, and includes any person presenting himself as the manufacturer by affixing to the product his name, trade mark or other distinctive mark, or the person who reconditions the product;

(b) when the manufacturer is not established in the Community—

(i) if the manufacturer does not have a representative established in the Community, the importer of the product;

(ii) in all other cases, the manufacturer's representative; and

(c) other professionals in the supply chain, insofar as their activities may affect the safety properties of a product placed on the market;

"product" means any product intended for consumers or likely to be used by consumers, supplied whether for consideration or not in the course of a commercial activity and whether new, used or reconditioned; provided, however, a product which is used exclusively in the context of a commercial activity even if it is used for or by a consumer shall not be regarded as a product for the purposes of these Regulations provided always and for the avoidance of doubt this exception shall not extend to the supply of such a product to a consumer;

"safe product" means any product which, under normal or reasonably foreseeable conditions of use, including duration, does not present any risk or only the minimum risks compatible with the product's use, considered as acceptable and consistent with a high level of protection for the safety and health of persons, taking into account in particular—

(a) the characteristics of the product, including its composition, packaging, instructions for assembly and maintenance;

(b) the effect on other products, where it is reasonably foreseeable that it will be used with other products;

(c) the presentation of the product, the labelling, any instructions for its use and disposal and any other indication or information provided by the producer; and

(d) the categories of consumers at serious risk when using the product, in particular children,

and the fact that higher levels of safety may be obtained or other products presenting a lesser degree of risk may be available shall not of itself cause the product to be considered other than a safe product.

(2) References in these Regulations to the "Community" are references to the European Economic Area established under the Agreement signed at Oporto on 2nd May 1992 as adjusted by the Protocol signed at Brussels on 17th March 1993.

3. Application and revocation.

These Regulations do not apply to—

(a) second-hand products which are antiques;

(b) products supplied for repair or reconditioning before use, provided the supplier clearly informs the person to whom he supplies the product to that effect; or

(c) any product where there are specific provisions in rules of Community law governing all aspects of the safety of the product.

4. The requirements of these Regulations apply to a product where the product is the subject of provisions of Community law other than the GPS Directive insofar as those provisions do not make specific provision governing an aspect of the safety of the product.

5. For the purposes of these Regulations the provisions of section 10 of the 1987 Act to the extent that they impose general safety requirements which must be complied with if products are to be—

(i) placed on the market, offered or agreed to be placed on the market or exposed or possessed to be placed on the market by producers; or

(ii) supplied, offered or agreed to be supplied or exposed or possessed to be supplied by distributors,

are hereby disapplied.

7. General safety requirement.
No producer shall place a product on the market unless the product is a safe product.

8. Requirement as to information.
(1) Within the limits of his activity, a producer shall—

(a) provide consumers with the relevant information to enable them to assess the risks inherent in a product throughout the normal or reasonably foreseeable period of its use, where such risks are not immediately obvious without adequate warnings, and to take precautions against those risks; and

(b) adopt measures commensurate with the characteristics of the products which he supplies, to enable him to be informed of the risks which these products might present and to take appropriate action, including, if necessary, withdrawing the product in question from the market to avoid those risks.

(2) The measures referred to in sub-paragraph (b) of paragraph (1) above may include, whenever appropriate—

(i) marking of the products or product batches in such a way that they can be identified;

(ii) sample testing of marketed products;

(iii) investigating complaints; and

(iv) keeping distributors informed of such monitoring.

9. Requirements of distributors.
A distributor shall act with due care in order to help ensure compliance with the requirements of regulation 7 above and, in particular, without limiting the generality of the foregoing—

(a) a distributor shall not supply products to any person which he knows, or should have presumed, on the basis of the information in his possession and as a professional, are dangerous products; and

(b) within the limits of his activities, a distributor shall participate in monitoring the safety of products placed on the market, in particular by passing on information on the product risks and cooperating in the action taken to avoid those risks.

10. Presumption of conformity and product assessment.
(1) Where in relation to any product such product conforms to the specific rules of the law of the United Kingdom laying down the health and safety requirements which the product must satisfy in order to be marketed there shall be a presumption that, until the contrary is proved, the product is a safe product.

(2) Where no specific rules as are mentioned or referred to in paragraph (1) exist, the conformity of a product to the general safety requirement shall be assessed taking into account—

(i) voluntary national standards of the United Kingdom giving effect to a European standard; or

(ii) Community technical specifications; or

(iii) if there are no such voluntary national standards of the United Kingdom or Community technical specifications—

(aa) standards drawn up in the United Kingdom; or

(bb) the codes of good practice in respect of health and safety in the product sector concerned; or

(cc) the state of the art and technology

and the safety which consumers may reasonably expect.

11. Enforcement.
For the purposes of providing for the enforcement of these Regulations—

(a) section 13 of the 1987 Act (prohibition notices and notices to warn) shall (to the extent that it does not already do so) apply to products as it applies to relevant goods under that section;

(b) the requirements of these Regulations shall constitute safety provisions for the purposes of sections 14 (suspension notices), 15 (appeals against suspension notices), 16 (forfeiture: England, Wales and Northern Ireland), 17 (forfeiture: Scotland) and 18 (power to obtain information) of the 1987 Act;

(c) (i) subject to paragraph (ii) below a weights and measures authority in Great Britain and a district council in Northern Ireland shall have the same duty to enforce these Regulations as they have in relation to Part II of the 1987 Act, and Part IV, sections 37 and 38 and subsections (3) and (4) of section 42 of that Act shall apply accordingly;

(ii) without prejudice to the provisions of paragraphs (a) and (b) above and sub-paragraph (i) above, insofar as these Regulations apply:—

(aa) to products licensed in accordance with the provisions of the 1968 Act [or which are the subject of a marketing authorisation within the meaning of the Medicines for Human Use (Marketing Authorisations Etc.) Regulations 1994], it shall be the duty of the enforcement authority as defined in section 132(1) of the 1968 Act to enforce or to secure the enforcement of these Regulations and sections 108 to 115 and section 119 of and Schedule 3 to that Act shall apply accordingly as if these Regulations were regulations made under the said Act;

(bb) in relation to food within the meaning of section 1 of the 1990 Act, it shall be the duty of each food authority as defined in section 5 of the 1990 Act to enforce or to secure the enforcement of these Regulations, within its area, in Great Britain and sections 9, 29, 30 and 32 of that Act shall apply accordingly as if these Regulations were food safety requirements made under the said Act and section 10 of that Act shall apply as if these Regulations were regulations made under Part II of that Act; and

(cc) in relation to food within the meaning of article 2 of the 1991 Order, it shall be the duty of the relevant enforcement authority as provided for in article 26 of that Order to enforce or to secure enforcement of these Regulations in Northern Ireland and articles 8, 29, 30, 31 and 33 of that Order shall apply accordingly as if these Regulations were food safety requirements made under that Order and article 9 of that Order shall apply as if these Regulations were regulations made under Part II of that Order;

(d) in sections 13(4) and 14(6) of the 1987 Act for the words "six months" there shall be substituted "three months"; and

(e) nothing in this regulation shall authorise any enforcement authority to bring proceedings in Scotland for an offence.

Offences and preparatory acts.
12. Any person who contravenes regulation 7 or 9(a) shall be guilty of an offence.

13. No producer or distributor shall—

(a) offer or agree to place on the market any dangerous product or expose or possess any such product for placing on the market; or

(b) offer or agree to supply any dangerous product or expose or possess any such product for supply,

and any person who contravenes the requirements of this regulation shall be guilty of an offence.

14. Defence of due diligence.

(1) Subject to the following paragraphs of this regulation, in proceedings against any person for an offence under these Regulations it shall be a defence for that person to show that he took all reasonable steps and exercised all due diligence to avoid committing the offence.

(2) Where in any proceedings against any person for such an offence the defence provided by paragraph (1) above involves an allegation that the commission of the offence was due—
   (a) to the act or default of another, or
   (b) to reliance on information given by another,
that person shall not, without leave of the court, be entitled to rely on the defence unless, not less than seven days before, in England, Wales and Northern Ireland, the hearing of the proceedings or, in Scotland, the trial diet, he has served a notice under paragraph (3) below on the person bringing the proceedings.

(3) A notice under this paragraph shall give such information identifying or assisting in the identification of the person who committed the act or default or gave the information as is in the possession of the person serving the notice at the time he serves it.

(4) It is hereby declared that a person shall not be entitled to rely on the defence provided in paragraph (1) above by reason of his reliance on information supplied by another, unless he shows that it was reasonable in all the circumstances for him to have relied on the information, having regard in particular—
   (a) to the steps which he took, and those which might reasonably have been taken, for the purpose of verifying the information; and
   (b) to whether he had any reason to disbelieve the information.

(5) It is hereby declared that a person shall not be entitled to rely on the defence provided by paragraph (1) above or by section 39(1) of the 1987 Act (defence of due diligence) if he has contravened regulation 9(b).

15. Liability of persons other than principal offender.

(1) Where the commission by any person of an offence to which regulation 14 above applies is due to the act or default committed by some other person in the course of a commercial activity of his, the other person shall be guilty of an offence and may be proceeded against and punished by virtue of this paragraph whether or not proceedings are taken against the first-mentioned person.

(2) Where a body corporate is guilty of an offence under these Regulations (including where it is so guilty by virtue of paragraph (1) above) in respect of any act or default which is shown to have been committed with the consent or connivance of, or to be attributable to any neglect on the part of any director, manager, secretary or other similar officer of the body corporate or any person who was purporting to act in any such capacity he, as well as the body corporate, shall be guilty of that offence and shall be liable to be proceeded against and punished accordingly.

(3) Where the affairs of a body corporate are managed by its members, paragraph (2) above shall apply in relation to the acts and defaults of a member in connection with his functions of management as if he were a director of the body corporate.

(4) Where a Scottish partnership is guilty of an offence under regulation 14 above (including where it is so guilty by virtue of paragraph (1) above) in respect of any act or default which is shown to have been committed with the consent or connivance of, or to be attributable to any neglect on the part of, a partner in the partnership, he, as well as the partnership, shall be guilty of that offence and shall be liable to be proceeded against and punished accordingly.

16. Extension of the time for bringing summary proceedings.

(1) Notwithstanding section 127 of the Magistrates' Courts Act 1980 and article 19 of the Magistrates' Courts (Northern Ireland) Order 1981, in England, Wales and

Northern Ireland a magistrates' court may try an information (in the case of England and Wales) or a complaint (in the case of Northern Ireland) in respect of proceedings for an offence under regulation 12 or 13 above if (in the case of England and Wales) the information is laid or (in the case of Northern Ireland) the complaint is made within twelve months from the date of the offence.

(2) Notwithstanding section 331 of the Criminal Procedure (Scotland) Act 1975, in Scotland summary proceedings for an offence under regulation 12 or 13 above may be commenced at any time within twelve months from the date of the offence.

(3) For the purposes of paragraph (2) above, section 331(3) of the Criminal Procedure (Scotland) Act 1975 shall apply as it applies for the purposes of that section.

17. Penalties.
A person guilty of an offence under regulation 12 or 13 above shall be liable on summary conviction to—
   (a) imprisonment for a term not exceeding three months; or
   (b) a fine not exceeding level 5 on the standard scale;
or to both.

18. Duties of enforcement authorities.
(1) Every enforcement authority shall give immediate notice to the Secretary of State of any action taken by it to prohibit or restrict the supply of any product or forfeit or do any other thing in respect of any product for the purposes of these Regulations.

(2) The requirements of paragraph (1) above shall not apply in the case of any action taken in respect of any second-hand product.

UNFAIR TERMS IN CONSUMER CONTRACTS REGULATIONS 1994
(SI 1994, No. 3159)

1. Citation and commencement.
These Regulations may be cited as the Unfair Terms in Consumer Contracts Regulations 1994 and shall come into force on 1st July 1995.

2. Interpretation.
(1) In these Regulations—

"business" includes a trade or profession and the activities of any government department or local or public authority;

"the Community" means the European Economic Community and the other States in the European Economic Area;

"consumer" means a natural person who, in making a contract to which these Regulations apply, is acting for purposes which are outside his business;

"court" in relation to England and Wales and Northern Ireland means the High Court, and in relation to Scotland, the Court of Session;

"Director" means the Director General of Fair Trading;

"EEA Agreement" means the Agreement on the European Economic Area signed at Oporto on 2 May 1992 as adjusted by the protocol signed at Brussels on 17 March 1993;

"member State" shall mean a State which is a contracting party to the EEA Agreement but until the EEA Agreement comes into force in relation to Liechtenstein does not include the State of Liechtenstein;

"seller" means a person who sells goods and who, in making a contract to which these Regulations apply, is acting for purposes relating to his business; and

"supplier" means a person who supplies goods or services and who, in making a contract to which these Regulations apply, is acting for purposes relating to his business.

3. **Terms to which these Regulations apply.**

(1) Subject to the provisions of Schedule 1, these Regulations apply to any term in a contract concluded between a seller or supplier and a consumer where the said term has not been individually negotiated.

(2) In so far as it is in plain, intelligible language, no assessment shall be made of the fairness of any term which—
   (a) defines the main subject matter of the contract, or
   (b) concerns the adequacy of the price or remuneration, as against the goods or services sold or supplied.

(3) For the purposes of these Regulations, a term shall always be regarded as not having been individually negotiated where it has been drafted in advance and the consumer has not been able to influence the substances of the term.

(4) Notwithstanding that a specific term or certain aspects of it in a contract has been individually negotiated, these Regulations shall apply to the rest of a contract if an overall assessment of the contract indicates that it is a pre-formulated standard contract.

(5) It shall be for any seller or supplier who claims that a term was individually negotiated to show that it was.

4. **Unfair terms.**

(1) In these Regulations, subject to paragraphs (2) and (3) below, "unfair term" means any term which contrary to the requirement of good faith causes a significant imbalance in the parties' rights and obligations under the contract to the detriment of the consumer.

(2) An assessment of the unfair nature of a term shall be made taking into account the nature of the goods or services for which the contract was concluded and referring, as at the time of the conclusion of the contract, to all circumstances attending the conclusion of the contract and to all the other terms of the contract or of another contract on which it is dependent.

(3) In determining whether a term satisfies the requirement of good faith, regard shall be had in particular to the matters specified in Schedule 2 to these Regulations.

(4) Schedule 3 to these Regulations contains an indicative and non-exhaustive list of the terms which may be regarded as unfair.

5. **Consequence of inclusion of unfair terms in contracts.**

(1) An unfair term in a contract concluded with a consumer by a seller of [*sic*] supplier shall not be binding on the consumer.

(2) The contract shall continue to bind the parties if it is capable of continuing in existence without the unfair term.

6. **Construction of written contracts.**

A seller or supplier shall ensure that any written term of a contract is expressed in plain, intelligible language, and if there is doubt about the meaning of a written term, the interpretation most favourable to the consumer shall prevail.

7. **Choice of law clauses.**

These Regulations shall apply notwithstanding any contract term which applies or purports to apply the law of a non member State, if the contract has a close connection with the territory of the member States.

8. **Prevention of continued use of unfair terms.**

(1) It shall be the duty of the Director to consider any complaint made to him that any contract term drawn up for general use is unfair, unless the complaint appears to the Director to be frivolous or vexatious.

(2) If having considered a complaint about any contract term pursuant to paragraph (1) above the Director considers that the contract term is unfair he may, if he considers

it appropriate to do so, bring proceedings for an injunction (in which proceedings he may also apply for an interlocutory injunction) against any person appearing to him to be using or recommending use of such a term in contracts concluded with consumers.

(3) The Director may, if he considers it appropriate to do so, have regard to any undertakings given to him by or on behalf of any person as to the continued use of such a term in contracts concluded with consumers.

(4) The Director shall give reasons for his decision to apply or not to apply, as the case may be, for an injunction in relation to any complaint which these Regulations require him to consider.

(5) The court on an application by the Director may grant an injunction on such terms as it thinks fit.

(6) An injunction may relate not only to use of a particular contract term drawn up for general use but to any similar term, or a term having like effect, used or recommended for use by any party to the proceedings.

(7) The Director may arrange for the dissemination in such form and manner as he considers appropriate of such information and advice concerning the operation of these Regulations as may appear to him to be expedient to give to the public and to all persons likely to be affected by these Regulations.

Regulation 3(1)   SCHEDULE 1
CONTRACTS AND PARTICULAR TERMS EXCLUDED FROM THE SCOPE OF THESE REGULATIONS

These Regulations do not apply to—
    (a) any contract relating to employment;
    (b) any contract relating to succession rights;
    (c) any contract relating to rights under family law;
    (d) any contract relating to the incorporation and organisation of companies or partnerships; and
    (e) any term incorporated in order to comply with or which reflects—
        (i) statutory or regulatory provisions of the United Kingdom; or
        (ii) the provisions or principles of international conventions to which the member States or the Community are party.

Regulation 4(3)   SCHEDULE 2
ASSESSMENT OF GOOD FAITH

In making an assessment of good faith, regard shall be had in particular to—
    (a) the strength of the bargaining positions of the parties;
    (b) whether the consumer had an inducement to agree to the term;
    (c) whether the goods or services were sold or supplied to the special order of the consumer, and
    (d) the extent to which the seller or supplier has dealt fairly and equitably with the consumer.

Regulation 4(4)   SCHEDULE 3
INDICATIVE AND ILLUSTRATIVE LIST OF TERMS WHICH MAY BE REGARDED AS UNFAIR

1. Terms which have the object or effect of—
    (a) excluding or limiting the legal liability of a seller or supplier in the event of the death of a consumer or personal injury to the latter resulting from an act or omission of that seller or supplier;
    (b) inappropriately excluding or limiting the legal rights of the consumer vis-à-vis the seller or supplier or another party in the event of total or partial non-performance or inadequate performance by the seller or supplier of any of the contractual obligations,

including the option of offsetting a debt owed to the seller or supplier against any claim which the consumer may have against him;

(c) making an agreement binding on the consumer whereas provision of services by the seller or supplier is subject to a condition whose realisation depends on his own will alone;

(d) permitting the seller or supplier to retain sums paid by the consumer where the latter decides not to conclude or perform the contract, without providing for the consumer to receive compensation of an equivalent amount from the seller or supplier where the latter is the party cancelling the contract;

(e) requiring any consumer who fails to fulfil his obligation to pay a disproportionately high sum in compensation;

(f) authorising the seller or supplier to dissolve the contract on a discretionary basis where the same facility is not granted to the consumer, or permitting the seller or supplier to retain the sums paid for services not yet supplied by him where it is the seller or supplier himself who dissolves the contract;

(g) enabling the seller or supplier to terminate a contract of indeterminate duration without reasonable notice except where there are serious grounds for doing so;

(h) automatically extending a contract of fixed duration where the consumer does not indicate otherwise, when the deadline fixed for the consumer to express this desire not to extend the contract is unreasonably early;

(i) irrevocably binding the consumer to terms with which he had no real opportunity of becoming acquainted before the conclusion of the contract;

(j) enabling the seller or supplier to alter the terms of the contract unilaterally without a valid reason which is specified in the contract;

(k) enabling the seller or supplier to alter unilaterally without a valid reason any characteristics of the product or service to be provided;

(l) providing for the price of goods to be determined at the time of delivery or allowing a seller of goods or supplier of services to increase their price without in both cases giving the consumer the corresponding right to cancel the contract if the final price is too high in relation to the price agreed when the contract was concluded;

(m) giving the seller or supplier the right to determine whether the goods or services supplied are in conformity with the contract, or giving him the exclusive right to interpret any term of the contract;

(n) limiting the seller's or supplier's obligation to respect commitments undertaken by his agents or making his commitments subject to compliance with a particular formality;

(o) obliging the consumer to fulfil all his obligations where the seller or supplier does not perform his;

(p) giving the seller or supplier the possibility of transferring his rights and obligations under the contract, where this may serve to reduce the guarantees for the consumer, without the latter's agreement;

(q) excluding or hindering the consumer's right to take legal action or exercise any other legal remedy, particularly by requiring the consumer to take disputes exclusively to arbitration not covered by legal provisions, unduly restricting the evidence available to him or imposing on him a burden of proof which, according to the applicable law, should lie with another party to the contract.

2. Scope of subparagraphs 1(g), (j) and (l)

(a) Subparagraph 1(g) is without hindrance to terms by which a supplier of financial services reserves the right to terminate unilaterally a contract of indeterminate duration without notice where there is a valid reason, provided that the supplier is required to inform the other contracting party or parties thereof immediately.

(b) Subparagraph 1(j) is without hindrance to terms under which a supplier of financial services reserves the right to alter the rate of interest payable by the consumer or due to the latter, or the amount of other charges for financial services without notice where there is a valid reason, provided that the supplier is required to inform the other contracting party or parties thereof at the earliest opportunity and that the latter are free to dissolve the contract immediately.

Subparagraph 1(j) is also without hindrance to terms under which a seller or supplier reserves the right to alter unilaterally the conditions of a contract of indeterminate duration, provided that he is required to inform the consumer with reasonable notice and that the consumer is free to dissolve the contract.

    (c)   Subparagraphs 1(g), (j) and (l) do not apply to:
— transactions in transferable securities, financial instruments and other products or services where the price is linked to fluctuations in a stock exchange quotation or index or a financial market rate that the seller or supplier does not control;
— contracts for the purchase or sale of foreign currency, traveller's cheques or international money orders denominated in foreign currency;

    (d)   Subparagraph 1(l) is without hindrance to price indexation clauses, where lawful, provided that the method by which prices vary is explicitly described.

PUBLIC SUPPLY CONTRACTS REGULATIONS 1995
(SI 1995, No. 201)

10. Selection of contract award procedure.

(1) For the purposes of seeking offers in relation to a proposed public supply contract a contracting authority shall use the open procedure, the restricted procedure or the negotiated procedure and shall decide which of those procedures to use in accordance with the following paragraphs of this regulation.

21. Criteria for the award of a public supply contract.

(1) Subject to paragraphs (5), (6) and (7) below, a contracting authority shall award a public supply contract on the basis of the offer which—

    (a)   is the most economically advantageous to the contracting authority, or

    (b)   offers the lowest price.

(2) The criteria which a contracting authority may use to determine that an offer is the most economically advantageous include delivery date, running costs, cost effectiveness, quality, aesthetic and functional characteristics, technical merit, after sales service, technical assistance and price.

(3) Where a contracting authority intends to award a public supply contract on the basis of the offer which is the most economically advantageous it shall state the criteria on which it intends to base its decision, where possible in descending order of importance, in the contract notice or in the contract documents.

(4) Where a contracting authority awards a public supply contract on the basis of the offer which is the most economically advantageous, it may take account of offers which offer variations on the requirements specified in the contract documents if—

    (a)   the offer meets the minimum requirements of the contracting authority, and

    (b)   it has stated those minimum requirements and any specific requirements for the presentation of an offer offering variations in the contract documents,

but if the contracting authority shall not take account of offers which offer such variations it shall state that fact in the contract notice.

(5) A contracting authority may not reject an offer which offers variations on the requirements specified in the contract documents on the ground that it would lead to the award of a public services contract within the meaning of the Public Services Contracts Regulations 1993.

(6) A contracting authority may not reject an offer on the ground that the technical specifications in the offer have been defined by reference to European specifications

(within the meaning of regulations 8(1)) or to the British technical specifications specified in regulation 8(7)(a) and (b).

(7) If an offer for a public supply contract is abnormally low the contracting authority may reject that offer but only if it has requested in writing an explanation of the offer, or of those parts which it considers contribute to the offer being abnormally low, and has—

(a) if awarding the public supply contract on the basis of the offer which offers the lowest price, examined the details of all the offers made, taking into account any explanation given to it of the abnormally low tender, before awarding the contract, or

(b) if awarding the public supply contract on the basis of the offer which is the most economically advantageous, taken any such explanation into account in assessing which is the most economically advantageous offer,

and, in considering that explanation, the contracting authority may take into account explanations relating to the economics of the manufacturing process, or to the technical solutions suggested by the supplier or the exceptionally favourable conditions available to the supplier for the provision of the supply of goods or the originality of the supplies proposed by the supplier.

(8) If a contracting authority which rejects an abnormally low offer is awarding the public supply contract on the basis of the offer which offers the lowest price, it shall send a report justifying the rejection to the Treasury for onward transmission to the Commission.

(9) For the purposes of this regulation an "offer" includes a bid by one part of a contracting authority to make available to another part of the contracting authority the goods required by it when the former part is invited by the latter part to compete with the offers sought from other persons.

PART IV
EC MATERIALS

TREATY
establishing
THE EUROPEAN ECONOMIC COMMUNITY
(Rome, 25 March 1957)

Art. 85. 1. The following shall be prohibited as incompatible with the common market: all agreements between undertakings, decisions by associations of undertakings and concerted practices which may affect trade between Member States and which have as their object or effect the prevention, restriction or distortion of competition within the common market, and in particular those which:

(a) directly or indirectly fix purchase or selling prices or any other trading conditions;

(b) limit or control production, markets, technical development, or investment;

(c) share markets or sources of supply;

(d) apply dissimilar conditions to equivalent transactions with other trading parties, thereby placing them at a competitive disadvantage;

(e) make the conclusion of contracts subject to acceptance by the other parties of supplementary obligations which, by their nature or according to commercial usage, have no connection with the subject of such contracts.

2. Any agreements or decisions prohibited pursuant to this Article shall be automatically void.

3. The provisions of paragraph 1 may, however, be declared inapplicable in the case of:
—any agreement or category of agreements between undertakings;
—any decision or category of decisions by associations of undertakings;
—any concerted practice or category of concerted practices;
which contributes to improving the production or distribution of goods or to promoting technical or economic progress, while allowing consumers a fair share of the resulting benefit, and which does not:

(a) impose on the undertakings concerned restrictions which are not indispensable to the attainment of these objectives;

(b) afford such undertakings the possibility of eliminating competition in respect of a substantial part of the products in question.

Art. 86. Any abuse by one or more undertakings of a dominant position within the common market or in a substantial part of it shall be prohibited as incompatible with the common market in so far as it may affect trade between Member States. Such abuse may, in particular, consist in:

(a) directly or indirectly imposing unfair purchase or selling prices or other unfair trading conditions;
(b) limiting production, markets or technical development to the prejudice of consumers;
(c) applying dissimilar conditions to equivalent transactions with other trading parties, thereby placing them at a competitive disadvantage;
(d) making the conclusion of contracts subject to acceptance by the other parties of supplementary obligations which, by their nature or according to commercial usage, have no connection with the subject of such contracts.

COUNCIL DIRECTIVE
of 25 July 1985
on the approximation of the laws, regulations and administrative provisions of the Member States concerning liability for defective products
(85/374/EEC:L 210/29)

THE COUNCIL OF THE EUROPEAN COMMUNITIES,

Having regard to the Treaty establishing the European Economic Community, and in particular Article 100 thereof,

Having regard to the proposal from the Commission,

Having regard to the opinion of the European Parliament,

Having regard to the opinion of the Economic and Social Committee,

Whereas approximation of the laws of the Member States concerning the liability of the producer for damage caused by the defectiveness of his products is necessary because the existing divergences may distort competition and affect the movement of goods within the common market and entail a differing degree of protection of the consumer against damage caused by a defective product to his health or property;

Whereas liability without fault on the part of the producer is the sole means of adequately solving the problem, peculiar to our age of increasing technicality, of a fair apportionment of the risks inherent in modern technological production;

Whereas liability without fault should apply only to movables which have been industrially produced; whereas, as a result, it is appropriate to exclude liability for agricultural products and game, except where they have undergone a processing of an industrial nature which could cause a defect in these products; whereas the liability provided for in this Directive should also apply to movables which are used in the construction of immovables or are installed in immovables;

Whereas protection of the consumer requires that all producers involved in the production process should be made liable, in so far as their finished product, component part or any raw material supplied by them was defective; whereas, for the same reason, liability should extend to importers of products into the Community and to persons who present themselves as producers by affixing their name, trade mark or other distinguishing feature or who supply a product the producer of which cannot be identified;

Whereas, in situations where several persons are liable for the same damage, the protection of the consumer requires that the injured person should be able to claim full compensation for the damage from any one of them;

Whereas, to protect the physical well-being and property of the consumer, the defectiveness of the product should be determined by reference not to its fitness for use but to the lack of the safety which the public at large is entitled to expect; whereas the safety is assessed by excluding any misuse of the product not reasonable under the circumstances;

Whereas a fair apportionment of risk between the injured person and the producer implies that the producer should be able to free himself from liability if he furnishes proof as to the existence of certain exonerating circumstances;

Whereas the protection of the consumer requires that the liability of the producer remains unaffected by acts or omissions of other persons having contributed to cause the damage; whereas, however, the contributory negligence of the injured person may be taken into account to reduce or disallow such liability;

Whereas the protection of the consumer requires compensation for death and personal injury as well as compensation for damage to property; whereas the latter should nevertheless be limited to goods for private use or consumption and be subject to a deduction of a lower threshold of a fixed amount in order to avoid litigation in an excessive number of cases; whereas this Directive should not prejudice compensation for pain and suffering and other non-material damages payable, where appropriate, under the law applicable to the case;

Whereas a uniform period of limitation for the bringing of action for compensation is in the interests both of the injured person and of the producer;

Whereas products age in the course of time, higher safety standards are developed and the state of science and technology progresses; whereas, therefore, it would not be reasonable to make the producer liable for an unlimited period for the defectiveness of his product; whereas therefore, liability should expire after a reasonable length of time, without prejudice to claims pending at law;

Whereas, to achieve effective protection of consumers, no contractual derogation should be permitted as regards the liability of the producer in relation to the injured person;

Whereas under the legal systems of the Member States an injured party may have a claim for damages based on grounds of contractual liability or on grounds of non-contractual liability other than that provided for in this Directive; in so far as these provisions also serve to attain the objective of effective protection of consumers, they should remain unaffected by this Directive; whereas, in so far as effective protection of consumers in the sector of pharmaceutical products is already also attained in a Member State under a special liability system, claims based on this system should similarly remain possible;

Whereas, to the extent that liability for nuclear injury or damage is already covered in all Member States by adequate special rules, it has been possible to exclude damage of this type from the scope of this Directive;

Whereas, since the exclusion of primary agricultural products and game from the scope of this Directive may be felt, in certain Member States, in view of what is expected for the protection of consumers, to restrict unduly such protection, it should be possible for a Member State to extend liability to such products;

Whereas, for similar reasons, the possibility offered to a producer to free himself from liability if he proves that the state of scientific and technical knowledge at the time when he put the product into circulation was not such as to enable the existence of a defect to be discovered may be felt in certain Member States to restrict unduly the protection of the consumer; whereas it should therefore be possible for a Member State to maintain in its legislation or to provide by new legislation that this exonerating circumstance is not admitted; whereas, in the case of new legislation, making use of this derogation should, however, be subject to a Community stand-still procedure, in order to raise, if possible, the level of protection in a uniform manner throughout the Community;

Whereas, taking into account the legal traditions in most of the Member States, it is inappropriate to set any financial ceiling on the producer's liability without fault; whereas, in so far as there are, however, differing traditions, it seems possible to admit that a Member State may derogate from the principle of unlimited liability by providing a limit for the total liability of the producer for damage resulting from a death or personal injury and caused by identical items with the same defect, provided that this limit is established at a level sufficiently high to guarantee adequate protection of the consumer and the correct functioning of the common market;

Whereas the harmonization resulting from this cannot be total at the present stage, but opens the way towards greater harmonization; whereas it is therefore necessary that the Council receive at regular intervals, reports from the Commission on the application of this Directive, accompanied, as the case may be, by appropriate proposals;

Whereas it is particularly important in this respect that a re-examination be carried out of those parts of the Directive relating to the derogations open to the Member States, at the expiry of a period of sufficient length to gather practical experience on the effects of these derogations on the protection of consumers and on the functioning of the common market,

HAS ADOPTED THIS DIRECTIVE:

Art. 1. The producer shall be liable for damage caused by a defect in his product.

Art. 2. For the purpose of this Directive "'product' means all movables, with the exception of primary agricultural products and game, even though incorporated into another movable or into an immovable. "Primary agricultural products' means the products of the soil, of stock-farming and of fisheries, excluding products which have undergone initial processing. "Product' includes electricity.

Art. 3. 1. "Producer" means the manufacturer of a finished product, the producer of any raw material or the manufacturer of a component part and any person who, by putting his name, trade mark or other distinguishing feature on the product presents himself as its producer.

Without prejudice to the liability of the producer, any person who imports into the Community a product for sale, hire, leasing or any form of distribution in the course of his business shall be deemed to be a producer within the meaning of this Directive and shall be responsible as a producer.

3. Where the producer of the product cannot be identified, each supplier of the product shall be treated as its producer unless he informs the injured person, within a reasonable time, of the identity of the producer or of the person who supplied him with the product. The same shall apply, in the case of an imported product, if this product does not indicate the identity of the importer referred to in paragraph 2, even if the name of the producer is indicated.

Art. 4. The injured person shall be required to prove the damage, the defect and the causal relationship between defect and damage.

Art. 5. Where, as a result of the provisions of this Directive, two or more persons are liable for the same damage, they shall be liable jointly and severally, without prejudice to the provisions of national law concerning the rights of contribution or recourse.

Art. 6. 1. A product is defective when it does not provide the safety which a person is entitled to expect, taking all circumstances into account, including:

(a) the presentation of the product;

(b) the use to which it could reasonably be expected that the product would be put;

(c) the time when the product was put into circulation.

2. A product shall not be considered defective for the sole reason that a better product is subsequently put into circulation.

Art. 7. The producer shall not be liable as a result of this Directive if he proves:

(a) that he did not put the product into circulation; or

(b) that, having regard to the circumstances, it is probable that the defect which caused the damage did not exist at the time when the product was put into circulation by him or that this defect came into being afterwards; or

(c) that the product was neither manufactured by him for sale or any form of distribution for economic purpose nor manufactured or distributed by him in the course of his business; or

(d) that the defect is due to compliance of the product with mandatory regulations issued by the public authorities; or

(e) that the state of scientific and technical knowledge at the time when he put the product into circulation was not such as to enable the existence of the defect to be discovered; or

(f) in the case of a manufacturer of a component, that the defect is attributable to the design of the product in which the component has been fitted or to the instructions given by the manufacturer of the product.

Art. 8. 1. Without prejudice to the provisions of national law concerning the right of contribution or recourse, the liability of the producer shall not be reduced when the damage is caused both by a defect in product and by the act or omission of a third party.

2. The liability of the producer may be reduced or disallowed when, having regard to all the circumstances, the damage is caused both by a defect in the product and by the fault of the injured person or any person for whom the injured person is responsible.

Art. 9. For the purpose of Article 1, "damage' means:
 (a) damage caused by death or by personal injuries;
 (b) damage to, or destruction of, any item of property other than the defective product itself, with a lower threshold of 500 ECU, provided that the item of property:
  (i) is of a type ordinarily intended for private use or consumption, and
  (ii) was used by the injured person mainly for his own private use or consumption.

This Article shall be without prejudice to national provisions relating to non-material damage.

Art. 10. 1. Member States shall provide in their legislation that a limitation period of three years shall apply to proceedings for the recovery of damages as provided for in this Directive. The limitation period shall begin to run from the day on which the plaintiff became aware, or should reasonably have become aware, of the damage, the defect and the identity of the producer.

2. The laws of Member States regulating suspension or interruption of the limitation period shall not be affected by this Directive.

Art. 11. Member States shall provide in their legislation that the rights conferred upon the injured person pursuant to this Directive shall be extinguished upon the expiry of a period of 10 years from the date on which the producer put into circulation the actual product which caused the damage, unless the injured person has in the meantime instituted proceedings against the producer.

Art. 12. The liability of the producer arising from this Directive may not, in relation to the injured person, be limited or excluded by a provision limiting his liability or exempting him from liability.

Art. 13. This Directive shall not affect any rights which an injured person may have according to the rules of the law of contractual or non-contractual liability or a special liability system existing at the moment when this Directive is notified.

Art. 14. This Directive shall not apply to injury or damage arising from nuclear accidents and covered by international conventions ratified by the Member States.

Art. 15. 1. Each Member State may:
 (a) by way of derogation from Article 2, provide in its legislation that within the meaning of Article 1 of this Directive "product' also means primary agricultural products and game;
 (b) by way of derogation from Article 7(e), maintain or, subject to the procedure set out in paragraph 2 of this Article, provide in this legislation that the producer shall be liable even if he proves that the state of scientific and technical knowledge at the time when he put the product into circulation was not such as to enable the existence of a defect to be discovered.

2. A Member State wishing to introduce the measure specified in paragraph 1(b) shall communicate the text of the proposed measure to the Commission. The Commission shall inform the other Member States thereof.

The Member State concerned shall hold the proposed measure in abeyance for nine months after the Commission is informed and provided that in the meantime the Commission has not submitted to the Council a proposal amending this Directive on the relevant matter. However, if within three months of receiving the said information, the Commission does not advise the Member State concerned that it intends submitting such a proposal to the Council, the Member State may take the proposed measure immediately.

If the Commission does submit to the Council such a proposal amending this Directive within the aforementioned nine months, the Member State concerned shall hold the proposed measure in abeyance for a further period of 18 months from the date on which the proposal is submitted.

3. Ten years after the date of notification of this Directive, the Commission shall submit to the Council a report on the effect that rulings by the courts as to the application of Article 7(e) and of paragraph 1(b) of this Article have on consumer protection and the functioning of the common market. In the light of this report the Council, acting on a proposal from the Commission and pursuant to the terms of Article 100 of the Treaty, shall decide whether to repeal Article 7(e).

Art. 16. 1. Any Member State may provide that a producer's total liability for damage resulting from a death or personal injury and caused by identical items with the same defect shall be limited to an amount which may not be less than 70 million ECU.

2. Ten years after the date of notification of this Directive, the Commission shall submit to the Council a report on the effect on consumer protection and the functioning of the common market of the implementation of the financial limit on liability by those Member States which have used the option provided for in paragraph 1. In the light of this report the Council, acting on a proposal from the Commission and pursuant to the terms of Article 100 of the Treaty, shall decide whether to repeal paragraph 1.

Art. 17. This Directive shall not apply to products put into circulation before the date on which the provisions referred to in Article 19 enter into force.

Art. 18. 1. For the purposes of this Directive, the ECU shall be that defined by Regulation (EEC) No. 3180/78, as amended by Regulation (EEC) No. 2626/84. The equivalent in national currency shall initially be calculated at the rate obtaining on the date of adoption of this Directive.

2. Every five years the Council, acting on a proposal from the Commission, shall examine and, if need be, revise the amounts in this Directive, in the light of economic and monetary trends in the Community.

Art. 19. 1. Member States shall bring into force, not later than three years from the date of notification of this Directive, the laws, regulations and administrative provisions necessary to comply with this Directive. They shall forthwith inform the Commission thereof.

2. The procedure set out in Article 15(2) shall apply from the date of notification of this Directive.

Art. 20. Member States shall communicate to the Commission the texts of the main provisions of national law which they subsequently adopt in the field governed by this Directive.

Art. 21. Every five years the Commission shall present a report to the Council on the application of this Directive and, if necessary, shall submit appropriate proposals to it.

Art. 22. This Directive is addressed to the Member States.
Done at Brussels, 25 July 1985.

COUNCIL DIRECTIVE
of 29 June 1992
on general product safety
(92/59/EEC:L 228/24)

THE COUNCIL OF THE EUROPEAN COMMUNITIES,

Having regard to the Treaty establishing the European Economic Community, and in particular Article 100a thereof,

Having regard to the proposal from the Commission,

In cooperation with the European Parliament,

Having regard to the opinion of the Economic and Social Committee,

Whereas it is important to adopt measures with the aim of progressively establishing the internal market over a period expiring on 31 December 1992; whereas the internal market is to comprise an area without internal frontiers in which the free movement of goods, persons, services and capital is ensured;

Whereas some Member States have adopted horizontal legislation on product safety, imposing, in particular, a general obligation on economic operators to market only safe products; whereas those legislations differ in the level of protection afforded to persons; whereas such disparities and the absence of horizontal legislation in other Member States are liable to create barriers to trade and distortions of competition within the internal market;

Whereas it is very difficult to adopt Community legislation for every product which exists or may be developed; whereas there is a need for a broadly-based, legislative framework of a horizontal nature to deal with those products, and also to cover lacunae in existing or forthcoming specific legislation, in particular with a view to ensuring a high level of protection of safety and health of persons, as required by Article 100a (3) of the Treaty;

Whereas it is therefore necessary to establish on a Community level a general safety requirement for any product placed on the market that is intended for consumers or likely to be used by consumers; whereas certain second-hand goods should nevertheless be excluded by their nature;

Whereas production equipment, capital goods and other products used exclusively in the context of a trade or business are not covered by this Directive;

Whereas, in the absence of more specific safety provisions, within the framework of Community regulations, covering the products concerned, the provisions of this Directive are to apply;

Whereas when there are specific rules of Community law, of the total harmonization type, and in particular rules adopted on the basis of the new approach, which lay down obligations regarding product safety, further obligations should not be imposed on economic operators as regards the placing on the market of products covered by such rules;

Whereas, when the provisions of specific Community regulations cover only certain aspects of safety or categories of risks in respect of the product concerned, the obligations of economic operators in respect of such aspects are determined solely by those provisions;

Whereas it is appropriate to supplement the duty to observe the general safety requirement by an obligation on economic operators to supply consumers with relevant information and adopt measures commensurate with the characteristics of the products, enabling them to be informed of the risks that these products might present;

Whereas in the absence of specific regulations, criteria should be defined whereby product safety can be assessed;

Whereas Member States must establish authorities responsible for monitoring product safety and with powers to take the appropriate measures;

Whereas it is necessary in particular for the appropriate measures to include the power for Member States to organise, immediately and efficiently, the withdrawal of dangerous products already placed on the market;

Whereas it is necessary for the preservation of the unity of the market to inform the Commission of any measure restricting the placing on the market of a product or requiring its withdrawal from the market except for those relating to an event which is local in effect and in any case limited to the territory of the Member State concerned; whereas such measures can be taken only in compliance with the provisions of the Treaty, and in particular Articles 30 to 36;

Whereas this Directive applies without prejudice to the notification procedures in Council Directive 83/189/EEC of 28 March 1983 laying down a procedure for the provision of information in the field of technical standards and regulations and in Commission Decision 88/383/EEC of 24 February 1988 providing for the improvement of information on safety, hygiene and health at work;

Whereas effective supervision of product safety requires the setting-up at national and Community levels of a system of rapid exchange of information in emergency situations in respect of the safety of a product and whereas the procedure laid down by Council Decision 89/45/EEC of 21 December 1988 on a Community system for the rapid exchange of information on dangers arising from the use of consumer products should therefore be incorporated into this Directive and the above Decision should be repealed; whereas it is also advisable for this Directive to take over the detailed procedures adopted under the above Decision and to give the Commission, assisted by a committee, power to adapt them;

Whereas, moreover, equivalent notification procedures already exist for pharmaceuticals, which come under Directives 75/319/EEC and 81/851/EEC, concerning animal diseases referred to in Directive 82/894/EEC, for products of animal origin covered by Directive 89/662/EEC, and in the form of the system for the rapid exchange of information in radiological emergencies under Decision 87/600/Euratom;

Whereas it is primarily for Member States, in compliance with the Treaty and in particular with Articles 30 to 36 thereof, to take appropriate measures with regard to dangerous products located within their territory;

Whereas in such a situation the decision taken on a particular product could differ from one Member State to another; whereas such a difference may entail unacceptable disparities in consumer protection and constitute a barrier to intra-Community trade;

Whereas it may be necessary to cope with serious product-safety problems which affect or could affect, in the immediate future, all or a large part of the Community and which, in view of the nature of the safety problem posed by the product cannot be dealt with effectively in a manner commensurate with the urgency of the problem under the procedures laid down in the specific rules of Community law applicable to the products or category of products in question;

Whereas it is therefore necessary to provide for an adequate mechanism allowing, in the last resort, for the adoption of measures applicable throughout the Community, in the form of a decision addressed to the Member States, in order to cope with emergency situations as mentioned above; whereas such a decision is not of direct application to economic operators and must be incorporated into a national instrument; whereas measures adopted under such a procedure can be no more than interim measures that have to be taken by the Commission assisted by a committee of representatives of the Member States; whereas, for reasons of cooperation with the Member States, it is appropriate to provide for a regulatory committee according to procedure III (b) of Decision 87/373/EEC;

Whereas this Directive does not affect victims' rights within the meaning of Council Directive 85/374/EEC of 25 July 1985 on the approximation of the laws, regulations and administrative provisions of the Member States concerning liability for defective products;

Whereas it is necessary that Member States provide for appropriate means of redress before the competent courts in respect of measures taken by the competent authorities which restrict the placing on the market of a product or require its withdrawal;

Whereas it is appropriate to consider, in the light of experience, possible adaptation of this Directive, particularly as regards extension of its scope and provisions on emergency situations and intervention at Community level;

Whereas, in addition, the adoption of measures concerning imported products with a view to preventing risks to the safety and health of persons must comply with the Community's international obligations,

HAS ADOPTED THIS DIRECTIVE:

TITLE I   Objective — Scope — Definitions

Art. 1.   1.   The purpose of the provisions of this Directive is to ensure that products placed on the market are safe.

2.   The provisions of this Directive shall apply in so far as there are no specific provisions in rules of Community law governing the safety of the products concerned.

In particular, where specific rules of Community law contain provisions imposing safety requirements on the products which they govern, the provisions of Articles 2 to 4 of this Directive shall not, in any event, apply to those products.

Where specific rules of Community law contain provisions governing only certain aspects of product safety or categories of risks for the products concerned, those are the provisions which shall apply to the products concerned with regard to the relevant safety aspects or risks.

Art. 2.   For the purposes of this Directive:

(a)   *product* shall mean any product intended for consumers or likely to be used by consumers, supplied whether for consideration or not in the course of a commercial activity and whether new, used or reconditioned.

However, this Directive shall not apply to second-hand products supplied as antiques or as products to be repaired or reconditioned prior to being used, provided that the supplier clearly informs the person to whom he supplies the product to that effect;

(b)   *safe product* shall mean any product which, under normal or reasonably foreseeable conditions of use, including duration, does not present any risk or only the minimum risks compatible with the product's use, considered as acceptable and consistent with a high level of protection for the safety and health of persons, taking into account the following points in particular:

— the characteristics of the product, including its composition, packaging, instructions for assembly and maintenance,

— the effect on other products, where it is reasonably foreseeable that it will be used with other products,

— the presentation of the product, the labelling, any instructions for its use and disposal and any other indication or information provided by the producer,

— the categories of consumers at serious risk when using the product, in particular children.

The feasibility of obtaining higher levels of safety or the availability of other products presenting a lesser degree of risk shall not constitute grounds for considering a product to be "unsafe" or "dangerous";

(c)   *dangerous product* shall mean any product which does not meet the definition of "safe product" according to point (b) hereof;

(d)   *producer* shall mean:

— the manufacturer of the product, when he is established in the Community, and any other person presenting himself as the manufacturer by affixing to the product his name, trade mark or other distinctive mark, or the person who reconditions the product,

— the manufacturer's representative, when the manufacturer is not established in the Community or, if there is no representative established in the Community, the importer of the product,

— other professionals in the supply chain, insofar as their activities may affect the safety properties of a product placed on the market.

(e) *distributor* shall mean any professional in the supply chain whose activity does not affect the safety properties of a product.

TITLE II General safety requirement

Art. 3. 1. Producers shall be obliged to place only safe products on the market.

2. Within the limits of their respective activities, producers shall:

— provide consumers with the relevant information to enable them to assess the risks inherent in a product throughout the normal or reasonably foreseeable period of its use, where such risks are not immediately obvious without adequate warnings, and to take precautions against those risks.

Provision of such warnings does not, however, exempt any person from compliance with the other requirements laid down in this Directive,

— adopt measures commensurate with the characteristics of the products which they supply, to enable them to be informed of risks which these products might present and to take appropriate action including, if necessary, withdrawing the product in question from the market to avoid these risks.

The above measures shall for example include, whenever appropriate, marking of the products or product batches in such a way that they can be identified, sample testing of marketed products, investigating complaints made and keeping distributors informed of such monitoring.

3. Distributors shall be required to act with due care in order to help to ensure compliance with the general safety requirement, in particular by not supplying products which they know or should have presumed, on the basis of the information in their possession and as professionals, do not comply with this requirement. In particular, within the limits of their respective activities, they shall participate in monitoring the safety of products placed on the market, especially by passing on information on product risks and cooperating in the action taken to avoid these risks.

Art. 4. 1. Where there are no specific Community provisions governing the safety of the products in question, a product shall be deemed safe when it conforms to the specific rules of national law of the Member State in whose territory the product is in circulation, such rules being drawn up in conformity with the Treaty, and in particular Articles 30 and 36 thereof, and laying down the health and safety requirements which the product must satisfy in order to be marketed.

2. In the absence of specific rules as referred to in paragraph 1, the conformity of a product to the general safety requirement shall be assessed having regard to voluntary national standards giving effect to a European standard or, where they exist, to Community technical specifications or, failing these, to standards drawn up in the Member State in which the product is in circulation, or to the codes of good practice in respect of health and safety in the sector concerned or to the state of the art and technology and to the safety which consumers may reasonably expect.

3. Conformity of a product with the provisions mentioned in paragraphs 1 or 2 shall not bar the competent authorities of the Member States from taking appropriate measures to impose restrictions on its being placed on the market or to require its withdrawal from the market where there is evidence that, despite such conformity, it is dangerous to the health and safety of consumers.

TITLE III Obligations and powers of the Member States

Art. 5. Member States shall adopt the necessary laws, regulations and administrative provisions to make producers and distributors comply with their obligations under this Directive in such a way that products placed on the market are safe.

In particular, Member States shall establish or nominate authorities to monitor the compliance of products with the obligation to place only safe products on the market and arrange for such authorities to have the necessary powers to take the appropriate measures incumbent upon them under this Directive, including the possibility of imposing suitable penalties in the event of failure to comply with the obligations deriving from this Directive. They shall notify the Commission of the said authorities; the Commission shall pass on the information to the other Member States.

Art. 6. 1. For the purposes of Article 5, Member States shall have the necessary powers, acting in accordance with the degree or risk and in conformity with the Treaty, and in particular Articles 30 and 36 thereof, to adopt appropriate measures with a view, *inter alia*, to:

   (a) organising appropriate checks on the safety properties of products, even after their being placed on the market as being safe, on an adequate scale, up to the final stage of use or consumption;

   (b) requiring all necessary information from the parties concerned;

   (c) taking samples of a product or a product line and subjecting them to safety checks;

   (d) subjecting product marketing to prior conditions designed to ensure product safety and requiring that suitable warnings be affixed regarding the risks which the product may present;

   (e) making arrangements to ensure that persons who might be exposed to a risk from a product are informed in good time and in a suitable manner of the said risk by, *inter alia*, the publication of special warnings;

   (f) temporarily prohibiting, for the period required to carry out the various checks, anyone from supplying, offering to supply or exhibiting a product or product batch, whenever there are precise and consistent indications that they are dangerous;

   (g) prohibiting the placing on the market of a product or product batch which has proved dangerous and establishing the accompanying measures needed to ensure that the ban is complied with;

   (h) organising the effective and immediate withdrawal of a dangerous product or product batch already on the market and, if necessary, its destruction under appropriate conditions.

2. The measures to be taken by the competent authorities of the Member States under this Article shall be addressed, as appropriate, to:

   (a) the producer;

   (b) within the limits of their respective activities, distributors and in particular the party responsible for the first stage of distribution on the national market;

   (c) any other person, where necessary, with regard to cooperation in action taken to avoid risks arising from a product.

TITLE IV Notification and Exchanges of Information

Art. 7. 1. Where a Member State takes measures which restrict the placing of a product or a product batch on the market or require its withdrawal from the market, such as provided for in Article 6(1)(d) to (h), the Member State shall, to the extent that such notification is not required under any specific Community legislation, inform the Commission of the said measures, specifying its reasons for adopting them. This obligation shall not apply where the measures relate to an event which is local in effect and in any case limited to the territory of the Member State concerned.

2. The Commission shall enter into consultations with the parties concerned as quickly as possible. Where the Commission concludes, after such consultations, that the measure is justified, it shall immediately inform the Member State which initiated the action and the other Member States. Where the Commission concludes, after such consultations, that the measures is not justified, it shall immediately inform the Member State which initiated the action.

TITLE V   Emergency situations and action at Community level

Art. 8. 1. Where a Member State adopts or decides to adopt emergency measures to prevent, restrict or impose specific conditions on the possible marketing or use, within its own territory, of a product or product batch by reason of a serious and immediate risk presented by the said product or product batch to the health and safety of consumers, it shall forthwith inform the Commission thereof, unless provision is made for this obligation in procedures of a similar nature in the context of other Community instruments.

This obligation shall not apply if the effects of the risk do not, or cannot, go beyond the territory of the Member State concerned.

Without prejudice to the provisions of the first subparagraph, Member States may pass on to the Commission any information in their possession regarding the existence of a serious and immediate risk before deciding to adopt the measures in question.

2. On receiving this information, the Commission shall check to see whether it complies with the provisions of this Directive and shall forward it to the other Member States, which, in turn, shall immediately inform the Commission of any measures adopted.

3. Detailed procedures for the Community information system described in this Article are set out in the Annex. They shall be adapted by the Commission in accordance with the procedure laid down in Article 11.

Art. 9. If the Commission becomes aware, through notification given by the Member States or through information provided by them, in particular under Article 7 or Article 8, of the existence of a serious and immediate risk from a product to the health and safety of consumers in various Member States and if:

(a)   one or more Member States have adopted measures entailing restrictions on the marketing of the product or requiring its withdrawal from the market, such as those provided for in Article 6(1)(d) to (h);

(b)   Member States differ on the adoption of measures to deal with the risk in question;

(c)   the risk cannot be dealt with, in view of the nature of the safety issue posed by the product and in a manner compatible with the urgency of the case, under the other procedures laid down by the specific Community legislation applicable to the product or category of products concerned; and

(d)   the risk can be eliminated effectively only by adopting appropriate measures applicable at Community level, in order to ensure the protection of the health and safety of consumers and the proper functioning of the common market;

the Commission, after consulting the Member States and at the request of at least one of them, may adopt a decision, in accordance with the procedure laid down in Article 11, requiring Member States to take temporary measures from among those listed in Article 6(1)(d) to (h).

Art. 10. 1. The Commission shall be assisted by a Committee on Product Safety Emergencies, hereinafter referred to as "the Committee", composed of the representatives of the Member States and chaired by a representative of the Commission.

2. Without prejudice to Article 9(c), there shall be close cooperation between the Committee referred to in paragraph 1 and the other Committees established by specific

rules of Community law to assist the Commission as regards the health and safety aspects of the product concerned.

Art. 11. 1. The Commission representative shall submit to the Committee a draft of the measures to be taken. The Committee, having verified that the conditions listed in Article 9 are fulfilled, shall deliver its opinion on the draft within a time limit which the Chairman may lay down according to the urgency of the matter but which may not exceed one month. The opinion shall be delivered by the majority laid down in Article 148(2) of the Treaty for adoption of decisions by the Council on a proposal from the Commission. The votes of the representatives of the Member States within the Committee shall be weighted in the manner set out in that Article. The Chairman shall not vote.

The Commission shall adopt the measures in question, if they are in accordance with the opinion of the Committee. If the measures proposed are not in accordance with the Committee's opinion, or in the absence of an opinion, the Commission shall forthwith submit to the Council a proposal regarding the measures to be taken. The Council shall act by a qualified majority.

If the Council has not acted within 15 days of the date on which the proposal was submitted to it, the measures proposed shall be adopted by the Commission unless the Council has decided against them by a simple majority.

2. Any measure adopted under this procedure shall be valid for no longer than three months. That period may be prolonged under the same procedure.

3. Member States shall take all necessary measures to implement the decisions adopted under this procedure within less than 10 days.

4. The competent authorities of the Member States responsible for carrying out measures adopted under this procedure shall, within one month, give the parties concerned an opportunity to submit their views and shall inform the Commission accordingly.

Art. 12. The Member States and the Commission shall take the steps necessary to ensure that their officials and agents are required not to disclose information obtained for the purposes of this Directive which, by its nature, is covered by professional secrecy, except for information relating to the safety properties of a given product which must be made public if circumstances so require, in order to protect the health and safety of persons.

TITLE VI   Miscellaneous and final provisions

Art. 13. This Directive shall be without prejudice to Directive 85/374/EEC.

Art. 14. 1. Any decision adopted under this Directive and involving restrictions on the placing of a product on the market, or requiring its withdrawal from the market, must state the appropriate reasons on which it is based. It shall be notified as soon as possible to the party concerned and shall indicate the remedies available under the provisions in force in the Member State in question and the time limits applying to such remedies.

The parties concerned shall, whenever feasible, be given an opportunity to submit their views before the adoption of the measure. If this has not been done in advance because of the urgency of the measures to be taken, such opportunity shall be given in due course after the measure has been implemented.

Measures requiring the withdrawal of a product from the market shall take into consideration the need to encourage distributors, users and consumers to contribute to the implementation of such measures.

2. Member States shall ensure that any measure taken by the competent authorities involving restrictions on the placing of a product on the market or requiring its withdrawal from the market can be challenged before the competent courts.

3. Any decision taken by virtue of this Directive and involving restrictions on the placing of a product on the market or requiring its withdrawal from the market shall be entirely without prejudice to assessment of the liability of the party concerned, in the light of the national criminal law applying in the case in question.

Art. 15. Every two years following the date of adoption, the Commission shall submit a report on the implementation of this Directive to the European Parliament and the Council.

Art. 16. Four years from the date referred to in Article 17(1), on the basis of a Commission report on the experience acquired, together with appropriate proposals, the Council shall decide whether to adjust this Directive, in particular with a view to extending its scope as laid down in Article 1(1) and Article 2(a), and whether the provisions of Title V should be amended.

Art. 17. 1. Member States shall adopt the laws, regulations and administrative provisions necessary to comply with this Directive by 29 June 1994 at the latest. They shall forthwith inform the Commission thereof. The provisions adopted shall apply with effect from 29 June 1994.

2. When these measures are adopted by the Member States, they shall contain a reference to this Directive or be accompanied by such a reference on the occasion of their official publication. The methods of making such a reference shall be laid down by the Member States.

3. Member States shall communicate to the Commission the text of the provisions of national law which they adopt in the area covered by this Directive.

Art. 18. Decision 89/45/EEC is hereby repealed on the date referred to in Article 17(1).

Art. 19. This Directive is addressed to the Member States.
Done at Luxembourg, 29 June 1992.

COUNCIL DIRECTIVE
of 5 April 1993
on unfair terms in consumer contracts
(93/13/EEC:L 95/29)

THE COUNCIL OF THE EUROPEAN COMMUNITIES,

Having regard to the Treaty establishing the European Economic Community, and in particular Article 100A thereof,

Having regard to the proposal from the Commission,

In cooperation with the European Parliament,

Having regard to the opinion of the Economic and Social Committee,

Whereas it is necessary to adopt measures with the aim of progressively establishing the internal market before 31 December 1992; whereas the internal market comprises an area without internal frontiers in which goods, persons, services and capital move freely;

Whereas the laws of Member States relating to the terms of contract between the seller of goods or supplier of services, on the one hand, and the consumer of them, on the other hand, show many disparities, with the result that the national markets for the sale of goods and services to consumers differ from each other and that distortions of competition may arise amongst the sellers and suppliers, notably when they sell and supply in other Member States;

Whereas, in particular, the laws of Member States relating to unfair terms in consumer contracts show marked divergences;

Whereas it is the responsibility of the Member States to ensure that contracts concluded with consumers do not contain unfair terms;

Whereas, generally speaking, consumers do not know the rules of law which, in Member States other than their own, govern contracts for the sale of goods or services; whereas this lack of awareness may deter them from direct transactions for the purchase of goods or services in another Member State;

Whereas, in order to facilitate the establishment of the internal market and to safeguard the citizen in his role as consumer when acquiring goods and services under contracts which are governed by the laws of Member States other than his own, it is essential to remove unfair terms from those contracts;

Whereas sellers of goods and suppliers of services will thereby be helped in their task of selling goods and supplying services, both at home and throughout the internal market; whereas competition will thus be stimulated, so contributing to increased choice for Community citizens as consumers;

Whereas the two Community programmes for a consumer protection and information policy underlined the importance of safeguarding consumers in the matter of unfair terms of contract; whereas this protection ought to be provided by laws and regulations which are either harmonised at Community level or adopted directly at that level;

Whereas in accordance with the principle laid down under the heading "Protection of the economic interests of the consumers", as stated in those programmes: "acquirers of goods and services should be protected against the abuse of power by the seller or supplier, in particular against one-sided standard contracts and the unfair exclusion of essential rights in contracts";

Whereas more effective protection of the consumer can be achieved by adopting uniform rules of law in the matter of unfair terms; whereas those rules should apply to all contracts concluded between sellers or suppliers and consumers; whereas as a result *inter alia* contracts relating to employment, contracts relating to succession rights, contracts relating to rights under family law and contracts relating to the incorporation and organisation of companies or partnership agreements must be excluded from this Directive;

Whereas the consumer must receive equal protection under contracts concluded by word of mouth and written contracts regardless, in the latter case, of whether the terms of the contract are contained in one or more documents;

Whereas, however, as they now stand, national laws allow only partial harmonisation to be envisaged; whereas, in particular, only contractual terms which have not been individually negotiated are covered by this Directive; whereas Member States should have the option, with due regard for the Treaty, to afford consumers a higher level of protection through national provisions that are more stringent than those of this Directive;

Whereas the statutory or regulatory provisions of the Member States which directly or indirectly determine the terms of consumer contracts are presumed not to contain unfair terms; whereas, therefore, it does not appear to be necessary to subject the terms which reflect mandatory statutory or regulatory provisions and the principles or provisions of international contraventions to which the Member States or the Community are party; whereas in that respect the wording "mandatory statutory or regulatory provisions" in Article 1 (2) also covers rules which, according to the law, shall apply between the contracting parties provided that no other arrangements have been established;

Whereas Member States must however ensure that unfair terms are not included, particularly because this Directive also applies to trades, business or professions of a public nature;

Whereas it is necessary to fix in a general way the criteria for assessing the unfair character of contract terms;

Whereas the assessment, according to the general criteria chosen, of the unfair character of terms, in particular in sale or supply activities of a public nature providing collective services which take account of solidarity among users, must be supplemented by a means of making an overall evaluation of the different interests involved; whereas this constitutes the requirement of good faith; whereas, in making an assessment of good faith, particular regard shall be had to the strength of the bargaining positions of the parties, whether the consumer had an inducement to agree to the term and whether the goods or services were sold or supplied to the special order of the consumer; whereas the requirement of good faith may be satisfied by the seller or supplier where he deals fairly and equitably with the other party whose legitimate interests he has to take into account;

Whereas, for the purposes of this Directive, the annexed list of terms can be of indicative value only and, because of the cause of the minimal character of the Directive, the scope of these terms may be the subject of amplification or more restrictive editing by the Member States in their national laws;

Whereas the nature of goods or services should have an influence on assessing the unfairness of contractual terms;

Whereas, for the purposes of this Directive, assessment of unfair character shall not be made of terms which describe the main subject matter of the contract nor the quality/price ratio of the goods or services supplied; whereas the main subject matter of the contract and the price/quality ratio may nevertheless be taken into account in assessing the fairness of other terms; whereas it follows, *inter alia*, that in insurance contracts, the terms which clearly define or circumscribe the insured risk and the insurer's liability shall not be subject to such assessment since these restrictions are taken into account in calculating the premium paid by the consumer;

Whereas contracts should be drafted in plain, intelligible language, the consumer should actually be given an opportunity to examine all the terms and, if in doubt, the interpretation most favourable to the consumer should prevail;

Whereas Member States should ensure that unfair terms are not used in contracts concluded with consumers by a seller or supplier and that if, nevertheless, such terms are so used, they will not bind the consumer, and the contract will continue to bind the parties upon those terms if it is capable of continuing in existence without the unfair provisions;

Whereas there is a risk that, in certain cases, the consumer may be deprived of protection under this Directive by designating the law of a non-Member country as the law applicable to the contract; whereas provisions should therefore be included in this Directive designed to avert this risk;

Whereas persons or organisations, if regarded under the law of a Member State as having a legitimate interest in the matter, must have facilities for initiating proceedings concerning terms of contract drawn up for general use in contracts concluded with consumers, and in particular unfair terms, either before a court or before an administrative authority competent to decide upon complaints or to initiate appropriate legal proceedings; whereas this possibility does not, however, entail prior verification of the general conditions obtaining in individual economic sectors;

Whereas the courts or administrative authorities of the Member States must have at their disposal adequate and effective means of preventing the continued application of unfair terms in consumer contracts,

HAS ADOPTED THIS DIRECTIVE:

Art. 1. 1. The purpose of this Directive is to approximate the laws, regulations and administrative provisions of the Member States relating to unfair terms in contracts concluded between a seller or supplier and a consumer.

2. The contractual terms which reflect mandatory statutory or regulatory provisions and the provisions or principles of international conventions to which the Member States or the Community are party, particularly in the transport area, shall not be subject to the provisions of this Directive.

Art. 2. For the purposes of this Directive:

(a) "unfair terms" means the contractual terms defined in Article 3;

(b) "consumer" means any natural person who, in contracts covered by this Directive, is acting for purposes which are outside his trade, business or profession;

(c) "seller or supplier" means any natural or legal person who, in contracts covered by this Directive, is acting for purposes relating to his trade, business or profession, whether publicly owned or privately owned.

Art. 3. 1. A contractual term which has not been individually negotiated shall be regarded as unfair if, contrary to the requirement of good faith, it causes a significant imbalance in the parties' rights and obligations arising under the contract, to the detriment of the consumer.

2. A term shall always be regarded as not individually negotiated where it has been drafted in advance and the consumer has therefore not been able to influence the substance of the term, particularly in the context of a pre-formulated standard contract.

The fact that certain aspects of a term or one specific term have been individually negotiated shall not exclude the application of this Article to the rest of a contract if an overall assessment of the contract indicates that it is nevertheless a pre-formulated standard contract.

Where any seller or supplier claims that a standard term has been individually negotiated, the burden of proof in this respect shall be incumbent on him.

3. The Annex shall contain an indicative and non-exhaustive list of the terms which may be regarded as unfair.

Art. 4. 1. Without prejudice to Article 7, the unfairness of a contractual term shall be assessed, taking into account the nature of the goods or services for which the contract was concluded and by referring, at the time of conclusion of the contract, to all the circumstances attending the conclusion of the contract and to all the other terms of the contract or of another contract on which it is dependent.

2. Assessment of the unfair nature of the terms shall relate neither to the definition of the main subject matter of the contract nor to the adequacy of the price and remuneration, on the one hand, as against the services or goods supplies in exchange, on the other, in so far as these terms are in plain intelligible language.

Art. 5. In the case of contracts where all or certain terms offered to the consumer are in writing, these terms must always be drafted in plain, intelligible language.

Where there is doubt about the meaning of a term, the interpretation most favourable to the consumer shall prevail. This rule on interpretation shall not apply in the context of the procedures laid down in Article 7(2).

Art. 6. 1. Member States shall lay down that unfair terms used in a contract concluded with a consumer by a seller or supplier shall, as provided for under their national law, not be binding on the consumer and that the contract shall continue to bind the parties upon those terms if it is capable of continuing in existence without the unfair terms.

2. Member States shall take the necessary measures to ensure that the consumer does not lose the protection granted by this Directive by virtue of the choice of the law of a non-Member country as the law applicable to the contract if the latter has a close connection with the territory of the Member States.

Art. 7. 1. Member States shall ensure that, in the interests of consumers and of competitors, adequate and effective means exist to prevent the continued use of unfair terms in contracts concluded with consumers by sellers or suppliers.

2. The means referred to in paragraph 1 shall include provisions whereby persons or organisations, having a legitimate interest under national law in protecting consumers, may take action according to the national law concerned before the courts or before competent administrative bodies for a decision as to whether contractual terms drawn up for general use are unfair, so that they can apply appropriate and effective means to prevent the continued use of such terms.

3. With due regard for national laws, the legal remedies referred to in paragraph 2 may be directed separately or jointly against a number of sellers or suppliers from the same economic sector or their associations which use or recommend the use of the same general contractual terms or similar terms.

Art. 8. Member States may adopt or retain the most stringent provisions compatible with the Treaty in the area covered by this Directive, to ensure a maximum degree of protection for the consumer.

Art. 9. The Commission shall present a report to the European Parliament and to the Council concerning the application of this Directive five years at the latest after the date in Article 10(1).

Art. 10. 1. Member States shall bring into force the laws, regulations and administrative provisions necessary to comply with this Directive no later than 31 Deccember 1994. They shall forthwith inform the Commission thereof.

These provisions shall be applicable to all contracts concluded after 31 December 1994.

2. When Member States adopt these measures, they shall contain a reference to this Directive or shall be accompanied by such reference on the occasion of their official publication. The methods of making such a reference shall be laid down by the Member States.

3. Member States shall communicate the main provisions of national law which they adopt in the field covered by this Directive to the Commission.

Art. 11. This Directive is addressed to the Member States.
Done at Luxembourg, 5 April 1993.

ANNEX
TERMS REFERRED TO IN ARTICLE 3(3)

1. **Terms which have the object or effect of:**

   (a) excluding or limiting the legal liability of a seller or supplier in the event of the death of a consumer or personal injury to the latter resulting from an act or omission of that seller or supplier;

   (b) inappropriately excluding or limiting the legal rights of the consumer *vis-à-vis* the seller or supplier or another party in the event of total or partial non-performance or inadequate performance by the seller or supplier of any of the contractual obligations, including the option of offsetting a debt owed to the seller or supplier against any claim which the consumer may have against him;

   (c) making an agreement binding on the consumer whereas provision of services by the seller or supplier is subject to a condition whose realisation depends on his own will alone;

   (d) permitting the seller or supplier to retain sums paid by the consumer where the latter decides not to conclude or perform the contract, without providing for the consumer to receive compensation of an equivalent amount from the seller or supplier where the latter is the party cancelling the contract;

   (e) requiring any consumer who fails to fulfil his obligation to pay a disproportionately high sum in compensation;

   (f) authorising the seller or supplier to dissolve the contract on a discretionary basis where the same facility is not granted to the consumer, or permitting the seller or supplier to retain the sums paid for services not yet supplied by him where it is the seller or supplier himself who dissolves the contract;

   (g) enabling the seller or supplier to terminate a contract of indeterminate duration without reasonable notice except where there are serious grounds for doing so;

   (h) automatically extending a contract of fixed duration where the consumer does not indicate otherwise, when the deadline fixed for the consumer to express this desire not to extend the contract is unreasonably early;

(i) irrevocably binding the consumer to terms with which he had no real opportunity of becoming acquainted before the conclusion of the contract;

(j) enabling the seller or supplier to alter the terms of the contract unilaterally without a valid reason which is specified in the contract;

(k) enabling the seller or supplier to alter unilaterally without a valid reason any characteristics of the product or service to be provided;

(l) providing for the price of goods to be determined at the time of delivery or allowing a seller of goods or supplier of services to increase their price without in both cases giving the consumer the corresponding right to cancel the contract if the final price is too high in relation to the price agreed when the contract was concluded;

(m) giving the seller or supplier the right to determine whether the goods or services supplied are in conformity with the contract, or giving him the exclusive right to interpret any term of the contract;

(n) limiting the seller's or supplier's obligation to respect commitments undertaken by his agents or making his commitments subject to compliance with a particular formality;

(o) obliging the consumer to fulfil all his obligations where the seller or supplier does not perform his;

(p) giving the seller or supplier the possibility of transferring his rights and obligations under the contract, where this may serve to reduce the guarantees for the consumer, without the latter's agreement;

(q) excluding or hindering the consumer's right to take legal action or exercise any other legal remedy, particularly by requiring the consumer to take disputes exclusively to arbitration not covered by legal provisions, unduly restricting the evidence available to him or imposing on him a burden of proof which, according to the applicable law, should lie with another party to the contract.

2. **Scope of subparagraphs (g), (j) and (l).**

(a) Subparagraph (g) is without hindrance to terms by which a supplier of financial services reserves the right to terminate unilaterally a contract of indeterminate duration without notice where there is a valid reason, provided that the supplier is required to inform the other contracting party or parties thereof immediately.

(b) Subparagraph (j) is without hindrance to terms under which a supplier of financial services reserves the right to alter the rate of interest payable by the consumer or due to the latter, or the amount of other charges for financial services without notice where there is a valid reason, provided that the supplier is required to inform the other contracting party or parties thereof at the earliest opportunity and that the latter are free to dissolve the contract immediately.

Subparagraph (j) is also without hindrance to terms under which a seller or supplier reserves the right to alter unilaterally the conditions of a contract of indeterminate duration, provided that he is required to inform the consumer with reasonable notice and that the consumer is free to dissolve the contract.

(c) Subparagraphs (g), (j) and (l) do not apply to:

— transactions in transferable securities, financial instruments and other products or services where the price is linked to fluctuations in a stock exchange quotation or index or a financial market rate that the seller or supplier does not control;

— contracts for the purchase or sale of foreign currency, traveller's cheques or international money orders denominated in foreign currency;

(d) Subparagraph (l) is without hindrance to price-indexation clauses, where lawful, provided that the method by which prices vary is explicitly described.

PART V
CODES

PRINCIPLES OF EUROPEAN CONTRACT LAW

[Permission is granted for unlimited reproduction for non-commercial purposes only of the text of the articles.]

Part I
Performance, Non-Performance and Remedies
CHAPTER 1
GENERAL PROVISIONS

1.101. Application of the principles.
(1) These Principles are intended to be applied as general rules of contract law in the European Community.
(2) These Principles will apply when the parties have agreed that their contract is to be governed by them.
(3) These Principles may be applied
   (a) when the parties have agreed that their contract is to be governed by "general principles of law", the "*lex mercatoria*" or the like; or
   (b) when the parties have not chosen any system or rules of law to govern their contract.
(4) These Principles may provide a solution to the issue raised where the system or rules of law applicable do not do so.

1.102. Exclusion or modification of the principles.
The parties may exclude the application of any of these Principles or derogate from or vary their effects except as otherwise provided in the Principles.

1.103. Usages and practices.
(1) The parties are bound by any usage to which they have agreed and by any practice they have established between themselves.
(2) The parties are bound by a usage which would be considered generally applicable by persons in the same situation as the parties, except where the application of such usage would be unreasonable.

1.104. Interpretation and supplementation.
(1) These Principles should be interpreted and developed in accordance with their purposes. In particular, regard should be had to the need to promote good faith and fair dealing, certainty in contractual relationships and uniformity of application.

(2) Issues within the scope of those Principles but not expressly settled by them are so far as possible to be settled in accordance with the ideas underlying the Principles. Failing this, the legal system applicable by virtue of the rules of private international law is to be applied.

1.105. Meaning of terms.
In these Principles, except where the context otherwise requires:
   (1) "act" includes omission;
   (2) "court" includes arbitral tribunal;
   (3) an "intentional" act includes an act done recklessly;
   (4) "non-performance" denotes any failure to perform an obligation under the contract, whether or not excused, and includes delayed performance, defective performance and failure to co-operate in order to give full effect to the contract.

1.106. Good faith and fair dealing.
   (1) In exercising his rights and performing his duties each party must act in accordance with good faith and fair dealing.
   (2) The parties may not exclude or limit this duty.

1.107. Duty to co-operate.
Each party owes to the other a duty to co-operate in order to give full effect to the contract.

1.108. Reasonableness.
Under these Principles reasonableness is to be judged by what persons acting in good faith and in the same situation as the parties would consider to be reasonable. In particular, in assessing what is reasonable the nature and purpose of the contract, the circumstances of the case, and the usages and practices of the trades or professions involved should be taken into account.

1.109. Imputed knowledge and intention.
   (1) A party is to be treated as having known or foreseen a fact, or as being in a position where he should have known or foreseen it, if any person for whom he was responsible knew or foresaw the fact, or should have known or foreseen it, unless that person was not involved in the making or performance of the contract.
   (2) A party is to be treated as having acted intentionally or with gross negligence or not in accordance with good faith and fair dealing if a person to whom he entrusted performance or who performed with his assent so acted.

1.110. Notice.
   (1) Notice given pursuant to these Principles has effect if given by any means, whether in writing or otherwise, appropriate to the circumstances.
   (2) If pursuant to these Principles one party gives notice to the other because of the other's non-performance or because such non-performance is reasonably anticipated by the first party and the notice is properly dispatched or given, a delay or error in the transmission of the notice or its failure to arrive does not prevent it from having effect. The notice shall have effect from the time at which it would have arrived under normal circumstances.
   (3) In any other case, notice does not have effect unless and until it reaches the person to whom it is given.
   (4) For the purpose of this Article, "notice" includes a declaration, demand, request or any other form of communication.

CHAPTER 2
TERM AND PERFORMANCE OF THE CONTRACT

2.101. Determination of price or other contractual terms.
Where the contract does not fix the price or the method of determining it, the parties are to be treated as having agreed on a reasonable price. The same rule applies to any other contractual term.

2.102. Unilateral determination by a party.
Where the price or any other contractual term is to be determined by one party whose determination is grossly unreasonable, then notwithstanding any provision to the contrary, a reasonable price or other term shall be substituted.

2.103. Determination by a third person.
(1) Where the price or any other contractual term is to be determined by a third person, and he cannot or will not do so, the parties are presumed to have empowered the court to appoint another person to determine it.

(2) If a price or other term fixed by a third person is grossly unreasonable, a reasonable price or term shall be substituted.

2.104. Reference to a non existent factor.
Where the price or any other contractual term is to be determined by reference to a factor which does not exist or has ceased to exist or to be accessible, the nearest equivalent factor shall be substituted.

2.105. Quality of performance.
If the contract does not specify the quality, a party must tender performance of at least average quality.

2.106. Place of performance.
(1) If the place of performance of a contractual obligation is not fixed by or determinable from the contract it shall be:

    (a) in the case of an obligation to pay money, the creditor's place of business at the time of the conclusion of the contract;

    (b) in the case of an obligation other than to pay money, the obligor's place of business at the time of conclusion of the contract.

(2) If a party has more than one place of business, the place of business for the purpose of the preceding paragraph is that which has the closest relationship to the contract, having regard to the circumstances known to or contemplated by the parties at the time of conclusion of the contract.

(3) If a party does not have a place of business his habitual residence is to be treated as his place of business.

2.107. Time of performance.
A party has to effect his performance:

    (1) if a time is fixed by or determinable from the contract, at that time;

    (2) if a period of time is fixed by or determinable from the contract, at any time within that period unless the circumstances of the case indicate that the other party is to choose the time;

    (3) in any other case, within a reasonable time after the conclusion of the contract.

2.108. Early performance.
(1) A party may decline a tender of performance made before it is due except where acceptance of the tender would not unreasonably prejudice his interests.

(2) A party's acceptance of early performance does not affect the time fixed for the performance of his own obligation.

2.109. Contract for an indefinite period.

A contract for an indefinite period may be ended by either party by giving notice of reasonable length.

2.110. Form of payment.

(1) Payment of money due may be made in any form used in the ordinary course of business.

(2) A creditor who, pursuant to the contract or voluntarily, accepts a cheque or other order to pay or a promise to pay is presumed to do so only on condition that it will be honoured. The creditor may not enforce the original obligation to pay unless the order or promise is not honoured.

2.111. Currency of payment.

(1) The parties may agree that payment shall be made only in a specified currency.

(2) In the absence of such agreement, a sum of money expressed in a currency other than that of the place where payment is due may be paid in the currency of that place according to the rate of exchange prevailing there at the time when payment is due.

(3) If, in a case falling within the preceding paragraph, the debtor has not paid at the time when payment is due, the creditor may require payment in the currency of the place where payment is due according to the rate of exchange prevailing there either at the time when payment is due or at the time of actual payment.

2.112. Appropriation of performance.

(1) Where a party has to perform several obligations of the same nature and the performance tendered does not suffice to discharge all of the obligations, then subject to paragraph (4) the party may at the time of his performance declare to which obligation the performance is to be appropriated.

(2) If the performing party does not make such a declaration, the other party may within a reasonable time appropriate the performance to such obligation as he chooses. He shall inform the performing party of the choice. However, any such appropriation to an obligation which:

    (a) is not yet due; or
    (b) is illegal; or
    (c) is disputed,

is invalid.

(3) In the absence of an appropriation by either party, and subject to paragraph (4), the performance is appropriated to that obligation which satisfies one of the following criteria in the sequence indicated:

    (a) the obligation which is due or is the first to fall due;
    (b) the obligation for which the obligee has the least security;
    (c) the obligation which is the most burdensome for the obligor;
    (d) the obligation which has arisen first.

If none of the preceding criteria applies, the performance is appropriated proportionately to all obligations.

(4) In the case of a monetary obligation, a payment by the debtor is to be appropriated, first, to expenses, secondly, to interest, and thirdly, to principal, unless the creditor makes a different appropriation.

2.113. Property not accepted.

(1) A party who is left in possession of tangible propety other than money because of the other party's failure to accept or retake the property must take reasonable steps to protect and preserve the property.

(2) The party left in possesion may discharge his duty to deliver or return:

    (a) by depositing the property on reasonable terms with a third person to be held to the order of the other party, and notifying the other party of this; or

(b) by selling the property on reasonable terms after notice to the other party, and paying the net proceeds to that party.

(3) Where, however, the property is liable to rapid deterioration or its preservation is unreasonably expensive, the party must take reasonable steps to dispose of it. He may discharge his duty to deliver or return by paying the net proceeds to the other party.

(4) The party left in possession is entitled to be reimbursed or to retain out of the proceeds of sale any expenses reasonably incurred.

2.114. Money not accepted.

Where a party fails to accept money properly tendered by the other party, that party may after notice to the first party discharge his obligation to pay by depositing the money to the order of the first party in accordance with the law of the place where payment is due.

2.115. Stipulation in favour of a third party.

(1) A third party may require performance of a contractual obligation when his right to do so has been expressly agreed upon between the promisor and the promisee, or when such agreement is to be inferred from the purpose of the contract or the circumstances of the case. The third party need not be identified at the time the agreement is concluded.

(2) If the third party renounces the right to performance the right is treated as never having accrued to him.

(3) The promisee may by notice to the promisor deprive the third party of the right to performance unless:

(a) the third party has received notice from the promisee that the right has been made irrevocable; or

(b) the promisor or the promisee has received notice from the third party that the latter accepts the right.

2.116. Performance by a third person.

(1) Except where the contract requires personal performance the obligee cannot refuse performance by a third person if:

(a) the third person acts with the assent of the obligor; or

(b) the third person has a legitimate interest in performance and the obligor has failed to perform or it is clear that he will not perform at the time performance is due.

(2) Performance by the third person in accordance with paragraph (1) discharges the obligor.

2.117. Change of circumstances.

(1) A party is bound to fulfil his obligations even if performance has become more onerous, whether because the cost of performance has increased or because the value of the performance he receives has diminished.

(2) If, however, performance of the contract becomes excessively onerous because of a change of circumstances, the parties are bound to enter into negotiations with a view to adapting the contract or terminating it provided that:

(a) the change of circumstances occurred after the time of conclusion of the contract, or had already occurred at that time but was not and could not reasonably have been known to the parties; and

(b) the possibility of a change of circumstances was not one which could reasonably have been taken into account at the time of conclusion of the contract; and

(c) the risk of the change of circumstances is not one which, according to the contract, the party affected should be required to bear.

(3) If the parties fail to reach agreement within a reasonable period, the court may:

(a) terminate the contract at a date and on terms to be determined by the court; or

(b) adapt the contract in order to distribute between the parties in a just and equitable manner the losses and gains resulting from the change of circumstances; and

(c) in either case, award damages for the loss suffered through the other party refusing to negotiate or breaking off negotiations in bad faith.

CHAPTER 3
NON-PERFORMANCE AND REMEDIES IN GENERAL

3.101. Remedies available.

(1) Whenever a party does not perform an obligation under the contract and the non-performance is not excused under Article 3.108, the aggrieved party may resort to any of the remedies set out in Chapter 4.

(2) Where a party's non-performance is excused under Article 3.108, the aggrieved party may resort to any of the remedies set out in Chapter 4 except claiming performance and damages.

(3) A party may not resort to any of the remedies set out in Chapter 4 to the extent that his own act caused the other party's non-performance.

3.102. Cumulation of remedies.

Remedies which are not incompatible may be cumulated. In particular, a party is not deprived of his right to damages by exercising his right to any other remedy.

3.103. Fundamental non-performance.

A non-performance of an obligation is fundamental to the contract if:

(a) strict compliance with the obligation is of the essence of the contract; or

(b) the non-performance substantially deprives the aggrieved party of what he was entitled to expect under the contract, unless the other party did not foresee and could not reasonably have foreseen that result; or

(c) the non-performance is intentional and gives the aggrieved party reason to believe that he cannot rely on the other party's future performance.

2.104. Cure by non-performing party.

A party whose tender of performance is not accepted by the other party because it does not conform to the contract may make a new and conforming tender where the time for performance has not yet arrived or the delay would not be such as to constitute a fundamental non-performance.

3.105. Assurance of performance.

(1) A party who reasonably believes that there will be a fundamental non-performance by the other party may demand adequate assurance of due performance and meanwhile may withhold performance of his own obligations so long as such reasonable belief continues.

(2) Where this assurance is not provided within a reasonable time, the party demanding it may terminate the contract if he still reasonably believes that there will be a fundamental non-performance by the other party and gives notice of termination without delay.

3.106. Notice fixing additional period for performance.

(1) In any case of non-performance the aggrieved party may by notice to the other party allow an additional period of time for performance.

(2) During the additional period the aggrieved party may withhold performance of his own reciprocal obligations and may claim damages, but he may not resort to any other remedy. If he receives notice from the other party that the latter will not perform within that period, or if upon expiry of that period due performance has not been made, the aggrieved party may resort to any of the remedies that may be available under Chapter 4.

(3) If in a case of delay in performance which is not fundamental the aggrieved party has given a notice fixing an additional period of time of reasonable length, he may

terminate the contract at the end of the period of notice. The aggrieved party may in his notice provide that if the other party does not perform within the period fixed by the notice the contract shall terminate automatically. If the period stated is too short, the aggrieved party may terminate, or, as the case may be, the contract shall terminate automatically, only after a reasonable period from the time of the notice.

3.107. Performance entrusted to another.
A party who entrusts performance of the contract to another person remains responsible for performance.

3.108. Excuse due to an impediment.
(1) A party's non-performance is excused if he proves that it is due to an impediment beyond his control and that he could not reasonably have been expected to take the impediment into account at the time of the conclusion of the contract, or to have avoided or overcome the impediment or its consequences.

(2) Where the impediment is only temporary the excuse provided by this article has effect for the period during which the impediment exists. However, if the delay amounts to a fundamental non-performance, the obligee may treat it as such.

(3) The non-performing party must ensure that notice of the impediment and of its effect on his ability to perform is received by the other party within a reasonable time after the non-performing party knew or ought to have known of these circumstances. The other party is entitled to damages for any loss resulting from the non-receipt of such notice.

3.109. Clause limiting or excluding liability.
The parties may agree in advance to limit or to exclude their liability for non-performance except where the non-performance is intentional or the limitation or exclusion is unreasonable.

CHAPTER 4
PARTICULAR REMEDIES FOR NON-PERFORMANCE

Section 1
Right to Performance

4.101. Monetary obligations.
(1) The creditor is entitled to recover money which is due.

(2) Where the creditor has not yet performed his obligation and it is clear that the debtor will be unwilling to receive performance, the creditor may nonetheless proceed with his performance and may recover any sum due under the contract unless:

    (a) he could have made a reasonable cover transaction without significant effort or expense; or

    (b) performance would be unreasonable in the circumstances.

4.102. Non-monetary obligations.
(1) The aggrieved party is entitled to specific performance of an obligation other than one to pay money, including the remedying of a defective performance.

(2) Specific performance cannot, however, be obtained where:

    (a) performance would be unlawful or impossible; or

    (b) performance would cause the obligor unreasonable effort or expense; or

    (c) the performance consists in the provision of services or work of a personal character or depends upon a personal relationship; or

    (d) the aggrieved party will lose the right to specific performance from another source.

(3) The aggrieved party will lose the right to specific performance if he fails to seek it within a reasonable time after he has or ought to have become aware of the non-performance.

4.103. Damages not precluded.
The fact that a right to performance is excluded under this Section does not preclude a claim for damages.

Section 2
Right to Withhold Performance

4.201. Right to withhold performance.
(1) A party who is to perform simultaneously with or after the other party may withhold performance until the other has tendered performance or has performed. The first party may withhold the whole of his performance or a part of it as may be reasonable in the circumstances.

(2) A party may similarly withhold performance for as long as it is clear that there will be a non-performance by the other party when the other party's performance becomes due.

Section 3
Termination of the Contract

4.301. Right to terminate the contract.
(1) A party may terminate the contract if the other party's non-performance is fundamental.

(2) In the case of delay the aggrieved party may also terminate the contract under Article 3.106(3).

4.302. Contract to be performed in parts.
If the contract is to be performed in separate parts and in relation to a part to which the counter performance can be apportioned, there is a fundamental non-performance, the aggrieved party may exercise his right to terminate under this Section in relation to the part concerned. He may terminate the contract as a whole only if the non-performance is fundamental to the contract as whole.

4.303. Notice of termination.
(1) A party's right to terminate the contract is to be exercised by notice to the other party.

(2) The aggrieved party loses his right to terminate the contract unless he gives notice within a reasonable time after he has or ought to have become aware of the non-performance.

(3)(a) When performance has not been tendered by the time it was due, the aggrieved party need not give notice of termination before a tender has been made. If a tender is later made he loses his right to terminate if he does not give such notice within a reasonable time after he has or ought to have become aware of the tender.

(b) If, however, the aggrieved party knows or has reason to know that the aggrieved party unreasonably fails to notify the other party that he will not accept performance, he loses his right to terminate if the other party in fact tenders within a reasonable time.

(4) If a party is excused under Article 3.108 through an impediment which is total and permanent, the contract is terminated automatically and without notice at the time the impediment arises.

4.304. Anticipatory non-performance.
Where prior to the time for performance by a party it is clear that there will be a fundamental non-performance by him the other party may terminate the contract.

4.305. Effects of termination in general.
(1) Termination of the contract releases both parties from their obligation to effect and to receive future performance, but, subject to Articles 4.306, 4.307 and 4.308, does not affect the rights and liabilities accrued up to the time of termination.

(2) Termination does not affect any provision of the contract for the settlement of disputes or any other provision which is to operate even after termination.

4.306. Property reduced in value.
A party who terminates the contract may reject property previously received from the other party if its value to the first party has been fundamentally reduced as a result of the other party's non-performance.

4.307. Recovery of money paid.
On termination of the contract a party may recover money paid for a performance which he did not receive or which he properly rejected.

4.308. Recovery of property.
On termination of the contract a party who has supplied property which can be returned and for which he has not received payment or other counter-performance may recover the property.

4.309. Recovery for performance that cannot be returned.
On termination of the contract a party who has rendered a performance which cannot be returned and for which he has not received payment or other counterperformance may recover a reasonable amount for the value of the performance to the other party.

Section 4
Price Reduction

4.401. Right to reduce price.
(1) A party who accepts a tender of performance not conforming to the contract may reduce the price. This reduction shall be proportionate to the decrease in the value of the performance at the time this was tendered compared to the value which a conforming tender would have had at that time.

(2) A party who is entitled to reduce the price under the preceding paragraph and who has already paid a sum exceeding the reduced price may recover the excess from the other party.

(3) A party who reduces the price cannot also recover damages for reduction in the value of the performance but remains entitled to damages for any further loss he has suffered so far as these are recoverable under Section 5 of this Chapter.

Section 5
Damages and Interest

4.501. Right to damages.
(1) The aggrieved party is entitled to damages for loss caused by the other party's non-performance which is not excused under Article 3.108.

(2) The loss for which damages are recoverable includes:
   (a) non-pecuniary loss; and
   (b) future loss which is reasonably likely to occur.

4.502. General measure of damages.
The general measure of damages is such sum as will put the aggrieved party as nearly as possible into the position in which he would have been if the contract had been duly performed. Such damages cover the loss which the aggrieved party has suffered and the gain of which he has been deprived.

4.503. Foreseeability.
The non-performing party is liable only for loss which he foresaw or could reasonably have foreseen at the time of conclusion of the contract as a likely result of his non-performance, unless the non-performance was intentional or grossly negligent.

4.504. Loss attributable to aggrieved party.

(1) The non-performing party is not liable for loss suffered by the aggrieved party to the extent that:
  (a) the aggrieved party contributed to the non-performance or its effects; or
  (b) his loss could have been reduced by his taking reasonable steps.

(2) The aggrieved party is entitled to recover any expenses reasonably incurred in attempting to reduce the loss.

4.505. Cover transaction.

Where the aggrieved party has terminated the contract and has made a cover transaction within a reasonable time and in a reasonable manner, he may recover the difference between the contract price and the price of the cover transaction as well as damages for any further loss so far as these are recoverable under this Section.

4.506. Current price.

Where the aggrieved party has terminated the contract and has not made a cover transaction but there is a current price for the performance contracted for, he may recover the difference betwen the contract price and the price current at the time the contract is terminated as well as damages for any further loss so far as these are recoverable under this Section.

4.507. Delay in payment of money.

(1) If payment of a sum of money is delayed, the aggrieved party is entitled to interest on that sum from the time when payment is due to the time of payment at the average commercial bank short-term lending rate to prime borrowers prevailing for the contractual currency of payment at the place where payment is due.

(2) The aggrieved party may in addition recover damages for any further loss so far as these are recoverable under this Section.

4.508. Agreed payment for non-performance.

(1) Where the contract provides that a party who fails to perform is to pay a specified sum to the aggrieved party for such non-performance, the aggrieved party shall be awarded that sum irrespective of his actual loss.

(2) However, despite any agreement to the contrary the specified sum may be reduced to a reasonable amount where it is grossly excessive in relation to the loss resulting from the non-performance and the other circumstances.

4.509. Currency by which damages to be measured.

Damages are to be measured by the currency which most appropriately reflects the aggrieved party's loss.

UNIDROIT PRINCIPLES FOR INTERNATIONAL COMMERCIAL CONTRACTS

[Reproduced from the *Unidroit Principles of International Commercial Contracts*, published by the International Institute for the Unification of Private Law (Unidroit), Rome, Italy, Copyright © Unidroit 1994, by permission of Unidroit. Readers are reminded that the official version of the *Unidroit Principles of International Commercial Contracts* also includes the Commentary thereto. The integral edition of the English, French, German, Italian and Spanish versions may be ordered directly from Unidroit Publications, Via Panisperna 28, 00184 Italy (fax: +39-6 69.94.13.94). The English version may also be ordered from Transnational Juris Publications, One Bridge Street, Irvington-on-Hudson, NY 10533 (fax: +1 (914) 591-2688).]

PREAMBLE (ex Arts. 1.1 and 1.2)
(Purpose of the Principles)

These Principles set forth general rules for international commercial contracts.

They shall be applied when the parties have agreed that their contract be governed by them.

They may be applied when the parties have agreed that their contract be governed by general principles of law, the *lex mercatoria* or the like.

They may provide a solution to an issue raised when it proves impossible to establish the relevant rule of the applicable law.

They may be used to interpret or supplement international uniform law instruments.

They may serve as a model for national and international legislators.

CHAPTER 1
GENERAL PROVISIONS

1.1. Freedom of contract.
The parties are free to enter into a contract and to determine its content.

1.2. No form required.
Nothing in these Principles requires a contract to be concluded in or evidenced by writing. It may be proved by any means, including witnesses.

1.3. Binding character of contract.
A contract validly entered into is binding upon the parties. It can only be modified or terminated in accordance with its terms or by agreement or as otherwise provided under these Principles.

1.4. Mandatory rules.
Nothing in these Principles shall restrict the application of mandatory rules, whether of national, international, or supranational origin, which are applicable in accordance with the relevant rules of private international law.

1.5. Exclusion or modification by the parties.
The parties may exclude the application of these Principles or derogate from or vary the effect of any of their provisions, except as otherwise provided in the Principles.

1.6. Interpretation and supplementation of the Principles.
(1) In the interpretation of these Principles, regard is to be had to their international character and to their purposes including the need to promote uniformity in their application.

(2) Issues within the scope of these Principles but not expressly settled by them are as far as possible to be settled in accordance with their underlying general principles.

1.7. Good faith and fair dealing.
(1) Each party must act in accordance with good faith and fair dealing in international trade.

(2). The parties may not exclude or limit this duty.

1.8. Usages and practices.
(1) The parties are bound by any usage to which they have agreed and by any practices which they have established between themselves.

(2) The parties are bound by a usage that is widely known to and regularly observed in international trade by parties in the particular trade concerned except where the application of such a usage would be unreasonable.

1.9. Notice.
(1) Where notice is required it may be given by any means appropriate to the circumstances.

(2) A notice is effective when it reaches the person to whom it is given.

(3) For the purpose of paragraph (2) a notice "reaches" a person when given to the person orally or delivered at that person's place of business or mailing address.

(4) For the purpose of this article "notice" includes a declaration, demand, request or any other communication of intention.

1.10. Definitions.
In these Principles
— "court" includes arbitration tribunal;
— where a party has more than one place of business the relevant "place of business" is that which has the closest relationship to the contract and its performance, having regard to the circumstances known to or contemplated by the parties at any time before or at the conclusion of the contract.
— "obligor" refers to the party who is to perform an obligation and "obligee" refers to the party who is entitled to performance of that obligation.
— "writing" means any mode of communication that preserves a record of the information contained therein and is capable of being reproduced in tangible form.

CHAPTER 2
FORMATION

2.1. Manner of formation.
A contract may be concluded either by the acceptance of an offer or by conduct of the parties that is sufficient to show agreement.

2.2. Definition of offer.
A proposal for concluding a contract constitutes an offer if it is sufficiently definite and indicates the intention of the offeror to be bound in case of acceptance.

2.3. Withdrawal of offer.
(1) An offer becomes effective when it reaches the offeree.
(2) An offer, even if it is irrevocable, may be withdrawn if the withdrawal reaches the offeree before or at the same time as the offer.

2.4. Revocation of offer.
(1) Until a contract is concluded an offer may be revoked if the revocation reaches the offeree before it has dispatched an acceptance.
(2) However, an offer cannot be revoked
    (a) if it indicates, whether by stating a fixed time for acceptance or otherwise, that it is irrevocable; or
    (b) if it was reasonable for the offeree to rely on the offer as being irrevocable and the offeree has acted in reliance on the offer.

2.5. Rejection of offer.
An offer is terminated when a rejection reaches the offeror.

2.6. Mode of acceptance.
(1) A statement made by or other conduct of the offeree indicating assent to an offer is an acceptance. Silence or inactivity does not in itself amount to acceptance.
(2) An acceptance of an offer becomes effective at the moment the indication of assent reaches the offeror.
(3) However, if, by virtue of the offer or as a result of practices which the parties have established between themselves or of usage, the offeree may indicate assent by performing an act without notice to the offeror, the acceptance is effective at the moment the act is performed.

2.7. Time of acceptance.
An offer must be accepted within the time the offeror has fixed or, if no time is fixed, within a reasonable time having regard to the circumstances, including the rapidity of the means of communication employed by the offeror. An oral offer must be accepted immediately unless the circumstances indicate otherwise.

2.8. Acceptance within a fixed period of time.

(1) A period of time for acceptance fixed by the offeror in a telegram or a letter begins to run from the moment the telegram is handed in for dispatch or from the date shown on the letter or, if no such date is shown, from the date shown on the envelope. A period of time for acceptance fixed by the offeror by means of instantaneous communication begins to run from the moment that the offer reaches the offeree.

(2) Official holidays or non-business days occurring during the period for acceptance are included in calculating the period. However, if a notice of acceptance cannot be delivered at the address of the offeror on the last day of the period because that day falls on an official holiday or a non-business day at the place of business of the offeror, the period is extended until the first business day which follows.

2.9. Late acceptance. Delay in transmission.

(1) A late acceptance is nevertheless effective as an acceptance if without undue delay the offeror so informs the offeree or gives a notice to that effect.

(2) If a letter or other writing containing a late acceptance shows that it has been sent in such circumstances that if its transmission had been normal it would have reached the offeror in due time, the late acceptance is effective as an acceptance unless, without undue delay, the offeror informs the offeree that it considers the offer as having lapsed.

2.10. Withdrawal of acceptance.

An acceptance may be withdrawn if the withdrawal reaches the offeror before or at the same time as the acceptance would have become effective.

2.11. Modified acceptance.

(1) A reply to an offer which purports to be an acceptance but contains additions, limitations or other modifications is a rejection of the offer and constitutes a counter-offer.

(2) However, a reply to an offer which purports to be an acceptance but contains additional or different terms which do not materially alter the terms of the offer constitutes an acceptance, unless the offeror, without undue delay, objects to the discrepancy. If the offeror does not object, the terms of the contract are the terms of the offer with the modifications contained in the acceptance.

2.12. Writings in confirmation.

If a writing which is sent within a reasonable time after the conclusion of the contract and which purports to be a confirmation of the contract contains additional or different terms, such terms become part of the contract, unless they materially alter the contract or the recipient, without undue delay, objects to the discrepancy.

2.13. Conclusion of contract dependent on agreement on specific matters or in a specific form.

Where in the course of negotiations one of the parties insists that the contract is not concluded until there is agreement on specific matters or in a specific form, no contract is concluded before there is agreement on those matters or in that form.

2.14. Contract with terms deliberately left open.

(1) If the parties intend to conclude a contract, the fact that they intentionally leave a term to be agreed upon in further negotiations or to be determined by a third person does not prevent a contract from coming into existence.

(2) The existence of the contract is not affected by the fact that subsequently
   (a) the parties reach no agreement on the term, or
   (b) the third person does not determine the term,
provided that there is an alternative means of rendering the term definite that is reasonable in the circumstances, having regard to the intention of the parties.

2.15. Negotiations in bad faith.

(1) A party is free to negotiate and is not liable for failure to reach an agreement.

(2) However, a party who has negotiated or breaks off negotiations in bad faith is liable for the losses caused to the other party.

(3) It is bad faith, in particular, for a party to enter into or continue negotiations when intending not to make an agreement with the other party.

2.16. Duty of confidentiality.

Where information is given as confidential by one party in the course of negotiations, the other party is under a duty not to disclose that information or to use it improperly for his own purposes, whether or not a contract is subsequently concluded. Where appropriate, the remedy for breach of that duty may include compensation based on the benefit received by the other party.

2.17. Merger clauses.

A contract in writing which contains a clause indicating that the writing completely embodies the terms on which the parties have agreed cannot be contradicted or supplemented by evidence of prior statement or agreements. However, such statements or agreements may be used to interpret the writing.

2.18. Written modification clauses.

A contract in writing which contains a clause requiring any modification or termination by agreement to be in writing may not be otherwise modified or terminated. However, a party may be precluded by its conduct from asserting such a clause to the extent that the other party has acted in reliance on that conduct.

2.19. Contracting under standard terms.

(1) Where one party or both parties use standard terms in concluding a contract, the general rules on formation apply, subject to Articles 2.20–2.22.

(2) Standard terms are provisions which are prepared in advance for general and repeated use by one party and which are actually used without negotiation with the other party.

2.20. Surprising terms.

(1) No term contained in standard terms which is of such a character that the other party could not reasonably have expected it, is effective unless it has been expressly accepted by that party.

(2) In determining whether a term is of such a character regard is to be had to its content, language and presentation.

2.21. Conflict between standard terms and non-standard terms.

In the case of conflict between a standard term and a term which is not a standard term the latter prevails.

2.22. Battle of forms.

Where both parties use standard terms and reach agreement except on those terms, a contract is concluded on the basis of the agreed terms and of any standard terms which are common in substance unless one party clearly indicates in advance, or later and without undue delay informs the other party that it does not intend to be bound by such a contract.

CHAPTER 3
VALIDITY

3.1. Matters not covered.

These Principles do not deal with invalidity arising from

    (a) lack of capacity;

(b) lack of authority;
(c) immorality or illegality.

3.2. Validity of mere agreement.
A contract is concluded, modified or terminated by the mere agreement of the parties, without any further requirement.

3.3. Initial impossibility.
(1) The mere fact that at the time of the conclusion of the contract the performance of the obligation assumed was impossible shall not effect the validity of the contract.

(2) The mere fact that at the time of the conclusion of the contract a party was not entitled to dispose of the assets to which the contract relates, does not effect the validity of the contract.

3.4. Definition of mistake.
Mistake is an erroneous assumption relating to facts or to law existing when the contract was concluded.

3.5. Relevant mistake.
(1) A party may only avoid the contract for mistake if, when the contract was concluded, the mistake was of such importance that a reasonable person in the same situation as the party in error would only have contracted the contract on materially different terms or would not have contracted at all if the true state of affairs had been known, and

(a) the other party made the same mistake, or caused the mistake, or knew or ought to have known of the mistake and it was contrary to reasonable commercial standards of fair dealing to leave the mistaken party in error; or

(b) the other party had not at the time of avoidance acted in reliance on the contract.

(2) However, a party may not avoid the contract, if
(a) it was grossly negligent in committing the mistake; or
(b) the mistake relates to a matter in regard to which the risk of mistake was assumed or, having regard to the circumstances, should be borne by the mistaken party.

3.6. Error in expression or transmission.
An error occurring in the expression or transmission of a declaration is considered to be a mistake of the person from whom the declaration emanated.

3.7. Remedies for non-performance.
A party is not entitled to avoid the contract on the ground of mistake if the circumstances on which that party relies afford, or could have afforded, him a remedy for non-performance.

3.8. Fraud.
A party may avoid the contract when it has been led to conclude the contract by the other party's fraudulent representation, including language or practices, or fraudulent non-disclosure of circumstances which, according to reasonable commercial standards of fair dealing, the latter party should have disclosed.

3.9. Threat.
A party may avoid the contract when he has been led to conclude the contract by the other party's unjustified threat which, having regard to the circumstances, is so imminent and serious as to leave the first party no reasonable alternative. In particular, a threat is unjustified if the act or omission with which a party has been threatened is wrongful in itself, or it is wrongful to use it as a means to obtain the conclusion of the contract.

3.10. Gross disparity.

(1) A party may avoid a contract or an individual term of it if, at the time of the conclusion of the contract, the contract or term unjustifiably gave the other party an excessive advantage. Regard is to be had, among other factors, to

   (a) the fact that the other party has taken unfair advantage of the first party's dependence, economic distress or urgent needs, or of its improvidence, ignorance, inexperience or lack of bargaining skill; and

   (b) the nature and purpose of the contract.

(2) Upon the request of the party entitled to avoidance, a court may adapt the contract or term in order to make it accord with reasonable commercial standards of fair dealing.

(3) A court may also adapt the contract or term upon the request of the party receiving notice of avoidance, provided that that party informs the other party of its request promptly after receiving such notice and before the other party has acted in reliance on it. The provisions of Article 3.13(2) apply accordingly.

3.11. Third persons.

(1) Where fraud, threat, gross disparity or a party's mistake is imputable to, or is known or ought to be known by, a third person for whose acts the other party is responsible, the contract may be avoided under the same conditions as if the behaviour or knowledge had been that of the party itself.

(2) Where fraud, threat or gross disparity is imputable to a third person for whose acts the other party is not responsible, the contract may be avoided if that party knew or ought to have known of the fraud, threat or disparity, or has not at the time of avoidance acted in reliance on the contract.

3.12. Confirmation.

If the party entitled to avoid the contract expressly or impliedly confirms the contract after the period of time for giving notice of avoidance has begun to run, avoidance of the contract is excluded.

3.13. Loss of right to avoid.

(1) If a party is entitled to avoid the contract for mistake but the other party declares itself willing to perform or performs the contract as it was understood by the party entitled to avoidance, the contract is considered to have been concluded as the latter party understood it. The other party must make such a declaration or render such performance promptly after having been informed of the manner in which the party entitled to avoidance had understood the contract and before that party has acted in reliance on a notice of avoidance.

(2) After such a declaration or performance the right to avoidance is lost and any earlier notice of avoidance is ineffective.

3.14. Notice of avoidance.

The right of a party to avoid the contract is exercised by notice to the other party.

3.15. Time limits.

(1) Notice of avoidance shall be given within a reasonable time, having regard to the circumstances, after the avoiding party knew or could not have been unaware of the relevant facts or became capable of acting freely.

(2) Where an individual term of the contract may be avoided by a party under Article 3.10, the period of time for giving notice of avoidance begins to run when that term is asserted by the other party.

3.16. Partial avoidance.

If a ground of avoidance affects only individual terms of the contract, the effect of avoidance is limited to those terms unless, having regard to the circumstances, it is unreasonable to uphold the remaining contract.

3.17. Retroactive effect of avoidance.
(1) Avoidance takes effect retroactively.

(2) On avoidance either party may claim restitution of whatever it has supplied under the contract or the part of it avoided, provided that it concurrently makes restitution of whatever it has received under the contract or the part of it avoided or, if it cannot make restitution in kind, it must make an allowance for what it has received.

3.18. Damages.
Irrespective of whether or not the contract has been avoided, the party who knew or ought to have known of the ground for avoidance is liable for damages so as to put the other party into the same position in which it would have been in if it had not concluded the contract.

3.19. Mandatory character of the provisions.
The provisions of this Chapter are mandatory, except insofar as they relate to the binding force of mere agreement, initial impossibility or mistake.

3.20. Unilateral declarations.
The provisions of this Chapter apply with appropriate adaptations to any communication of intention addressed by one party to the other.

CHAPTER 4
INTERPRETATION

4.1. Intention of parties.
(1) A contract shall be interpreted according to the common intention of the parties.

(2) If such an intention cannot be established, the contract shall be interpreted according to the meaning that reasonable persons of the same kind as the parties would give to it in the same circumstances.

4.2. Interpretation of statements and other conduct.
(1) The statements and other conduct of a party shall be interpreted according to that party's intention if the other party knew or could not have been unaware of that intention.

(2) If the preceding paragraph is not applicable, such statements and other conduct shall be interpreted according to the meaning that a reasonable person of the same kind as the other party would give to it in the same circumstances.

4.3. Relevant circumstances.
(1) In applying Articles 4.1 and 4.2, regard shall be had to all the circumstances, including
  (a) any preliminary negotiations between the parties;
  (b) any practices which the parties have established between themselves;
  (c) any conduct of the parties subsequent to the conclusion of the contract;
  (d) the nature and purpose of the contract;
  (e) the meaning commonly given to terms and expressions in the trade concerned; and
  (f) usages.

4.4. Reference to contract or statement as a whole.
Terms and expressions shall be inerpreted in the light of the whole contract or statement in which they appear.

4.5. All terms to be given effect.
Contract terms shall be interpreted so as to give effect to all the terms rather than to deprive some of them of effect.

4.6. *Contra proferentem* rule.
If contract terms supplied by one party are unclear, an interpretation against that party is preferred.

4.7. Linguistic discrepancies.
Where a contract is drawn up in two or more language versions which are equally authoritative there is, in case of discrepancy between the versions, a preference for the interpretation according to the version in which the contract was originally drawn up.

4.8. Supplying an omitted term.
(1) Where the parties to a contract have not agreed with respect to a term which is important for a determination of their rights and duties, a term which is appropriate in the circumstances shall be supplied.

(2) In determining what is an appropriate term regard shall be had, among other factors, to
    (a) the intention of the parties;
    (b) the nature and purpose of the contract;
    (c) good faith and fair dealing;
    (d) reasonableness.

CHAPTER 5
CONTENT

5.1. Express and implied obligations.
The contractual obligations of the parties may be express or implied.

5.2. Implied obligations.
Implied obligations stem from
    (a) the nature and purpose of the contract;
    (b) practices established between the parties and usages;
    (c) good faith and fair dealing;
    (d) reasonableness.

5.3. Co-operation between the parties.
Each party shall co-operate with the other party, when such co-operation may reasonably be expected for the performance of that party's obligations.

5.4. Duty to achieve a specific result, duty of best efforts.
(1) To the extent that an obligation of a party involves a duty to achieve a specific result, that party is bound to achieve that result.

(2) To the extent that an obligation of a party involves a duty of best efforts in the performance of an activity, that party is bound to make such efforts as would be made by a reasonable person of the same kind in the same circumstances.

5.5. Determination of kind of duty involved.
In determining the extent to which an obligation of a party involves a duty of best efforts in the performance of an activity or a duty to achieve a specific result, regard shall be had, among other factors, to
    (a) the way in which the obligation is expressed in the contract;
    (b) the contractual price and other terms of the contract;
    (c) the degree of risk normally involved in achieving the expected result;
    (d) the ability of the other party to influence the performance of the obligation.

5.6. Determination of quality of performance.
Where the quality of performance is neither fixed by, nor determinable from, the contract, a party is bound to render a performance of a quality that is reasonable and not less than average in the circumstances.

5.7. Price determination.

(1) Where a contract does not fix or make provision for determining the price, the parties are considered, in the absence of any indication to the contrary, to have made reference to the price generally charged at the time of the conclusion of the contract for such performance under comparable circumstances in the trade concerned or, if no such price is available, to a reasonable price.

(2) Where the price is to be determined by one party and that determination is manifestly unreasonable, a reasonable price shall be substituted notwithstanding any contract term to the contrary.

(3) Where the price is to be fixed by a third person, and that person cannot or will not do so, the price shall be a reasonable price.

(4) Where the price is to be fixed by reference to factors which do not exist or have ceased to exist or to be accessible, the nearest equivalent factor shall be treated as a substitute.

5.8. Contract for an indefinite period.

A contract for an indefinite period may be ended by either party by giving notice a reasonable time in advance.

CHAPTER 6
PERFORMANCE

Section 1
Performance in General

6.1.1. Time of performance.

A party must perform its obligations:

    (a) if a time is fixed by or determinable from the contract, at that time;

    (b) if a period of time is fixed by or determinable from the contract, at any time within that period unless circumstances indicate that the other party is to choose a time; or

    (c) in any other case, within a reasonable time after the conclusion of the contract.

6.1.2. Performance at one time or in instalments.

In cases under Article 6.1.1(b) or (c), a party must perform its obligations at one time if that performance can be rendered at one time and the circumstances do not indicate otherwise.

6.1.3. Partial performance.

(1) The obligee may reject an offer to perform in part at the time performance is due, whether or not such offer is coupled with an assurance as to the balance of the performance, unless the obligee has no legitimate interest in so doing.

(2) Additional expenses caused to the obligee by partial performance are to be borne by the obligor without prejudice to any other remedy.

6.1.4. Order of performance.

(1) To the extent that the performances of the parties can be rendered simultaneously, the parties are bound to render them simultaneously unless the circumstances indicate otherwise.

(2) To the extent that the performance of only one party requires a period of time, that party is bound to render its performance first, unless the circumstances indicate otherwise.

6.1.5. Earlier performance.

(1) The obligee may reject an earlier performance unless it has no legitimate interest in so doing.

(2) Acceptance by a party of an earlier performance does not affect the time for the performance of its own obligation if that time has been fixed irrespective of the performance of the other party's obligations.

(3) Additional expenses caused to the obligee by earlier performance are to be borne by the obligor, without prejudice to any other remedy.

6.1.6. Place of performance.

(1) If the place of performance is neither fixed by, nor determinable from, the contract, a party is to perform:
  (a) a monetary obligation, at the obligee's place of business;
  (b) any other obligation, at its own place of business.

(2) A party must bear any increase in the expenses incidental to performance which is caused by a change in its place of business subsequent to the conclusion of the contract.

6.1.7. Payment by cheque or other instruments.

(1) Payment may be made in any form used in the ordinary course of business at the place for payment.

(2) However, an obligee who accepts, either by virtue of paragraph (1) or voluntarily, a cheque, an other order to pay or a promise to pay, is presumed to do so only on condition that it will be honoured.

6.1.8. Payment by funds transfer.

(1) Unless the obligee has indicated a particular account, payment may be made by a transfer to any of the financial institutions in which the obligee has made it known that it has an account.

(2) In case of payment by a transfer the obligation of the obligor is discharged when the transfer to the obligee's financial institution becomes effective.

6.1.9. Currency of payment.

(1) If a monetary obligation is expressed in a currency other than that of the place for payment, it may be paid by the obligor in the currency of the place for payment unless
  (a) that currency is not freely convertible; or
  (b) the parties have agreed that payment should be made only in the currency in which the monetary obligation is expressed.

(2) If it is impossible for the obligor to make payment in the currency in which the monetary obligation is expressed, the obligee may require payment in the currency of the place for payment, even in the case referred to in paragraph (1)(b).

(3) Payment in the currency of the place for payment is to be made according to the applicable rate of exchange prevailing there when payment is due.

(4) However, if the obligor has not paid at the time when payment is due, the obligee may require payment according to the applicable rate of exchange prevailing either when payment is due or at the time of actual payment.

6.1.10. Currency not expressed.

Where a monetary obligation is not expressed in a particular currency, payment must be made in the currency of the place where payment is to be made.

6.1.11. Costs of performance.

Each party shall bear the costs of performance of its obligations.

6.1.12. Imputation of payments.

(1) An obligor owing several monetary obligations to the same obligee may specify at the time of payment the debt to which it intends the payment to be applied. However, the payment discharges first any expenses, then interests due and finally the principal.

(2) If the obligor makes no such specification, the obligee may, within a reasonable time after payment, declare to the obligor the obligation to which it imputes the payment, provided that the obligation is due and undisputed.

(3) In the absence of imputation under paragraphs (1) or (2), payment is imputed to that obligation which satisfies one of the following criteria in the order indicated:
  (a) an obligation which is due or which is the first to fall due;
  (b) an obligation for which the obligee has least security;
  (c) the obligation which is the most burdensome for the obligor;
  (d) the obligation which has arisen first.

If none of the preceding criteria applies, payment is imputed to all the obligations proportionally.

6.1.13. Imputation of non-monetary obligations.

Article 6.1.11 applies with appropriate adaptions to the imputation of performances of non-monetary obligations.

6.1.14. Application for public permission.

Where the law of a State requires a public permission affecting the validity of the contract or its performance and neither that law nor the circumstances indicate otherwise
  (a) if only one party has his place of business in that State, that party shall take the measures necessary to obtain the permission;
  (b) in any other case the party whose performances requires permission shall take the necessary measures.

6.1.15. Procedure in applying for permission.

(1) The party required to take the measures necessary to obtain the permission shall do so without undue delay and shall bear any expenses incurred.

(2) That party shall whenever appropriate give the other party notice of the grant or refusal of such permission without undue delay.

6.1.16. Permission neither granted nor refused.

(1) If, notwithstanding the fact that the party responsible has taken all measures required, permission is neither granted nor refused within an agreed period or, where no period has been agreed, within a reasonable time from the conclusion of the contract, either party is entitled to terminate the contract.

(2) Where the permission affects some terms only, paragraph (1) does not apply if, having regard to the circumstances, it is reasonable to uphold the remaining contract even if the permission is refused.

6.1.17. Permission refused.

(1) The refusal of a permission affecting the validity of the contract renders the contract void. If the refusal affects the validity of some terms only, only such terms are void if, having regard to the circumstances of the case, it is reasonable to uphold the remaining contract.

(2) Where the refusal of a permission renders the performance of the contract impossible in whole or in part, the rules on non-performance apply.

Section 2
Hardship

6.2.1. Contract to be observed.

Where the performance of a contract becomes more onerous for one of the parties, that party is nevertheless bound to perform its obligations subject to the following provisions on hardship.

6.2.2. Definition of hardship.
There is hardship where the occurrence of events fundamentally alters the equilibrium of the contract either because the cost of a party's performance has increased or because the value of the performance a party receives has diminished, and
> (a) the events occur or become known to the disadvantaged party after the conclusion of the contract;
> (b) the events could not reasonably have been taken into account by the disadvantaged party at the time of the conclusion of the contract;
> (c) the events are beyond the control of the disadvantaged party; and
> (d) the risk of the events was not assumed by the disadvantaged party.

6.2.3. Effects of hardship.
(1) In a case of hardship the disadvantaged party is entitled to request renegotiations. The request shall be made without undue delay and shall indicate the grounds on which it is based.

(2) The request for renegotiation does not in itself entitle the disadvantaged party to withhold performance.

(3) Upon failure to reach agreement within a reasonable time either party may resort to the court.

(4) If a court finds hardship it may, if reasonable,
> (a) terminate the contract at a date and on terms to be fixed; or
> (b) adapt the contract with a view to restoring its equilibrium.

CHAPTER 7
NON-PERFORMANCE

Section 1
General Provisions

7.1.1. Non-performance defined.
Non-performance is failure by a party to perform any of its obligations under the contract, including defective performance or late performance.

7.1.2. Interference by the other party.
A party may not rely on the non-performance of the other party to the extent that such non-performance was caused by the first party's act or omission or by another event as to which the first party bears the risk.

7.1.3. Withholding performance.
(1) Where the parties are to perform simultaneously, either party may withhold performance until the other party tenders its performance.

(2) Where the parties are to perform consecutively, the party that is to perform later may withhold its performance until the first party has performed.

7.1.4. Cure by non-performing party.
(1) The non-performing party may, at its own expense, cure any non-performance, provided that
> (a) without undue delay, it gives notice indicating the proposed manner and timing of the cure;
> (b) cure is appropriate in the circumstances;
> (c) the aggrieved party has no legitimate interest in refusing cure; and
> (d) cure is effected promptly.

(2) The right to cure is not precluded by notice of termination.

(3) Upon effective notice of cure, rights of the aggrieved party that are inconsistent with the non-performing party's performance are suspended until the time for cure has expired.

(4) The aggrieved party may withhold performance pending cure.

(5) Notwithstanding cure, the aggrieved party retains the right to claim damages for delay as well as for any harm caused or not prevented by the cure.

7.1.5. Additional period for performance.

(1) In a case of non-performance the aggrieved party may by notice to the other party allow an additional period of time for performance.

(2) During the additional period the aggrieved party may withhold performance of its own reciprocal obligations and may claim damages but may not resort to any other remedy. If it receives notice from the other party that the latter will not perform within that period, or if upon expiry of that period due performance has not been made, the aggrieved party may resort to any of the remedies that may be available under this Chapter.

(3) Where in a case of delay in performance which is not fundamental the aggrieved party has given notice allowing an additional period of time of reasonable length, it may terminate the contract at the end of that period. If the additional period is not of reasonable length it shall be extended to a reasonable length. The aggrieved party may in its notice provide that if the other party fails to perform within the period allowed by the notice the contract shall automatically terminate.

(4) Paragraph (3) does not apply when the obligation which has not been performed is only a minor part of the non-performing party.

7.1.6. Exemption clauses.

A term which limits or excludes one party's liability for non-performance or which permits one party to render performance substantially different from what the other party reasonably expected may not be invoked if it would be grossly unfair to do so, having regard to the purpose of the contract.

7.1.7. Force majeure.

(1) Non-performance by a party is excused if that party proves that the non-performance was due to an impediment beyond its control and that it could not reasonably be expected to have taken the impediment into account at the time of the conclusion of the contract or to have avoided or overcome it or its consequences.

(2) When the impediment is only temporary, the excuse shall have effect for such period as is reasonable having regard to the effect of the impediment on performance of the contract.

(3) A party who fails to perform must give notice to the other party of the impediment and its effect on its ability to perform. If the notice is not received by the other party within a reasonable time after the party who fails to perform knew or ought to have known of the impediment, it is liable for damages resulting from such non-receipt;

(4) Nothing in this article prevents a party from exercising a right to terminate the contract or withhold performance or request interest on money due.

Section 2
Right to Performance

7.2.1. Performance of monetary obligation.

Where a party who is obliged to pay money does not do so, the other party may require payment.

7.2.2. Performance of non-monetary obligation.

Where a party who owes an obligation other than one to pay money does not perform, the other party may require performance, unless
    (a) performance is impossible in law or in fact;

(b) performance or, when relevant, enforcement is unreasonably burdensome or expensive;
(c) the party entitled to performance may reasonably obtain performance from another source;
(d) performance is of an exclusively personal character; or
(e) the party entitled to performance does not require performance within a reasonable time after it has, or ought to have, become aware of the non-performance.

7.2.3. Repair and replacement of defective performance.
The right to performance includes in appropriate cases the right to require repair, replacement or other cure of a defective performance. The provisions of Articles 7.2.1 and 7.2.2 apply accordingly.

7.2.4. Judicial penalty.
(1) Where the court orders a party to perform, it may also direct that this party pay a penalty if it does not comply with the order.
(2) The penalty shall be paid to the aggrieved party unless mandatory provisions of the law of the forum provide otherwise. Payment of the penalty to the aggrieved party does not exclude any claim for damages.

7.2.5. Change of remedy.
(1) An aggrieved party who has required performance of a non-monetary obligation and who has not received performance within a period fixed or otherwise within a reasonable period of time may invoke any other remedy.
(2) Where the decision of a court for performance of a non-monetary obligation cannot be enforced, the aggrieved party may invoke any other remedy.

Section 3
Termination

7.3.1. Right to terminate the contract.
(1) A party may terminate the contract where the failure of the other party to perform an obligation under the contract amounts to a fundamental non-performance.
(2) In determining whether a failure to perform an obligation amounts to a fundamental non-performance regard shall be had, in particular, to whether
(a) the non-performance substantially deprives the aggrieved party of what it was entitled to expect under the contract unless the other party did not foresee and could not reasonably have foreseen such result;
(b) strict compliance with the obligation which has not been performed is of essence under the contract;
(c) the non-performance is intentional or reckless;
(d) the non-performance gives the aggrieved party reason to believe that it cannot rely on the other party's future performance;
(e) the non-performing party will suffer disproportionate loss as a result of the preparation or performance if the contract is terminated.
(3) In the case of delay the aggrieved party may also terminate the contract if the other party fails to perform before the time allowed it under Article 7.1.5 has expired.

7.3.2. Notice of termination.
(1) The right of a party to terminate the contract is to be exercised by notice to the other party.
(2) If performance has been offered late or otherwise does not conform to the contract the aggrieved party will lose its right to terminate the contract unless it gives notice to the other party within a reasonable time after it has or ought to have become aware of the offer or of the non-conforming performance.

7.3.3. Anticipatory non-performance.
Where prior to the date for performance by one of the parties it is clear that there will be a fundamental non-performance by that party, the other party may terminate the contract.

7.3.4. Adequate assurance of due performance.
A party who reasonably believes that there will be a fundamental non-performance by the other party may demand adequate assurance of due performance and may meanwhile withhold its own performance. Where this assurance is not provided within a reasonable time the party demanding it may terminate the contract.

7.3.5. Effects of termination in general.
(1) Termination of the contract releases both parties from their obligation to effect and to receive future performance.

(2) Termination does not preclude a claim for damages for non-performance.

(3) Termination does not affect any provision in the contract for the settlement of disputes or any other term of the contract which is to operate even after termination.

7.3.6. Restitution.
(1) On termination of the contract either party may claim restitution of whatever it has supplied, provided that such party concurrently makes restitution of whatever it has received. If restitution in kind is not possible or appropriate allowance should be made in money whenever reasonable.

(2) However, if performance of the contract has extended over a period of time and the contract is divisible, such restitution can only be claimed for the period after termination has taken effect.

Section 4
Damages

7.4.1. Right to damages.
Any non-performance gives the aggrieved party a right to damages either exclusively or in conjunction with any other remedies except where the non-performance is excused under these Principles.

7.4.2. Full compensation.
(1) The aggrieved party is entitled to full compensation for harm as a result of the non-performance. Such harm includes both any loss which it suffered and any gain of which it was deprived, taking into account any gain to the aggrieved party resulting from its avoidance of cost or harm.

(2) Such harm may be non-pecuniary and includes, for instance, physical suffering or emotional distress.

7.4.3. Certainty of harm.
(1) Compensation is due only for harm, including future harm, that is established with a reasonable degree of certainty.

(2) Compensation may be due for the loss of a chance in proportion to the probability of its occurrence.

(3) Where the amount of damages cannot be established with a sufficient degree of certainty, the assessment is at the discretion of the court.

7.4.4. Foreseeability of harm.
The non-performing party is liable only for harm which it foresaw or could reasonably have foreseen at the time of the conclusion of the contract as being likely to result from its non-performance.

7.4.5. Proof of harm in case of replacement transaction.
Where the aggrieved party has terminated the contract and has made a replacement transaction within a reasonable time and in a reasonable manner it may recover the difference between the contract price and the price of the replacement transaction as well as damages for any further harm.

7.4.6. Proof of harm by current price.
(1) Where the aggrieved party has terminated the contract and has not made a replacement transaction but there is a current price for the performance contracted for, it may recover the difference between the contract price and the price current at the time the contract is terminated as well as damages for any further harm.

(2) Current price is the price generally charged for goods delivered or services rendered in comparable circumstances at the place where the contract should have been performed or, if there is no current price at that place, the current price at such other place that appears reasonable to take as a reference.

7.4.7. Harm due in part to aggrieved party.
Where the harm is due in part to an act or omission of the aggrieved party or to another event as to which that party bears the risk, the amount of damages shall be reduced to the extent these factors have contributed to the harm, having regard to the conduct of each of the parties.

7.4.8. Mitigation of harm.
(1) The non-performing party is not liable for harm suffered by the aggrieved party to the extent that the harm could have been reduced by the latter party's taking reasonable steps.

(2) The aggrieved party is entitled to recover any expenses reasonably incurred in attempting to reduce the harm.

7.4.9. Interest for failure to pay money.
(1) If a party does not pay a sum of money when it falls due the aggrieved party is entitled to interest upon that sum from the time when payment is due to the time of payment whether or not the non-payment is excused.

(2) The rate of interest shall be the average bank short-term lending rate to prime borrowers prevailing for the currency of payment at the place for payment, or where no such rate exists at that place, then the same rate in the State of the currency of payment. In the absence of such a rate at either place the rate of interest shall be the appropriate rate fixed by the law of the State of the currency of payment.

(3) The aggrieved party is entitled to additional damages if the non-payment caused it a greater harm.

7.4.10. Interest on damages.
Unless otherwise agreed, interests on damages for non-performance of non-monetary obligations accrues as from the time of non-performance.

7.4.11. Manner of monetary redress.
(1) Damages are to be paid in a lump sum. However, they may be payable in instalments when the nature of the harm makes this appropriate.

(2) Damages to be paid in instalments may be indexed.

7.4.12. Currency in which to assess damages.
Damages are to be assessed either in the currency in which the monetary obligation was expressed or in the currency in which the harm was suffered, whichever is more appropriate.

7.4.13. Agreed payment for non-performance.

(1) Where the contract provides that a party who does not perform is to pay a specified sum to the aggrieved party for such non-performance, the aggrieved party is entitled to that sum irrespective of its actual harm.

(2) However, notwithstanding any agreement to the contrary the specified sum may be reduced to a reasonable amount where it is grossly excessive in relation to the harm resulting from the non-performance and to the other circumstances.

DRAFT RULES ON UNJUSTIFIED ENRICHMENT
(Scot. Law Com. D.P. No. 99, Appendix)

1. General principle.

A person who has been enriched at the expense of another person is bound, if the enrichment is unjustified, to redress the enrichment.

2. Enrichment.

(1) A person is enriched if he acquires an economic benefit.

(2) A person acquires an economic benefit if his net worth is increased or is prevented from being decreased, and accordingly a person may be enriched, among other ways, by
   (a) acquiring money or other property
   (b) having value added to property
   (c) being freed, in whole or in part, from an obligation, or
   (d) being saved from a loss or expenditure

(3) A person is treated as acquiring an economic benefit under a void contract, or under a voidable contract which has been reduced, rescinded or otherwise set aside, or under a contract which has been terminated by frustration or rescission for breach or by some other means (apart from full performance) or under any other transaction or purported transaction which does not provide legal cause for the acquisition, if he would have acquired an economic benefit but for the fact that he gave consideration, and accordingly in such circumstances both parties to the transaction or purported transaction may be regarded as being enriched.

3. At the expense of another person.

(1) The enrichment of one person is at the expense of another person if it is the direct result of
   (a) a payment, grant, transfer, incurring of liability, or rendering of services by the other person
      (i) to the enriched person
      (ii) in fulfilment of an obligation of the enriched person
      (iii) in adding value to the enriched person's property, or
      (iv) in acquiring some other economic benefit for the enriched person, or
   (b) in any case not covered by paragraph (a), an interference with the patrionial rights of the other person otherwise than by the operation of natural forces.

(2) A person interferes with the patrimonial rights of another person if, among other things, he
   (a) extinguishes those rights or acts in such a way that they are extinguished
   (b) disposes or purports to dispose of property belonging to that other person
   (c) uses property which that other person has the right to use to the exclusion of the interferer, or
   (d) actively intercepts a benefit due to the other person
but a person does not interfere with the partrimonial rights of another person merely because he breaches a contract between himself and the other person.

Draft Rules on Unjustified Enrichment

(3) A person who claims redress or any unjustified enrichment resulting from an interference with his patrimonial rights is treated for the purpose of any claims by or against third parties as thereby ratifying the interference.

(4) A person who purchases property in good faith from someone who is not the owner of the property is not treated as being enriched at the expense of the owner or of any former owner by reason only of any economic benefit derived by him from the purchase of the property; and the same rule applies to any other acquirer, in good faith and for value, of the right, or of what purports to be the right, to deal with the property or rights of another, and to anyone deriving title from such a purchaser or acquirer.

(5) Where a person (E) has been enriched indirectly as a result of performance by another person (C) under a contract between C and a third party (T), E's enrichment is not regarded as being at the expense of C, even if C is unable to recover under his contract with T.

(6) This rule is subject to rule 8 (which deals with certain exceptional cases where redress is due for indirect enrichment).

4. Unjustified.

An enrichment is unjustified unless it is justified under rules 5 or 6.

5. Enrichment justified by legal cause.

(1) An enrichment is justified if the enriched person is entitled to it by virtue of
   (a) an enactment
   (b) a rule of law
   (c) a court decree
   (d) a contract (whether or not the person claiming redress is a party) or unilateral voluntary obligation
   (e) a will or trust
   (f) a gift, or
   (g) some other legal cause.

(2) The reference to an enactment or rule of law in rule 5(1) is to an enactment or rule of law which confers rights directly and not to an enactment or rule of law in so far as it operates indirectly by regulating the effects of court decrees, contracts, wills, trusts, gifts or other legal causes.

(3) A purported or apparent legal cause does not justify an enrichment if it is void or if, being voidable, it has been reduced, rescinded or otherwise set aside.

(4) An acquisition of property is not a justified enrichment merely because legal title to the property has been acquired.

6. Enrichment justified by public policy.

(1) An enrichment is justified if it is the result of
   (a) work or expenditure which was undertaken or incurred by the other person for his own benefit, or for the benefit of a third party or the public at large, which has incidentally conferred a benefit on the enriched person, and which was undertaken or incurred when the person knew or could reasonably have been expected to know that there would be a benefit to the enriched person and accepted, or could reasonably be supposed to have accepted, the risk that the enriched person would not pay for the benefit
   (b) the voluntary and deliberate conferring by the other person of a benefit on the enriched person, in the knowledge that it is not due and in acceptance of the risk that the enriched person may choose not to pay or do anything in return
   (c) a voluntary performance by the other person of an obligation which has prescribed, even if he erroneously believed that the obligation was still due, provided that any due counter-performance has been given

(d) a voluntary performance by the other person of an obligation which is invalid for some formal reason only, even if he erroneously believed that the obligation was valid, provided that any due counter-performance has been given
or if there is some other consideration of public policy which requires it to be regarded as justified.

(2) For the purpose of rule 6(1)(a) "benefit", in relation to a person who has done work or provided services in tendering for a contract or in the anticipation of obtaining a contract, includes the benefit to the person of having, or improving, the chance of obtaining the contract.

7. Exceptions to rules 5 and 6.

(1) Rule 5(1)(b) does not apply in so far as the enrichment is the result of any rule of law on the acquisition of property by accession or specification, or any analogous rule whereby one person may acquire another's property when it becomes attached to or mixed with his own.

(2) Rule 5(1)(d) does not apply in so far as the contract or obligation,

(a) is unenforceable because of an enactment or rule of law (whether or not it is also illegal), unless allowing redress for the enrichment would contravene the policy underlying the enactment or rule of law.

(b) has been terminated by rescission or frustration or some other means (apart from full performance) and the contract or obligation does not, expressly or impliedly, exclude redress in respect of the benefit in question.

(3) For the purpose of rule 7(2)(b) a contract which provides for performance in several parts or stages is presumed, unless the contract indicates the contrary, to exclude redress in so far as performance by one party under, and substantially in accordance with, the contract has been met by performance by the other party under, and substantially in accordance with, the contract.

(4) Rule 5(1)(f) does not apply where the gift

(a) was made in error, whether of fact or law, or

(b) was subject to a condition, which has been met, that it would be returned.

(5) Rule 6(1)(a) and (b) do not apply where the other person has, in circumstances where it was reasonable to do so,

(a) paid a monetary debt due by the enriched person

(b) fulfilled an alimentary obligation due by the enriched person

(c) incurred expenditure or performed services necessary for preserving the life, health or welfare of the enriched person, or

(d) incurred expenditure or performed services urgently necessary for preserving the property of the enriched person or preventing it from being dangerous.

8. Redress for indirect enrichment.

(1)(a) Where a person (E) has acquired money or money's worth from a third party (T) by disposing or purporting to dispose of property belonging to another person (C), or by otherwise interfering with C's patrimonial rights, or by disposing of property acquired by him from C under a transaction voidable at C's instance, E's enrichment is treated, notwithstanding anything in the preceding rules, as being at the expense of C and as not being justified by any contract between himself and T.

(b) Paragraph (a) does not apply if E was a purchaser in good faith of the property in question, or had otherwise acquired, in good faith and for value, the right, or what purported to be the right, to deal with the property or rights in question, or had derived title from such a purchaser or acquirer.

(2) Where a person (T) has been enriched at the expense of another person (C) and T has transferred to another person (E) any benefit arising out of the enrichment then, notwithstanding anything in the preceding rules, E is taken to be enriched at the expense

of C and neither the transfer by T to E, nor any voluntary obligation underlying the transfer, justifies the enrichment if

(a) T's enrichment at the expense of C was unjustified or was justified only by a transaction voidable at C's instance

(b) C is unable to recover from T, or cannot reasonably be expected to attempt to recover from T, and

(c) the acquisition by E from T was not in good faith and for value.

(3) Where a person (E) has been enriched by receiving a benefit from a trust estate or from the estate of a deceased person, the fact that E's enrichment is the result of a transfer from a trustee or executor does not prevent him from being liable to make redress to

(a) a creditor of the estate to the extent that the creditor, because of the transfer to the beneficiary, has been unable to recover from the trustee or executor, or

(b) a person (the true beneficiary) who is legally entitled to the benefit in question.

(4) Where a debtor pays the wrong person, that person is enriched at the expense of the true creditor in so far as the payment extinguishes the liability of the debtor to the true creditor.

(5) Nothing in these rules affects any procedural rule designed to avoid duplication of proceedings.

9. Redress due.

(1) The redress due by an enriched person under these rules is such transfer of property or payment of money, or both, as is required to redress the enriched person's unjustified enrichment at the expense of the claimant.

(2) The redress due is assessed in accordance with the rules in the schedule in any case where those rules are applicable.

(3) Where the enriched person has been enriched at the expense of the claimant in more than one way, the rules in the schedule apply cumulatively unless there would be double redress in respect of the same enrichment.

(4) This rule is subject to the provisions of rule 10.

10. Court's powers to refuse or modify award.

(1) Where, in an action for unjustified enrichment, it appears to the court that each party is bound to make redress to the other, the court may

(a) refuse to grant decree against the defender until satisfied that the pursuer has made, or will make, the redress due by him, or

(b) where both obligations are to pay money, set off one entitlement against the other and grant decree for the difference.

(2) Where, in an action for unjustified enrichment based on the passive receipt of a benefit by the enriched person, it appears to the court.

(a) that the enriched person had no reasonable opportunity to refuse the benefit

(b) that the enriched person would have refused the benefit if he had had such an opportunity

(c) that the enriched person cannot, or cannot reasonably be expected to, convert the value of the benefit into money or money's worth, and

(d) that it would be inequitable to make a full award

the court may refuse or modify the award accordingly.

(3) Where, in an action for unjustified enrichment based on the defender's acquisition of the pursuer's property by accession or specification or any analogous rule, it appears to the court that the pursuer has acted in good faith and that, having regard to the respective values of the properties involved, the conduct of the parties and all other relevant factors, the most appropriate and equitable solution would be for the defender to be ordered to sell to the pursuer such property at such a price as would

enable the pursuer to regain his property without prejudice to the defender, the court may grant decree accordingly.

(4) Notwithstanding anything in the preceding rules, a court deciding an action for unjustified enrichment may refuse to make an award, or may make a reduced award, or may grant decree subject to conditions, if it considers

 (a) that the person enriched, where he did not know, and could not reasonably be expected to know, that redress was due, changed his position (whether by spending money, disposing of property, consuming property or its fruits, abandoning rights, failing to exercise rights in time, or otherwise) in reliance on his enrichment, and it would for that reason be inequitable to make a full award or grant decree unconditionally

 (b) that the claimant was so culpable or negligent in causing the unjustified enrichment that it would be inequitable or contrary to public policy to make a full award or grant decree unconditionally

 (c) that the claimant would be unjustly enriched if a full award were made or if decree were granted unconditionally, or

 (d) that, for any other reason, it would be inequitable or contrary to public policy to make a full award or grant decree unconditionally.

11. Bars to proceedings.

(1)(a) An action for unjustified enrichment cannot be brought under these rules if there is, or was,

 (i) a special statutory or contractual procedure for dealing with the situation giving rise to the enrichment or

 (ii) another legal remedy for the enrichment

and if the claimant could reasonably have been expected to use that procedure or remedy.

 (b) Paragraph (a) does not apply if the enactment or contract providing the other procedure or remedy indicates expressly or impliedly that it is intended to be in addition to any remedy available under the general law on unjustified enrichment.

 (c) The availability of damages for loss does not preclude an action for redress of unjustified enrichment but, without prejudice to his right to claim damages for any consequential or other loss, the claimant cannot claim both redress of the other party's unjustified enrichment and damages for his corresponding loss.

(2)(a) A person who, before a court decision in proceedings to which he was not a party, has made a payment or transfer which was apparently due under the law as it was commonly supposed to be at that time cannot bring an action for unjustified enrichment in respect of that payment or transfer on the ground that the decision has shown that the law was not as it was commonly supposed to be and that the payment or transfer was accordingly not in fact due.

 (b) In the preceding paragraph, "decision" in any case where a decision is affirmed or restored on appeal means the decision so affirmed or restored and not the decision affirming or restoring it.

(3) The bars mentioned in this rule are in addition to any bar resulting from the operation of the general law on personal bar.

12. Areas of law not affected.

(1) These rules replace the existing Scottish common law on unjustified enrichment, including

 (a) the common law on restitution in so far as it is part of the law on unjustified enrichment

 (b) the common law on repetition and recompense, and

 (c) the *condictio indebiti*; the *condictio causa data causa non secuta*; the *condictio ob turpem vel iniustam causam*; the *condictio ob non causam*; the *condictio sine causa*; the *actio in quantum locupletior factus est*; and the *actio de in rem verso* in so far as they form part of the existing law.

(2) Nothing in these rules affects
   (a) any enacted law
   (b) the law on rights of relief of cautioners and co-obligants
   (c) the law on subrogation of insurers or those who have paid an indemnity
   (d) the law derived from the case of *Walker* v *Milne* (whereby loss suffered or expenditure incurred in the expectation of a contract may in certain circumstances be recovered)
   (e) the law on the rights of a defrauded person as against the creditors of the person who defrauded him
   (f) the law on the recovery by a person of the possession or control of his own property or of any other property to the possession or control of which he is entitled
   (g) the law on the special obligations of those in a fiduciary position
   (h) the law on general average or salvage
   (i) the law on *negotiorum gestio*.

13. Interpretation.
(1) In these rules, and in the schedule where applicable,
   (a) "court decree" includes the decision of any tribunal, quasi-judicial body or arbiter having jurisdiction
   (b) "enactment" includes subordinate legislation
   (c) "gift" includes a gratuitous waiver, renunciation or discharge of a right
   (d) "he" means he, she or it; "him" means him, her or it; and "his" means his, hers or its
   (e) "patrimonial rights" include rights flowing from the ownership of property, rights to protect confidential information and other rights having an economic value but do not include purely personal rights, such as the rights to life, liberty, bodily integrity or reputation, and
   (f) "property" means property of any kind, corporeal or incorporeal, heritable or moveable.

(2) Any reference in these rules to a contract which has been terminated by rescission or frustration includes a reference to a contract which has been substantially terminated by rescission or frustration and a reference to a severable part of a contract which has been terminated by rescission or frustration.

SCHEDULE

REDRESS DUE

PART I

E acquires benefit directly from C

1. This part of the schedule applies where the enriched person (E) has been enriched by acquiring a benefit directly from the claimant (C).

2.—(1) Where the unjustified enrichment resulted from the acquisition of money by E from C, the redress due by E to C is the amount acquired, with interest from the time of acquisition.

(2) Where the unjustified enrichment resulted from the acquisition of other property by E from C, the redress due by E to C is
   (a) if the property is corporeal and can be returned in substantially the same condition as it was in at the time of the acquisition, the return of the property in that condition along with a sum of money to take account of any benefit derived by E from the ownership, use or possession of the property and interest on that sum where appropriate

(b) if the property is corporeal and cannot be returned in substantially the same condition as it was in at the time of the acquisition, the amount which it would have been reasonable to expect E to pay C for the property at the time of its acquisition by E, with interest on that amount from the time of acquisition

(c) if the property is incorporeal, the return of the property where possible and, whether or not return is possible, a sum of money to take account of any benefit derived by E from the ownership of the property and interest on that sum where appropriate.

3. Where the unjustified enrichment resulted from the addition of value by C to E's property, the redress due by E to C is the amount which it would have been reasonable to expect E to pay C for his work or expenditure in adding that value, or the amount of value added (at the time when the addition was made), if less, with interest where appropriate.

4. Where the unjustified enrichment resulted from the discharge or reduction of any liability of E by means of a payment by C, the redress due by E to C is the amount paid, with interest from the date of payment.

5. Where the unjustified enrichment resulted from E's being saved a loss or expenditure by receiving C's services, the redress due by E to C is the amount which it would have been reasonable to expect E to pay for those services, or the amount of loss or expenditure saved, if less, with interest where appropriate.

6.—(1) Where the unjustified enrichment resulted from E's being saved a loss or expenditure by using or possessing C's property, the redress due by E to C is the amount which it would have been reasonable to expect E to pay for that use or possession, or the amount of loss or expenditure saved, if less, with interest where appropriate.

(2) Where the unjustified enrichment resulted from E's being saved a loss or expenditure by consuming C's property, the redress due by E to C is the amount which it would have been reasonable to expect E to pay for the property at the time of consumption, or the amount of loss or expenditure saved, if less, with interest where appropriate.

(3) Where the unjustified enrichment resulted from E's being saved a loss or expenditure by interfering with C's patrimonial rights in any other way, the redress due by E to C is the amount which it would have been reasonable to expect E to pay C, at the time of the interference, for permission to interfere with those rights in that way in the circumstances, or the amount of loss or expenditure saved, if less, with interest where appropriate.

7. Where the unjustified enrichment resulted from the acquisition of any other benefit by E from C, the redress due by E to C is the amount which it would have been reasonable to expect E to pay C for the benefit at the time or acquisition, or the amount of E's actual enrichment, if less, with interest where appropriate.

PART II

E acquires benefit from T at indirect expense of C

8. This part of the schedule applies where the enriched person (E) has been enriched indirectly at the expense of the claimant (C).

9. Where E has enriched himself by using or disposing of C's property, or otherwise interfering with C's patrimonial rights, in order to obtain money or money's worth from a third party (T) the redress due by E to C is the amount which it would have been reasonable for E to pay C at the time of the use, disposal or interference for permission to use or dispose of C's property or to interfere with his rights in that way, or the amount of E's actual enrichment attributable to the use, disposal or interference, if less, with interest where appropriate.

10. Where E has been indirectly enriched at the expense of C as a result of the transfer of a benefit from a third party (T) in the circumstances covered by rule 8(2)

(transfer of benefit arising from unjustified enrichment to person taking otherwise than in good faith and for value) T is treated as if he had been acting as E's agent and accordingly the redress due by E to C is the same, and is due on the same conditions, as it would have been if E had acquired the benefit directly from C.

11. Where E has been indirectly enriched at the expense of C in the circumstances covered by rule 8(3) (transfers from trusts or executries) the redress due by E to C is

(1) where C is a creditor claiming under rule 8(3)(a) the amount of the debt due to C out of the estate or the amount of E's enrichment out of the estate, whichever is the less, with interest where appropriate

(2) where C is a true beneficiary claiming under rule 8(3)(b), and the benefit due to him out of the estate and received by E was a special legacy, the transfer of the subject matter of the legacy along with a sum to take account of any benefit derived by E from its use or possession or, if the subject matter of the legacy cannot be transferred in substantially the same condition as it was in when acquired by E, an amount representing its value when acquired by E, with interest from that date

(3) where C is a true beneficiary claiming under rule 8(3)(b), and the benefit due to him out of the estate and received by E was not a special legacy, the amount of the benefit due to C out of the estate or the amount of E's unjustified enrichment out of the estate, whichever is the less, with interest where appropriate.

PART III

General

12. Any reference in this schedule to the return of property includes a reference to a return by reconveyance or by any other means by which ownership can be restored to the other person.

13. For the purposes of paragraph 2(2) corporeal property acquired by the enriched person by accession or specification, or any analogous rule whereby one person may acquire another's property when it becomes attached to or mixed with his own, is treated as property which cannot be returned in substantially the same condition as it was in at the time of acquisition.

14. Where property is to be returned or transferred to the claimant by the enriched person under these rules, the expenses of the return or transfer are to be borne

(1) by the claimant if the enrichment was in good faith, or

(2) by the enriched person if the enrichment was in bad faith

unless a court dealing with the claim orders otherwise.

15. In assessing what it would have been reasonable for E to pay C for any interference with C's rights or for permission to interfere with those rights regard may be had to any factors which would have made C reluctant or unwilling to permit the interference.

INDEX

Access to Health Records Act 1990
  ss 3, 9 *222*
Access to Neighbouring Land Act 1992
  ss 1-4, 6 *252–7*
Administration of Justice Act 1970
  s 40 *35–6*
Administration of Justice Act 1982
  ss 1, 2, 5 *140–1*
Administration of Justice Act 1985
  ss 12, 21 *156*
Agricultural Holdings Act 1986
  s 24 *161*
Agricultural Tenancies Act 1995
  ss 16, 17, 20, 22, 26 *297–8*
Animals Act 1971
  ss 1-12 *39–43*
Apportionment Act 1870
  ss 2, 3, 5-7 *5–6*
Arbitration Act 1950
  s 13A *21*
Arbitration Act 1996
  ss 8, 29, 40, 41, 74, 87, 89–91 *309–10*
Banking Act 1987
  s 3 *167*
British Telecommunications Act 1981
  s 23 *138*
Broadcasting Act 1990
  ss 166, 201, Sch 20 *222–3*
Broadcasting Act 1996
  ss 99, 106, 107, 121 *310–1*
Building Act 1984
  ss 1, 38 *151–2*
Business Names Act 1985
  ss 4, 5 *156*
Building Societies Act 1986
  s 66A *161*
Carriage of Goods by Sea Act 1971
  ss 1-6, Sch art I-X *43–9*
Carriage of Goods by Sea Act 1992
  ss 1-5 *257–60*
Child Support Act 1991
  ss 9, 41B *242–3*
Children Act 1989
  s 2 *217*
Civil Aviation Act 1982
  ss 76, 77 *141–2*
Civil Evidence Act 1968
  ss 11, 13 *31–2*
Civil Liability (Contribution) Act 1978
  ss 1-7 *98–100*
Civil Procedure Act 1997
  s 7 *340–1*
Clean Air Act 1993
  ss 1, 34, 51 *281*
Coal Mining Subsidence Act 1991
  ss 2, 8, 12, 37 *244–5*
Companies Act 1985
  ss 3A, 14, 35, 35A, 35B, 36, 36A, 36C, 111A, 322A *157–9*
Companies Act 1989
  s 48 *217–8*
Congenital Disabilities (Civil Liability) Act 1976
  ss 1, 1A-5 *78–80*
Consumer Credit Act 1974
  ss 46, 55-7, 60, 65, 67-71, 75, 76, 87, 88, 94, 96, 99, 100, 113, 127, 129, 132, 137-9, 162, 163, 165, 170, 173, 175, 181, 189 *61–8*
Consumer Protection Act 1987
  ss 1-16, 18-35, 37-42, 45, 46, Sch 2 *167–97*
Consumer Transactions (Restrictions on Statements) Order 1976
  ss 3-5 *373–5*
Contempt of Court Act 1981
  s 4 *138*
Contract (Scotland) Act 1997
  ss 1-4 *341*
Contracts (Applicable Law) Act 1990
  ss 1, 2, Sch 1 *223–4*
Contracts (Rights of Third Parties) Bill (Draft)
  ss 1-9 *369–72*
Contributory Negligence Bill (Draft)
  ss 1-3 *367–8*
Council Directive (of 25 July 1985)
  400–4
Council Directive (of 29 June 1992)
  405–12
Council Directive (of 5 April 1993)
  412–17

Index   453

Courts and Legal Services Act 1990
   ss 34, 44, 61, 62, 69 *224–5*
Criminal Injuries Compensation Act 1995
   ss 1, 2, 3, 7, 9 *298–300*
Criminal Justice Act 1988
   ss 71, 72, 72AA, 74B, 74C, 98, 133, 134
   198–203
Criminal Justice and Public Order Act 1994
   ss 60–6, 68–9 *286–9*
Criminal Law Act 1967
   ss 3, 14 *29–30*
Crown Proceedings Act 1947
   ss 2, 10 *18–9*
Crown Proceedings (Armed Forces) Act 1987
   ss 1, 2 *197–8*
Customs and Excise Management Act 1979
   s 137A *100–1*
Damages Act 1996
   ss 1–8 *311–4*
Dangerous Wild Animals Act 1976
   ss 1, 4 *80–1*
Data Protection Act 1984
   s 22 *152*
Defamation Act 1952
   ss 2, 3, 5, 6, 9–13, 16, 17 *21–2*
Defamation Act 1996
   ss 1–4, 7–10, 13–15, 17, 20, Sch 1 *314–23*
Defective Premises Act 1972
   ss 1–6 *53–6*
Draft Rules on Unjustified Enrichment
   444–51
Drug Trafficking Act 1994
   s 2 *289*
Education Act 1996
   ss 206–7, 256–8, 492–4, 521–3, 548–50,
   550A, 550B *323–30*
Electricity Act 1989
   ss 1, 39 *218*
Employers' Liability (Compulsory
   Insurance) Act 1969
   ss 1, 2 *34–5*
Employers' Liability (Compulsory
   Insurance) General Regulations 1971
   ss 2, 3 *373*
Employer's Liability (Defective
   Equipment) Act 1969
   s 1 *35*
Employment Act 1989
   s 11 *218–9*
Employment Rights Act 1996
   ss 15, 16 *330*
Environmental Protection Act 1990
   ss 18, 33, 34, 70, 73, 78A–H, 78J–N, 78P–T,
   78YC, 79, 80, 82 *225–40*
Equal Pay Act 1970
   s 1 *36*
Factors Act 1889
   ss 1, 2 *6–7*

Fatal Accidents Act 1976
   ss 1, 1A, 2-5 *81–3*
Finance Act 1989
   s 29 *219*
Finance Act 1997
   ss 47, 50, 51, Sch 5 *341–7*
Financial Services Act 1986
   ss 3, 6, 61-62A, 63, 132, 150, 151,
   154, 162, 163, 166 *162–5*
Fires Prevention (Metropolis) Act 1774
   s 86 *1*
Food Safety Act 1990
   s 44 *241*
Forfeiture Act 1982
   ss 1, 2, 5 *142*
Further and Higher Education Act 1992
   ss 41, 42, 49 *260–1*
Gaming Act 1845
   s 18 *4*
Gaming Act 1892
   s 1 *8*
General Product Safety Regulations 1994
   regs 1–5, 7–18 *388–93*
Guard Dogs Act 1975
   ss 1, 2, 5 *74–5*
Health and Safety at Work Act 1974
   ss 2–4, 10, 15, 17, 47 *68–71*
Highways Act 1980
   ss 41, 58, 102, 165 *121–2*
Housing Act 1985
   ss 118, 164, 179 *159–60*
Housing Act 1988
   ss 16, 27, 28 *204–5*
Housing Act 1996
   ss 11, 12, 152, 153, 211 *330–2*
Housing Grants, Construction and
   Regeneration Act 1996
   ss 43, 45, 51, 52, 55 *332–4*
Human Fertilisation and Embryology
   Act 1990
   ss 27-29, 35 *241*
Human Organ Transplants Act 1989
   s 1 *219*
Income and Corporation Taxes Act 1988
   ss 148, 329AA, 329AB, 824–6 *205–8*
Inheritance Tax Act 1984
   s 241 *152*
Insolvency Act 1986
   s 238 *165*
Insurance Companies Act 1982
   s 2 *143*
Intelligence Services Act 1994
   s 5 *289*
International Transport Conventions Act
   1983
   ss 1, 3 *150*
Jobseekers Act 1995
   s 23 *300*

Justices of the Peace Act 1997
  s 51, 52   *348*
Land Drainage Act 1991
  ss 21, 24   *245*
Landlord and Tenant Act 1985
  s 8   *160*
Landlord and Tenant Act 1988
  ss 1, 4, 6   *208–9*
Landlord and Tenant (Covenants) Act 1995
  ss 3–7, 9–11, 13, 23–25   *300–5*
Latent Damage Act 1986
  ss 1-4   *165–7*
Law of Libel Amendment Act 1888
  s 4   *6*
Law of Property Act 1925
  ss 41, 49, 56, 136, 146, 205   *11–12*
Law of Property (Miscellaneous Provisions) Act 1989
  ss 1-3   *220–1*
Law Reform (Contributory Negligence) Act 1945
  ss 1, 4   *17–8*
Law Reform (Frustrated Contracts) Act 1943
  ss 1-3   *16–7*
Law Reform (Husband and Wife) Act 1962
  s 1   *24–5*
Law Reform (Married Women and Tortfeasors) Act 1935
  ss 3, 4   *15*
Law Reform (Miscellaneous Provisions) Act 1934
  s 1   *14–5*
Law Reform (Personal Injuries) Act 1948
  ss 1-3   *19*
Leasehold Reform, Housing and Urban Development Act 1993
  ss 158, 163, 168   *282*
Libel Act 1792
  ss 1, 2   *2*
Libel Act 1843
  ss 1, 2   *3*
Libel Act 1845
  s 2   *4*
Limitation Act 1623
  s 5   *1*
Limitation Act 1980
  ss 1-4, 4A, 5, 6, 8-11, 11A, 12-14, 14A, 14B, 15–24, 26, 28, 28A, 29-32, 32A, 33, 35-9   *122–37*
Malicious Communications Act 1988
  s 1   *209*
Marine Insurance Act 1906
  ss 4, 17, 18, 20, 22, 30, 33, 34, 35, 48, 49, 82–4, 87   *8–11*
Mental Health Act 1983
  ss 95, 139   *151*
Mercantile Law Amendment Act 1856
  ss 3, 5   *4*

Merchant Shipping Act 1995
  ss 39, 70, 92, 93, 185, 231, 234, Sch 7   *305–8*
Mineral Workings (Offshore Installations) Act 1971
  ss 6, 11   *50*
Minors' Contracts Act 1987
  ss 2, 3   *198*
Misrepresentation Act 1967
  ss 1-5   *30*
National Parks and Access to the Countryside Act 1949
  ss 60, 66   *20*
NHS and Community Care Act 1990
  s 4   *241–2*
Noise Act 1996
  ss 1–5, 10, 12, Sch 10   *334–9*
Noise and Statutory Nuisance Act 1993
  s 9, sch 3   *282–3*
Nuclear Installations Act 1965
  ss 7, 9, 12, 13, 15, 16, 18, 19   *25–29*
Occupiers' Liability Act 1957
  ss 1-3, 5   *22–4*
Occupiers' Liability Act 1984
  ss 1, 3   *152–3*
Offences against the Person Act 1861
  ss 44, 45   *5*
Package Travel, Package Holidays and Package Tours Regulations 1992
  ss 2–15, 23–28, Sch 1–3   *375–83*
Parliamentary Commissioner Act 1967
  s 10   *31*
Parliamentary Papers Act 1840
  ss 1-4   *2–3*
Party Wall etc. Act 1996
  ss 7, 8   *339*
Pension Schemes Act 1993
  ss 61, 62, 127   *283–4*
Pensions Act 1995
  ss 1, 14, 48, 91   *308–9*
Petroleum and Submarine Pipe-Lines Act 1975
  s 30   *75*
Pilotage Act 1987
  ss 16, 22   *198*
Plant Varieties and Seeds Act 1964
  s 17   *25*
Pneumoconiosis etc. (Workers' Compensation) Act 1979
  ss 1, 2, 5, 9   *101–2*
Police Act 1996
  s 88   *339–40*
Police Act 1997
  aa 1, 42, 86, 92–101, Sch 7   *348–53*
Police and Criminal Evidence Act 1984
  ss 17, 19, 22, 24, 25, 32, 34, 55, 62, 65   *153–5*
Powers of Criminal Courts Act 1973
  ss 35, 38   *56–7*

Index   455

Prevention of Terrorism (Temporary
  Provisions) Act 1989
  s 12, Sch 4   *221–2*
Principles of European Contract Law
  418–27
Property Misdescriptions Act 1991
  ss 1, 2   *245–7*
Protection from Eviction Act 1977
  ss 1–3   *84–5*
Protection from Harassment Act 1997
  ss 1–5, 7, 12   *353–5*
Provision and Use of Work Equipment
  Regulations 1992
  ss 1, 2, 5-24   *383–8*
Public Bodies (Admission to Meetings)
  Act 1960
  s 1   *24*
Public Supply Contracts Regulations 1995
  regs 10, 21   *397–8*
Race Relations Act 1976   *83*
Railways Act 1993
  ss 1, 50, 93, 122, 151   *285–6*
Rehabilitation of Offenders Act 1974
  ss 4, 8   *71–2*
Resale Prices Act 1976
  ss 1, 5, 25   *83–4*
Reserve and Auxiliary Forces (Protection
  of Civil Interests) Act 1951
  s 13   *21*
Reservoirs (Safety Provisions) Act 1930
  s 7   *12*
Restitution (Mistakes of Law) (Draft) Bill
  ss 1–5   *368–9*
Road Traffic Act 1988
  ss 16, 38, 143-5, 148, 149, 151,
  153, 157-9   *209–17*
Road Traffic (Consequential Provisions)
  Act 1988
  s 7   *217*
Sale of Goods Act 1979
  ss 1–15, *15A, 15B,* 16–20, 20A-B, 21–35,
  35A, 36–39, 41–53, *53A,*
  54–64   *102–120*
Security Service Act 1989
  ss 1, 3   *222*
Sex Discrimination Act 1975
  ss 1, 2, 29, 41, 66, 71, 77   *75–7*
Slander of Women Act 1891
  s 1   *7*
Social Security Administration Act 1992
  ss 61A, 74A, 75, 76, 78, 106, 119,
  140C, 187   *261–5*
Social Security (Recovery of Benefits) Act 1997
  ss 1–24, 28–32, Sch 1–2   *355–66*
Social Security Contributions and
  Benefits Act 1992
  ss 94, 97, 98, 100, 101, 174
  265–6

Solicitors Act 1974
  ss 37, 37A, 87, Sch 1A   *72–4*
State Immunity Act 1978
  ss 1, 3, 5   *100*
Statute of Frauds 1677
  s 4   *1*
Statute of Frauds Amendment Act 1828
  s 6   *2*
Supply of Goods (Implied Terms) Act 1973
  ss 8–11, 11A, 12, 12A, 14, 15   *57–60*
Supply of Goods and Services Act 1982
  ss 1–5, *5A,* 6–10, *10A,* 11-16, 18-20
  143–50
Supreme Court Act 1981
  ss 32, 32A, 35, 35A, 37, 49, 50, 69   *138–40*
Surrogacy Arrangements Act 1985
  ss 1, 1A, 2   *160*
Taxes Management Act 1970
  ss 30, 33, 33A   *36–9*
Telecommunications Act 1984
  ss 27F, 106   *155–6*
Theatres Act 1968
  ss 4, 7   *32*
Theft Act 1968
  s 28   *32–3*
Third Parties (Rights against Insurers)
  Act 1930
  ss 1–3   *12–4*
Timeshare Act 1992
  ss 7   *266–7*
Torts (Interference with Goods) Act 1977
  ss 1-14, 16, Sch 1 Part I, II   *85–91*
Town and Country Planning Act 1990
  s 336   *242*
Trade Descriptions Act 1968
  ss 1-3, 6, 35   *33–4*
Trade Marks Act 1994
  ss 16, 19   *289*
Trade Union and Labour Relations
  (Consolidation) Act 1992
  ss 1, 5, 10, 11, 15, 16, 20-22, 113,
  127, 128, 137, 138, 140, 142-45,
  152, 153, 155-57, 164, 166, 167,
  178-80, 186, 187, 219, 220, 222,
  224-26, 236, 237, 240, 241, 244,
  245, 266, 273-75, 280, 288   *267–81*
Transfer of Undertakings (Protection of
  Employment) Regulations 1981
  s 5   *375*
Treaty of Rome, 1957   *399–400*
Unfair Contract Terms Act 1977
  ss 1–7, 9-14, 26-29,
  Sch 1, 2   *91–8*
Unfair Terms in Consumer Contracts
  Regulations 1994
  regs 1–8, Schs 1–3   *393–73*
Unidroit Principles for International
  Commercial Contracts   *427–44*

Unsolicited Goods and Services Act 1971
    ss 1-3, 3A, 4-6   *50–3*
Unsolicited Goods and Services
    (Amendment) Act 1975
    ss 2-4   *77–8*
Vaccine Damage Payments Act 1979
    ss 1-3, 6, 12   *120–1*
Value Added Tax Act 1994
    ss 78, 78A, 79, 80, 80A, 80B, 81, 89   *290–6*

Vehicle Excise and Registration
    Act 1994
    s 50   *296*
Water Industry Act 1991
    ss 1, 3, 45, 98, 107, 118, 180, 181, 209,
    Sch 6   *247–9*
Water Resources Act 1991
    ss 70, 100, 161, 161A, 161B, 161D, 208,
    221   *250–2*

BLACKSTONE'S STATUTES
TITLES IN THE SERIES

Contract, Tort & Restitution Statutes
Public Law Statutes
Employment Law Statutes
Criminal Law Statutes
Evidence Statutes
Family Law Statutes
Property Law Statutes
Commercial and Consumer Law Statutes
English Legal System Statutes
EC Legislation
International Law Documents
Landlord and Tenant Statutes
Medical Law Statutes
Planning Law Statutes
Intellectual Property Statutes
Environmental Law Statutes
International Human Rights Documents
Company Law Statutes